PUBLIC ENEMY
#2

ALSO BY AARON McGRUDER

The Boondocks: Because I Know You Don't Read the Newspaper

Fresh for '01 . . . You Suckas!: A Boondocks Collection

A Right to Be Hostile: The Boondocks Treasury

Birth of a Nation: A Comic Novel
with Reginald Hudlin • illustrated by Kyle Baker

PUBLIC ENEMY #2

AN ALL-NEW BOONDOCKS COLLECTION

Known Aliases: "Angry Kid with Afro"
Height: Varies with length of hair
Age: Unknown (Young, yet ... old)
Eyes: Noticeably scornful

Race: Black as the Ace of Spades
Hair: Completely out of control
Complexion: Kinda brownish
Nationality: (Un)American

AARON McGRUDER

 THREE RIVERS PRESS • NEW YORK

Published in the United States by Three Rivers Press,
an imprint of the Crown Publishing Group, a division of Random House, Inc, New York.
www.crownpublishing.com

All comic strips have previously appeared in syndication.

Library of Congress Cataloging-in-Publication Data
McGruder, Aaron.
[Boondocks. Selections]
Public enemy #2 : an all new Boondocks collection / Aaron McGruder.—1st ed.
I. Title: Public enemy number two. II. Title.
PN6728.B63M395 2005
741.5'973—dc22 2004063736

ISBN 1-4000-8258-7

Printed in the United States of America

Design by Max Werner

10 9 8 7 6 5 4 3 2

First Edition

For Dedric, Mom and Bill, Anthony, Cole, Arielle, and Alice

For Michelle . . .

And for the fans . . .

SPECIAL THANKS

To Greg and Shawn for putting up with me week after week.

To Rashon Khan and "Khanditioning" for keeping me sane and healthy.

To Harriet Choice . . . Hope you can live with what you've done!

To Rodney Barnes, Jen Seng, and Carl Jones on the help out.

To John McMeel, Lee Salem, John Vivona, and everyone at Universal Press Syndicate.

To Stephen Barnes and to Norman Aladjem and Paradigm.

To the late, great Bill Liebowitz of Golden Apple Comics.

To Todd, John Landis, Quincy Jones, Bill Maher, Michael Moore, Dr. Heather Lyons, Team Johnson, Big George and Terri,
Caroline and Bill, Lonnae, and my girlfriend's entire family for feeding me on holidays.

To Yair, Sandy, Penney, and Russ. Because I really wasn't doing enough.

To Denys and the entire production team for the show.

To De La Soul for that *Grind Date* album. Man . . .

And to the two people who *really* made this book possible: Chris Jackson and Lydia Wills.
See, it's this funny story where I forgot both of their names on the last book—well, never mind . . .

INTRODUCTION

Doing a TV show is like being stuck in a "making of" documentary for 72 weeks without the boring parts cut out. And it takes lots and lots of time. But if there's one lesson you learn early on in Hollywood it's never to quit your day job. So I spend just about all of my time trying to make sure that the strip and the show don't suck.

Many of the strips in this book were done while we were making *The Boondocks* pilot last year. I had hired an artist to help me on some of the art duties. People think I stopped drawing the strip, but that's never been the case. To this day there has never been a single *Boondocks* strip that I did not personally touch—I still obsess over the details of Huey, Riley, Caesar, and Granddad. I still go over every panel, I still care what it looks like, and I always will. In the eternal words of Memphis Bleek, "Anything left out, you can blame it on the brain, not the heart." He also said, "Just about the best out, any nigga realer than me is in a mess hall with their chest out." That part has nothing to do with me.

In the still depressing weeks and months that have followed the election, let this book be your reminder that you're really not the only one still pissed off about what's happening in the world, and that as long as Huey is on the page, you never will be. In the meantime, I'm going to write a book called *Profits of Rage,* and it'll be about all the wonderful, amazing, surreal things that have happened to me since this whole wild ride started, from getting religious advice from Snoop at the Playboy mansion to the lunch I attended with Fidel Castro in Havana.

All I'll have to do is find the time to write it.

As always, thanks for reading.

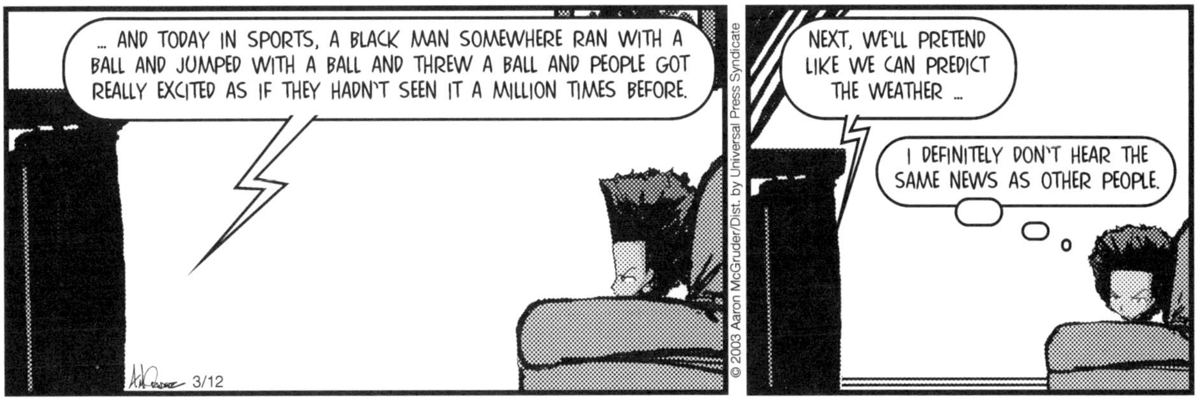
... AND TODAY IN SPORTS, A BLACK MAN SOMEWHERE RAN WITH A BALL AND JUMPED WITH A BALL AND THREW A BALL AND PEOPLE GOT REALLY EXCITED AS IF THEY HADN'T SEEN IT A MILLION TIMES BEFORE.
3/12
© 2003 Aaron McGruder/Dist. by Universal Press Syndicate
NEXT, WE'LL PRETEND LIKE WE CAN PREDICT THE WEATHER ...
I DEFINITELY DON'T HEAR THE SAME NEWS AS OTHER PEOPLE.

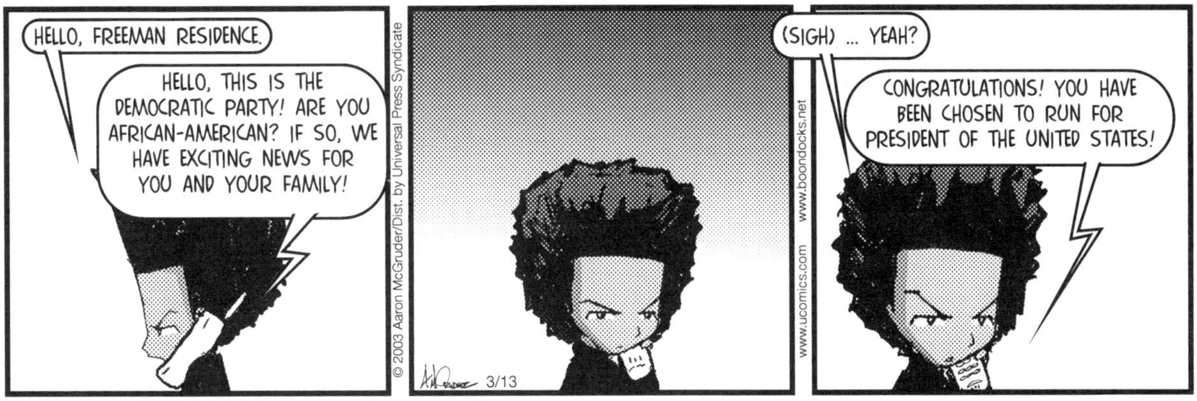
HELLO, FREEMAN RESIDENCE.
HELLO, THIS IS THE DEMOCRATIC PARTY! ARE YOU AFRICAN-AMERICAN? IF SO, WE HAVE EXCITING NEWS FOR YOU AND YOUR FAMILY!
© 2003 Aaron McGruder/Dist. by Universal Press Syndicate
3/13
www.ucomics.com www.boondocks.net
(SIGH) ... YEAH?
CONGRATULATIONS! YOU HAVE BEEN CHOSEN TO RUN FOR PRESIDENT OF THE UNITED STATES!

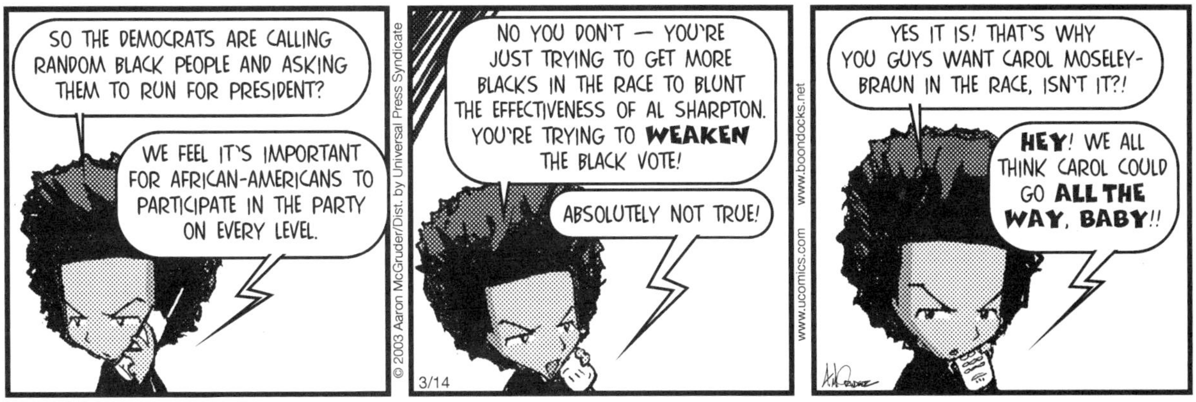
SO THE DEMOCRATS ARE CALLING RANDOM BLACK PEOPLE AND ASKING THEM TO RUN FOR PRESIDENT?
WE FEEL IT'S IMPORTANT FOR AFRICAN-AMERICANS TO PARTICIPATE IN THE PARTY ON EVERY LEVEL.
© 2003 Aaron McGruder/Dist. by Universal Press Syndicate
NO YOU DON'T — YOU'RE JUST TRYING TO GET MORE BLACKS IN THE RACE TO BLUNT THE EFFECTIVENESS OF AL SHARPTON. YOU'RE TRYING TO **WEAKEN** THE BLACK VOTE!
ABSOLUTELY NOT TRUE!
3/14
www.ucomics.com www.boondocks.net
YES IT IS! THAT'S WHY YOU GUYS WANT CAROL MOSELEY-BRAUN IN THE RACE, ISN'T IT?!
HEY! WE ALL THINK CAROL COULD GO **ALL THE WAY, BABY**!!

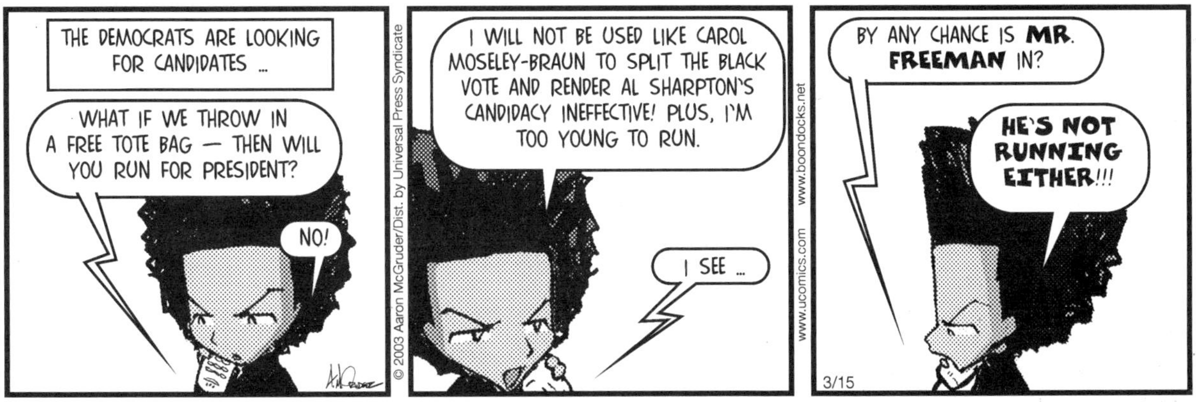
THE DEMOCRATS ARE LOOKING FOR CANDIDATES ...
WHAT IF WE THROW IN A FREE TOTE BAG — THEN WILL YOU RUN FOR PRESIDENT?
NO!
© 2003 Aaron McGruder/Dist. by Universal Press Syndicate
I WILL NOT BE USED LIKE CAROL MOSELEY-BRAUN TO SPLIT THE BLACK VOTE AND RENDER AL SHARPTON'S CANDIDACY INEFFECTIVE! PLUS, I'M TOO YOUNG TO RUN.
I SEE ...
www.ucomics.com www.boondocks.net
BY ANY CHANCE IS **MR. FREEMAN** IN?
HE'S NOT RUNNING EITHER!!!
3/15

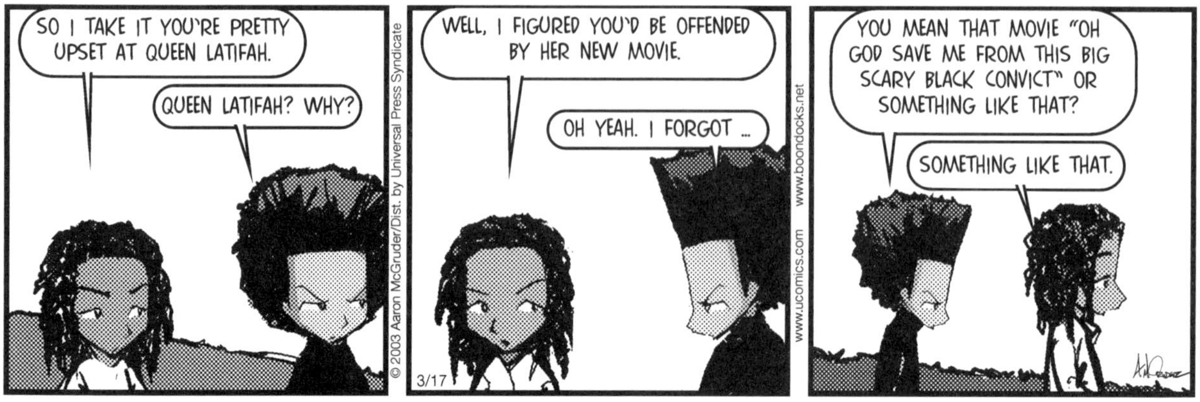
SO I TAKE IT YOU'RE PRETTY UPSET AT QUEEN LATIFAH.
QUEEN LATIFAH? WHY?
WELL, I FIGURED YOU'D BE OFFENDED BY HER NEW MOVIE.
OH YEAH. I FORGOT ...
YOU MEAN THAT MOVIE "OH GOD SAVE ME FROM THIS BIG SCARY BLACK CONVICT" OR SOMETHING LIKE THAT?
SOMETHING LIKE THAT.
3/17
© 2003 Aaron McGruder/Dist. by Universal Press Syndicate
www.ucomics.com www.boondocks.net

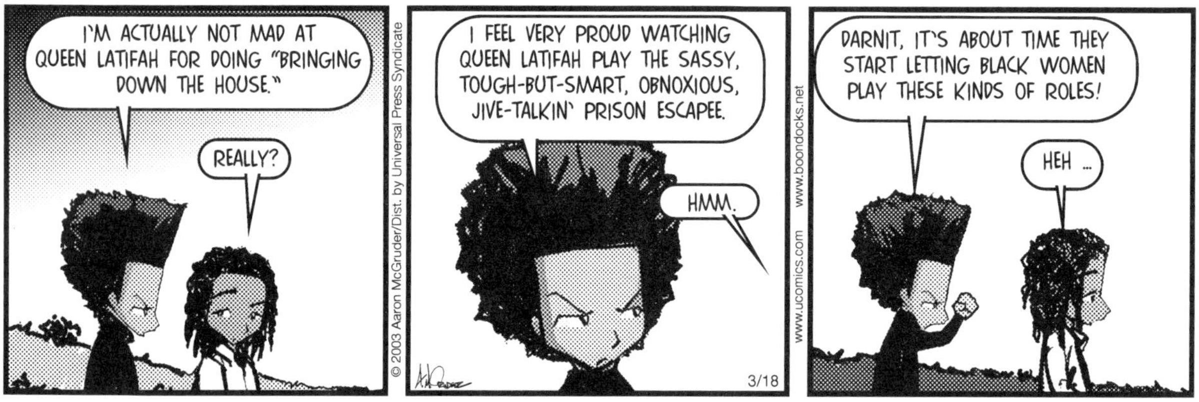
I'M ACTUALLY NOT MAD AT QUEEN LATIFAH FOR DOING "BRINGING DOWN THE HOUSE."
REALLY?
I FEEL VERY PROUD WATCHING QUEEN LATIFAH PLAY THE SASSY, TOUGH-BUT-SMART, OBNOXIOUS, JIVE-TALKIN' PRISON ESCAPEE.
HMM.
DARNIT, IT'S ABOUT TIME THEY START LETTING BLACK WOMEN PLAY THESE KINDS OF ROLES!
HEH ...
3/18
© 2003 Aaron McGruder/Dist. by Universal Press Syndicate
www.ucomics.com www.boondocks.net

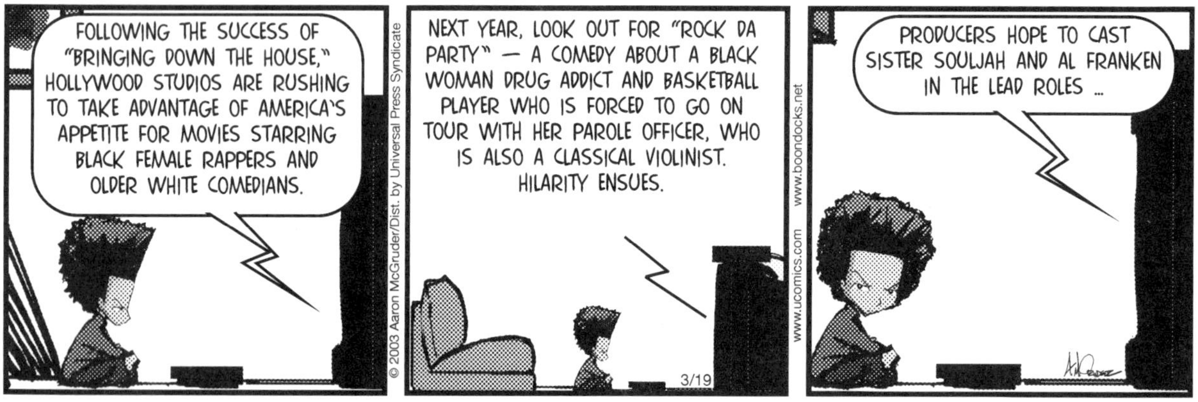
FOLLOWING THE SUCCESS OF "BRINGING DOWN THE HOUSE," HOLLYWOOD STUDIOS ARE RUSHING TO TAKE ADVANTAGE OF AMERICA'S APPETITE FOR MOVIES STARRING BLACK FEMALE RAPPERS AND OLDER WHITE COMEDIANS.
NEXT YEAR, LOOK OUT FOR "ROCK DA PARTY" — A COMEDY ABOUT A BLACK WOMAN DRUG ADDICT AND BASKETBALL PLAYER WHO IS FORCED TO GO ON TOUR WITH HER PAROLE OFFICER, WHO IS ALSO A CLASSICAL VIOLINIST. HILARITY ENSUES.
PRODUCERS HOPE TO CAST SISTER SOULJAH AND AL FRANKEN IN THE LEAD ROLES ...
3/19
© 2003 Aaron McGruder/Dist. by Universal Press Syndicate
www.ucomics.com www.boondocks.net

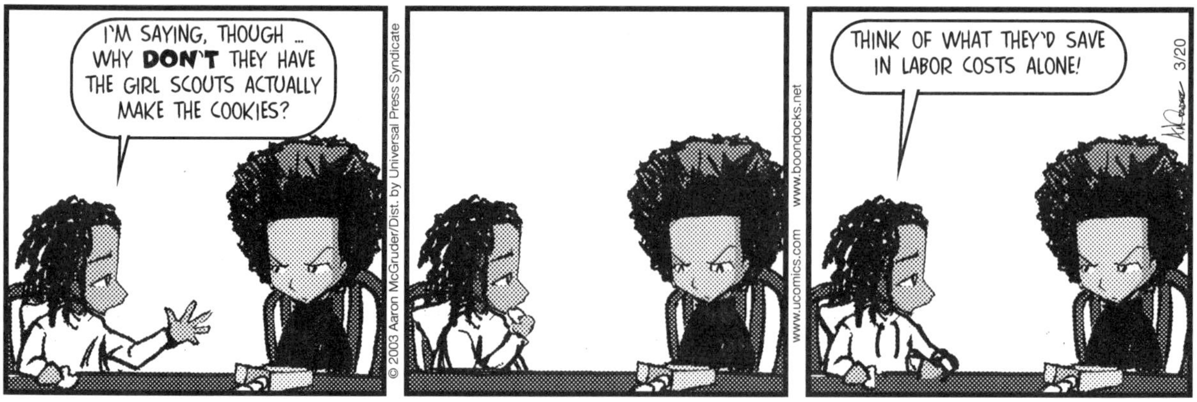
I'M SAYING, THOUGH ... WHY DON'T THEY HAVE THE GIRL SCOUTS ACTUALLY MAKE THE COOKIES?
THINK OF WHAT THEY'D SAVE IN LABOR COSTS ALONE!
3/20
© 2003 Aaron McGruder/Dist. by Universal Press Syndicate
www.ucomics.com www.boondocks.net

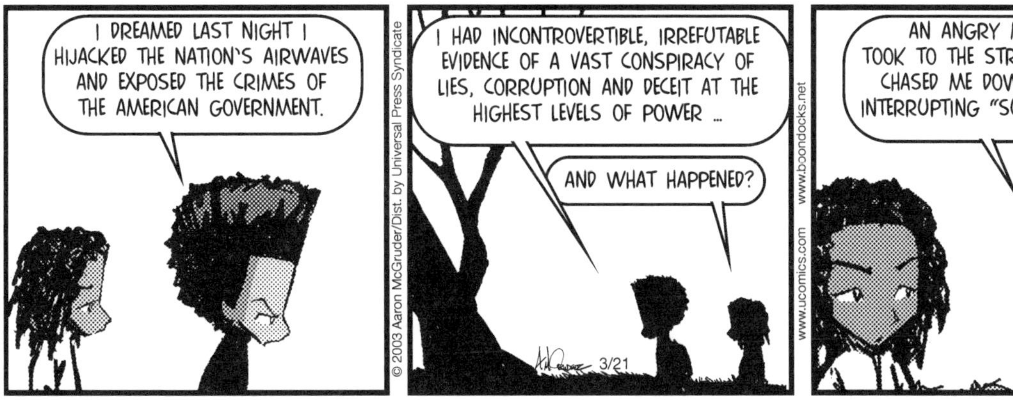
I DREAMED LAST NIGHT I HIJACKED THE NATION'S AIRWAVES AND EXPOSED THE CRIMES OF THE AMERICAN GOVERNMENT.
I HAD INCONTROVERTIBLE, IRREFUTABLE EVIDENCE OF A VAST CONSPIRACY OF LIES, CORRUPTION AND DECEIT AT THE HIGHEST LEVELS OF POWER ...
AND WHAT HAPPENED?
AN ANGRY MOB TOOK TO THE STREETS AND CHASED ME DOWN FOR INTERRUPTING "SURVIVOR."
© 2003 Aaron McGruder/Dist. by Universal Press Syndicate
3/21
www.ucomics.com www.boondocks.net

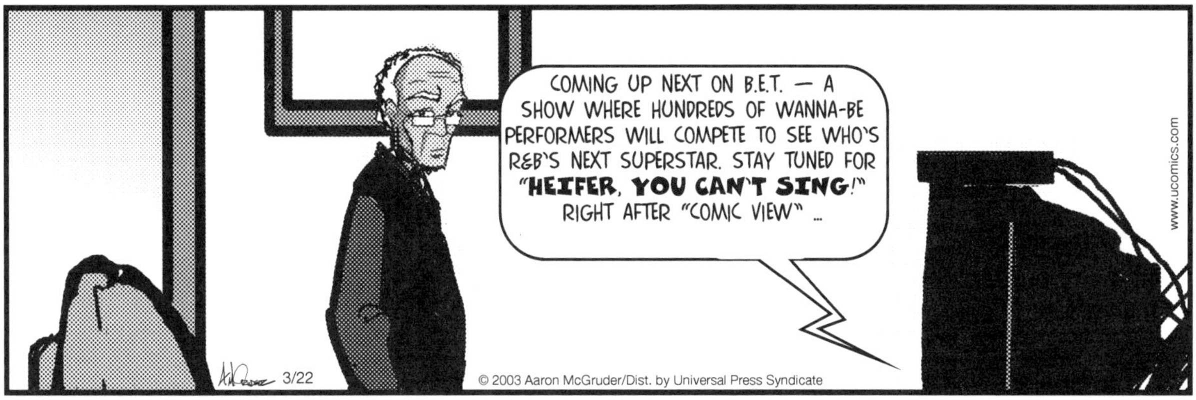
COMING UP NEXT ON B.E.T. — A SHOW WHERE HUNDREDS OF WANNA-BE PERFORMERS WILL COMPETE TO SEE WHO'S R&B'S NEXT SUPERSTAR. STAY TUNED FOR "HEIFER, YOU CAN'T SING!" RIGHT AFTER "COMIC VIEW" ...
3/22
© 2003 Aaron McGruder/Dist. by Universal Press Syndicate
www.ucomics.com

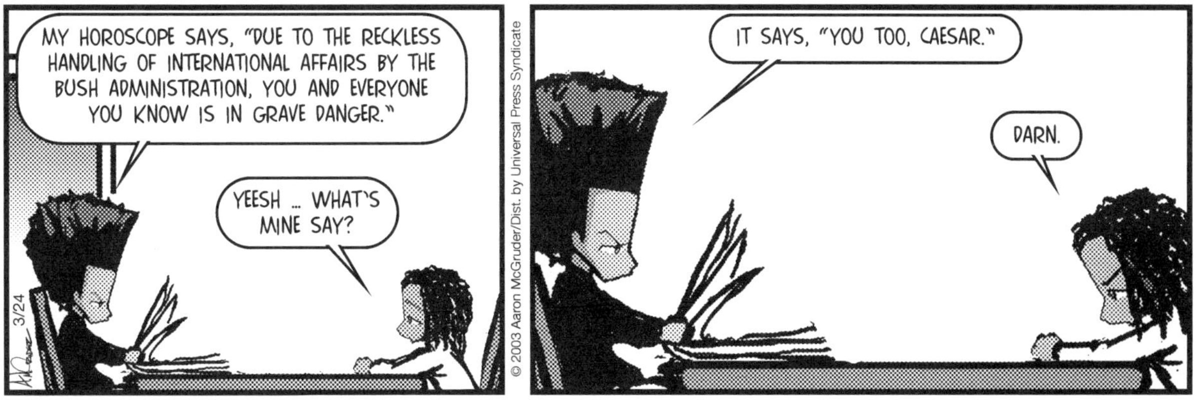
MY HOROSCOPE SAYS, "DUE TO THE RECKLESS HANDLING OF INTERNATIONAL AFFAIRS BY THE BUSH ADMINISTRATION, YOU AND EVERYONE YOU KNOW IS IN GRAVE DANGER."
YEESH ... WHAT'S MINE SAY?
IT SAYS, "YOU TOO, CAESAR."
DARN.
3/24
© 2003 Aaron McGruder/Dist. by Universal Press Syndicate

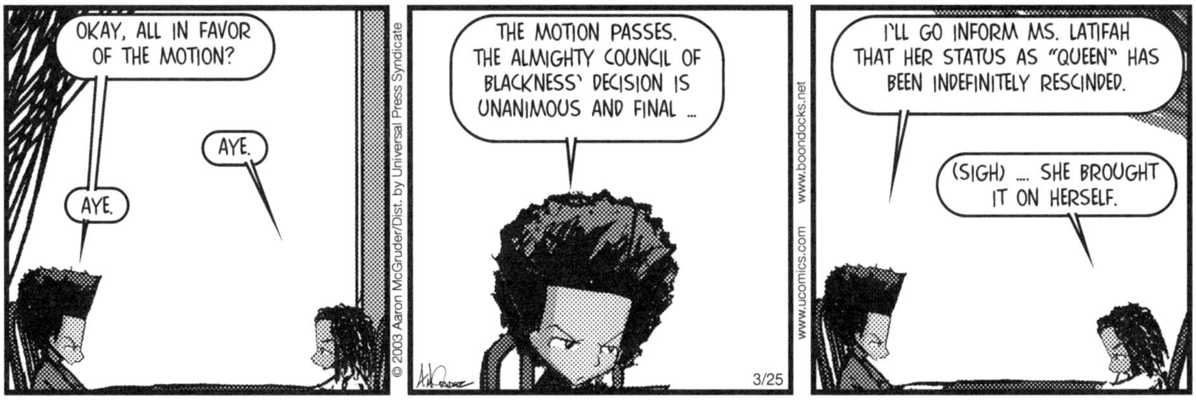
OKAY, ALL IN FAVOR OF THE MOTION?
AYE.
AYE.
THE MOTION PASSES. THE ALMIGHTY COUNCIL OF BLACKNESS' DECISION IS UNANIMOUS AND FINAL ...
I'LL GO INFORM MS. LATIFAH THAT HER STATUS AS "QUEEN" HAS BEEN INDEFINITELY RESCINDED.
(SIGH) .... SHE BROUGHT IT ON HERSELF.
© 2003 Aaron McGruder/Dist. by Universal Press Syndicate
3/25
www.ucomics.com www.boondocks.net

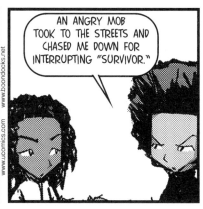

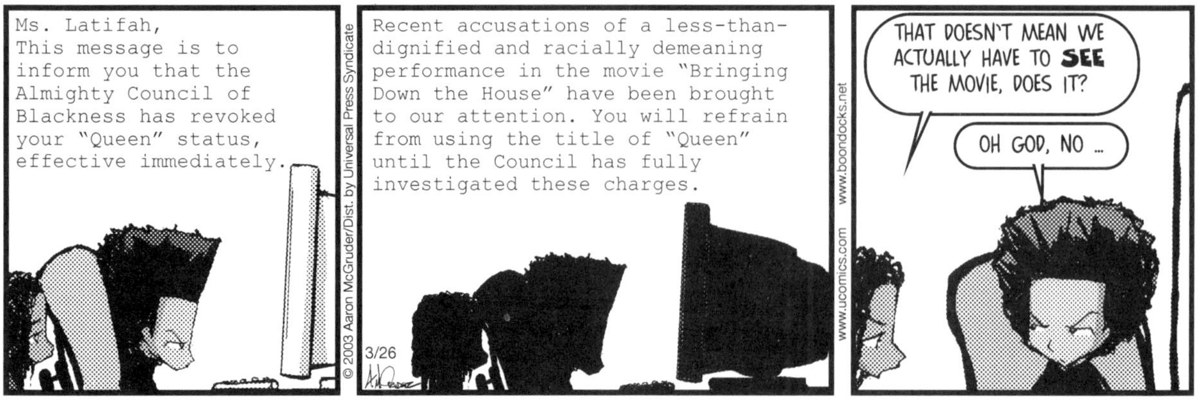
Ms. Latifah,
This message is to inform you that the Almighty Council of Blackness has revoked your "Queen" status, effective immediately.
© 2003 Aaron McGruder/Dist. by Universal Press Syndicate
3/26
Recent accusations of a less-than-dignified and racially demeaning performance in the movie "Bringing Down the House" have been brought to our attention. You will refrain from using the title of "Queen" until the Council has fully investigated these charges.
www.ucomics.com www.boondocks.net
THAT DOESN'T MEAN WE ACTUALLY HAVE TO SEE THE MOVIE, DOES IT?
OH GOD, NO ...

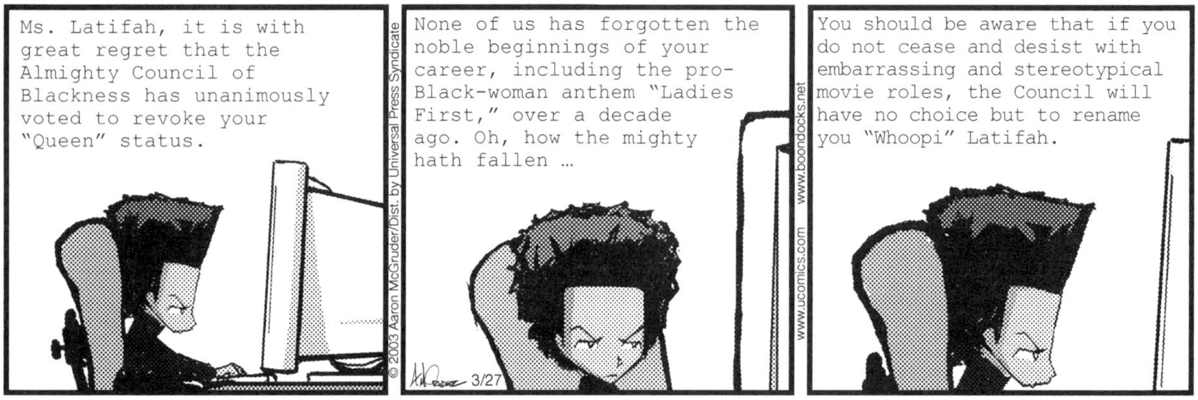
Ms. Latifah, it is with great regret that the Almighty Council of Blackness has unanimously voted to revoke your "Queen" status.
© 2003 Aaron McGruder/Dist. by Universal Press Syndicate
3/27
None of us has forgotten the noble beginnings of your career, including the pro-Black-woman anthem "Ladies First," over a decade ago. Oh, how the mighty hath fallen ...
www.ucomics.com www.boondocks.net
You should be aware that if you do not cease and desist with embarrassing and stereotypical movie roles, the Council will have no choice but to rename you "Whoopi" Latifah.

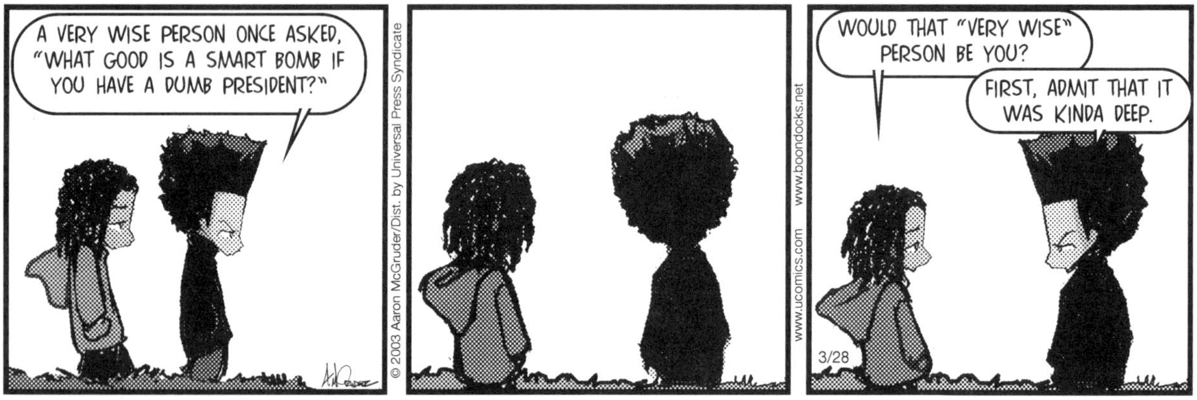
A VERY WISE PERSON ONCE ASKED, "WHAT GOOD IS A SMART BOMB IF YOU HAVE A DUMB PRESIDENT?"
© 2003 Aaron McGruder/Dist. by Universal Press Syndicate
www.ucomics.com www.boondocks.net
3/28
WOULD THAT "VERY WISE" PERSON BE YOU?
FIRST, ADMIT THAT IT WAS KINDA DEEP.

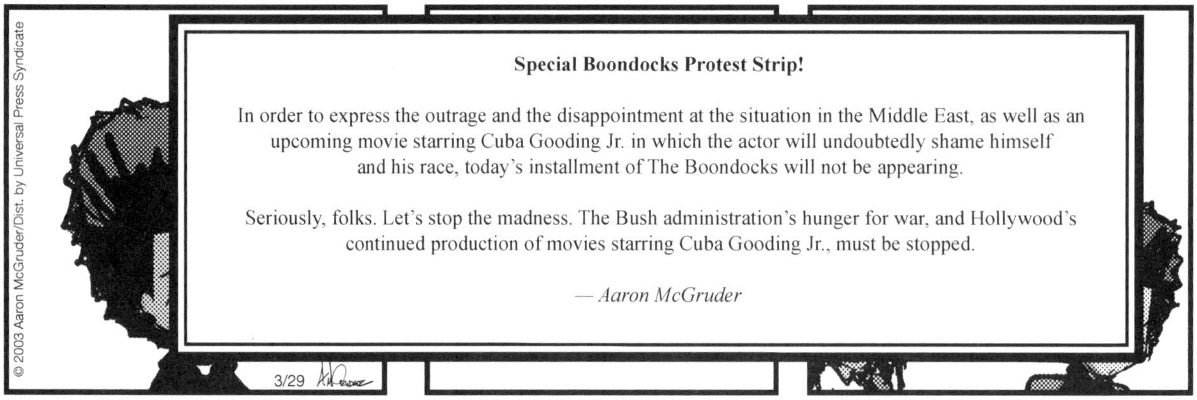
© 2003 Aaron McGruder/Dist. by Universal Press Syndicate
Special Boondocks Protest Strip!
In order to express the outrage and the disappointment at the situation in the Middle East, as well as an upcoming movie starring Cuba Gooding Jr. in which the actor will undoubtedly shame himself and his race, today's installment of The Boondocks will not be appearing.
Seriously, folks. Let's stop the madness. The Bush administration's hunger for war, and Hollywood's continued production of movies starring Cuba Gooding Jr., must be stopped.
— Aaron McGruder
3/29

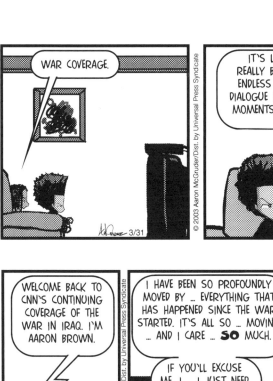

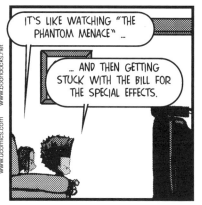

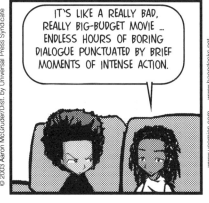

WAR COVERAGE.
© 2003 Aaron McGruder/Dist. by Universal Press Syndicate
IT'S LIKE A REALLY BAD, REALLY BIG-BUDGET MOVIE ... ENDLESS HOURS OF BORING DIALOGUE PUNCTUATED BY BRIEF MOMENTS OF INTENSE ACTION.
www.ucomics.com www.boondocks.net
IT'S LIKE WATCHING "THE PHANTOM MENACE" ...
... AND THEN GETTING STUCK WITH THE BILL FOR THE SPECIAL EFFECTS.
3/31

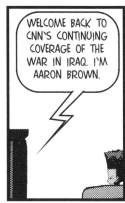

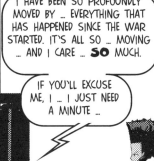

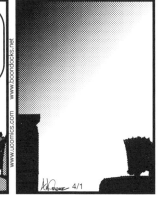

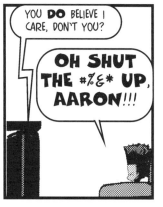

WELCOME BACK TO CNN'S CONTINUING COVERAGE OF THE WAR IN IRAQ. I'M AARON BROWN.
© 2003 Aaron McGruder/Dist. by Universal Press Syndicate
I HAVE BEEN SO PROFOUNDLY MOVED BY ... EVERYTHING THAT HAS HAPPENED SINCE THE WAR STARTED. IT'S ALL SO ... MOVING ... AND I CARE ... SO MUCH.
IF YOU'LL EXCUSE ME, I ... I JUST NEED A MINUTE ...
www.ucomics.com www.boondocks.net
4/1
YOU DO BELIEVE I CARE, DON'T YOU?
OH SHUT THE #%&* UP, AARON!!!

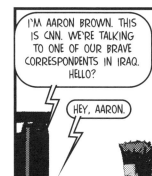

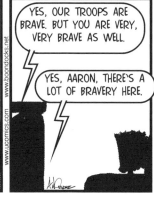

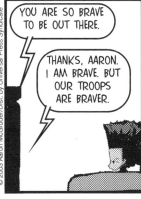

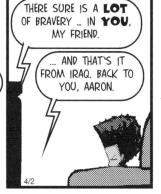

I'M AARON BROWN. THIS IS CNN. WE'RE TALKING TO ONE OF OUR BRAVE CORRESPONDENTS IN IRAQ. HELLO?
HEY, AARON.
© 2003 Aaron McGruder/Dist. by Universal Press Syndicate
YOU ARE SO BRAVE TO BE OUT THERE.
THANKS, AARON. I AM BRAVE. BUT OUR TROOPS ARE BRAVER.
www.ucomics.com www.boondocks.net
YES, OUR TROOPS ARE BRAVE. BUT YOU ARE VERY, VERY BRAVE AS WELL.
YES, AARON, THERE'S A LOT OF BRAVERY HERE.
THERE SURE IS A LOT OF BRAVERY ... IN YOU, MY FRIEND.
... AND THAT'S IT FROM IRAQ. BACK TO YOU, AARON.
4/2

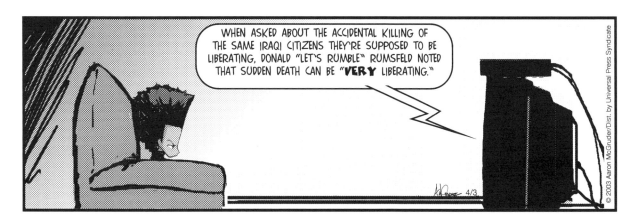

WHEN ASKED ABOUT THE ACCIDENTAL KILLING OF THE SAME IRAQI CITIZENS THEY'RE SUPPOSED TO BE LIBERATING, DONALD "LET'S RUMBLE" RUMSFELD NOTED THAT SUDDEN DEATH CAN BE "VERY LIBERATING."
4/3
© 2003 Aaron McGruder/Dist. by Universal Press Syndicate

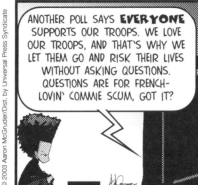

A NEW POLL SHOWS THAT EVERYONE, INCLUDING YOU, SUPPORTS PRESIDENT BUSH AND SUPPORTS THIS WAR. EVERYONE EXCEPT FRENCH-LOVIN' COMMIE SCUM. YOU'RE NOT FRENCH-LOVIN' COMMIE SCUM, ARE YOU?
© 2003 Aaron McGruder/Dist. by Universal Press Syndicate
ANOTHER POLL SAYS EVERYONE SUPPORTS OUR TROOPS. WE LOVE OUR TROOPS, AND THAT'S WHY WE LET THEM GO AND RISK THEIR LIVES WITHOUT ASKING QUESTIONS. QUESTIONS ARE FOR FRENCH-LOVIN' COMMIE SCUM, GOT IT?
www.ucomics.com www.boondocks.net
THIS IS CNN. I'M AARON BROWN ...
4/4

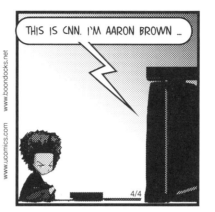

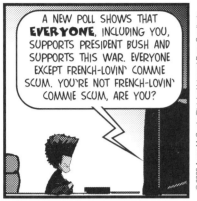

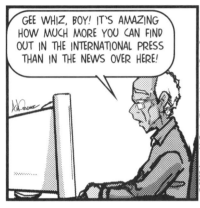

GEE WHIZ, BOY! IT'S AMAZING HOW MUCH MORE YOU CAN FIND OUT IN THE INTERNATIONAL PRESS THAN IN THE NEWS OVER HERE!
© 2003 Aaron McGruder/Dist. by Universal Press Syndicate
www.ucomics.com www.boondocks.net
DID YOU KNOW BUSH LOST THE ELECTION?!
I HADN'T HEARD THAT.
4/5

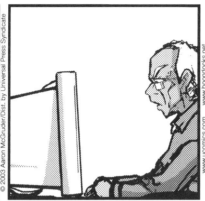

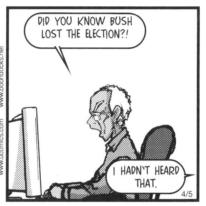

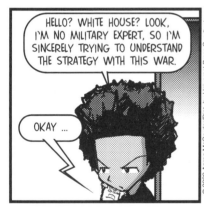

HELLO? WHITE HOUSE? LOOK, I'M NO MILITARY EXPERT, SO I'M SINCERELY TRYING TO UNDERSTAND THE STRATEGY WITH THIS WAR.
OKAY ...
© 2003 Aaron McGruder/Dist. by Universal Press Syndicate
NOW ... THE PLAN WAS TO BOMB IRAQ ON A SIZE AND SCALE HERETOFORE UNSEEN IN THE HISTORY OF WARFARE ...
RIGHT ...
4/7
www.ucomics.com www.boondocks.net
AND THAT WAS SUPPOSED TO GET THE IRAQIS MAD AT ... WHO?
I KNOW IT'S WEIRD, BUT SOMEHOW IT MADE GREAT SENSE AT THE TIME ...

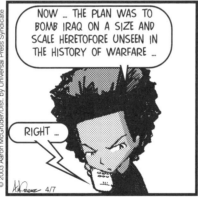

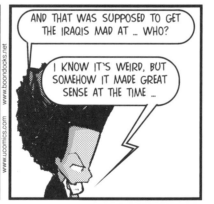

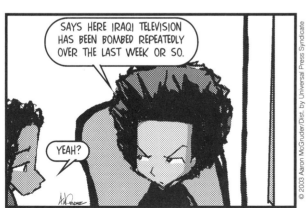

SAYS HERE IRAQI TELEVISION HAS BEEN BOMBED REPEATEDLY OVER THE LAST WEEK OR SO.
YEAH?
© 2003 Aaron McGruder/Dist. by Universal Press Syndicate
www.ucomics.com www.boondocks.net
HOWEVER, AN IRAQI SPOKESMAN SAID THE SMOLDERING RUINS OF THE STATION ARE STILL MORE ENTERTAINING THAN B.E.T.
4/8

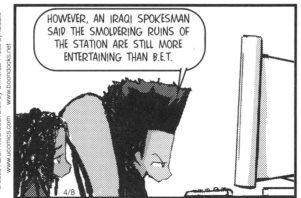

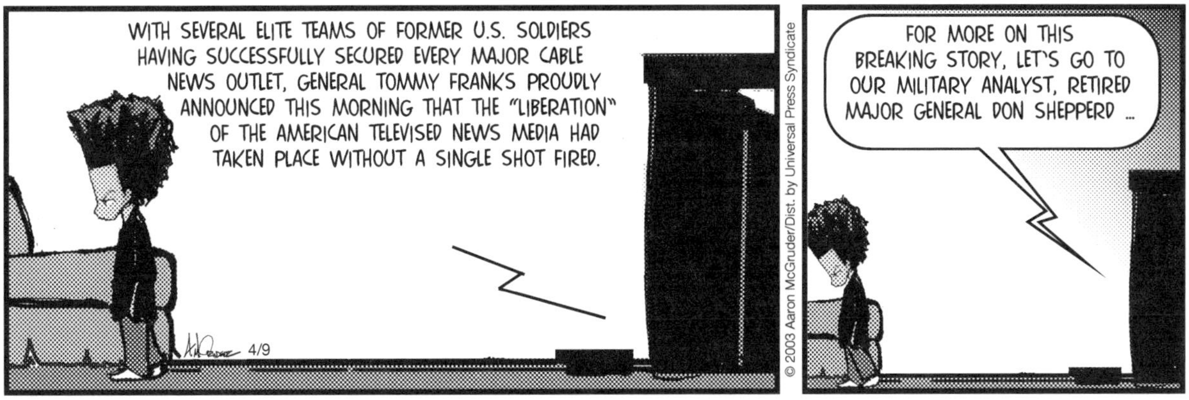
WITH SEVERAL ELITE TEAMS OF FORMER U.S. SOLDIERS HAVING SUCCESSFULLY SECURED EVERY MAJOR CABLE NEWS OUTLET, GENERAL TOMMY FRANKS PROUDLY ANNOUNCED THIS MORNING THAT THE "LIBERATION" OF THE AMERICAN TELEVISED NEWS MEDIA HAD TAKEN PLACE WITHOUT A SINGLE SHOT FIRED.
4/9
© 2003 Aaron McGruder/Dist. by Universal Press Syndicate
FOR MORE ON THIS BREAKING STORY, LET'S GO TO OUR MILITARY ANALYST, RETIRED MAJOR GENERAL DON SHEPPERD ...

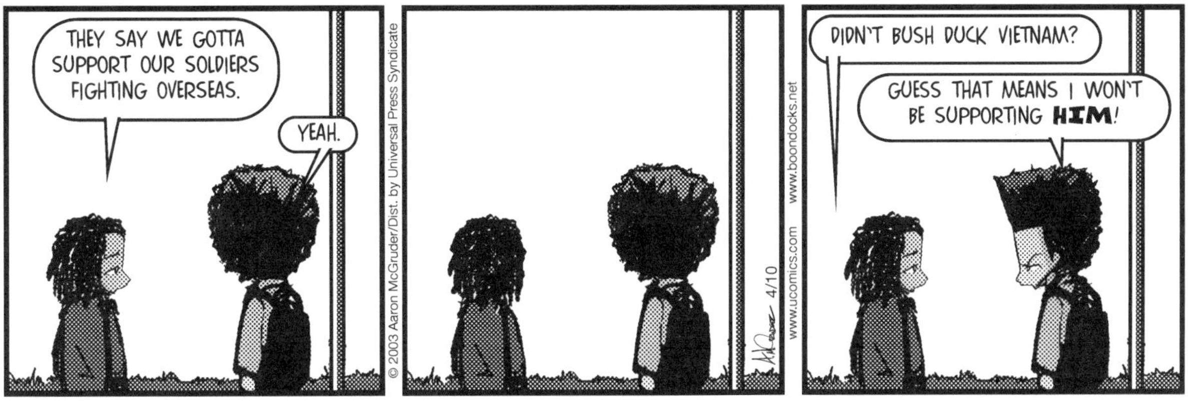
THEY SAY WE GOTTA SUPPORT OUR SOLDIERS FIGHTING OVERSEAS.
YEAH.
© 2003 Aaron McGruder/Dist. by Universal Press Syndicate
4/10
www.ucomics.com
www.boondocks.net
DIDN'T BUSH DUCK VIETNAM?
GUESS THAT MEANS I WON'T BE SUPPORTING **HIM**!

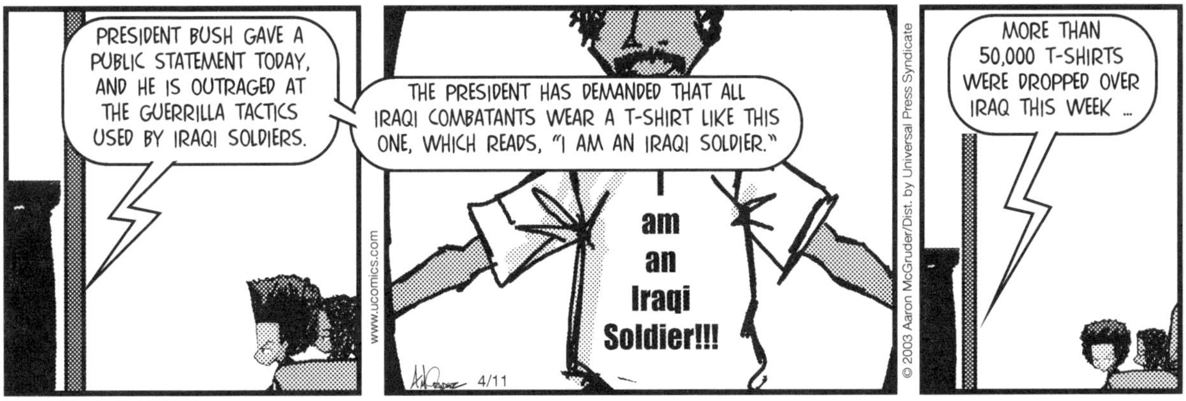
PRESIDENT BUSH GAVE A PUBLIC STATEMENT TODAY, AND HE IS OUTRAGED AT THE GUERRILLA TACTICS USED BY IRAQI SOLDIERS.
www.ucomics.com
THE PRESIDENT HAS DEMANDED THAT ALL IRAQI COMBATANTS WEAR A T-SHIRT LIKE THIS ONE, WHICH READS, "I AM AN IRAQI SOLDIER."
I am an Iraqi Soldier!!!
4/11
© 2003 Aaron McGruder/Dist. by Universal Press Syndicate
MORE THAN 50,000 T-SHIRTS WERE DROPPED OVER IRAQ THIS WEEK ...

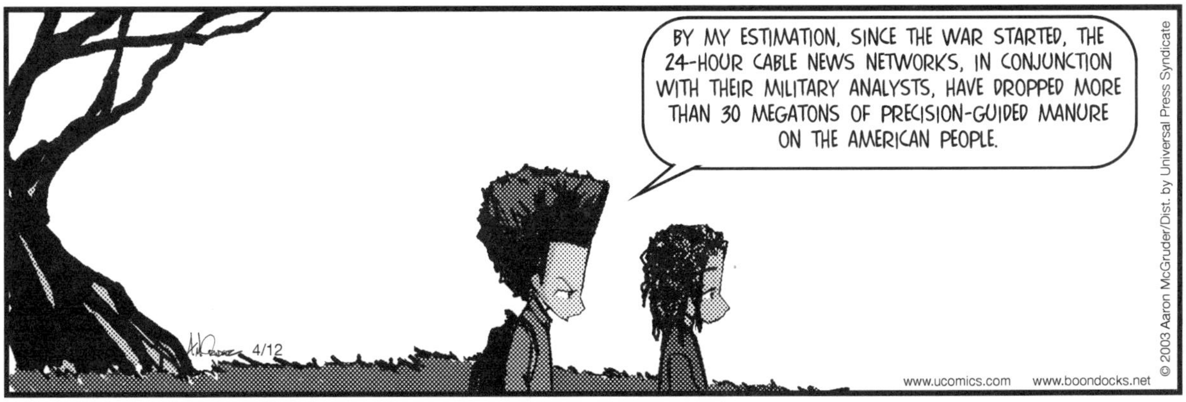
BY MY ESTIMATION, SINCE THE WAR STARTED, THE 24-HOUR CABLE NEWS NETWORKS, IN CONJUNCTION WITH THEIR MILITARY ANALYSTS, HAVE DROPPED MORE THAN 30 MEGATONS OF PRECISION-GUIDED MANURE ON THE AMERICAN PEOPLE.
4/12
www.ucomics.com www.boondocks.net
© 2003 Aaron McGruder/Dist. by Universal Press Syndicate

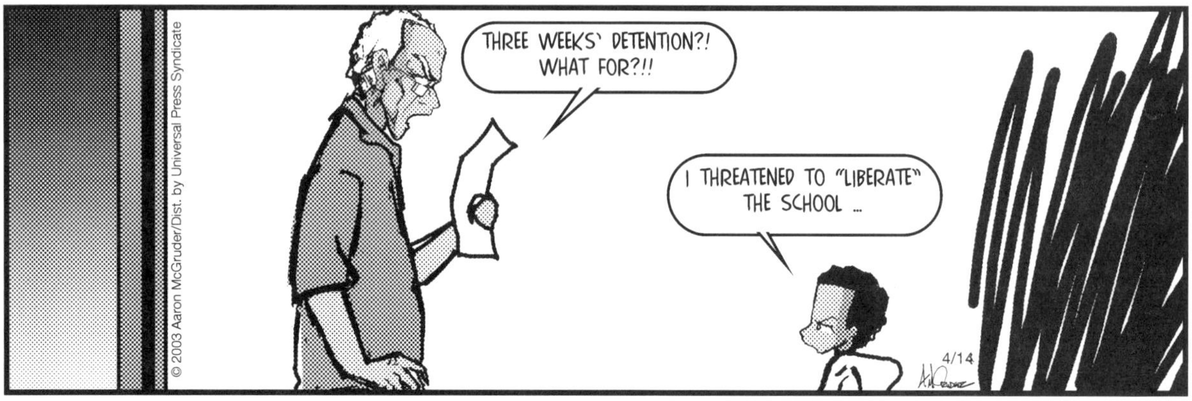
© 2003 Aaron McGruder/Dist. by Universal Press Syndicate
THREE WEEKS' DETENTION?! WHAT FOR?!!
I THREATENED TO "LIBERATE" THE SCHOOL ...
4/14

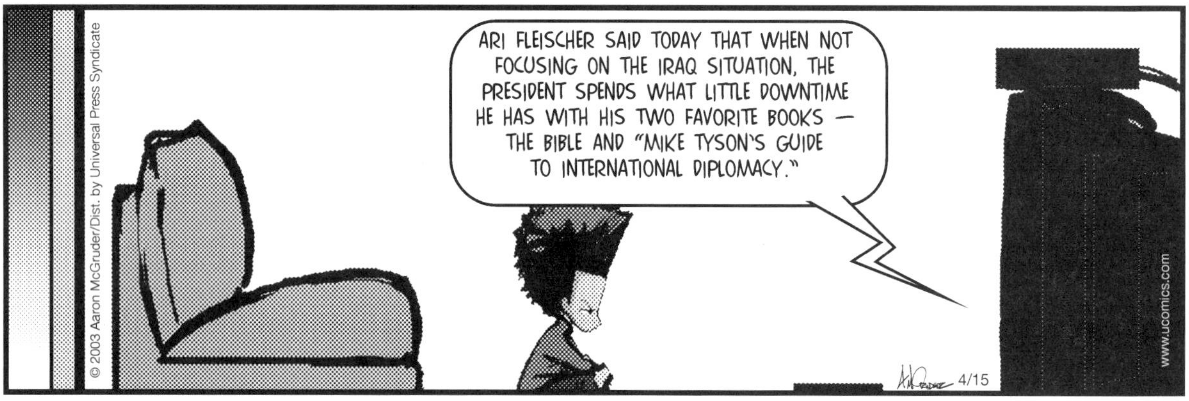
© 2003 Aaron McGruder/Dist. by Universal Press Syndicate
ARI FLEISCHER SAID TODAY THAT WHEN NOT FOCUSING ON THE IRAQ SITUATION, THE PRESIDENT SPENDS WHAT LITTLE DOWNTIME HE HAS WITH HIS TWO FAVORITE BOOKS — THE BIBLE AND "MIKE TYSON'S GUIDE TO INTERNATIONAL DIPLOMACY."
4/15
www.ucomics.com

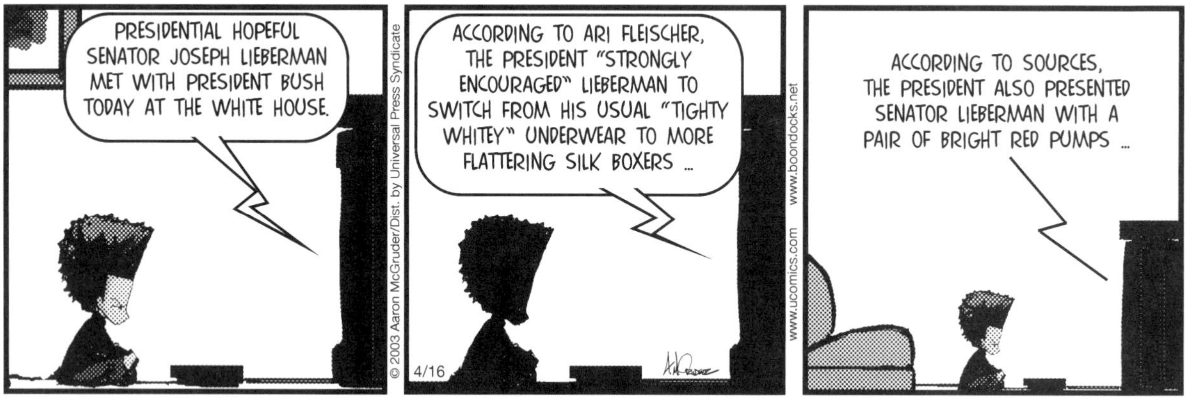
PRESIDENTIAL HOPEFUL SENATOR JOSEPH LIEBERMAN MET WITH PRESIDENT BUSH TODAY AT THE WHITE HOUSE.
© 2003 Aaron McGruder/Dist. by Universal Press Syndicate
ACCORDING TO ARI FLEISCHER, THE PRESIDENT "STRONGLY ENCOURAGED" LIEBERMAN TO SWITCH FROM HIS USUAL "TIGHTY WHITEY" UNDERWEAR TO MORE FLATTERING SILK BOXERS ...
4/16
www.ucomics.com www.boondocks.net
ACCORDING TO SOURCES, THE PRESIDENT ALSO PRESENTED SENATOR LIEBERMAN WITH A PAIR OF BRIGHT RED PUMPS ...

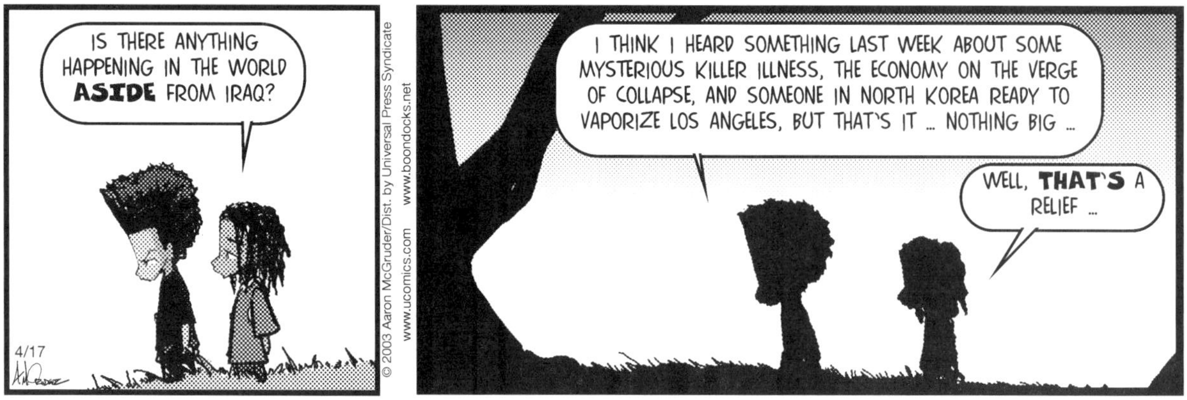
IS THERE ANYTHING HAPPENING IN THE WORLD **ASIDE** FROM IRAQ?
4/17
© 2003 Aaron McGruder/Dist. by Universal Press Syndicate
www.ucomics.com www.boondocks.net
I THINK I HEARD SOMETHING LAST WEEK ABOUT SOME MYSTERIOUS KILLER ILLNESS, THE ECONOMY ON THE VERGE OF COLLAPSE, AND SOMEONE IN NORTH KOREA READY TO VAPORIZE LOS ANGELES, BUT THAT'S IT ... NOTHING BIG ...
WELL, **THAT'S** A RELIEF ...

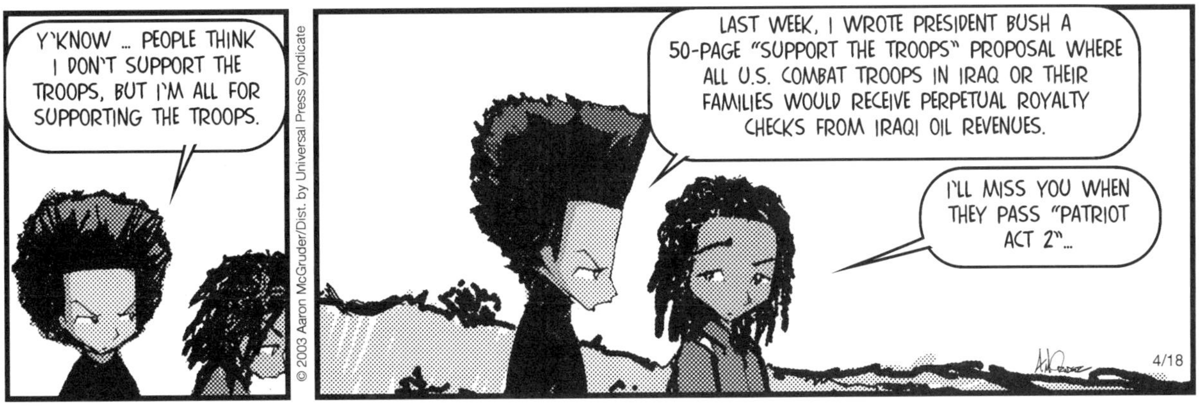
Y'KNOW ... PEOPLE THINK I DON'T SUPPORT THE TROOPS, BUT I'M ALL FOR SUPPORTING THE TROOPS.
LAST WEEK, I WROTE PRESIDENT BUSH A 50-PAGE "SUPPORT THE TROOPS" PROPOSAL WHERE ALL U.S. COMBAT TROOPS IN IRAQ OR THEIR FAMILIES WOULD RECEIVE PERPETUAL ROYALTY CHECKS FROM IRAQI OIL REVENUES.
I'LL MISS YOU WHEN THEY PASS "PATRIOT ACT 2"...
© 2003 Aaron McGruder/Dist. by Universal Press Syndicate
4/18

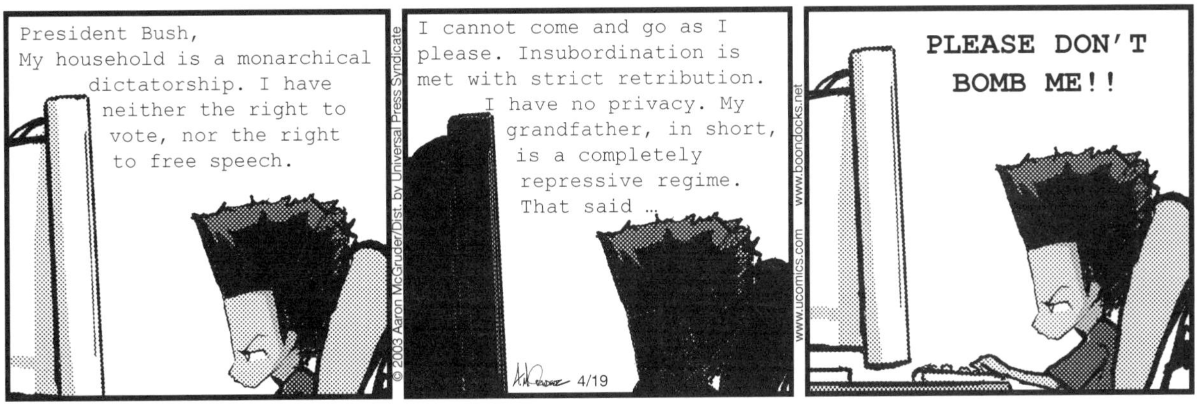
President Bush,
My household is a monarchical dictatorship. I have neither the right to vote, nor the right to free speech.
I cannot come and go as I please. Insubordination is met with strict retribution. I have no privacy. My grandfather, in short, is a completely repressive regime. That said ...
PLEASE DON'T BOMB ME!!
© 2003 Aaron McGruder/Dist. by Universal Press Syndicate
www.ucomics.com www.boondocks.net
4/19

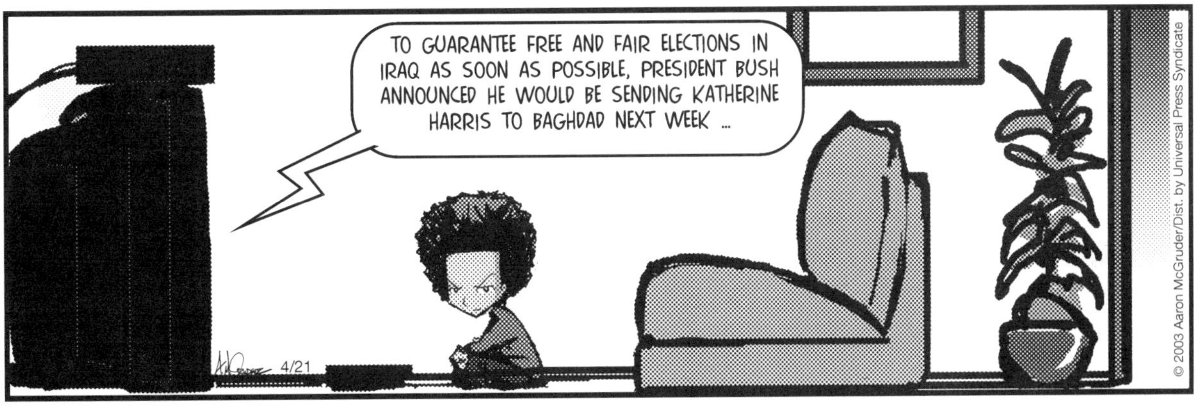
TO GUARANTEE FREE AND FAIR ELECTIONS IN IRAQ AS SOON AS POSSIBLE, PRESIDENT BUSH ANNOUNCED HE WOULD BE SENDING KATHERINE HARRIS TO BAGHDAD NEXT WEEK ...
© 2003 Aaron McGruder/Dist. by Universal Press Syndicate
4/21

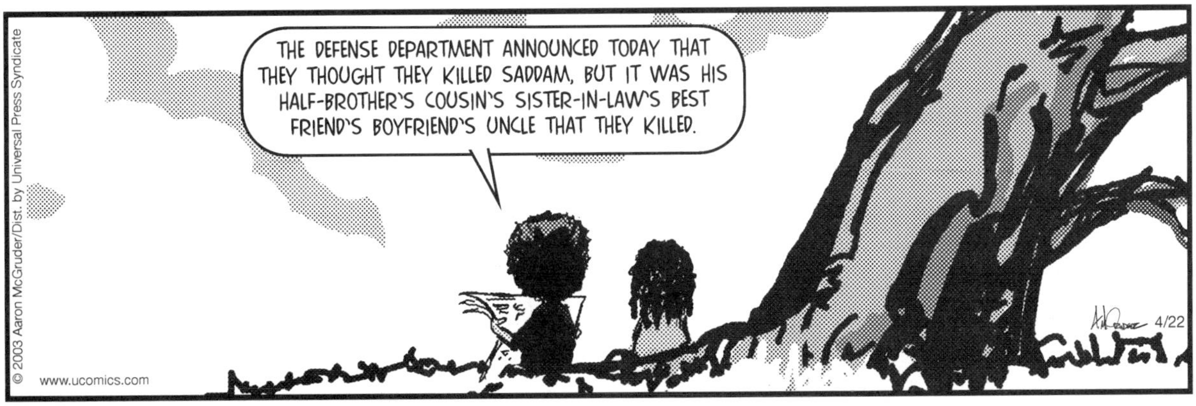
THE DEFENSE DEPARTMENT ANNOUNCED TODAY THAT THEY THOUGHT THEY KILLED SADDAM, BUT IT WAS HIS HALF-BROTHER'S COUSIN'S SISTER-IN-LAW'S BEST FRIEND'S BOYFRIEND'S UNCLE THAT THEY KILLED.
© 2003 Aaron McGruder/Dist. by Universal Press Syndicate
www.ucomics.com
4/22

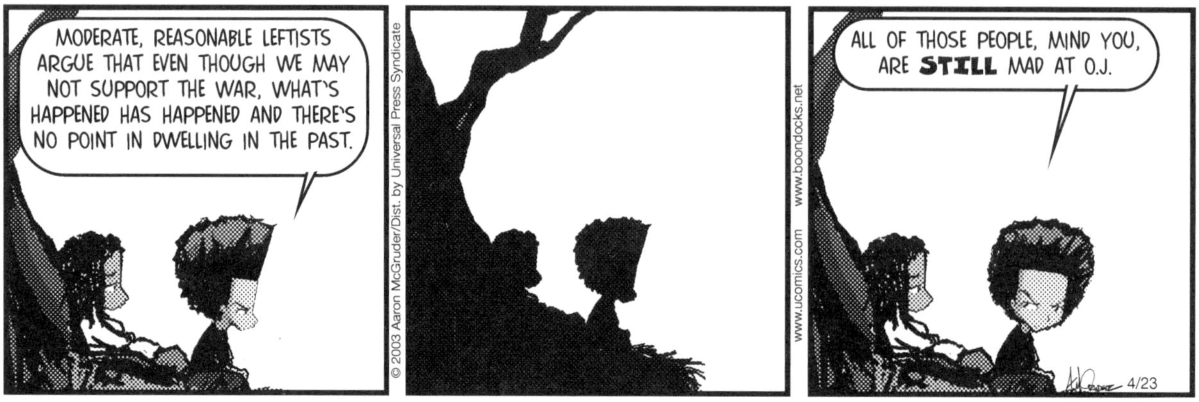
MODERATE, REASONABLE LEFTISTS ARGUE THAT EVEN THOUGH WE MAY NOT SUPPORT THE WAR, WHAT'S HAPPENED HAS HAPPENED AND THERE'S NO POINT IN DWELLING IN THE PAST.
© 2003 Aaron McGruder/Dist. by Universal Press Syndicate
ALL OF THOSE PEOPLE, MIND YOU, ARE **STILL** MAD AT O.J.
www.ucomics.com www.boondocks.net
4/23

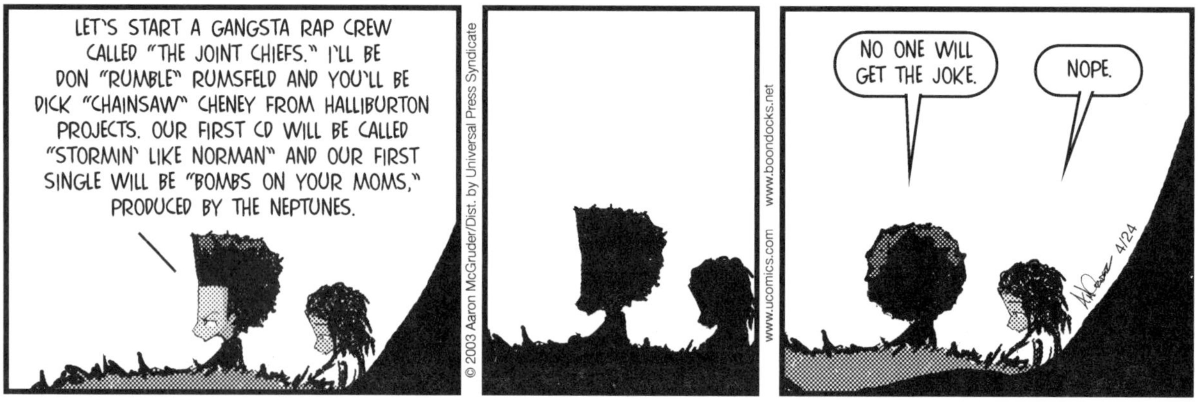
LET'S START A GANGSTA RAP CREW CALLED "THE JOINT CHIEFS." I'LL BE DON "RUMBLE" RUMSFELD AND YOU'LL BE DICK "CHAINSAW" CHENEY FROM HALLIBURTON PROJECTS. OUR FIRST CD WILL BE CALLED "STORMIN' LIKE NORMAN" AND OUR FIRST SINGLE WILL BE "BOMBS ON YOUR MOMS," PRODUCED BY THE NEPTUNES.
© 2003 Aaron McGruder/Dist. by Universal Press Syndicate
www.ucomics.com www.boondocks.net
NO ONE WILL GET THE JOKE.
NOPE.
4/24

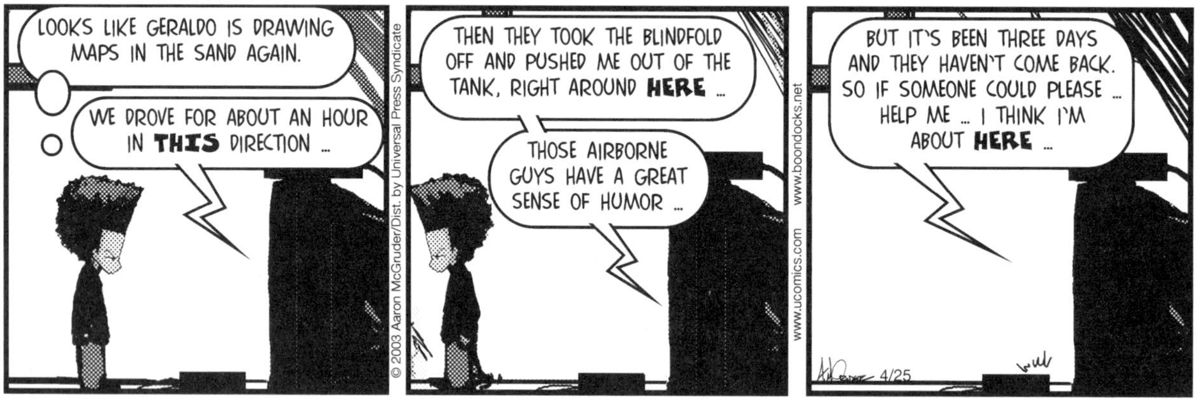
LOOKS LIKE GERALDO IS DRAWING MAPS IN THE SAND AGAIN.
WE DROVE FOR ABOUT AN HOUR IN **THIS** DIRECTION ...
© 2003 Aaron McGruder/Dist. by Universal Press Syndicate
THEN THEY TOOK THE BLINDFOLD OFF AND PUSHED ME OUT OF THE TANK, RIGHT AROUND **HERE** ...
THOSE AIRBORNE GUYS HAVE A GREAT SENSE OF HUMOR ...
www.ucomics.com www.boondocks.net
BUT IT'S BEEN THREE DAYS AND THEY HAVEN'T COME BACK. SO IF SOMEONE COULD PLEASE ... HELP ME ... I THINK I'M ABOUT **HERE** ...
4/25

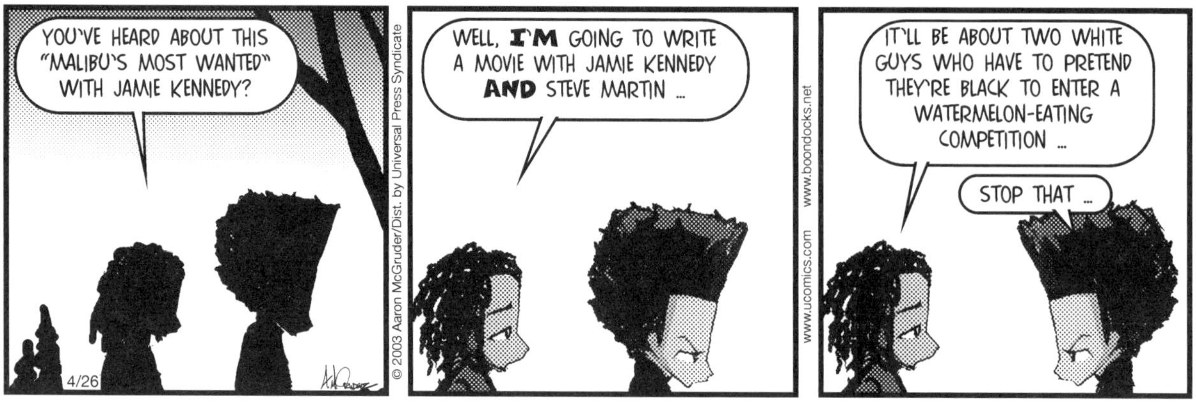
YOU'VE HEARD ABOUT THIS "MALIBU'S MOST WANTED" WITH JAMIE KENNEDY?
4/26
© 2003 Aaron McGruder/Dist. by Universal Press Syndicate
WELL, **I'M** GOING TO WRITE A MOVIE WITH JAMIE KENNEDY **AND** STEVE MARTIN ...
www.ucomics.com www.boondocks.net
IT'LL BE ABOUT TWO WHITE GUYS WHO HAVE TO PRETEND THEY'RE BLACK TO ENTER A WATERMELON-EATING COMPETITION ...
STOP THAT ...

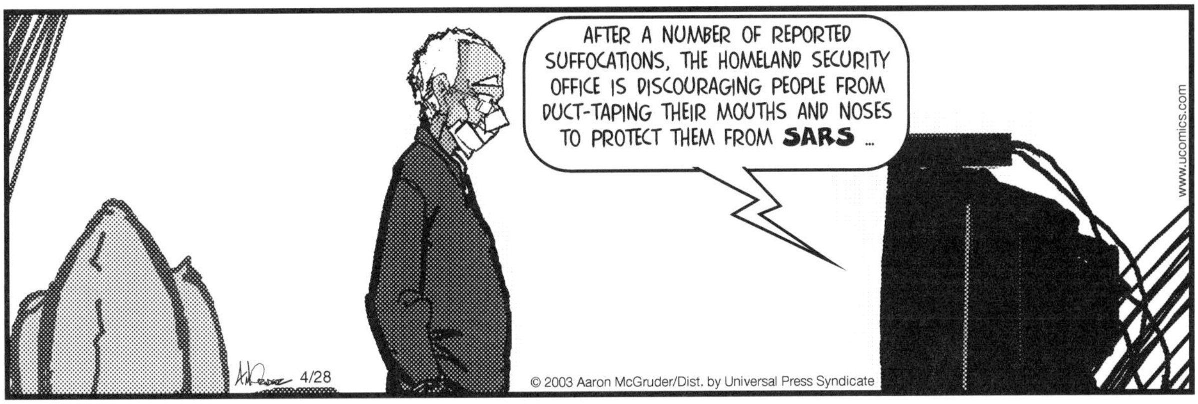
AFTER A NUMBER OF REPORTED SUFFOCATIONS, THE HOMELAND SECURITY OFFICE IS DISCOURAGING PEOPLE FROM DUCT-TAPING THEIR MOUTHS AND NOSES TO PROTECT THEM FROM SARS ...
4/28
© 2003 Aaron McGruder/Dist. by Universal Press Syndicate
www.ucomics.com

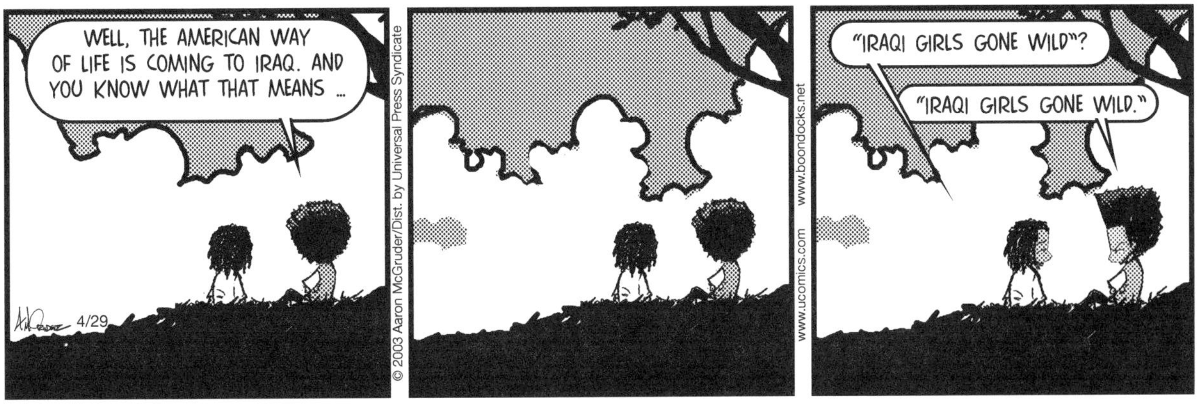
WELL, THE AMERICAN WAY OF LIFE IS COMING TO IRAQ. AND YOU KNOW WHAT THAT MEANS ...
4/29
© 2003 Aaron McGruder/Dist. by Universal Press Syndicate
www.ucomics.com www.boondocks.net
"IRAQI GIRLS GONE WILD"?
"IRAQI GIRLS GONE WILD."

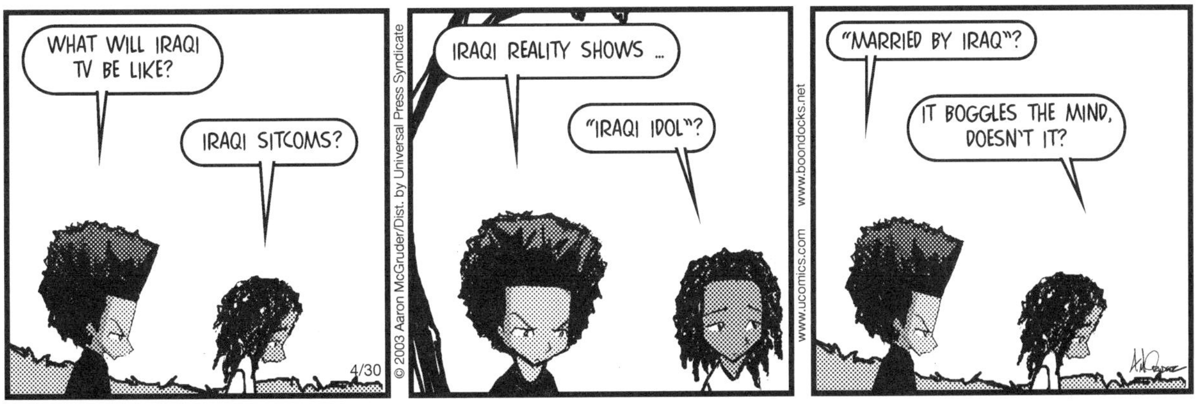
WHAT WILL IRAQI TV BE LIKE?
IRAQI SITCOMS?
4/30
© 2003 Aaron McGruder/Dist. by Universal Press Syndicate
IRAQI REALITY SHOWS ...
"IRAQI IDOL"?
www.ucomics.com www.boondocks.net
"MARRIED BY IRAQ"?
IT BOGGLES THE MIND, DOESN'T IT?

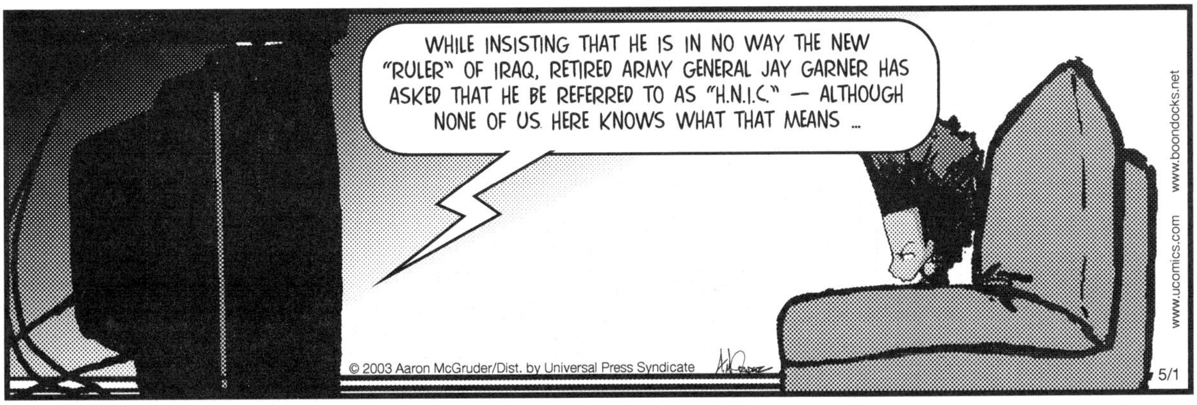
WHILE INSISTING THAT HE IS IN NO WAY THE NEW "RULER" OF IRAQ, RETIRED ARMY GENERAL JAY GARNER HAS ASKED THAT HE BE REFERRED TO AS "H.N.I.C." — ALTHOUGH NONE OF US HERE KNOWS WHAT THAT MEANS ...
© 2003 Aaron McGruder/Dist. by Universal Press Syndicate
5/1
www.ucomics.com www.boondocks.net

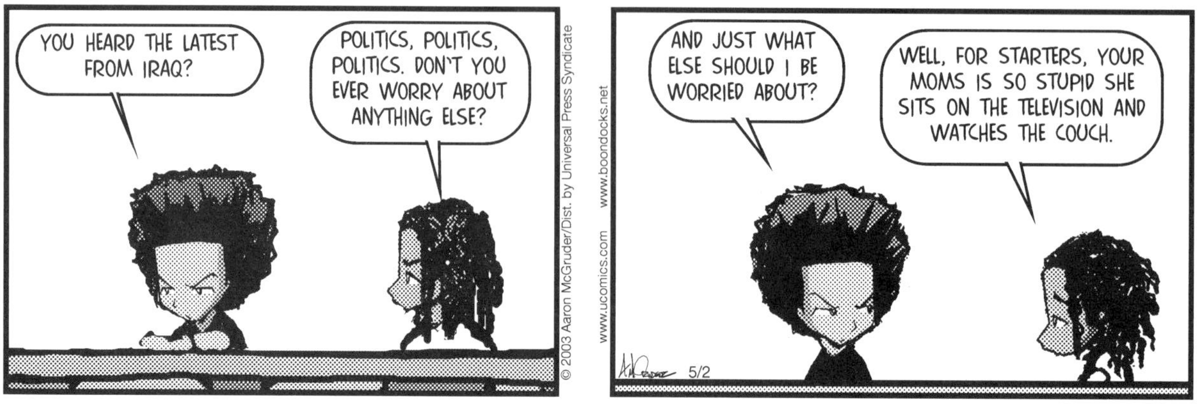
YOU HEARD THE LATEST FROM IRAQ?
POLITICS, POLITICS, POLITICS. DON'T YOU EVER WORRY ABOUT ANYTHING ELSE?
© 2003 Aaron McGruder/Dist. by Universal Press Syndicate
www.ucomics.com www.boondocks.net
AND JUST WHAT ELSE SHOULD I BE WORRIED ABOUT?
WELL, FOR STARTERS, YOUR MOMS IS SO STUPID SHE SITS ON THE TELEVISION AND WATCHES THE COUCH.
5/2

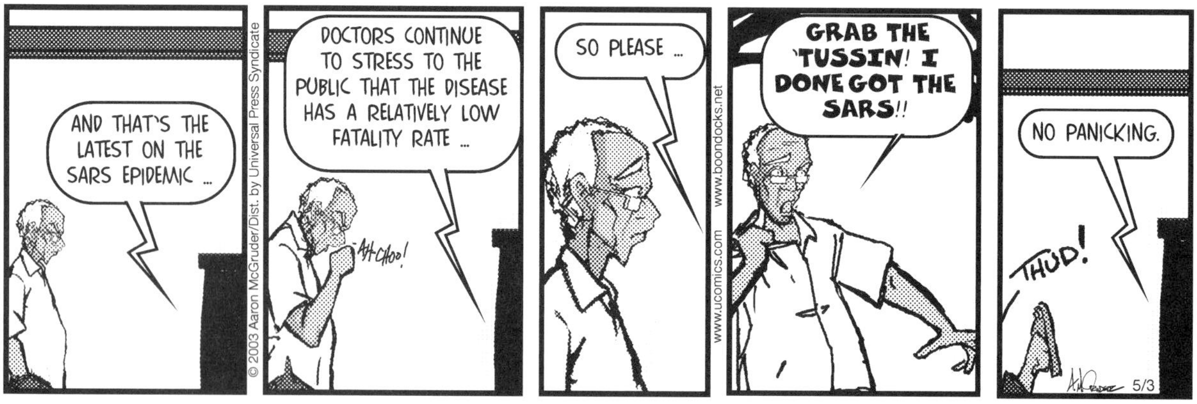
AND THAT'S THE LATEST ON THE SARS EPIDEMIC ...
© 2003 Aaron McGruder/Dist. by Universal Press Syndicate
DOCTORS CONTINUE TO STRESS TO THE PUBLIC THAT THE DISEASE HAS A RELATIVELY LOW FATALITY RATE ...
AH-CHOO!
SO PLEASE ...
www.ucomics.com www.boondocks.net
GRAB THE 'TUSSIN! I DONE GOT THE SARS!!
NO PANICKING.
THUD!
5/3

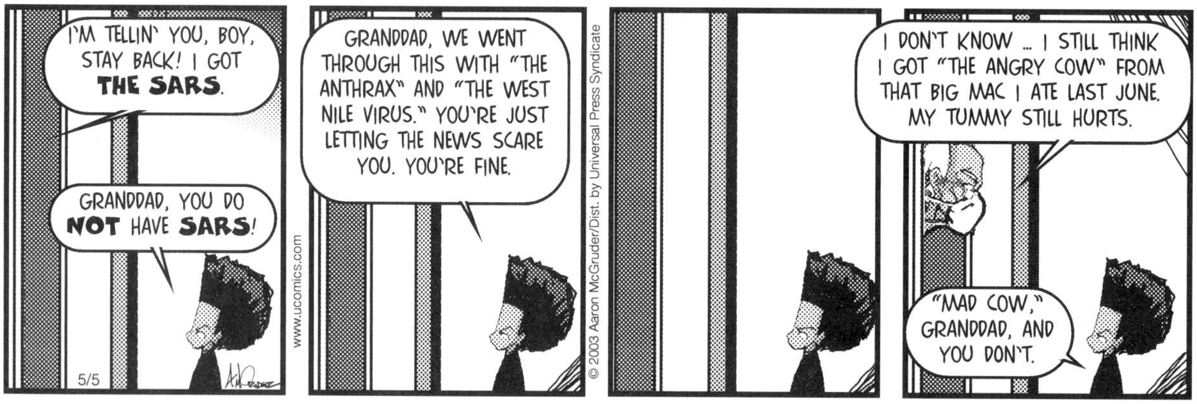
I'M TELLIN' YOU, BOY, STAY BACK! I GOT THE SARS.
GRANDDAD, YOU DO NOT HAVE SARS!
5/5
www.ucomics.com
GRANDDAD, WE WENT THROUGH THIS WITH "THE ANTHRAX" AND "THE WEST NILE VIRUS." YOU'RE JUST LETTING THE NEWS SCARE YOU. YOU'RE FINE.
© 2003 Aaron McGruder/Dist. by Universal Press Syndicate
I DON'T KNOW ... I STILL THINK I GOT "THE ANGRY COW" FROM THAT BIG MAC I ATE LAST JUNE. MY TUMMY STILL HURTS.
"MAD COW," GRANDDAD, AND YOU DON'T.

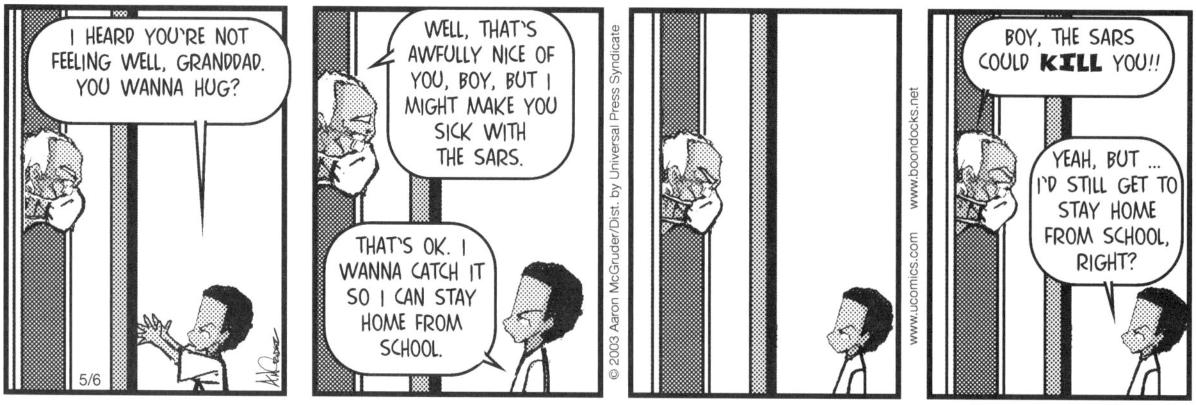
I HEARD YOU'RE NOT FEELING WELL, GRANDDAD. YOU WANNA HUG?
5/6
WELL, THAT'S AWFULLY NICE OF YOU, BOY, BUT I MIGHT MAKE YOU SICK WITH THE SARS.
THAT'S OK. I WANNA CATCH IT SO I CAN STAY HOME FROM SCHOOL.
© 2003 Aaron McGruder/Dist. by Universal Press Syndicate
www.ucomics.com www.boondocks.net
BOY, THE SARS COULD KILL YOU!!
YEAH, BUT ... I'D STILL GET TO STAY HOME FROM SCHOOL, RIGHT?

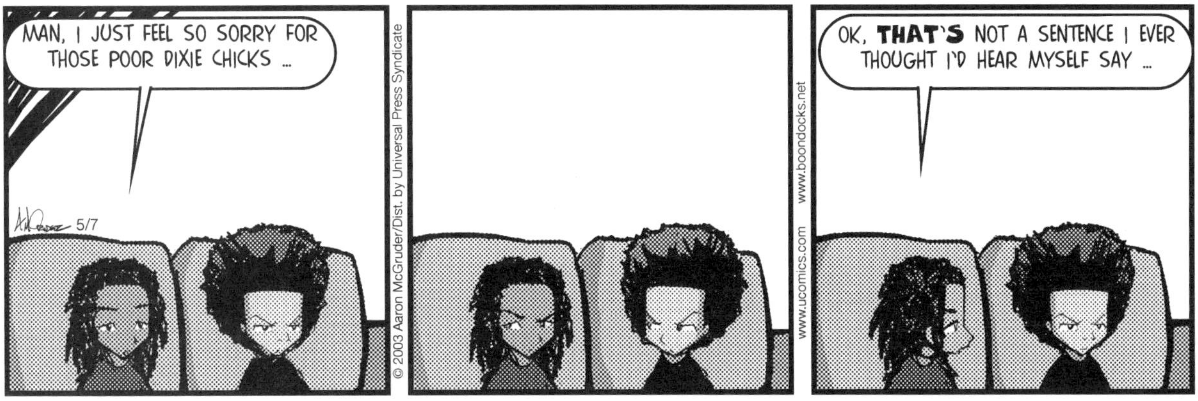
MAN, I JUST FEEL SO SORRY FOR THOSE POOR DIXIE CHICKS ...
5/7
© 2003 Aaron McGruder/Dist. by Universal Press Syndicate
OK, **THAT'S** NOT A SENTENCE I EVER THOUGHT I'D HEAR MYSELF SAY ...
www.ucomics.com www.boondocks.net

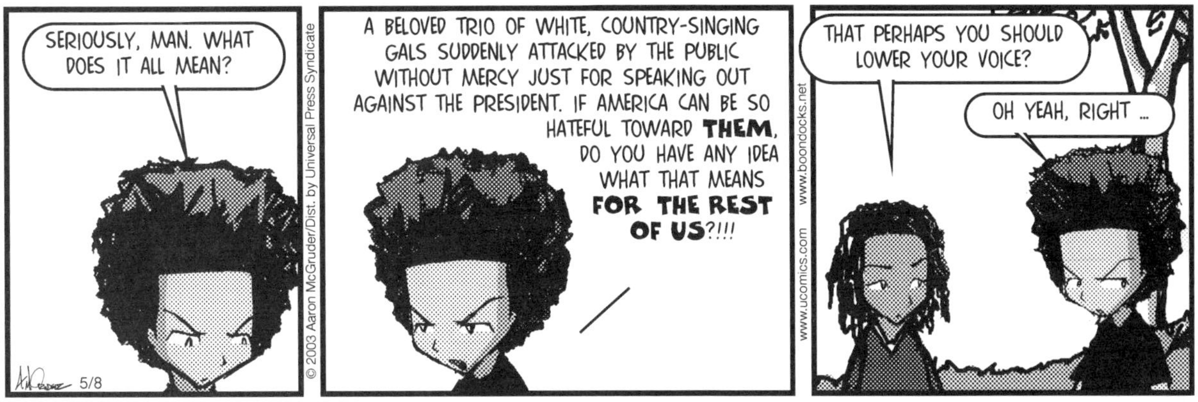
SERIOUSLY, MAN. WHAT DOES IT ALL MEAN?
5/8
© 2003 Aaron McGruder/Dist. by Universal Press Syndicate
A BELOVED TRIO OF WHITE, COUNTRY-SINGING GALS SUDDENLY ATTACKED BY THE PUBLIC WITHOUT MERCY JUST FOR SPEAKING OUT AGAINST THE PRESIDENT. IF AMERICA CAN BE SO HATEFUL TOWARD **THEM**, DO YOU HAVE ANY IDEA WHAT THAT MEANS **FOR THE REST OF US**?!!!
THAT PERHAPS YOU SHOULD LOWER YOUR VOICE?
OH YEAH, RIGHT ...
www.ucomics.com www.boondocks.net

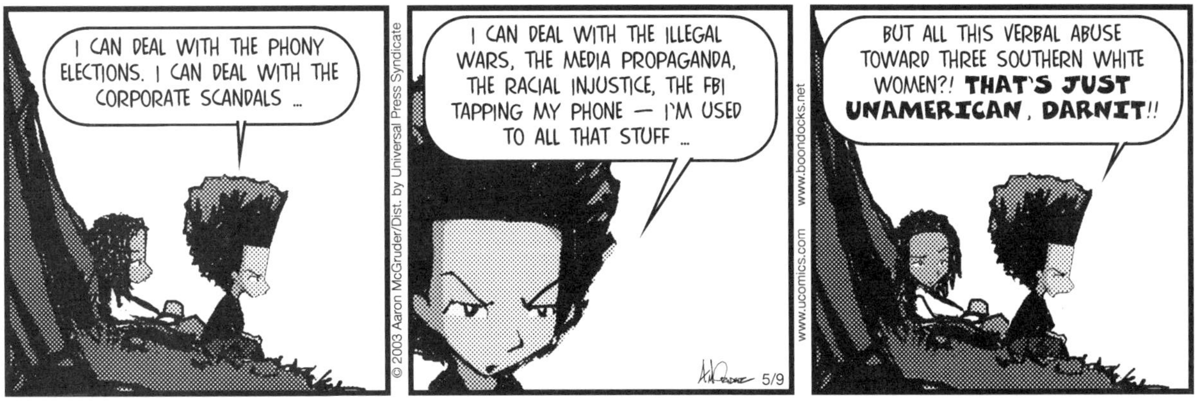
I CAN DEAL WITH THE PHONY ELECTIONS. I CAN DEAL WITH THE CORPORATE SCANDALS ...
© 2003 Aaron McGruder/Dist. by Universal Press Syndicate
I CAN DEAL WITH THE ILLEGAL WARS, THE MEDIA PROPAGANDA, THE RACIAL INJUSTICE, THE FBI TAPPING MY PHONE — I'M USED TO ALL THAT STUFF ...
5/9
BUT ALL THIS VERBAL ABUSE TOWARD THREE SOUTHERN WHITE WOMEN?! **THAT'S JUST UNAMERICAN, DARNIT**!!
www.ucomics.com www.boondocks.net

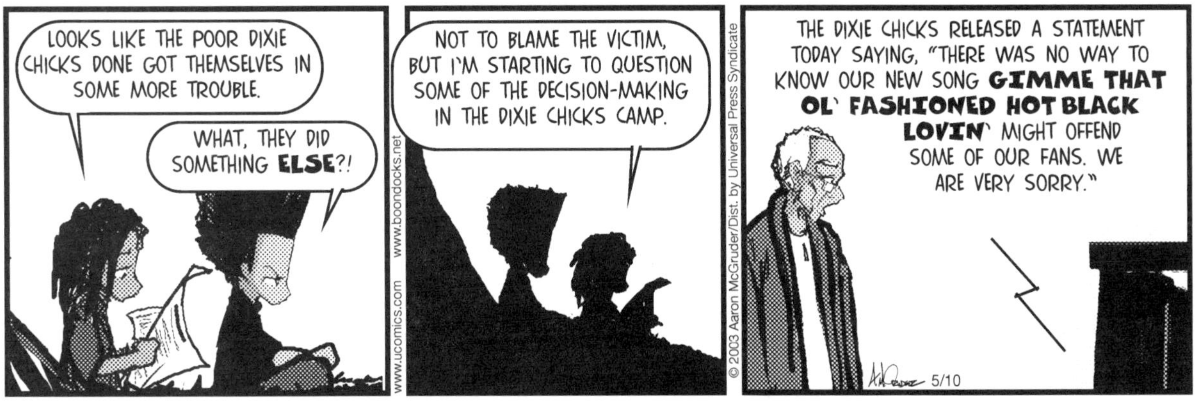
LOOKS LIKE THE POOR DIXIE CHICKS DONE GOT THEMSELVES IN SOME MORE TROUBLE.
WHAT, THEY DID SOMETHING **ELSE**?!
www.ucomics.com www.boondocks.net
NOT TO BLAME THE VICTIM, BUT I'M STARTING TO QUESTION SOME OF THE DECISION-MAKING IN THE DIXIE CHICKS CAMP.
© 2003 Aaron McGruder/Dist. by Universal Press Syndicate
THE DIXIE CHICKS RELEASED A STATEMENT TODAY SAYING, "THERE WAS NO WAY TO KNOW OUR NEW SONG **GIMME THAT OL' FASHIONED HOT BLACK LOVIN'** MIGHT OFFEND SOME OF OUR FANS. WE ARE VERY SORRY."
5/10

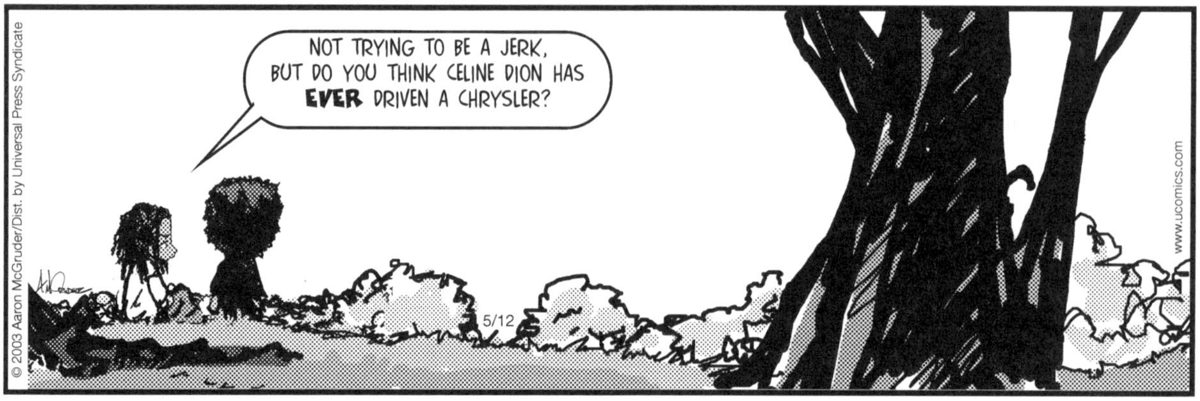
NOT TRYING TO BE A JERK, BUT DO YOU THINK CELINE DION HAS **EVER** DRIVEN A CHRYSLER?
5/12
© 2003 Aaron McGruder/Dist. by Universal Press Syndicate
www.ucomics.com

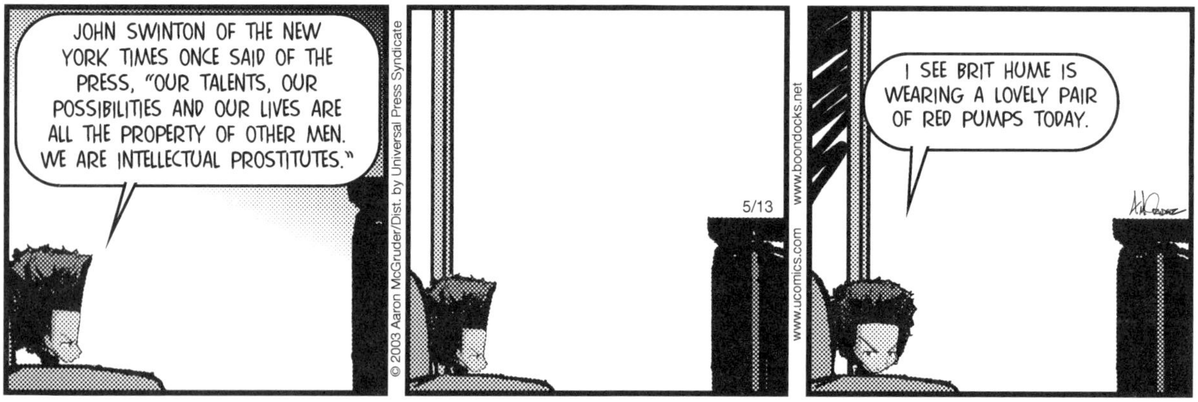
JOHN SWINTON OF THE NEW YORK TIMES ONCE SAID OF THE PRESS, "OUR TALENTS, OUR POSSIBILITIES AND OUR LIVES ARE ALL THE PROPERTY OF OTHER MEN. WE ARE INTELLECTUAL PROSTITUTES."
I SEE BRIT HUME IS WEARING A LOVELY PAIR OF RED PUMPS TODAY.
5/13
© 2003 Aaron McGruder/Dist. by Universal Press Syndicate
www.boondocks.net
www.ucomics.com

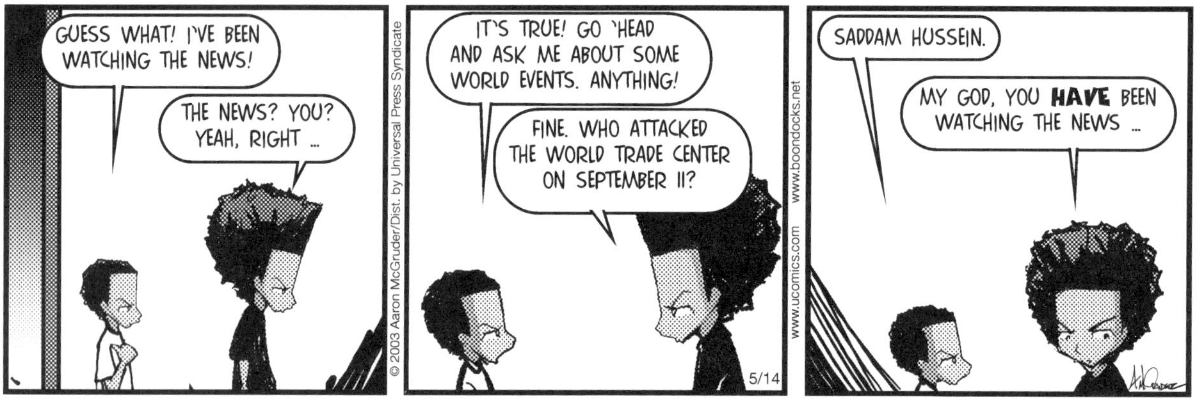
GUESS WHAT! I'VE BEEN WATCHING THE NEWS!
THE NEWS? YOU? YEAH, RIGHT ...
IT'S TRUE! GO 'HEAD AND ASK ME ABOUT SOME WORLD EVENTS. ANYTHING!
FINE. WHO ATTACKED THE WORLD TRADE CENTER ON SEPTEMBER 11?
SADDAM HUSSEIN.
MY GOD, YOU **HAVE** BEEN WATCHING THE NEWS ...
5/14
© 2003 Aaron McGruder/Dist. by Universal Press Syndicate
www.boondocks.net
www.ucomics.com

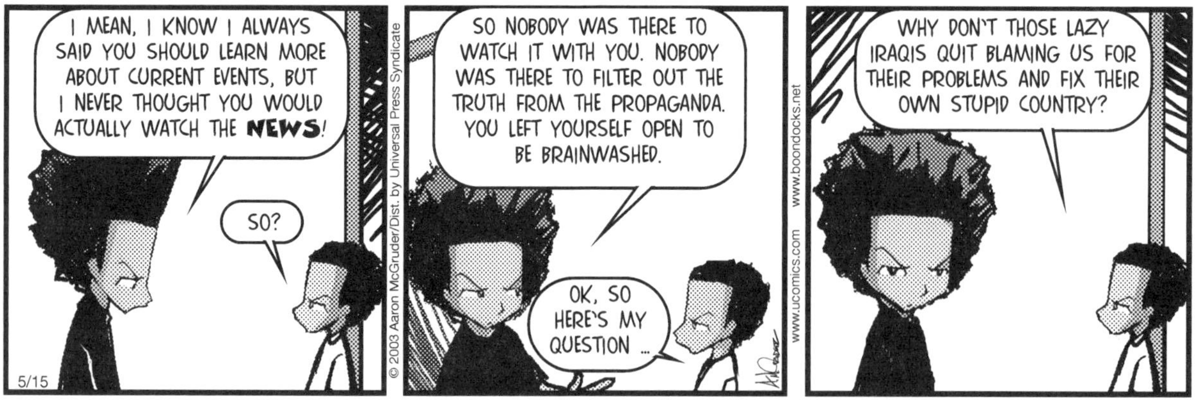
I MEAN, I KNOW I ALWAYS SAID YOU SHOULD LEARN MORE ABOUT CURRENT EVENTS, BUT I NEVER THOUGHT YOU WOULD ACTUALLY WATCH THE **NEWS**!
SO?
SO NOBODY WAS THERE TO WATCH IT WITH YOU. NOBODY WAS THERE TO FILTER OUT THE TRUTH FROM THE PROPAGANDA. YOU LEFT YOURSELF OPEN TO BE BRAINWASHED.
OK, SO HERE'S MY QUESTION ...
WHY DON'T THOSE LAZY IRAQIS QUIT BLAMING US FOR THEIR PROBLEMS AND FIX THEIR OWN STUPID COUNTRY?
5/15
© 2003 Aaron McGruder/Dist. by Universal Press Syndicate
www.boondocks.net
www.ucomics.com

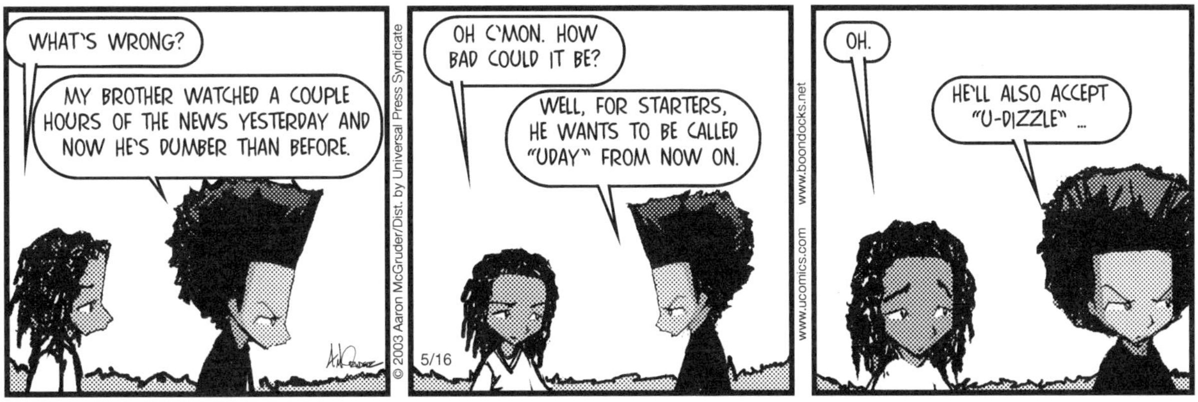
WHAT'S WRONG?
MY BROTHER WATCHED A COUPLE HOURS OF THE NEWS YESTERDAY AND NOW HE'S DUMBER THAN BEFORE.
OH C'MON. HOW BAD COULD IT BE?
WELL, FOR STARTERS, HE WANTS TO BE CALLED "UDAY" FROM NOW ON.
OH.
HE'LL ALSO ACCEPT "U-DIZZLE" ...
5/16
© 2003 Aaron McGruder/Dist. by Universal Press Syndicate
www.ucomics.com www.boondocks.net

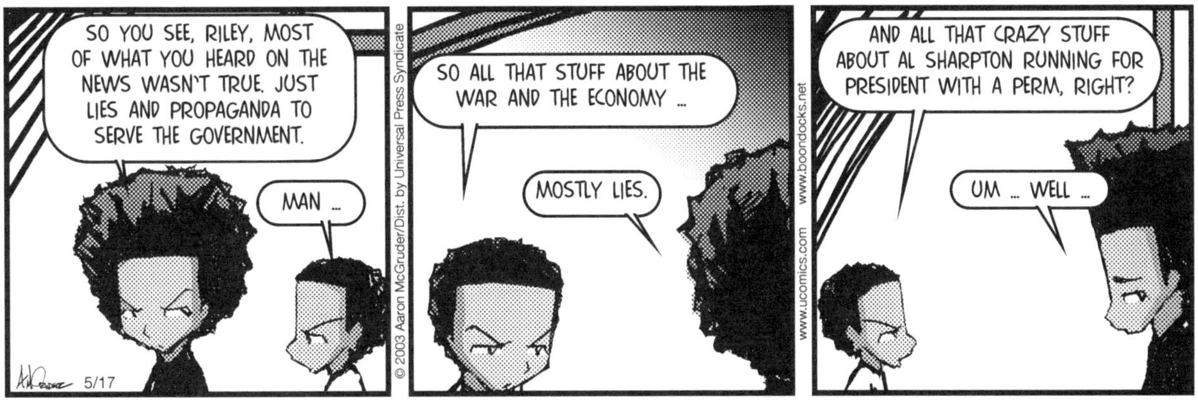
SO YOU SEE, RILEY, MOST OF WHAT YOU HEARD ON THE NEWS WASN'T TRUE. JUST LIES AND PROPAGANDA TO SERVE THE GOVERNMENT.
MAN ...
SO ALL THAT STUFF ABOUT THE WAR AND THE ECONOMY ...
MOSTLY LIES.
AND ALL THAT CRAZY STUFF ABOUT AL SHARPTON RUNNING FOR PRESIDENT WITH A PERM, RIGHT?
UM ... WELL ...
5/17
© 2003 Aaron McGruder/Dist. by Universal Press Syndicate
www.ucomics.com www.boondocks.net

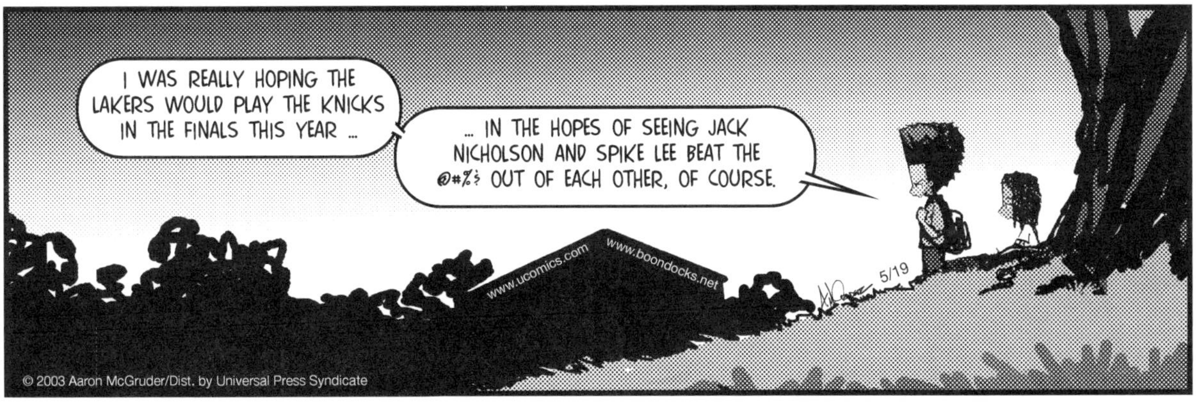
I WAS REALLY HOPING THE LAKERS WOULD PLAY THE KNICKS IN THE FINALS THIS YEAR ...
... IN THE HOPES OF SEEING JACK NICHOLSON AND SPIKE LEE BEAT THE @#%$ OUT OF EACH OTHER, OF COURSE.
www.ucomics.com www.boondocks.net
5/19
© 2003 Aaron McGruder/Dist. by Universal Press Syndicate

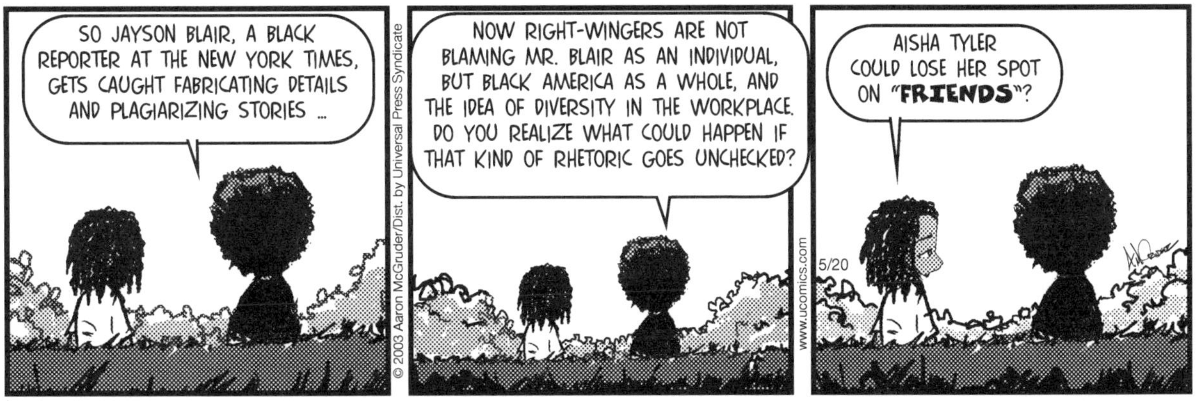
SO JAYSON BLAIR, A BLACK REPORTER AT THE NEW YORK TIMES, GETS CAUGHT FABRICATING DETAILS AND PLAGIARIZING STORIES ...
NOW RIGHT-WINGERS ARE NOT BLAMING MR. BLAIR AS AN INDIVIDUAL, BUT BLACK AMERICA AS A WHOLE, AND THE IDEA OF DIVERSITY IN THE WORKPLACE. DO YOU REALIZE WHAT COULD HAPPEN IF THAT KIND OF RHETORIC GOES UNCHECKED?
AISHA TYLER COULD LOSE HER SPOT ON "FRIENDS"?
5/20
© 2003 Aaron McGruder/Dist. by Universal Press Syndicate
www.ucomics.com

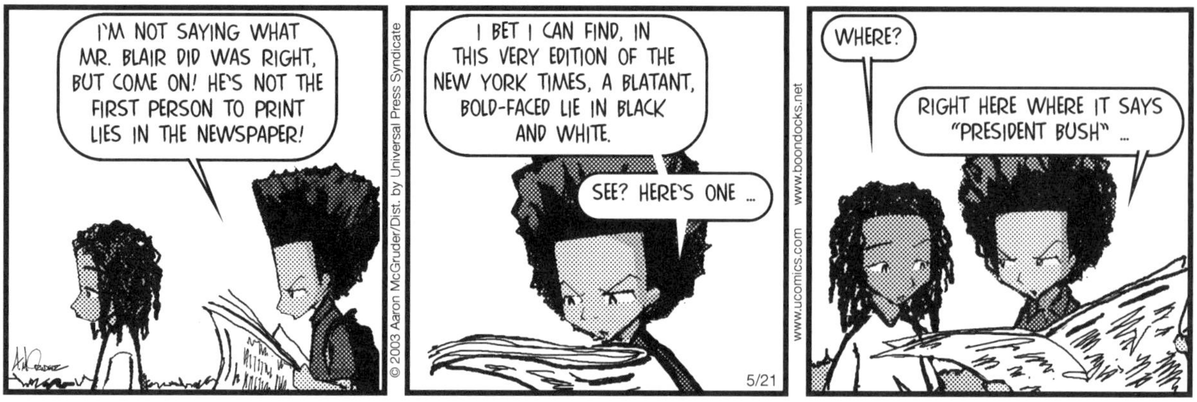
I'M NOT SAYING WHAT MR. BLAIR DID WAS RIGHT, BUT COME ON! HE'S NOT THE FIRST PERSON TO PRINT LIES IN THE NEWSPAPER!
© 2003 Aaron McGruder/Dist. by Universal Press Syndicate
I BET I CAN FIND, IN THIS VERY EDITION OF THE NEW YORK TIMES, A BLATANT, BOLD-FACED LIE IN BLACK AND WHITE.
SEE? HERE'S ONE ...
5/21
www.ucomics.com www.boondocks.net
WHERE?
RIGHT HERE WHERE IT SAYS "PRESIDENT BUSH" ...

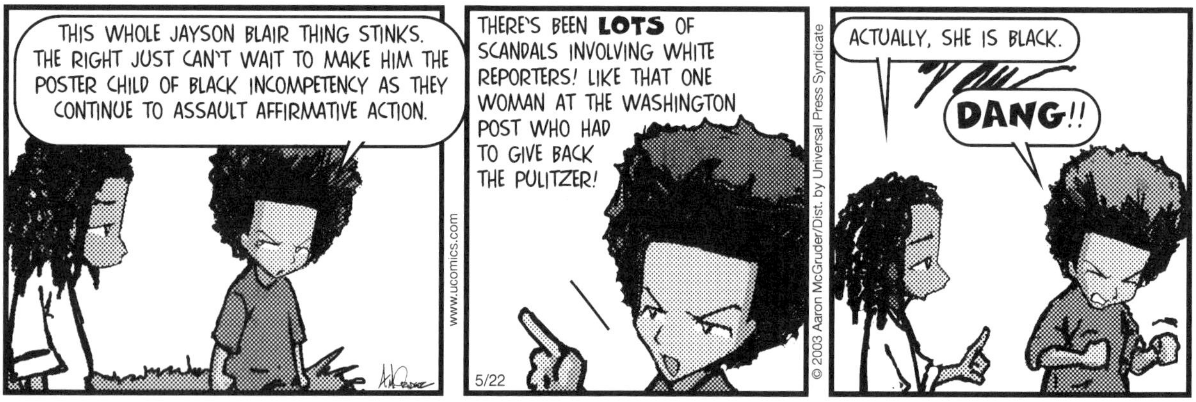
THIS WHOLE JAYSON BLAIR THING STINKS. THE RIGHT JUST CAN'T WAIT TO MAKE HIM THE POSTER CHILD OF BLACK INCOMPETENCY AS THEY CONTINUE TO ASSAULT AFFIRMATIVE ACTION.
www.ucomics.com
THERE'S BEEN LOTS OF SCANDALS INVOLVING WHITE REPORTERS! LIKE THAT ONE WOMAN AT THE WASHINGTON POST WHO HAD TO GIVE BACK THE PULITZER!
5/22
© 2003 Aaron McGruder/Dist. by Universal Press Syndicate
ACTUALLY, SHE IS BLACK.
DANG!!

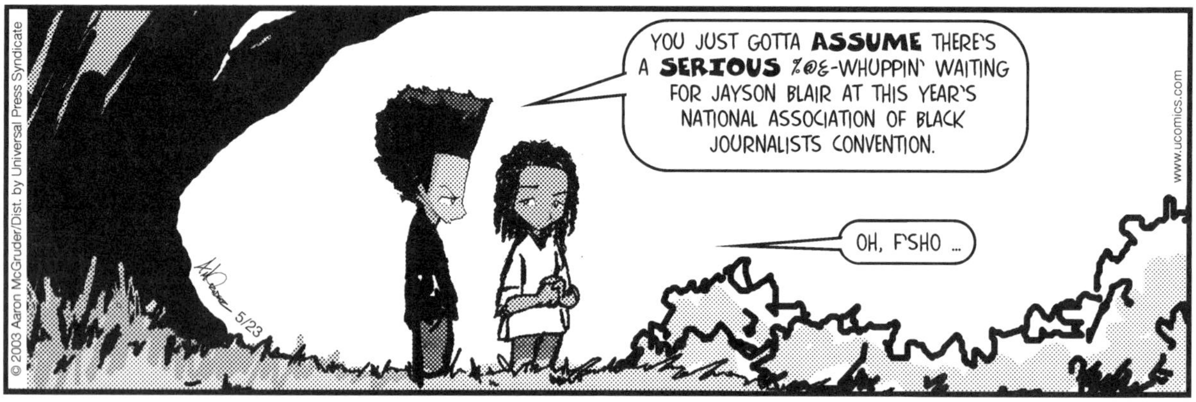
© 2003 Aaron McGruder/Dist. by Universal Press Syndicate
YOU JUST GOTTA ASSUME THERE'S A SERIOUS %@&-WHUPPIN' WAITING FOR JAYSON BLAIR AT THIS YEAR'S NATIONAL ASSOCIATION OF BLACK JOURNALISTS CONVENTION.
OH, F'SHO ...
5/23
www.ucomics.com

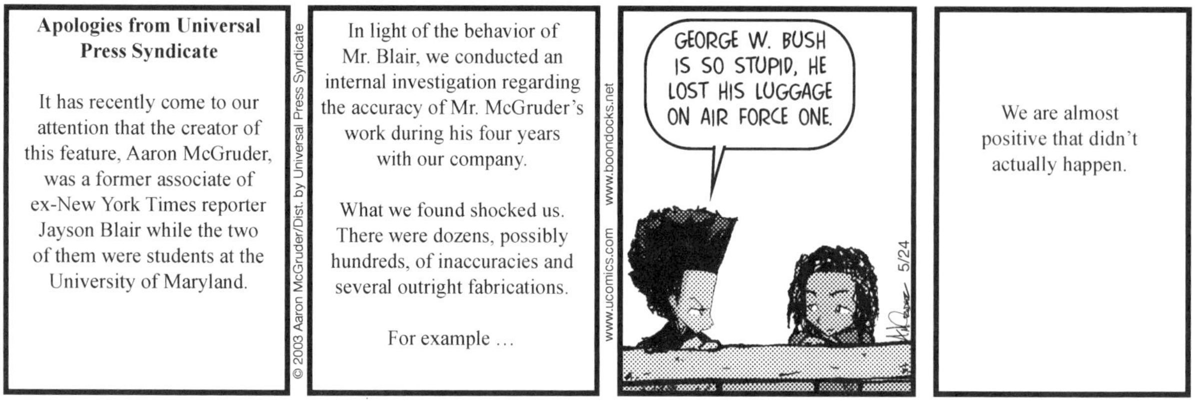
Apologies from Universal Press Syndicate
It has recently come to our attention that the creator of this feature, Aaron McGruder, was a former associate of ex-New York Times reporter Jayson Blair while the two of them were students at the University of Maryland.
© 2003 Aaron McGruder/Dist. by Universal Press Syndicate
In light of the behavior of Mr. Blair, we conducted an internal investigation regarding the accuracy of Mr. McGruder's work during his four years with our company.
What we found shocked us. There were dozens, possibly hundreds, of inaccuracies and several outright fabrications.
For example ...
www.ucomics.com www.boondocks.net
GEORGE W. BUSH IS SO STUPID, HE LOST HIS LUGGAGE ON AIR FORCE ONE.
5/24
We are almost positive that didn't actually happen.

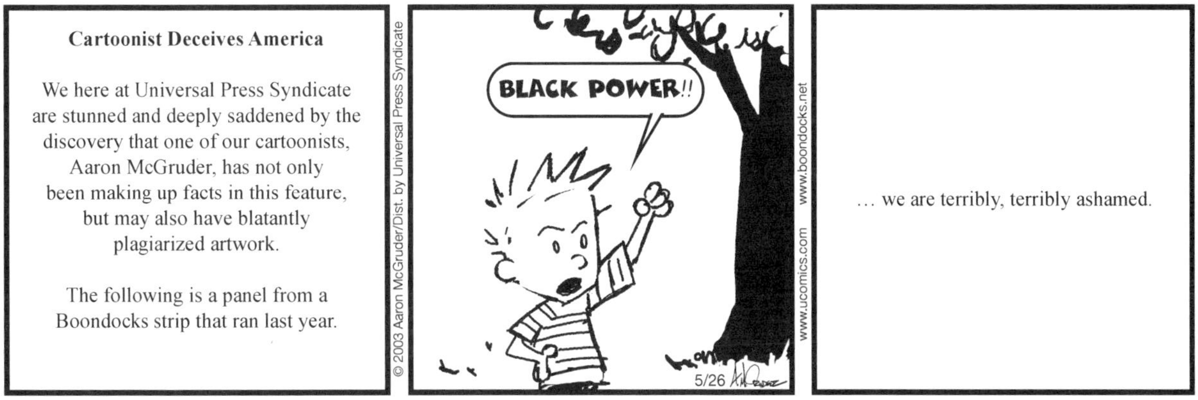
Cartoonist Deceives America
We here at Universal Press Syndicate are stunned and deeply saddened by the discovery that one of our cartoonists, Aaron McGruder, has not only been making up facts in this feature, but may also have blatantly plagiarized artwork.
The following is a panel from a Boondocks strip that ran last year.
© 2003 Aaron McGruder/Dist. by Universal Press Syndicate
BLACK POWER!!
www.ucomics.com www.boondocks.net
5/26
… we are terribly, terribly ashamed.

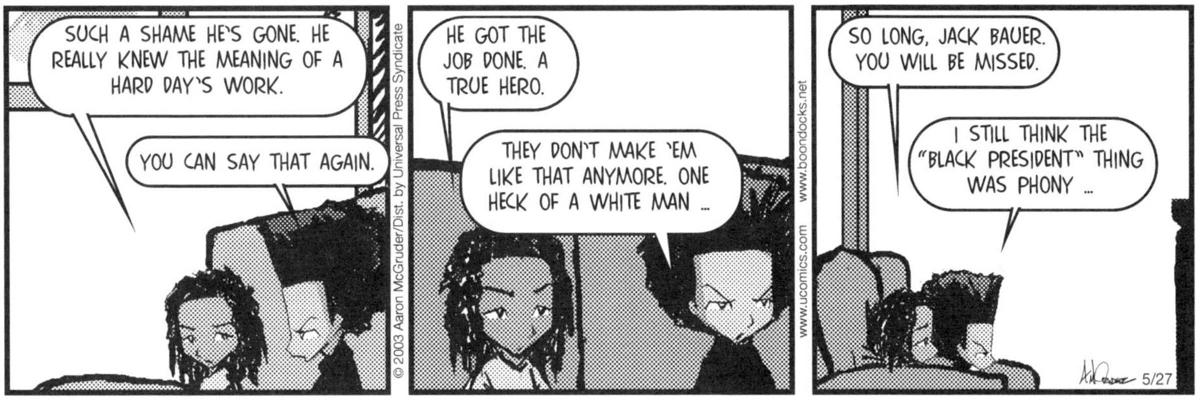
SUCH A SHAME HE'S GONE. HE REALLY KNEW THE MEANING OF A HARD DAY'S WORK.
YOU CAN SAY THAT AGAIN.
© 2003 Aaron McGruder/Dist. by Universal Press Syndicate
HE GOT THE JOB DONE. A TRUE HERO.
THEY DON'T MAKE 'EM LIKE THAT ANYMORE. ONE HECK OF A WHITE MAN …
www.ucomics.com www.boondocks.net
SO LONG, JACK BAUER. YOU WILL BE MISSED.
I STILL THINK THE "BLACK PRESIDENT" THING WAS PHONY …
5/27

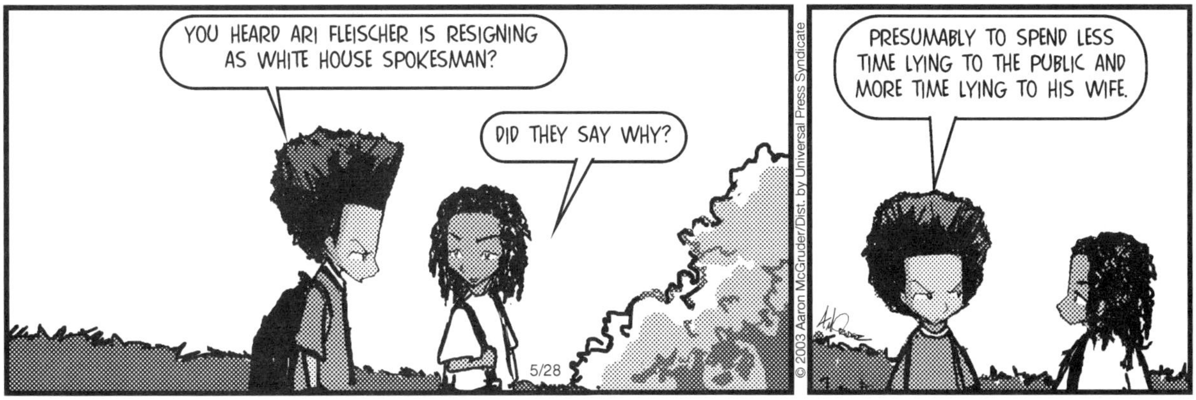
YOU HEARD ARI FLEISCHER IS RESIGNING AS WHITE HOUSE SPOKESMAN?
DID THEY SAY WHY?
5/28
© 2003 Aaron McGruder/Dist. by Universal Press Syndicate
PRESUMABLY TO SPEND LESS TIME LYING TO THE PUBLIC AND MORE TIME LYING TO HIS WIFE.

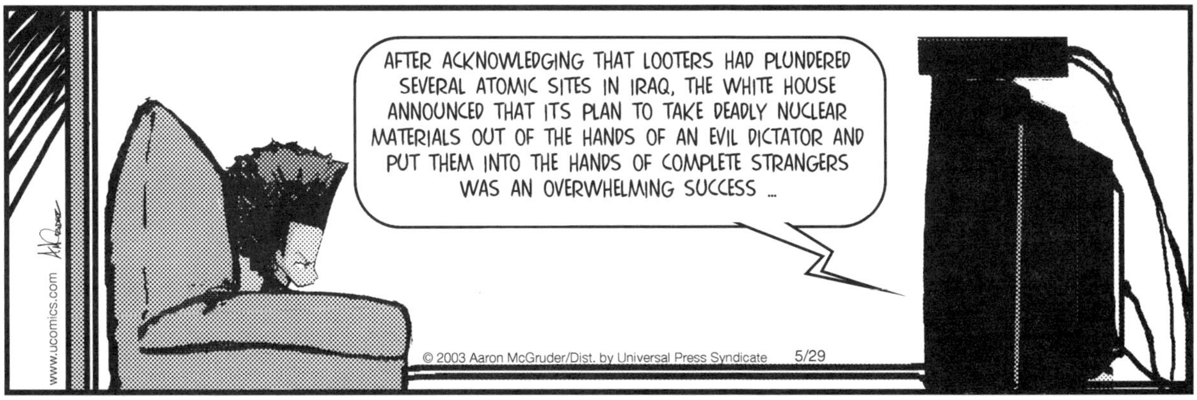
AFTER ACKNOWLEDGING THAT LOOTERS HAD PLUNDERED SEVERAL ATOMIC SITES IN IRAQ, THE WHITE HOUSE ANNOUNCED THAT ITS PLAN TO TAKE DEADLY NUCLEAR MATERIALS OUT OF THE HANDS OF AN EVIL DICTATOR AND PUT THEM INTO THE HANDS OF COMPLETE STRANGERS WAS AN OVERWHELMING SUCCESS …
www.ucomics.com
© 2003 Aaron McGruder/Dist. by Universal Press Syndicate 5/29

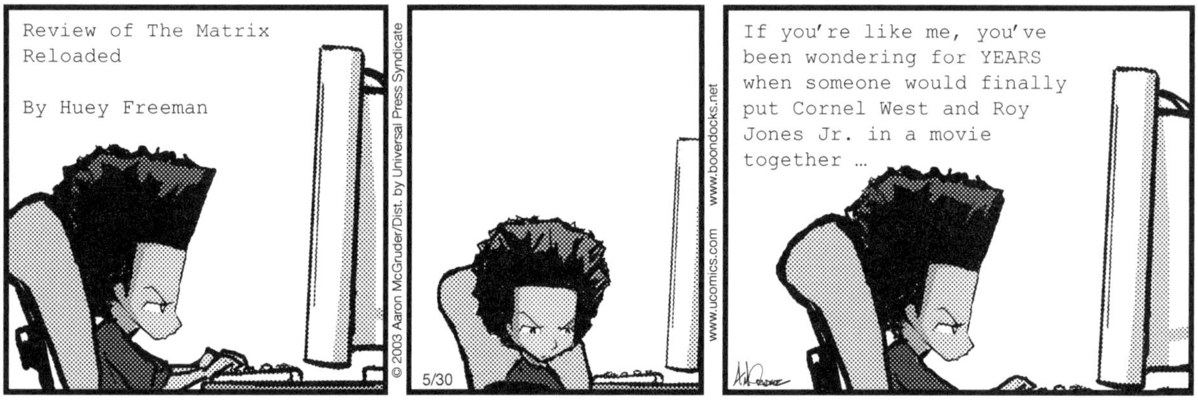
Review of The Matrix Reloaded
By Huey Freeman
© 2003 Aaron McGruder/Dist. by Universal Press Syndicate
5/30
www.ucomics.com www.boondocks.net
If you're like me, you've been wondering for YEARS when someone would finally put Cornel West and Roy Jones Jr. in a movie together …

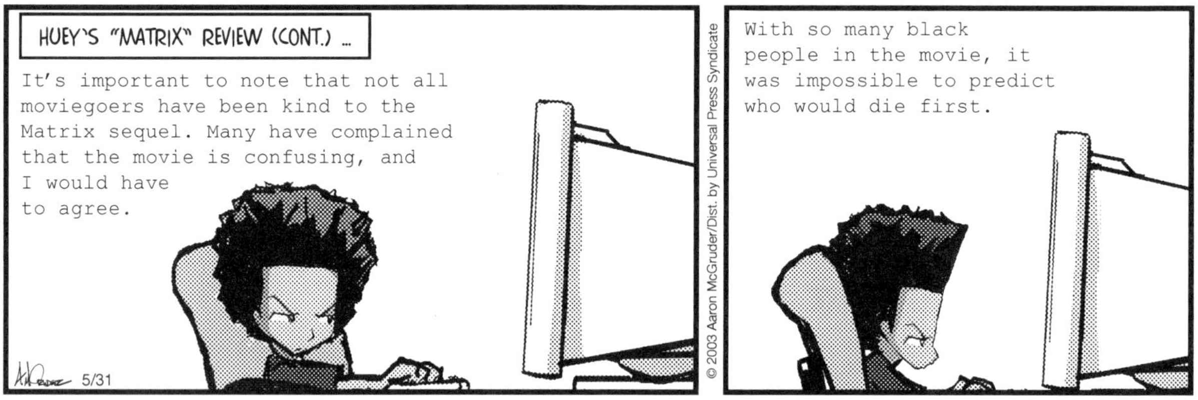
HUEY'S "MATRIX" REVIEW (CONT.) …
It's important to note that not all moviegoers have been kind to the Matrix sequel. Many have complained that the movie is confusing, and I would have to agree.
5/31
© 2003 Aaron McGruder/Dist. by Universal Press Syndicate
With so many black people in the movie, it was impossible to predict who would die first.

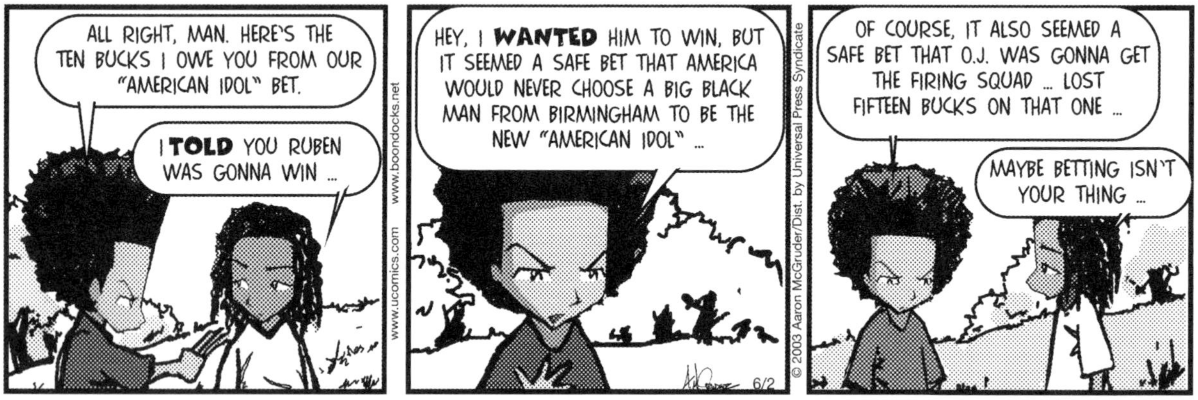
ALL RIGHT, MAN. HERE'S THE TEN BUCKS I OWE YOU FROM OUR "AMERICAN IDOL" BET.
I **TOLD** YOU RUBEN WAS GONNA WIN …
www.ucomics.com www.boondocks.net
HEY, I **WANTED** HIM TO WIN, BUT IT SEEMED A SAFE BET THAT AMERICA WOULD NEVER CHOOSE A BIG BLACK MAN FROM BIRMINGHAM TO BE THE NEW "AMERICAN IDOL" …
6/2
© 2003 Aaron McGruder/Dist. by Universal Press Syndicate
OF COURSE, IT ALSO SEEMED A SAFE BET THAT O.J. WAS GONNA GET THE FIRING SQUAD … LOST FIFTEEN BUCKS ON THAT ONE …
MAYBE BETTING ISN'T YOUR THING …

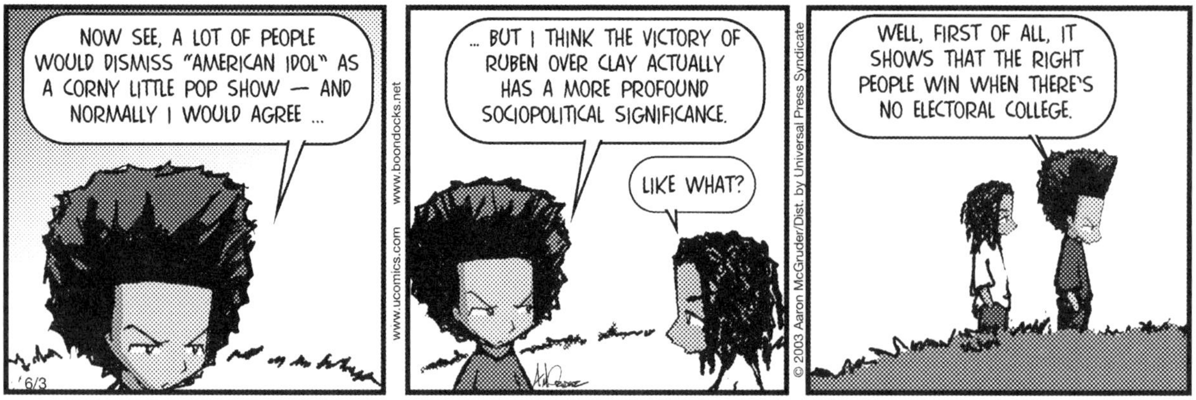
NOW SEE, A LOT OF PEOPLE WOULD DISMISS "AMERICAN IDOL" AS A CORNY LITTLE POP SHOW — AND NORMALLY I WOULD AGREE …
6/3
www.ucomics.com www.boondocks.net
… BUT I THINK THE VICTORY OF RUBEN OVER CLAY ACTUALLY HAS A MORE PROFOUND SOCIOPOLITICAL SIGNIFICANCE.
LIKE WHAT?
© 2003 Aaron McGruder/Dist. by Universal Press Syndicate
WELL, FIRST OF ALL, IT SHOWS THAT THE RIGHT PEOPLE WIN WHEN THERE'S NO ELECTORAL COLLEGE.

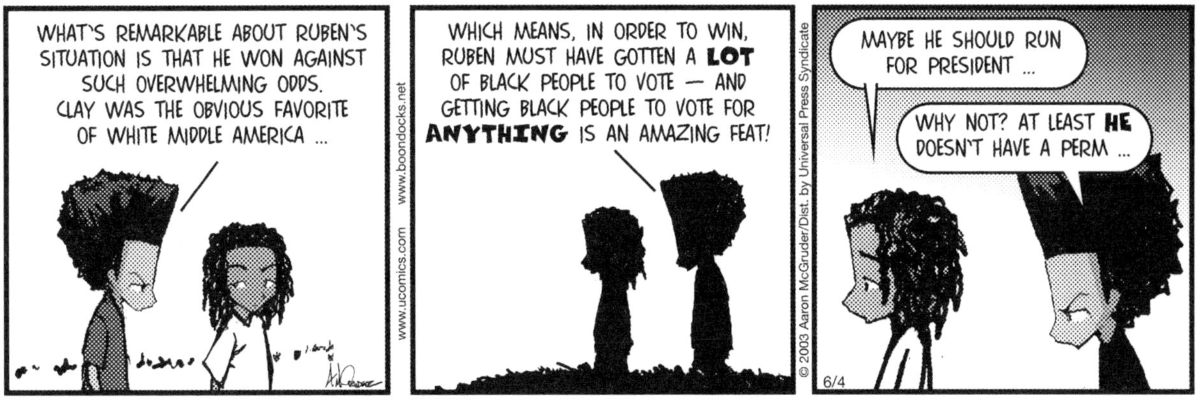
WHAT'S REMARKABLE ABOUT RUBEN'S SITUATION IS THAT HE WON AGAINST SUCH OVERWHELMING ODDS. CLAY WAS THE OBVIOUS FAVORITE OF WHITE MIDDLE AMERICA ...
WHICH MEANS, IN ORDER TO WIN, RUBEN MUST HAVE GOTTEN A **LOT** OF BLACK PEOPLE TO VOTE — AND GETTING BLACK PEOPLE TO VOTE FOR **ANYTHING** IS AN AMAZING FEAT!
MAYBE HE SHOULD RUN FOR PRESIDENT ...
WHY NOT? AT LEAST **HE** DOESN'T HAVE A PERM ...
www.ucomics.com www.boondocks.net
© 2003 Aaron McGruder/Dist. by Universal Press Syndicate
6/4

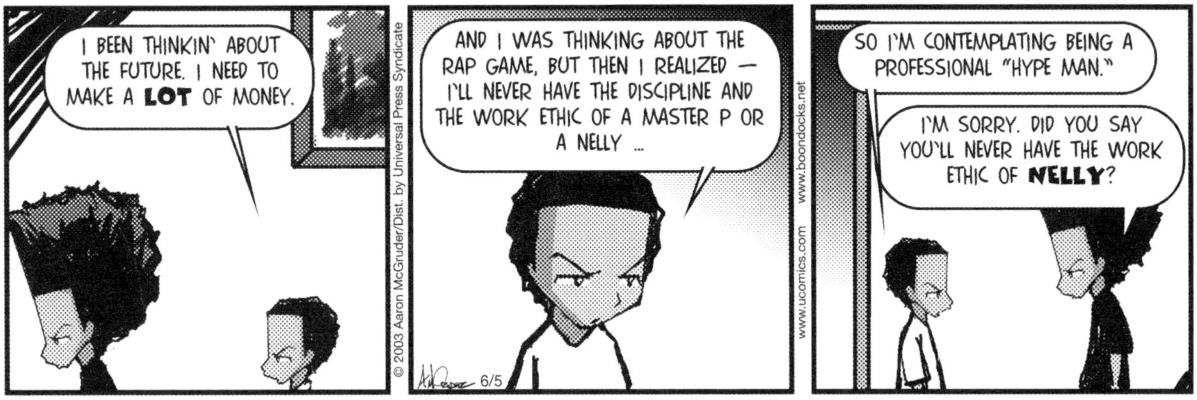
I BEEN THINKIN' ABOUT THE FUTURE. I NEED TO MAKE A **LOT** OF MONEY.
AND I WAS THINKING ABOUT THE RAP GAME, BUT THEN I REALIZED — I'LL NEVER HAVE THE DISCIPLINE AND THE WORK ETHIC OF A MASTER P OR A NELLY ...
SO I'M CONTEMPLATING BEING A PROFESSIONAL "HYPE MAN."
I'M SORRY. DID YOU SAY YOU'LL NEVER HAVE THE WORK ETHIC OF **NELLY**?
© 2003 Aaron McGruder/Dist. by Universal Press Syndicate
6/5
www.ucomics.com www.boondocks.net

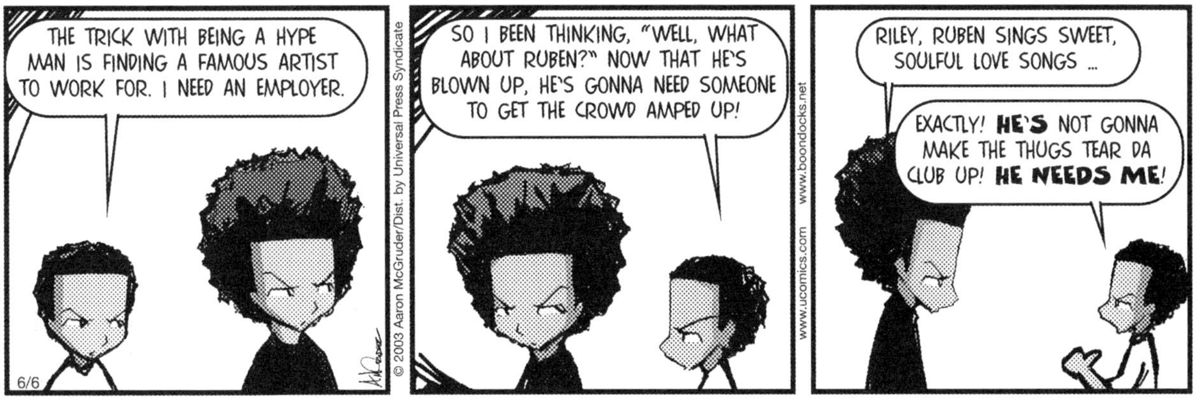
THE TRICK WITH BEING A HYPE MAN IS FINDING A FAMOUS ARTIST TO WORK FOR. I NEED AN EMPLOYER.
6/6
SO I BEEN THINKING, "WELL, WHAT ABOUT RUBEN?" NOW THAT HE'S BLOWN UP, HE'S GONNA NEED SOMEONE TO GET THE CROWD AMPED UP!
© 2003 Aaron McGruder/Dist. by Universal Press Syndicate
RILEY, RUBEN SINGS SWEET, SOULFUL LOVE SONGS ...
EXACTLY! **HE'S** NOT GONNA MAKE THE THUGS TEAR DA CLUB UP! **HE NEEDS ME**!
www.ucomics.com www.boondocks.net

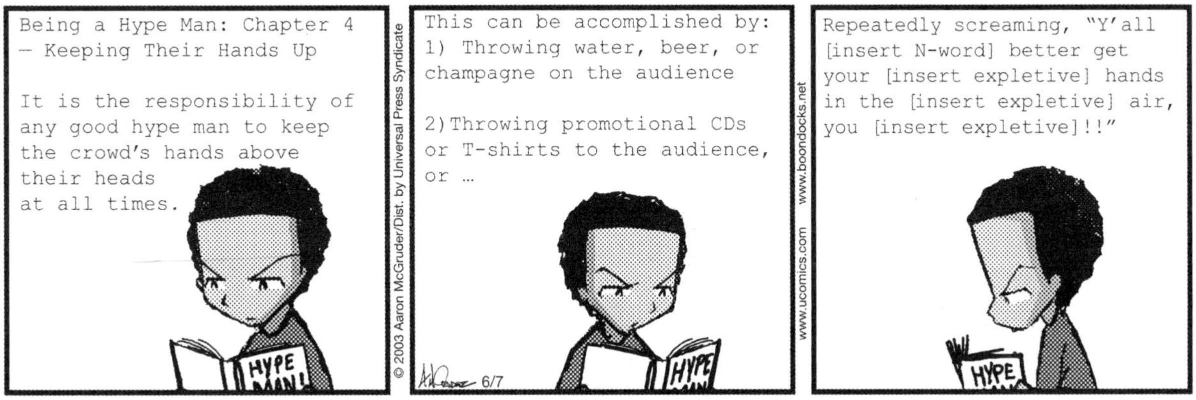
Being a Hype Man: Chapter 4 – Keeping Their Hands Up
It is the responsibility of any good hype man to keep the crowd's hands above their heads at all times.
HYPE MAN!
This can be accomplished by:
1) Throwing water, beer, or champagne on the audience
2)Throwing promotional CDs or T-shirts to the audience, or …
© 2003 Aaron McGruder/Dist. by Universal Press Syndicate
6/7
Repeatedly screaming, "Y'all [insert N-word] better get your [insert expletive] hands in the [insert expletive] air, you [insert expletive]!!"
www.ucomics.com www.boondocks.net

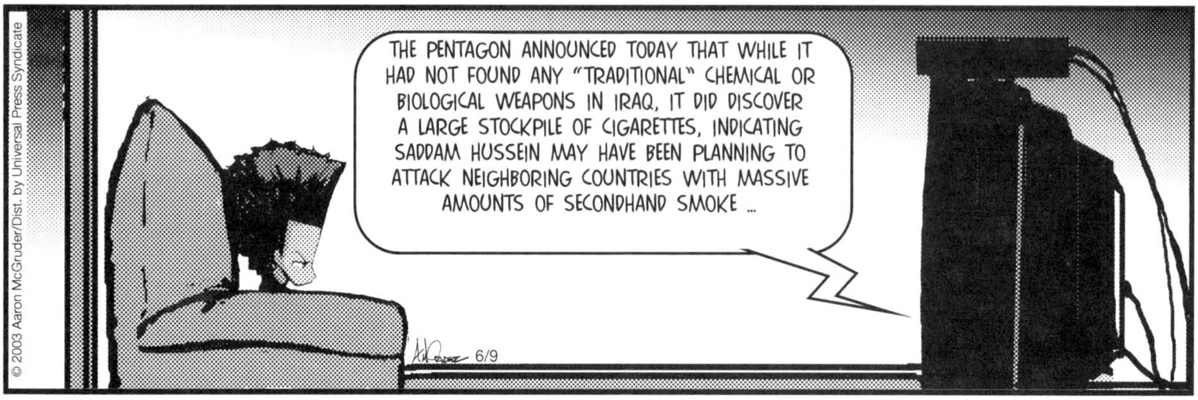
THE PENTAGON ANNOUNCED TODAY THAT WHILE IT HAD NOT FOUND ANY "TRADITIONAL" CHEMICAL OR BIOLOGICAL WEAPONS IN IRAQ, IT DID DISCOVER A LARGE STOCKPILE OF CIGARETTES, INDICATING SADDAM HUSSEIN MAY HAVE BEEN PLANNING TO ATTACK NEIGHBORING COUNTRIES WITH MASSIVE AMOUNTS OF SECONDHAND SMOKE ...
6/9
© 2003 Aaron McGruder/Dist. by Universal Press Syndicate

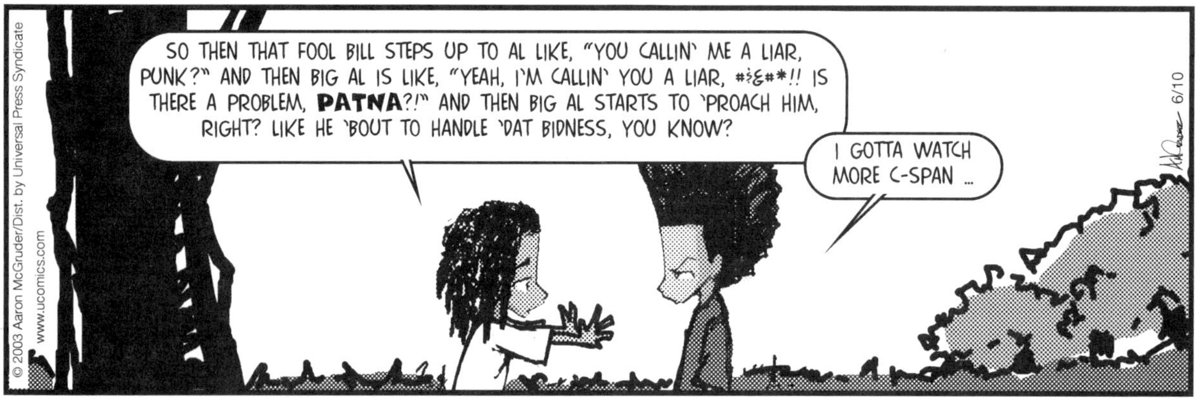
SO THEN THAT FOOL BILL STEPS UP TO AL LIKE, "YOU CALLIN' ME A LIAR, PUNK?" AND THEN BIG AL IS LIKE, "YEAH, I'M CALLIN' YOU A LIAR, #$&#*!! IS THERE A PROBLEM, **PATNA**?!" AND THEN BIG AL STARTS TO 'PROACH HIM, RIGHT? LIKE HE 'BOUT TO HANDLE 'DAT BIDNESS, YOU KNOW?
I GOTTA WATCH MORE C-SPAN ...
6/10
© 2003 Aaron McGruder/Dist. by Universal Press Syndicate
www.ucomics.com

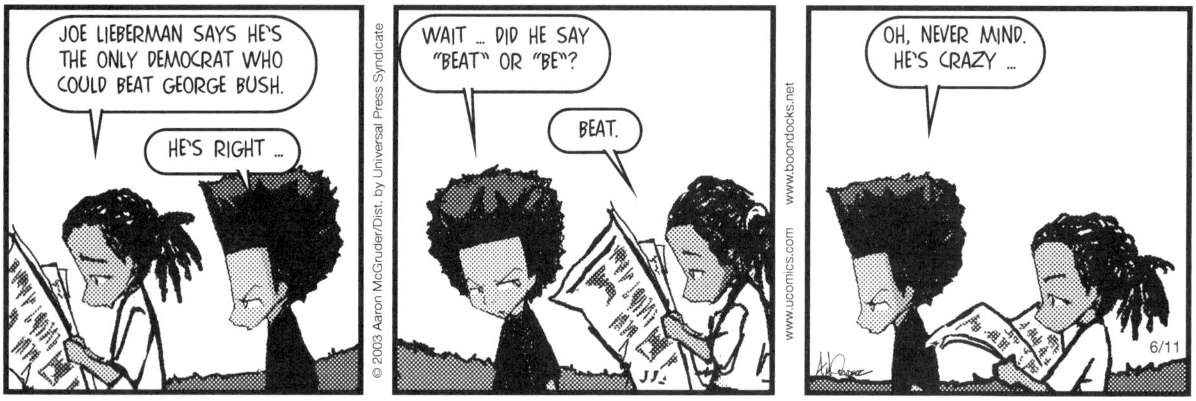
JOE LIEBERMAN SAYS HE'S THE ONLY DEMOCRAT WHO COULD BEAT GEORGE BUSH.
HE'S RIGHT ...
WAIT ... DID HE SAY "BEAT" OR "BE"?
BEAT.
OH, NEVER MIND. HE'S CRAZY ...
6/11
© 2003 Aaron McGruder/Dist. by Universal Press Syndicate
www.ucomics.com www.boondocks.net

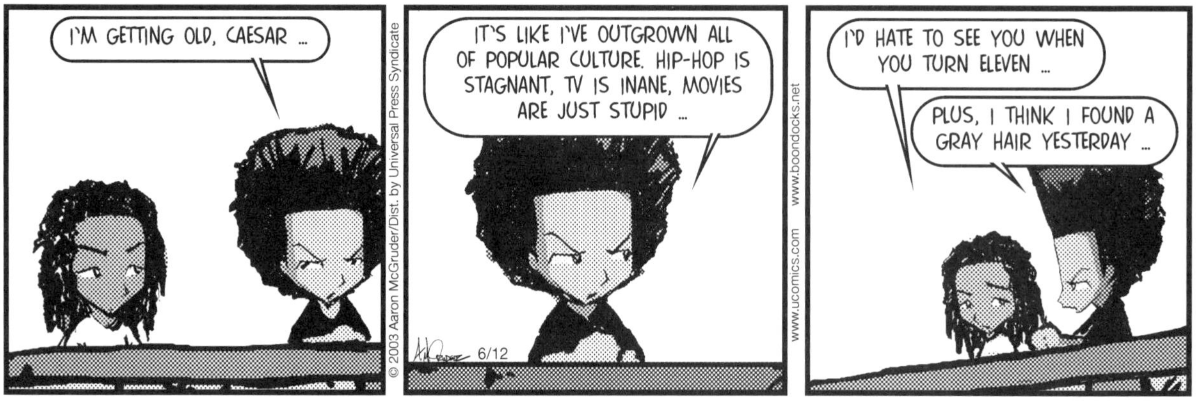
I'M GETTING OLD, CAESAR ...
IT'S LIKE I'VE OUTGROWN ALL OF POPULAR CULTURE. HIP-HOP IS STAGNANT, TV IS INANE, MOVIES ARE JUST STUPID ...
I'D HATE TO SEE YOU WHEN YOU TURN ELEVEN ...
PLUS, I THINK I FOUND A GRAY HAIR YESTERDAY ...
6/12
© 2003 Aaron McGruder/Dist. by Universal Press Syndicate
www.ucomics.com www.boondocks.net

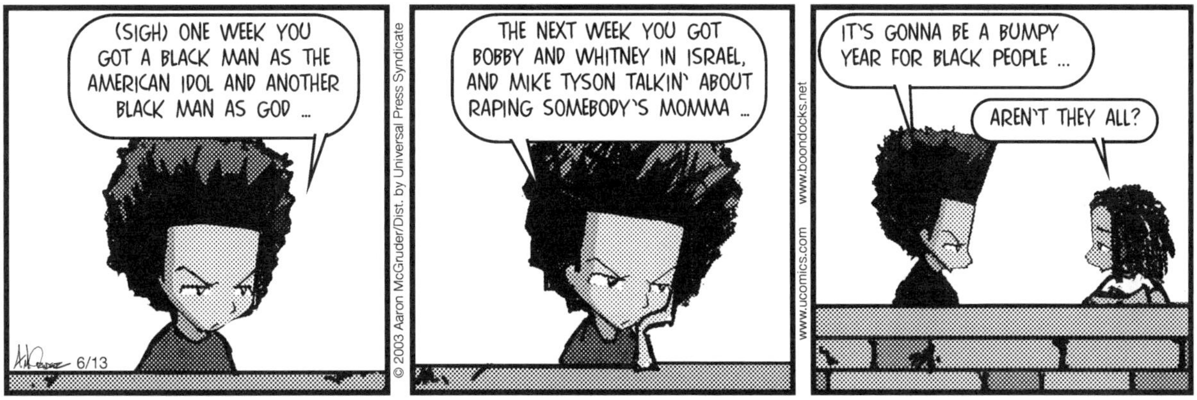
(SIGH) ONE WEEK YOU GOT A BLACK MAN AS THE AMERICAN IDOL AND ANOTHER BLACK MAN AS GOD ...
6/13
© 2003 Aaron McGruder/Dist. by Universal Press Syndicate
THE NEXT WEEK YOU GOT BOBBY AND WHITNEY IN ISRAEL, AND MIKE TYSON TALKIN' ABOUT RAPING SOMEBODY'S MOMMA ...
www.ucomics.com www.boondocks.net
IT'S GONNA BE A BUMPY YEAR FOR BLACK PEOPLE ...
AREN'T THEY ALL?

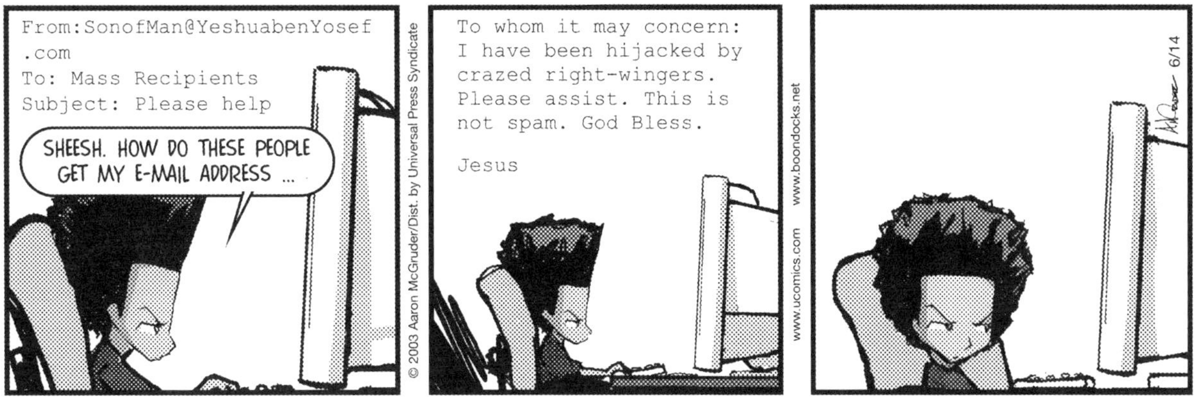
From:SonofMan@YeshuabenYosef.com
To: Mass Recipients
Subject: Please help
SHEESH. HOW DO THESE PEOPLE GET MY E-MAIL ADDRESS ...
© 2003 Aaron McGruder/Dist. by Universal Press Syndicate
To whom it may concern: I have been hijacked by crazed right-wingers. Please assist. This is not spam. God Bless.
Jesus
www.ucomics.com www.boondocks.net
6/14

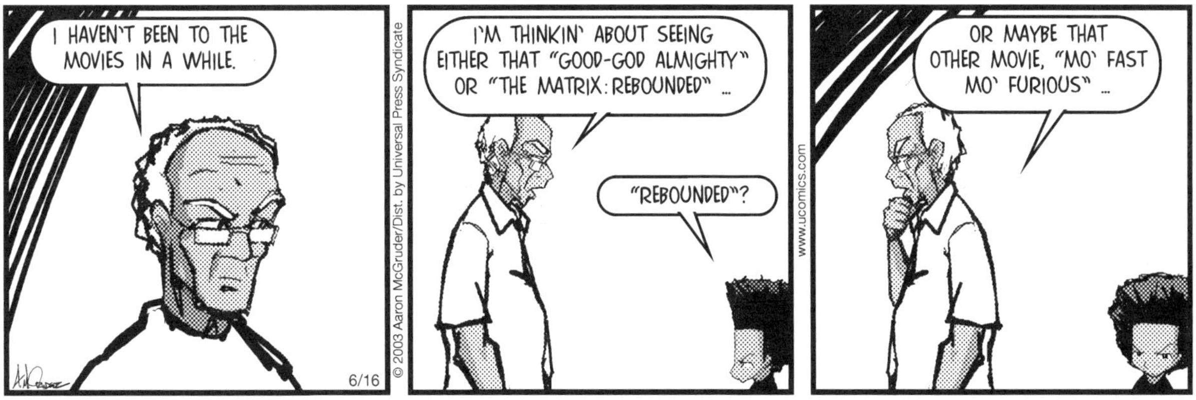
I HAVEN'T BEEN TO THE MOVIES IN A WHILE.
6/16
© 2003 Aaron McGruder/Dist. by Universal Press Syndicate
I'M THINKIN' ABOUT SEEING EITHER THAT "GOOD-GOD ALMIGHTY" OR "THE MATRIX: REBOUNDED" ...
"REBOUNDED"?
www.ucomics.com
OR MAYBE THAT OTHER MOVIE, "MO' FAST MO' FURIOUS" ...

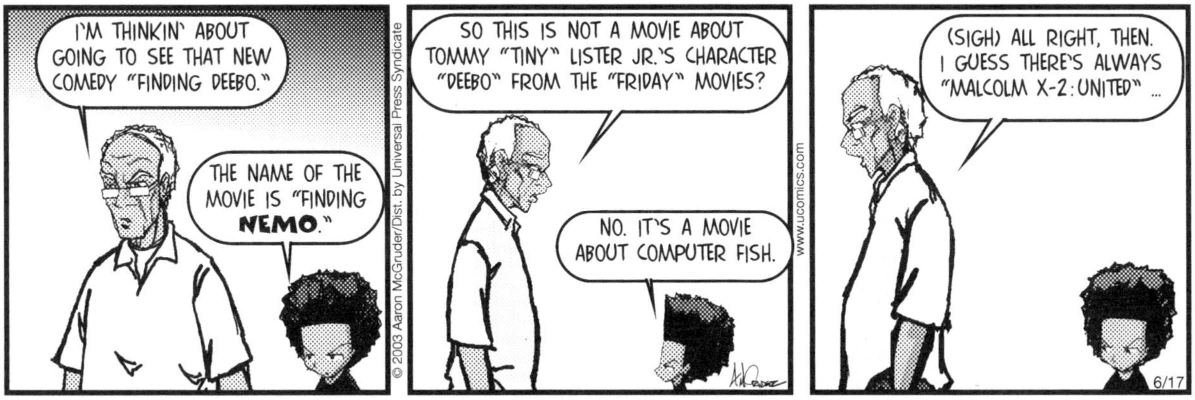
I'M THINKIN' ABOUT GOING TO SEE THAT NEW COMEDY "FINDING DEEBO."
THE NAME OF THE MOVIE IS "FINDING NEMO."
© 2003 Aaron McGruder/Dist. by Universal Press Syndicate
SO THIS IS NOT A MOVIE ABOUT TOMMY "TINY" LISTER JR.'S CHARACTER "DEEBO" FROM THE "FRIDAY" MOVIES?
NO. IT'S A MOVIE ABOUT COMPUTER FISH.
www.ucomics.com
(SIGH) ALL RIGHT, THEN. I GUESS THERE'S ALWAYS "MALCOLM X-2: UNITED" ...
6/17

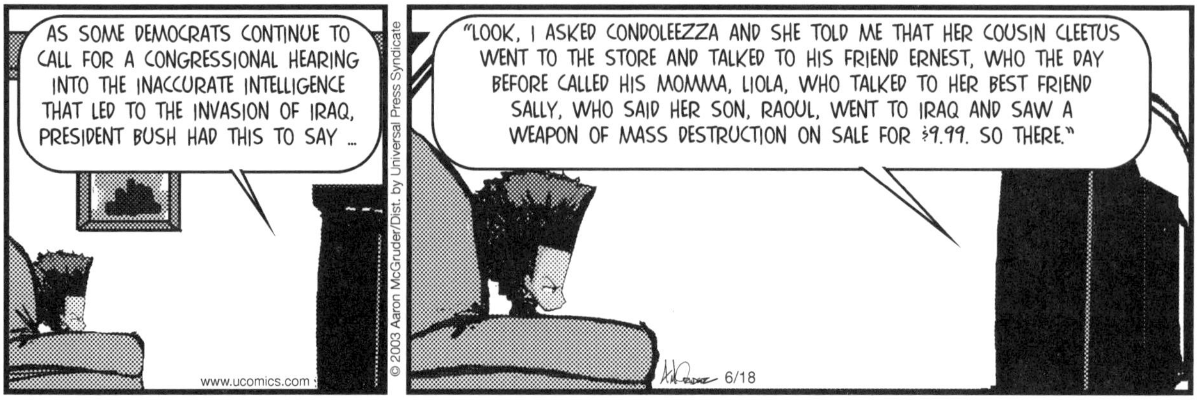
AS SOME DEMOCRATS CONTINUE TO CALL FOR A CONGRESSIONAL HEARING INTO THE INACCURATE INTELLIGENCE THAT LED TO THE INVASION OF IRAQ, PRESIDENT BUSH HAD THIS TO SAY ...
www.ucomics.com
© 2003 Aaron McGruder/Dist. by Universal Press Syndicate
"LOOK, I ASKED CONDOLEEZZA AND SHE TOLD ME THAT HER COUSIN CLEETUS WENT TO THE STORE AND TALKED TO HIS FRIEND ERNEST, WHO THE DAY BEFORE CALLED HIS MOMMA, LIOLA, WHO TALKED TO HER BEST FRIEND SALLY, WHO SAID HER SON, RAOUL, WENT TO IRAQ AND SAW A WEAPON OF MASS DESTRUCTION ON SALE FOR $9.99. SO THERE."
6/18

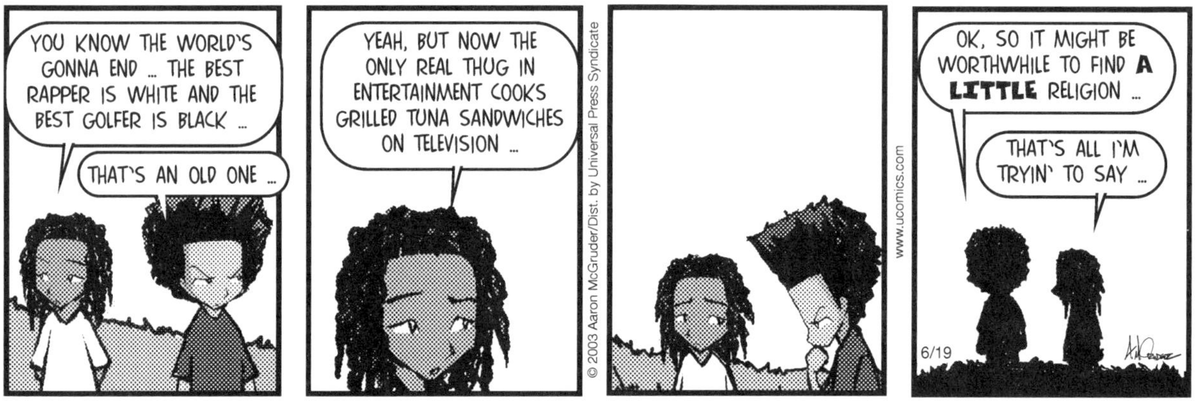
YOU KNOW THE WORLD'S GONNA END ... THE BEST RAPPER IS WHITE AND THE BEST GOLFER IS BLACK ...
THAT'S AN OLD ONE ...
YEAH, BUT NOW THE ONLY REAL THUG IN ENTERTAINMENT COOKS GRILLED TUNA SANDWICHES ON TELEVISION ...
© 2003 Aaron McGruder/Dist. by Universal Press Syndicate
www.ucomics.com
OK, SO IT MIGHT BE WORTHWHILE TO FIND **A LITTLE** RELIGION ...
THAT'S ALL I'M TRYIN' TO SAY ...
6/19

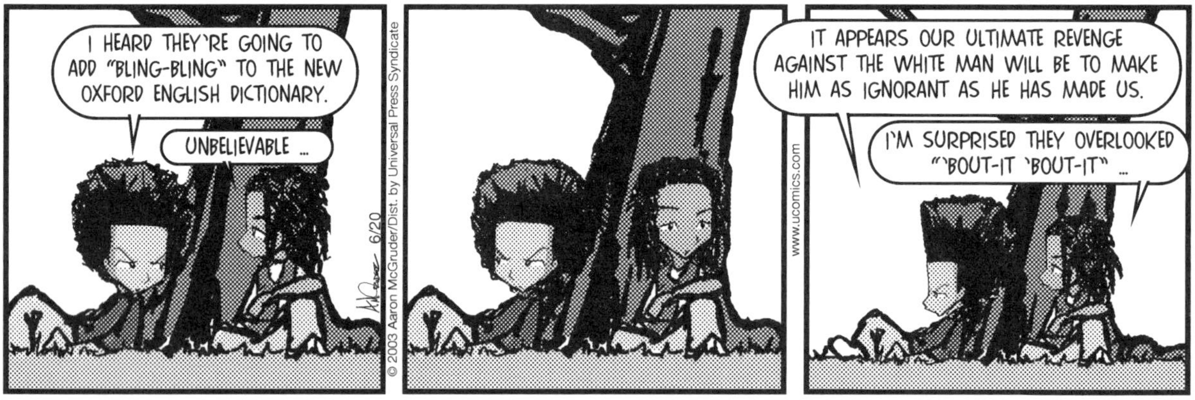
I HEARD THEY'RE GOING TO ADD "BLING-BLING" TO THE NEW OXFORD ENGLISH DICTIONARY.
UNBELIEVABLE ...
6/20
© 2003 Aaron McGruder/Dist. by Universal Press Syndicate
www.ucomics.com
IT APPEARS OUR ULTIMATE REVENGE AGAINST THE WHITE MAN WILL BE TO MAKE HIM AS IGNORANT AS HE HAS MADE US.
I'M SURPRISED THEY OVERLOOKED "'BOUT-IT 'BOUT-IT" ...

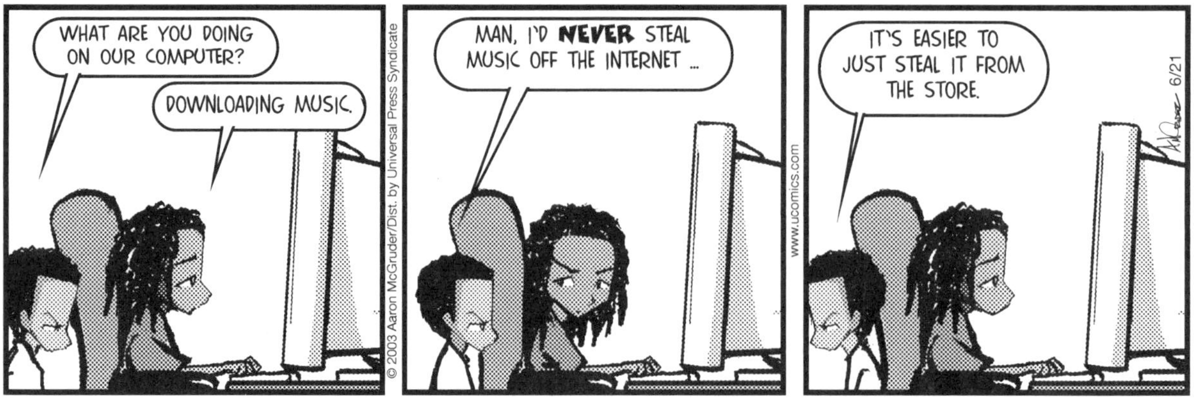
WHAT ARE YOU DOING ON OUR COMPUTER?
DOWNLOADING MUSIC.
© 2003 Aaron McGruder/Dist. by Universal Press Syndicate
MAN, I'D **NEVER** STEAL MUSIC OFF THE INTERNET ...
www.ucomics.com
IT'S EASIER TO JUST STEAL IT FROM THE STORE.
6/21

NOW WHERE IS THAT BOY? DRIVEWAY SHOULD HAVE BEEN CLEARED AN HOUR AGO, AND I I DON'T EVEN SEE HIM OUT THERE ...
I JUST DON'T KNOW ABOUT THESE KIDS NOWADAYS. NO RESPECT ... NO DISCIPLINE ... NO WORK ETHIC ...
IT MUST BE THAT RAP MUSIC 'CAUSE I SURE WASN'T LIKE THIS WHEN I WAS YOUNG ...
1/5
© 2000 Aaron McGruder/Dist. by Universal Press Syndicate
... WHEN YA ELDERS TOLD YOU TO SHOVEL SOME SNOW, YOU SHOVELED SOME SNOW!
BUT THAT SHIFTLESS GRANDSON OF MINE COULDN'T DO THAT ONE SIMPLE TASK ... AND WHY?
www.uexpress.com www.boondocks.net
"CAUSE HE LAZY!"

UGH ... THIS VIDEO IS TERRIBLE. TURN IT.
YOU SAY EVERYTHING IS TERRIBLE. YOU'RE A HATER.
© 2003 Aaron McGruder/Dist. by Universal Press Syndicate
Y'KNOW ... THE BRUTALLY HONEST CRITIQUES THAT YOU CALL "HATING" ARE WHY BLACK PEOPLE HAVE ALWAYS BEEN AT THE FOREFRONT OF MUSIC AND CULTURE. ARTISTS KNEW THAT IF THEY DIDN'T EXCEL, BLACK PEOPLE WOULD YELL AND BOO AND HECKLE THEM OFF THE STAGE. TOUGH AUDIENCES HAVE ALWAYS MADE OUR ARTISTS BETTER ...
UH-HUH ...
www.ucomics.com www.boondocks.net
NOW IF WE COULD ONLY GET BLACK PEOPLE TO START BOOING EACH OTHER IN MATH CLASS ...
WHATEVER, HATER.
1/12

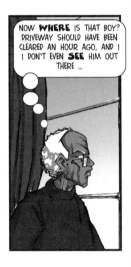

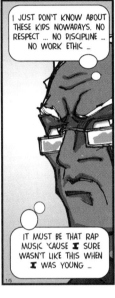

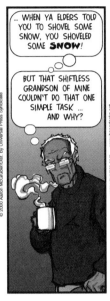

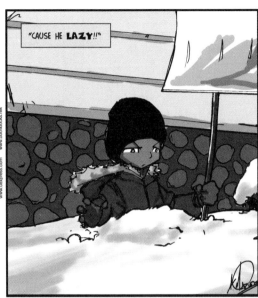

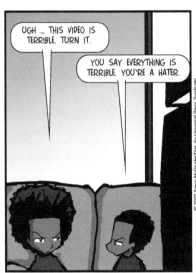

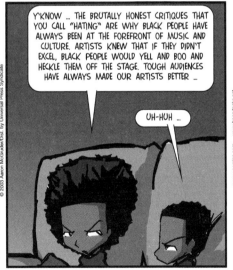

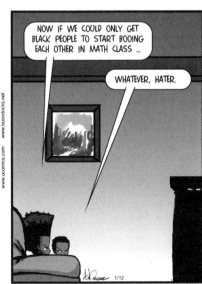

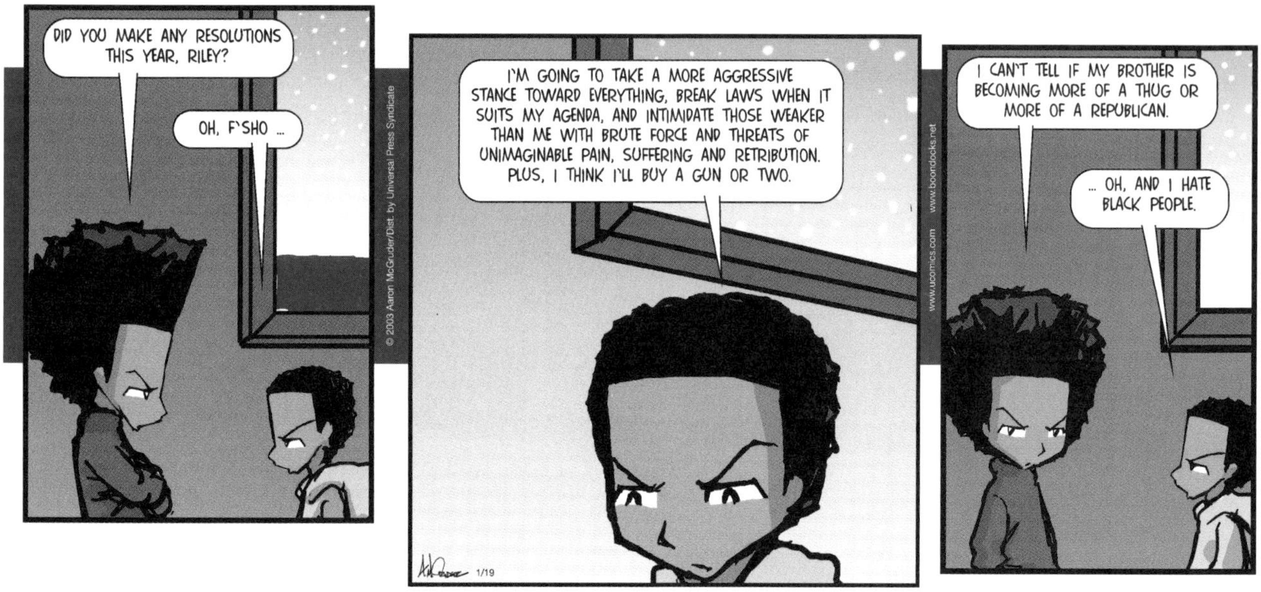
DID YOU MAKE ANY RESOLUTIONS THIS YEAR, RILEY?
OH, F'SHO ...
I'M GOING TO TAKE A MORE AGGRESSIVE STANCE TOWARD EVERYTHING, BREAK LAWS WHEN IT SUITS MY AGENDA, AND INTIMIDATE THOSE WEAKER THAN ME WITH BRUTE FORCE AND THREATS OF UNIMAGINABLE PAIN, SUFFERING AND RETRIBUTION. PLUS, I THINK I'LL BUY A GUN OR TWO.
I CAN'T TELL IF MY BROTHER IS BECOMING MORE OF A THUG OR MORE OF A REPUBLICAN.
... OH, AND I HATE BLACK PEOPLE.
© 2003 Aaron McGruder/Dist. by Universal Press Syndicate
www.ucomics.com www.boondocks.net
1/19

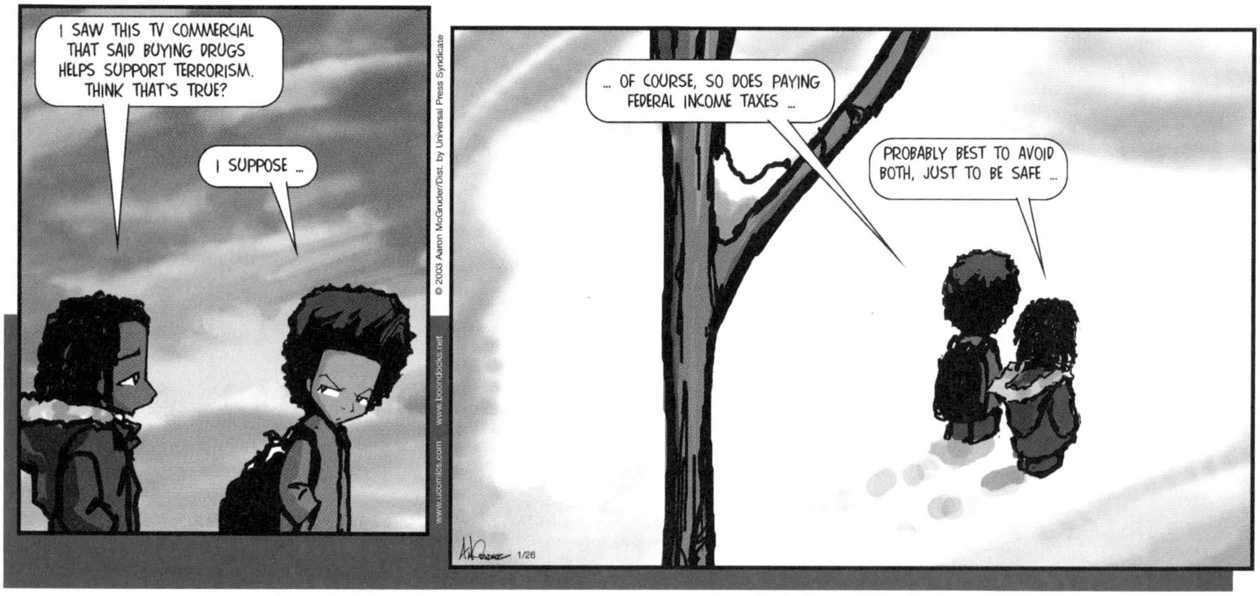
I SAW THIS TV COMMERCIAL THAT SAID BUYING DRUGS HELPS SUPPORT TERRORISM. THINK THAT'S TRUE?
I SUPPOSE ...
... OF COURSE, SO DOES PAYING FEDERAL INCOME TAXES ...
PROBABLY BEST TO AVOID BOTH, JUST TO BE SAFE ...
© 2003 Aaron McGruder/Dist. by Universal Press Syndicate
www.ucomics.com www.boondocks.net
1/26

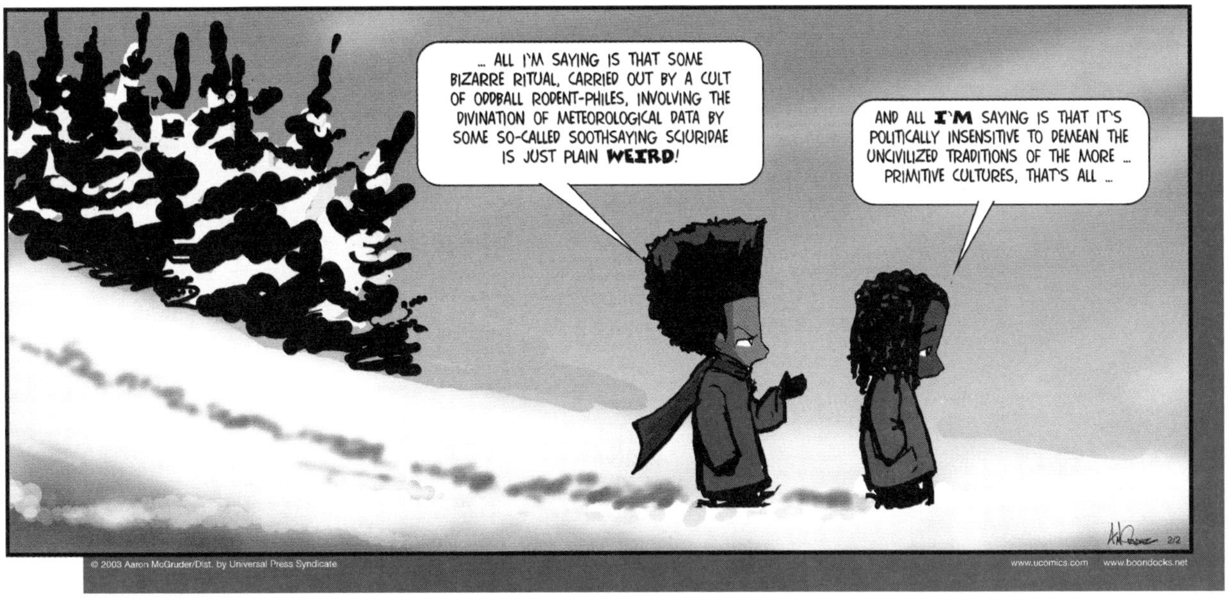
... ALL I'M SAYING IS THAT SOME BIZARRE RITUAL, CARRIED OUT BY A CULT OF ODDBALL RODENT-PHILES, INVOLVING THE DIVINATION OF METEOROLOGICAL DATA BY SOME SO-CALLED SOOTHSAYING SCIURIDAE IS JUST PLAIN WEIRD!
AND ALL I'M SAYING IS THAT IT'S POLITICALLY INSENSITIVE TO DEMEAN THE UNCIVILIZED TRADITIONS OF THE MORE ... PRIMITIVE CULTURES, THAT'S ALL ...
2/2
© 2003 Aaron McGruder/Dist. by Universal Press Syndicate
www.ucomics.com www.boondocks.net

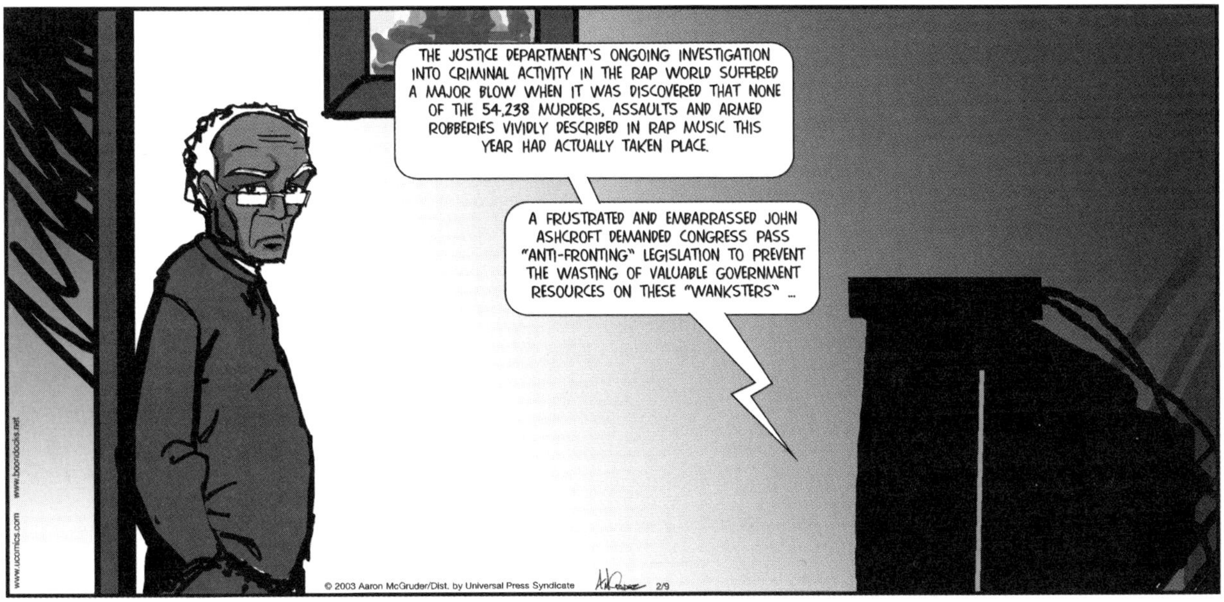
THE JUSTICE DEPARTMENT'S ONGOING INVESTIGATION INTO CRIMINAL ACTIVITY IN THE RAP WORLD SUFFERED A MAJOR BLOW WHEN IT WAS DISCOVERED THAT NONE OF THE 54,238 MURDERS, ASSAULTS AND ARMED ROBBERIES VIVIDLY DESCRIBED IN RAP MUSIC THIS YEAR HAD ACTUALLY TAKEN PLACE.
A FRUSTRATED AND EMBARRASSED JOHN ASHCROFT DEMANDED CONGRESS PASS "ANTI-FRONTING" LEGISLATION TO PREVENT THE WASTING OF VALUABLE GOVERNMENT RESOURCES ON THESE "WANKSTERS" ...
www.ucomics.com www.boondocks.net
© 2003 Aaron McGruder/Dist. by Universal Press Syndicate
2/9

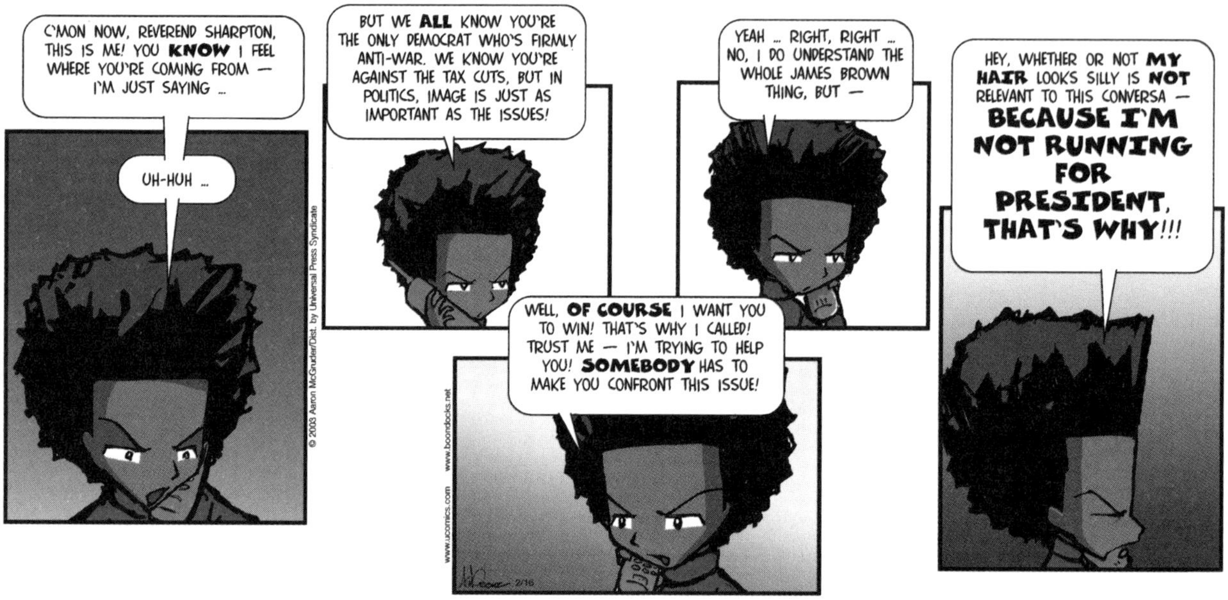
C'MON NOW, REVEREND SHARPTON, THIS IS ME! YOU **KNOW** I FEEL WHERE YOU'RE COMING FROM — I'M JUST SAYING ...
UH-HUH ...
BUT WE **ALL** KNOW YOU'RE THE ONLY DEMOCRAT WHO'S FIRMLY ANTI-WAR. WE KNOW YOU'RE AGAINST THE TAX CUTS, BUT IN POLITICS, IMAGE IS JUST AS IMPORTANT AS THE ISSUES!
YEAH ... RIGHT, RIGHT ... NO, I DO UNDERSTAND THE WHOLE JAMES BROWN THING, BUT —
WELL, **OF COURSE** I WANT YOU TO WIN! THAT'S WHY I CALLED! TRUST ME — I'M TRYING TO HELP YOU! **SOMEBODY** HAS TO MAKE YOU CONFRONT THIS ISSUE!
HEY, WHETHER OR NOT **MY HAIR** LOOKS SILLY IS **NOT** RELEVANT TO THIS CONVERSA — **BECAUSE I'M NOT RUNNING FOR PRESIDENT, THAT'S WHY!!!**
© 2003 Aaron McGruder/Dist. by Universal Press Syndicate
www.ucomics.com www.boondocks.net
2/16

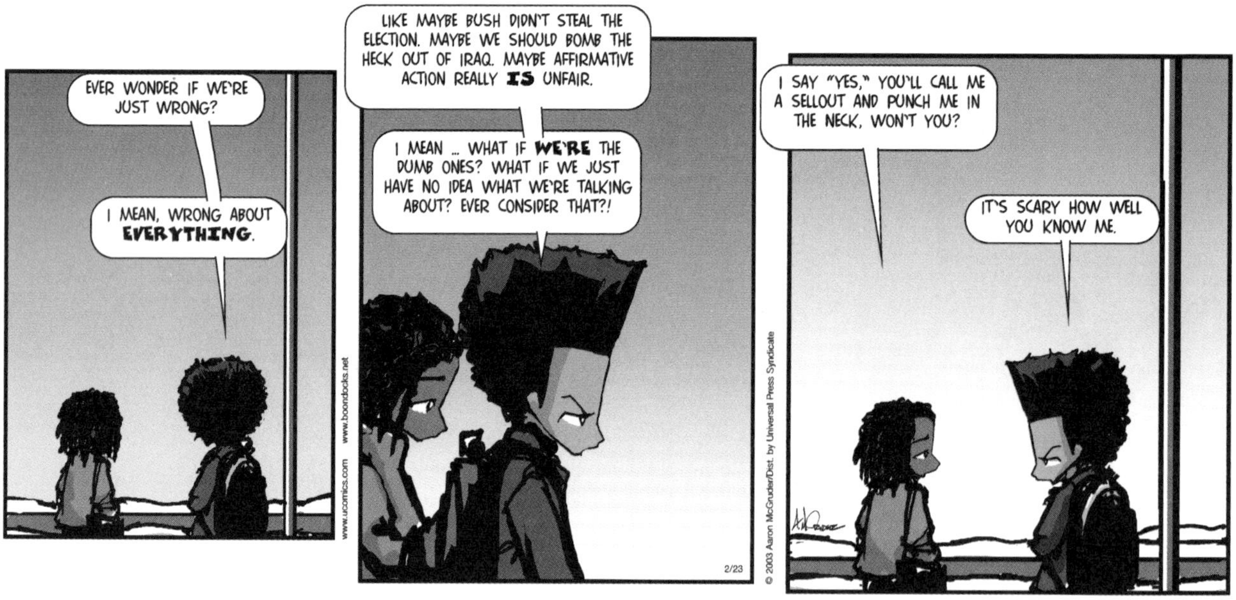
EVER WONDER IF WE'RE JUST WRONG?
I MEAN, WRONG ABOUT **EVERYTHING**.
LIKE MAYBE BUSH DIDN'T STEAL THE ELECTION. MAYBE WE SHOULD BOMB THE HECK OUT OF IRAQ. MAYBE AFFIRMATIVE ACTION REALLY **IS** UNFAIR.
I MEAN ... WHAT IF **WE'RE** THE DUMB ONES? WHAT IF WE JUST HAVE NO IDEA WHAT WE'RE TALKING ABOUT? EVER CONSIDER THAT?!
I SAY "YES," YOU'LL CALL ME A SELLOUT AND PUNCH ME IN THE NECK, WON'T YOU?
IT'S SCARY HOW WELL YOU KNOW ME.
www.ucomics.com www.boondocks.net
2/23
© 2003 Aaron McGruder/Dist. by Universal Press Syndicate

SO WHAT DO YOU THINK, CAESAR? WHAT'S THE SECRET TO HAPPINESS?
© 2003 Aaron McGruder/Dist. by Universal Press Syndicate
www.ucomics.com www.boondocks.net
WHITE WOMEN?
STOP THAT.

SOMETIMES I THINK MY BRAIN WORKS DIFFERENTLY THAN MOST PEOPLE'S ...
FOR EXAMPLE, DO YOU EVER, LIKE, NARRATE YOUR LIFE IN YOUR OWN HEAD AS IT HAPPENS — LIKE IT WAS A HISTORY CHANNEL-TYPE DOCUMENTARY?
NOPE.
"AND THEN ... CAESAR'S BEST FRIEND, HUEY, ASKED HIM YET ANOTHER WEIRD AND STUPID QUESTION ... IT WOULD NOT BE THE LAST ..."
3/9 © 2003 Aaron McGruder/Dist. by Universal Press Syndicate
www.ucomics.com www.boondocks.net

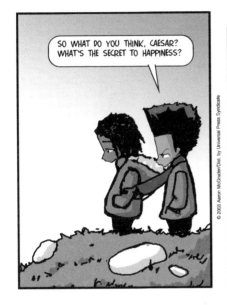

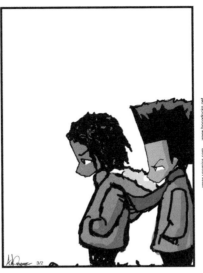

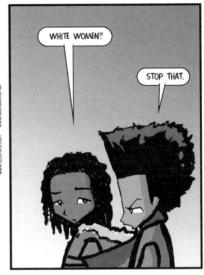

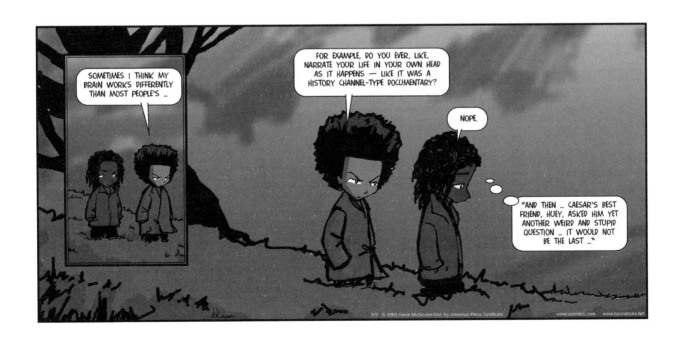

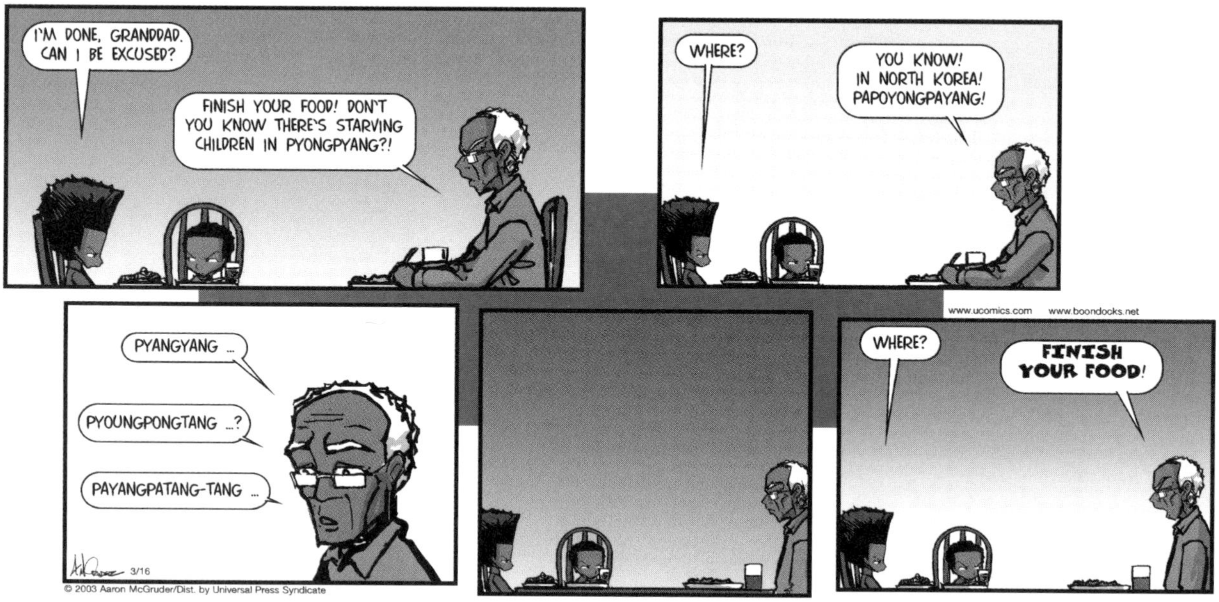
I'M DONE, GRANDDAD. CAN I BE EXCUSED?
FINISH YOUR FOOD! DON'T YOU KNOW THERE'S STARVING CHILDREN IN PYONGPYANG?!
WHERE?
YOU KNOW! IN NORTH KOREA! PAPOYONGPAYANG!
www.ucomics.com www.boondocks.net
PYANGYANG ...
PYOUNGPONGTANG ...?
PAYANGPATANG-TANG ...
3/16
© 2003 Aaron McGruder/Dist. by Universal Press Syndicate
WHERE?
FINISH YOUR FOOD!

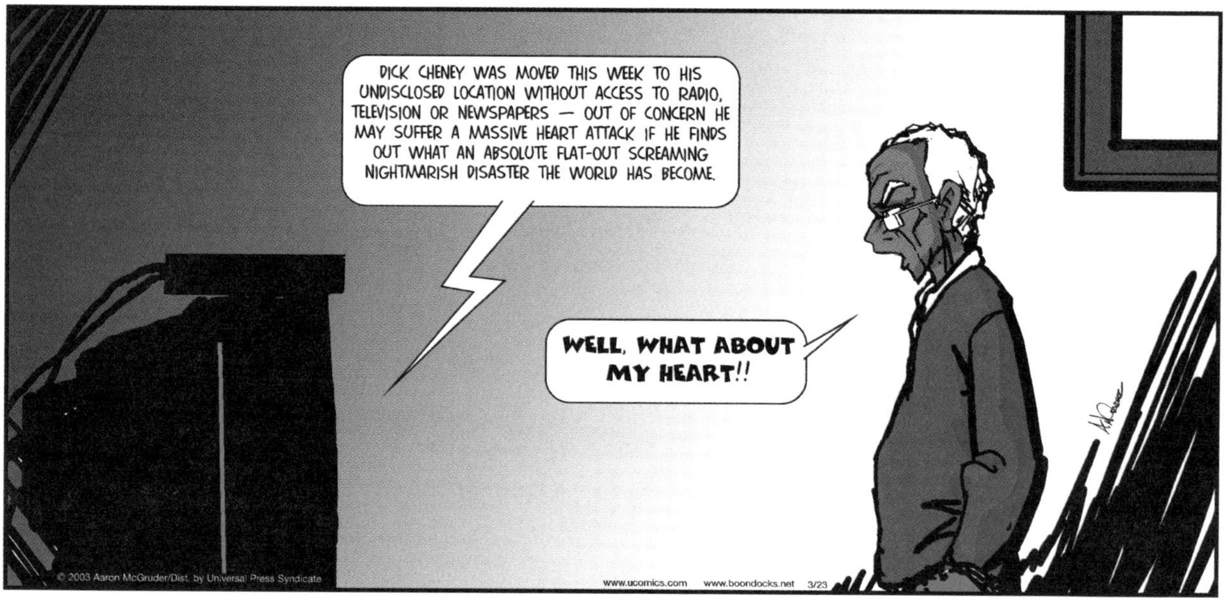
DICK CHENEY WAS MOVED THIS WEEK TO HIS UNDISCLOSED LOCATION WITHOUT ACCESS TO RADIO, TELEVISION OR NEWSPAPERS — OUT OF CONCERN HE MAY SUFFER A MASSIVE HEART ATTACK IF HE FINDS OUT WHAT AN ABSOLUTE FLAT-OUT SCREAMING NIGHTMARISH DISASTER THE WORLD HAS BECOME.
WELL, WHAT ABOUT MY HEART!!
© 2003 Aaron McGruder/Dist. by Universal Press Syndicate
www.ucomics.com www.boondocks.net 3/23

AMERICAN DEMOCRACY IS A THING OF THE PAST. THE MEDIA CONSPIRE WITH THIS ADMINISTRATION TO MISINFORM A PUBLIC THAT IS EITHER TOO SCARED OR TOO STUPID TO RECLAIM THEIR GOVERNMENT.
SOMEONE ONCE SAID, "THE CYNIC KNOWS THE PRICE OF EVERYTHING AND THE VALUE OF NOTHING."
AND PEOPLE NEED TO STOP WASTING PRECIOUS TIME COMING UP WITH WORTHLESS SAYINGS ...
3/30
© 2003 Aaron McGruder/Dist. by Universal Press Syndicate www.ucomics.com www.boondocks.net

SO WHAT HAPPENS NOW THAT HISPANICS HAVE PASSED BLACKS AS AMERICA'S LARGEST MINORITY GROUP?
WELL, IT'S ONLY A MATTER OF TIME BEFORE CORPORATIONS RESPOND TO THE NEWS AND WE SEE GREAT CHANGES IN THE AMERICAN CULTURAL LANDSCAPE.
4/6
© 2003 Aaron McGruder/Dist. by Universal Press Syndicate www.ucomics.com www.boondocks.net
OH NO!! YOU DON'T THINK THEY'D REPLACE THE "McRIB" WITH THE "McTACO," DO YOU?!
IT'S A POSSIBILITY ...

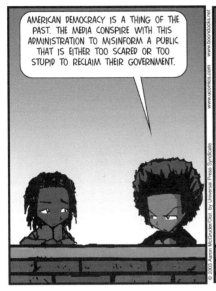

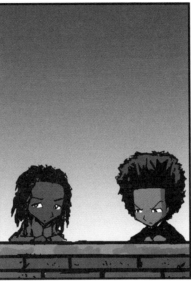

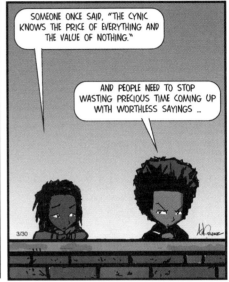

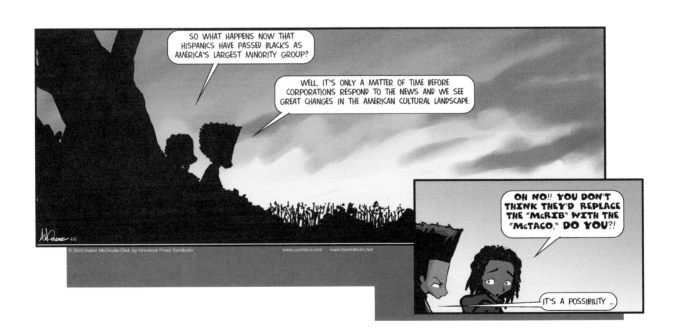

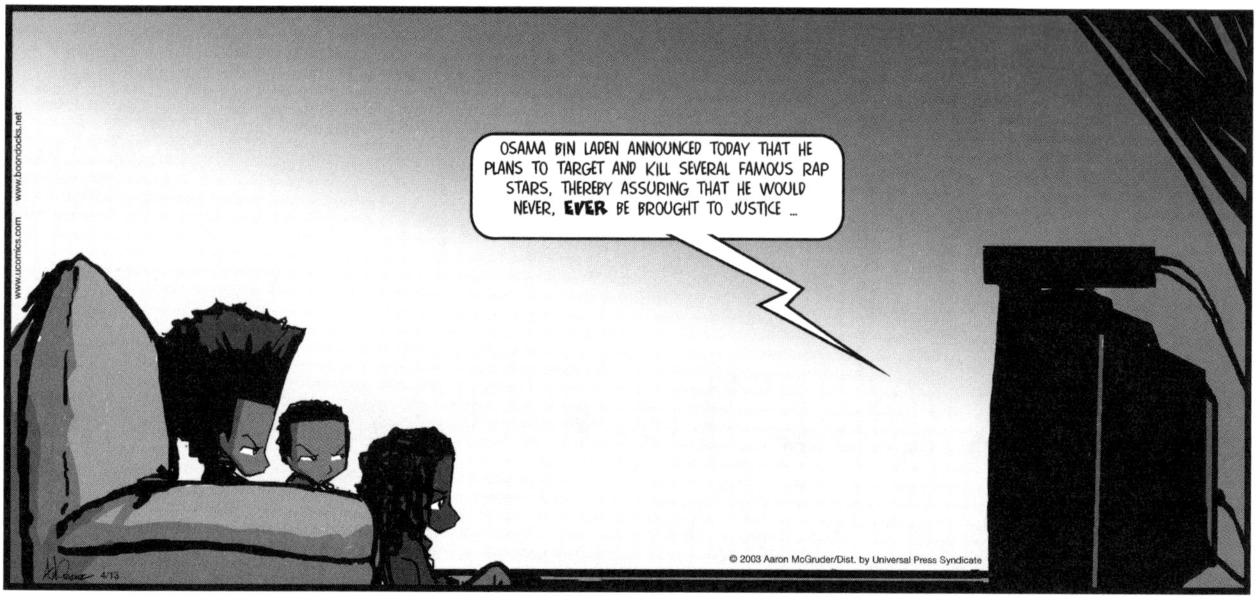
OSAMA BIN LADEN ANNOUNCED TODAY THAT HE PLANS TO TARGET AND KILL SEVERAL FAMOUS RAP STARS, THEREBY ASSURING THAT HE WOULD NEVER, EVER BE BROUGHT TO JUSTICE ...
www.ucomics.com www.boondocks.net
© 2003 Aaron McGruder/Dist. by Universal Press Syndicate

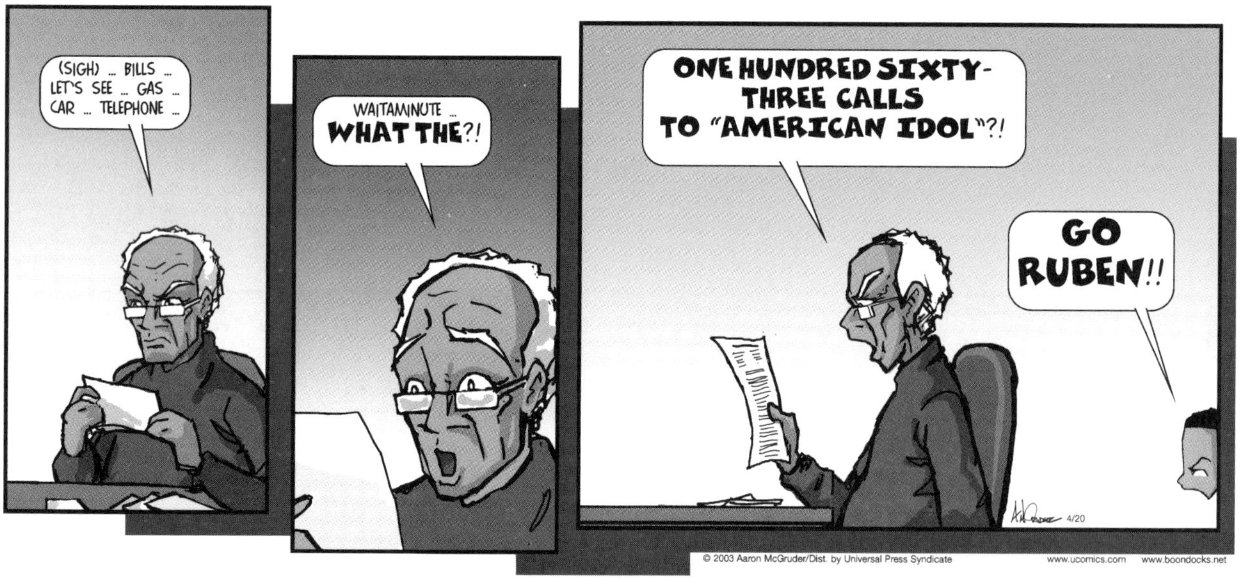
(SIGH) ... BILLS ... LET'S SEE ... GAS ... CAR ... TELEPHONE ...
WAITAMINUTE ... WHAT THE?!
ONE HUNDRED SIXTY-THREE CALLS TO "AMERICAN IDOL"?!
GO RUBEN!!
© 2003 Aaron McGruder/Dist. by Universal Press Syndicate
www.ucomics.com www.boondocks.net

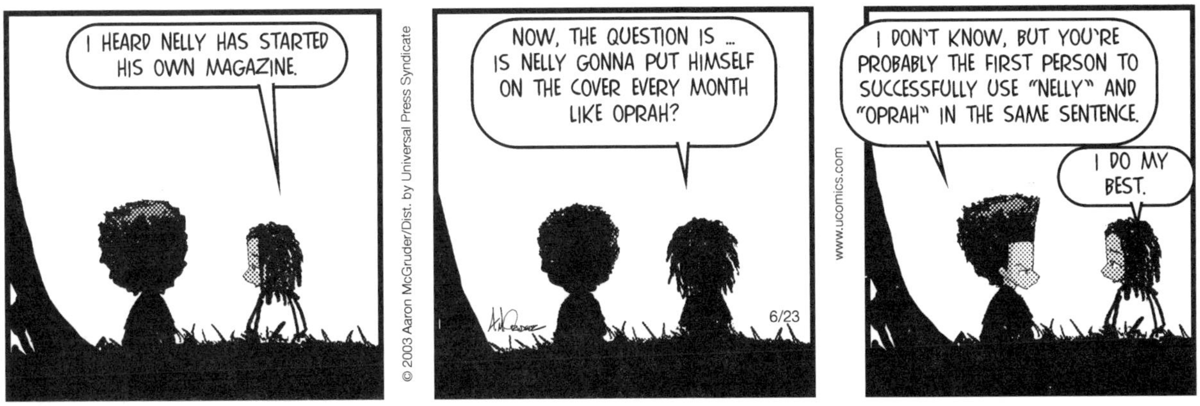
I HEARD NELLY HAS STARTED HIS OWN MAGAZINE.
© 2003 Aaron McGruder/Dist. by Universal Press Syndicate
NOW, THE QUESTION IS ... IS NELLY GONNA PUT HIMSELF ON THE COVER EVERY MONTH LIKE OPRAH?
6/23
www.ucomics.com
I DON'T KNOW, BUT YOU'RE PROBABLY THE FIRST PERSON TO SUCCESSFULLY USE "NELLY" AND "OPRAH" IN THE SAME SENTENCE.
I DO MY BEST.

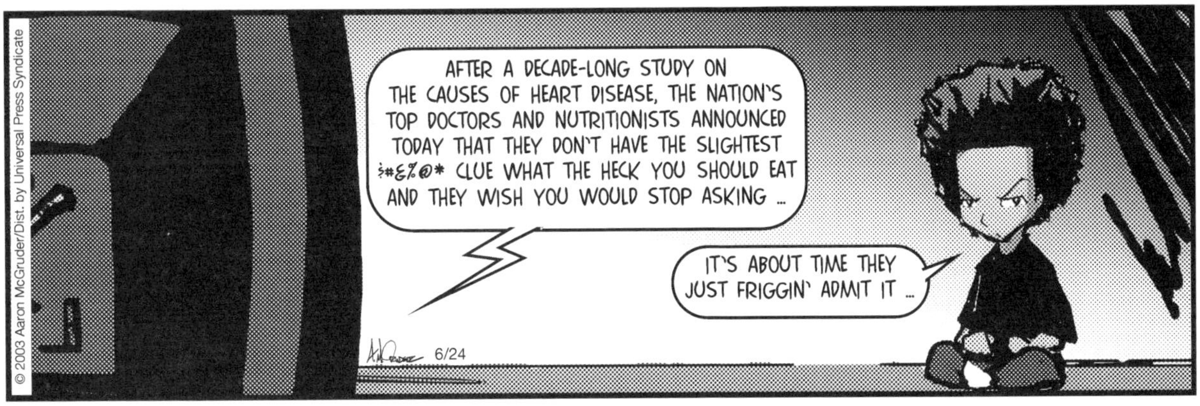
© 2003 Aaron McGruder/Dist. by Universal Press Syndicate
AFTER A DECADE-LONG STUDY ON THE CAUSES OF HEART DISEASE, THE NATION'S TOP DOCTORS AND NUTRITIONISTS ANNOUNCED TODAY THAT THEY DON'T HAVE THE SLIGHTEST $#&%@* CLUE WHAT THE HECK YOU SHOULD EAT AND THEY WISH YOU WOULD STOP ASKING ...
IT'S ABOUT TIME THEY JUST FRIGGIN' ADMIT IT ...
6/24

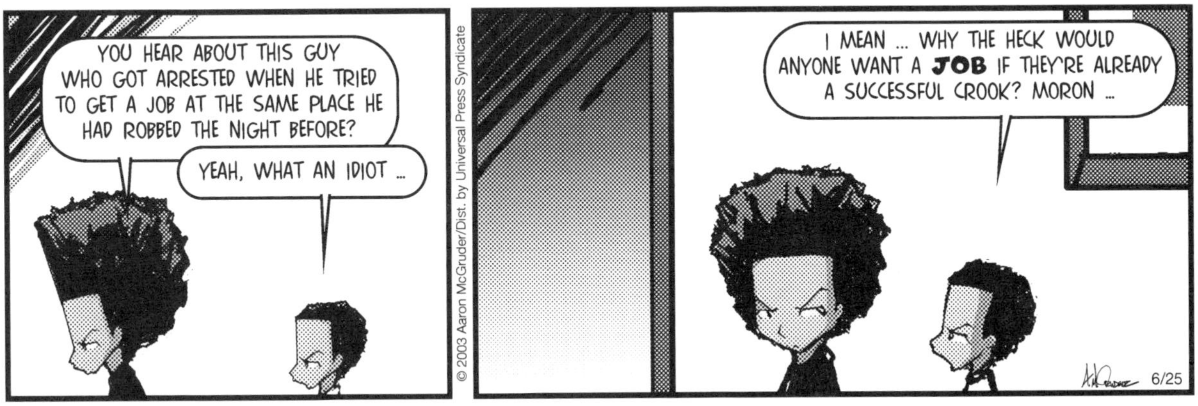
YOU HEAR ABOUT THIS GUY WHO GOT ARRESTED WHEN HE TRIED TO GET A JOB AT THE SAME PLACE HE HAD ROBBED THE NIGHT BEFORE?
YEAH, WHAT AN IDIOT ...
© 2003 Aaron McGruder/Dist. by Universal Press Syndicate
I MEAN ... WHY THE HECK WOULD ANYONE WANT A JOB IF THEY'RE ALREADY A SUCCESSFUL CROOK? MORON ...
6/25

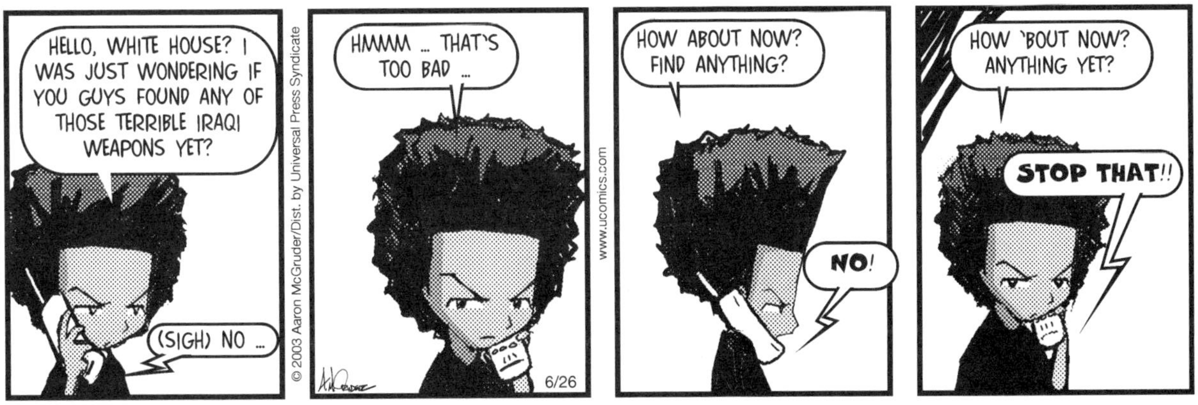
HELLO, WHITE HOUSE? I WAS JUST WONDERING IF YOU GUYS FOUND ANY OF THOSE TERRIBLE IRAQI WEAPONS YET?
(SIGH) NO ...
© 2003 Aaron McGruder/Dist. by Universal Press Syndicate
HMMM ... THAT'S TOO BAD ...
6/26
www.ucomics.com
HOW ABOUT NOW? FIND ANYTHING?
NO!
HOW 'BOUT NOW? ANYTHING YET?
STOP THAT!!

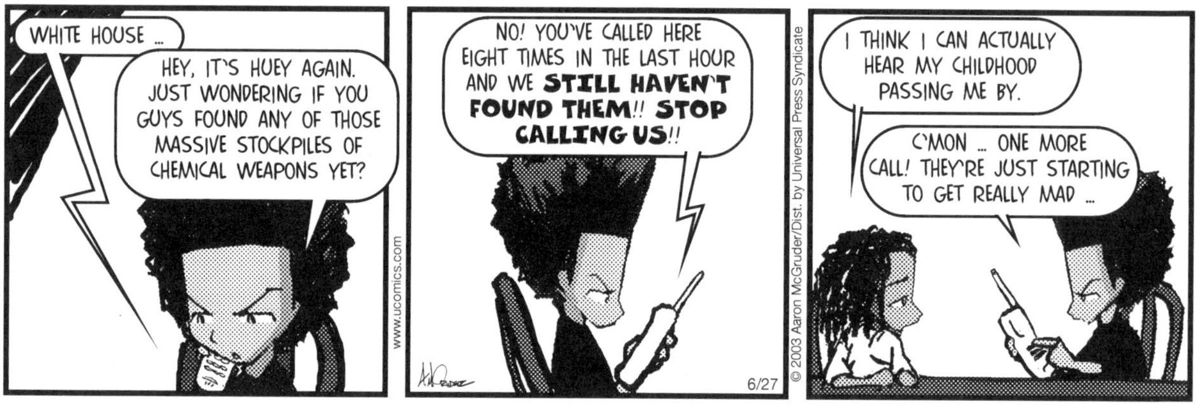
WHITE HOUSE ...
HEY, IT'S HUEY AGAIN. JUST WONDERING IF YOU GUYS FOUND ANY OF THOSE MASSIVE STOCKPILES OF CHEMICAL WEAPONS YET?
NO! YOU'VE CALLED HERE EIGHT TIMES IN THE LAST HOUR AND WE **STILL HAVEN'T FOUND THEM!! STOP CALLING US!!**
I THINK I CAN ACTUALLY HEAR MY CHILDHOOD PASSING ME BY.
C'MON ... ONE MORE CALL! THEY'RE JUST STARTING TO GET REALLY MAD ...
6/27

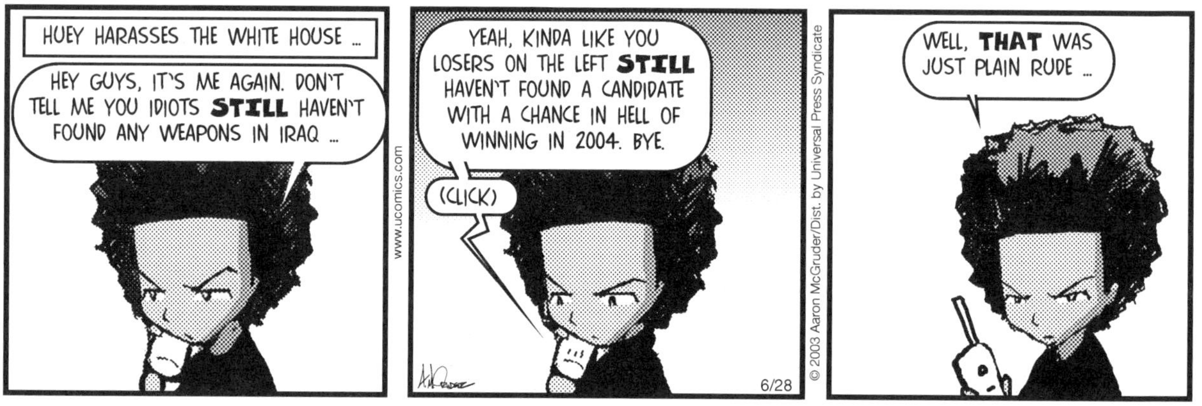
HUEY HARASSES THE WHITE HOUSE ...
HEY GUYS, IT'S ME AGAIN. DON'T TELL ME YOU IDIOTS **STILL** HAVEN'T FOUND ANY WEAPONS IN IRAQ ...
YEAH, KINDA LIKE YOU LOSERS ON THE LEFT **STILL** HAVEN'T FOUND A CANDIDATE WITH A CHANCE IN HELL OF WINNING IN 2004. BYE.
(CLICK)
WELL, **THAT** WAS JUST PLAIN RUDE ...
6/28

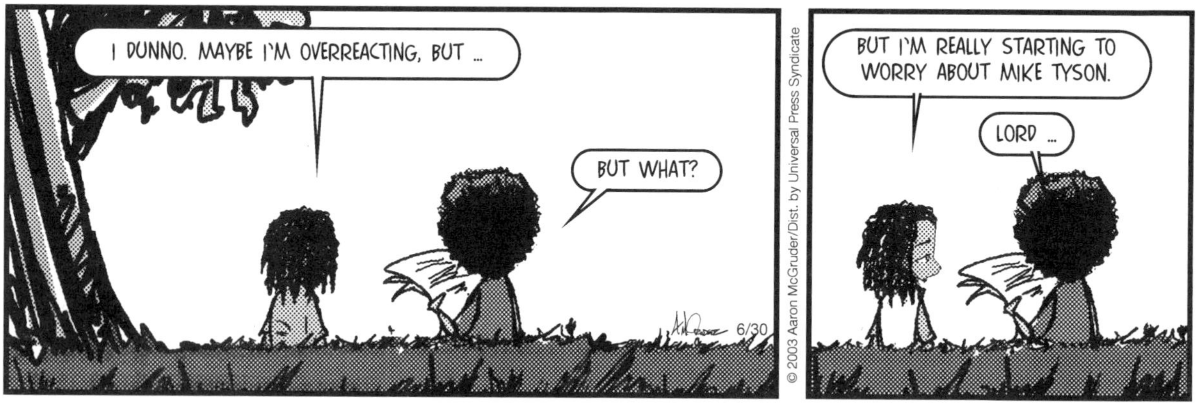
I DUNNO. MAYBE I'M OVERREACTING, BUT ...
BUT WHAT?
6/30
BUT I'M REALLY STARTING TO WORRY ABOUT MIKE TYSON.
LORD ...

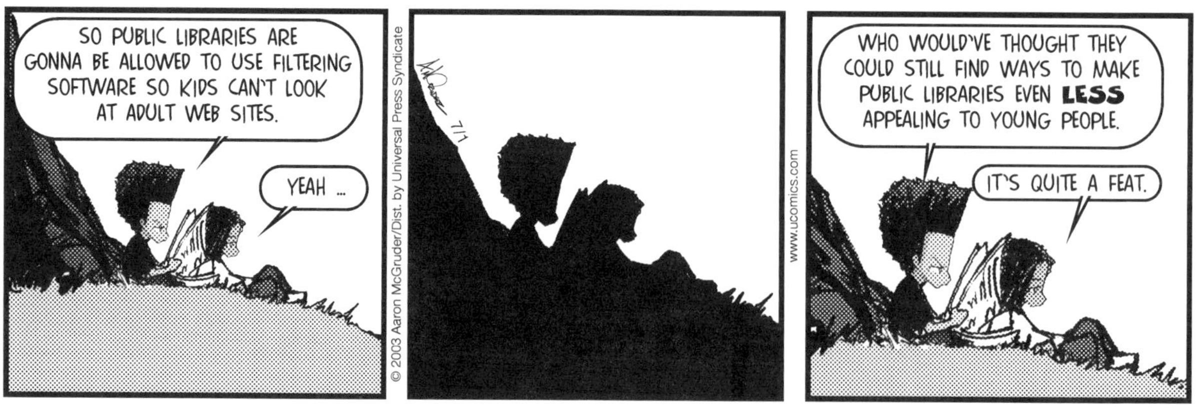
SO PUBLIC LIBRARIES ARE GONNA BE ALLOWED TO USE FILTERING SOFTWARE SO KIDS CAN'T LOOK AT ADULT WEB SITES.
YEAH ...
7/1
WHO WOULD'VE THOUGHT THEY COULD STILL FIND WAYS TO MAKE PUBLIC LIBRARIES EVEN **LESS** APPEALING TO YOUNG PEOPLE.
IT'S QUITE A FEAT.

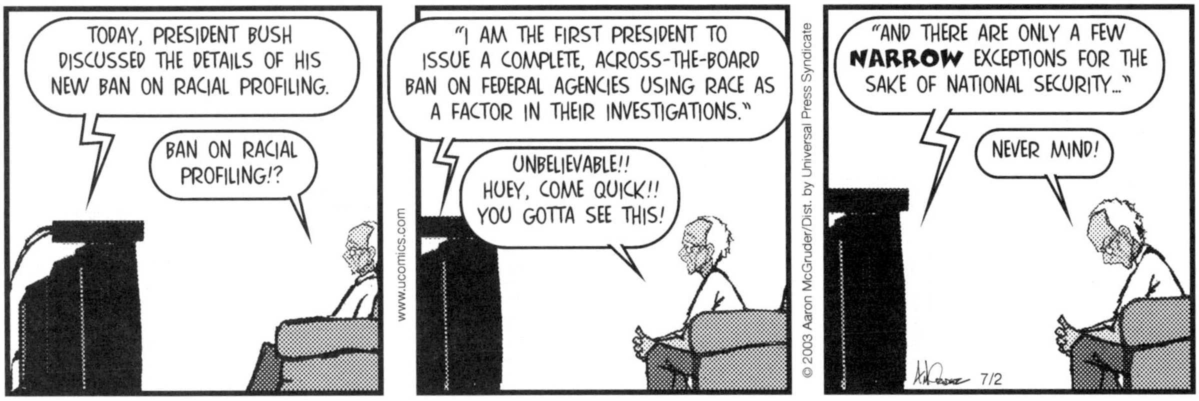
TODAY, PRESIDENT BUSH DISCUSSED THE DETAILS OF HIS NEW BAN ON RACIAL PROFILING.
BAN ON RACIAL PROFILING!?
"I AM THE FIRST PRESIDENT TO ISSUE A COMPLETE, ACROSS-THE-BOARD BAN ON FEDERAL AGENCIES USING RACE AS A FACTOR IN THEIR INVESTIGATIONS."
UNBELIEVABLE!! HUEY, COME QUICK!! YOU GOTTA SEE THIS!
"AND THERE ARE ONLY A FEW **NARROW** EXCEPTIONS FOR THE SAKE OF NATIONAL SECURITY..."
NEVER MIND!
www.ucomics.com
© 2003 Aaron McGruder/Dist. by Universal Press Syndicate
7/2

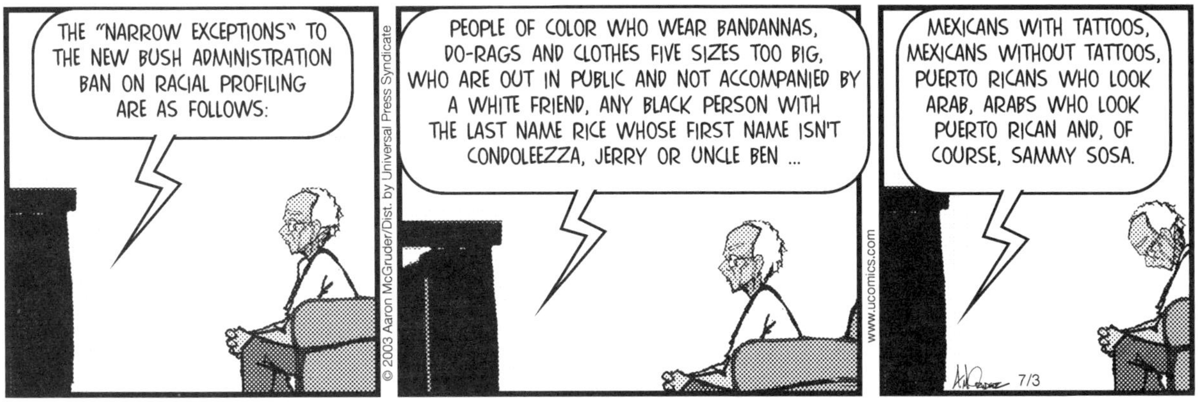
THE "NARROW EXCEPTIONS" TO THE NEW BUSH ADMINISTRATION BAN ON RACIAL PROFILING ARE AS FOLLOWS:
PEOPLE OF COLOR WHO WEAR BANDANNAS, DO-RAGS AND CLOTHES FIVE SIZES TOO BIG, WHO ARE OUT IN PUBLIC AND NOT ACCOMPANIED BY A WHITE FRIEND, ANY BLACK PERSON WITH THE LAST NAME RICE WHOSE FIRST NAME ISN'T CONDOLEEZZA, JERRY OR UNCLE BEN ...
MEXICANS WITH TATTOOS, MEXICANS WITHOUT TATTOOS, PUERTO RICANS WHO LOOK ARAB, ARABS WHO LOOK PUERTO RICAN AND, OF COURSE, SAMMY SOSA.
© 2003 Aaron McGruder/Dist. by Universal Press Syndicate
www.ucomics.com
7/3

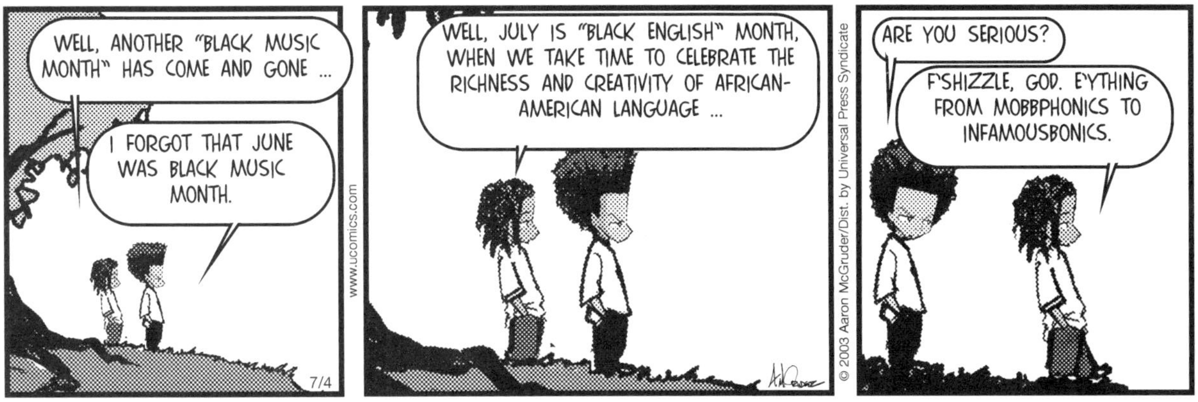
WELL, ANOTHER "BLACK MUSIC MONTH" HAS COME AND GONE ...
I FORGOT THAT JUNE WAS BLACK MUSIC MONTH.
www.ucomics.com
7/4
WELL, JULY IS "BLACK ENGLISH" MONTH, WHEN WE TAKE TIME TO CELEBRATE THE RICHNESS AND CREATIVITY OF AFRICAN-AMERICAN LANGUAGE ...
© 2003 Aaron McGruder/Dist. by Universal Press Syndicate
ARE YOU SERIOUS?
F'SHIZZLE, GOD. E'YTHING FROM MOBBPHONICS TO INFAMOUSBONICS.

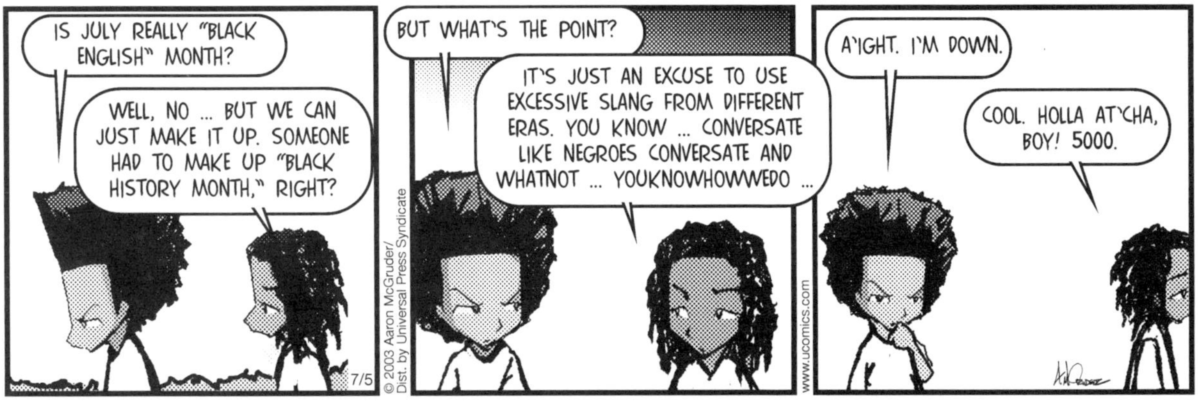
IS JULY REALLY "BLACK ENGLISH" MONTH?
WELL, NO ... BUT WE CAN JUST MAKE IT UP. SOMEONE HAD TO MAKE UP "BLACK HISTORY MONTH," RIGHT?
7/5
© 2003 Aaron McGruder/ Dist. by Universal Press Syndicate
BUT WHAT'S THE POINT?
IT'S JUST AN EXCUSE TO USE EXCESSIVE SLANG FROM DIFFERENT ERAS. YOU KNOW ... CONVERSATE LIKE NEGROES CONVERSATE AND WHATNOT ... YOUKNOWHOWWEDO ...
www.ucomics.com
A'IGHT. I'M DOWN.
COOL. HOLLA AT'CHA, BOY! 5000.

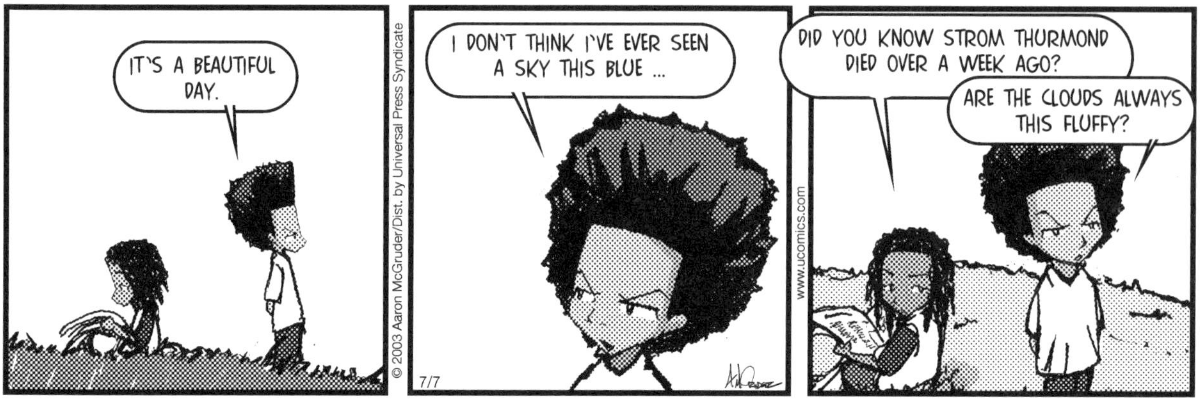
IT'S A BEAUTIFUL DAY.
I DON'T THINK I'VE EVER SEEN A SKY THIS BLUE ...
© 2003 Aaron McGruder/Dist. by Universal Press Syndicate
7/7
DID YOU KNOW STROM THURMOND DIED OVER A WEEK AGO?
ARE THE CLOUDS ALWAYS THIS FLUFFY?
www.ucomics.com

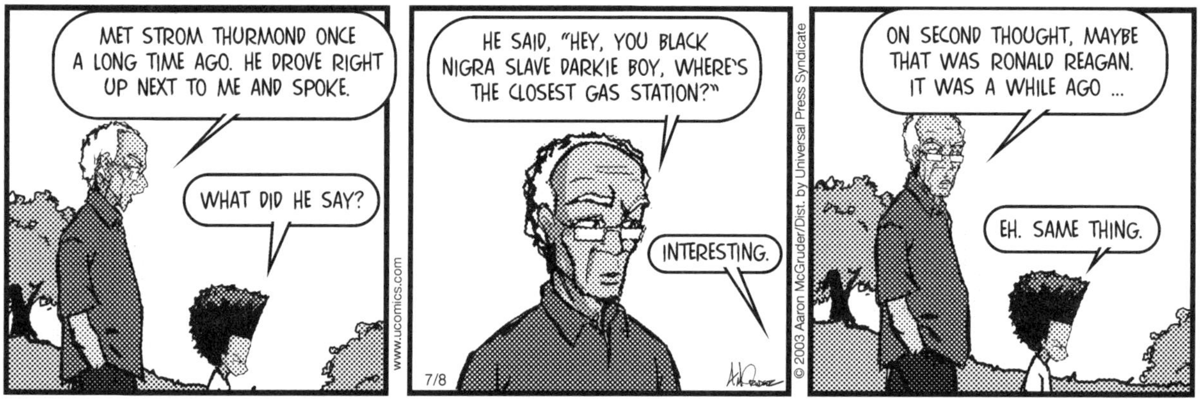
MET STROM THURMOND ONCE A LONG TIME AGO. HE DROVE RIGHT UP NEXT TO ME AND SPOKE.
WHAT DID HE SAY?
www.ucomics.com
HE SAID, "HEY, YOU BLACK NIGRA SLAVE DARKIE BOY, WHERE'S THE CLOSEST GAS STATION?"
INTERESTING.
7/8
© 2003 Aaron McGruder/Dist. by Universal Press Syndicate
ON SECOND THOUGHT, MAYBE THAT WAS RONALD REAGAN. IT WAS A WHILE AGO ...
EH. SAME THING.

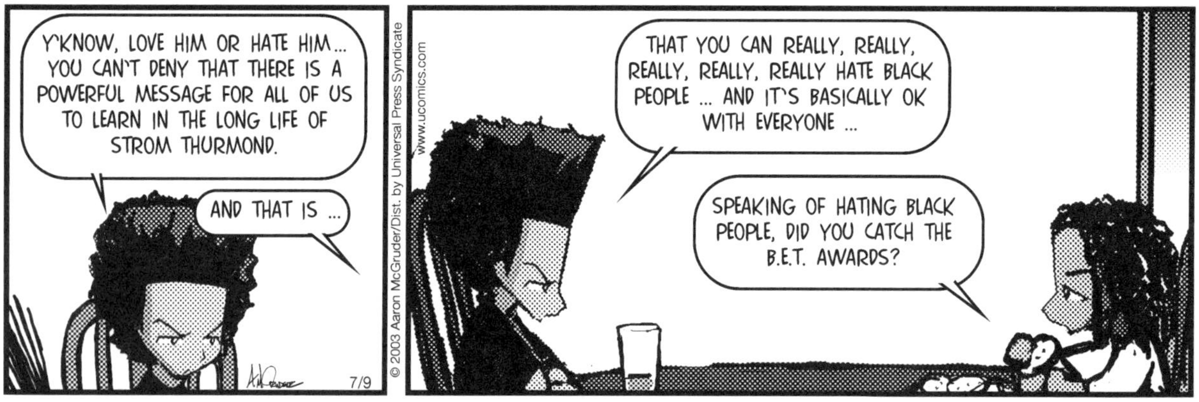
Y'KNOW, LOVE HIM OR HATE HIM... YOU CAN'T DENY THAT THERE IS A POWERFUL MESSAGE FOR ALL OF US TO LEARN IN THE LONG LIFE OF STROM THURMOND.
AND THAT IS ...
7/9
© 2003 Aaron McGruder/Dist. by Universal Press Syndicate
www.ucomics.com
THAT YOU CAN REALLY, REALLY, REALLY, REALLY, REALLY HATE BLACK PEOPLE ... AND IT'S BASICALLY OK WITH EVERYONE ...
SPEAKING OF HATING BLACK PEOPLE, DID YOU CATCH THE B.E.T. AWARDS?

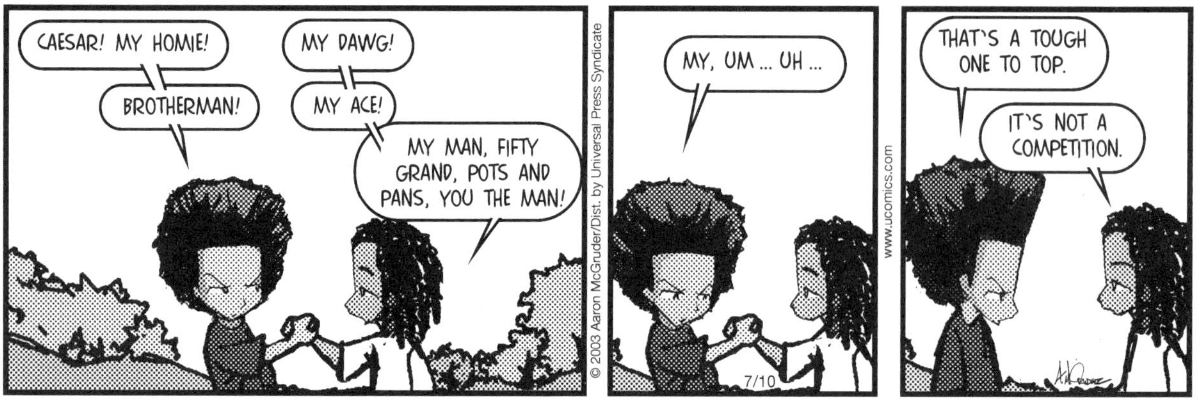
CAESAR! MY HOMIE!
MY DAWG!
BROTHERMAN!
MY ACE!
MY MAN, FIFTY GRAND, POTS AND PANS, YOU THE MAN!
© 2003 Aaron McGruder/Dist. by Universal Press Syndicate
MY, UM ... UH ...
7/10
www.ucomics.com
THAT'S A TOUGH ONE TO TOP.
IT'S NOT A COMPETITION.

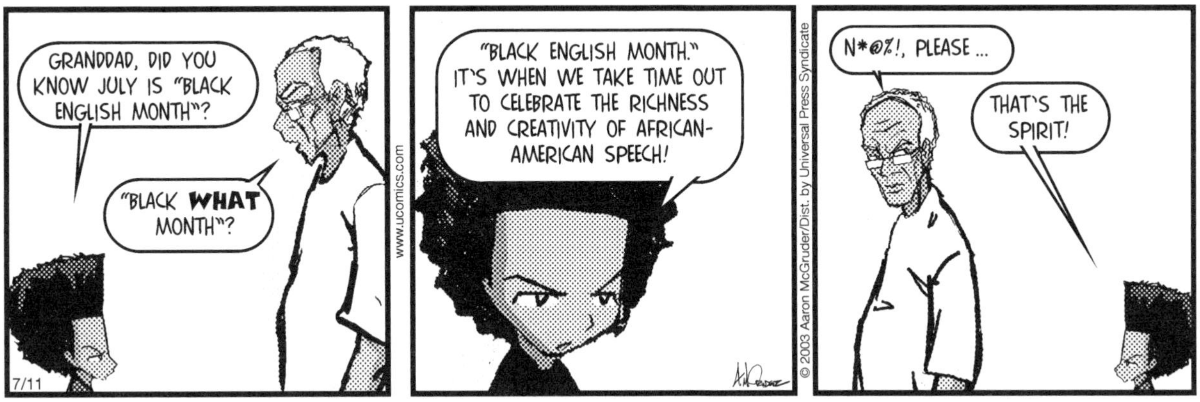
GRANDDAD, DID YOU KNOW JULY IS "BLACK ENGLISH MONTH"?
"BLACK **WHAT** MONTH"?
www.ucomics.com
7/11
"BLACK ENGLISH MONTH." IT'S WHEN WE TAKE TIME OUT TO CELEBRATE THE RICHNESS AND CREATIVITY OF AFRICAN-AMERICAN SPEECH!
© 2003 Aaron McGruder/Dist. by Universal Press Syndicate
N*@%!, PLEASE ...
THAT'S THE SPIRIT!

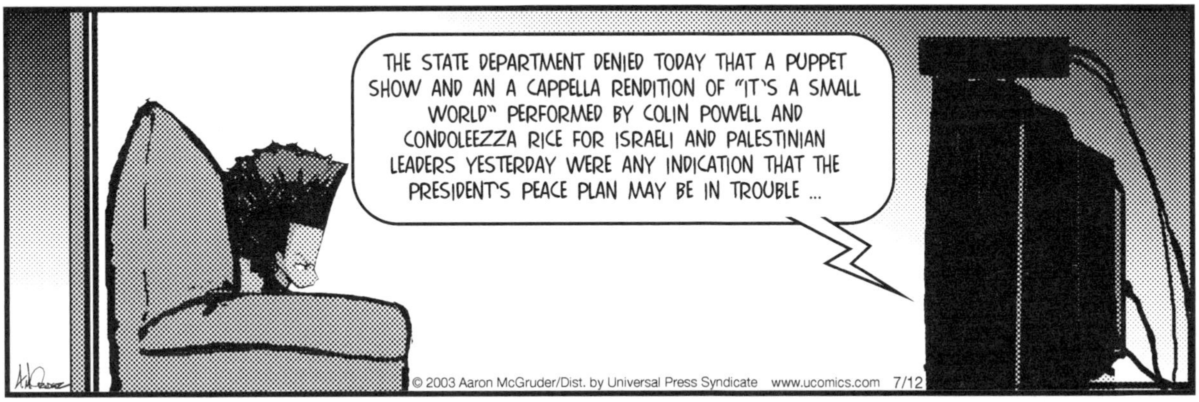
THE STATE DEPARTMENT DENIED TODAY THAT A PUPPET SHOW AND AN A CAPPELLA RENDITION OF "IT'S A SMALL WORLD" PERFORMED BY COLIN POWELL AND CONDOLEEZZA RICE FOR ISRAELI AND PALESTINIAN LEADERS YESTERDAY WERE ANY INDICATION THAT THE PRESIDENT'S PEACE PLAN MAY BE IN TROUBLE ...
© 2003 Aaron McGruder/Dist. by Universal Press Syndicate www.ucomics.com 7/12

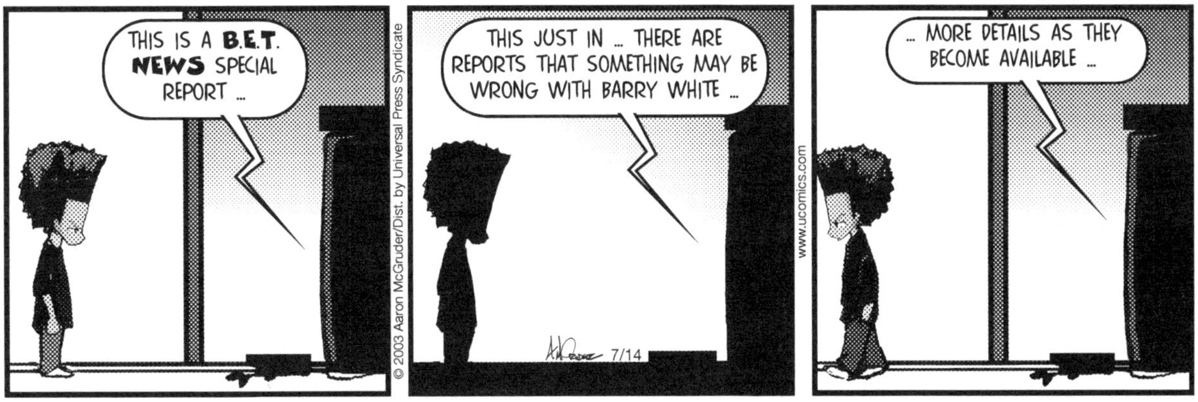
THIS IS A **B.E.T. NEWS** SPECIAL REPORT ...
© 2003 Aaron McGruder/Dist. by Universal Press Syndicate
THIS JUST IN ... THERE ARE REPORTS THAT SOMETHING MAY BE WRONG WITH BARRY WHITE ...
7/14
www.ucomics.com
... MORE DETAILS AS THEY BECOME AVAILABLE ...

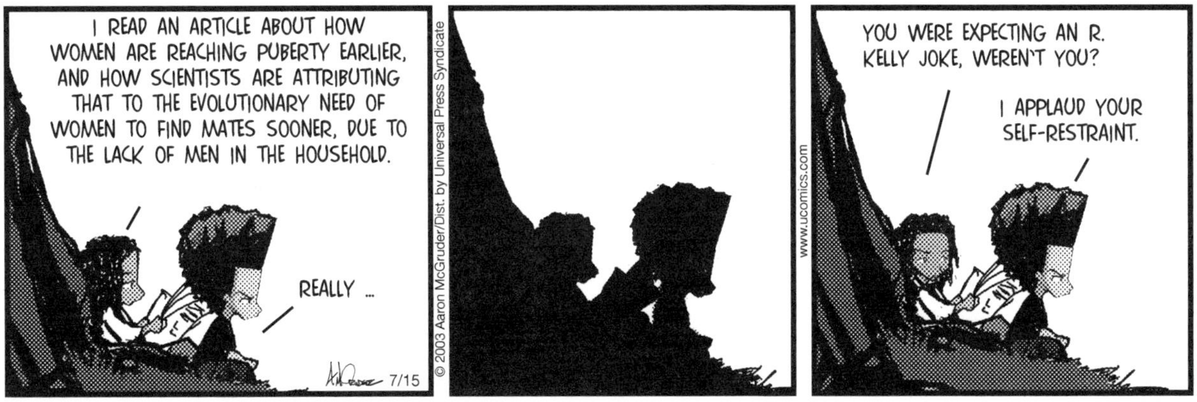
I READ AN ARTICLE ABOUT HOW WOMEN ARE REACHING PUBERTY EARLIER, AND HOW SCIENTISTS ARE ATTRIBUTING THAT TO THE EVOLUTIONARY NEED OF WOMEN TO FIND MATES SOONER, DUE TO THE LACK OF MEN IN THE HOUSEHOLD.
REALLY ...
7/15
© 2003 Aaron McGruder/Dist. by Universal Press Syndicate
www.ucomics.com
YOU WERE EXPECTING AN R. KELLY JOKE, WEREN'T YOU?
I APPLAUD YOUR SELF-RESTRAINT.

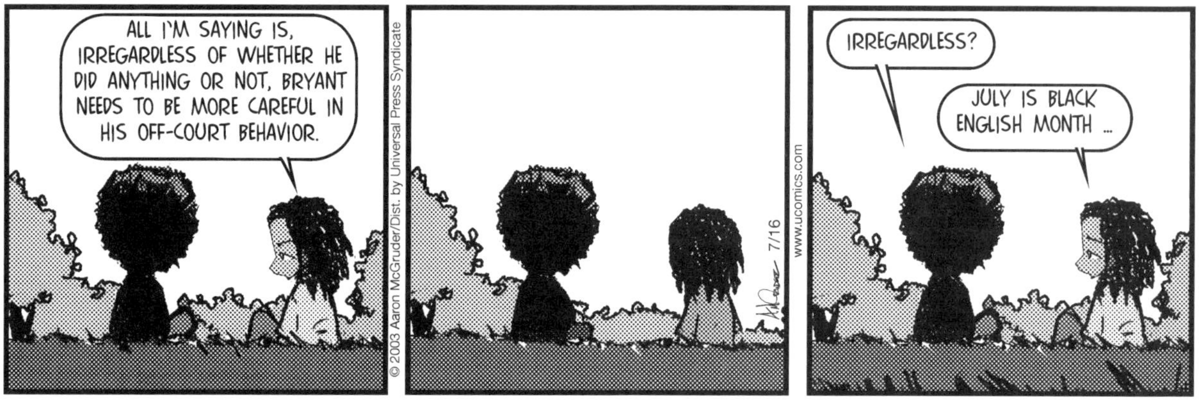
ALL I'M SAYING IS, IRREGARDLESS OF WHETHER HE DID ANYTHING OR NOT, BRYANT NEEDS TO BE MORE CAREFUL IN HIS OFF-COURT BEHAVIOR.
IRREGARDLESS?
JULY IS BLACK ENGLISH MONTH ...
7/16
© 2003 Aaron McGruder/Dist. by Universal Press Syndicate
www.ucomics.com

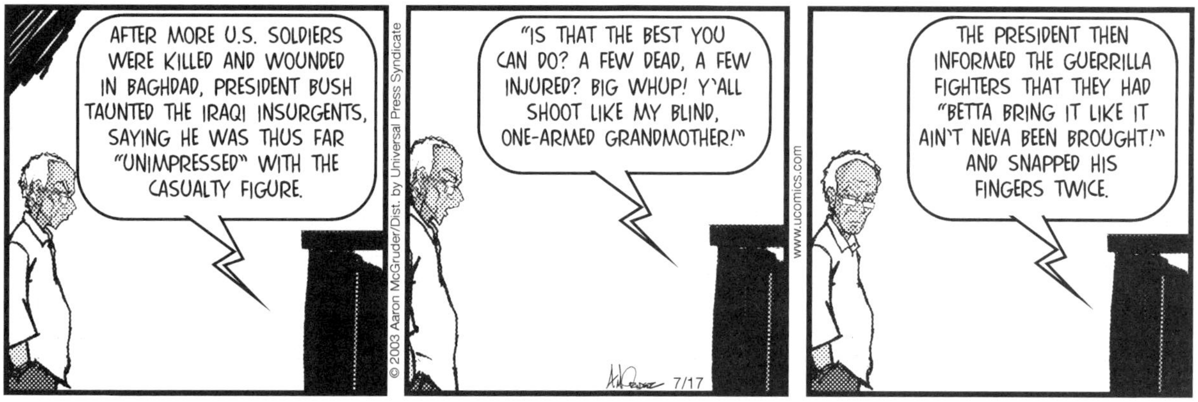
AFTER MORE U.S. SOLDIERS WERE KILLED AND WOUNDED IN BAGHDAD, PRESIDENT BUSH TAUNTED THE IRAQI INSURGENTS, SAYING HE WAS THUS FAR "UNIMPRESSED" WITH THE CASUALTY FIGURE.
"IS THAT THE BEST YOU CAN DO? A FEW DEAD, A FEW INJURED? BIG WHUP! Y'ALL SHOOT LIKE MY BLIND, ONE-ARMED GRANDMOTHER!"
THE PRESIDENT THEN INFORMED THE GUERRILLA FIGHTERS THAT THEY HAD "BETTA BRING IT LIKE IT AIN'T NEVA BEEN BROUGHT!" AND SNAPPED HIS FINGERS TWICE.
7/17
© 2003 Aaron McGruder/Dist. by Universal Press Syndicate
www.ucomics.com

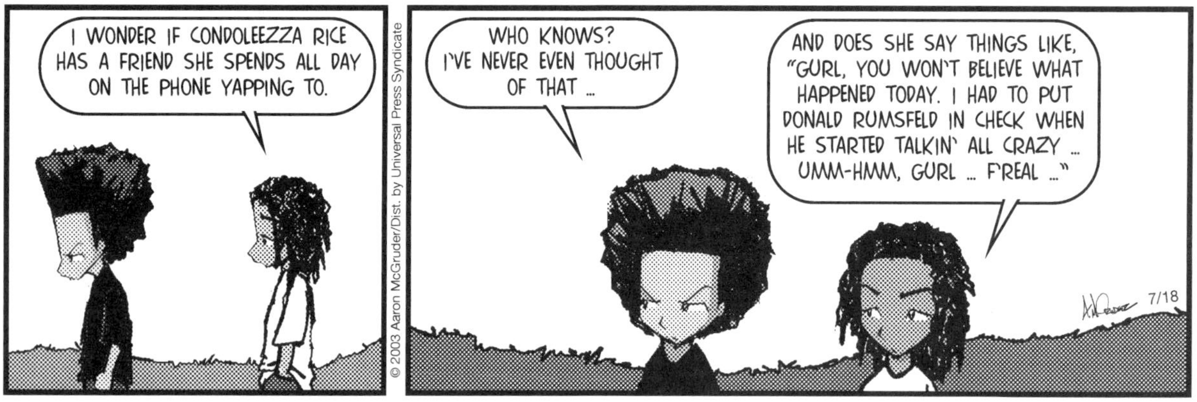
I WONDER IF CONDOLEEZZA RICE HAS A FRIEND SHE SPENDS ALL DAY ON THE PHONE YAPPING TO.
WHO KNOWS? I'VE NEVER EVEN THOUGHT OF THAT ...
AND DOES SHE SAY THINGS LIKE, "GURL, YOU WON'T BELIEVE WHAT HAPPENED TODAY. I HAD TO PUT DONALD RUMSFELD IN CHECK WHEN HE STARTED TALKIN' ALL CRAZY ... UMM-HMM, GURL ... F'REAL ..."
7/18
© 2003 Aaron McGruder/Dist. by Universal Press Syndicate

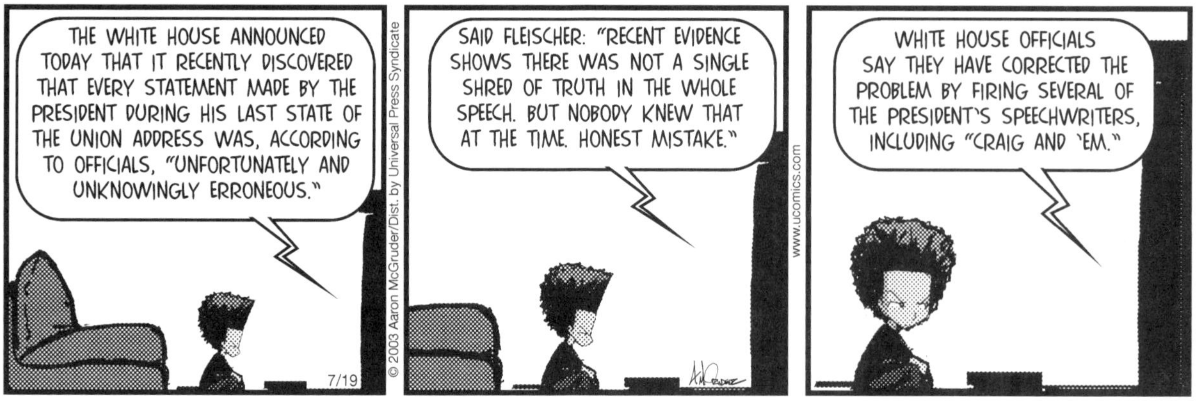
THE WHITE HOUSE ANNOUNCED TODAY THAT IT RECENTLY DISCOVERED THAT EVERY STATEMENT MADE BY THE PRESIDENT DURING HIS LAST STATE OF THE UNION ADDRESS WAS, ACCORDING TO OFFICIALS, "UNFORTUNATELY AND UNKNOWINGLY ERRONEOUS."
SAID FLEISCHER: "RECENT EVIDENCE SHOWS THERE WAS NOT A SINGLE SHRED OF TRUTH IN THE WHOLE SPEECH. BUT NOBODY KNEW THAT AT THE TIME. HONEST MISTAKE."
WHITE HOUSE OFFICIALS SAY THEY HAVE CORRECTED THE PROBLEM BY FIRING SEVERAL OF THE PRESIDENT'S SPEECHWRITERS, INCLUDING "CRAIG AND 'EM."
7/19
© 2003 Aaron McGruder/Dist. by Universal Press Syndicate
www.ucomics.com

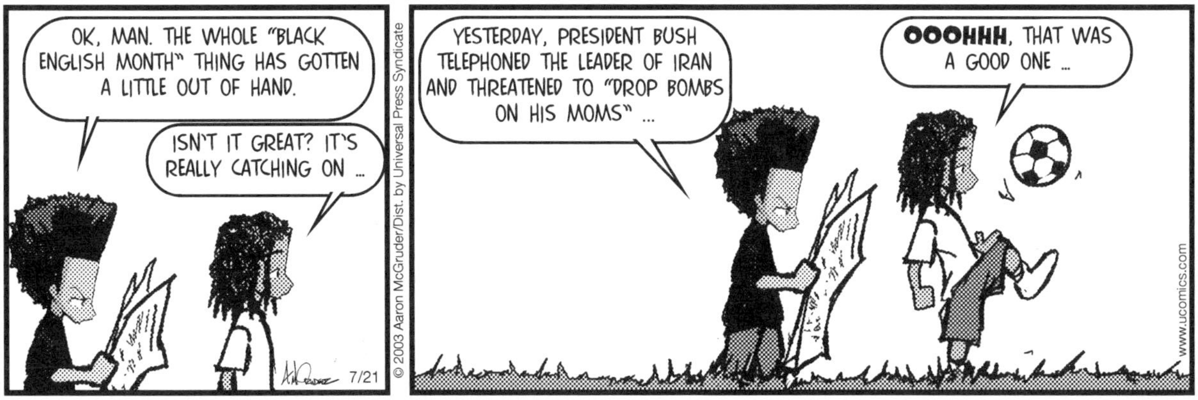
OK, MAN. THE WHOLE "BLACK ENGLISH MONTH" THING HAS GOTTEN A LITTLE OUT OF HAND.
ISN'T IT GREAT? IT'S REALLY CATCHING ON ...
YESTERDAY, PRESIDENT BUSH TELEPHONED THE LEADER OF IRAN AND THREATENED TO "DROP BOMBS ON HIS MOMS" ...
OOOHHH, THAT WAS A GOOD ONE ...
7/21
© 2003 Aaron McGruder/Dist. by Universal Press Syndicate
www.ucomics.com

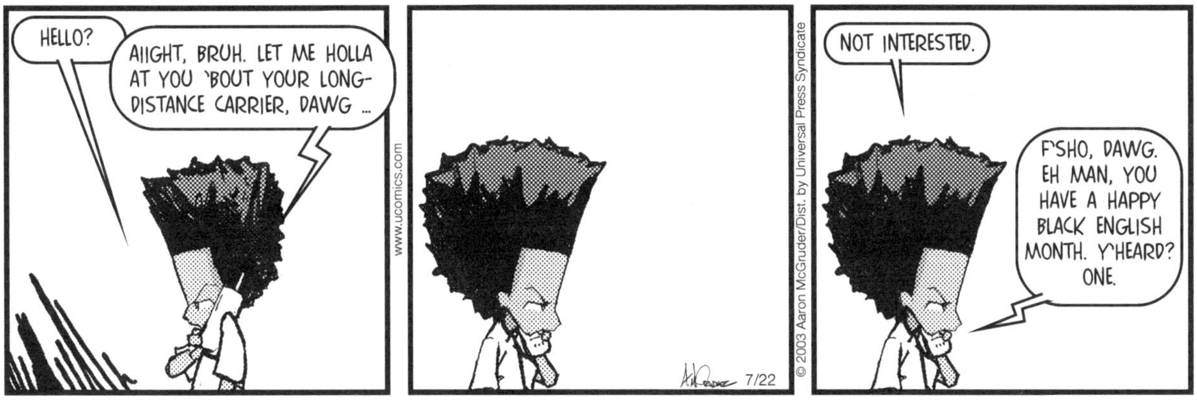
HELLO?
AIIGHT, BRUH. LET ME HOLLA AT YOU 'BOUT YOUR LONG-DISTANCE CARRIER, DAWG ...
NOT INTERESTED.
F'SHO, DAWG. EH MAN, YOU HAVE A HAPPY BLACK ENGLISH MONTH. Y'HEARD? ONE.
7/22
www.ucomics.com
© 2003 Aaron McGruder/Dist. by Universal Press Syndicate

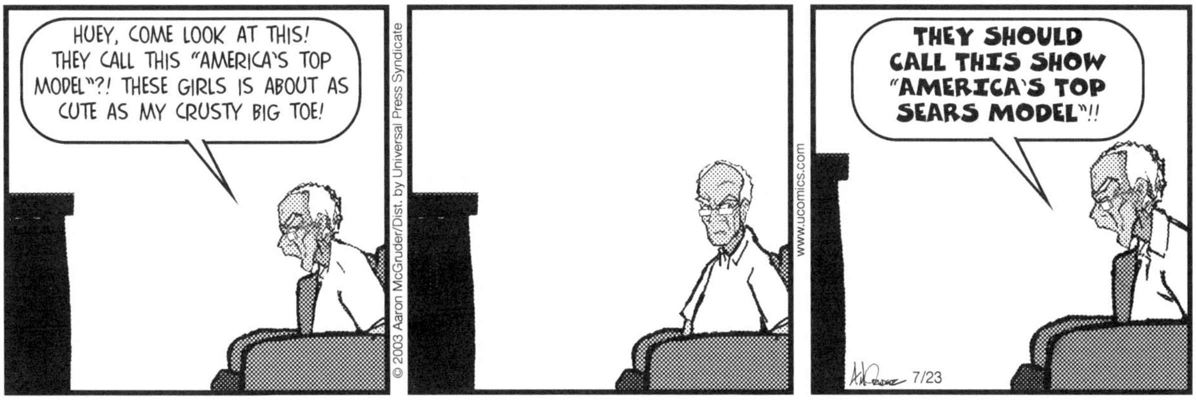
HUEY, COME LOOK AT THIS! THEY CALL THIS "AMERICA'S TOP MODEL"?! THESE GIRLS IS ABOUT AS CUTE AS MY CRUSTY BIG TOE!
THEY SHOULD CALL THIS SHOW "AMERICA'S TOP SEARS MODEL"!!
7/23
© 2003 Aaron McGruder/Dist. by Universal Press Syndicate
www.ucomics.com

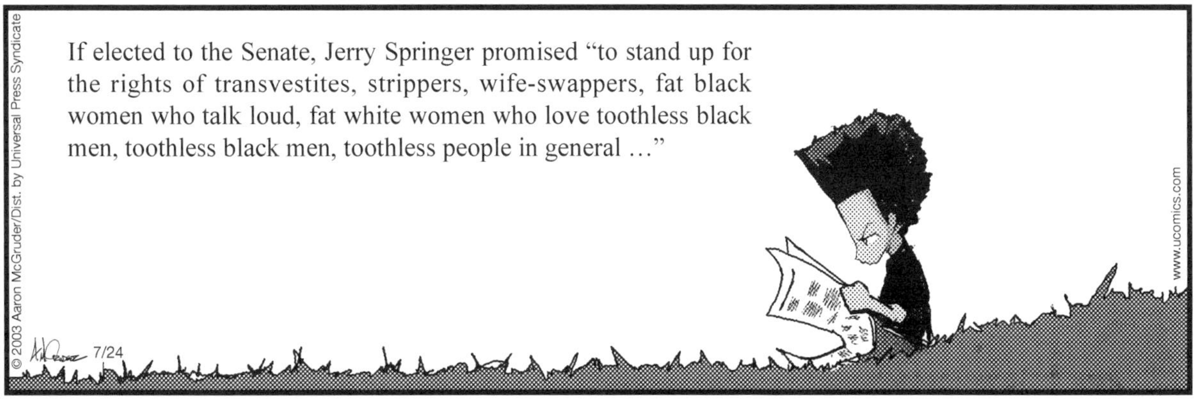
If elected to the Senate, Jerry Springer promised "to stand up for the rights of transvestites, strippers, wife-swappers, fat black women who talk loud, fat white women who love toothless black men, toothless black men, toothless people in general ..."
7/24
© 2003 Aaron McGruder/Dist. by Universal Press Syndicate
www.ucomics.com

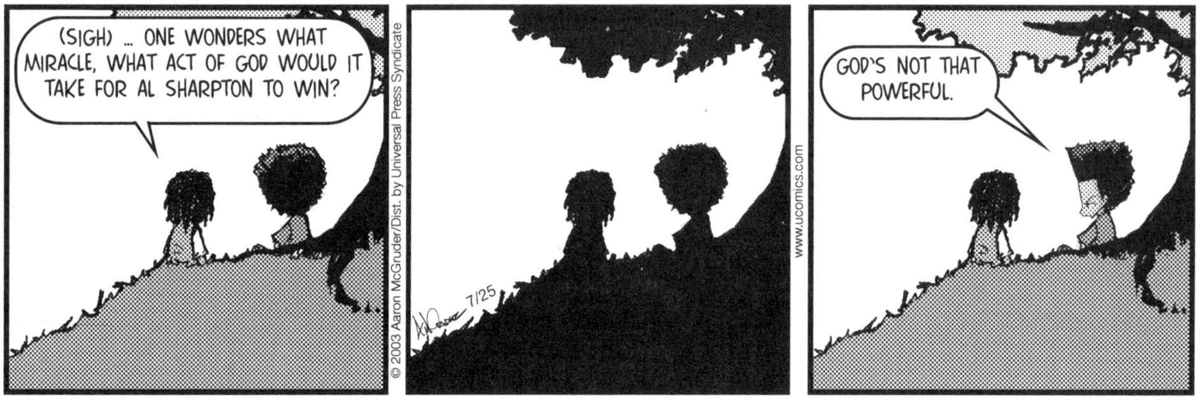
(SIGH) ... ONE WONDERS WHAT MIRACLE, WHAT ACT OF GOD WOULD IT TAKE FOR AL SHARPTON TO WIN?
© 2003 Aaron McGruder/Dist. by Universal Press Syndicate
7/25
www.ucomics.com
GOD'S NOT THAT POWERFUL.

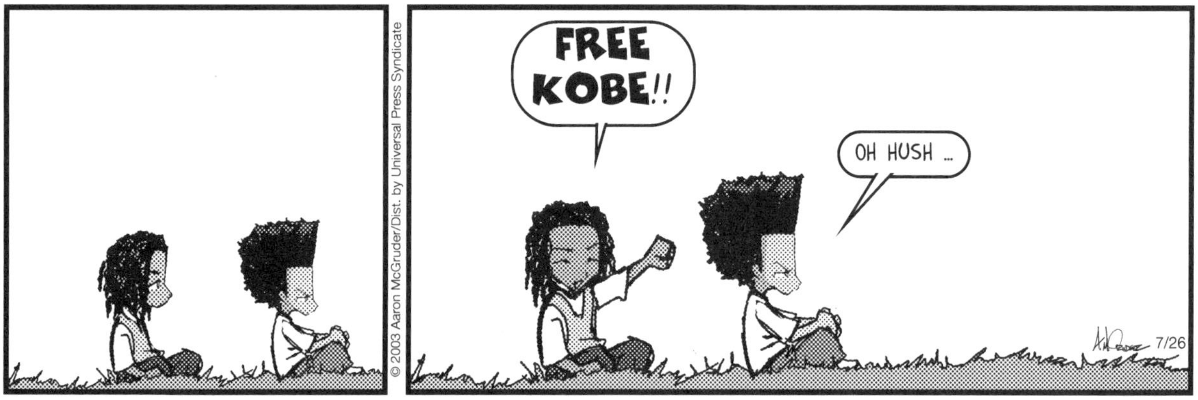
© 2003 Aaron McGruder/Dist. by Universal Press Syndicate
FREE KOBE!!
OH HUSH ...
7/26

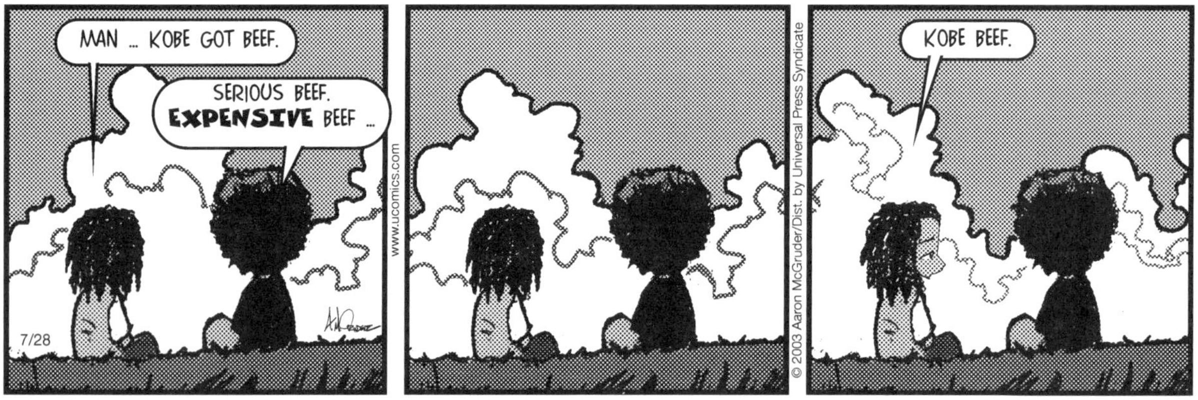
MAN ... KOBE GOT BEEF.
SERIOUS BEEF. EXPENSIVE BEEF ...
7/28
www.ucomics.com
© 2003 Aaron McGruder/Dist. by Universal Press Syndicate
KOBE BEEF.

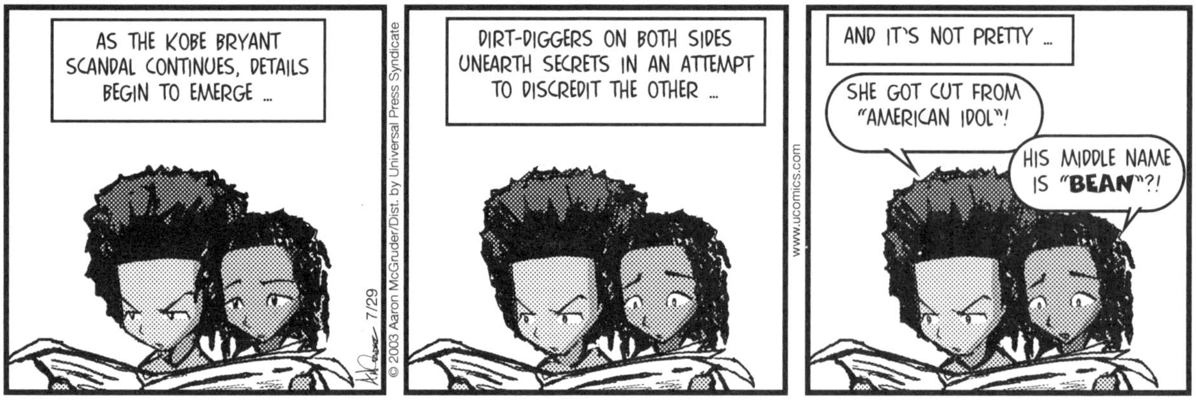
AS THE KOBE BRYANT SCANDAL CONTINUES, DETAILS BEGIN TO EMERGE ...
7/29
© 2003 Aaron McGruder/Dist. by Universal Press Syndicate
DIRT-DIGGERS ON BOTH SIDES UNEARTH SECRETS IN AN ATTEMPT TO DISCREDIT THE OTHER ...
www.ucomics.com
AND IT'S NOT PRETTY ...
SHE GOT CUT FROM "AMERICAN IDOL"!
HIS MIDDLE NAME IS "BEAN"?!

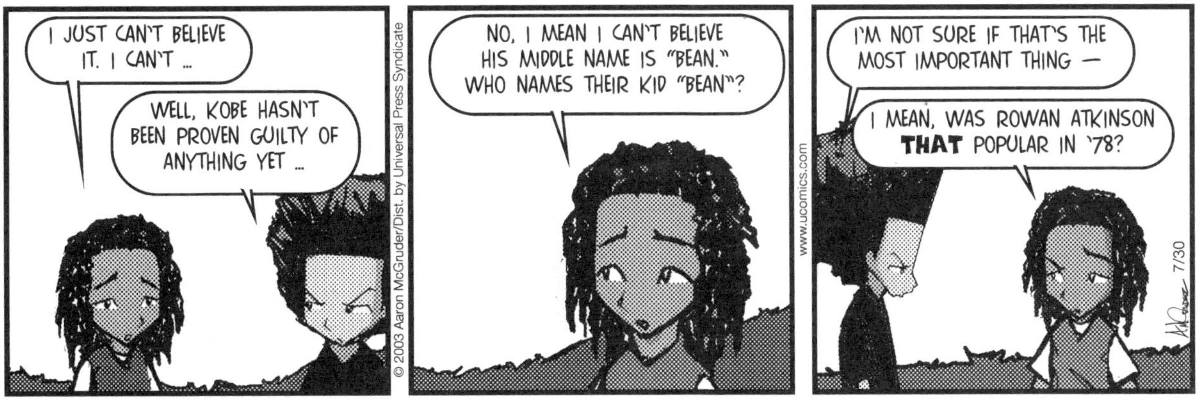
I JUST CAN'T BELIEVE IT. I CAN'T ...
WELL, KOBE HASN'T BEEN PROVEN GUILTY OF ANYTHING YET ...
© 2003 Aaron McGruder/Dist. by Universal Press Syndicate
NO, I MEAN I CAN'T BELIEVE HIS MIDDLE NAME IS "BEAN." WHO NAMES THEIR KID "BEAN"?
www.ucomics.com
I'M NOT SURE IF THAT'S THE MOST IMPORTANT THING —
I MEAN, WAS ROWAN ATKINSON **THAT** POPULAR IN '78?
7/30

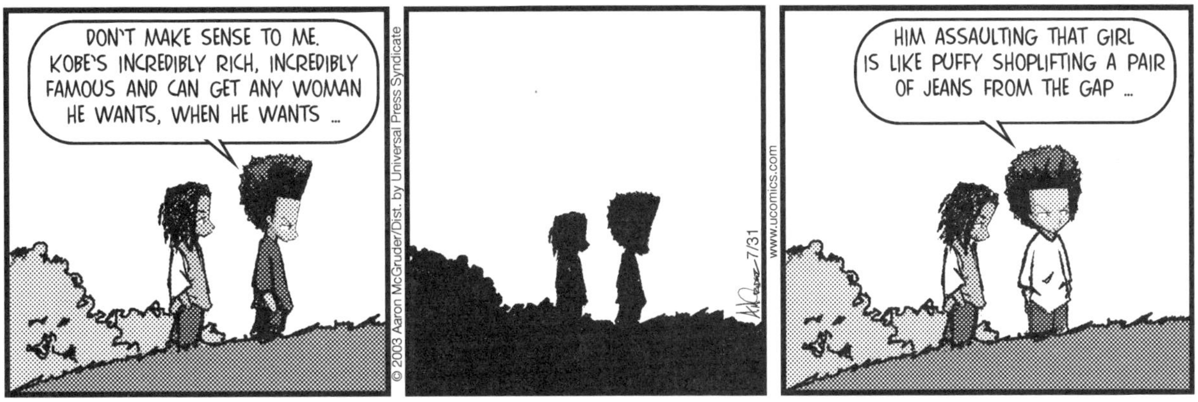
DON'T MAKE SENSE TO ME. KOBE'S INCREDIBLY RICH, INCREDIBLY FAMOUS AND CAN GET ANY WOMAN HE WANTS, WHEN HE WANTS ...
© 2003 Aaron McGruder/Dist. by Universal Press Syndicate
7/31
www.ucomics.com
HIM ASSAULTING THAT GIRL IS LIKE PUFFY SHOPLIFTING A PAIR OF JEANS FROM THE GAP ...

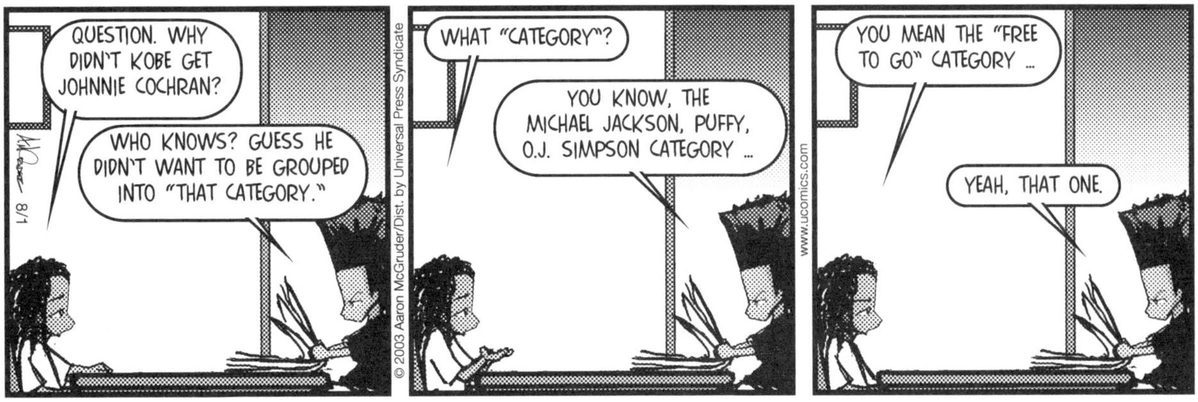
QUESTION. WHY DIDN'T KOBE GET JOHNNIE COCHRAN?
8/1
WHO KNOWS? GUESS HE DIDN'T WANT TO BE GROUPED INTO "THAT CATEGORY."
© 2003 Aaron McGruder/Dist. by Universal Press Syndicate
WHAT "CATEGORY"?
YOU KNOW, THE MICHAEL JACKSON, PUFFY, O.J. SIMPSON CATEGORY ...
www.ucomics.com
YOU MEAN THE "FREE TO GO" CATEGORY ...
YEAH, THAT ONE.

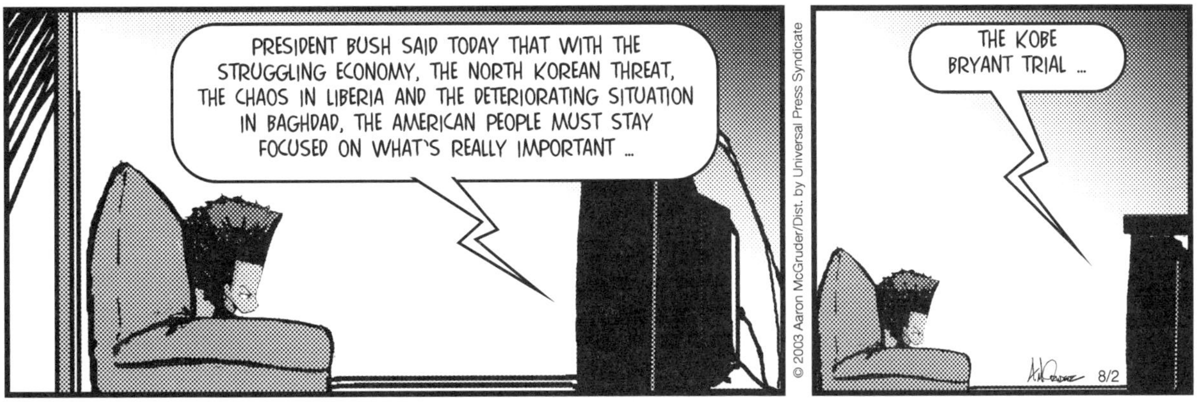
PRESIDENT BUSH SAID TODAY THAT WITH THE STRUGGLING ECONOMY, THE NORTH KOREAN THREAT, THE CHAOS IN LIBERIA AND THE DETERIORATING SITUATION IN BAGHDAD, THE AMERICAN PEOPLE MUST STAY FOCUSED ON WHAT'S REALLY IMPORTANT ...
© 2003 Aaron McGruder/Dist. by Universal Press Syndicate
THE KOBE BRYANT TRIAL ...
8/2

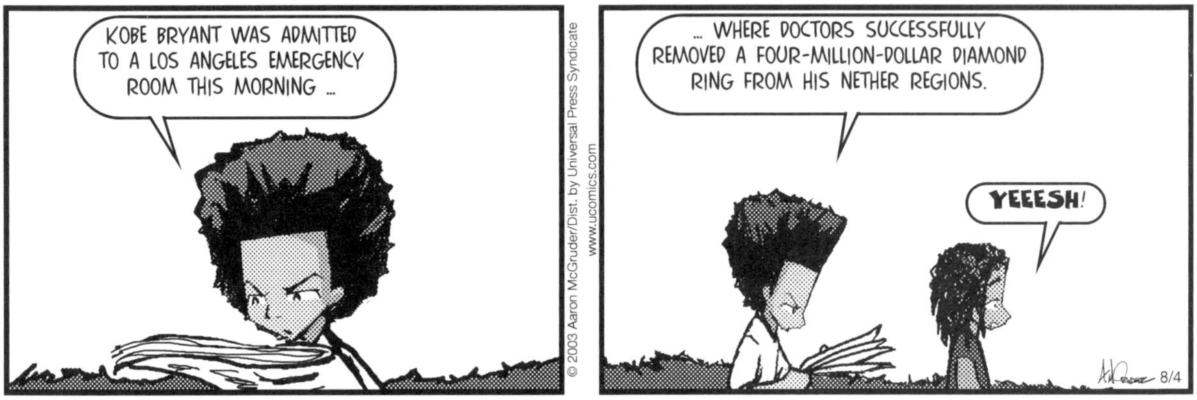
KOBE BRYANT WAS ADMITTED TO A LOS ANGELES EMERGENCY ROOM THIS MORNING ...
... WHERE DOCTORS SUCCESSFULLY REMOVED A FOUR-MILLION-DOLLAR DIAMOND RING FROM HIS NETHER REGIONS.
YEEESH!
8/4
© 2003 Aaron McGruder/Dist. by Universal Press Syndicate
www.ucomics.com

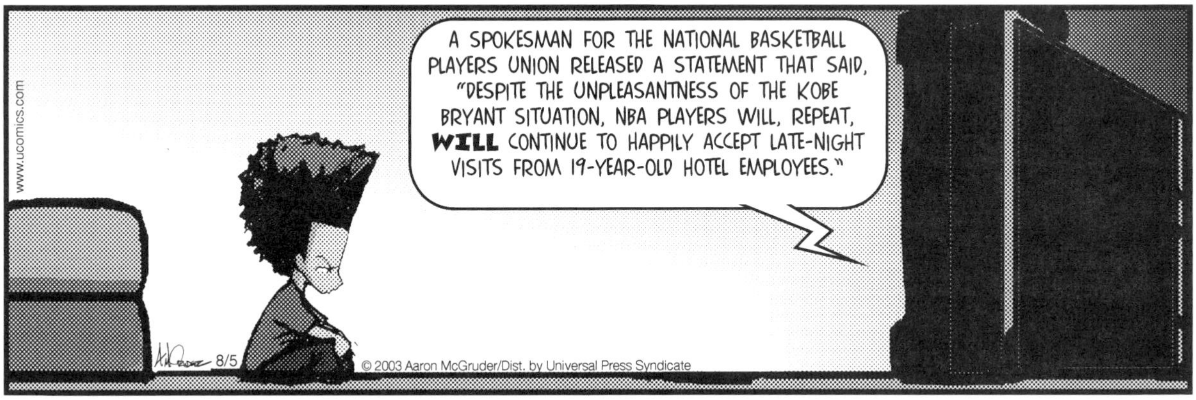
A SPOKESMAN FOR THE NATIONAL BASKETBALL PLAYERS UNION RELEASED A STATEMENT THAT SAID, "DESPITE THE UNPLEASANTNESS OF THE KOBE BRYANT SITUATION, NBA PLAYERS WILL, REPEAT, WILL CONTINUE TO HAPPILY ACCEPT LATE-NIGHT VISITS FROM 19-YEAR-OLD HOTEL EMPLOYEES."
8/5
© 2003 Aaron McGruder/Dist. by Universal Press Syndicate
www.ucomics.com

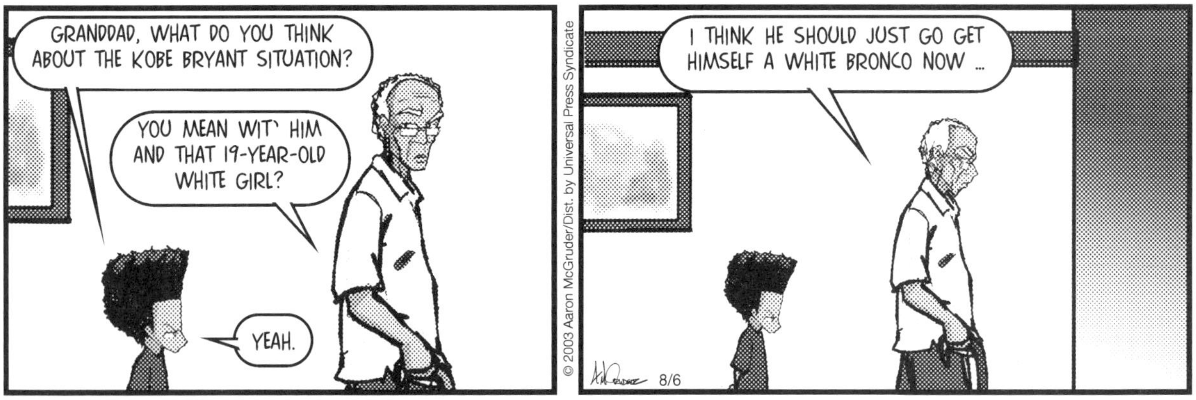
GRANDDAD, WHAT DO YOU THINK ABOUT THE KOBE BRYANT SITUATION?
YOU MEAN WIT' HIM AND THAT 19-YEAR-OLD WHITE GIRL?
YEAH.
I THINK HE SHOULD JUST GO GET HIMSELF A WHITE BRONCO NOW ...
8/6
© 2003 Aaron McGruder/Dist. by Universal Press Syndicate

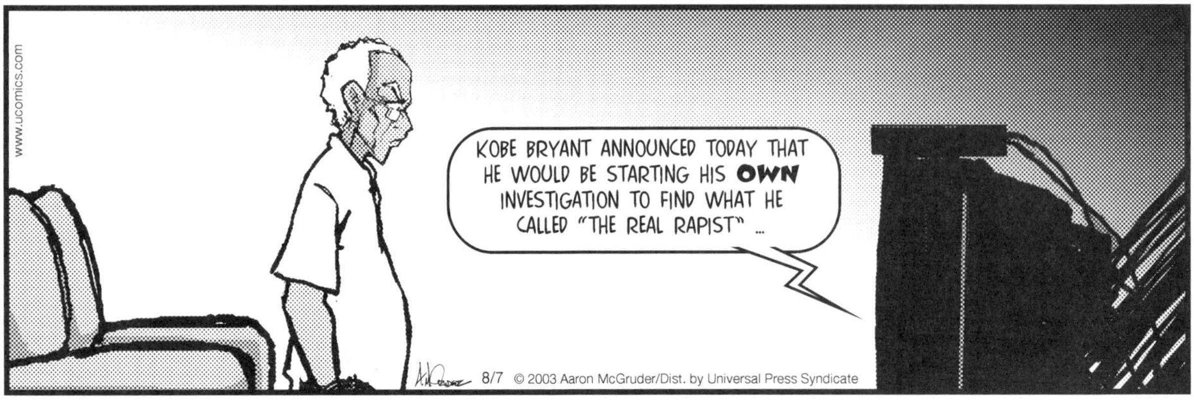
KOBE BRYANT ANNOUNCED TODAY THAT HE WOULD BE STARTING HIS OWN INVESTIGATION TO FIND WHAT HE CALLED "THE REAL RAPIST" ...
8/7
© 2003 Aaron McGruder/Dist. by Universal Press Syndicate
www.ucomics.com

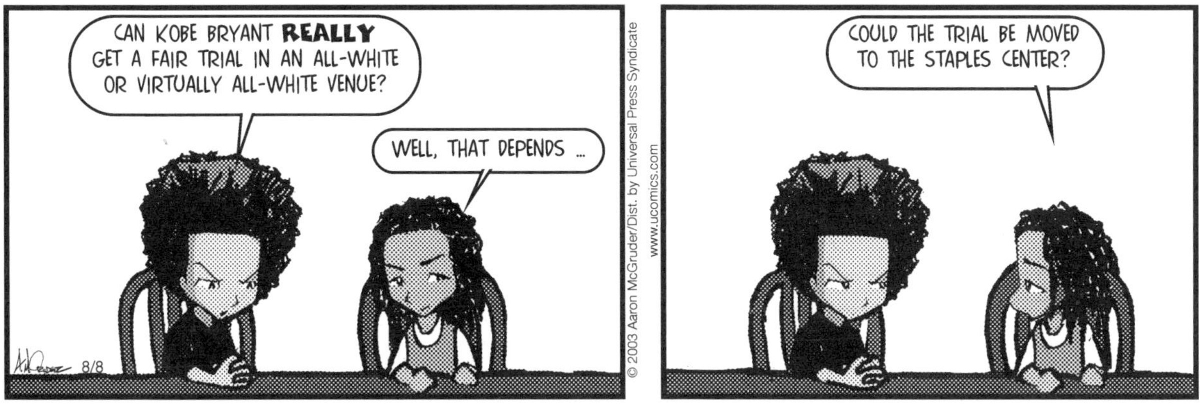
CAN KOBE BRYANT **REALLY** GET A FAIR TRIAL IN AN ALL-WHITE OR VIRTUALLY ALL-WHITE VENUE?
WELL, THAT DEPENDS ...
8/8
COULD THE TRIAL BE MOVED TO THE STAPLES CENTER?

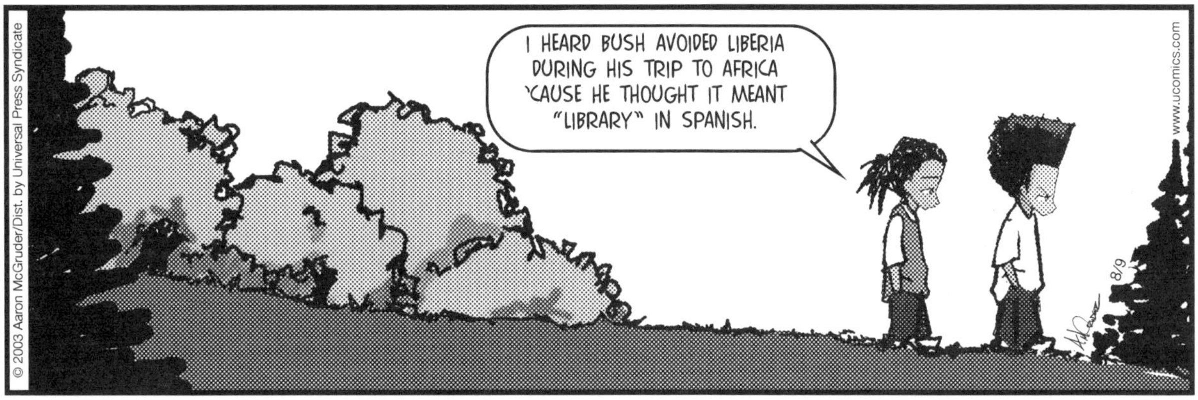
I HEARD BUSH AVOIDED LIBERIA DURING HIS TRIP TO AFRICA 'CAUSE HE THOUGHT IT MEANT "LIBRARY" IN SPANISH.
8/9

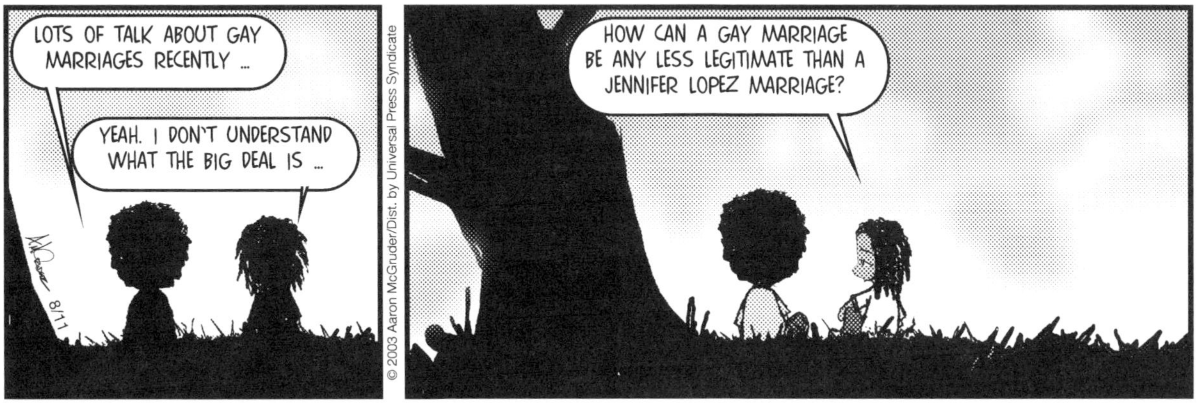
LOTS OF TALK ABOUT GAY MARRIAGES RECENTLY ...
YEAH. I DON'T UNDERSTAND WHAT THE BIG DEAL IS ...
8/11
HOW CAN A GAY MARRIAGE BE ANY LESS LEGITIMATE THAN A JENNIFER LOPEZ MARRIAGE?

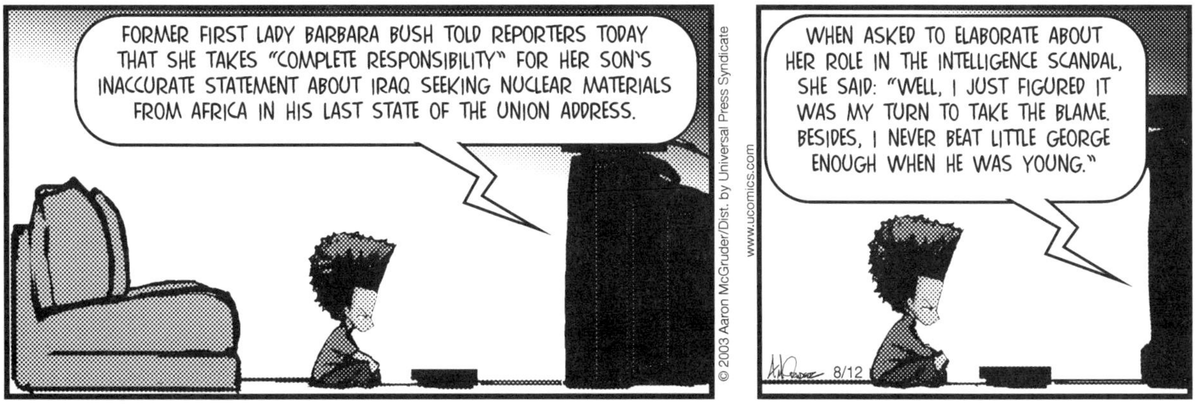
FORMER FIRST LADY BARBARA BUSH TOLD REPORTERS TODAY THAT SHE TAKES "COMPLETE RESPONSIBILITY" FOR HER SON'S INACCURATE STATEMENT ABOUT IRAQ SEEKING NUCLEAR MATERIALS FROM AFRICA IN HIS LAST STATE OF THE UNION ADDRESS.
WHEN ASKED TO ELABORATE ABOUT HER ROLE IN THE INTELLIGENCE SCANDAL, SHE SAID: "WELL, I JUST FIGURED IT WAS MY TURN TO TAKE THE BLAME. BESIDES, I NEVER BEAT LITTLE GEORGE ENOUGH WHEN HE WAS YOUNG."
8/12

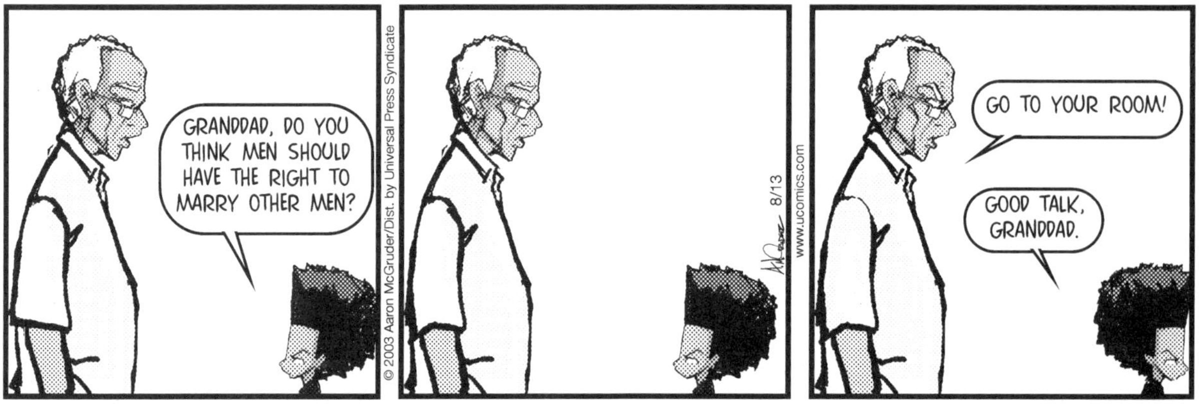
GRANDDAD, DO YOU THINK MEN SHOULD HAVE THE RIGHT TO MARRY OTHER MEN?
© 2003 Aaron McGruder/Dist. by Universal Press Syndicate
8/13
www.ucomics.com
GO TO YOUR ROOM!
GOOD TALK, GRANDDAD.

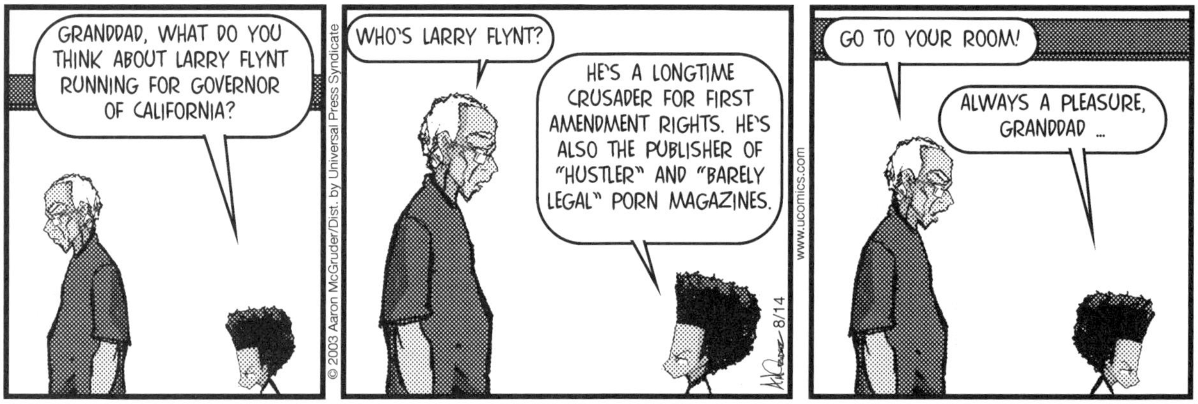
GRANDDAD, WHAT DO YOU THINK ABOUT LARRY FLYNT RUNNING FOR GOVERNOR OF CALIFORNIA?
© 2003 Aaron McGruder/Dist. by Universal Press Syndicate
WHO'S LARRY FLYNT?
HE'S A LONGTIME CRUSADER FOR FIRST AMENDMENT RIGHTS. HE'S ALSO THE PUBLISHER OF "HUSTLER" AND "BARELY LEGAL" PORN MAGAZINES.
8/14
www.ucomics.com
GO TO YOUR ROOM!
ALWAYS A PLEASURE, GRANDDAD ...

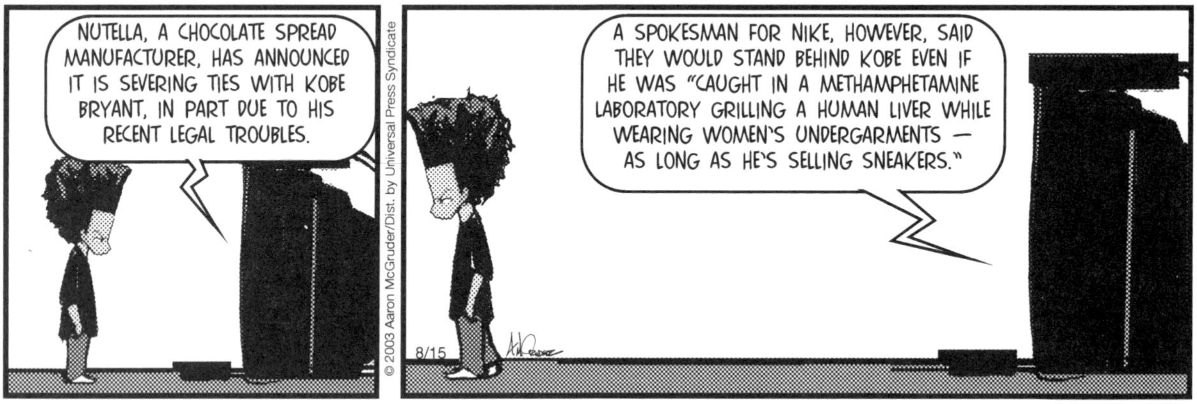
NUTELLA, A CHOCOLATE SPREAD MANUFACTURER, HAS ANNOUNCED IT IS SEVERING TIES WITH KOBE BRYANT, IN PART DUE TO HIS RECENT LEGAL TROUBLES.
© 2003 Aaron McGruder/Dist. by Universal Press Syndicate
8/15
A SPOKESMAN FOR NIKE, HOWEVER, SAID THEY WOULD STAND BEHIND KOBE EVEN IF HE WAS "CAUGHT IN A METHAMPHETAMINE LABORATORY GRILLING A HUMAN LIVER WHILE WEARING WOMEN'S UNDERGARMENTS — AS LONG AS HE'S SELLING SNEAKERS."

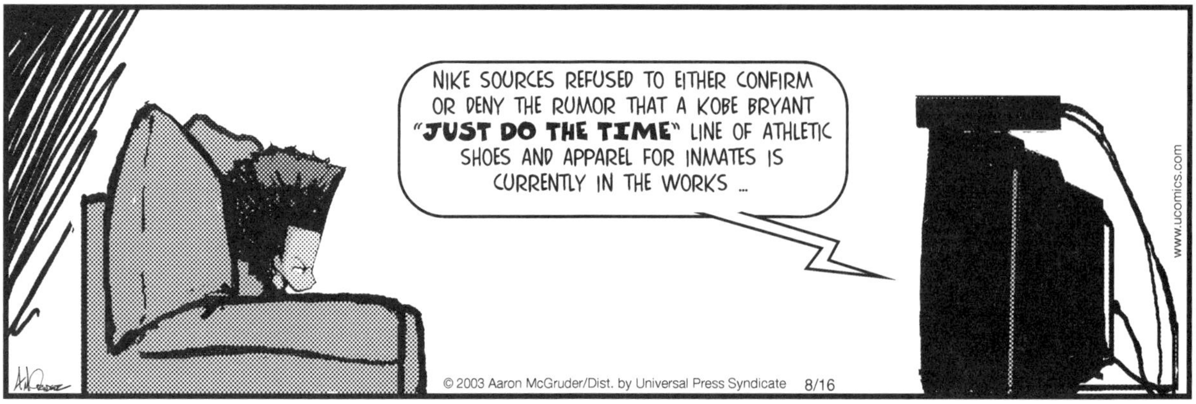
NIKE SOURCES REFUSED TO EITHER CONFIRM OR DENY THE RUMOR THAT A KOBE BRYANT "JUST DO THE TIME" LINE OF ATHLETIC SHOES AND APPAREL FOR INMATES IS CURRENTLY IN THE WORKS ...
www.ucomics.com
© 2003 Aaron McGruder/Dist. by Universal Press Syndicate 8/16

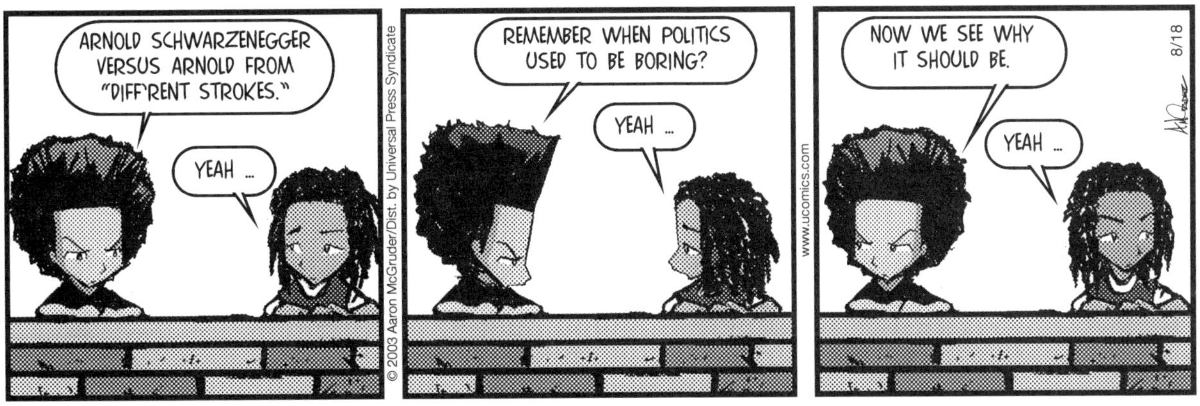
ARNOLD SCHWARZENEGGER VERSUS ARNOLD FROM "DIFF'RENT STROKES."
YEAH ...
REMEMBER WHEN POLITICS USED TO BE BORING?
YEAH ...
NOW WE SEE WHY IT SHOULD BE.
YEAH ...
© 2003 Aaron McGruder/Dist. by Universal Press Syndicate
www.ucomics.com
8/18

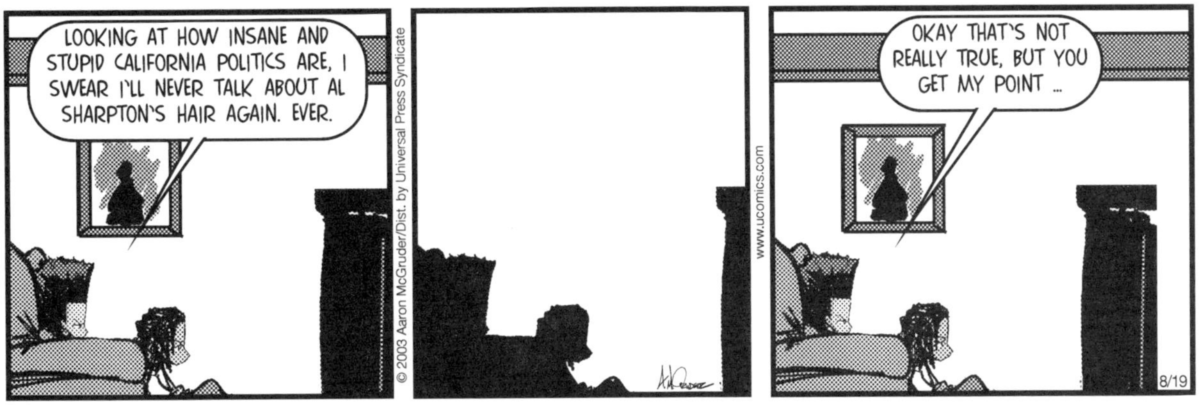
LOOKING AT HOW INSANE AND STUPID CALIFORNIA POLITICS ARE, I SWEAR I'LL NEVER TALK ABOUT AL SHARPTON'S HAIR AGAIN. EVER.
OKAY THAT'S NOT REALLY TRUE, BUT YOU GET MY POINT ...
© 2003 Aaron McGruder/Dist. by Universal Press Syndicate
www.ucomics.com
8/19

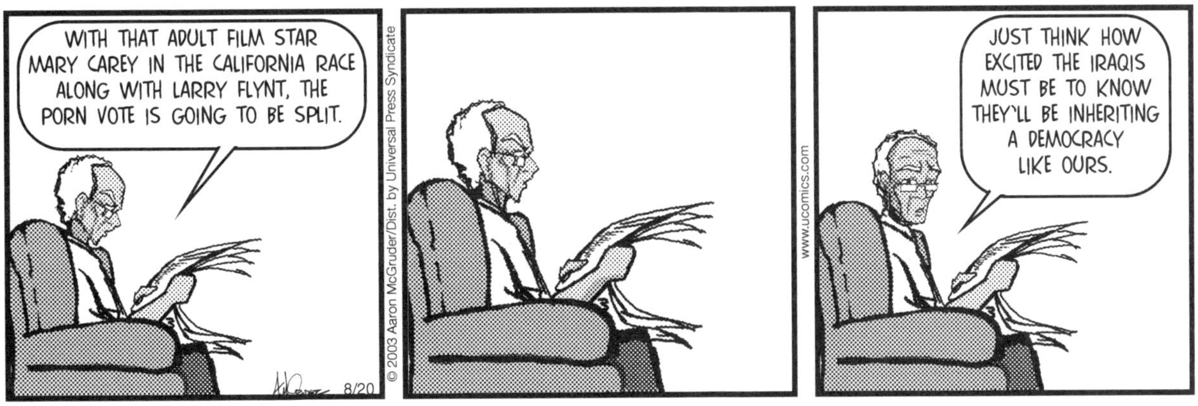
WITH THAT ADULT FILM STAR MARY CAREY IN THE CALIFORNIA RACE ALONG WITH LARRY FLYNT, THE PORN VOTE IS GOING TO BE SPLIT.
JUST THINK HOW EXCITED THE IRAQIS MUST BE TO KNOW THEY'LL BE INHERITING A DEMOCRACY LIKE OURS.
© 2003 Aaron McGruder/Dist. by Universal Press Syndicate
www.ucomics.com
8/20

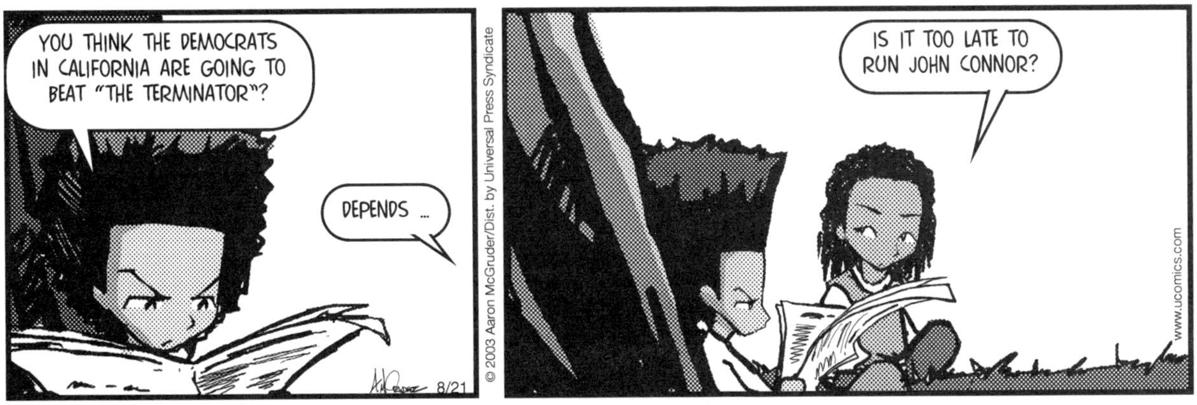
YOU THINK THE DEMOCRATS IN CALIFORNIA ARE GOING TO BEAT "THE TERMINATOR"?
DEPENDS ...
IS IT TOO LATE TO RUN JOHN CONNOR?
© 2003 Aaron McGruder/Dist. by Universal Press Syndicate
www.ucomics.com
8/21

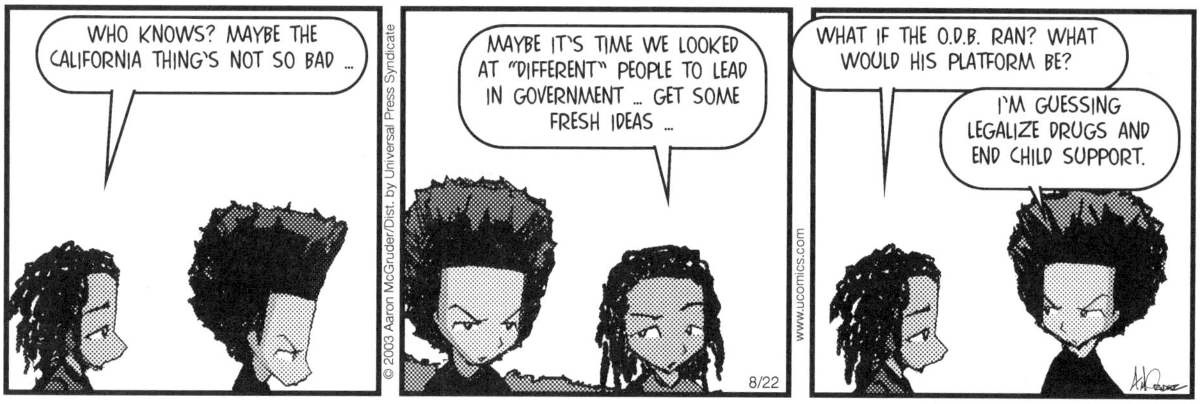
WHO KNOWS? MAYBE THE CALIFORNIA THING'S NOT SO BAD ...
MAYBE IT'S TIME WE LOOKED AT "DIFFERENT" PEOPLE TO LEAD IN GOVERNMENT ... GET SOME FRESH IDEAS ...
WHAT IF THE O.D.B. RAN? WHAT WOULD HIS PLATFORM BE?
I'M GUESSING LEGALIZE DRUGS AND END CHILD SUPPORT.
© 2003 Aaron McGruder/Dist. by Universal Press Syndicate
8/22
www.ucomics.com

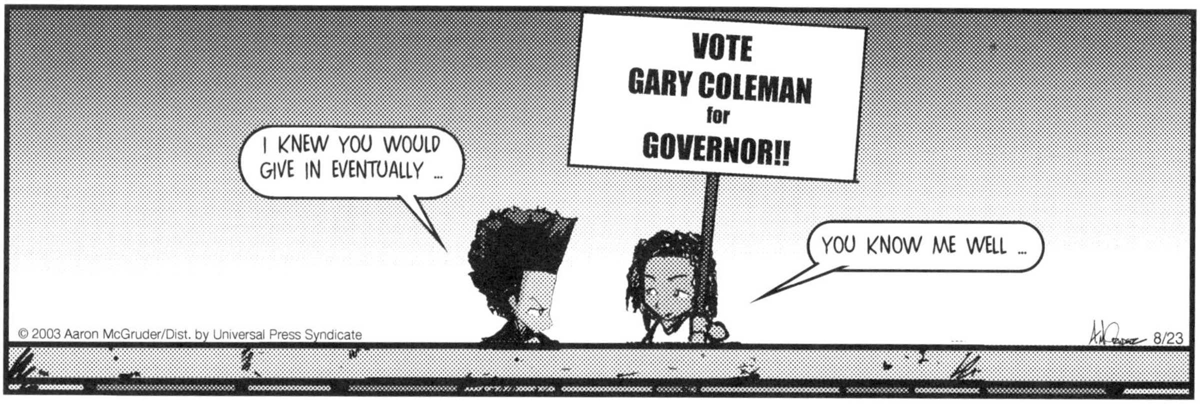
VOTE GARY COLEMAN for GOVERNOR!!
I KNEW YOU WOULD GIVE IN EVENTUALLY ...
YOU KNOW ME WELL ...
© 2003 Aaron McGruder/Dist. by Universal Press Syndicate
8/23

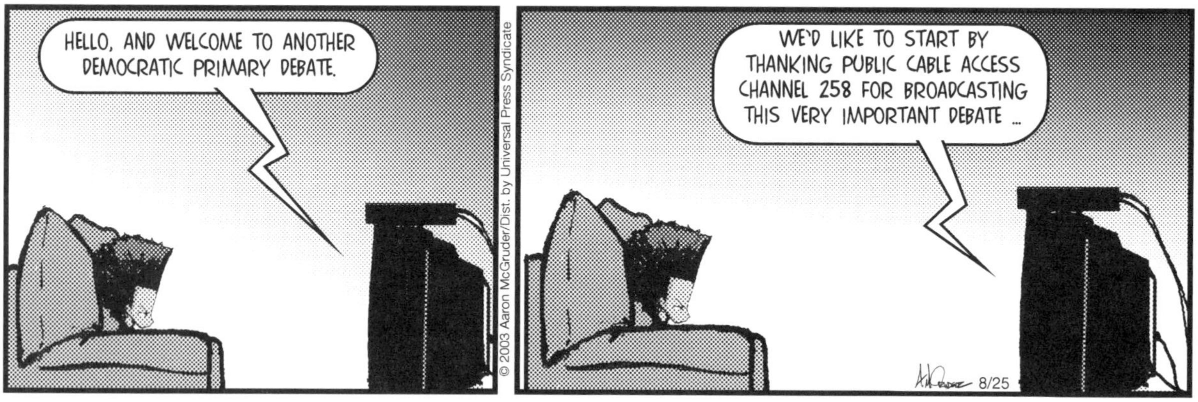
HELLO, AND WELCOME TO ANOTHER DEMOCRATIC PRIMARY DEBATE.
WE'D LIKE TO START BY THANKING PUBLIC CABLE ACCESS CHANNEL 258 FOR BROADCASTING THIS VERY IMPORTANT DEBATE ...
© 2003 Aaron McGruder/Dist. by Universal Press Syndicate
8/25

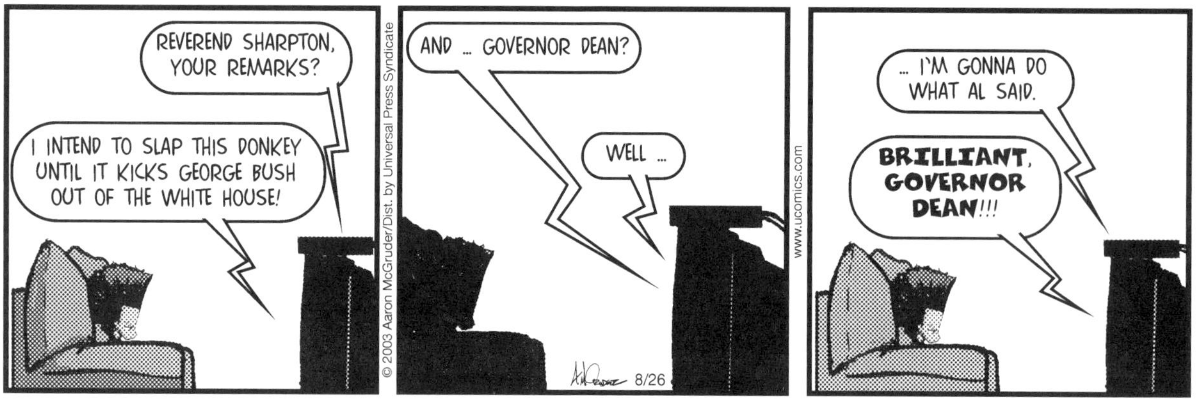
REVEREND SHARPTON, YOUR REMARKS?
I INTEND TO SLAP THIS DONKEY UNTIL IT KICKS GEORGE BUSH OUT OF THE WHITE HOUSE!
AND ... GOVERNOR DEAN?
WELL ...
... I'M GONNA DO WHAT AL SAID.
BRILLIANT, GOVERNOR DEAN!!!
© 2003 Aaron McGruder/Dist. by Universal Press Syndicate
8/26
www.ucomics.com

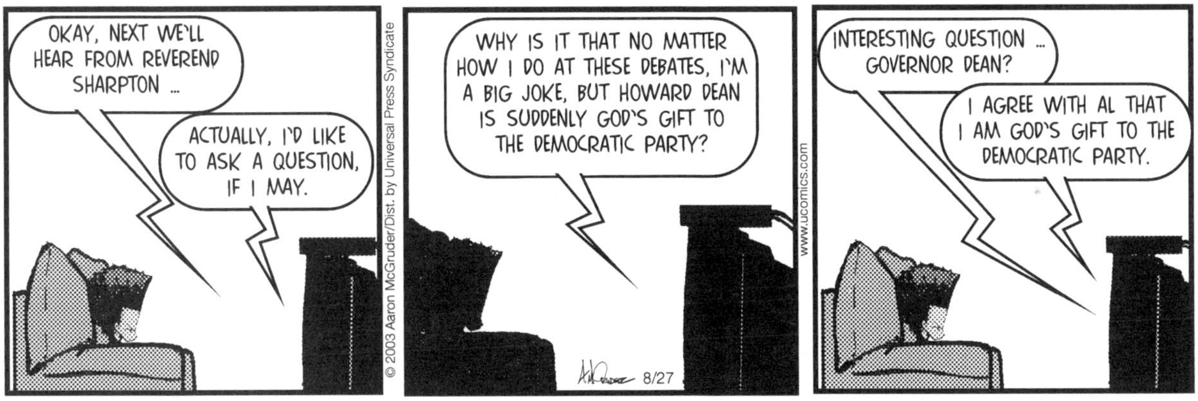
OKAY, NEXT WE'LL HEAR FROM REVEREND SHARPTON ...
ACTUALLY, I'D LIKE TO ASK A QUESTION, IF I MAY.
© 2003 Aaron McGruder/Dist. by Universal Press Syndicate
WHY IS IT THAT NO MATTER HOW I DO AT THESE DEBATES, I'M A BIG JOKE, BUT HOWARD DEAN IS SUDDENLY GOD'S GIFT TO THE DEMOCRATIC PARTY?
8/27
www.ucomics.com
INTERESTING QUESTION ... GOVERNOR DEAN?
I AGREE WITH AL THAT I AM GOD'S GIFT TO THE DEMOCRATIC PARTY.

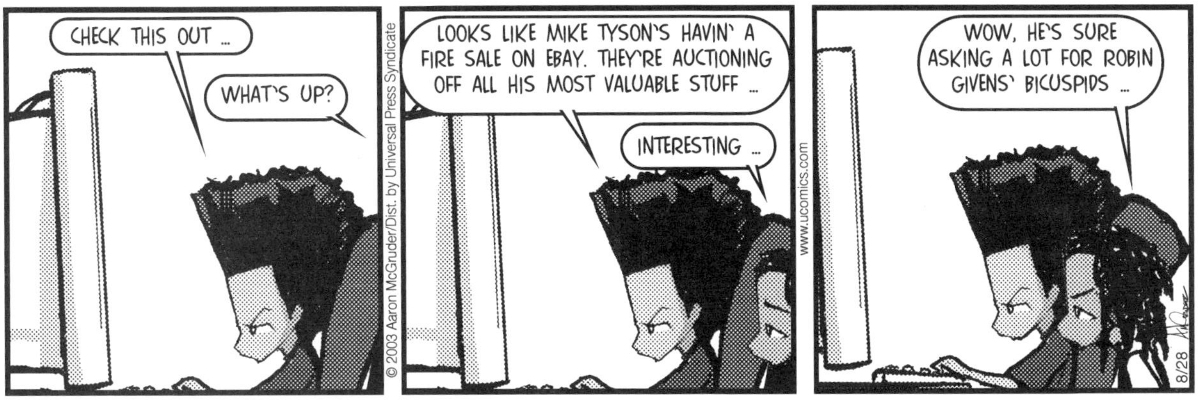
CHECK THIS OUT ...
WHAT'S UP?
© 2003 Aaron McGruder/Dist. by Universal Press Syndicate
LOOKS LIKE MIKE TYSON'S HAVIN' A FIRE SALE ON EBAY. THEY'RE AUCTIONING OFF ALL HIS MOST VALUABLE STUFF ...
INTERESTING ...
www.ucomics.com
WOW, HE'S SURE ASKING A LOT FOR ROBIN GIVENS' BICUSPIDS ...
8/28

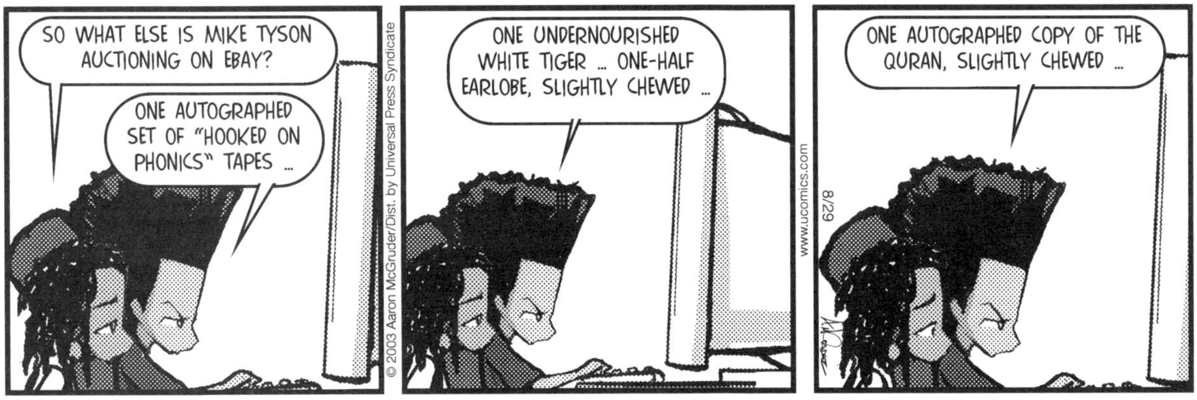
SO WHAT ELSE IS MIKE TYSON AUCTIONING ON EBAY?
ONE AUTOGRAPHED SET OF "HOOKED ON PHONICS" TAPES ...
© 2003 Aaron McGruder/Dist. by Universal Press Syndicate
ONE UNDERNOURISHED WHITE TIGER ... ONE-HALF EARLOBE, SLIGHTLY CHEWED ...
8/29
www.ucomics.com
ONE AUTOGRAPHED COPY OF THE QURAN, SLIGHTLY CHEWED ...

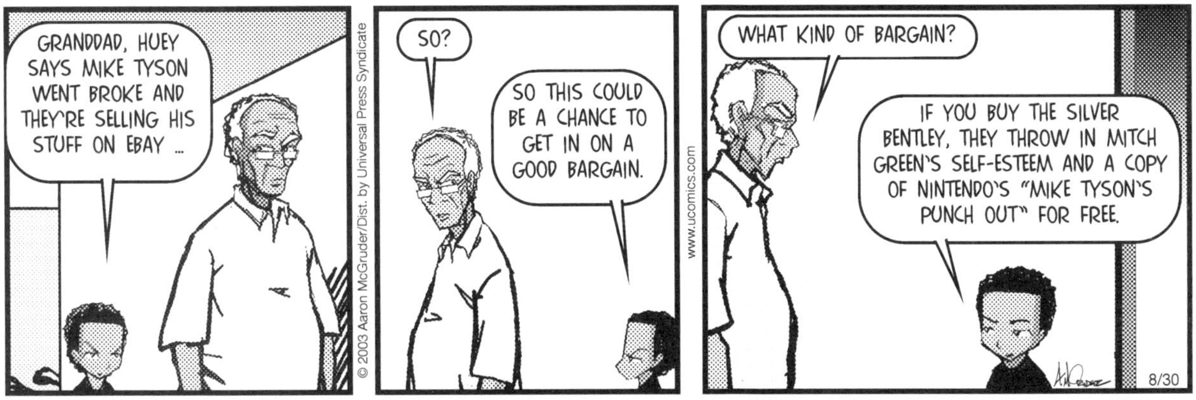
GRANDDAD, HUEY SAYS MIKE TYSON WENT BROKE AND THEY'RE SELLING HIS STUFF ON EBAY ...
© 2003 Aaron McGruder/Dist. by Universal Press Syndicate
SO?
SO THIS COULD BE A CHANCE TO GET IN ON A GOOD BARGAIN.
www.ucomics.com
WHAT KIND OF BARGAIN?
IF YOU BUY THE SILVER BENTLEY, THEY THROW IN MITCH GREEN'S SELF-ESTEEM AND A COPY OF NINTENDO'S "MIKE TYSON'S PUNCH OUT" FOR FREE.
8/30

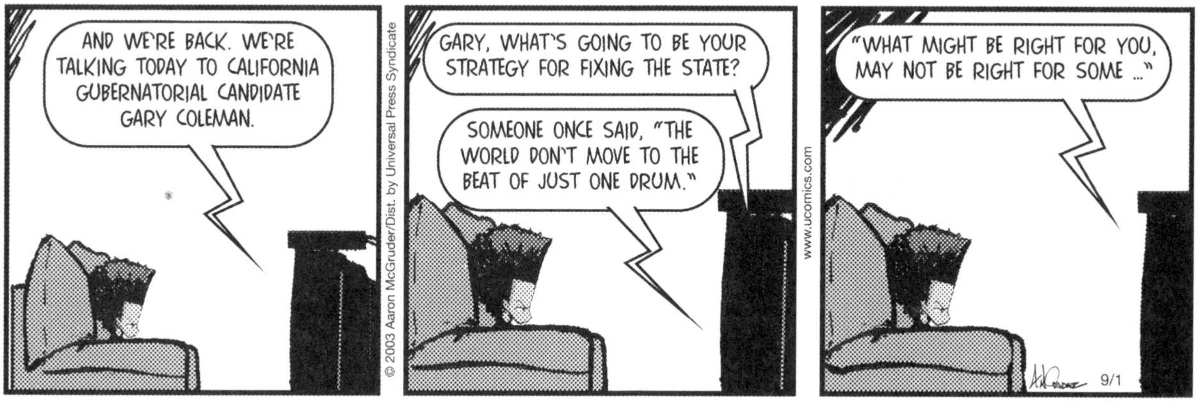
AND WE'RE BACK. WE'RE TALKING TODAY TO CALIFORNIA GUBERNATORIAL CANDIDATE GARY COLEMAN.
GARY, WHAT'S GOING TO BE YOUR STRATEGY FOR FIXING THE STATE?
SOMEONE ONCE SAID, "THE WORLD DON'T MOVE TO THE BEAT OF JUST ONE DRUM."
"WHAT MIGHT BE RIGHT FOR YOU, MAY NOT BE RIGHT FOR SOME ..."
© 2003 Aaron McGruder/Dist. by Universal Press Syndicate
www.ucomics.com
9/1

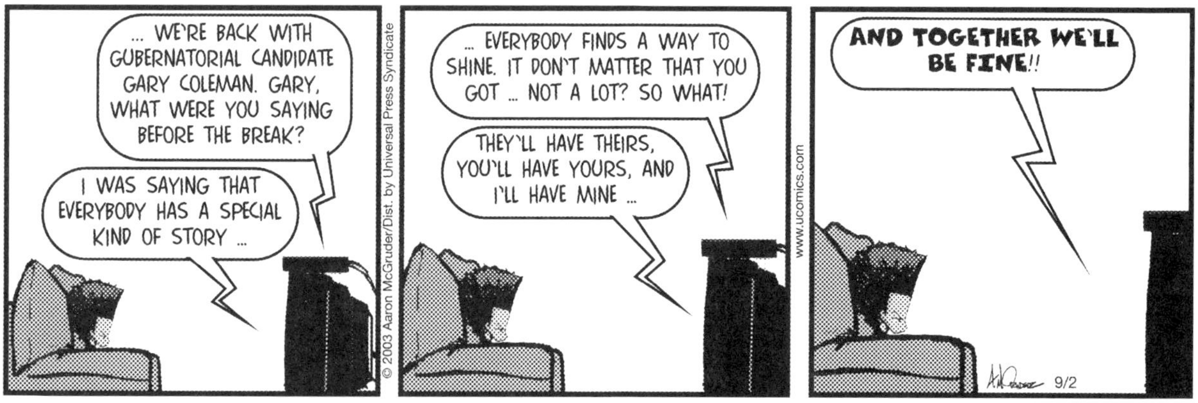
... WE'RE BACK WITH GUBERNATORIAL CANDIDATE GARY COLEMAN. GARY, WHAT WERE YOU SAYING BEFORE THE BREAK?
I WAS SAYING THAT EVERYBODY HAS A SPECIAL KIND OF STORY ...
... EVERYBODY FINDS A WAY TO SHINE. IT DON'T MATTER THAT YOU GOT ... NOT A LOT? SO WHAT!
THEY'LL HAVE THEIRS, YOU'LL HAVE YOURS, AND I'LL HAVE MINE ...
AND TOGETHER WE'LL BE FINE!!
© 2003 Aaron McGruder/Dist. by Universal Press Syndicate
www.ucomics.com
9/2

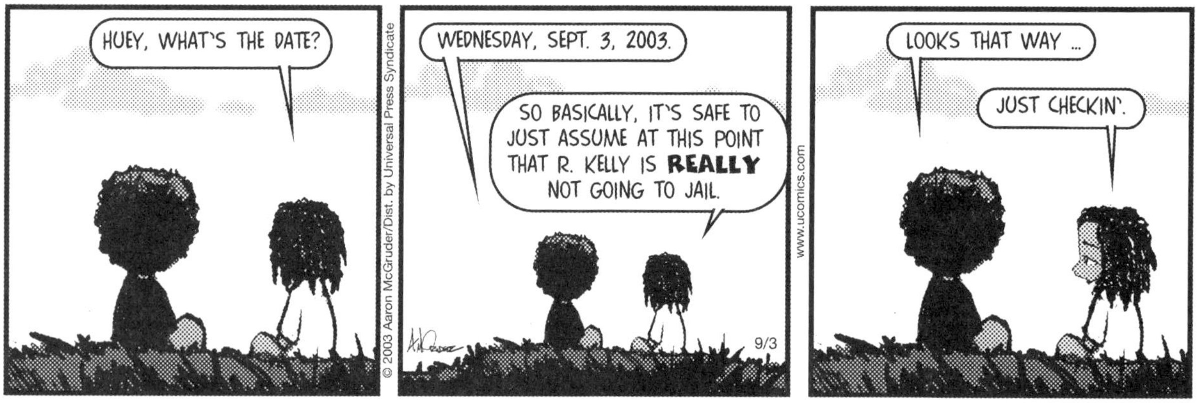
HUEY, WHAT'S THE DATE?
WEDNESDAY, SEPT. 3, 2003.
SO BASICALLY, IT'S SAFE TO JUST ASSUME AT THIS POINT THAT R. KELLY IS REALLY NOT GOING TO JAIL.
LOOKS THAT WAY ...
JUST CHECKIN'.
© 2003 Aaron McGruder/Dist. by Universal Press Syndicate
www.ucomics.com
9/3

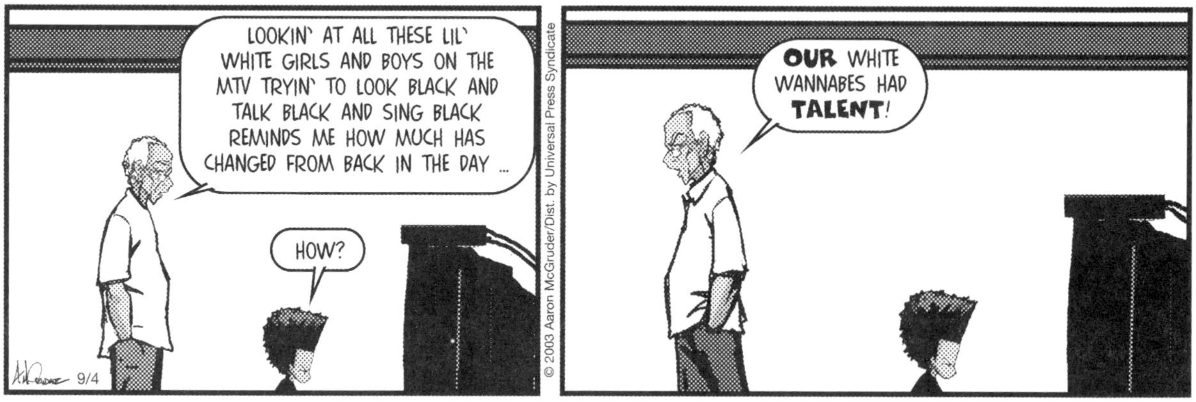
LOOKIN' AT ALL THESE LIL' WHITE GIRLS AND BOYS ON THE MTV TRYIN' TO LOOK BLACK AND TALK BLACK AND SING BLACK REMINDS ME HOW MUCH HAS CHANGED FROM BACK IN THE DAY ...
HOW?
OUR WHITE WANNABES HAD TALENT!
© 2003 Aaron McGruder/Dist. by Universal Press Syndicate
9/4

WELL, I DON'T CARE WHAT ANYONE SAYS ...
I LIKE R. KELLY'S LATEST VIDEO ...
WHAT?!
THAT'S DISGUSTING!!
I MEANT HIS LATEST MUSIC VIDEO!!
OH, RIGHT. NEVER MIND.
© 2003 Aaron McGruder/Dist. by Universal Press Syndicate www.ucomics.com www.boondocks.net
4/27

THAT'S IT, GRANDDAD. I'M NEVER GOING TO THE MOVIES WITH YOU AGAIN ...
WHY NOT?!
© 2003 Aaron McGruder/Dist. by Universal Press Syndicate www.ucomics.com www.boondocks.net
BECAUSE YOU START YELLING IN THE THEATER ABOUT HOW YOU'RE OLD AND YOU DON'T HAVE MUCH TIME LEFT AND YOU DON'T WANT YOUR PRECIOUS LAST HOURS WASTED BY A BAD MOVIE!
IT'S TERRIBLY, TERRIBLY EMBARRASSING!
5/4
BUT YOU YELL THE SAME THING!!
IT'S HUMOROUSLY IRONIC WHEN I DO IT ...

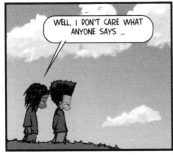

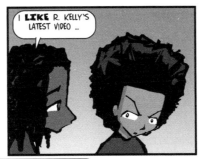

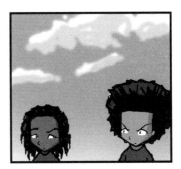

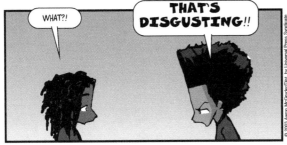

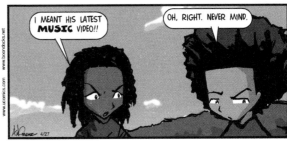

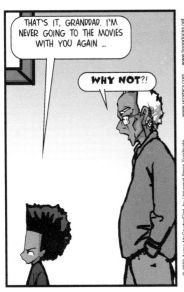

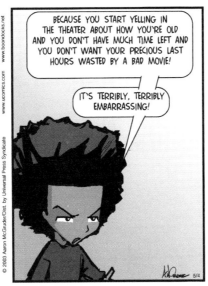

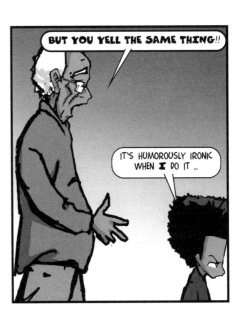

ACCORDING TO THE DEPARTMENT OF JUSTICE, ONE OUT OF EVERY THREE BLACK MEN WILL GO TO JAIL SOMETIME IN HIS LIFE.
5/11
© 2003 Aaron McGruder/Dist. by Universal Press Syndicate
www.ucomics.com www.boondocks.net
WHAT?!
NOTHING ...

THE BURDEN OF BRINGING THE TRUTH TO THE IGNORANT MASSES IS BOTH HEAVY AND COMPLICATED. THE KEY IS NOT JUST **WHAT** YOU SAY, IT'S **HOW** YOU SAY IT.
© 2003 Aaron McGruder/Dist. by Universal Press Syndicate
www.ucomics.com www.boondocks.net
PROBLEM IS, PEOPLE SOMETIMES CONFUSE MY CONFIDENT RIGHTEOUSNESS FOR ARROGANCE, AT WHICH POINT THEY STOP LISTENING ...
IF I WERE TO COMMUNICATE IN A HUMBLE, LESS AGGRESSIVE FASHION, I WONDER IF I MIGHT BE MORE EFFECTIVE?
5/18
BUT THEN AGAIN, HUMILITY IN THE FACE OF MY OVERWHELMING GENIUS WOULD OBVIOUSLY AMOUNT TO HYPOCRISY.
I'M SORRY ... WERE YOU SAYING SOMETHING?

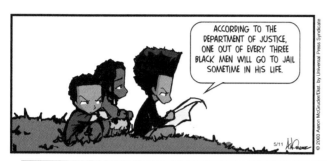

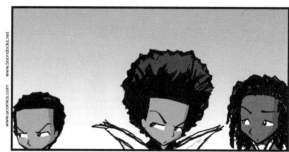

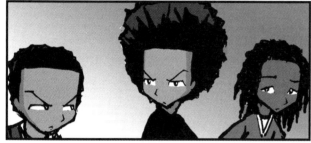

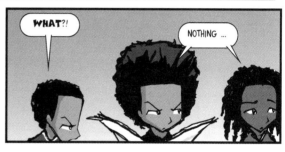

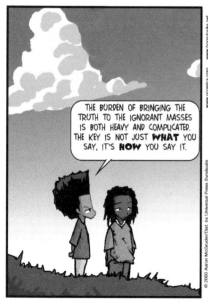

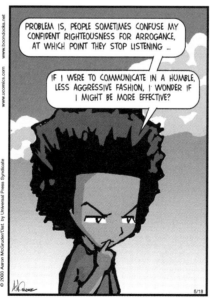

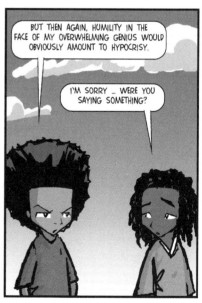

"IT DOES NOT REQUIRE A MAJORITY TO PREVAIL, BUT RATHER AN IRATE, TIRELESS MINORITY KEEN TO SET BRUSHFIRES IN PEOPLE'S MINDS."
SAMUEL ADAMS SAID THAT.
PRETTY DEEP FOR A GUY WHO MAKES BEER FOR A LIVING.
© 2003 Aaron McGruder/Dist. by Universal Press Syndicate www.ucomics.com www.boondocks.net
5/25

DON'T GET ME WRONG — I COMPLETELY AND TOTALLY OPPOSE U.S. INVOLVEMENT IN IRAQ IN EVERY WAY. I'M JUST SAYING ...
IF ANYBODY WAS GOING TO BE PUT IN CHARGE OF REBUILDING IRAQ, IT SHOULD HAVE BEEN MAGIC JOHNSON ...
© 2003 Aaron McGruder/Dist. by Universal Press Syndicate www.ucomics.com www.boondocks.net
6/1

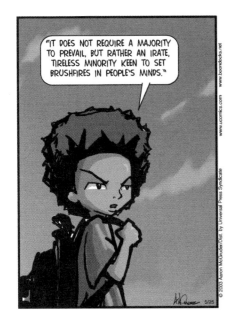

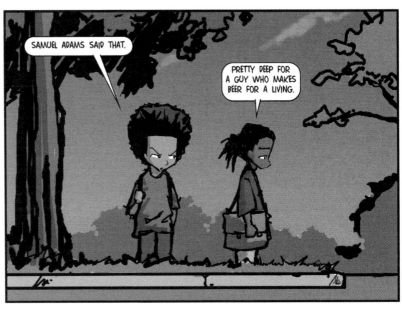

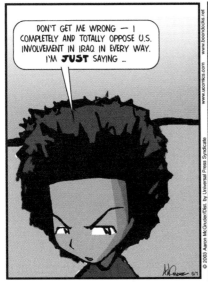

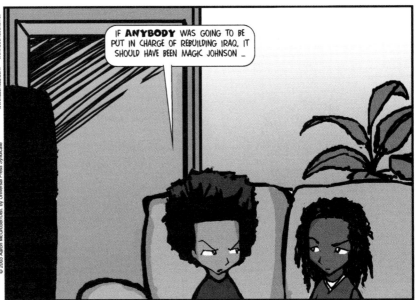

HUEY HELPS HIS GRANDFATHER NAVIGATE THE SOMETIMES CONFUSING WORLD OF THE INTERNET ...
WHY DOES IT KEEP ASKING ME IF I WANT TO BE SPANKED? DID I DO SOMETHING WRONG?
(SIGH)
© 2003 Aaron McGruder/Dist. by Universal Press Syndicate
www.ucomics.com www.boondocks.net

WHAT'S THIS? A LETTER?
To Whichever Grandchild It May Concern,
I have left on a one-week vacation to Brazil to spend quality time with those gals from the new Snoop Dogg "Beautiful" video. If you get hungry you know where the store is ...
Happy Father's Day to Me!
Granddad
www.ucomics.com www.boondocks.net
© 2003 Aaron McGruder/Dist. by Universal Press Syndicate

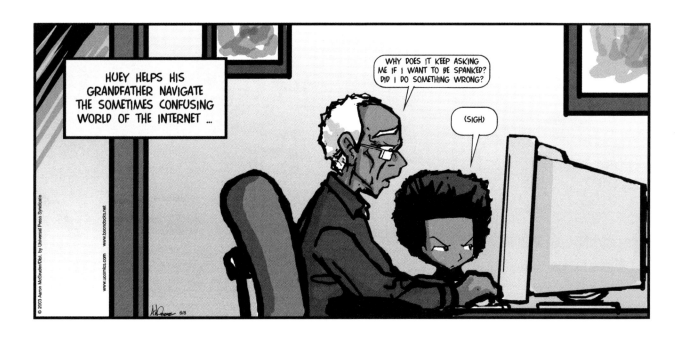

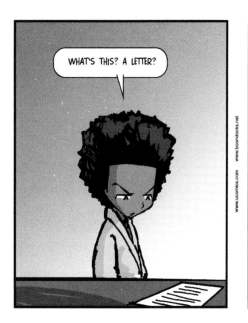

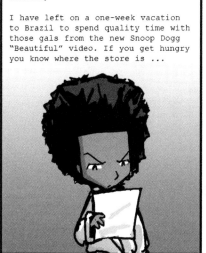

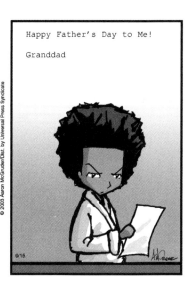

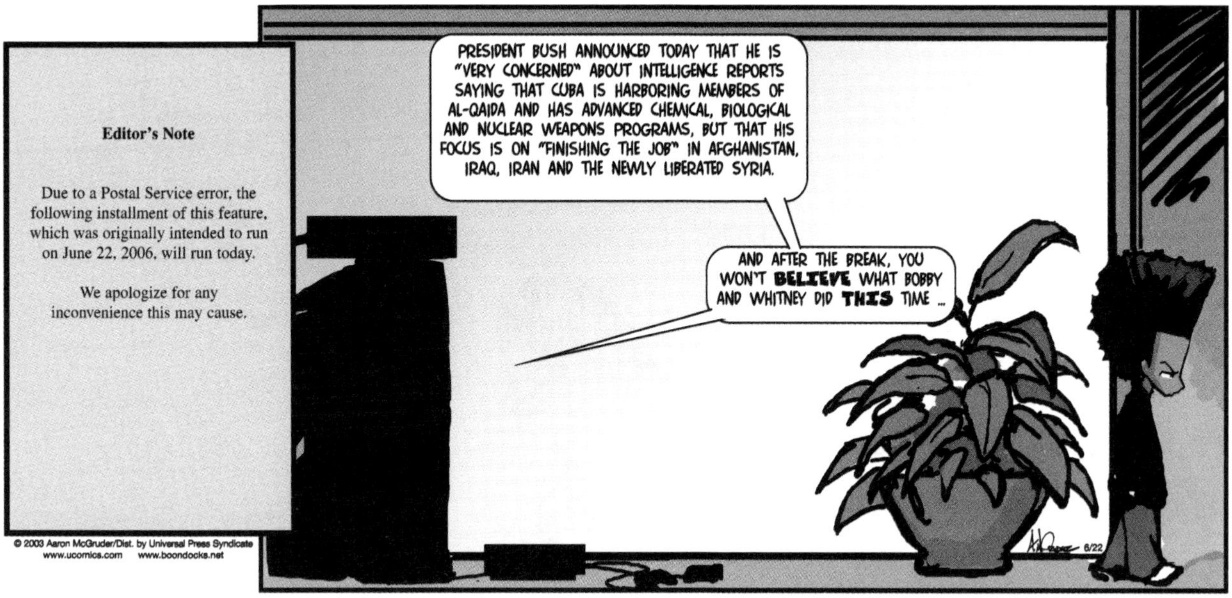
Editor's Note
Due to a Postal Service error, the following installment of this feature, which was originally intended to run on June 22, 2006, will run today.
We apologize for any inconvenience this may cause.
PRESIDENT BUSH ANNOUNCED TODAY THAT HE IS "VERY CONCERNED" ABOUT INTELLIGENCE REPORTS SAYING THAT CUBA IS HARBORING MEMBERS OF AL-QAIDA AND HAS ADVANCED CHEMICAL, BIOLOGICAL AND NUCLEAR WEAPONS PROGRAMS, BUT THAT HIS FOCUS IS ON "FINISHING THE JOB" IN AFGHANISTAN, IRAQ, IRAN AND THE NEWLY LIBERATED SYRIA.
AND AFTER THE BREAK, YOU WON'T BELIEVE WHAT BOBBY AND WHITNEY DID THIS TIME ...
© 2003 Aaron McGruder/Dist. by Universal Press Syndicate
www.ucomics.com www.boondocks.net
6/22

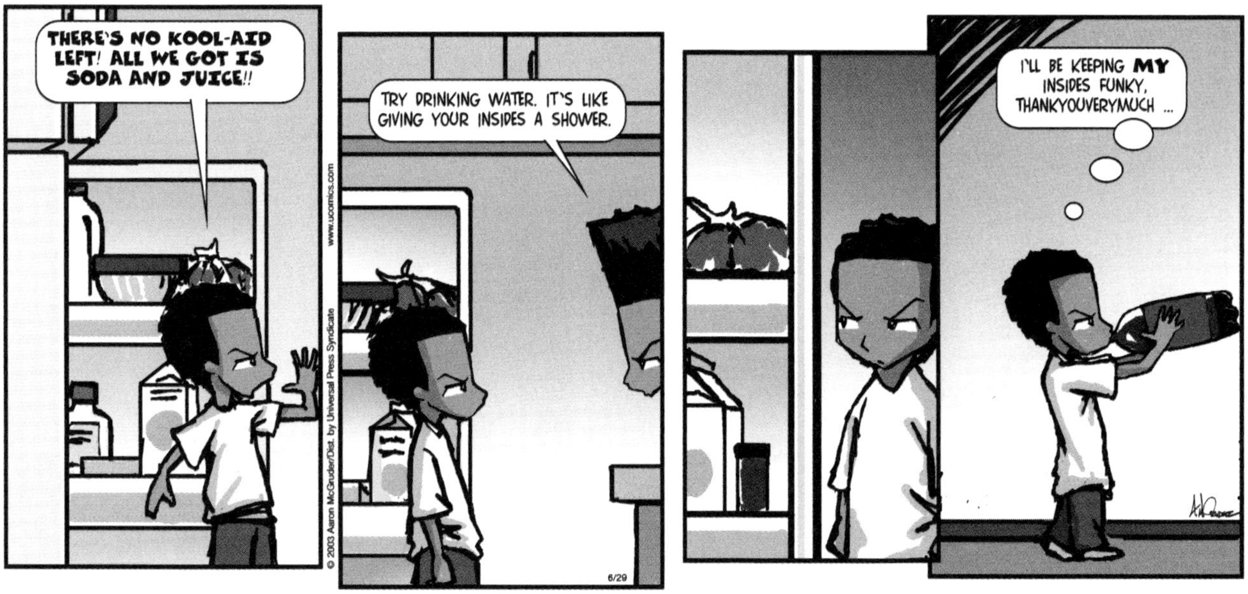
THERE'S NO KOOL-AID LEFT! ALL WE GOT IS SODA AND JUICE!!
© 2003 Aaron McGruder/Dist. by Universal Press Syndicate www.ucomics.com
TRY DRINKING WATER. IT'S LIKE GIVING YOUR INSIDES A SHOWER.
6/29
I'LL BE KEEPING MY INSIDES FUNKY, THANKYOUVERYMUCH ...

IS ARNOLD SCHWARZENEGGER ACTUALLY GONNA RUN FOR GOVERNOR OF CALIFORNIA?
IF HE DOES, I THINK HE'S GOT A PRETTY GOOD SHOT ...
© 2003 Aaron McGruder/Dist. by Universal Press Syndicate
www.ucomics.com
ESPECIALLY SINCE NONE OF THE VOTING PUBLIC HAS SEEN HIS LAST TEN MOVIES ...
7/6

WHO'S ON TOP OF THE RAP GAME RIGHT NOW? 50 CENT, THAT'S WHO. AND YOU KNOW WHY? STREET CREDIBILITY, THAT'S WHY!
© 2003 Aaron McGruder/Dist. by Universal Press Syndicate
www.ucomics.com
SEE, WHILE EVERYONE ELSE WAS JUST **TALKIN'** ABOUT GETTIN' SHOT, HE REALLY **DID** GET SHOT. **NINE TIMES**! HE RAISED THE THUG BAR! AND NOW HE'S RICH AND FAMOUS.
7/13
AND YOUR THINKING IS ... MAYBE IF **YOU** COULD GET SHOT A FEW TIMES, YOU'D BE RICH, TOO?
NO DOUBT! THE THUG BAR HAS BEEN RAISED, AND IN **THIS** NEIGHBORHOOD IT'S GONNA BE HARD TO COMPETE.
A NEW DEFINITION OF "DISADVANTAGED YOUTH."
I MEAN, I'VE BEEN SHOT AT ONCE, **MAYBE** TWICE SINCE WE MOVED HERE? IT'S JUST NOT FAIR ...

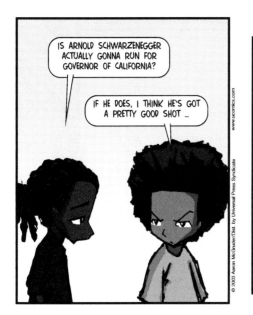

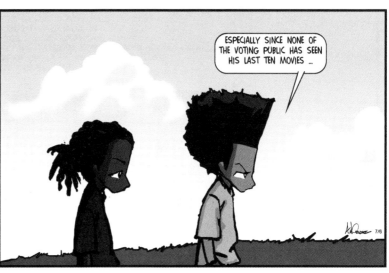

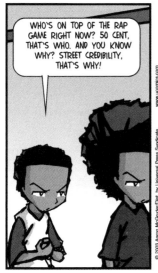

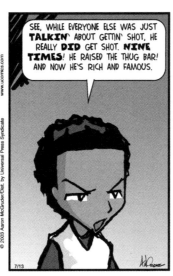

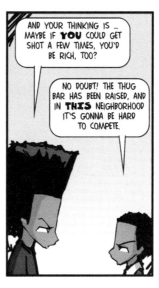

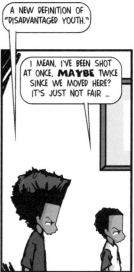

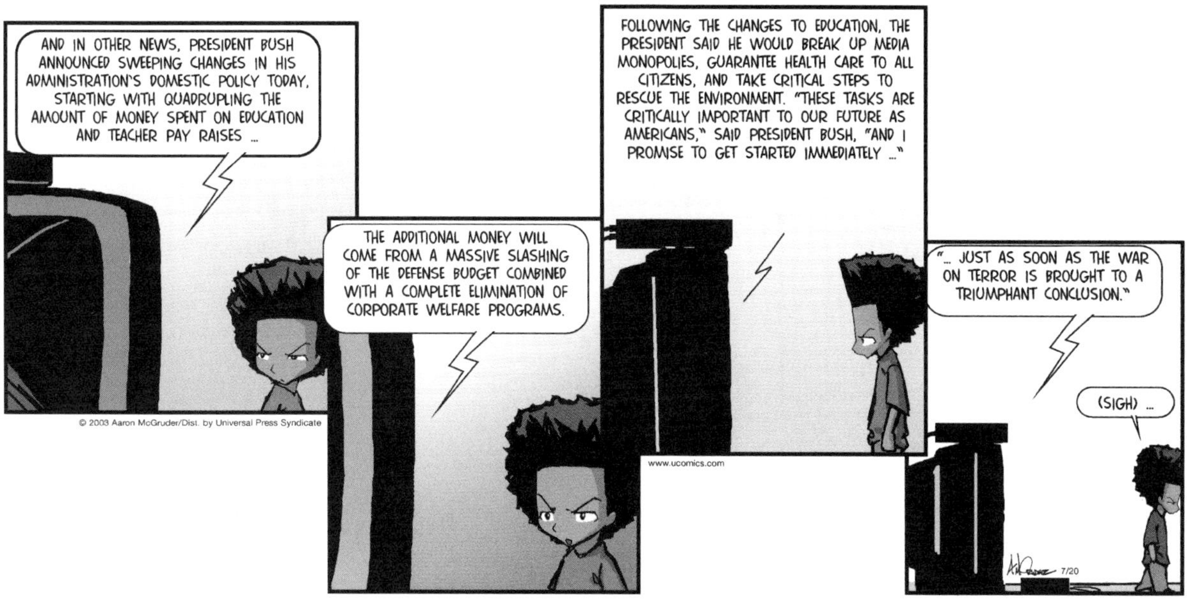
AND IN OTHER NEWS, PRESIDENT BUSH ANNOUNCED SWEEPING CHANGES IN HIS ADMINISTRATION'S DOMESTIC POLICY TODAY, STARTING WITH QUADRUPLING THE AMOUNT OF MONEY SPENT ON EDUCATION AND TEACHER PAY RAISES ...
© 2003 Aaron McGruder/Dist. by Universal Press Syndicate
THE ADDITIONAL MONEY WILL COME FROM A MASSIVE SLASHING OF THE DEFENSE BUDGET COMBINED WITH A COMPLETE ELIMINATION OF CORPORATE WELFARE PROGRAMS.
FOLLOWING THE CHANGES TO EDUCATION, THE PRESIDENT SAID HE WOULD BREAK UP MEDIA MONOPOLIES, GUARANTEE HEALTH CARE TO ALL CITIZENS, AND TAKE CRITICAL STEPS TO RESCUE THE ENVIRONMENT. "THESE TASKS ARE CRITICALLY IMPORTANT TO OUR FUTURE AS AMERICANS," SAID PRESIDENT BUSH, "AND I PROMISE TO GET STARTED IMMEDIATELY ..."
www.ucomics.com
"... JUST AS SOON AS THE WAR ON TERROR IS BROUGHT TO A TRIUMPHANT CONCLUSION."
(SIGH) ...
7/20

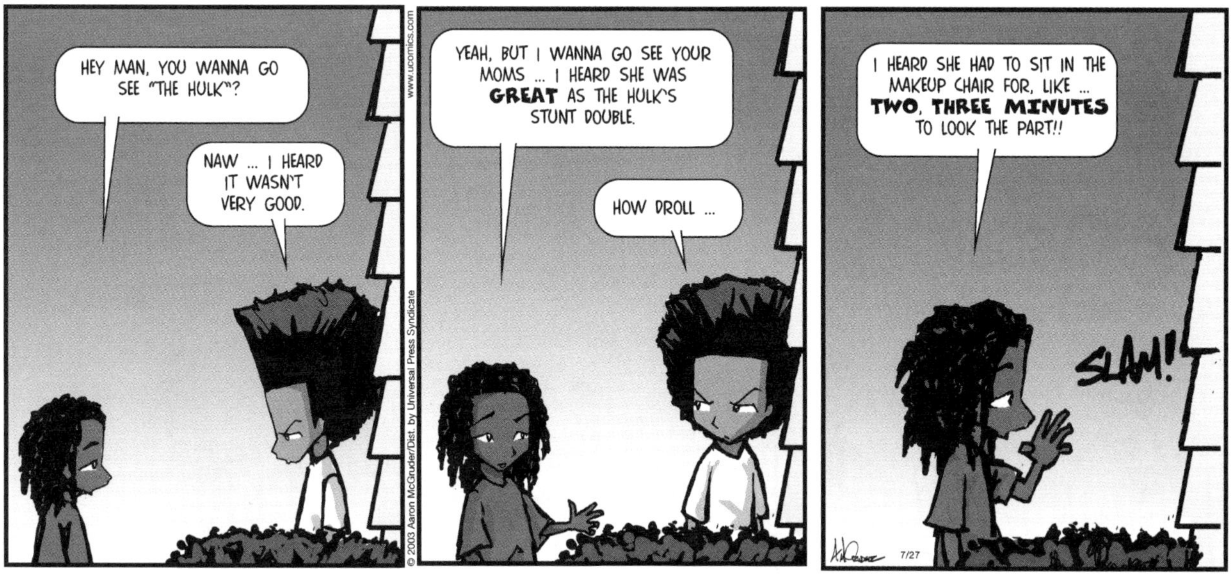
HEY MAN, YOU WANNA GO SEE "THE HULK"?
NAW ... I HEARD IT WASN'T VERY GOOD.
www.ucomics.com
© 2003 Aaron McGruder/Dist. by Universal Press Syndicate
YEAH, BUT I WANNA GO SEE YOUR MOMS ... I HEARD SHE WAS GREAT AS THE HULK'S STUNT DOUBLE.
HOW DROLL ...
I HEARD SHE HAD TO SIT IN THE MAKEUP CHAIR FOR, LIKE ... TWO, THREE MINUTES TO LOOK THE PART!!
SLAM!
7/27

YOU KNOW, PEOPLE SAY THE BEST WAY TO MAKE GOOD THINGS HAPPEN IS TO PUT POSITIVE THOUGHTS OUT INTO THE UNIVERSE.
© 2003 Aaron McGruder/Dist. by Universal Press Syndicate www.ucomics.com
8/3
QUEEN LATIFAH VERSUS ANN COULTER IN A STEEL CAGE DEATHMATCH ... QUEEN LATIFAH VERSUS ANN COULTER IN A STEEL CAGE DEATHMATCH ...

DON'T YOU HATE HAVING LOTS OF HAIR IN THE SUMMER? IT FEELS ALL HOT AND ITCHY ...
YEAH ...
© 2003 Aaron McGruder/Dist. by Universal Press Syndicate www.ucomics.com
I WONDER IF YOUR MOMS HAS THIS PROBLEM WITH HER FULL BEARD AND HAIRY BACK?
8/10

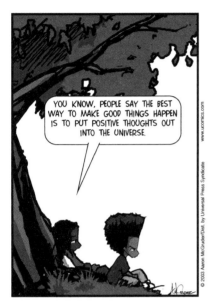

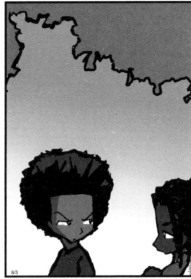

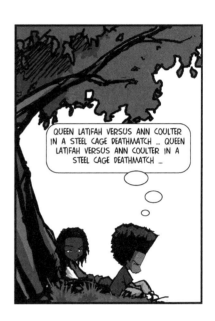

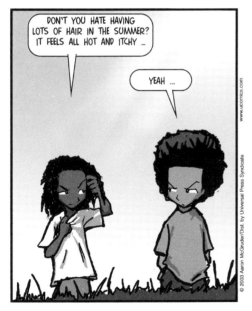

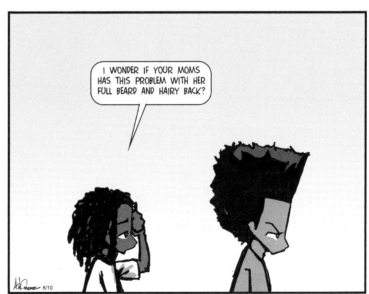

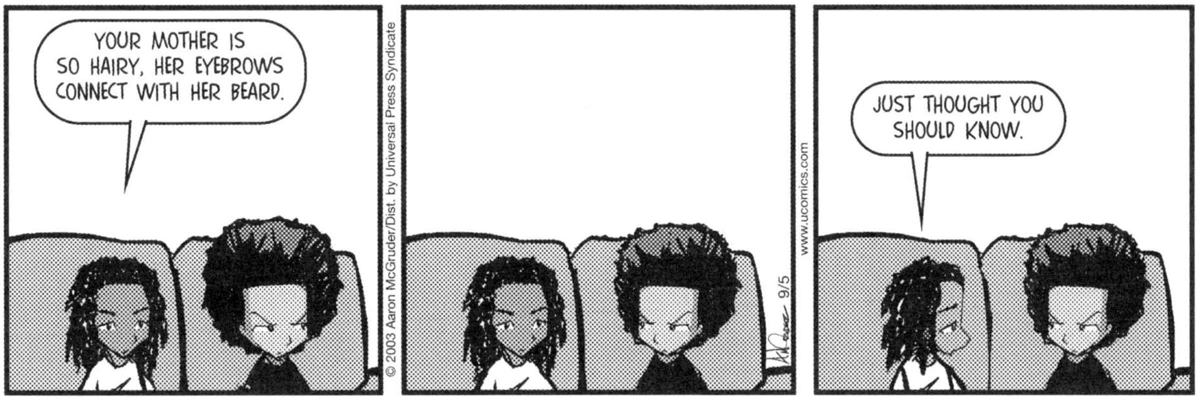
YOUR MOTHER IS SO HAIRY, HER EYEBROWS CONNECT WITH HER BEARD.
JUST THOUGHT YOU SHOULD KNOW.
© 2003 Aaron McGruder/Dist. by Universal Press Syndicate
www.ucomics.com
9/5

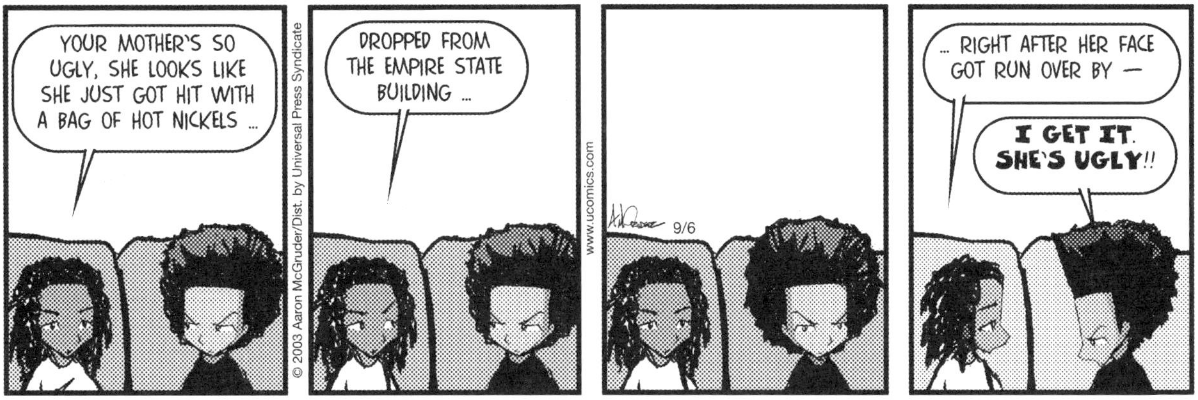
YOUR MOTHER'S SO UGLY, SHE LOOKS LIKE SHE JUST GOT HIT WITH A BAG OF HOT NICKELS ...
DROPPED FROM THE EMPIRE STATE BUILDING ...
... RIGHT AFTER HER FACE GOT RUN OVER BY —
I GET IT. SHE'S UGLY!!
© 2003 Aaron McGruder/Dist. by Universal Press Syndicate
www.ucomics.com
9/6

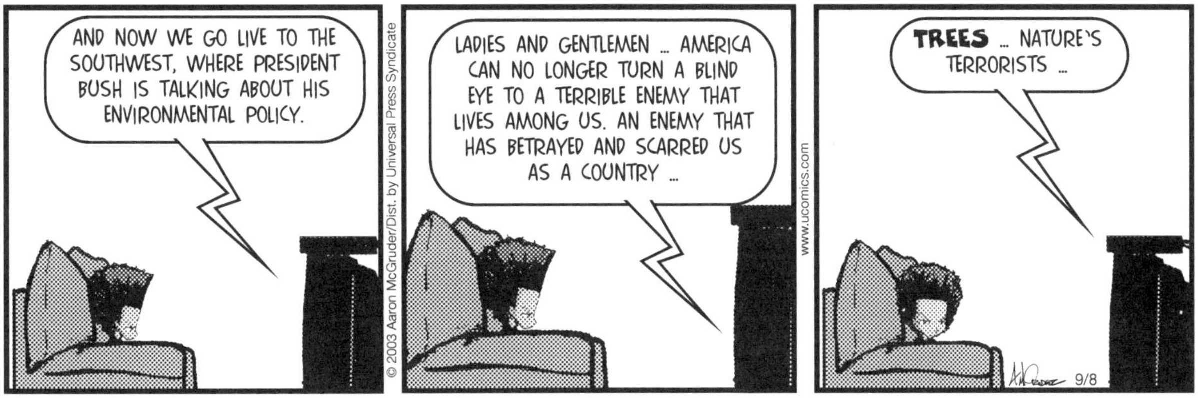
AND NOW WE GO LIVE TO THE SOUTHWEST, WHERE PRESIDENT BUSH IS TALKING ABOUT HIS ENVIRONMENTAL POLICY.
LADIES AND GENTLEMEN ... AMERICA CAN NO LONGER TURN A BLIND EYE TO A TERRIBLE ENEMY THAT LIVES AMONG US. AN ENEMY THAT HAS BETRAYED AND SCARRED US AS A COUNTRY ...
TREES ... NATURE'S TERRORISTS ...
© 2003 Aaron McGruder/Dist. by Universal Press Syndicate
www.ucomics.com
9/8

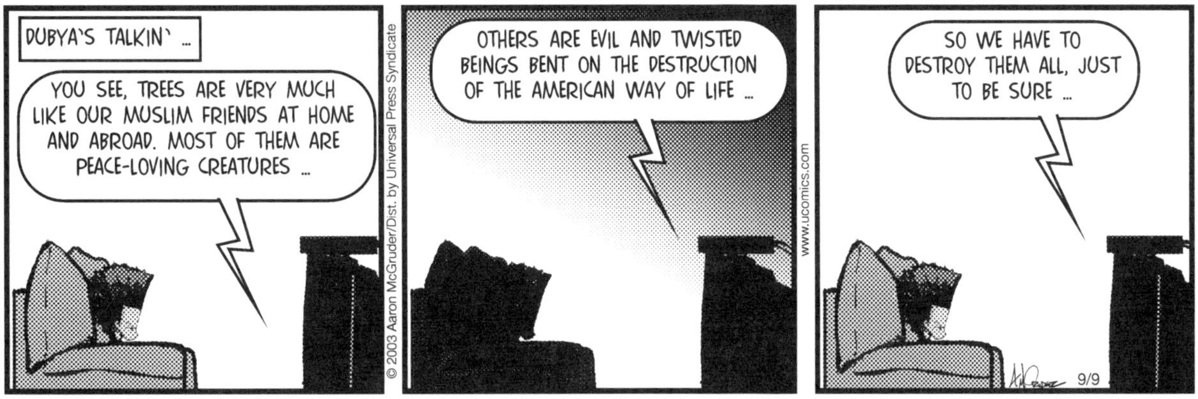
DUBYA'S TALKIN' ...
YOU SEE, TREES ARE VERY MUCH LIKE OUR MUSLIM FRIENDS AT HOME AND ABROAD. MOST OF THEM ARE PEACE-LOVING CREATURES ...
OTHERS ARE EVIL AND TWISTED BEINGS BENT ON THE DESTRUCTION OF THE AMERICAN WAY OF LIFE ...
SO WE HAVE TO DESTROY THEM ALL, JUST TO BE SURE ...
© 2003 Aaron McGruder/Dist. by Universal Press Syndicate
www.ucomics.com
9/9

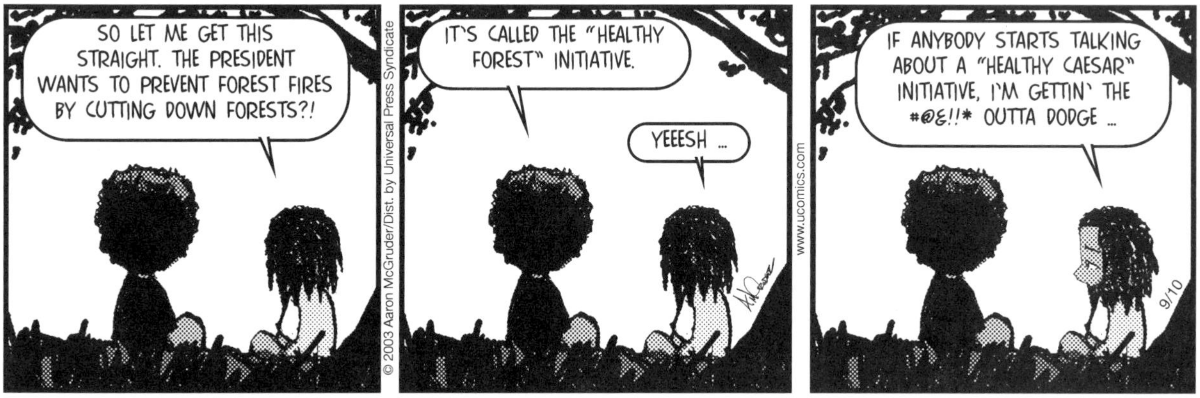
SO LET ME GET THIS STRAIGHT. THE PRESIDENT WANTS TO PREVENT FOREST FIRES BY CUTTING DOWN FORESTS?!
IT'S CALLED THE "HEALTHY FOREST" INITIATIVE.
YEEESH ...
IF ANYBODY STARTS TALKING ABOUT A "HEALTHY CAESAR" INITIATIVE, I'M GETTIN' THE #@&!!* OUTTA DODGE ...
© 2003 Aaron McGruder/Dist. by Universal Press Syndicate
www.ucomics.com
9/10

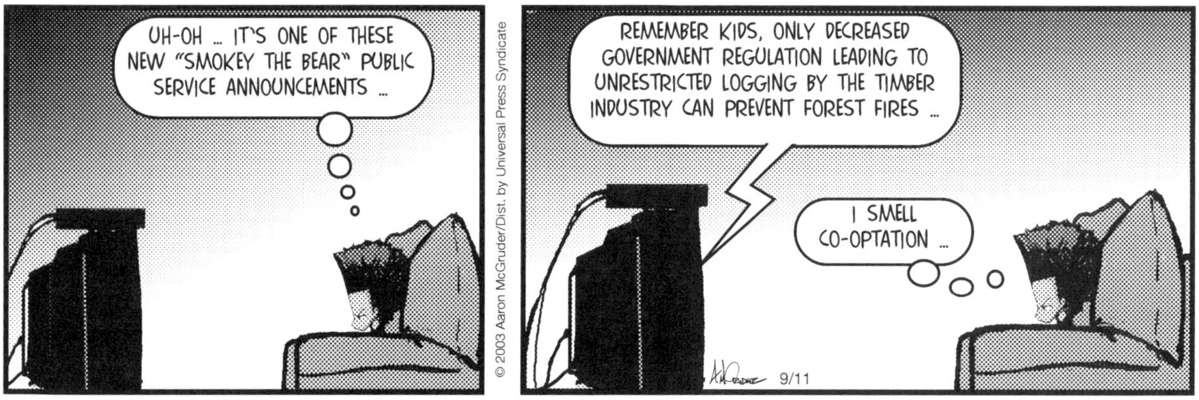
UH-OH ... IT'S ONE OF THESE NEW "SMOKEY THE BEAR" PUBLIC SERVICE ANNOUNCEMENTS ...
REMEMBER KIDS, ONLY DECREASED GOVERNMENT REGULATION LEADING TO UNRESTRICTED LOGGING BY THE TIMBER INDUSTRY CAN PREVENT FOREST FIRES ...
I SMELL CO-OPTATION ...
© 2003 Aaron McGruder/Dist. by Universal Press Syndicate
9/11

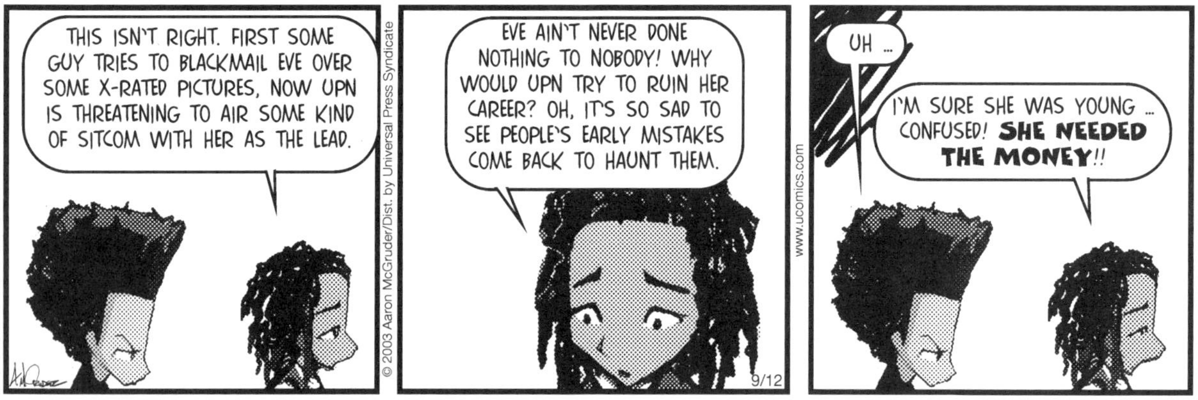
THIS ISN'T RIGHT. FIRST SOME GUY TRIES TO BLACKMAIL EVE OVER SOME X-RATED PICTURES, NOW UPN IS THREATENING TO AIR SOME KIND OF SITCOM WITH HER AS THE LEAD.
EVE AIN'T NEVER DONE NOTHING TO NOBODY! WHY WOULD UPN TRY TO RUIN HER CAREER? OH, IT'S SO SAD TO SEE PEOPLE'S EARLY MISTAKES COME BACK TO HAUNT THEM.
UH ...
I'M SURE SHE WAS YOUNG ... CONFUSED! SHE NEEDED THE MONEY!!
© 2003 Aaron McGruder/Dist. by Universal Press Syndicate
www.ucomics.com
9/12

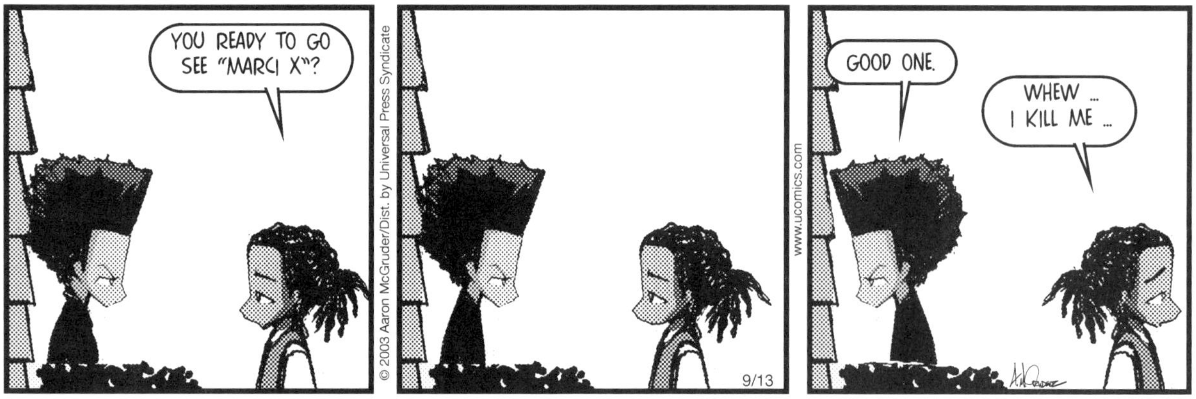
YOU READY TO GO SEE "MARCI X"?
GOOD ONE.
WHEW ... I KILL ME ...
© 2003 Aaron McGruder/Dist. by Universal Press Syndicate
www.ucomics.com
9/13

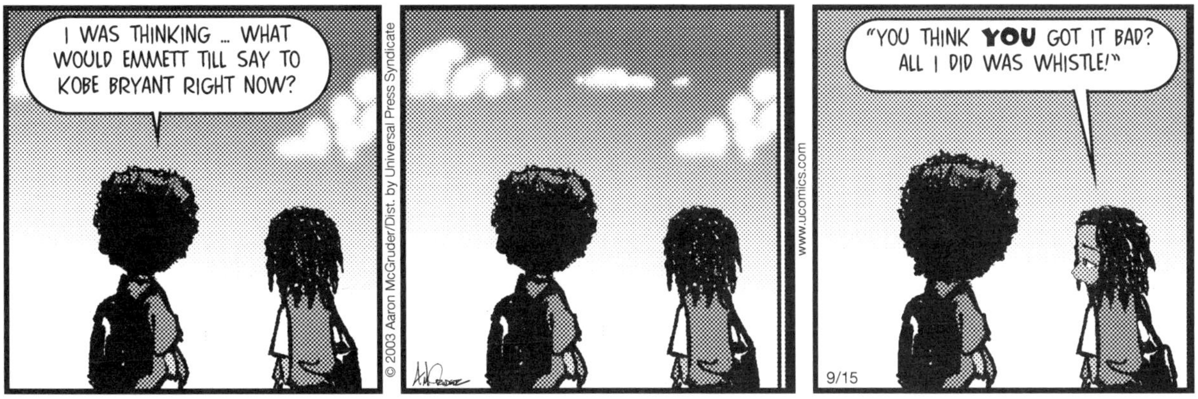
I WAS THINKING ... WHAT WOULD EMMETT TILL SAY TO KOBE BRYANT RIGHT NOW?
"YOU THINK **YOU** GOT IT BAD? ALL I DID WAS WHISTLE!"
© 2003 Aaron McGruder/Dist. by Universal Press Syndicate
www.ucomics.com
9/15

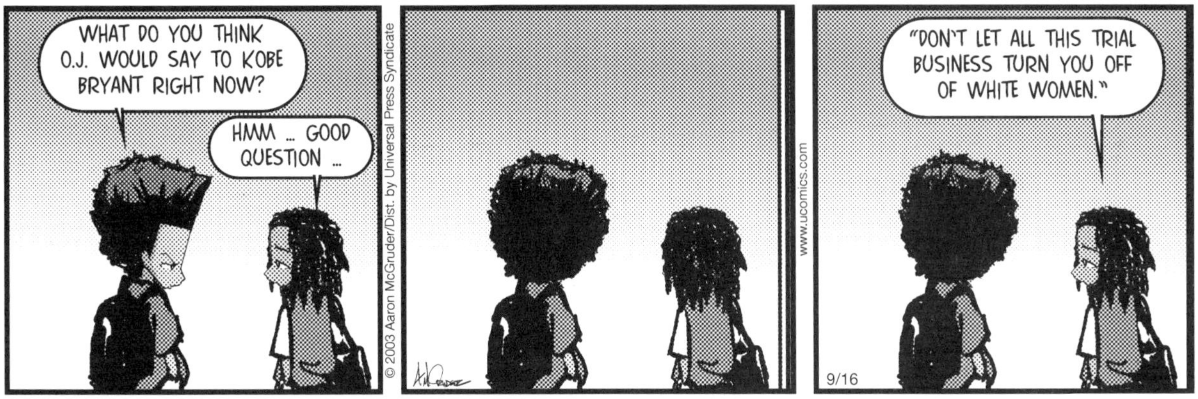
WHAT DO YOU THINK O.J. WOULD SAY TO KOBE BRYANT RIGHT NOW?
HMM ... GOOD QUESTION ...
"DON'T LET ALL THIS TRIAL BUSINESS TURN YOU OFF OF WHITE WOMEN."
© 2003 Aaron McGruder/Dist. by Universal Press Syndicate
www.ucomics.com
9/16

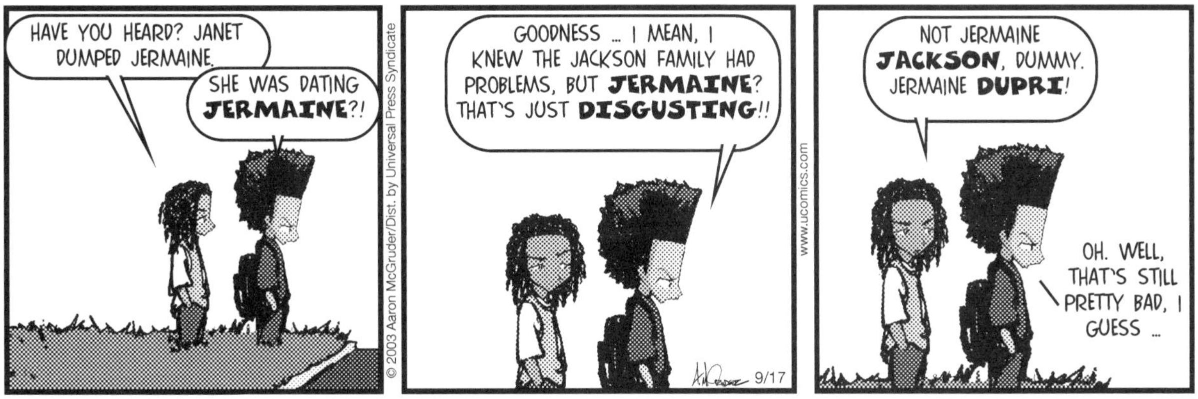
HAVE YOU HEARD? JANET DUMPED JERMAINE.
SHE WAS DATING **JERMAINE**?!
GOODNESS ... I MEAN, I KNEW THE JACKSON FAMILY HAD PROBLEMS, BUT **JERMAINE**? THAT'S JUST **DISGUSTING**!!
NOT JERMAINE **JACKSON**, DUMMY. JERMAINE **DUPRI**!
OH. WELL, THAT'S STILL PRETTY BAD, I GUESS ...
© 2003 Aaron McGruder/Dist. by Universal Press Syndicate
www.ucomics.com
9/17

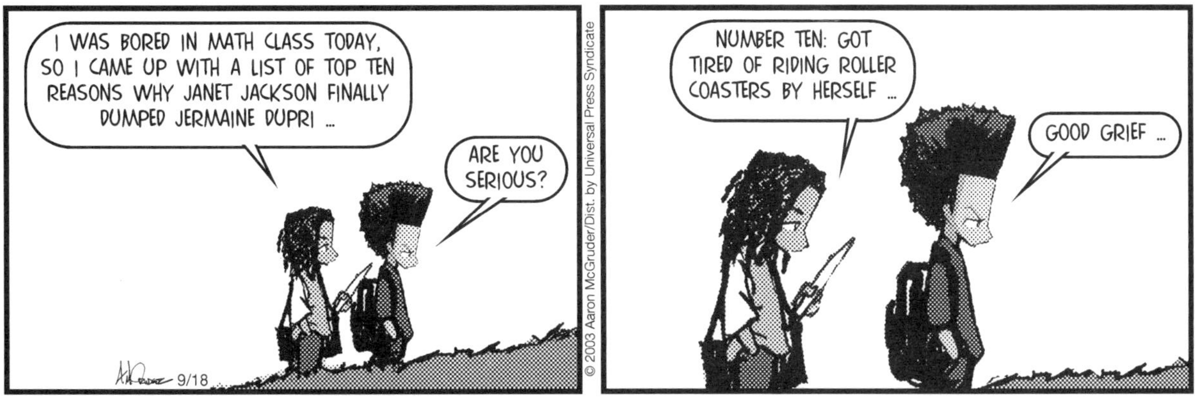
I WAS BORED IN MATH CLASS TODAY, SO I CAME UP WITH A LIST OF TOP TEN REASONS WHY JANET JACKSON FINALLY DUMPED JERMAINE DUPRI ...
ARE YOU SERIOUS?
NUMBER TEN: GOT TIRED OF RIDING ROLLER COASTERS BY HERSELF ...
GOOD GRIEF ...
9/18
© 2003 Aaron McGruder/Dist. by Universal Press Syndicate

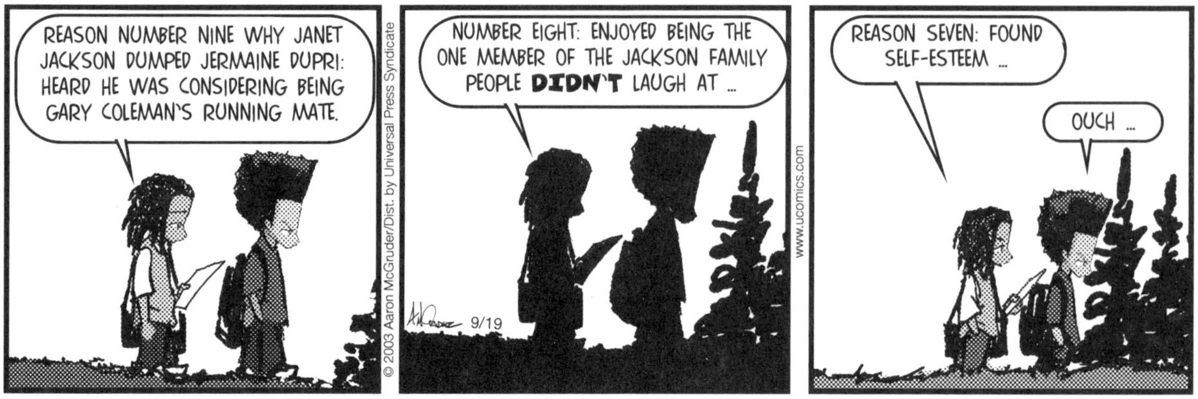
REASON NUMBER NINE WHY JANET JACKSON DUMPED JERMAINE DUPRI: HEARD HE WAS CONSIDERING BEING GARY COLEMAN'S RUNNING MATE.
NUMBER EIGHT: ENJOYED BEING THE ONE MEMBER OF THE JACKSON FAMILY PEOPLE **DIDN'T** LAUGH AT ...
REASON SEVEN: FOUND SELF-ESTEEM ...
OUCH ...
9/19
© 2003 Aaron McGruder/Dist. by Universal Press Syndicate
www.ucomics.com

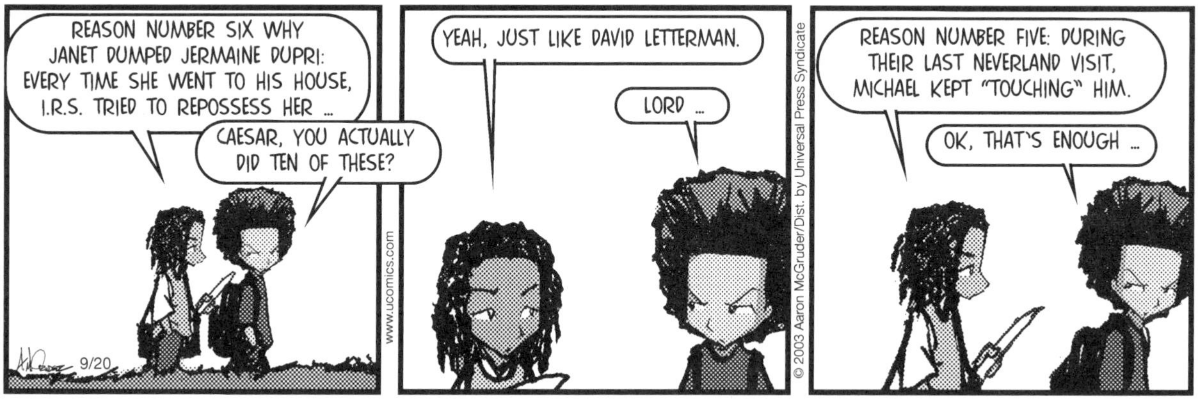
REASON NUMBER SIX WHY JANET DUMPED JERMAINE DUPRI: EVERY TIME SHE WENT TO HIS HOUSE, I.R.S. TRIED TO REPOSSESS HER ...
CAESAR, YOU ACTUALLY DID TEN OF THESE?
YEAH, JUST LIKE DAVID LETTERMAN.
LORD ...
REASON NUMBER FIVE: DURING THEIR LAST NEVERLAND VISIT, MICHAEL KEPT "TOUCHING" HIM.
OK, THAT'S ENOUGH ...
9/20
www.ucomics.com
© 2003 Aaron McGruder/Dist. by Universal Press Syndicate

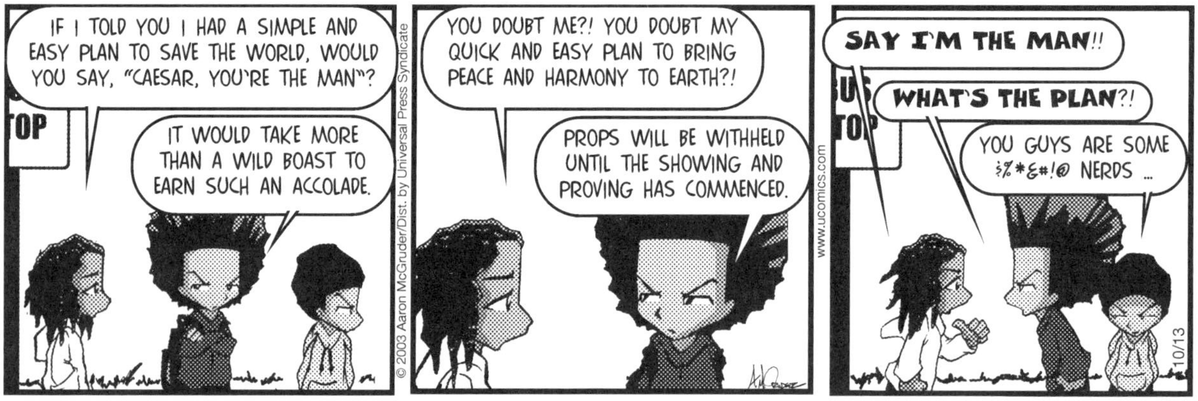
IF I TOLD YOU I HAD A SIMPLE AND EASY PLAN TO SAVE THE WORLD, WOULD YOU SAY, "CAESAR, YOU'RE THE MAN"?
IT WOULD TAKE MORE THAN A WILD BOAST TO EARN SUCH AN ACCOLADE.
YOU DOUBT ME?! YOU DOUBT MY QUICK AND EASY PLAN TO BRING PEACE AND HARMONY TO EARTH?!
PROPS WILL BE WITHHELD UNTIL THE SHOWING AND PROVING HAS COMMENCED.
SAY I'M THE MAN!!
WHAT'S THE PLAN?!
YOU GUYS ARE SOME $%*&#!@ NERDS ...
10/13
© 2003 Aaron McGruder/Dist. by Universal Press Syndicate
www.ucomics.com

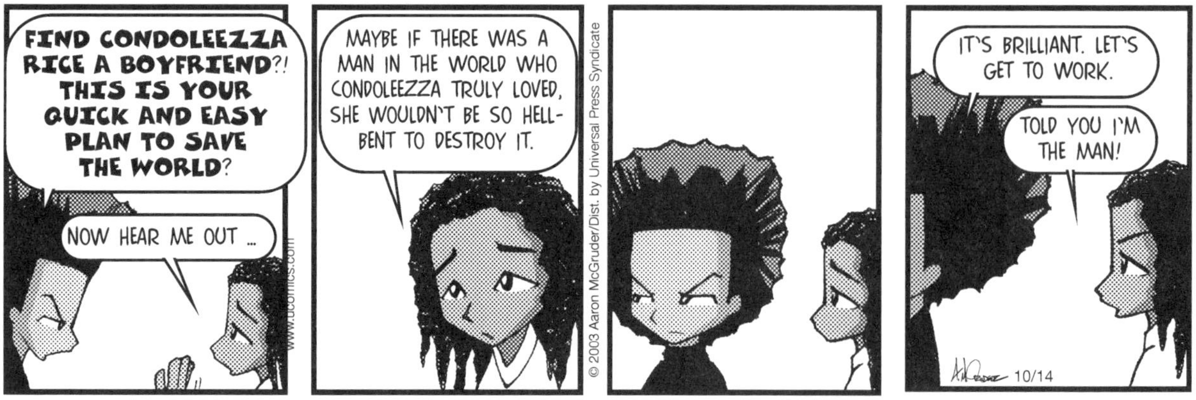
FIND CONDOLEEZZA RICE A BOYFRIEND?! THIS IS YOUR QUICK AND EASY PLAN TO SAVE THE WORLD?
NOW HEAR ME OUT ...
MAYBE IF THERE WAS A MAN IN THE WORLD WHO CONDOLEEZZA TRULY LOVED, SHE WOULDN'T BE SO HELL-BENT TO DESTROY IT.
IT'S BRILLIANT. LET'S GET TO WORK.
TOLD YOU I'M THE MAN!
10/14
www.ucomics.com
© 2003 Aaron McGruder/Dist. by Universal Press Syndicate

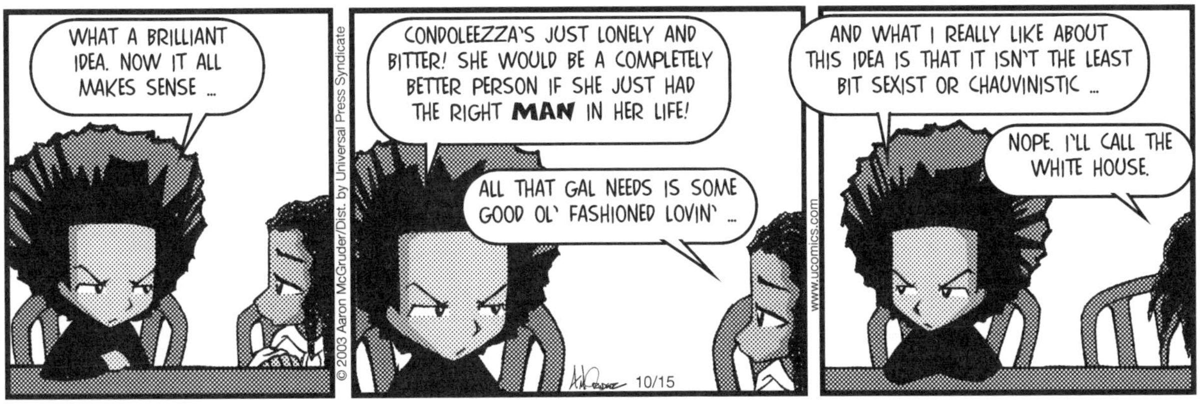
WHAT A BRILLIANT IDEA. NOW IT ALL MAKES SENSE ...
© 2003 Aaron McGruder/Dist. by Universal Press Syndicate
CONDOLEEZZA'S JUST LONELY AND BITTER! SHE WOULD BE A COMPLETELY BETTER PERSON IF SHE JUST HAD THE RIGHT MAN IN HER LIFE!
ALL THAT GAL NEEDS IS SOME GOOD OL' FASHIONED LOVIN' ...
10/15
www.ucomics.com
AND WHAT I REALLY LIKE ABOUT THIS IDEA IS THAT IT ISN'T THE LEAST BIT SEXIST OR CHAUVINISTIC ...
NOPE. I'LL CALL THE WHITE HOUSE.

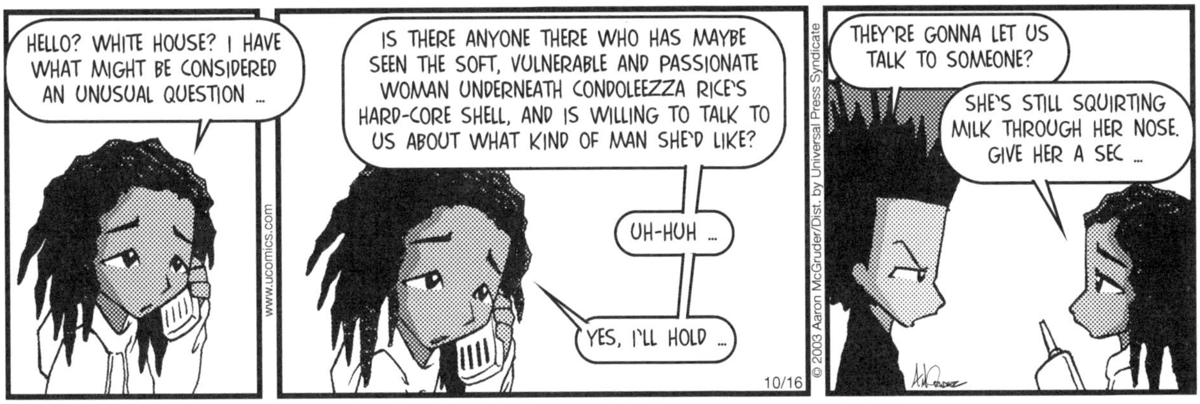
HELLO? WHITE HOUSE? I HAVE WHAT MIGHT BE CONSIDERED AN UNUSUAL QUESTION ...
www.ucomics.com
IS THERE ANYONE THERE WHO HAS MAYBE SEEN THE SOFT, VULNERABLE AND PASSIONATE WOMAN UNDERNEATH CONDOLEEZZA RICE'S HARD-CORE SHELL, AND IS WILLING TO TALK TO US ABOUT WHAT KIND OF MAN SHE'D LIKE?
UH-HUH ...
YES, I'LL HOLD ...
10/16
© 2003 Aaron McGruder/Dist. by Universal Press Syndicate
THEY'RE GONNA LET US TALK TO SOMEONE?
SHE'S STILL SQUIRTING MILK THROUGH HER NOSE. GIVE HER A SEC ...

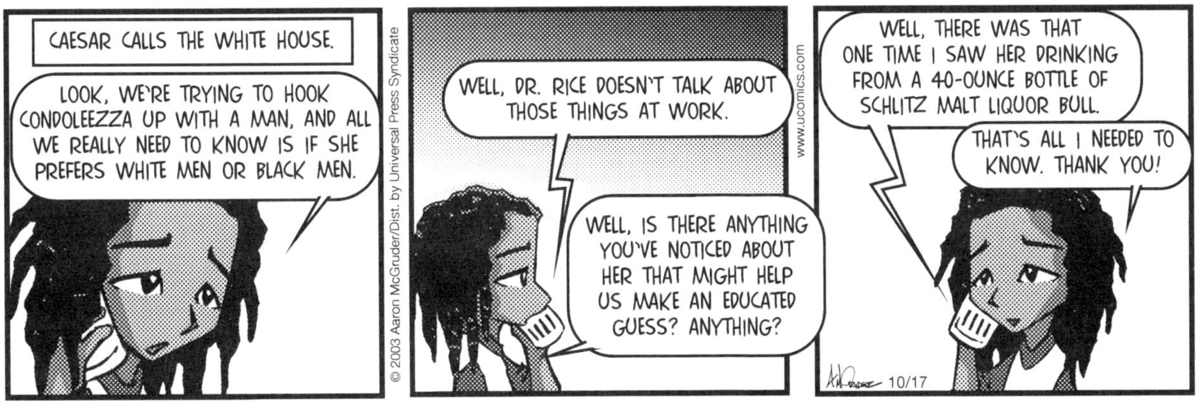
CAESAR CALLS THE WHITE HOUSE.
LOOK, WE'RE TRYING TO HOOK CONDOLEEZZA UP WITH A MAN, AND ALL WE REALLY NEED TO KNOW IS IF SHE PREFERS WHITE MEN OR BLACK MEN.
© 2003 Aaron McGruder/Dist. by Universal Press Syndicate
WELL, DR. RICE DOESN'T TALK ABOUT THOSE THINGS AT WORK.
WELL, IS THERE ANYTHING YOU'VE NOTICED ABOUT HER THAT MIGHT HELP US MAKE AN EDUCATED GUESS? ANYTHING?
www.ucomics.com
WELL, THERE WAS THAT ONE TIME I SAW HER DRINKING FROM A 40-OUNCE BOTTLE OF SCHLITZ MALT LIQUOR BULL.
THAT'S ALL I NEEDED TO KNOW. THANK YOU!
10/17

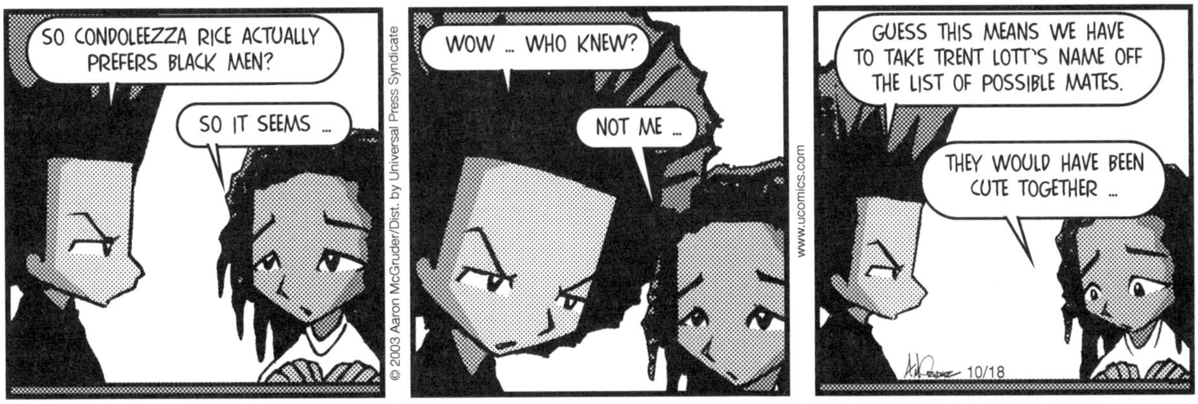
SO CONDOLEEZZA RICE ACTUALLY PREFERS BLACK MEN?
SO IT SEEMS ...
© 2003 Aaron McGruder/Dist. by Universal Press Syndicate
WOW ... WHO KNEW?
NOT ME ...
www.ucomics.com
GUESS THIS MEANS WE HAVE TO TAKE TRENT LOTT'S NAME OFF THE LIST OF POSSIBLE MATES.
THEY WOULD HAVE BEEN CUTE TOGETHER ...
10/18

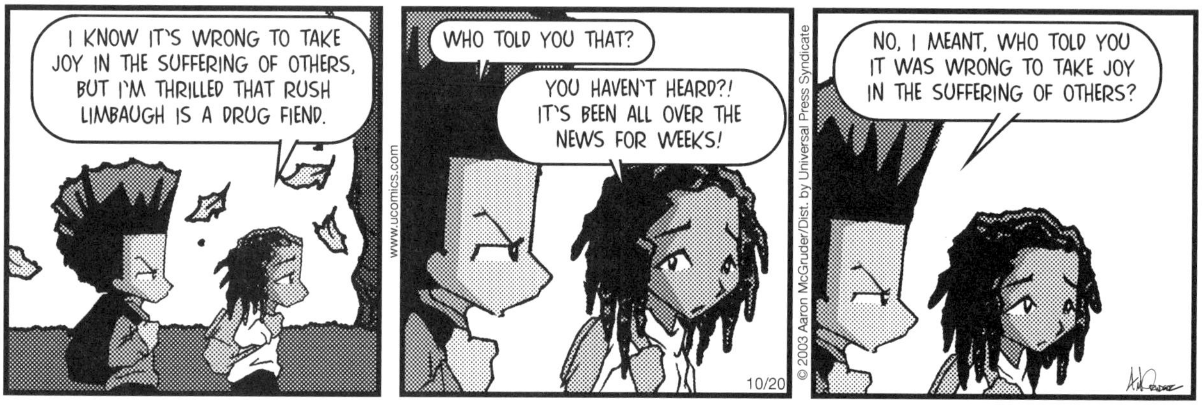
I KNOW IT'S WRONG TO TAKE JOY IN THE SUFFERING OF OTHERS, BUT I'M THRILLED THAT RUSH LIMBAUGH IS A DRUG FIEND.
WHO TOLD YOU THAT?
YOU HAVEN'T HEARD?! IT'S BEEN ALL OVER THE NEWS FOR WEEKS!
NO, I MEANT, WHO TOLD YOU IT WAS WRONG TO TAKE JOY IN THE SUFFERING OF OTHERS?
www.ucomics.com
10/20
© 2003 Aaron McGruder/Dist. by Universal Press Syndicate

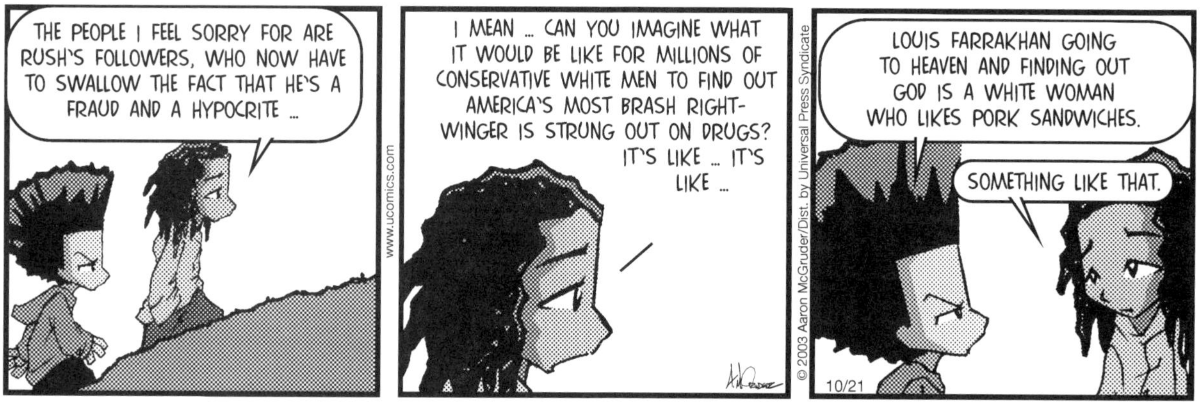
THE PEOPLE I FEEL SORRY FOR ARE RUSH'S FOLLOWERS, WHO NOW HAVE TO SWALLOW THE FACT THAT HE'S A FRAUD AND A HYPOCRITE ...
I MEAN ... CAN YOU IMAGINE WHAT IT WOULD BE LIKE FOR MILLIONS OF CONSERVATIVE WHITE MEN TO FIND OUT AMERICA'S MOST BRASH RIGHT-WINGER IS STRUNG OUT ON DRUGS?
IT'S LIKE ... IT'S LIKE ...
LOUIS FARRAKHAN GOING TO HEAVEN AND FINDING OUT GOD IS A WHITE WOMAN WHO LIKES PORK SANDWICHES.
SOMETHING LIKE THAT.
www.ucomics.com
© 2003 Aaron McGruder/Dist. by Universal Press Syndicate
10/21

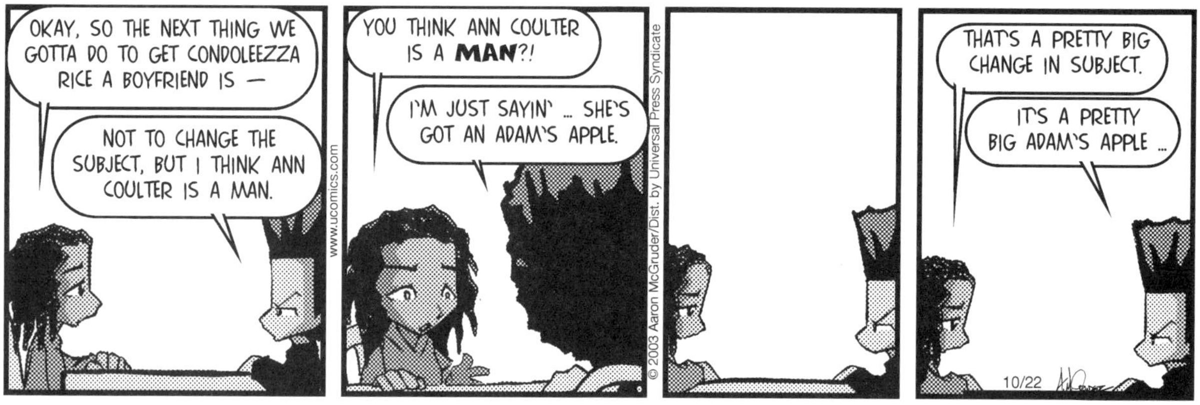
OKAY, SO THE NEXT THING WE GOTTA DO TO GET CONDOLEEZZA RICE A BOYFRIEND IS —
NOT TO CHANGE THE SUBJECT, BUT I THINK ANN COULTER IS A MAN.
YOU THINK ANN COULTER IS A **MAN**?!
I'M JUST SAYIN' ... SHE'S GOT AN ADAM'S APPLE.
THAT'S A PRETTY BIG CHANGE IN SUBJECT.
IT'S A PRETTY BIG ADAM'S APPLE ...
www.ucomics.com
© 2003 Aaron McGruder/Dist. by Universal Press Syndicate
10/22

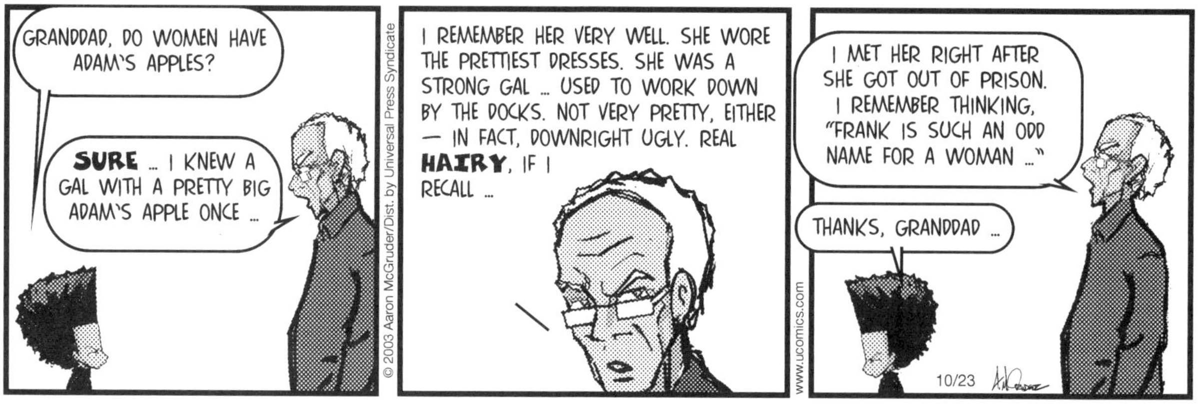
GRANDDAD, DO WOMEN HAVE ADAM'S APPLES?
SURE ... I KNEW A GAL WITH A PRETTY BIG ADAM'S APPLE ONCE ...
I REMEMBER HER VERY WELL. SHE WORE THE PRETTIEST DRESSES. SHE WAS A STRONG GAL ... USED TO WORK DOWN BY THE DOCKS. NOT VERY PRETTY, EITHER — IN FACT, DOWNRIGHT UGLY. REAL **HAIRY**, IF I RECALL ...
I MET HER RIGHT AFTER SHE GOT OUT OF PRISON. I REMEMBER THINKING, "FRANK IS SUCH AN ODD NAME FOR A WOMAN ..."
THANKS, GRANDDAD ...
© 2003 Aaron McGruder/Dist. by Universal Press Syndicate
www.ucomics.com
10/23

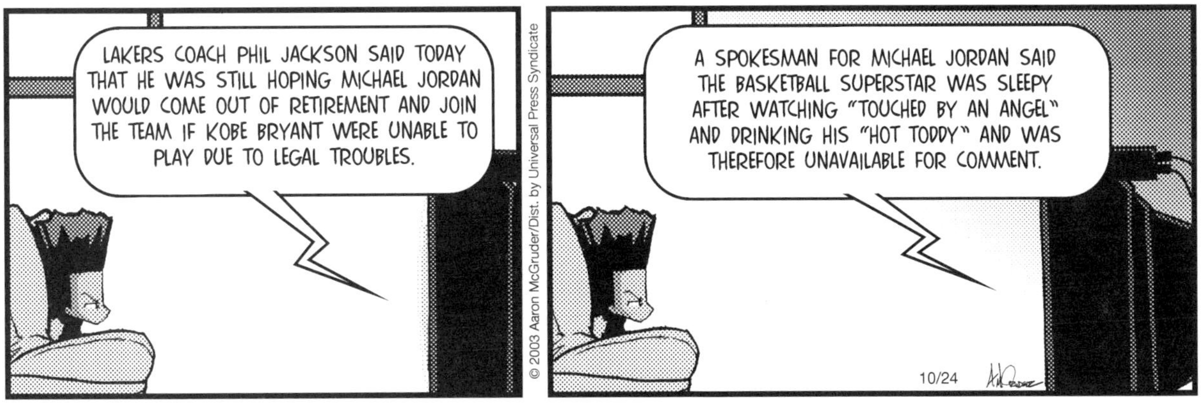
LAKERS COACH PHIL JACKSON SAID TODAY THAT HE WAS STILL HOPING MICHAEL JORDAN WOULD COME OUT OF RETIREMENT AND JOIN THE TEAM IF KOBE BRYANT WERE UNABLE TO PLAY DUE TO LEGAL TROUBLES.
© 2003 Aaron McGruder/Dist. by Universal Press Syndicate
A SPOKESMAN FOR MICHAEL JORDAN SAID THE BASKETBALL SUPERSTAR WAS SLEEPY AFTER WATCHING "TOUCHED BY AN ANGEL" AND DRINKING HIS "HOT TODDY" AND WAS THEREFORE UNAVAILABLE FOR COMMENT.
10/24

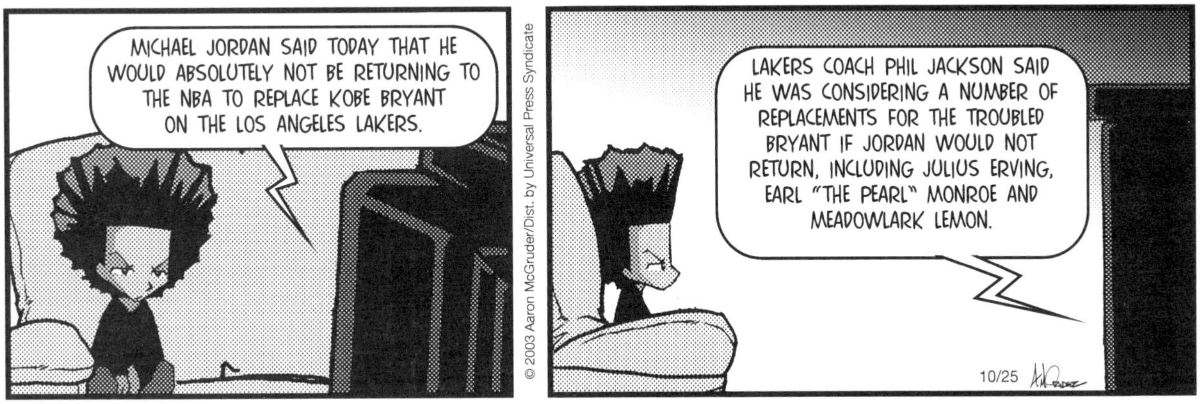
MICHAEL JORDAN SAID TODAY THAT HE WOULD ABSOLUTELY NOT BE RETURNING TO THE NBA TO REPLACE KOBE BRYANT ON THE LOS ANGELES LAKERS.
© 2003 Aaron McGruder/Dist. by Universal Press Syndicate
LAKERS COACH PHIL JACKSON SAID HE WAS CONSIDERING A NUMBER OF REPLACEMENTS FOR THE TROUBLED BRYANT IF JORDAN WOULD NOT RETURN, INCLUDING JULIUS ERVING, EARL "THE PEARL" MONROE AND MEADOWLARK LEMON.
10/25

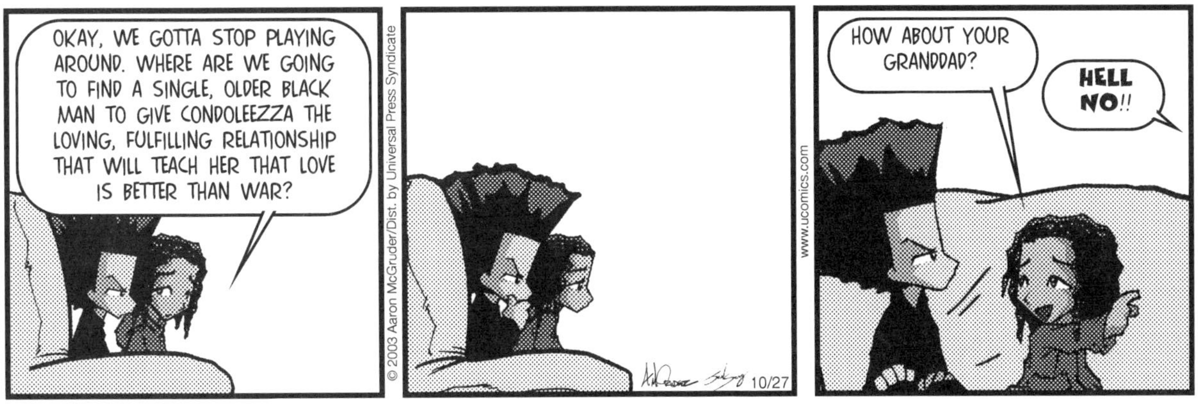
OKAY, WE GOTTA STOP PLAYING AROUND. WHERE ARE WE GOING TO FIND A SINGLE, OLDER BLACK MAN TO GIVE CONDOLEEZZA THE LOVING, FULFILLING RELATIONSHIP THAT WILL TEACH HER THAT LOVE IS BETTER THAN WAR?
© 2003 Aaron McGruder/Dist. by Universal Press Syndicate
10/27
www.ucomics.com
HOW ABOUT YOUR GRANDDAD?
HELL NO!!

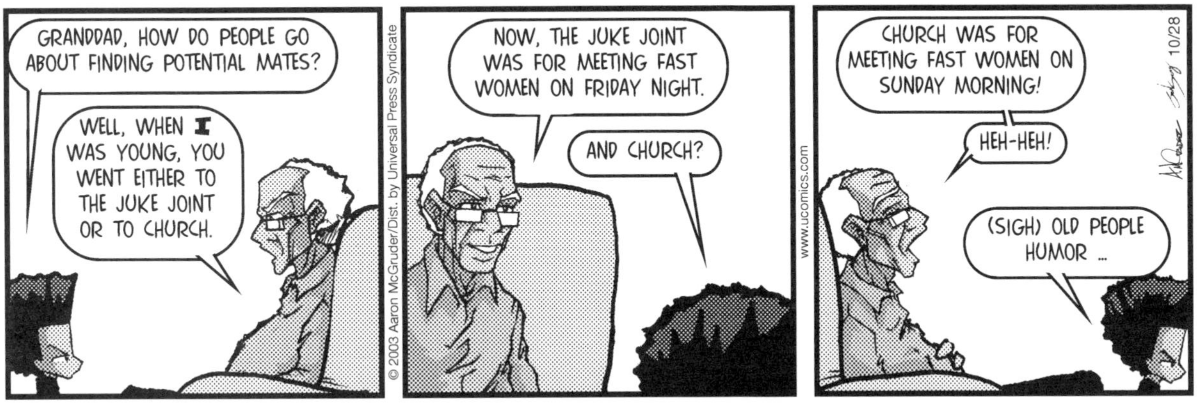
GRANDDAD, HOW DO PEOPLE GO ABOUT FINDING POTENTIAL MATES?
WELL, WHEN I WAS YOUNG, YOU WENT EITHER TO THE JUKE JOINT OR TO CHURCH.
© 2003 Aaron McGruder/Dist. by Universal Press Syndicate
NOW, THE JUKE JOINT WAS FOR MEETING FAST WOMEN ON FRIDAY NIGHT.
AND CHURCH?
www.ucomics.com
CHURCH WAS FOR MEETING FAST WOMEN ON SUNDAY MORNING!
HEH-HEH!
(SIGH) OLD PEOPLE HUMOR ...
10/28

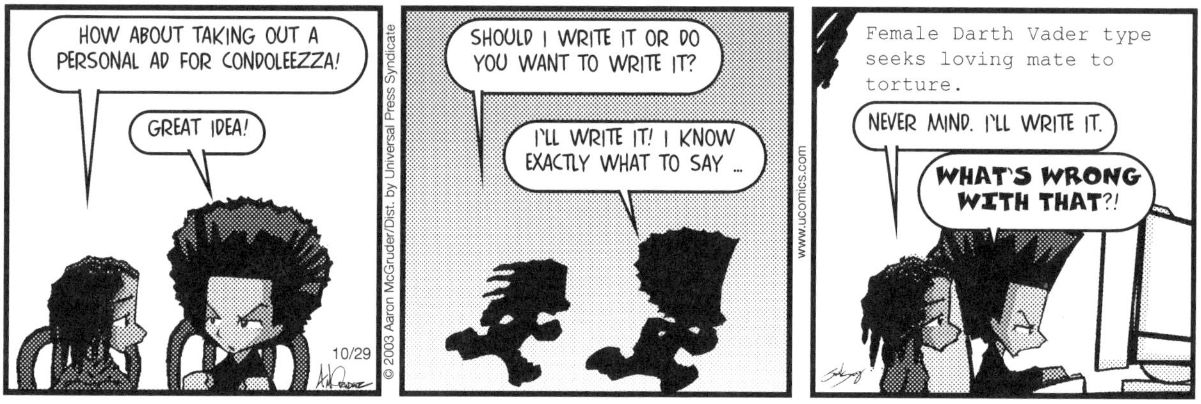
HOW ABOUT TAKING OUT A PERSONAL AD FOR CONDOLEEZZA!
GREAT IDEA!
10/29
© 2003 Aaron McGruder/Dist. by Universal Press Syndicate
SHOULD I WRITE IT OR DO YOU WANT TO WRITE IT?
I'LL WRITE IT! I KNOW EXACTLY WHAT TO SAY ...
www.ucomics.com
Female Darth Vader type seeks loving mate to torture.
NEVER MIND. I'LL WRITE IT.
WHAT'S WRONG WITH THAT?!

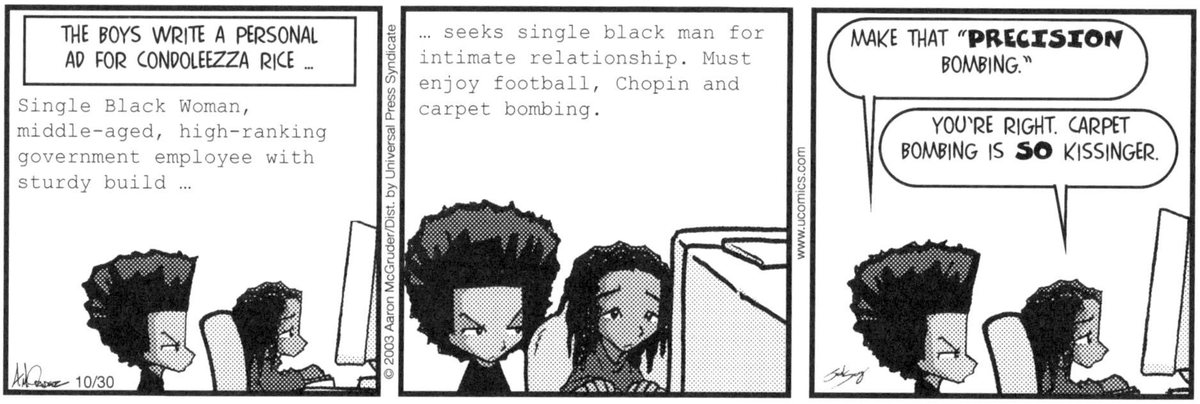
THE BOYS WRITE A PERSONAL AD FOR CONDOLEEZZA RICE ...
Single Black Woman, middle-aged, high-ranking government employee with sturdy build ...
10/30
© 2003 Aaron McGruder/Dist. by Universal Press Syndicate
... seeks single black man for intimate relationship. Must enjoy football, Chopin and carpet bombing.
www.ucomics.com
MAKE THAT "PRECISION BOMBING."
YOU'RE RIGHT. CARPET BOMBING IS SO KISSINGER.

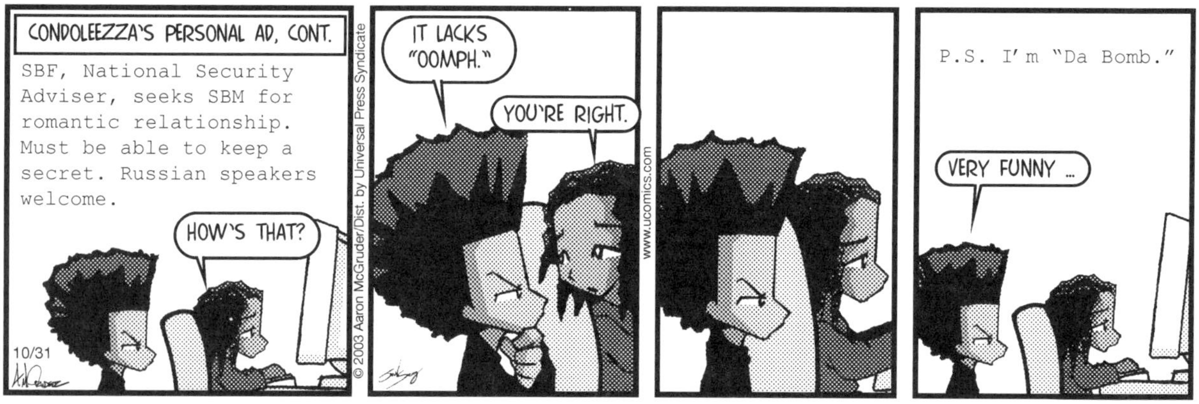
CONDOLEEZZA'S PERSONAL AD, CONT.
SBF, National Security Adviser, seeks SBM for romantic relationship. Must be able to keep a secret. Russian speakers welcome.
HOW'S THAT?
10/31
© 2003 Aaron McGruder/Dist. by Universal Press Syndicate
IT LACKS "OOMPH."
YOU'RE RIGHT.
www.ucomics.com
P.S. I'm "Da Bomb."
VERY FUNNY ...

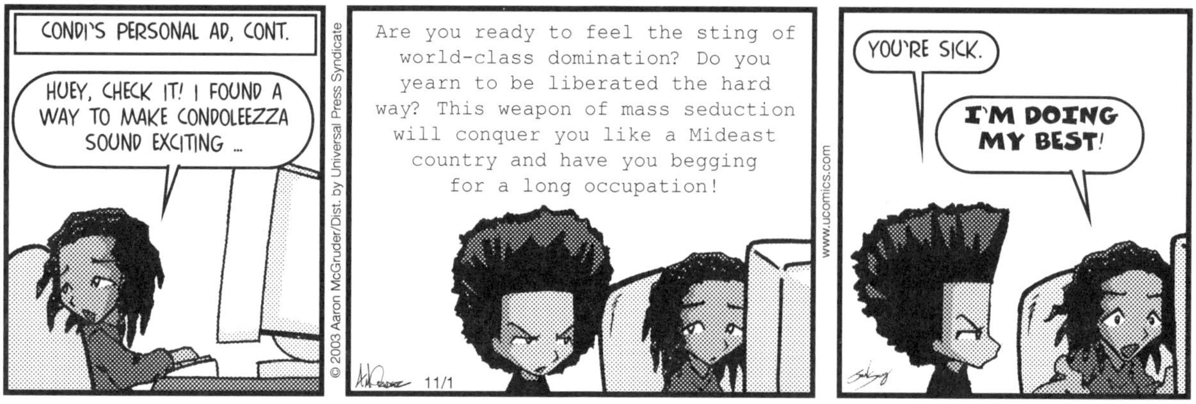
CONDI'S PERSONAL AD, CONT.
HUEY, CHECK IT! I FOUND A WAY TO MAKE CONDOLEEZZA SOUND EXCITING ...
© 2003 Aaron McGruder/Dist. by Universal Press Syndicate
Are you ready to feel the sting of world-class domination? Do you yearn to be liberated the hard way? This weapon of mass seduction will conquer you like a Mideast country and have you begging for a long occupation!
11/1
www.ucomics.com
YOU'RE SICK.
I'M DOING MY BEST!

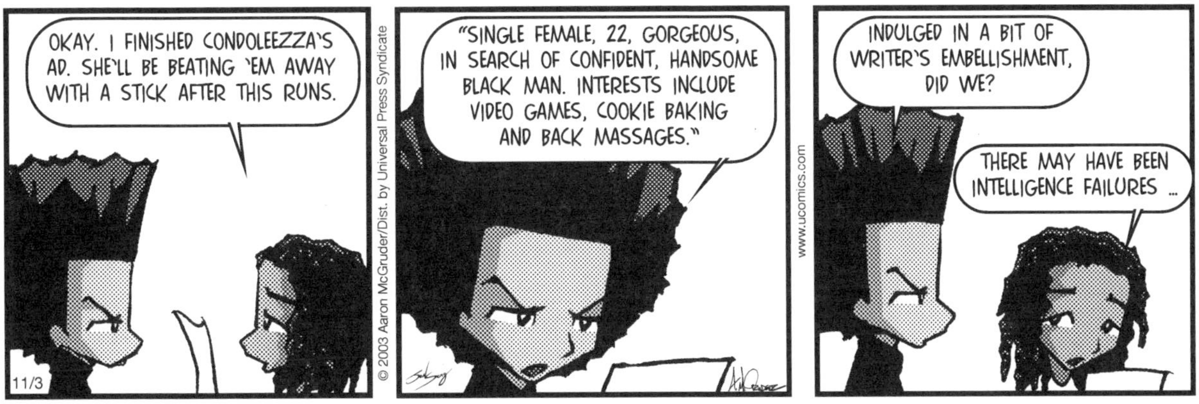
OKAY. I FINISHED CONDOLEEZZA'S AD. SHE'LL BE BEATING 'EM AWAY WITH A STICK AFTER THIS RUNS.
11/3
© 2003 Aaron McGruder/Dist. by Universal Press Syndicate
"SINGLE FEMALE, 22, GORGEOUS, IN SEARCH OF CONFIDENT, HANDSOME BLACK MAN. INTERESTS INCLUDE VIDEO GAMES, COOKIE BAKING AND BACK MASSAGES."
www.ucomics.com
INDULGED IN A BIT OF WRITER'S EMBELLISHMENT, DID WE?
THERE MAY HAVE BEEN INTELLIGENCE FAILURES ...

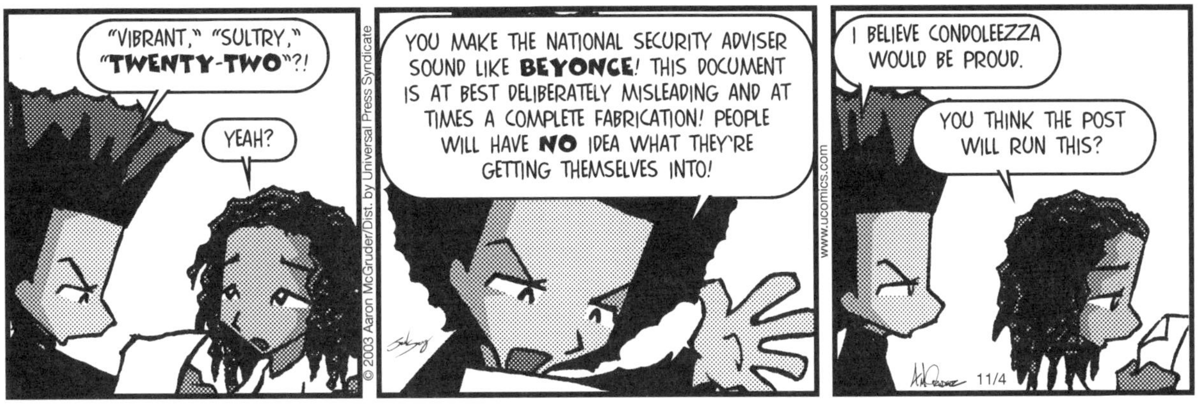
"VIBRANT," "SULTRY," "TWENTY-TWO"?!
YEAH?
© 2003 Aaron McGruder/Dist. by Universal Press Syndicate
YOU MAKE THE NATIONAL SECURITY ADVISER SOUND LIKE BEYONCE! THIS DOCUMENT IS AT BEST DELIBERATELY MISLEADING AND AT TIMES A COMPLETE FABRICATION! PEOPLE WILL HAVE NO IDEA WHAT THEY'RE GETTING THEMSELVES INTO!
www.ucomics.com
I BELIEVE CONDOLEEZZA WOULD BE PROUD.
YOU THINK THE POST WILL RUN THIS?
11/4

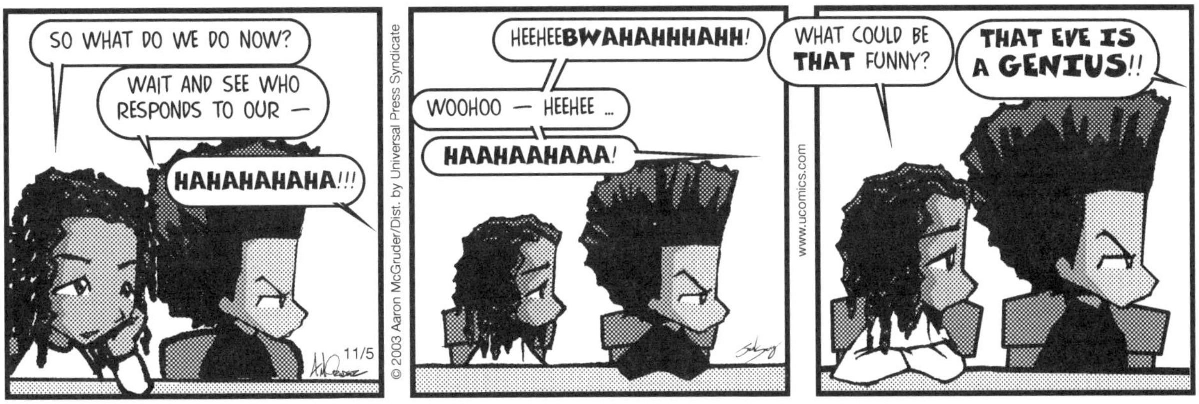
SO WHAT DO WE DO NOW?
WAIT AND SEE WHO RESPONDS TO OUR —
HAHAHAHAHA!!!
11/5
© 2003 Aaron McGruder/Dist. by Universal Press Syndicate
HEEHEEBWAHAHHHAHH!
WOOHOO — HEEHEE ...
HAAHAAHAAA!
www.ucomics.com
WHAT COULD BE THAT FUNNY?
THAT EVE IS A GENIUS!!

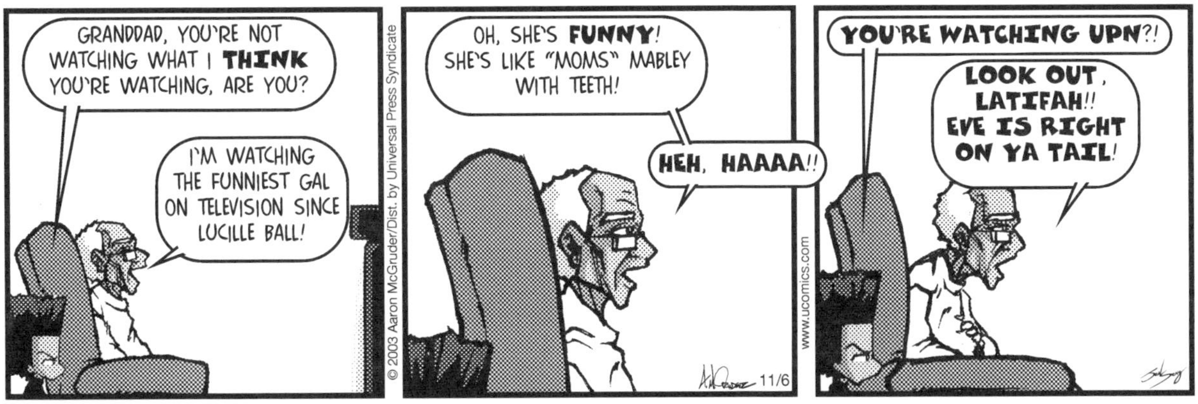
GRANDDAD, YOU'RE NOT WATCHING WHAT I THINK YOU'RE WATCHING, ARE YOU?
I'M WATCHING THE FUNNIEST GAL ON TELEVISION SINCE LUCILLE BALL!
© 2003 Aaron McGruder/Dist. by Universal Press Syndicate
OH, SHE'S FUNNY! SHE'S LIKE "MOMS" MABLEY WITH TEETH!
HEH, HAAAA!!
11/6
www.ucomics.com
YOU'RE WATCHING UPN?!
LOOK OUT, LATIFAH!! EVE IS RIGHT ON YA TAIL!

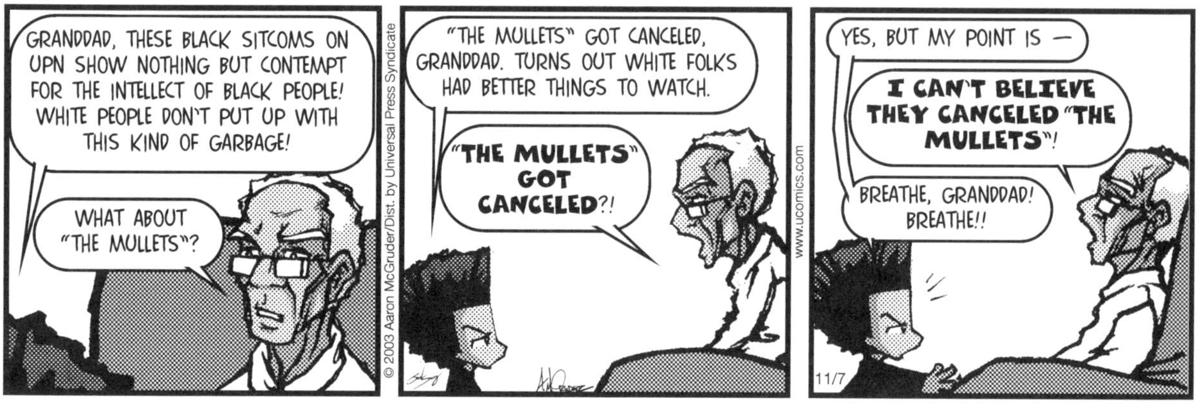
GRANDDAD, THESE BLACK SITCOMS ON UPN SHOW NOTHING BUT CONTEMPT FOR THE INTELLECT OF BLACK PEOPLE! WHITE PEOPLE DON'T PUT UP WITH THIS KIND OF GARBAGE!
WHAT ABOUT "THE MULLETS"?
© 2003 Aaron McGruder/Dist. by Universal Press Syndicate
"THE MULLETS" GOT CANCELED, GRANDDAD. TURNS OUT WHITE FOLKS HAD BETTER THINGS TO WATCH.
"THE MULLETS" GOT CANCELED?!
www.ucomics.com
YES, BUT MY POINT IS —
I CAN'T BELIEVE THEY CANCELED "THE MULLETS"!
BREATHE, GRANDDAD! BREATHE!!
11/7

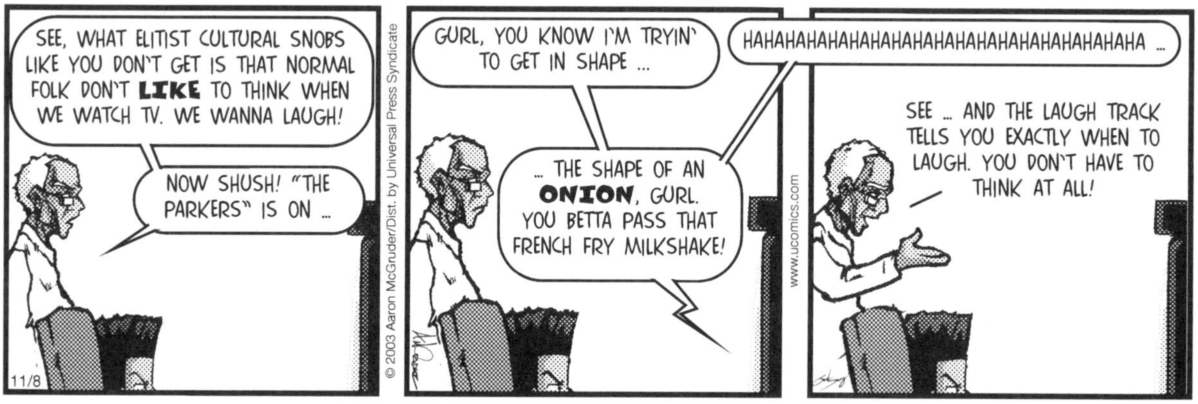
SEE, WHAT ELITIST CULTURAL SNOBS LIKE YOU DON'T GET IS THAT NORMAL FOLK DON'T LIKE TO THINK WHEN WE WATCH TV. WE WANNA LAUGH!
NOW SHUSH! "THE PARKERS" IS ON ...
11/8
© 2003 Aaron McGruder/Dist. by Universal Press Syndicate
GURL, YOU KNOW I'M TRYIN' TO GET IN SHAPE ...
... THE SHAPE OF AN ONION, GURL. YOU BETTA PASS THAT FRENCH FRY MILKSHAKE!
HAHAHAHAHAHAHAHAHAHAHAHAHAHAHAHAHAHA ...
www.ucomics.com
SEE ... AND THE LAUGH TRACK TELLS YOU EXACTLY WHEN TO LAUGH. YOU DON'T HAVE TO THINK AT ALL!

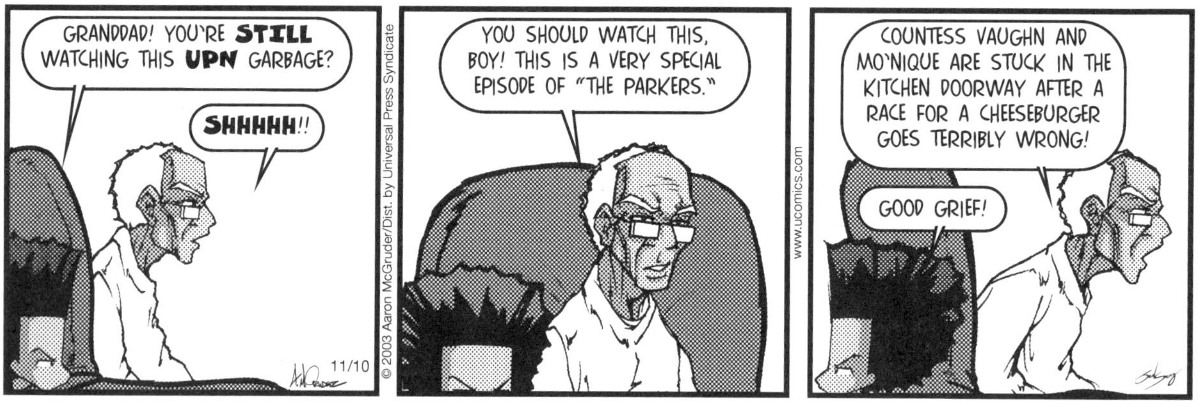
GRANDDAD! YOU'RE STILL WATCHING THIS UPN GARBAGE?
SHHHHH!!
11/10
© 2003 Aaron McGruder/Dist. by Universal Press Syndicate
YOU SHOULD WATCH THIS, BOY! THIS IS A VERY SPECIAL EPISODE OF "THE PARKERS."
www.ucomics.com
COUNTESS VAUGHN AND MO'NIQUE ARE STUCK IN THE KITCHEN DOORWAY AFTER A RACE FOR A CHEESEBURGER GOES TERRIBLY WRONG!
GOOD GRIEF!

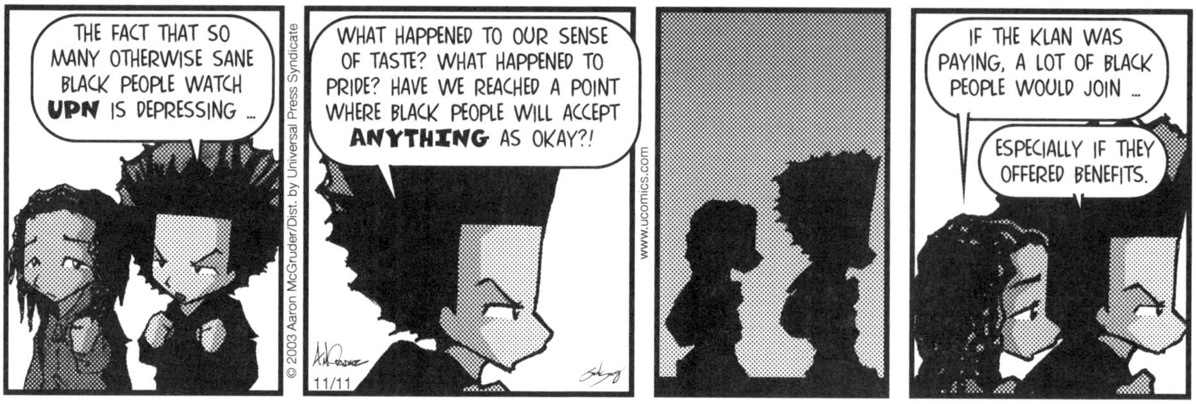
THE FACT THAT SO MANY OTHERWISE SANE BLACK PEOPLE WATCH UPN IS DEPRESSING ...
© 2003 Aaron McGruder/Dist. by Universal Press Syndicate
WHAT HAPPENED TO OUR SENSE OF TASTE? WHAT HAPPENED TO PRIDE? HAVE WE REACHED A POINT WHERE BLACK PEOPLE WILL ACCEPT ANYTHING AS OKAY?!
11/11
www.ucomics.com
IF THE KLAN WAS PAYING, A LOT OF BLACK PEOPLE WOULD JOIN ...
ESPECIALLY IF THEY OFFERED BENEFITS.

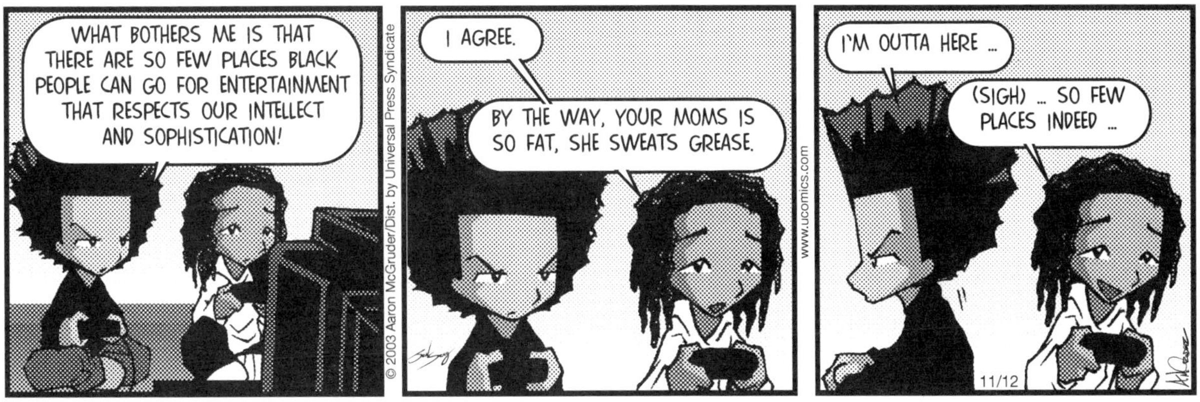
WHAT BOTHERS ME IS THAT THERE ARE SO FEW PLACES BLACK PEOPLE CAN GO FOR ENTERTAINMENT THAT RESPECTS OUR INTELLECT AND SOPHISTICATION!
© 2003 Aaron McGruder/Dist. by Universal Press Syndicate
I AGREE.
BY THE WAY, YOUR MOMS IS SO FAT, SHE SWEATS GREASE.
www.ucomics.com
I'M OUTTA HERE ...
(SIGH) ... SO FEW PLACES INDEED ...
11/12

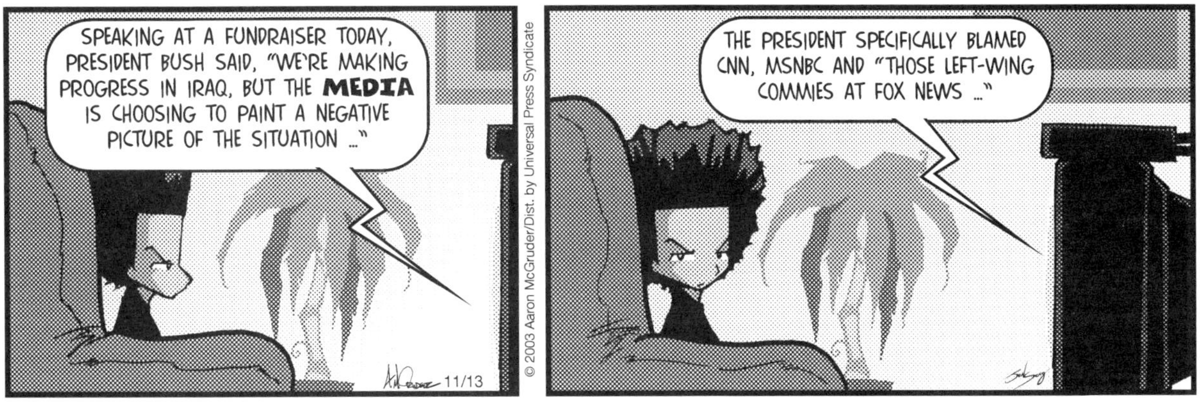
SPEAKING AT A FUNDRAISER TODAY, PRESIDENT BUSH SAID, "WE'RE MAKING PROGRESS IN IRAQ, BUT THE MEDIA IS CHOOSING TO PAINT A NEGATIVE PICTURE OF THE SITUATION ..."
11/13
© 2003 Aaron McGruder/Dist. by Universal Press Syndicate
THE PRESIDENT SPECIFICALLY BLAMED CNN, MSNBC AND "THOSE LEFT-WING COMMIES AT FOX NEWS ..."

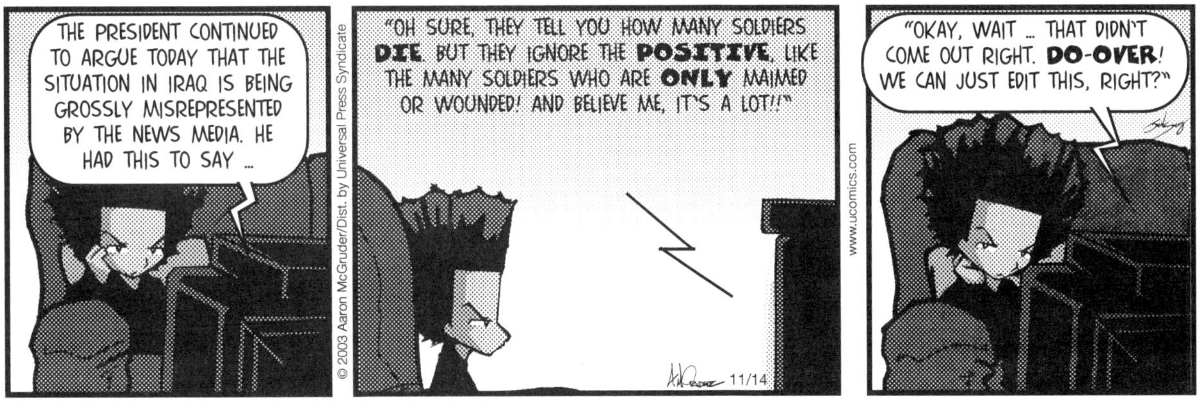
THE PRESIDENT CONTINUED TO ARGUE TODAY THAT THE SITUATION IN IRAQ IS BEING GROSSLY MISREPRESENTED BY THE NEWS MEDIA. HE HAD THIS TO SAY ...
© 2003 Aaron McGruder/Dist. by Universal Press Syndicate
"OH SURE, THEY TELL YOU HOW MANY SOLDIERS DIE, BUT THEY IGNORE THE POSITIVE, LIKE THE MANY SOLDIERS WHO ARE ONLY MAIMED OR WOUNDED! AND BELIEVE ME, IT'S A LOT!!"
11/14
www.ucomics.com
"OKAY, WAIT ... THAT DIDN'T COME OUT RIGHT. DO-OVER! WE CAN JUST EDIT THIS, RIGHT?"

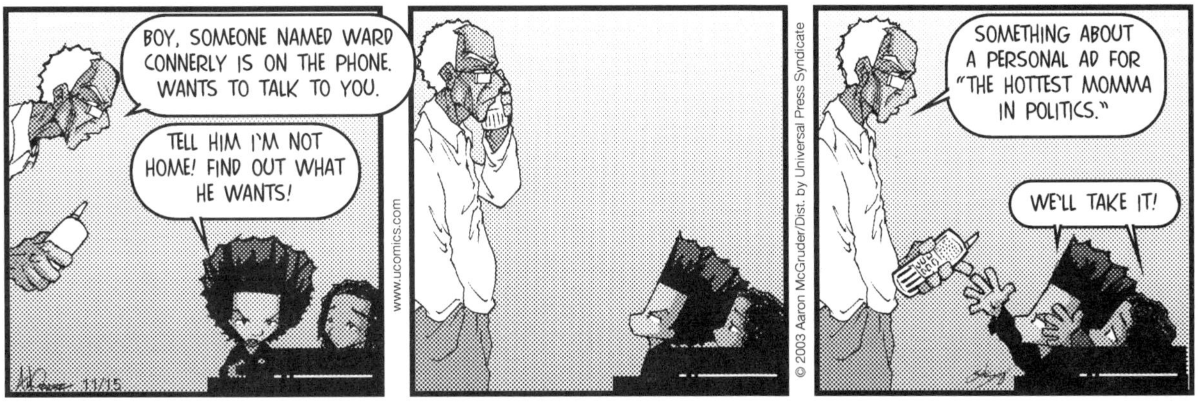
BOY, SOMEONE NAMED WARD CONNERLY IS ON THE PHONE. WANTS TO TALK TO YOU.
TELL HIM I'M NOT HOME! FIND OUT WHAT HE WANTS!
11/15
www.ucomics.com
© 2003 Aaron McGruder/Dist. by Universal Press Syndicate
SOMETHING ABOUT A PERSONAL AD FOR "THE HOTTEST MOMMA IN POLITICS."
WE'LL TAKE IT!

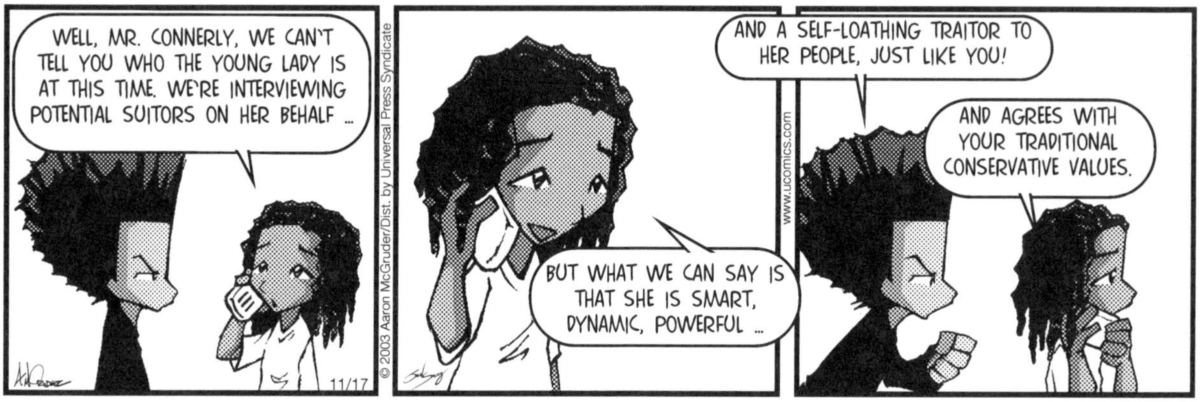
WELL, MR. CONNERLY, WE CAN'T TELL YOU WHO THE YOUNG LADY IS AT THIS TIME. WE'RE INTERVIEWING POTENTIAL SUITORS ON HER BEHALF ...
11/17
© 2003 Aaron McGruder/Dist. by Universal Press Syndicate
BUT WHAT WE CAN SAY IS THAT SHE IS SMART, DYNAMIC, POWERFUL ...
www.ucomics.com
AND A SELF-LOATHING TRAITOR TO HER PEOPLE, JUST LIKE YOU!
AND AGREES WITH YOUR TRADITIONAL CONSERVATIVE VALUES.

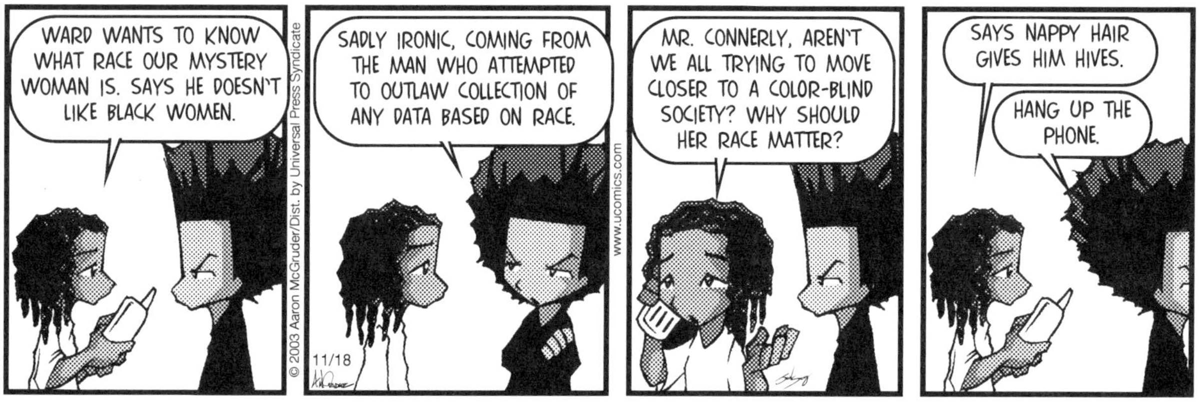
WARD WANTS TO KNOW WHAT RACE OUR MYSTERY WOMAN IS. SAYS HE DOESN'T LIKE BLACK WOMEN.
© 2003 Aaron McGruder/Dist. by Universal Press Syndicate
SADLY IRONIC, COMING FROM THE MAN WHO ATTEMPTED TO OUTLAW COLLECTION OF ANY DATA BASED ON RACE.
11/18
www.ucomics.com
MR. CONNERLY, AREN'T WE ALL TRYING TO MOVE CLOSER TO A COLOR-BLIND SOCIETY? WHY SHOULD HER RACE MATTER?
SAYS NAPPY HAIR GIVES HIM HIVES.
HANG UP THE PHONE.

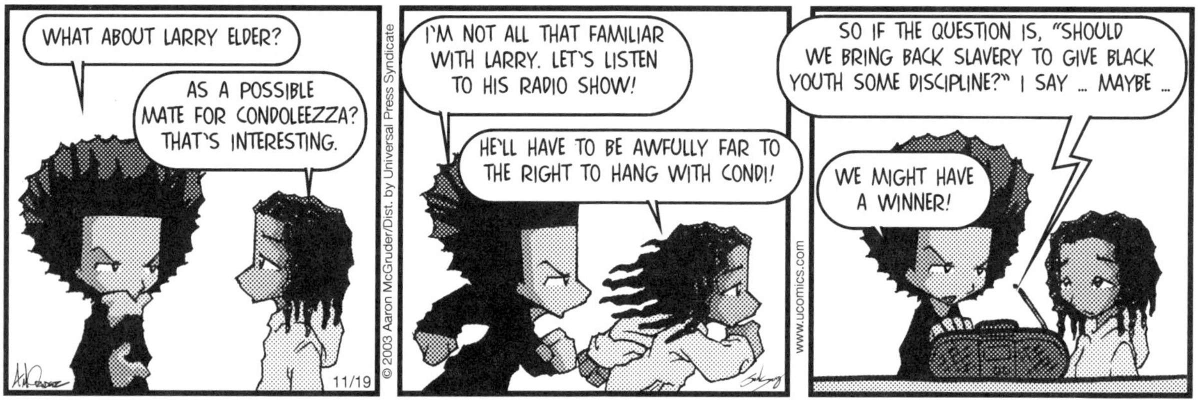
WHAT ABOUT LARRY ELDER?
AS A POSSIBLE MATE FOR CONDOLEEZZA? THAT'S INTERESTING.
11/19
© 2003 Aaron McGruder/Dist. by Universal Press Syndicate
I'M NOT ALL THAT FAMILIAR WITH LARRY. LET'S LISTEN TO HIS RADIO SHOW!
HE'LL HAVE TO BE AWFULLY FAR TO THE RIGHT TO HANG WITH CONDI!
www.ucomics.com
SO IF THE QUESTION IS, "SHOULD WE BRING BACK SLAVERY TO GIVE BLACK YOUTH SOME DISCIPLINE?" I SAY ... MAYBE ...
WE MIGHT HAVE A WINNER!

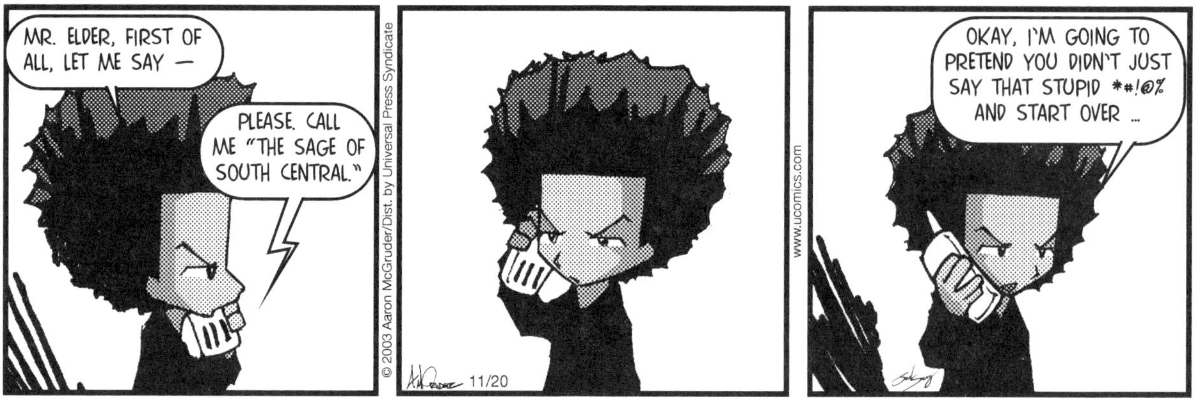
MR. ELDER, FIRST OF ALL, LET ME SAY —
PLEASE. CALL ME "THE SAGE OF SOUTH CENTRAL."
© 2003 Aaron McGruder/Dist. by Universal Press Syndicate
11/20
www.ucomics.com
OKAY, I'M GOING TO PRETEND YOU DIDN'T JUST SAY THAT STUPID *#!@% AND START OVER ...

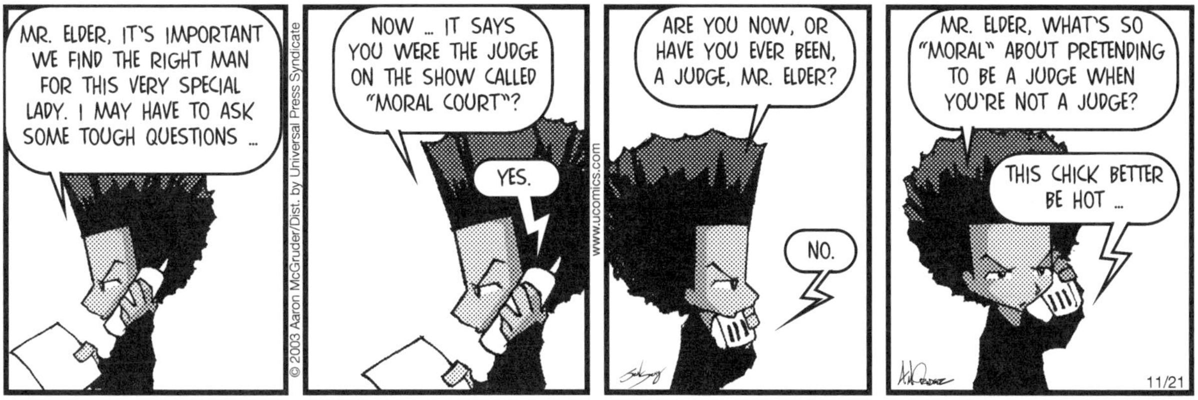
MR. ELDER, IT'S IMPORTANT WE FIND THE RIGHT MAN FOR THIS VERY SPECIAL LADY. I MAY HAVE TO ASK SOME TOUGH QUESTIONS ...
© 2003 Aaron McGruder/Dist. by Universal Press Syndicate
NOW ... IT SAYS YOU WERE THE JUDGE ON THE SHOW CALLED "MORAL COURT"?
YES.
www.ucomics.com
ARE YOU NOW, OR HAVE YOU EVER BEEN, A JUDGE, MR. ELDER?
NO.
MR. ELDER, WHAT'S SO "MORAL" ABOUT PRETENDING TO BE A JUDGE WHEN YOU'RE NOT A JUDGE?
THIS CHICK BETTER BE HOT ...
11/21

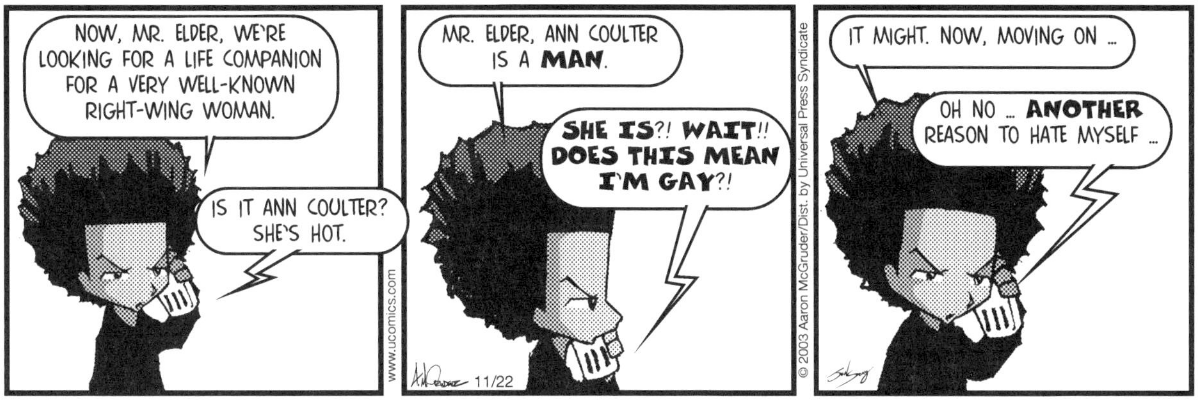
NOW, MR. ELDER, WE'RE LOOKING FOR A LIFE COMPANION FOR A VERY WELL-KNOWN RIGHT-WING WOMAN.
IS IT ANN COULTER? SHE'S HOT.
www.ucomics.com
11/22
MR. ELDER, ANN COULTER IS A MAN.
SHE IS?! WAIT!! DOES THIS MEAN I'M GAY?!
© 2003 Aaron McGruder/Dist. by Universal Press Syndicate
IT MIGHT. NOW, MOVING ON ...
OH NO ... ANOTHER REASON TO HATE MYSELF ...

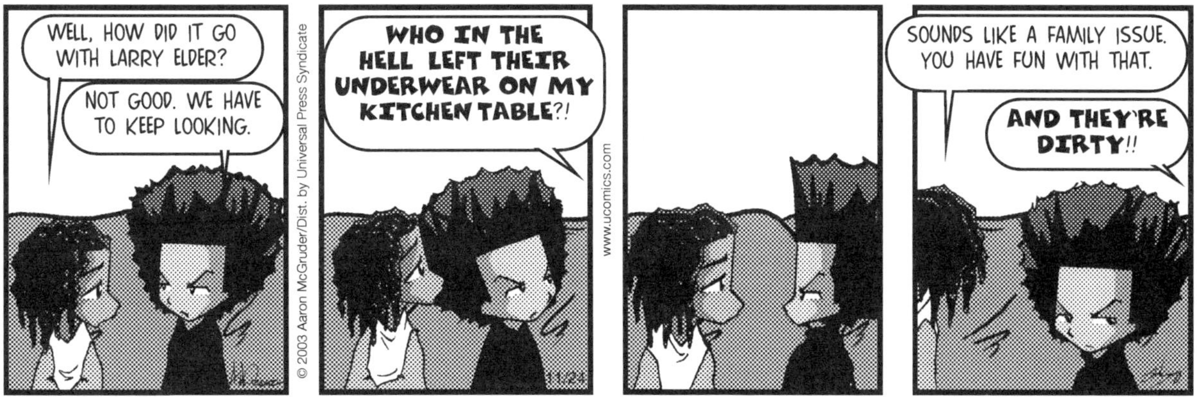
WELL, HOW DID IT GO WITH LARRY ELDER?
NOT GOOD. WE HAVE TO KEEP LOOKING.
© 2003 Aaron McGruder/Dist. by Universal Press Syndicate
WHO IN THE HELL LEFT THEIR UNDERWEAR ON MY KITCHEN TABLE?!
11/24
www.ucomics.com
SOUNDS LIKE A FAMILY ISSUE. YOU HAVE FUN WITH THAT.
AND THEY'RE DIRTY!!

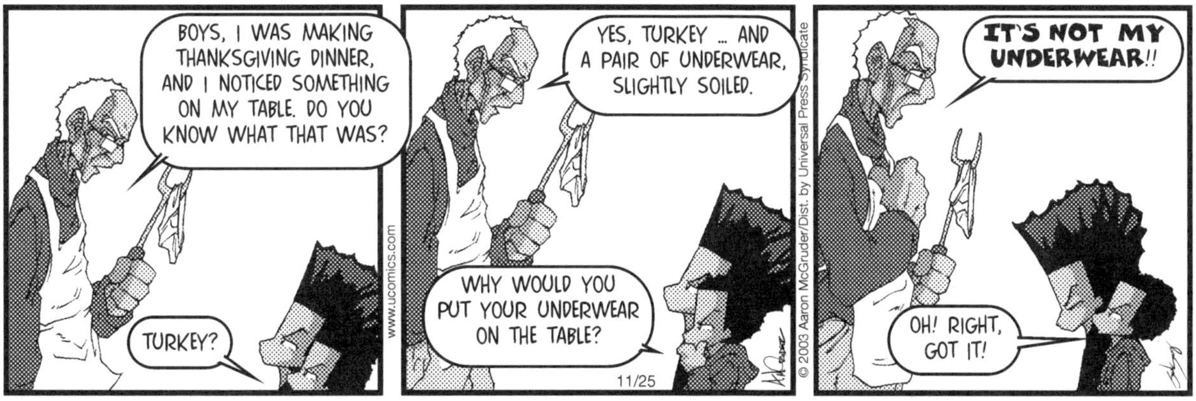
BOYS, I WAS MAKING THANKSGIVING DINNER, AND I NOTICED SOMETHING ON MY TABLE. DO YOU KNOW WHAT THAT WAS?
TURKEY?
www.ucomics.com
YES, TURKEY ... AND A PAIR OF UNDERWEAR, SLIGHTLY SOILED.
WHY WOULD YOU PUT YOUR UNDERWEAR ON THE TABLE?
11/25
© 2003 Aaron McGruder/Dist. by Universal Press Syndicate
IT'S NOT MY UNDERWEAR!!
OH! RIGHT, GOT IT!

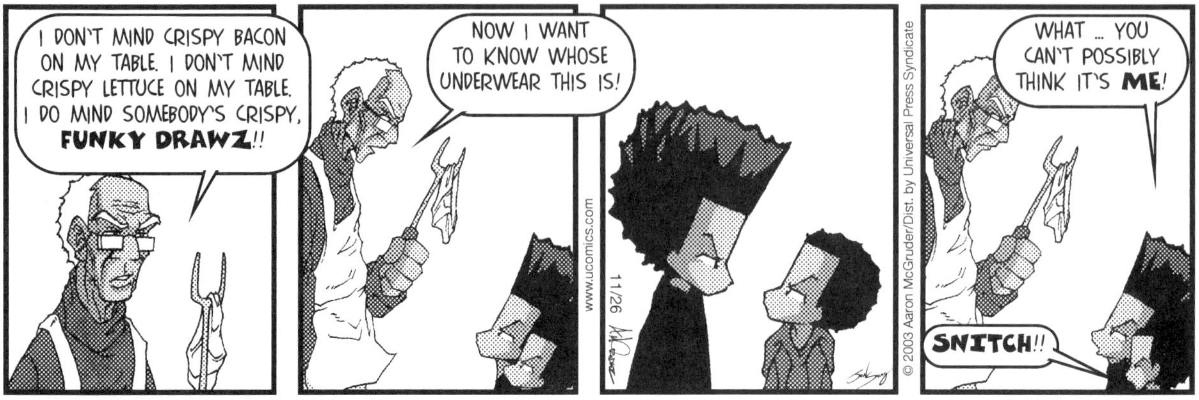
I DON'T MIND CRISPY BACON ON MY TABLE. I DON'T MIND CRISPY LETTUCE ON MY TABLE. I DO MIND SOMEBODY'S CRISPY, **FUNKY DRAWZ**!!
NOW I WANT TO KNOW WHOSE UNDERWEAR THIS IS!
www.ucomics.com 11/26
© 2003 Aaron McGruder/Dist. by Universal Press Syndicate
WHAT ... YOU CAN'T POSSIBLY THINK IT'S **ME**!
SNITCH!!

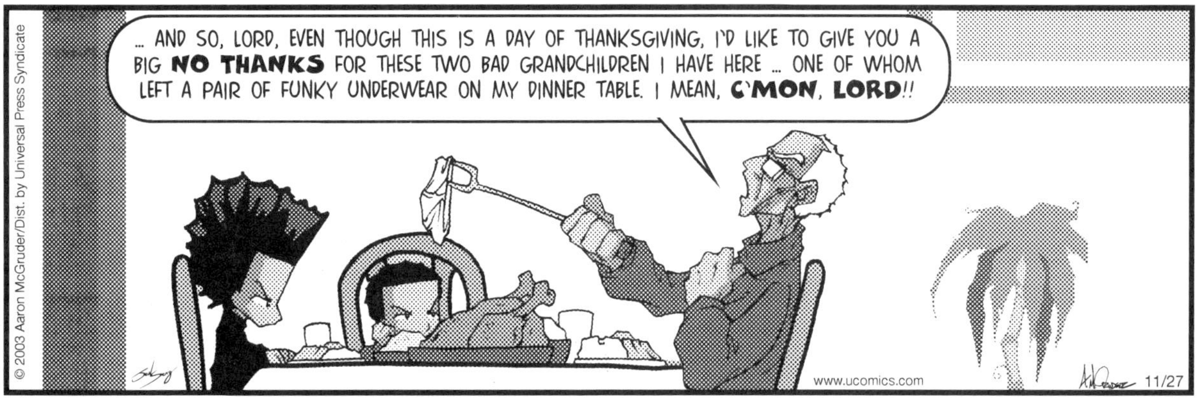
© 2003 Aaron McGruder/Dist. by Universal Press Syndicate
... AND SO, LORD, EVEN THOUGH THIS IS A DAY OF THANKSGIVING, I'D LIKE TO GIVE YOU A BIG **NO THANKS** FOR THESE TWO BAD GRANDCHILDREN I HAVE HERE ... ONE OF WHOM LEFT A PAIR OF FUNKY UNDERWEAR ON MY DINNER TABLE. I MEAN, **C'MON, LORD**!!
www.ucomics.com
11/27

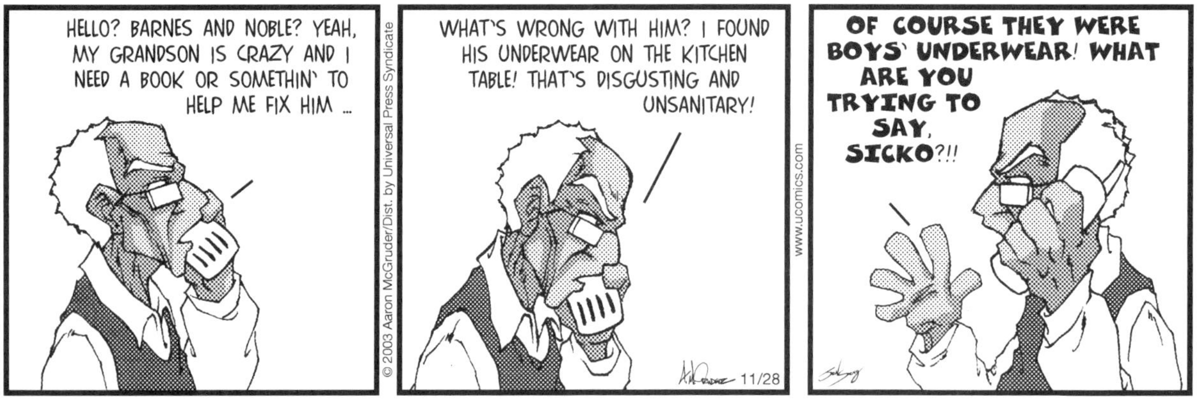
HELLO? BARNES AND NOBLE? YEAH, MY GRANDSON IS CRAZY AND I NEED A BOOK OR SOMETHIN' TO HELP ME FIX HIM ...
© 2003 Aaron McGruder/Dist. by Universal Press Syndicate
WHAT'S WRONG WITH HIM? I FOUND HIS UNDERWEAR ON THE KITCHEN TABLE! THAT'S DISGUSTING AND UNSANITARY!
11/28
www.ucomics.com
OF COURSE THEY WERE BOYS' UNDERWEAR! WHAT ARE YOU TRYING TO SAY, SICKO?!!

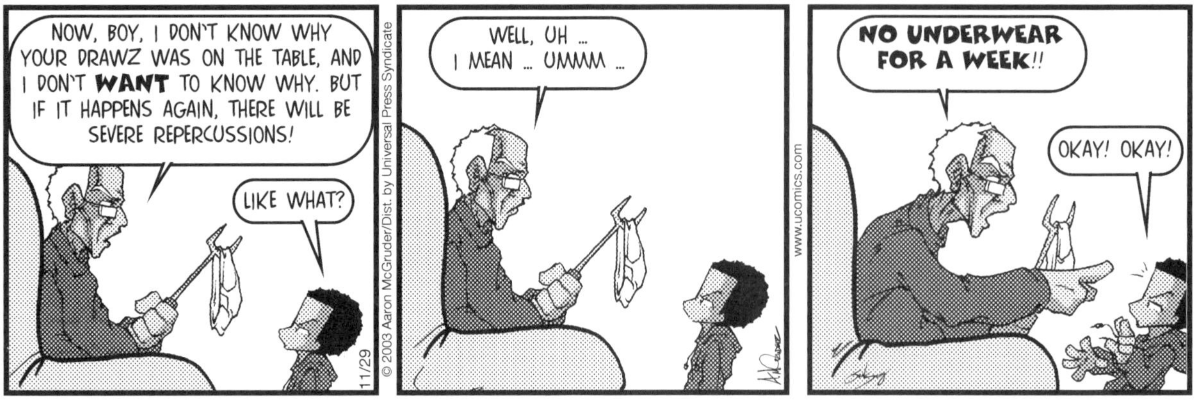
NOW, BOY, I DON'T KNOW WHY YOUR DRAWZ WAS ON THE TABLE, AND I DON'T **WANT** TO KNOW WHY. BUT IF IT HAPPENS AGAIN, THERE WILL BE SEVERE REPERCUSSIONS!
LIKE WHAT?
11/29
© 2003 Aaron McGruder/Dist. by Universal Press Syndicate
WELL, UH ... I MEAN ... UMMM ...
www.ucomics.com
NO UNDERWEAR FOR A WEEK!!
OKAY! OKAY!

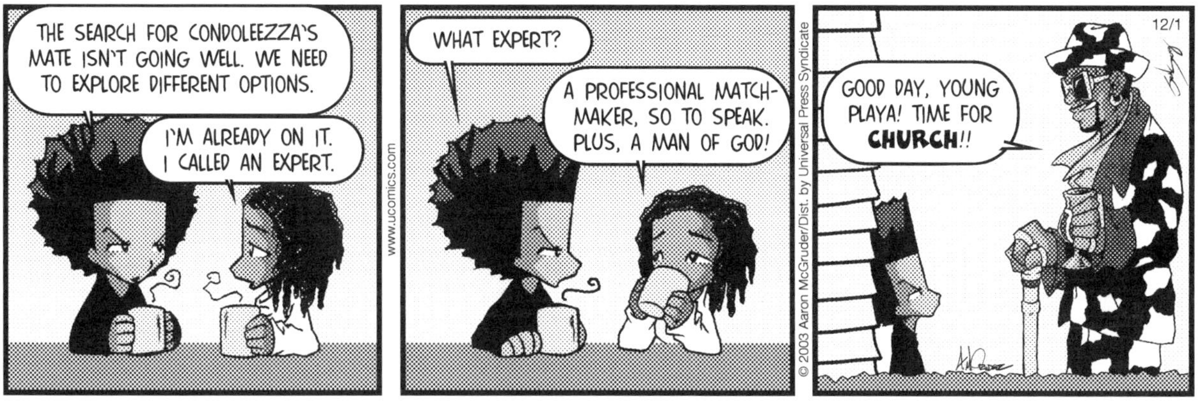
THE SEARCH FOR CONDOLEEZZA'S MATE ISN'T GOING WELL. WE NEED TO EXPLORE DIFFERENT OPTIONS.
I'M ALREADY ON IT. I CALLED AN EXPERT.
www.ucomics.com
WHAT EXPERT?
A PROFESSIONAL MATCH-MAKER, SO TO SPEAK. PLUS, A MAN OF GOD!
© 2003 Aaron McGruder/Dist. by Universal Press Syndicate
12/1
GOOD DAY, YOUNG PLAYA! TIME FOR **CHURCH**!!

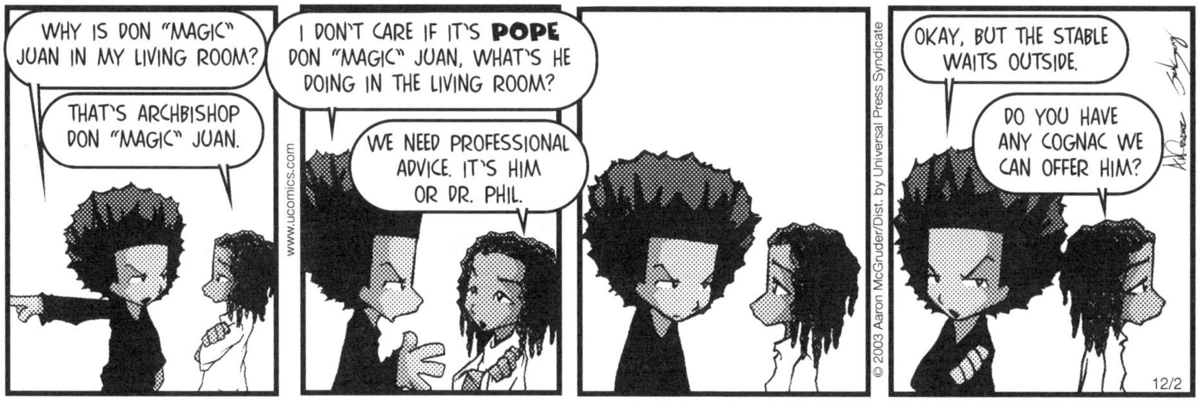
WHY IS DON "MAGIC" JUAN IN MY LIVING ROOM?
THAT'S ARCHBISHOP DON "MAGIC" JUAN.
www.ucomics.com
I DON'T CARE IF IT'S **POPE** DON "MAGIC" JUAN, WHAT'S HE DOING IN THE LIVING ROOM?
WE NEED PROFESSIONAL ADVICE. IT'S HIM OR DR. PHIL.
© 2003 Aaron McGruder/Dist. by Universal Press Syndicate
OKAY, BUT THE STABLE WAITS OUTSIDE.
DO YOU HAVE ANY COGNAC WE CAN OFFER HIM?
12/2

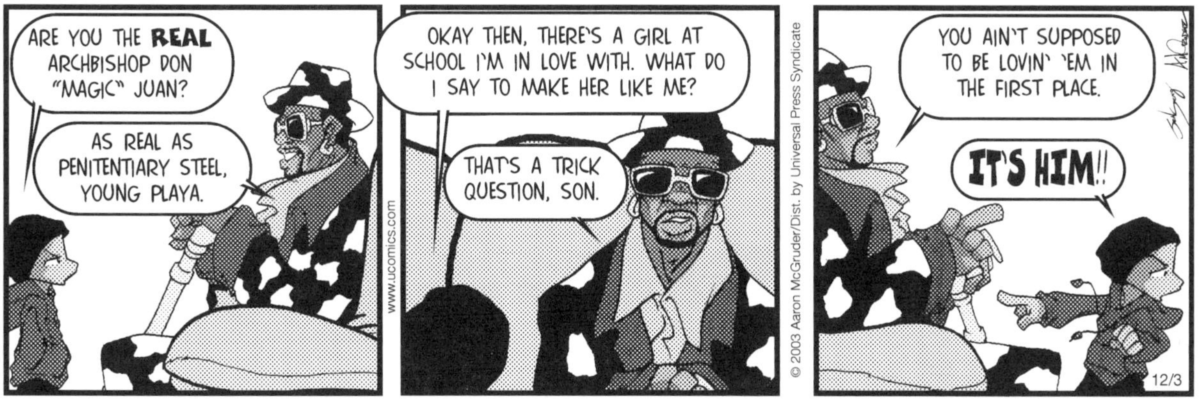
ARE YOU THE **REAL** ARCHBISHOP DON "MAGIC" JUAN?
AS REAL AS PENITENTIARY STEEL, YOUNG PLAYA.
www.ucomics.com
OKAY THEN, THERE'S A GIRL AT SCHOOL I'M IN LOVE WITH. WHAT DO I SAY TO MAKE HER LIKE ME?
THAT'S A TRICK QUESTION, SON.
© 2003 Aaron McGruder/Dist. by Universal Press Syndicate
YOU AIN'T SUPPOSED TO BE LOVIN' 'EM IN THE FIRST PLACE.
IT'S HIM!!
12/3

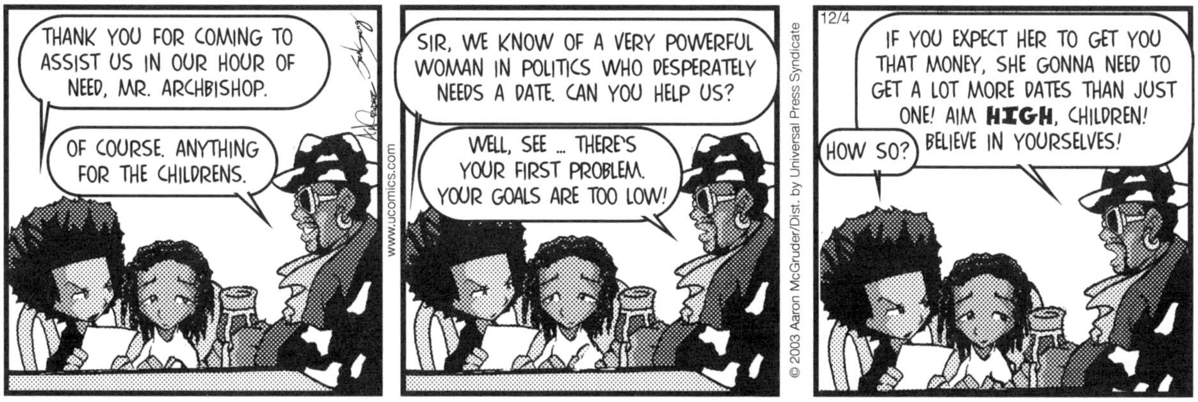
THANK YOU FOR COMING TO ASSIST US IN OUR HOUR OF NEED, MR. ARCHBISHOP.
OF COURSE. ANYTHING FOR THE CHILDRENS.
www.ucomics.com
SIR, WE KNOW OF A VERY POWERFUL WOMAN IN POLITICS WHO DESPERATELY NEEDS A DATE. CAN YOU HELP US?
WELL, SEE ... THERE'S YOUR FIRST PROBLEM. YOUR GOALS ARE TOO LOW!
© 2003 Aaron McGruder/Dist. by Universal Press Syndicate
12/4
HOW SO?
IF YOU EXPECT HER TO GET YOU THAT MONEY, SHE GONNA NEED TO GET A LOT MORE DATES THAN JUST ONE! AIM **HIGH**, CHILDREN! BELIEVE IN YOURSELVES!

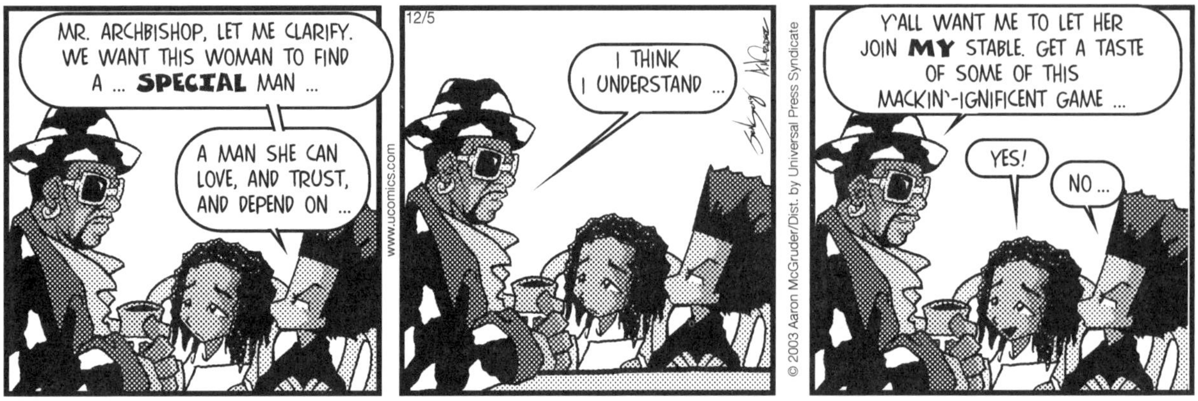
MR. ARCHBISHOP, LET ME CLARIFY. WE WANT THIS WOMAN TO FIND A ... **SPECIAL** MAN ...
A MAN SHE CAN LOVE, AND TRUST, AND DEPEND ON ...
12/5
I THINK I UNDERSTAND ...
© 2003 Aaron McGruder/Dist. by Universal Press Syndicate
www.ucomics.com
Y'ALL WANT ME TO LET HER JOIN **MY** STABLE. GET A TASTE OF SOME OF THIS MACKIN'-IGNIFICENT GAME ...
YES!
NO ...

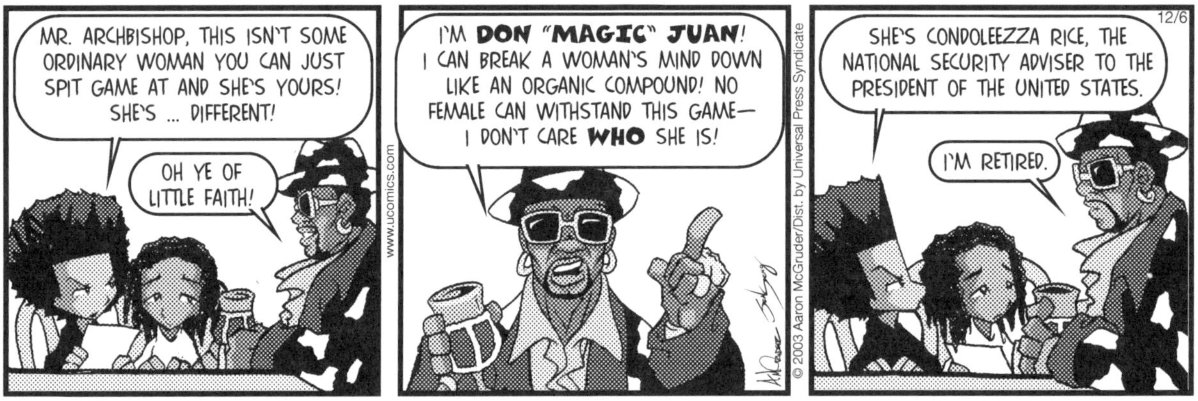
MR. ARCHBISHOP, THIS ISN'T SOME ORDINARY WOMAN YOU CAN JUST SPIT GAME AT AND SHE'S YOURS! SHE'S ... DIFFERENT!
OH YE OF LITTLE FAITH!
www.ucomics.com
I'M **DON "MAGIC" JUAN**! I CAN BREAK A WOMAN'S MIND DOWN LIKE AN ORGANIC COMPOUND! NO FEMALE CAN WITHSTAND THIS GAME— I DON'T CARE **WHO** SHE IS!
© 2003 Aaron McGruder/Dist. by Universal Press Syndicate
12/6
SHE'S CONDOLEEZZA RICE, THE NATIONAL SECURITY ADVISER TO THE PRESIDENT OF THE UNITED STATES.
I'M RETIRED.

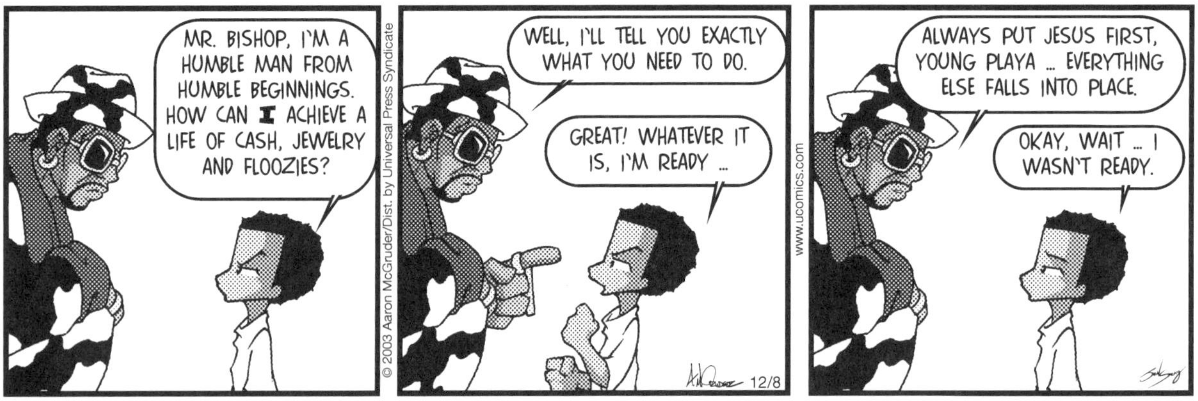
MR. BISHOP, I'M A HUMBLE MAN FROM HUMBLE BEGINNINGS. HOW CAN **I** ACHIEVE A LIFE OF CASH, JEWELRY AND FLOOZIES?
© 2003 Aaron McGruder/Dist. by Universal Press Syndicate
WELL, I'LL TELL YOU EXACTLY WHAT YOU NEED TO DO.
GREAT! WHATEVER IT IS, I'M READY ...
12/8
www.ucomics.com
ALWAYS PUT JESUS FIRST, YOUNG PLAYA ... EVERYTHING ELSE FALLS INTO PLACE.
OKAY, WAIT ... I WASN'T READY.

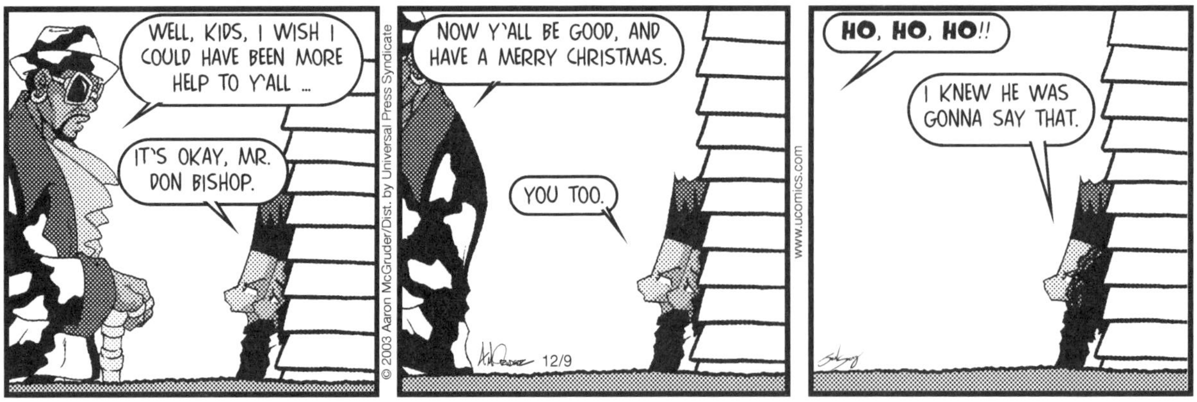
WELL, KIDS, I WISH I COULD HAVE BEEN MORE HELP TO Y'ALL ...
IT'S OKAY, MR. DON BISHOP.
© 2003 Aaron McGruder/Dist. by Universal Press Syndicate
NOW Y'ALL BE GOOD, AND HAVE A MERRY CHRISTMAS.
YOU TOO.
12/9
www.ucomics.com
HO, HO, HO!!
I KNEW HE WAS GONNA SAY THAT.

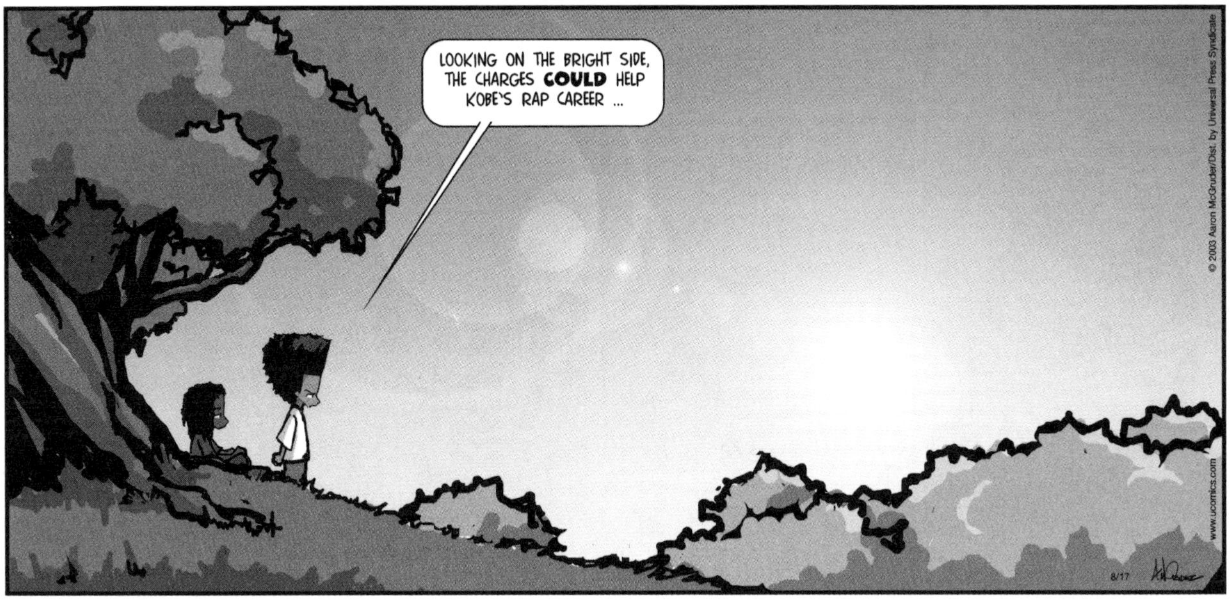
LOOKING ON THE BRIGHT SIDE, THE CHARGES **COULD** HELP KOBE'S RAP CAREER ...
© 2003 Aaron McGruder/Dist. by Universal Press Syndicate
www.ucomics.com
8/17

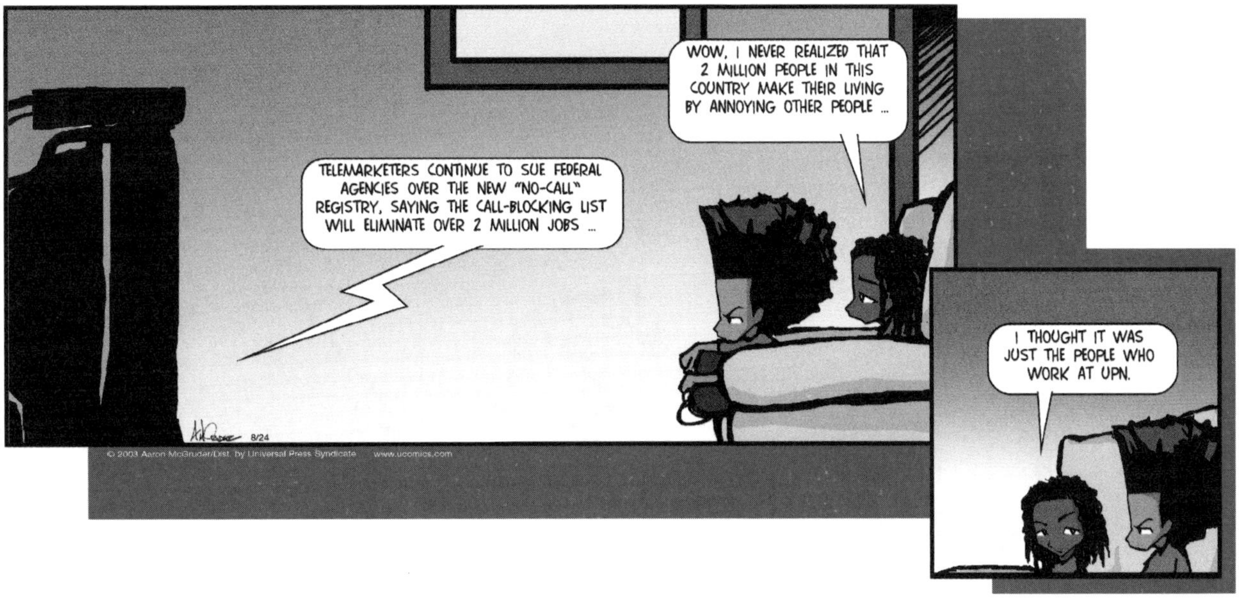
TELEMARKETERS CONTINUE TO SUE FEDERAL AGENCIES OVER THE NEW "NO-CALL" REGISTRY, SAYING THE CALL-BLOCKING LIST WILL ELIMINATE OVER 2 MILLION JOBS ...
WOW, I NEVER REALIZED THAT 2 MILLION PEOPLE IN THIS COUNTRY MAKE THEIR LIVING BY ANNOYING OTHER PEOPLE ...
I THOUGHT IT WAS JUST THE PEOPLE WHO WORK AT UPN.
8/24
© 2003 Aaron McGruder/Dist. by Universal Press Syndicate www.ucomics.com

CAN SOMEONE EXPLAIN TO ME HOW, IN THE YEAR 2003, I'M **STILL** READING ABOUT HOW ADMIRAL POINDEXTER IS MESSING UP THE COUNTRY?
IRAN-CONTRA ADMIRAL POINDEXTER?!! **CONVICTED FELON** ADMIRAL POINDEXTER?!! TWENTY YEARS LATER WE'RE **STILL** TALKIN' ABOUT THIS FOOL!! **STILL**?!
WHAT IS THIS, "BLOOM COUNTY"?!
8/31
© 2003 Aaron McGruder/Dist. by Universal Press Syndicate
www.ucomics.com

THAT'S IT!! I'M NOT BUYING YOU NO MORE FORTY-DOLLAR GEORGE BUSH DOLLS IF YOU'RE GONNA TREAT 'EM LIKE THIS!!
AND THIS BETTER BE MUD!!
9/7
© 2003 Aaron McGruder/Dist. by Universal Press Syndicate
www.ucomics.com

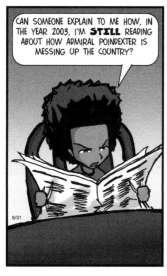

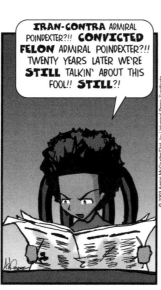

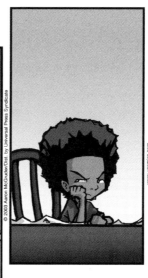

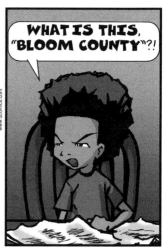

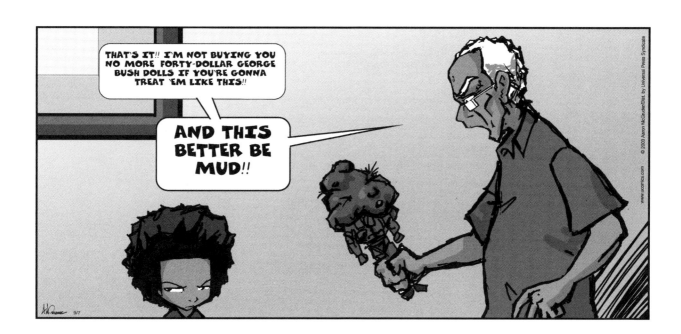

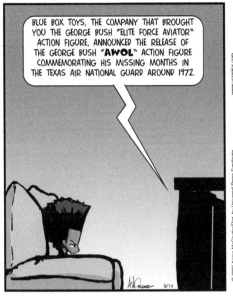

BLUE BOX TOYS, THE COMPANY THAT BROUGHT YOU THE GEORGE BUSH "ELITE FORCE AVIATOR" ACTION FIGURE, ANNOUNCED THE RELEASE OF THE GEORGE BUSH "AWOL" ACTION FIGURE COMMEMORATING HIS MISSING MONTHS IN THE TEXAS AIR NATIONAL GUARD AROUND 1972.
9/14
© 2003 Aaron McGruder/Dist. by Universal Press Syndicate www.ucomics.com
DUBYA'S SPORTING NEON GREEN SHORTS, A "BIKINI INSPECTOR" T-SHIRT AND THE "BEER HELMET" SEEN BELOW ...
BIKINI INSPECTOR
AWOL BUSH SAYS, "COWABUNGA," "BEER RUN!" AND "WOOOOO!!"

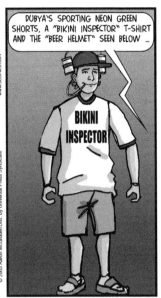

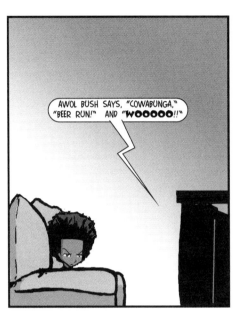

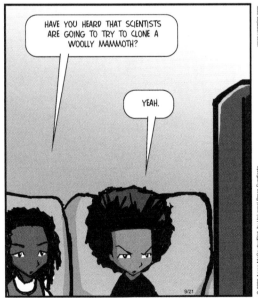

HAVE YOU HEARD THAT SCIENTISTS ARE GOING TO TRY TO CLONE A WOOLLY MAMMOTH?
YEAH.
9/21
© 2003 Aaron McGruder/Dist. by Universal Press Syndicate www.ucomics.com
WELL, I THINK IT'S REALLY GOOD OF YOUR MOTHER TO DONATE THE DNA SAMPLE.

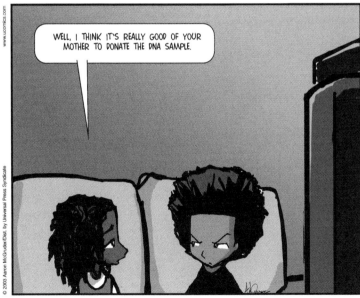

I CAN SEE IT!! I CAN SEE IT!! CAESAR, COME HERE!!
11/2
© 2003 Aaron McGruder/Dist. by Universal Press Syndicate
WHAT?! WHAT IS IT?!
ANN COULTER'S ADAM'S APPLE! LOOK!
YOU CALLED ME IN HERE TO LOOK AT ANN COULTER'S ADAM'S APPLE?!
IT'S MASSIVE! IT'S GIGANTIC! IT'S ABSOLUTELY HUMONGOUS!!
www.ucomics.com
I THINK IT'S TIME YOU TOOK UP AN INSTRUMENT OR SOMETHING ...
IT LOOKS LIKE LOU FERRIGNO'S ADAM'S APPLE!

IT'S A DISGUSTING SOCIETAL DOUBLE STANDARD. POOR PEOPLE GET HOOKED ON CRACK AND THEY'RE THE GARBAGE OF SOCIETY. THE ELITES GET ADDICTED TO PAINKILLERS AND THEY MAKE THE COVER OF NEWSWEEK.
11/9
© 2003 Aaron McGruder/Dist. by Universal Press Syndicate
www.ucomics.com
AND WHAT IS IT ABOUT WHITE PEOPLE THAT THEY GET HOOKED ON PAINKILLERS, ANYWAY?
I MEAN, YOU DON'T SEE BLACK PEOPLE GETTIN' HOOKED ON ROBITUSSIN?

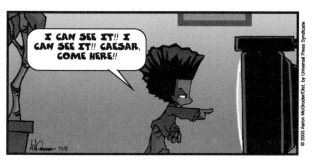

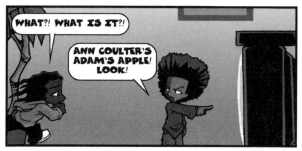

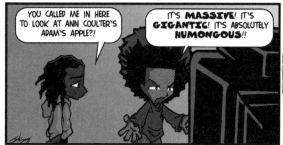

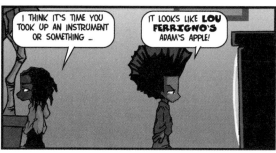

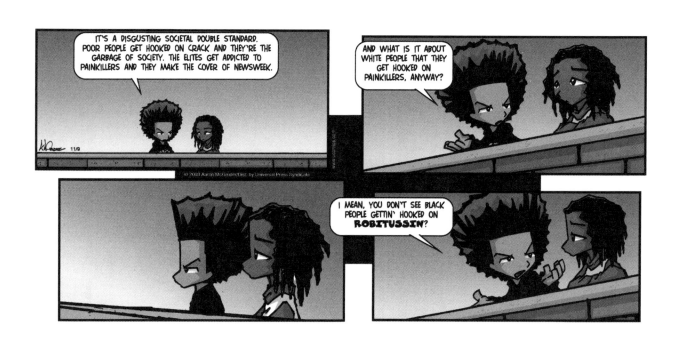

MY GOODNESS.
LOOK AT THE TIME!
11/16
GET UP!! YOU BOYS ARE GONNA BE LATE FOR SCHOOL!!
C'MON NOW, BOYS. GET YOUR TEETH BRUSHED! DON'T FORGET YOUR BOOKS NOW. C'MON NOW, HURRY ON UP ...
© 2003 Aaron McGruder/Dist. by Universal Press Syndicate
SLAM!
www.ucomics.com
WHAT TIME IS IT?
IT'S SIX THIRTY-FIVE ON SUNDAY MORNING!!
GO 'HEAD AND GET YOURSELVES GOOD SEATS!

WAKE UP.
HEY! WAKE UP!
WHY? IT'S SUNDAY.
I DON'T KNOW. GRANDDAD TOLD ME TO WAKE YOU UP, SO GET UP!
SO, WHAT ... YOU'RE MY ALARM CLOCK NOW?
I GUESS SO.
FINE.
11/23
© 2003 Aaron McGruder/Dist. by Universal Press Syndicate
OW!! HEY!!!
SMACK
www.ucomics.com
SNOOZE.

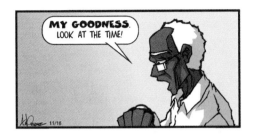

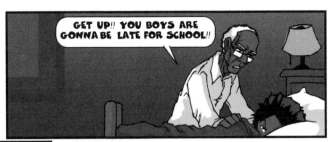

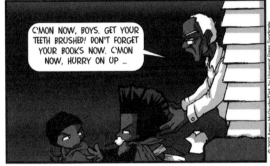

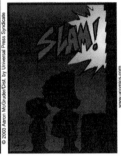

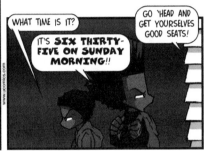

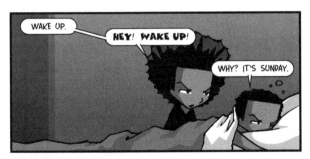

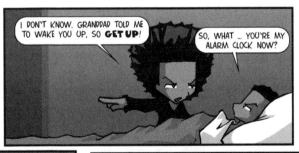

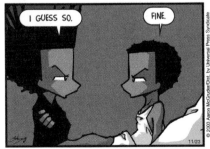

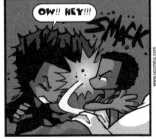

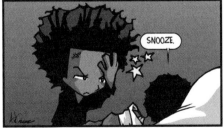

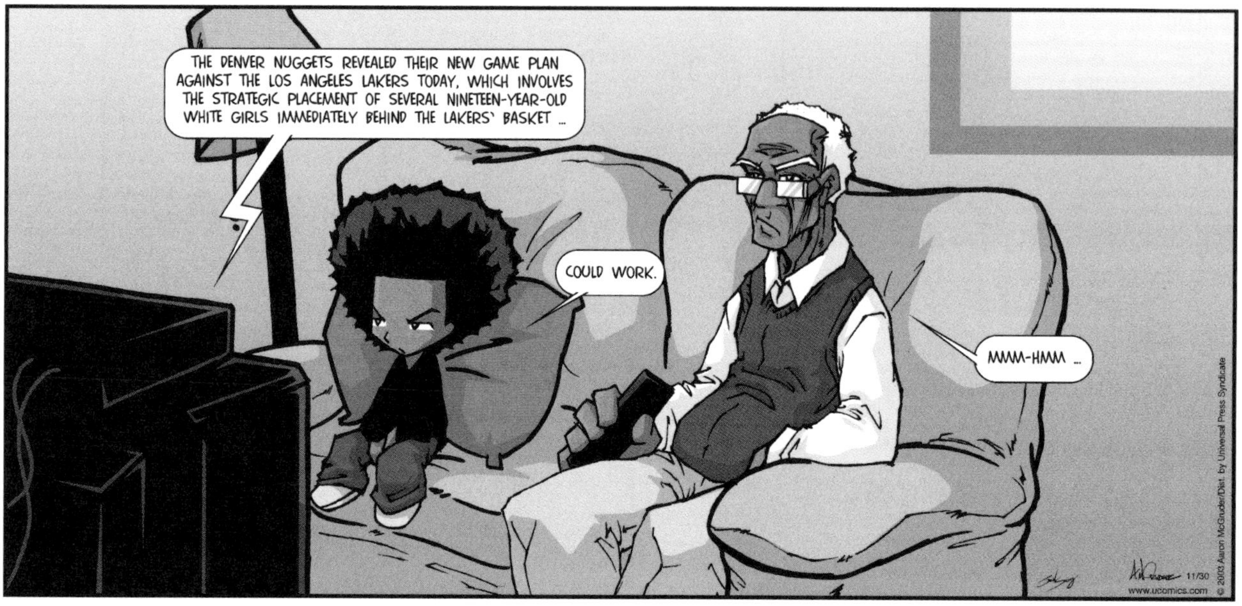
THE DENVER NUGGETS REVEALED THEIR NEW GAME PLAN AGAINST THE LOS ANGELES LAKERS TODAY, WHICH INVOLVES THE STRATEGIC PLACEMENT OF SEVERAL NINETEEN-YEAR-OLD WHITE GIRLS IMMEDIATELY BEHIND THE LAKERS' BASKET ...
COULD WORK.
MMM-HMM ...
11/30
© 2003 Aaron McGruder/Dist. by Universal Press Syndicate
www.ucomics.com

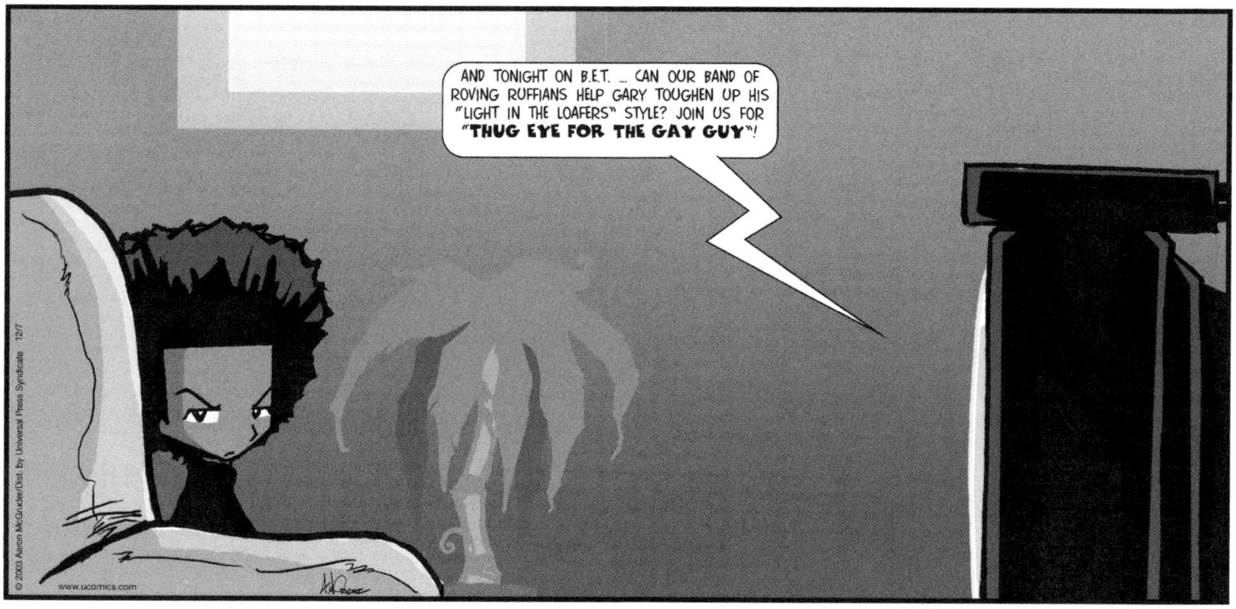
AND TONIGHT ON B.E.T. ... CAN OUR BAND OF ROVING RUFFIANS HELP GARY TOUGHEN UP HIS "LIGHT IN THE LOAFERS" STYLE? JOIN US FOR "THUG EYE FOR THE GAY GUY"!
© 2003 Aaron McGruder/Dist. by Universal Press Syndicate 12/7
www.ucomics.com

WHY THEY ALWAYS MESSIN' WITH MICHAEL JACKSON?!
© 2003 Aaron McGruder/Dist. by Universal Press Syndicate
www.ucomics.com
BECAUSE HE HAS SLEEPOVERS WITH TWELVE-YEAR-OLD BOYS AND THEN CASUALLY TALKS ABOUT IT ON NATIONAL TELEVISION.
AND THAT'S A CRIME ALL OF A SUDDEN?!!
12/14

... WELL, IF HE IS DUMB ENOUGH TO SHOW HIS FACE AROUND HERE, THE BAG AND THE SLEIGH ARE MINE ...
AND I WISH THEM REINDEER WOULD TRY SOMETHIN' ...
© 2003 Aaron McGruder/Dist. by Universal Press Syndicate www.ucomics.com
12/21

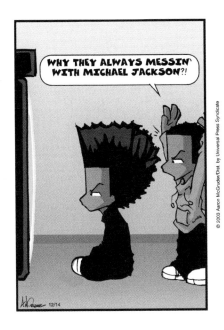

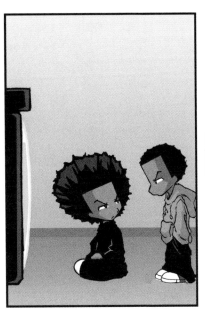

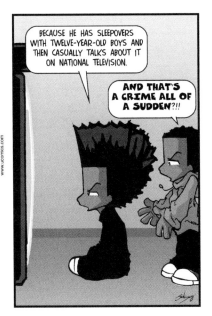

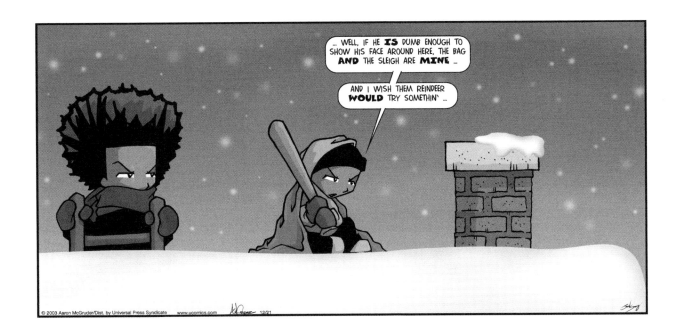

I'M MAKING A NEW YEAR'S RESOLUTION. YOU KNOW THOSE RIMS THAT KEEP SPINNING EVEN AFTER THE CAR STOPS?
www.ucomics.com
WELL, I'M RESOLVING TO GET A DIAMOND THAT SPINS AROUND IN MY FRONT TOOTH.
12/28
SPINNING DIAMOND?
SPINNING DIAMOND.
© 2003 Aaron McGruder/Dist. by Universal Press Syndicate
I'M RESOLVING NEVER TO VISIT THE LAND OF "NEGRONIA," FROM WHENCE YOU COME.
AND YOU **BETTER** NOT STEAL MY TOOTH IDEA!

CHECK IT OUT, HUEY! I BOUGHT A "BLACKBERRY" WITH ALL MY CHRISTMAS MONEY.
THAT'S AN EXPENSIVE PIECE OF FRUIT.
THIS IS THE LATEST IN PORTABLE TELECOMMUNICATIONS! I CAN MAKE PHONE CALLS, SEND E-MAILS, PLUS ORGANIZE MY VARIOUS APPOINTMENTS!
AND IT PLAYS A DIFFERENT 50 CENT SONG EVERY TIME SOMEONE SENDS ME A MESSAGE.
1/4
WITHOUT ONE OF THESE, YOU MIGHT AS WELL BE IN THE STONE AGE, LOSER!
BUT WHO YOU GONNA TALK TO, RILEY? YOU DON'T HAVE ANY FRIENDS.
© 2004 Aaron McGruder/Dist. by Universal Press Syndicate
Y'KNOW, **YOU** SHOULD GET ONE OF THESE! THEN WE COULD —
NOPE. COMMUNICATING WITH YOU IS AGGRAVATING ENOUGH WITHOUT HAVING TO PAY FOR IT.
www.ucomics.com

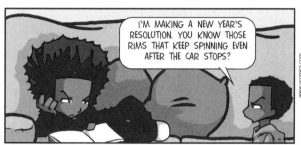

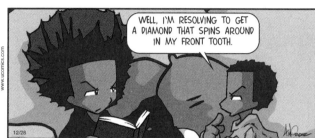

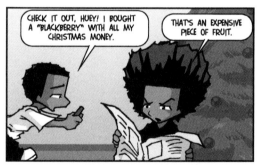

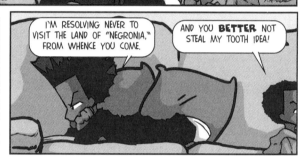

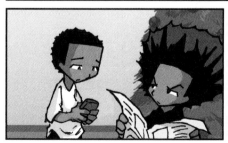

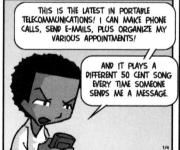

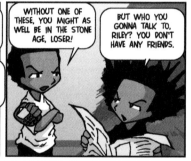

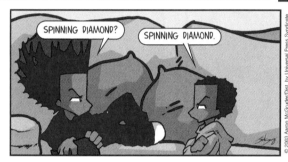

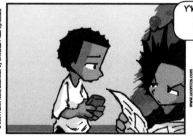

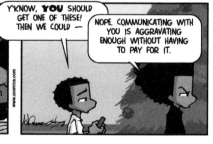

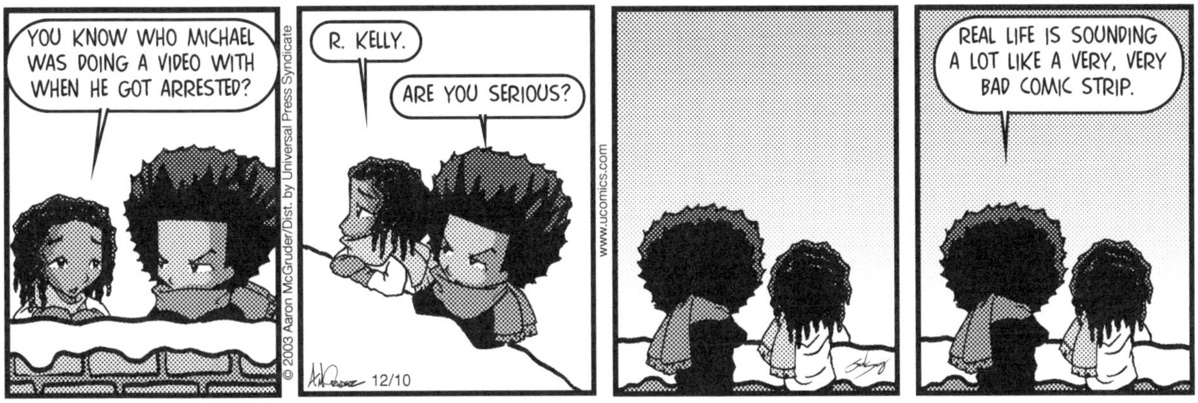
YOU KNOW WHO MICHAEL WAS DOING A VIDEO WITH WHEN HE GOT ARRESTED?
R. KELLY.
ARE YOU SERIOUS?
REAL LIFE IS SOUNDING A LOT LIKE A VERY, VERY BAD COMIC STRIP.
© 2003 Aaron McGruder/Dist. by Universal Press Syndicate
www.ucomics.com
12/10

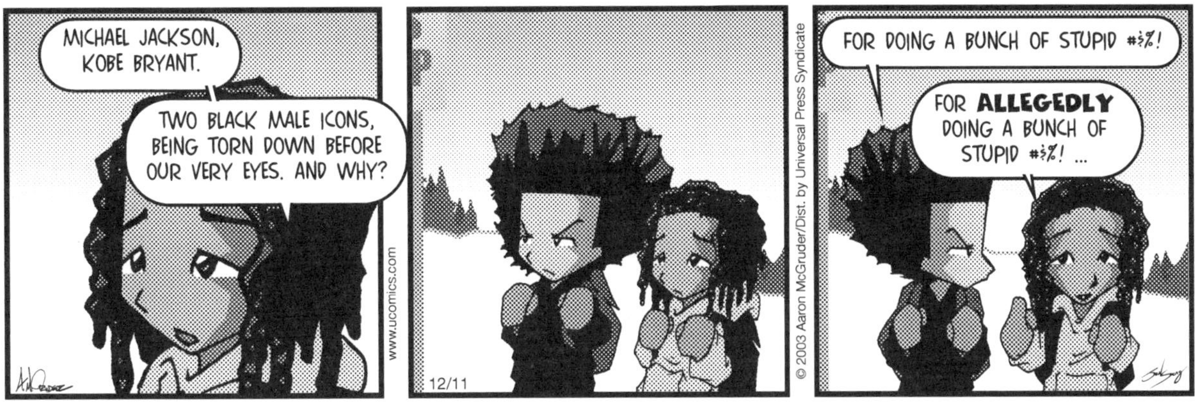
MICHAEL JACKSON, KOBE BRYANT.
TWO BLACK MALE ICONS, BEING TORN DOWN BEFORE OUR VERY EYES. AND WHY?
FOR DOING A BUNCH OF STUPID #$%!
FOR **ALLEGEDLY** DOING A BUNCH OF STUPID #$%! ...
www.ucomics.com
12/11
© 2003 Aaron McGruder/Dist. by Universal Press Syndicate

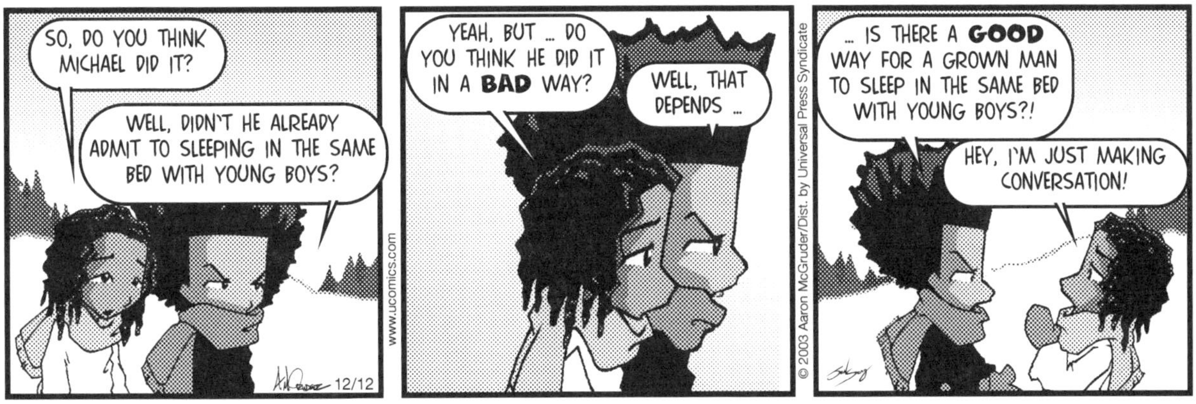
SO, DO YOU THINK MICHAEL DID IT?
WELL, DIDN'T HE ALREADY ADMIT TO SLEEPING IN THE SAME BED WITH YOUNG BOYS?
YEAH, BUT ... DO YOU THINK HE DID IT IN A **BAD** WAY?
WELL, THAT DEPENDS ...
... IS THERE A **GOOD** WAY FOR A GROWN MAN TO SLEEP IN THE SAME BED WITH YOUNG BOYS?!
HEY, I'M JUST MAKING CONVERSATION!
12/12
www.ucomics.com
© 2003 Aaron McGruder/Dist. by Universal Press Syndicate

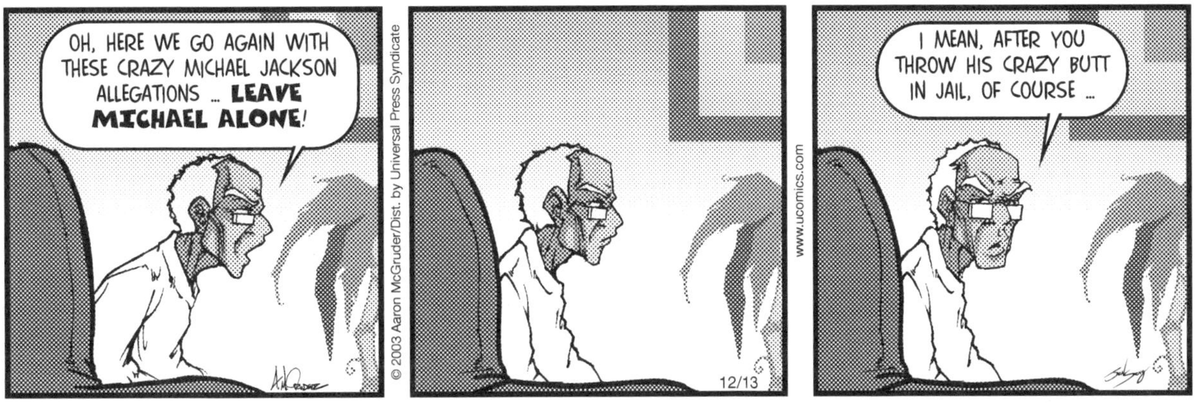
OH, HERE WE GO AGAIN WITH THESE CRAZY MICHAEL JACKSON ALLEGATIONS ... **LEAVE MICHAEL ALONE**!
© 2003 Aaron McGruder/Dist. by Universal Press Syndicate
12/13
www.ucomics.com
I MEAN, AFTER YOU THROW HIS CRAZY BUTT IN JAIL, OF COURSE ...

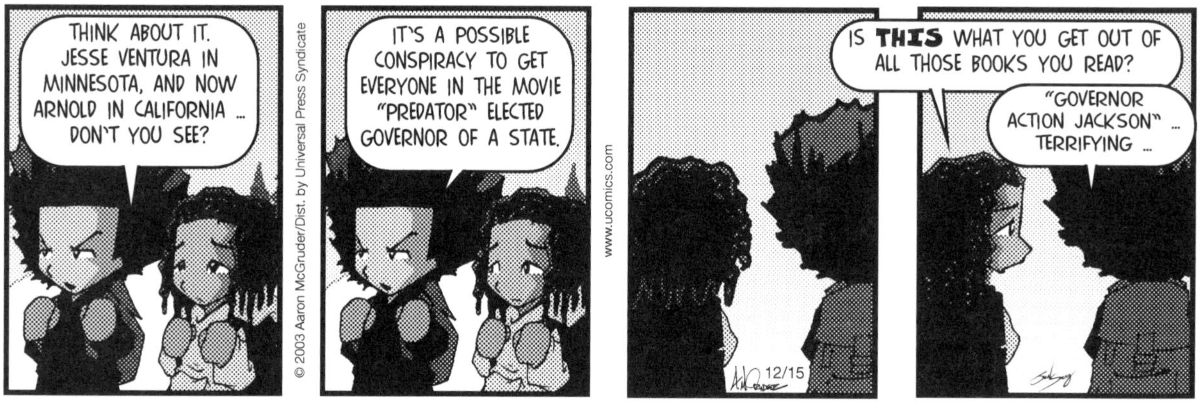
THINK ABOUT IT. JESSE VENTURA IN MINNESOTA, AND NOW ARNOLD IN CALIFORNIA ... DON'T YOU SEE?
IT'S A POSSIBLE CONSPIRACY TO GET EVERYONE IN THE MOVIE "PREDATOR" ELECTED GOVERNOR OF A STATE.
IS THIS WHAT YOU GET OUT OF ALL THOSE BOOKS YOU READ?
"GOVERNOR ACTION JACKSON" ... TERRIFYING ...
© 2003 Aaron McGruder/Dist. by Universal Press Syndicate
www.ucomics.com
12/15

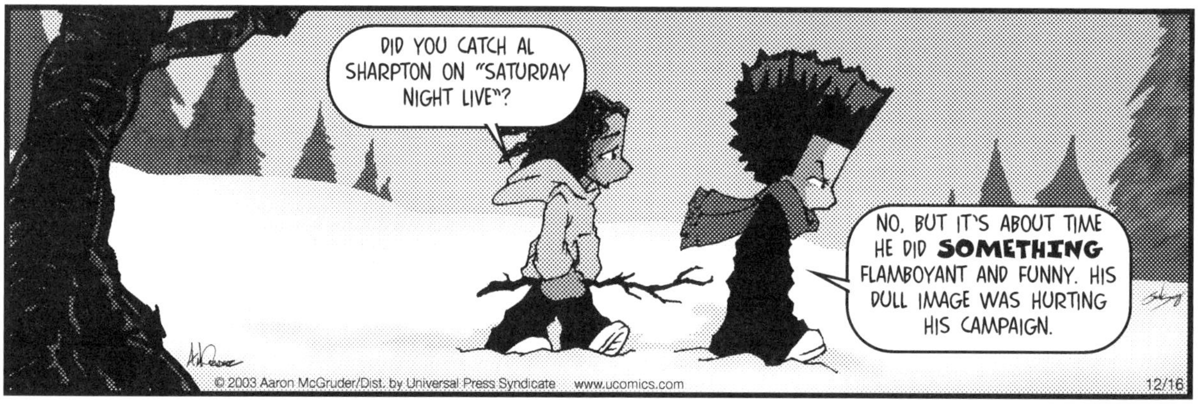
DID YOU CATCH AL SHARPTON ON "SATURDAY NIGHT LIVE"?
NO, BUT IT'S ABOUT TIME HE DID SOMETHING FLAMBOYANT AND FUNNY. HIS DULL IMAGE WAS HURTING HIS CAMPAIGN.
© 2003 Aaron McGruder/Dist. by Universal Press Syndicate www.ucomics.com
12/16

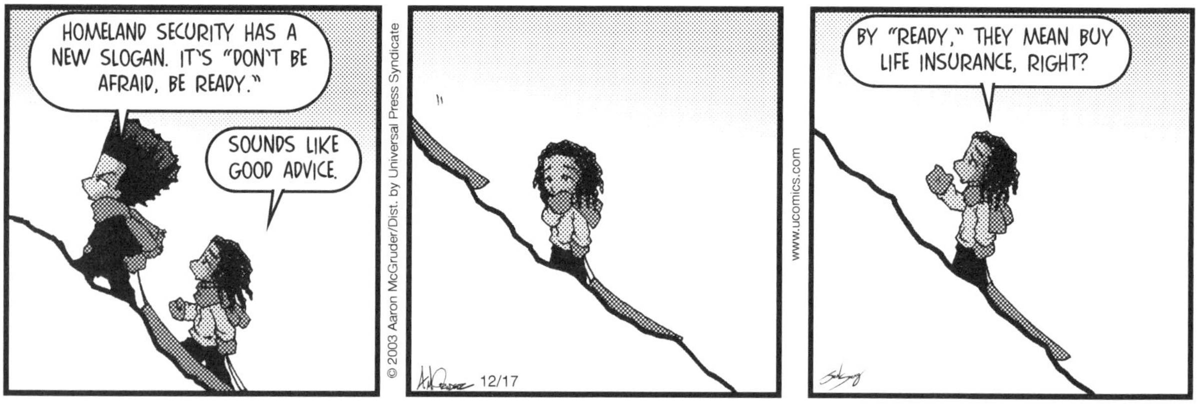
HOMELAND SECURITY HAS A NEW SLOGAN. IT'S "DON'T BE AFRAID, BE READY."
SOUNDS LIKE GOOD ADVICE.
BY "READY," THEY MEAN BUY LIFE INSURANCE, RIGHT?
© 2003 Aaron McGruder/Dist. by Universal Press Syndicate
www.ucomics.com
12/17

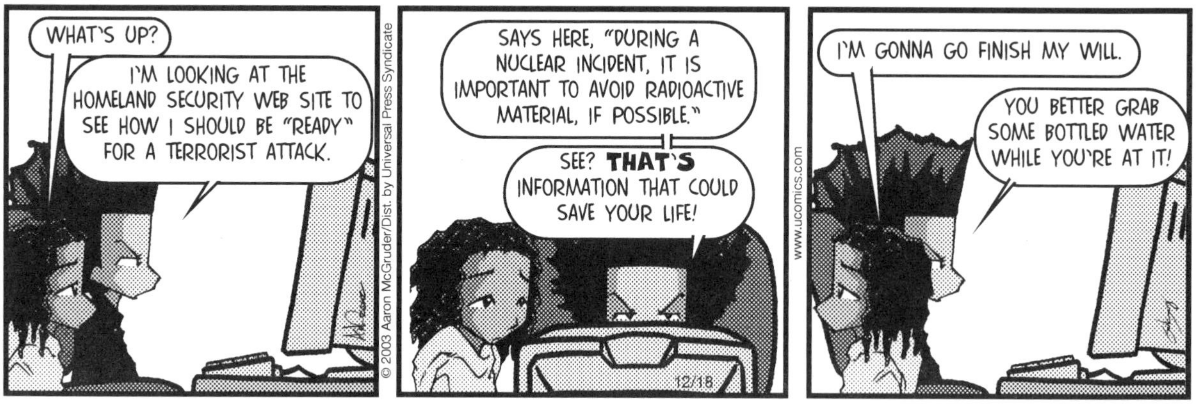
WHAT'S UP?
I'M LOOKING AT THE HOMELAND SECURITY WEB SITE TO SEE HOW I SHOULD BE "READY" FOR A TERRORIST ATTACK.
SAYS HERE, "DURING A NUCLEAR INCIDENT, IT IS IMPORTANT TO AVOID RADIOACTIVE MATERIAL, IF POSSIBLE."
SEE? THAT'S INFORMATION THAT COULD SAVE YOUR LIFE!
I'M GONNA GO FINISH MY WILL.
YOU BETTER GRAB SOME BOTTLED WATER WHILE YOU'RE AT IT!
© 2003 Aaron McGruder/Dist. by Universal Press Syndicate
www.ucomics.com
12/18

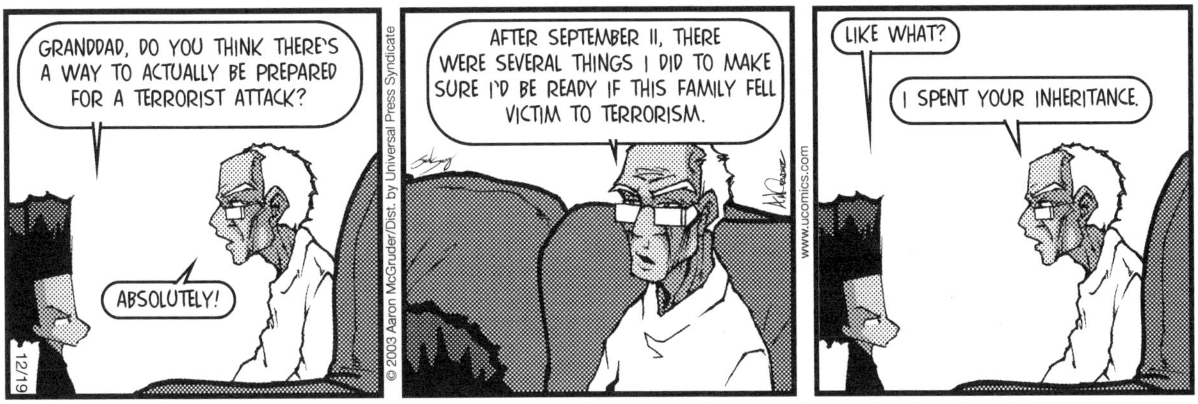
GRANDDAD, DO YOU THINK THERE'S A WAY TO ACTUALLY BE PREPARED FOR A TERRORIST ATTACK?
ABSOLUTELY!
AFTER SEPTEMBER 11, THERE WERE SEVERAL THINGS I DID TO MAKE SURE I'D BE READY IF THIS FAMILY FELL VICTIM TO TERRORISM.
LIKE WHAT?
I SPENT YOUR INHERITANCE.
12/19
© 2003 Aaron McGruder/Dist. by Universal Press Syndicate
www.ucomics.com

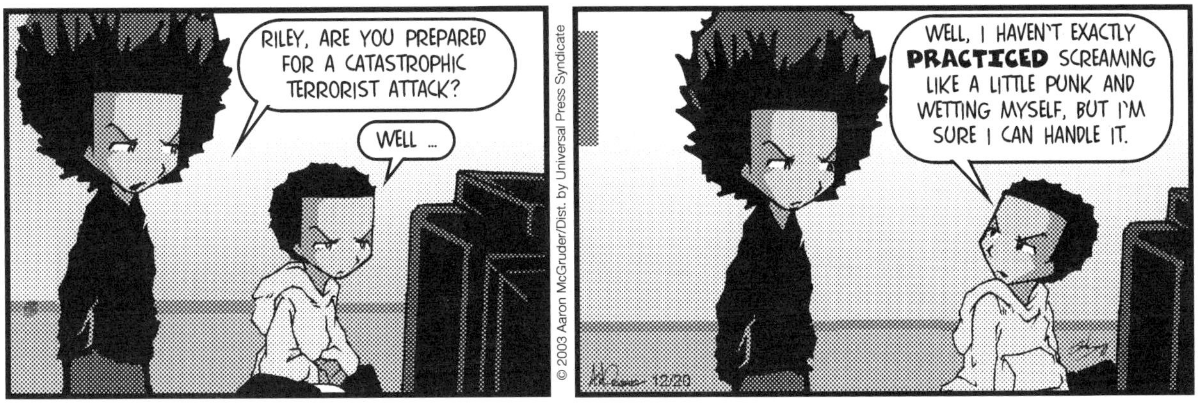
RILEY, ARE YOU PREPARED FOR A CATASTROPHIC TERRORIST ATTACK?
WELL ...
WELL, I HAVEN'T EXACTLY **PRACTICED** SCREAMING LIKE A LITTLE PUNK AND WETTING MYSELF, BUT I'M SURE I CAN HANDLE IT.
© 2003 Aaron McGruder/Dist. by Universal Press Syndicate
12/20

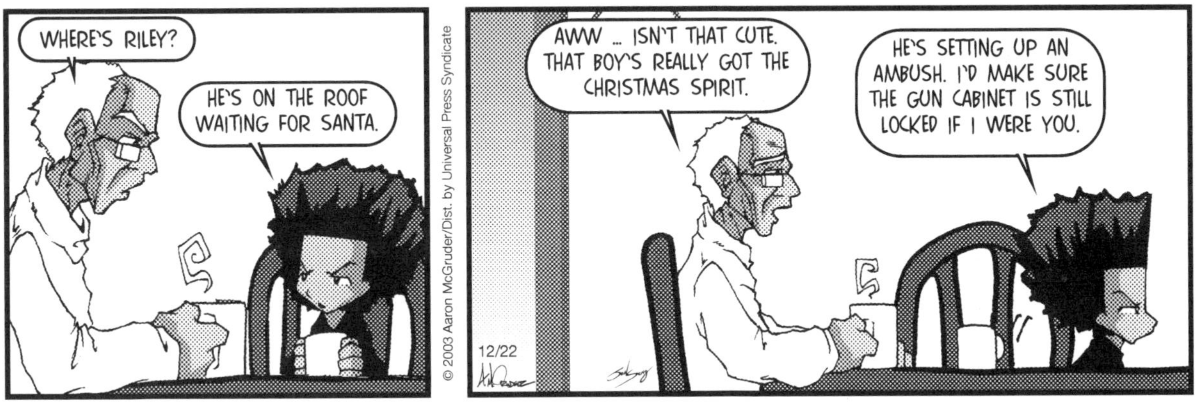
WHERE'S RILEY?
HE'S ON THE ROOF WAITING FOR SANTA.
AWW ... ISN'T THAT CUTE. THAT BOY'S REALLY GOT THE CHRISTMAS SPIRIT.
HE'S SETTING UP AN AMBUSH. I'D MAKE SURE THE GUN CABINET IS STILL LOCKED IF I WERE YOU.
© 2003 Aaron McGruder/Dist. by Universal Press Syndicate
12/22

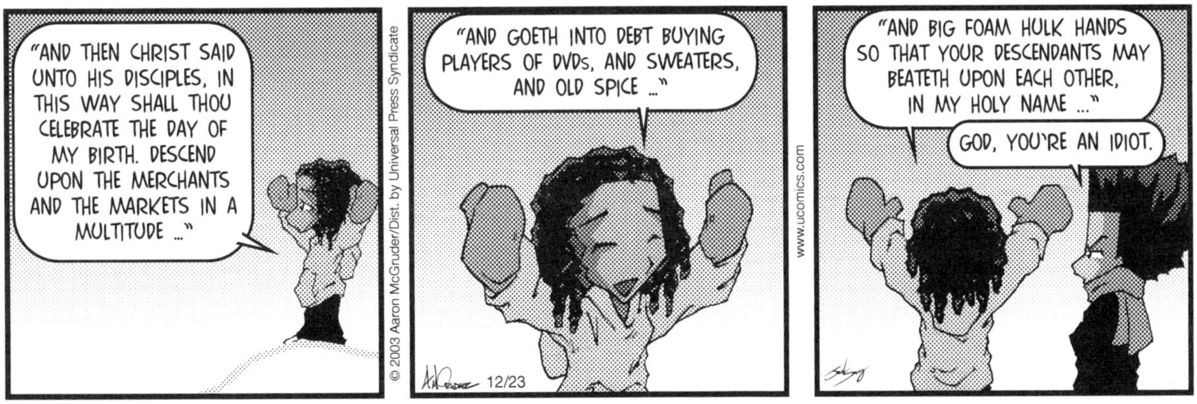
"AND THEN CHRIST SAID UNTO HIS DISCIPLES, IN THIS WAY SHALL THOU CELEBRATE THE DAY OF MY BIRTH. DESCEND UPON THE MERCHANTS AND THE MARKETS IN A MULTITUDE ..."
"AND GOETH INTO DEBT BUYING PLAYERS OF DVDs, AND SWEATERS, AND OLD SPICE ..."
"AND BIG FOAM HULK HANDS SO THAT YOUR DESCENDANTS MAY BEATETH UPON EACH OTHER, IN MY HOLY NAME ..."
GOD, YOU'RE AN IDIOT.
© 2003 Aaron McGruder/Dist. by Universal Press Syndicate
12/23
www.ucomics.com

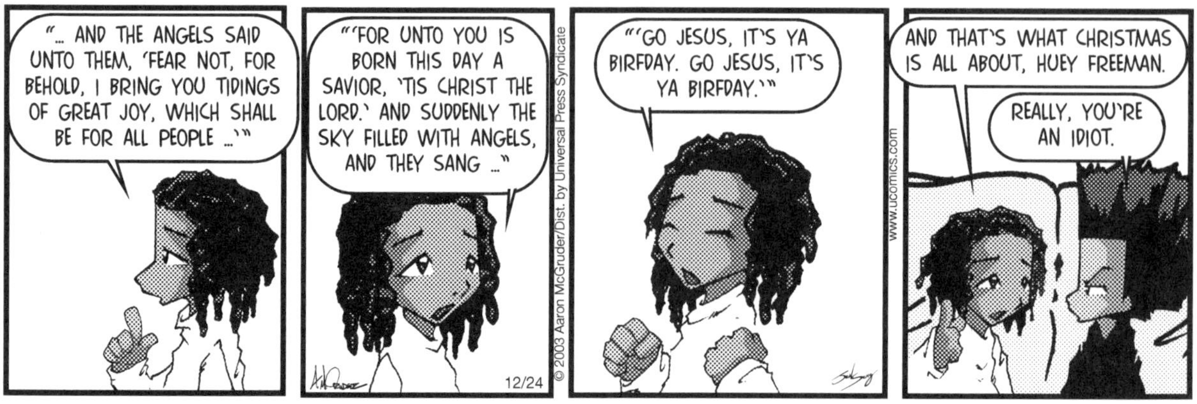
"... AND THE ANGELS SAID UNTO THEM, 'FEAR NOT, FOR BEHOLD, I BRING YOU TIDINGS OF GREAT JOY, WHICH SHALL BE FOR ALL PEOPLE ...'"
"'FOR UNTO YOU IS BORN THIS DAY A SAVIOR, 'TIS CHRIST THE LORD.' AND SUDDENLY THE SKY FILLED WITH ANGELS, AND THEY SANG ..."
12/24
© 2003 Aaron McGruder/Dist. by Universal Press Syndicate
"'GO JESUS, IT'S YA BIRFDAY. GO JESUS, IT'S YA BIRFDAY.'"
AND THAT'S WHAT CHRISTMAS IS ALL ABOUT, HUEY FREEMAN.
REALLY, YOU'RE AN IDIOT.
www.ucomics.com

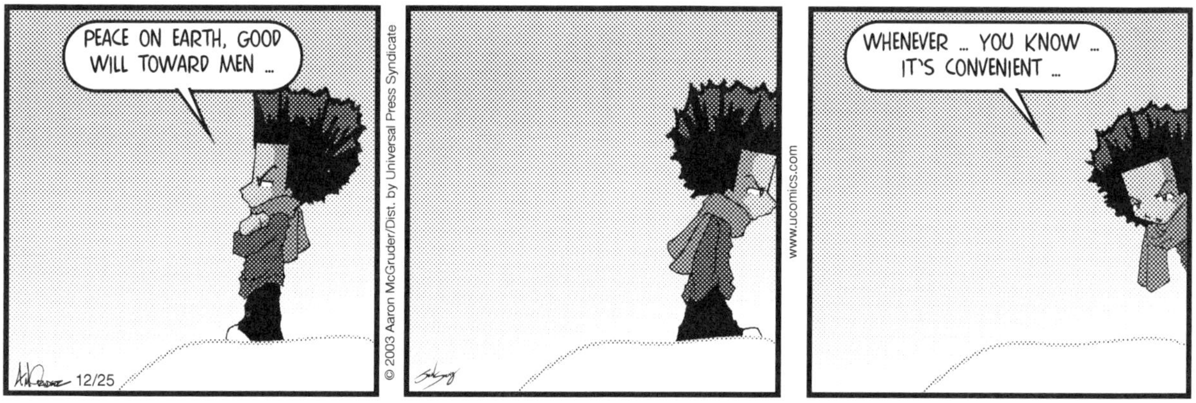
PEACE ON EARTH, GOOD WILL TOWARD MEN ...
12/25
© 2003 Aaron McGruder/Dist. by Universal Press Syndicate
www.ucomics.com
WHENEVER ... YOU KNOW ... IT'S CONVENIENT ...

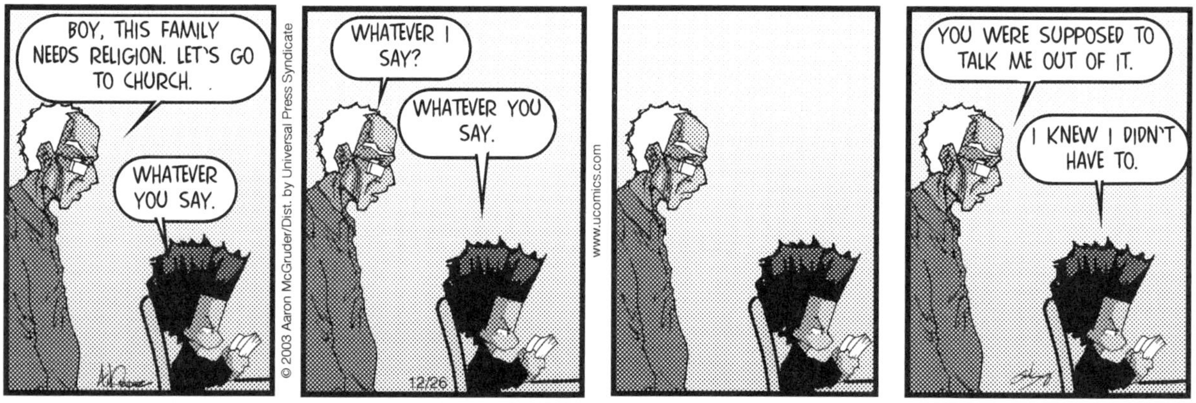
BOY, THIS FAMILY NEEDS RELIGION. LET'S GO TO CHURCH.
WHATEVER YOU SAY.
© 2003 Aaron McGruder/Dist. by Universal Press Syndicate
WHATEVER I SAY?
WHATEVER YOU SAY.
12/26
www.ucomics.com
YOU WERE SUPPOSED TO TALK ME OUT OF IT.
I KNEW I DIDN'T HAVE TO.

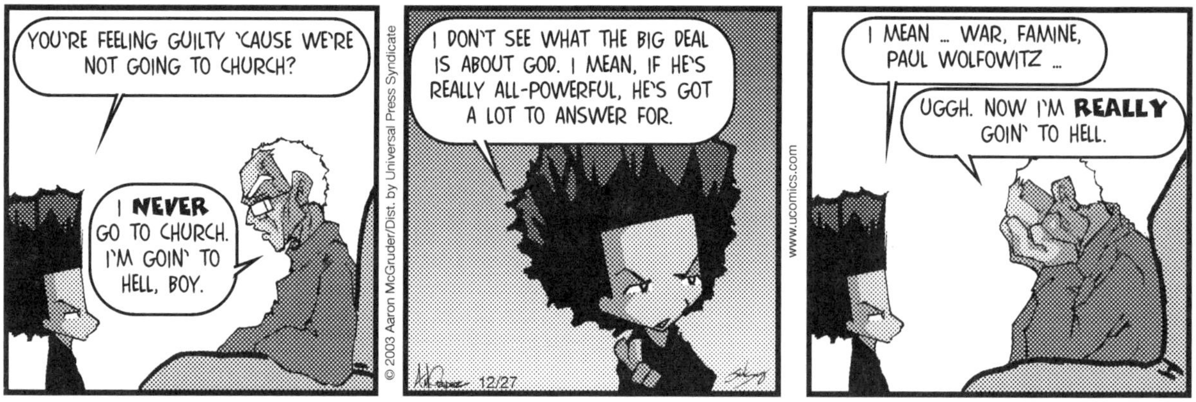
YOU'RE FEELING GUILTY 'CAUSE WE'RE NOT GOING TO CHURCH?
I **NEVER** GO TO CHURCH. I'M GOIN' TO HELL, BOY.
© 2003 Aaron McGruder/Dist. by Universal Press Syndicate
I DON'T SEE WHAT THE BIG DEAL IS ABOUT GOD. I MEAN, IF HE'S REALLY ALL-POWERFUL, HE'S GOT A LOT TO ANSWER FOR.
12/27
www.ucomics.com
I MEAN ... WAR, FAMINE, PAUL WOLFOWITZ ...
UGGH. NOW I'M **REALLY** GOIN' TO HELL.

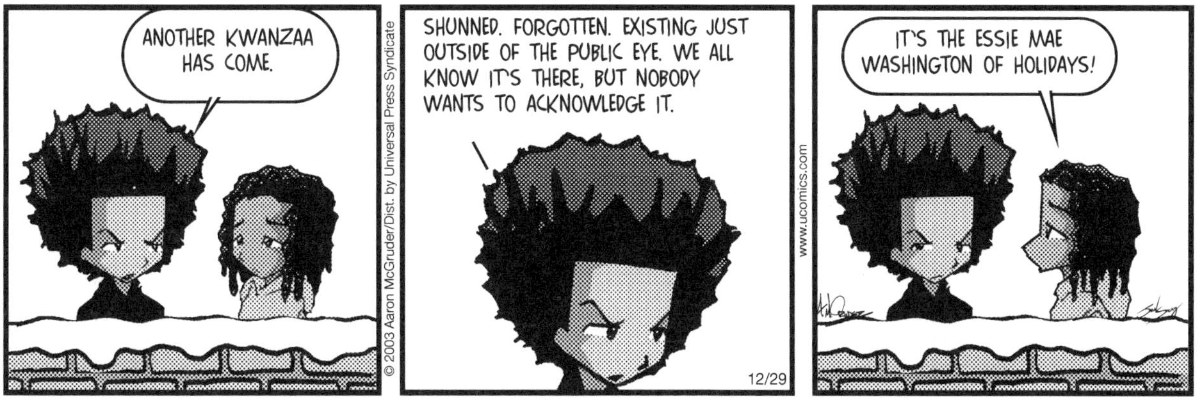
ANOTHER KWANZAA HAS COME.
SHUNNED. FORGOTTEN. EXISTING JUST OUTSIDE OF THE PUBLIC EYE. WE ALL KNOW IT'S THERE, BUT NOBODY WANTS TO ACKNOWLEDGE IT.
IT'S THE ESSIE MAE WASHINGTON OF HOLIDAYS!
© 2003 Aaron McGruder/Dist. by Universal Press Syndicate
www.ucomics.com
12/29

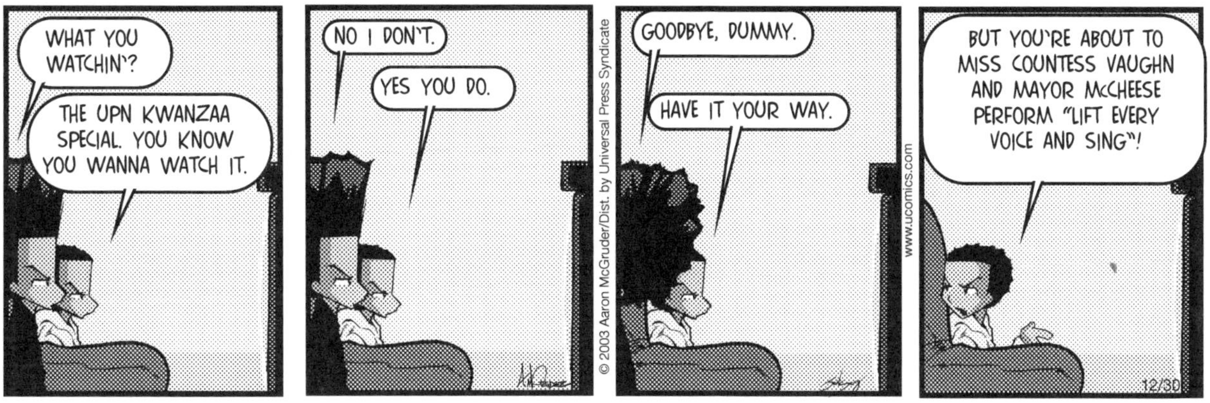
WHAT YOU WATCHIN'?
THE UPN KWANZAA SPECIAL. YOU KNOW YOU WANNA WATCH IT.
NO I DON'T.
YES YOU DO.
GOODBYE, DUMMY.
HAVE IT YOUR WAY.
BUT YOU'RE ABOUT TO MISS COUNTESS VAUGHN AND MAYOR McCHEESE PERFORM "LIFT EVERY VOICE AND SING"!
© 2003 Aaron McGruder/Dist. by Universal Press Syndicate
www.ucomics.com
12/30

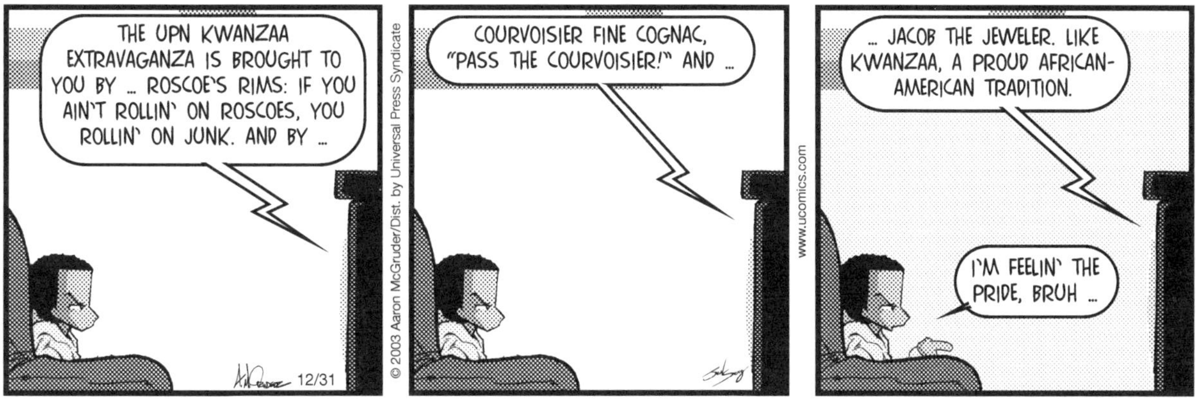
THE UPN KWANZAA EXTRAVAGANZA IS BROUGHT TO YOU BY ... ROSCOE'S RIMS: IF YOU AIN'T ROLLIN' ON ROSCOES, YOU ROLLIN' ON JUNK. AND BY ...
COURVOISIER FINE COGNAC, "PASS THE COURVOISIER!" AND ...
... JACOB THE JEWELER. LIKE KWANZAA, A PROUD AFRICAN-AMERICAN TRADITION.
I'M FEELIN' THE PRIDE, BRUH ...
12/31
© 2003 Aaron McGruder/Dist. by Universal Press Syndicate
www.ucomics.com

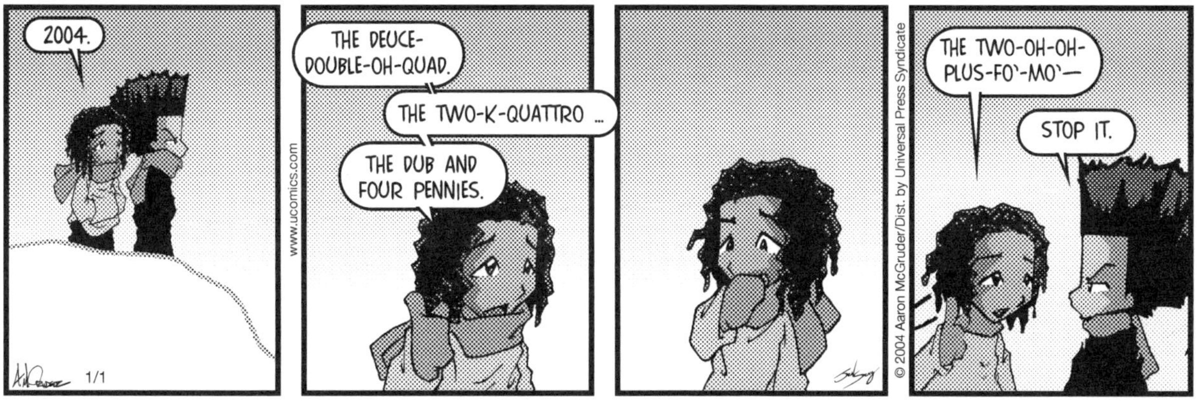
2004.
THE DEUCE-DOUBLE-OH-QUAD.
THE TWO-K-QUATTRO ...
THE DUB AND FOUR PENNIES.
THE TWO-OH-OH-PLUS-FO'-MO'—
STOP IT.
1/1
www.ucomics.com
© 2004 Aaron McGruder/Dist. by Universal Press Syndicate

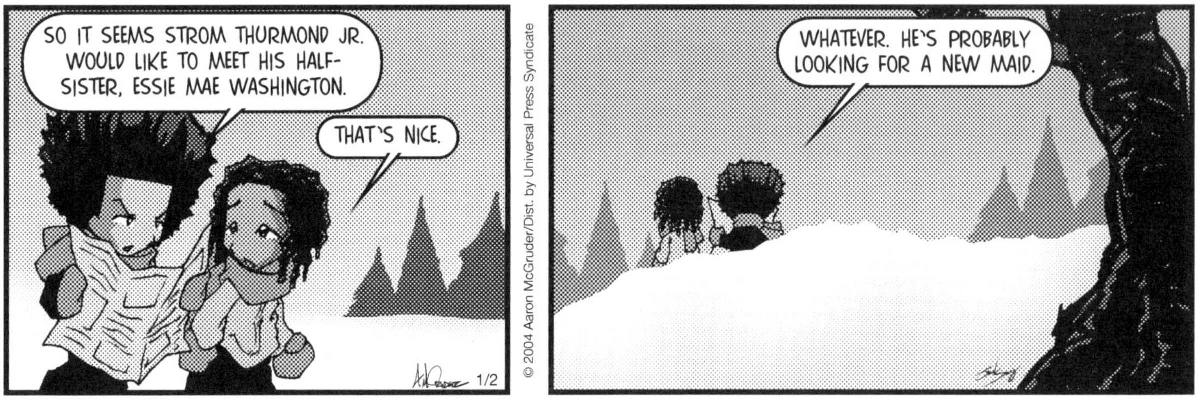
SO IT SEEMS STROM THURMOND JR. WOULD LIKE TO MEET HIS HALF-SISTER, ESSIE MAE WASHINGTON.
THAT'S NICE.
1/2
© 2004 Aaron McGruder/Dist. by Universal Press Syndicate
WHATEVER. HE'S PROBABLY LOOKING FOR A NEW MAID.

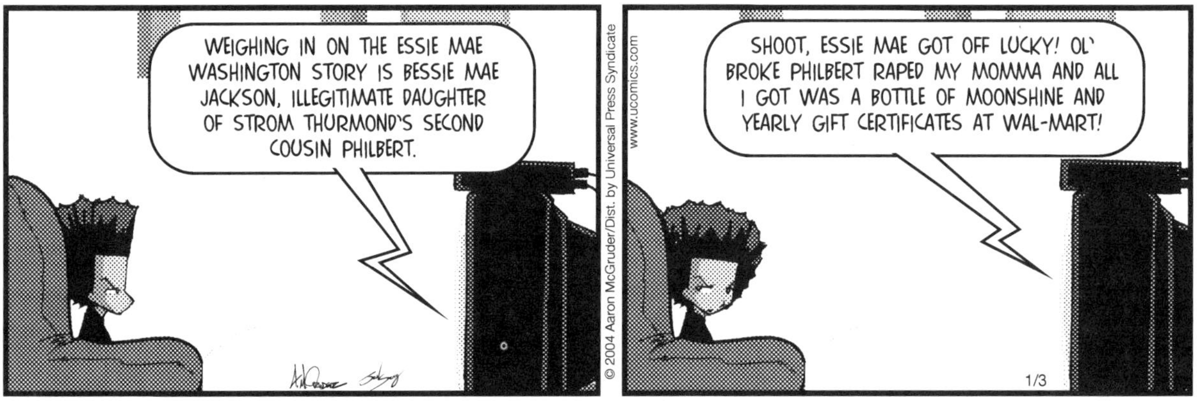
WEIGHING IN ON THE ESSIE MAE WASHINGTON STORY IS BESSIE MAE JACKSON, ILLEGITIMATE DAUGHTER OF STROM THURMOND'S SECOND COUSIN PHILBERT.
© 2004 Aaron McGruder/Dist. by Universal Press Syndicate
www.ucomics.com
SHOOT, ESSIE MAE GOT OFF LUCKY! OL' BROKE PHILBERT RAPED MY MOMMA AND ALL I GOT WAS A BOTTLE OF MOONSHINE AND YEARLY GIFT CERTIFICATES AT WAL-MART!
1/3

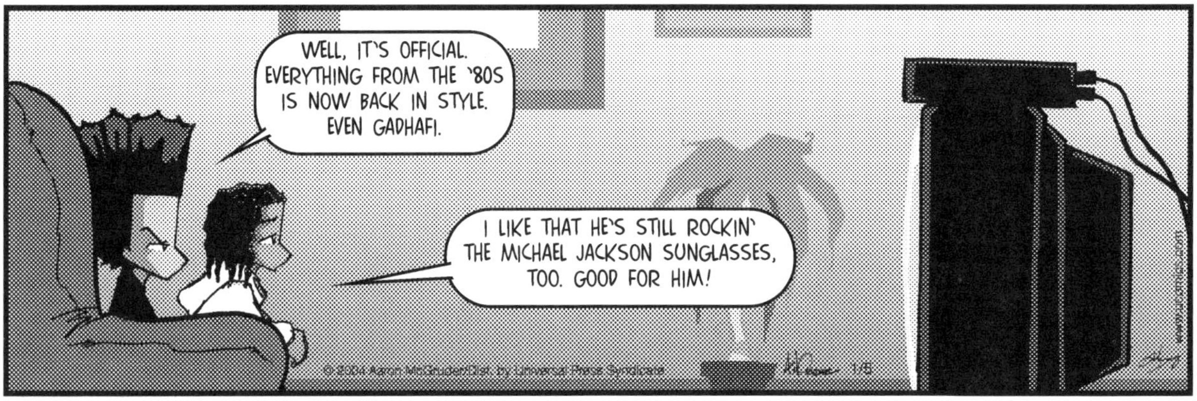
WELL, IT'S OFFICIAL. EVERYTHING FROM THE '80S IS NOW BACK IN STYLE. EVEN GADHAFI.
I LIKE THAT HE'S STILL ROCKIN' THE MICHAEL JACKSON SUNGLASSES, TOO. GOOD FOR HIM!
© 2004 Aaron McGruder/Dist. by Universal Press Syndicate
1/5
www.ucomics.com

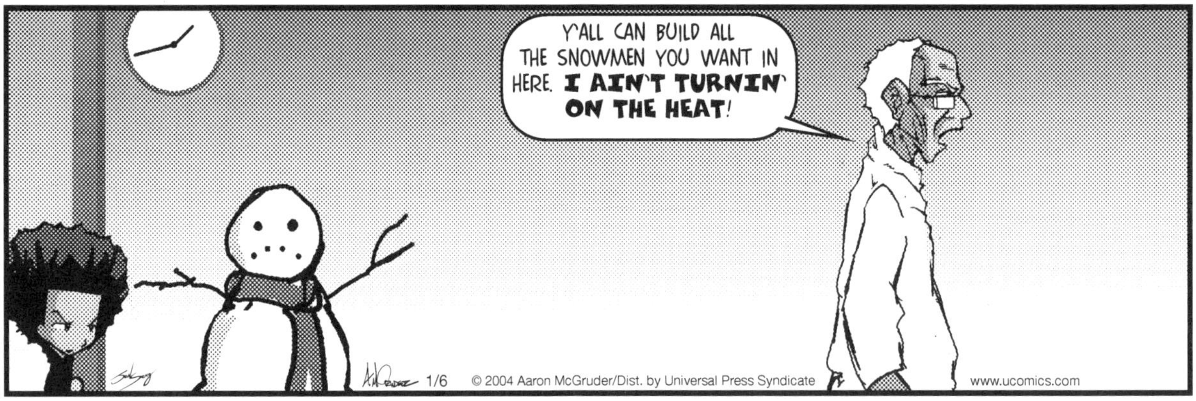
Y'ALL CAN BUILD ALL THE SNOWMEN YOU WANT IN HERE. **I AIN'T TURNIN' ON THE HEAT**!
1/6
© 2004 Aaron McGruder/Dist. by Universal Press Syndicate
www.ucomics.com

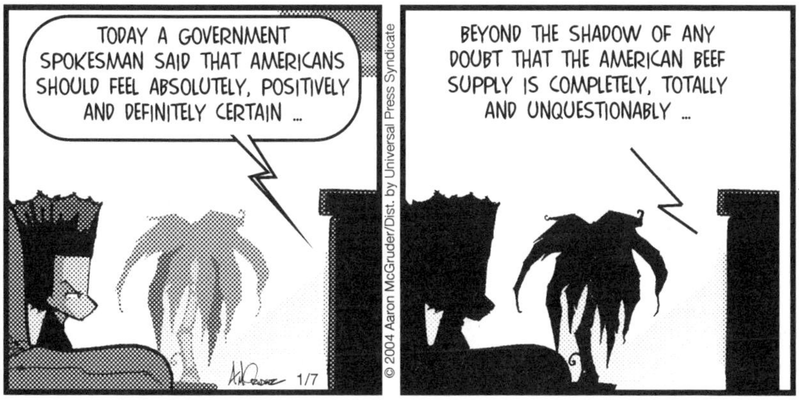
TODAY A GOVERNMENT SPOKESMAN SAID THAT AMERICANS SHOULD FEEL ABSOLUTELY, POSITIVELY AND DEFINITELY CERTAIN ...
BEYOND THE SHADOW OF ANY DOUBT THAT THE AMERICAN BEEF SUPPLY IS COMPLETELY, TOTALLY AND UNQUESTIONABLY ...
... NOT GONNA GIVE YOU A FATAL BRAIN-EATING DISEASE, PROBABLY. THANK YOU, AND EAT WELL.
1/7
© 2004 Aaron McGruder/Dist. by Universal Press Syndicate
www.ucomics.com

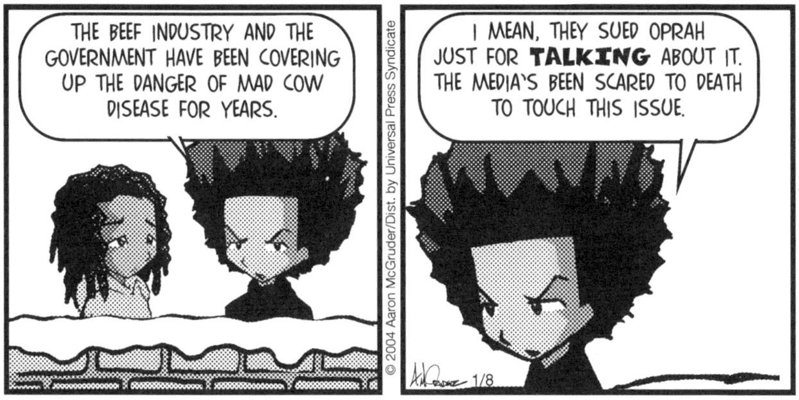
THE BEEF INDUSTRY AND THE GOVERNMENT HAVE BEEN COVERING UP THE DANGER OF MAD COW DISEASE FOR YEARS.
I MEAN, THEY SUED OPRAH JUST FOR **TALKING** ABOUT IT. THE MEDIA'S BEEN SCARED TO DEATH TO TOUCH THIS ISSUE.
THE PRESIDENT DOESN'T SEEM TOO WORRIED.
SURE, IF **HE** CATCHES A BRAIN-EATING DISEASE, WHO'S GONNA NOTICE?
1/8
© 2004 Aaron McGruder/Dist. by Universal Press Syndicate
www.ucomics.com

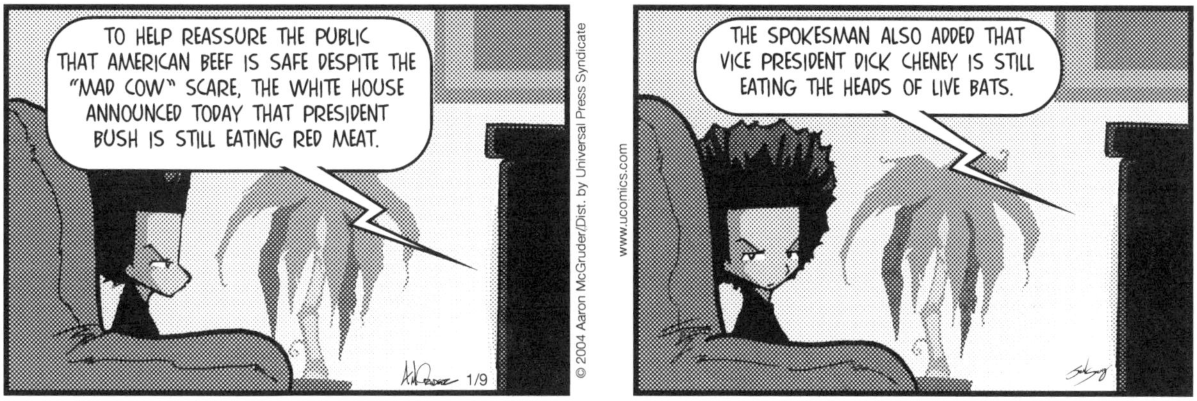
TO HELP REASSURE THE PUBLIC THAT AMERICAN BEEF IS SAFE DESPITE THE "MAD COW" SCARE, THE WHITE HOUSE ANNOUNCED TODAY THAT PRESIDENT BUSH IS STILL EATING RED MEAT.
THE SPOKESMAN ALSO ADDED THAT VICE PRESIDENT DICK CHENEY IS STILL EATING THE HEADS OF LIVE BATS.
1/9
© 2004 Aaron McGruder/Dist. by Universal Press Syndicate
www.ucomics.com

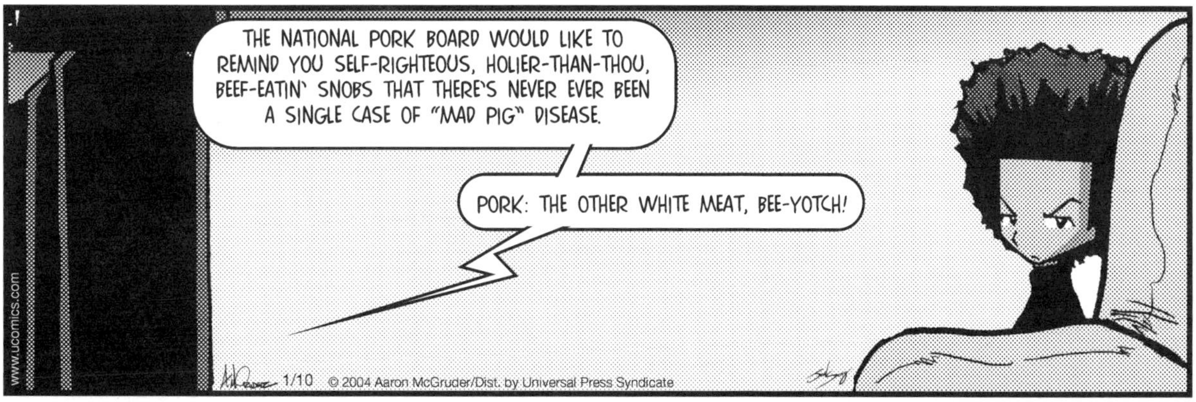
THE NATIONAL PORK BOARD WOULD LIKE TO REMIND YOU SELF-RIGHTEOUS, HOLIER-THAN-THOU, BEEF-EATIN' SNOBS THAT THERE'S NEVER EVER BEEN A SINGLE CASE OF "MAD PIG" DISEASE.
PORK: THE OTHER WHITE MEAT, BEE-YOTCH!
1/10
© 2004 Aaron McGruder/Dist. by Universal Press Syndicate
www.ucomics.com

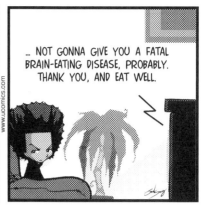

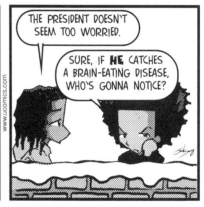

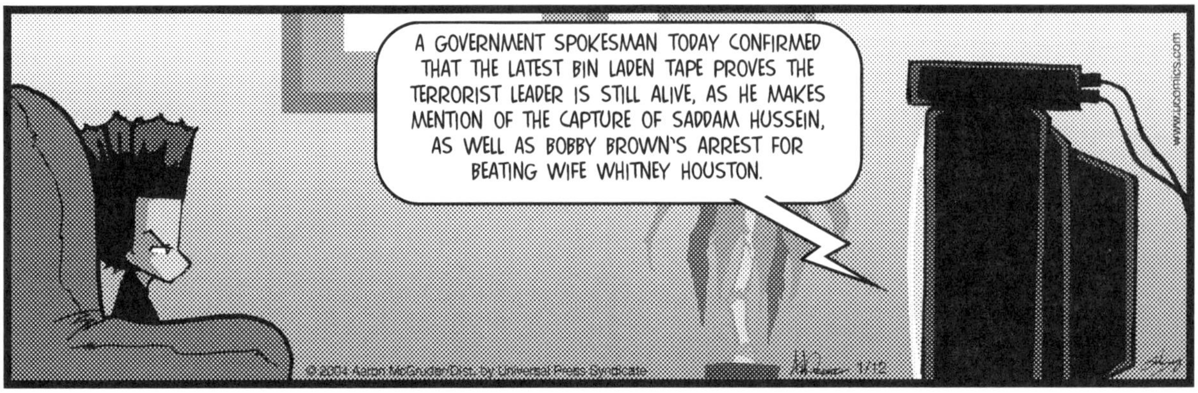
A GOVERNMENT SPOKESMAN TODAY CONFIRMED THAT THE LATEST BIN LADEN TAPE PROVES THE TERRORIST LEADER IS STILL ALIVE, AS HE MAKES MENTION OF THE CAPTURE OF SADDAM HUSSEIN, AS WELL AS BOBBY BROWN'S ARREST FOR BEATING WIFE WHITNEY HOUSTON.
© 2004 Aaron McGruder/Dist. by Universal Press Syndicate
1/12
www.ucomics.com

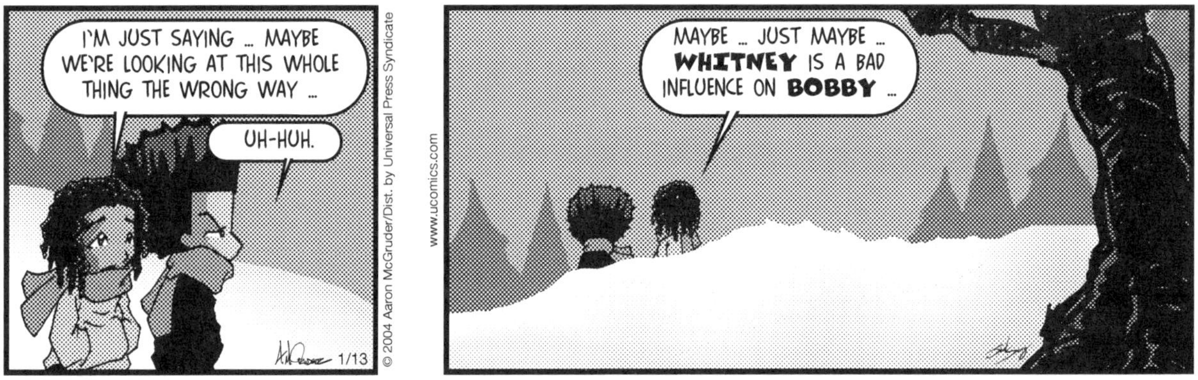
I'M JUST SAYING ... MAYBE WE'RE LOOKING AT THIS WHOLE THING THE WRONG WAY ...
UH-HUH.
1/13
© 2004 Aaron McGruder/Dist. by Universal Press Syndicate
www.ucomics.com
MAYBE ... JUST MAYBE ... **WHITNEY** IS A BAD INFLUENCE ON **BOBBY** ...

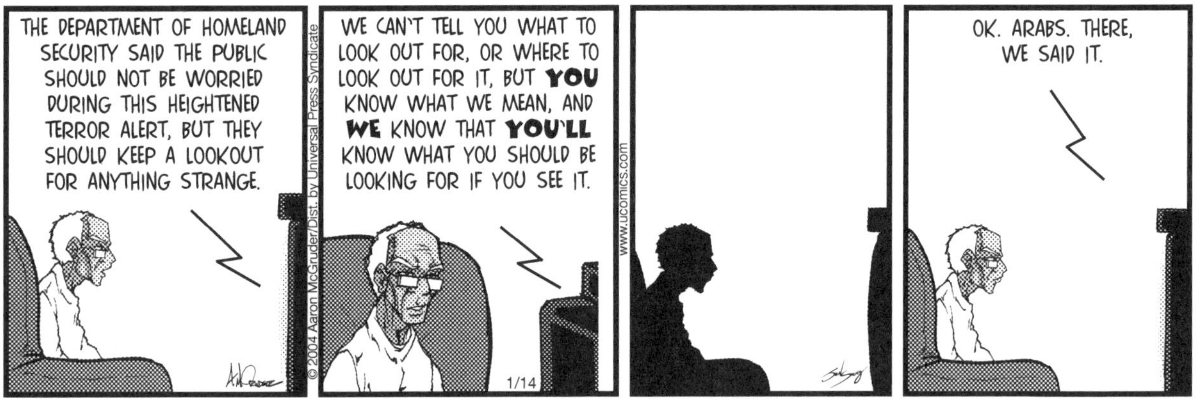
THE DEPARTMENT OF HOMELAND SECURITY SAID THE PUBLIC SHOULD NOT BE WORRIED DURING THIS HEIGHTENED TERROR ALERT, BUT THEY SHOULD KEEP A LOOKOUT FOR ANYTHING STRANGE.
© 2004 Aaron McGruder/Dist. by Universal Press Syndicate
WE CAN'T TELL YOU WHAT TO LOOK OUT FOR, OR WHERE TO LOOK OUT FOR IT, BUT **YOU** KNOW WHAT WE MEAN, AND **WE** KNOW THAT **YOU'LL** KNOW WHAT YOU SHOULD BE LOOKING FOR IF YOU SEE IT.
1/14
www.ucomics.com
OK. ARABS. THERE, WE SAID IT.

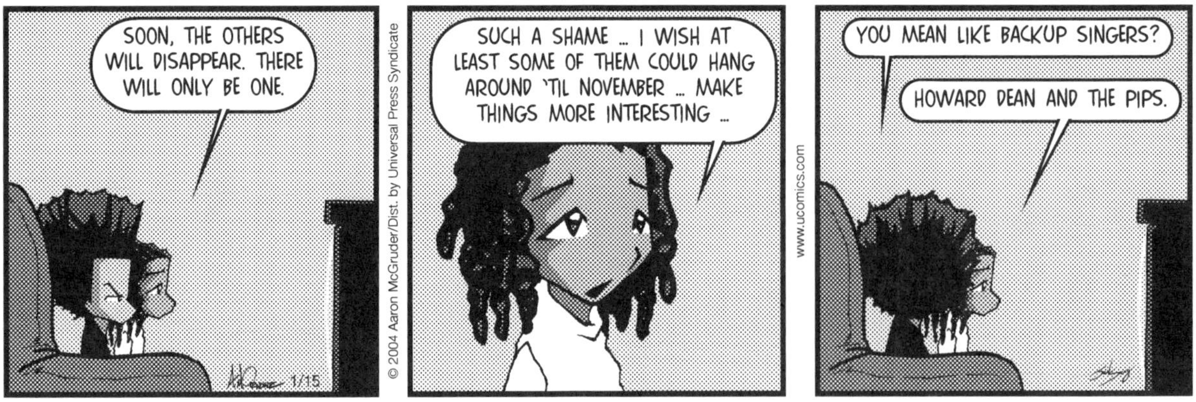
SOON, THE OTHERS WILL DISAPPEAR. THERE WILL ONLY BE ONE.
1/15
© 2004 Aaron McGruder/Dist. by Universal Press Syndicate
SUCH A SHAME ... I WISH AT LEAST SOME OF THEM COULD HANG AROUND 'TIL NOVEMBER ... MAKE THINGS MORE INTERESTING ...
www.ucomics.com
YOU MEAN LIKE BACKUP SINGERS?
HOWARD DEAN AND THE PIPS.

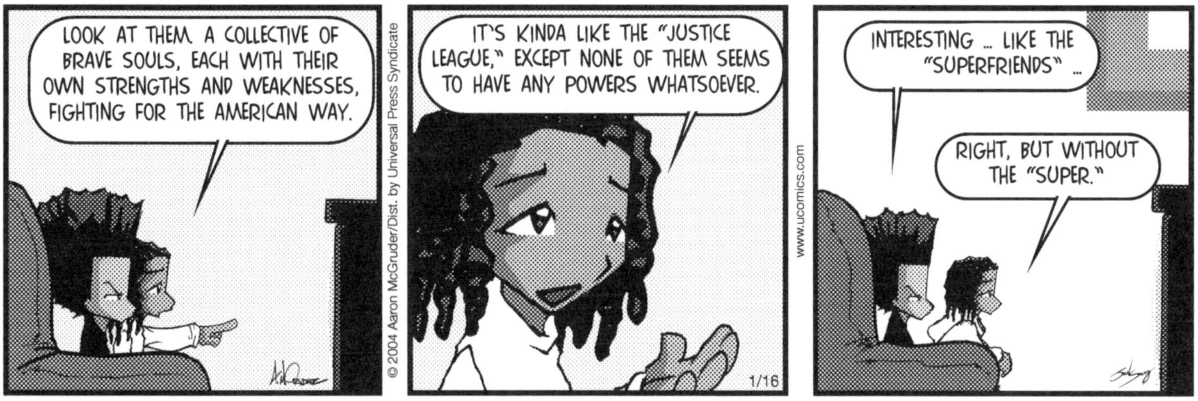
LOOK AT THEM. A COLLECTIVE OF BRAVE SOULS, EACH WITH THEIR OWN STRENGTHS AND WEAKNESSES, FIGHTING FOR THE AMERICAN WAY.
© 2004 Aaron McGruder/Dist. by Universal Press Syndicate
IT'S KINDA LIKE THE "JUSTICE LEAGUE," EXCEPT NONE OF THEM SEEMS TO HAVE ANY POWERS WHATSOEVER.
1/16
www.ucomics.com
INTERESTING ... LIKE THE "SUPERFRIENDS" ...
RIGHT, BUT WITHOUT THE "SUPER."

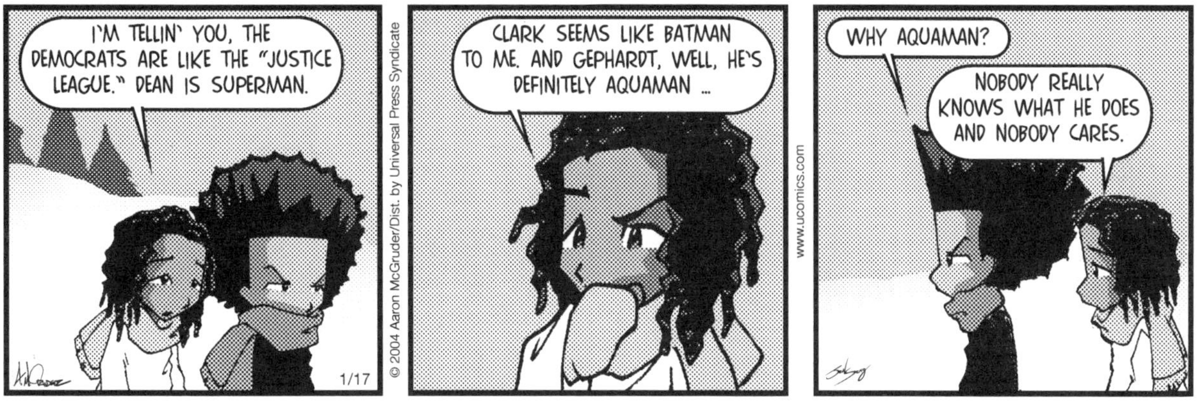
I'M TELLIN' YOU, THE DEMOCRATS ARE LIKE THE "JUSTICE LEAGUE." DEAN IS SUPERMAN.
1/17
© 2004 Aaron McGruder/Dist. by Universal Press Syndicate
CLARK SEEMS LIKE BATMAN TO ME. AND GEPHARDT, WELL, HE'S DEFINITELY AQUAMAN ...
www.ucomics.com
WHY AQUAMAN?
NOBODY REALLY KNOWS WHAT HE DOES AND NOBODY CARES.

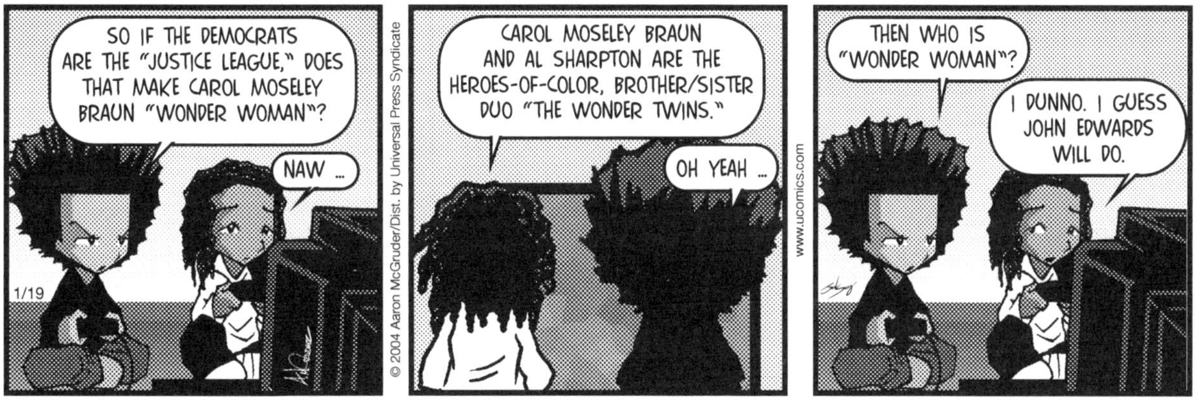
SO IF THE DEMOCRATS ARE THE "JUSTICE LEAGUE," DOES THAT MAKE CAROL MOSELEY BRAUN "WONDER WOMAN"?
NAW ...
1/19
© 2004 Aaron McGruder/Dist. by Universal Press Syndicate
CAROL MOSELEY BRAUN AND AL SHARPTON ARE THE HEROES-OF-COLOR, BROTHER/SISTER DUO "THE WONDER TWINS."
OH YEAH ...
www.ucomics.com
THEN WHO IS "WONDER WOMAN"?
I DUNNO. I GUESS JOHN EDWARDS WILL DO.

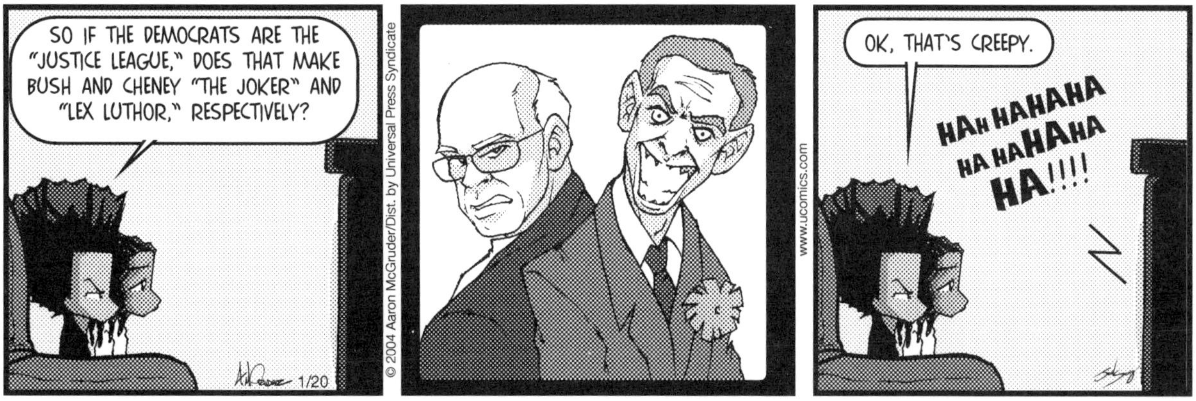
SO IF THE DEMOCRATS ARE THE "JUSTICE LEAGUE," DOES THAT MAKE BUSH AND CHENEY "THE JOKER" AND "LEX LUTHOR," RESPECTIVELY?
1/20
© 2004 Aaron McGruder/Dist. by Universal Press Syndicate
www.ucomics.com
OK, THAT'S CREEPY.
HAHHAHAHA HA HAHAHA HA!!!!

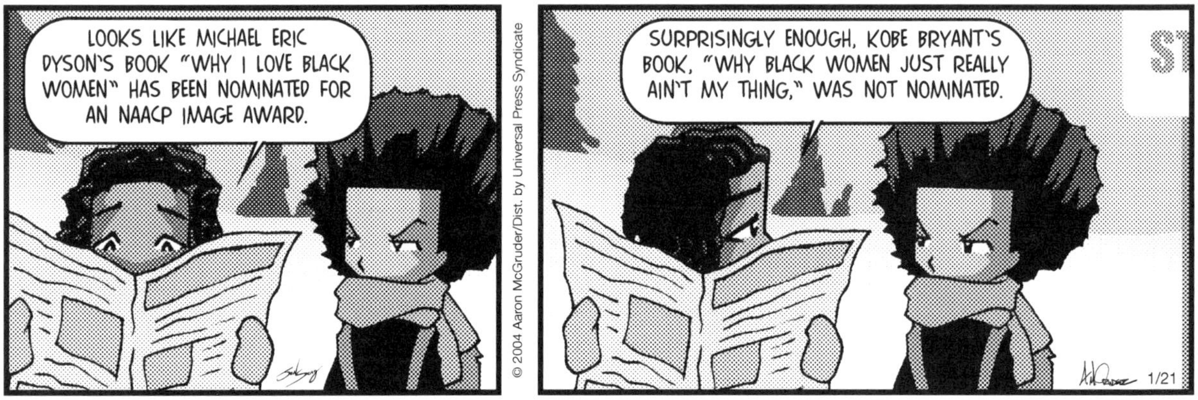
LOOKS LIKE MICHAEL ERIC DYSON'S BOOK "WHY I LOVE BLACK WOMEN" HAS BEEN NOMINATED FOR AN NAACP IMAGE AWARD.
© 2004 Aaron McGruder/Dist. by Universal Press Syndicate
SURPRISINGLY ENOUGH, KOBE BRYANT'S BOOK, "WHY BLACK WOMEN JUST REALLY AIN'T MY THING," WAS NOT NOMINATED.
1/21

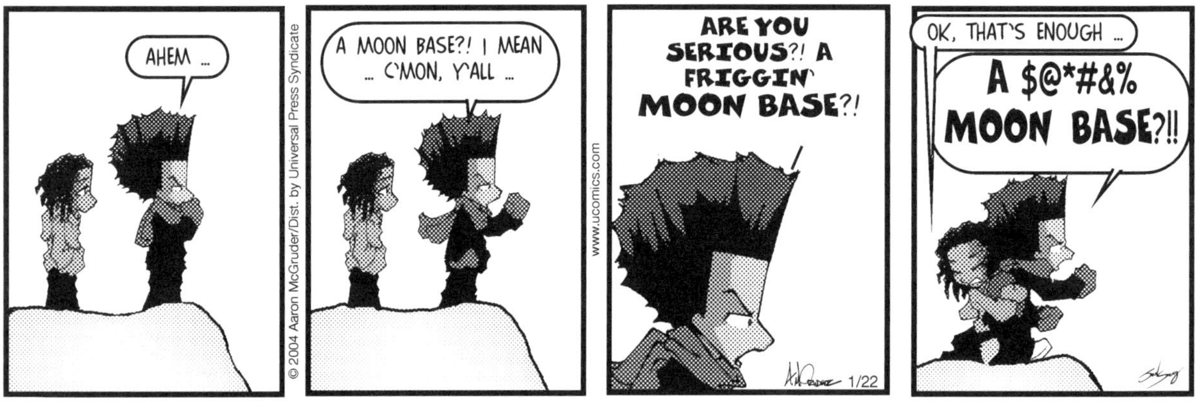
AHEM ...
© 2004 Aaron McGruder/Dist. by Universal Press Syndicate
A MOON BASE?! I MEAN ... C'MON, Y'ALL ...
www.ucomics.com
ARE YOU SERIOUS?! A FRIGGIN' MOON BASE?!
1/22
OK, THAT'S ENOUGH ...
A $@*#&% MOON BASE?!!

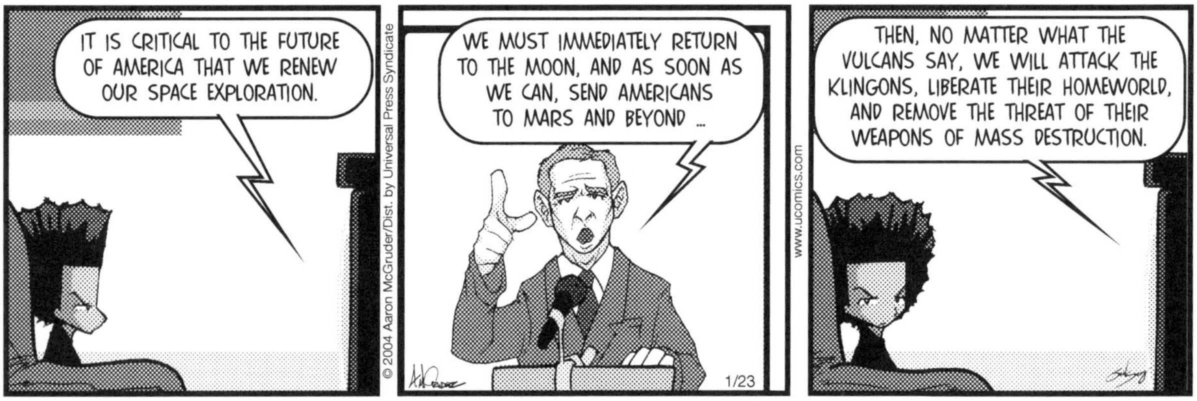
IT IS CRITICAL TO THE FUTURE OF AMERICA THAT WE RENEW OUR SPACE EXPLORATION.
© 2004 Aaron McGruder/Dist. by Universal Press Syndicate
WE MUST IMMEDIATELY RETURN TO THE MOON, AND AS SOON AS WE CAN, SEND AMERICANS TO MARS AND BEYOND ...
1/23
www.ucomics.com
THEN, NO MATTER WHAT THE VULCANS SAY, WE WILL ATTACK THE KLINGONS, LIBERATE THEIR HOMEWORLD, AND REMOVE THE THREAT OF THEIR WEAPONS OF MASS DESTRUCTION.

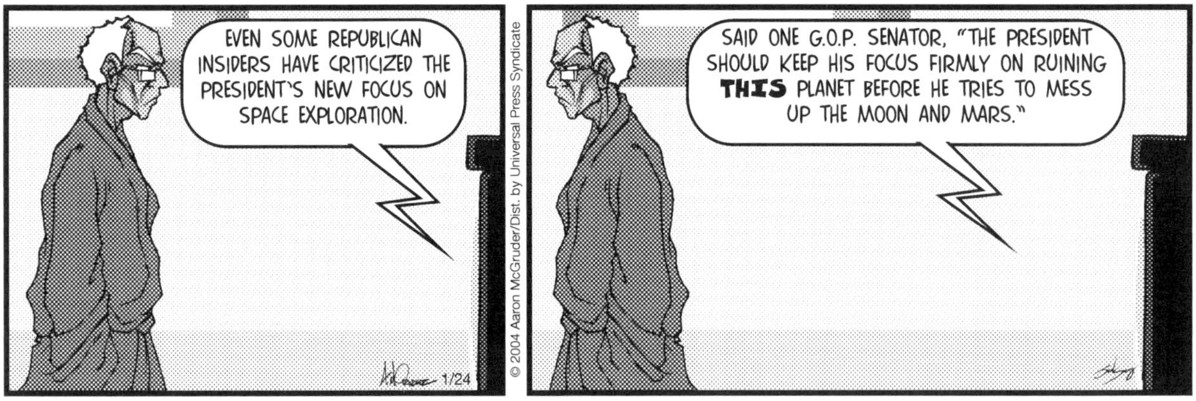
EVEN SOME REPUBLICAN INSIDERS HAVE CRITICIZED THE PRESIDENT'S NEW FOCUS ON SPACE EXPLORATION.
1/24
© 2004 Aaron McGruder/Dist. by Universal Press Syndicate
SAID ONE G.O.P. SENATOR, "THE PRESIDENT SHOULD KEEP HIS FOCUS FIRMLY ON RUINING THIS PLANET BEFORE HE TRIES TO MESS UP THE MOON AND MARS."

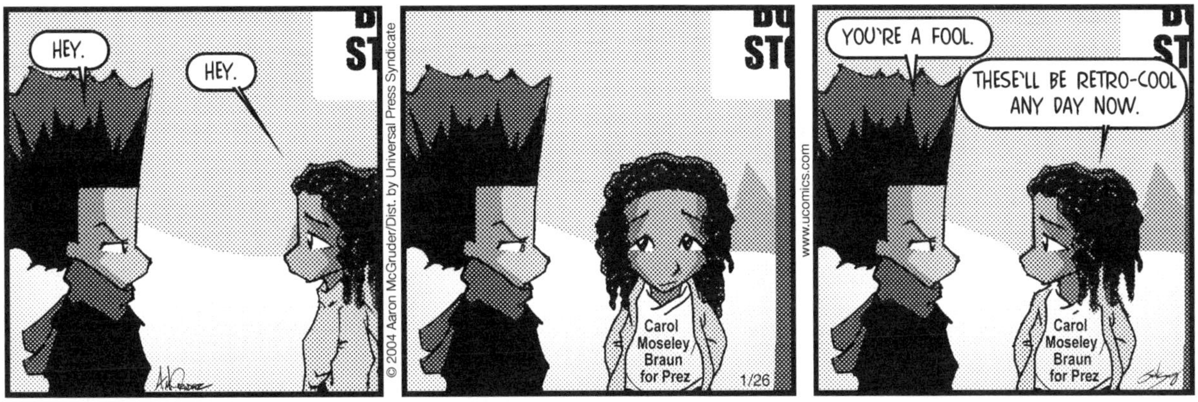
HEY.
HEY.
© 2004 Aaron McGruder/Dist. by Universal Press Syndicate
Carol Moseley Braun for Prez
1/26
www.ucomics.com
YOU'RE A FOOL.
THESE'LL BE RETRO-COOL ANY DAY NOW.
Carol Moseley Braun for Prez

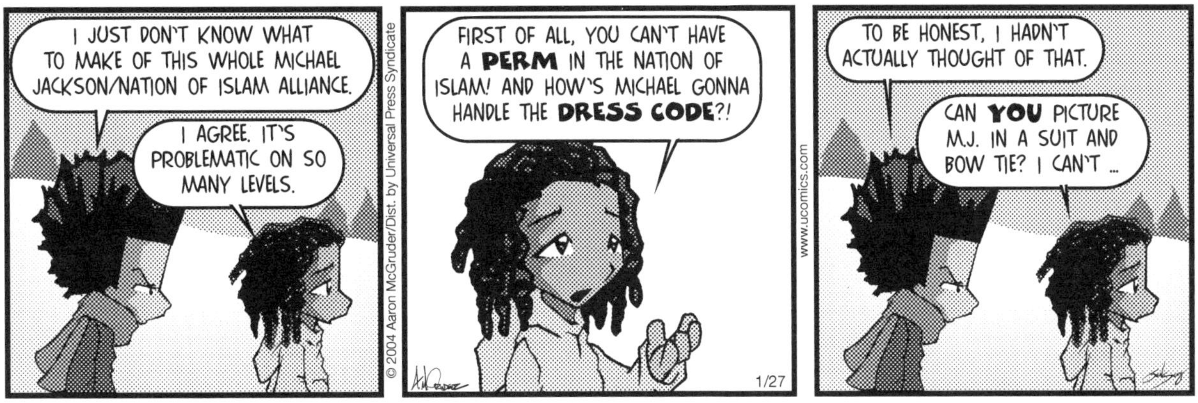
I JUST DON'T KNOW WHAT TO MAKE OF THIS WHOLE MICHAEL JACKSON/NATION OF ISLAM ALLIANCE.
I AGREE. IT'S PROBLEMATIC ON SO MANY LEVELS.
© 2004 Aaron McGruder/Dist. by Universal Press Syndicate
FIRST OF ALL, YOU CAN'T HAVE A **PERM** IN THE NATION OF ISLAM! AND HOW'S MICHAEL GONNA HANDLE THE **DRESS CODE**?!
1/27
www.ucomics.com
TO BE HONEST, I HADN'T ACTUALLY THOUGHT OF THAT.
CAN **YOU** PICTURE M.J. IN A SUIT AND BOW TIE? I CAN'T ...

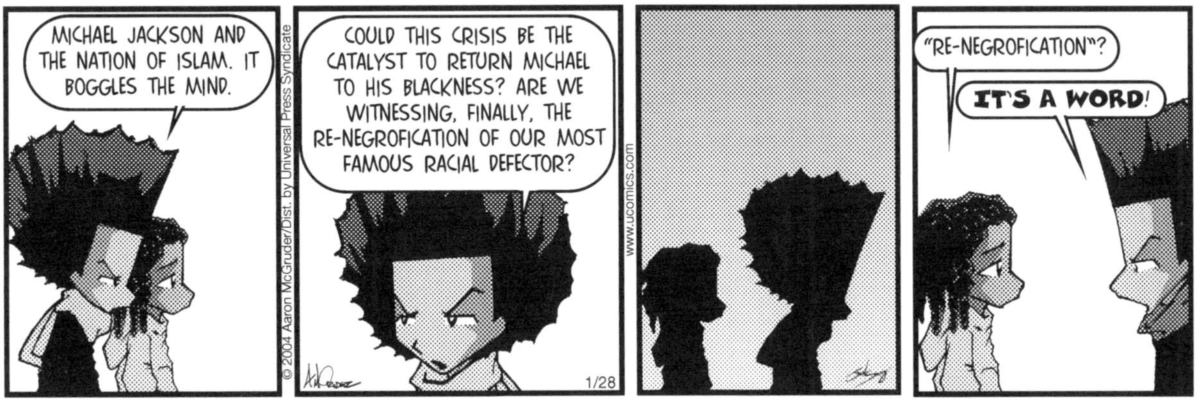
MICHAEL JACKSON AND THE NATION OF ISLAM. IT BOGGLES THE MIND.
© 2004 Aaron McGruder/Dist. by Universal Press Syndicate
COULD THIS CRISIS BE THE CATALYST TO RETURN MICHAEL TO HIS BLACKNESS? ARE WE WITNESSING, FINALLY, THE RE-NEGROFICATION OF OUR MOST FAMOUS RACIAL DEFECTOR?
1/28
www.ucomics.com
"RE-NEGROFICATION"?
IT'S A WORD!

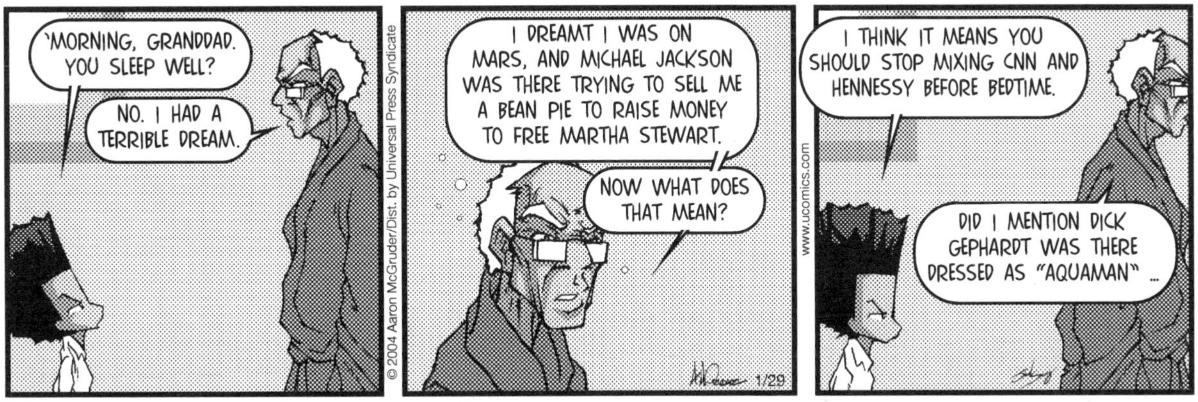
'MORNING, GRANDDAD. YOU SLEEP WELL?
NO. I HAD A TERRIBLE DREAM.
© 2004 Aaron McGruder/Dist. by Universal Press Syndicate
I DREAMT I WAS ON MARS, AND MICHAEL JACKSON WAS THERE TRYING TO SELL ME A BEAN PIE TO RAISE MONEY TO FREE MARTHA STEWART.
NOW WHAT DOES THAT MEAN?
1/29
www.ucomics.com
I THINK IT MEANS YOU SHOULD STOP MIXING CNN AND HENNESSY BEFORE BEDTIME.
DID I MENTION DICK GEPHARDT WAS THERE DRESSED AS "AQUAMAN" ...

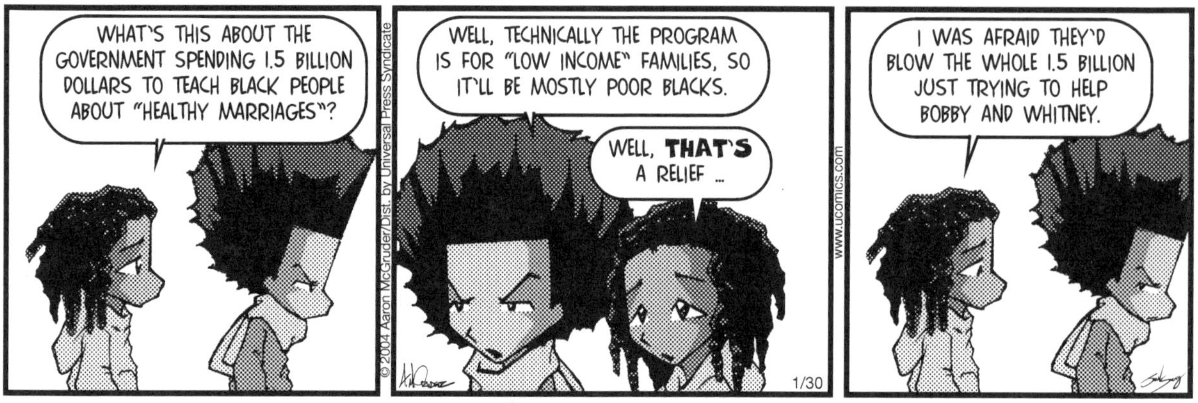
WHAT'S THIS ABOUT THE GOVERNMENT SPENDING 1.5 BILLION DOLLARS TO TEACH BLACK PEOPLE ABOUT "HEALTHY MARRIAGES"?
WELL, TECHNICALLY THE PROGRAM IS FOR "LOW INCOME" FAMILIES, SO IT'LL BE MOSTLY POOR BLACKS.
WELL, THAT'S A RELIEF ...
I WAS AFRAID THEY'D BLOW THE WHOLE 1.5 BILLION JUST TRYING TO HELP BOBBY AND WHITNEY.
© 2004 Aaron McGruder/Dist. by Universal Press Syndicate
1/30
www.ucomics.com

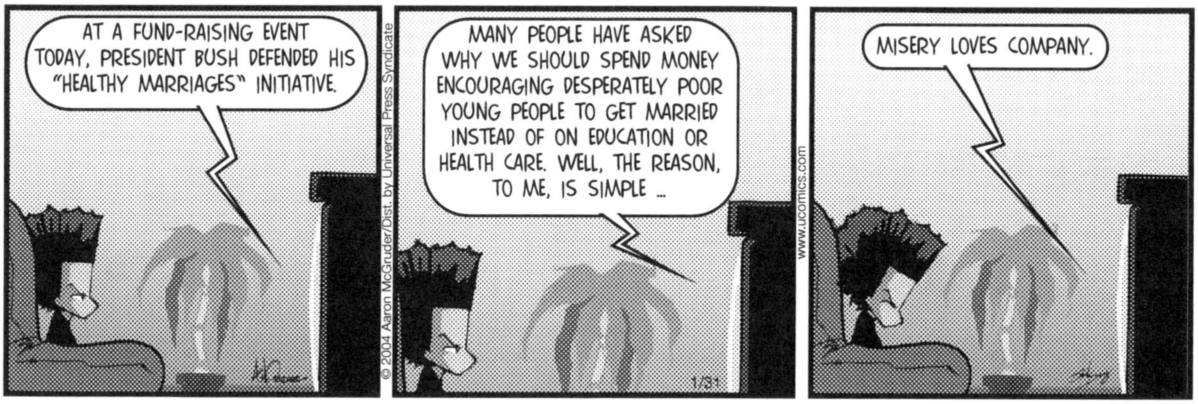
AT A FUND-RAISING EVENT TODAY, PRESIDENT BUSH DEFENDED HIS "HEALTHY MARRIAGES" INITIATIVE.
MANY PEOPLE HAVE ASKED WHY WE SHOULD SPEND MONEY ENCOURAGING DESPERATELY POOR YOUNG PEOPLE TO GET MARRIED INSTEAD OF ON EDUCATION OR HEALTH CARE. WELL, THE REASON, TO ME, IS SIMPLE ...
MISERY LOVES COMPANY.
© 2004 Aaron McGruder/Dist. by Universal Press Syndicate
1/31
www.ucomics.com

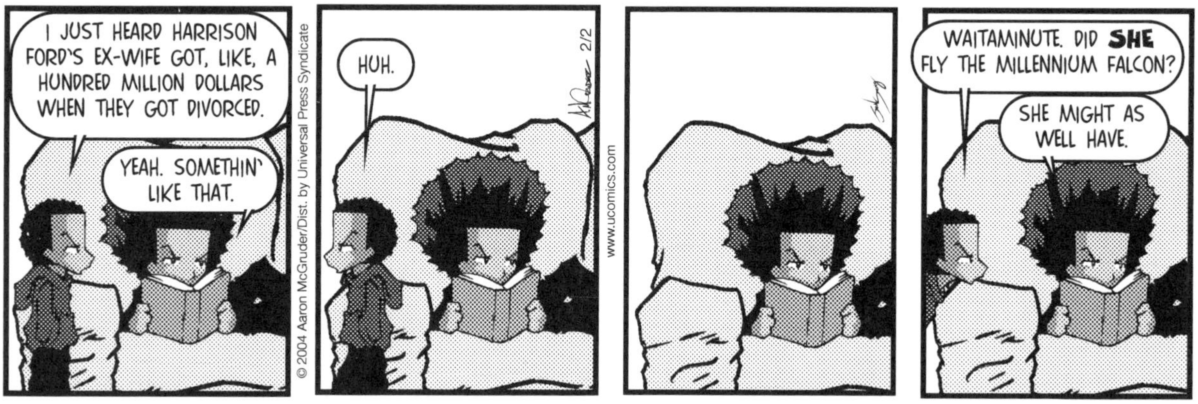
I JUST HEARD HARRISON FORD'S EX-WIFE GOT, LIKE, A HUNDRED MILLION DOLLARS WHEN THEY GOT DIVORCED.
YEAH. SOMETHIN' LIKE THAT.
HUH.
WAITAMINUTE. DID SHE FLY THE MILLENNIUM FALCON?
SHE MIGHT AS WELL HAVE.
© 2004 Aaron McGruder/Dist. by Universal Press Syndicate
2/2
www.ucomics.com

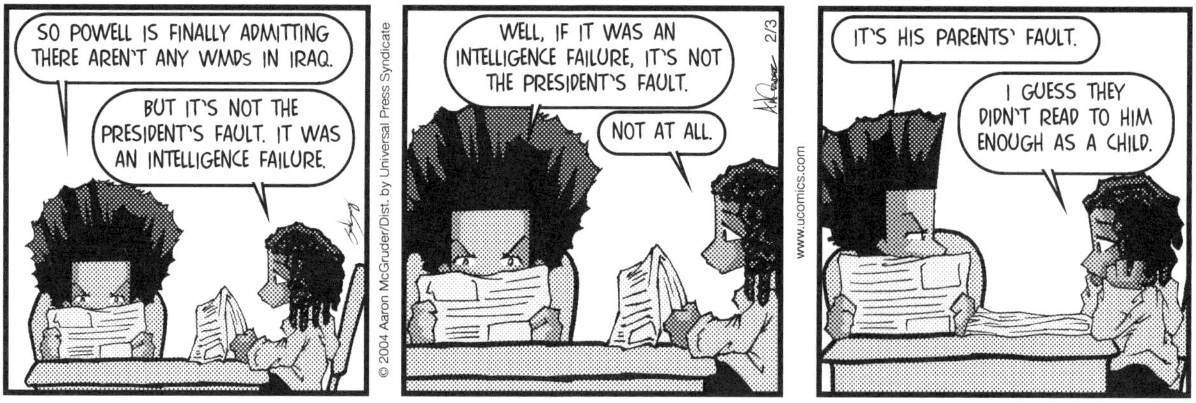
SO POWELL IS FINALLY ADMITTING THERE AREN'T ANY WMDs IN IRAQ.
BUT IT'S NOT THE PRESIDENT'S FAULT. IT WAS AN INTELLIGENCE FAILURE.
WELL, IF IT WAS AN INTELLIGENCE FAILURE, IT'S NOT THE PRESIDENT'S FAULT.
NOT AT ALL.
IT'S HIS PARENTS' FAULT.
I GUESS THEY DIDN'T READ TO HIM ENOUGH AS A CHILD.
© 2004 Aaron McGruder/Dist. by Universal Press Syndicate
2/3
www.ucomics.com

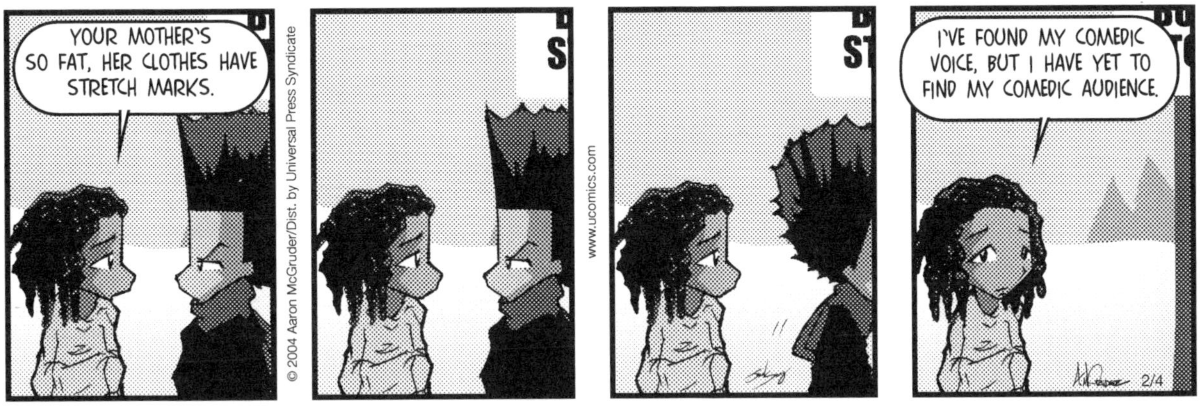
YOUR MOTHER'S SO FAT, HER CLOTHES HAVE STRETCH MARKS.
I'VE FOUND MY COMEDIC VOICE, BUT I HAVE YET TO FIND MY COMEDIC AUDIENCE.
2/4
www.ucomics.com

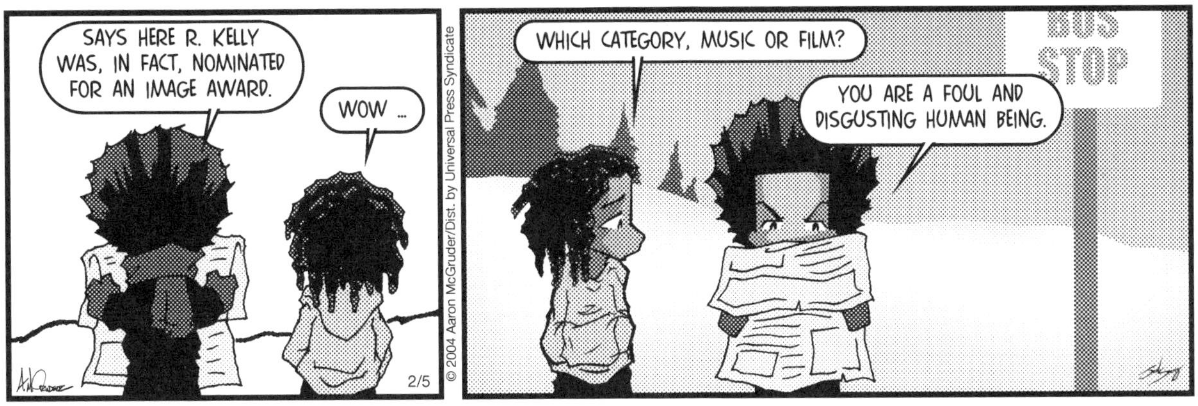
SAYS HERE R. KELLY WAS, IN FACT, NOMINATED FOR AN IMAGE AWARD.
WOW ...
2/5
WHICH CATEGORY, MUSIC OR FILM?
YOU ARE A FOUL AND DISGUSTING HUMAN BEING.
BUS STOP

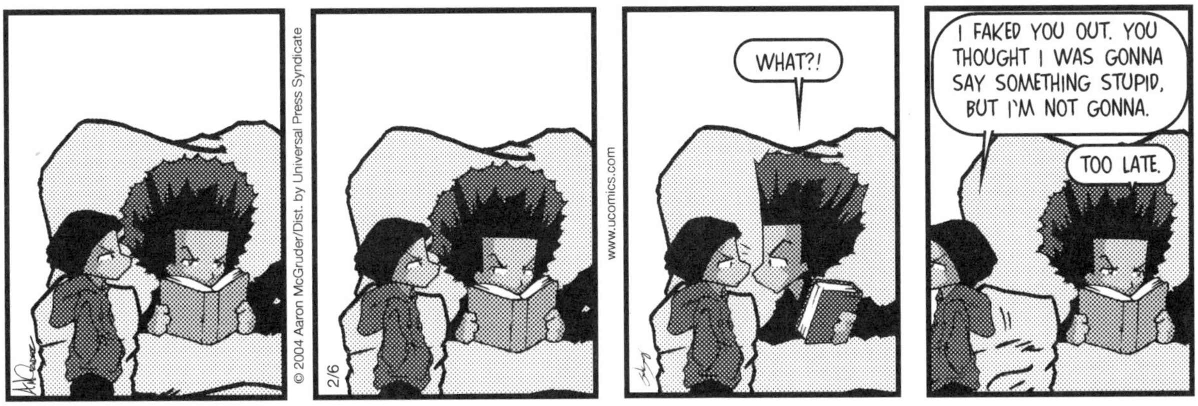
2/6
WHAT?!
I FAKED YOU OUT. YOU THOUGHT I WAS GONNA SAY SOMETHING STUPID, BUT I'M NOT GONNA.
TOO LATE.
www.ucomics.com

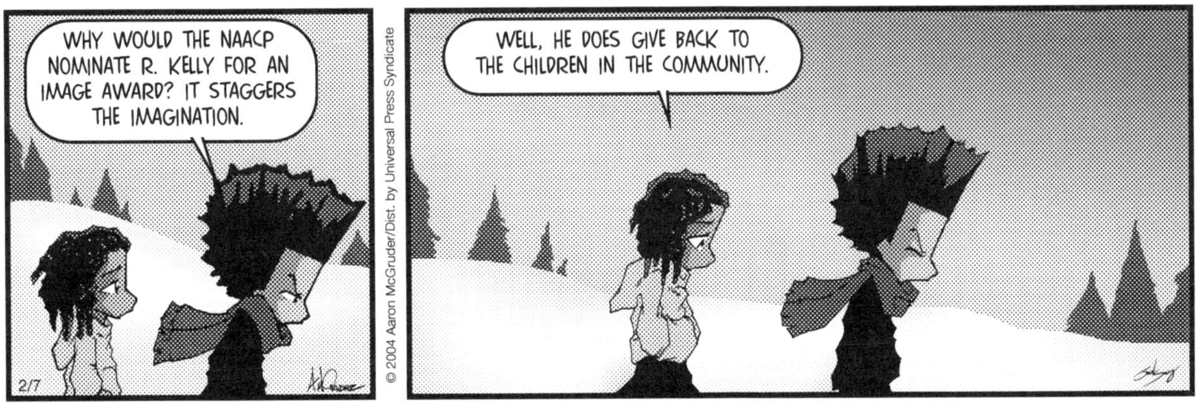
WHY WOULD THE NAACP NOMINATE R. KELLY FOR AN IMAGE AWARD? IT STAGGERS THE IMAGINATION.
2/7
WELL, HE DOES GIVE BACK TO THE CHILDREN IN THE COMMUNITY.

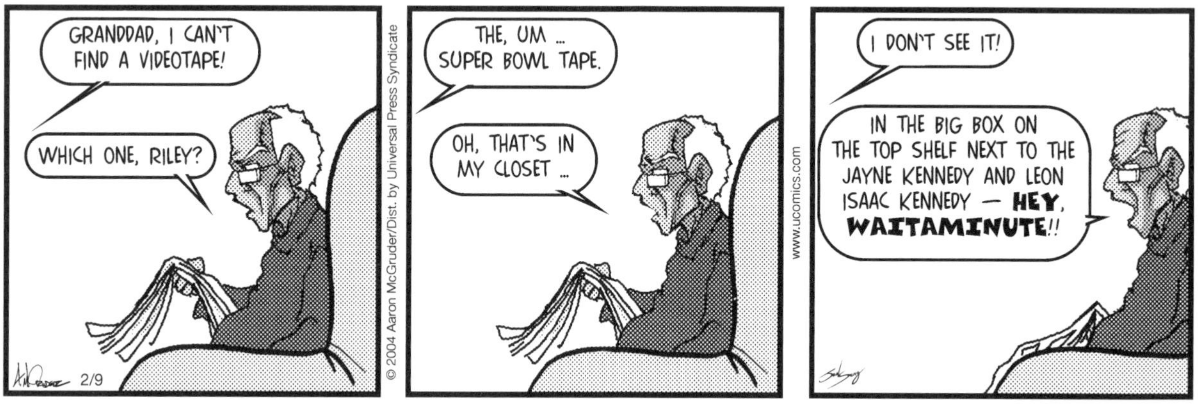
GRANDDAD, I CAN'T FIND A VIDEOTAPE!
WHICH ONE, RILEY?
2/9
© 2004 Aaron McGruder/Dist. by Universal Press Syndicate
THE, UM ... SUPER BOWL TAPE.
OH, THAT'S IN MY CLOSET ...
www.ucomics.com
I DON'T SEE IT!
IN THE BIG BOX ON THE TOP SHELF NEXT TO THE JAYNE KENNEDY AND LEON ISAAC KENNEDY — HEY, WAITAMINUTE!!

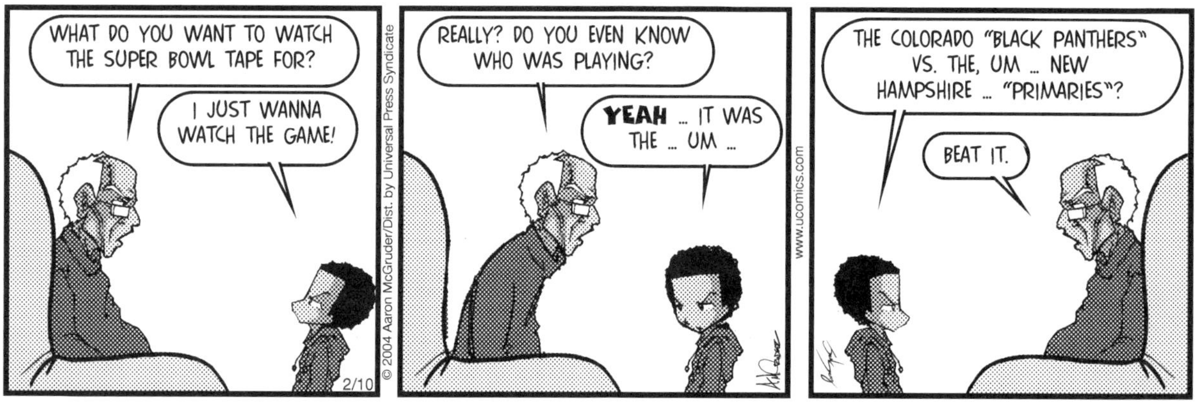
WHAT DO YOU WANT TO WATCH THE SUPER BOWL TAPE FOR?
I JUST WANNA WATCH THE GAME!
2/10
© 2004 Aaron McGruder/Dist. by Universal Press Syndicate
REALLY? DO YOU EVEN KNOW WHO WAS PLAYING?
YEAH ... IT WAS THE ... UM ...
www.ucomics.com
THE COLORADO "BLACK PANTHERS" VS. THE, UM ... NEW HAMPSHIRE ... "PRIMARIES"?
BEAT IT.

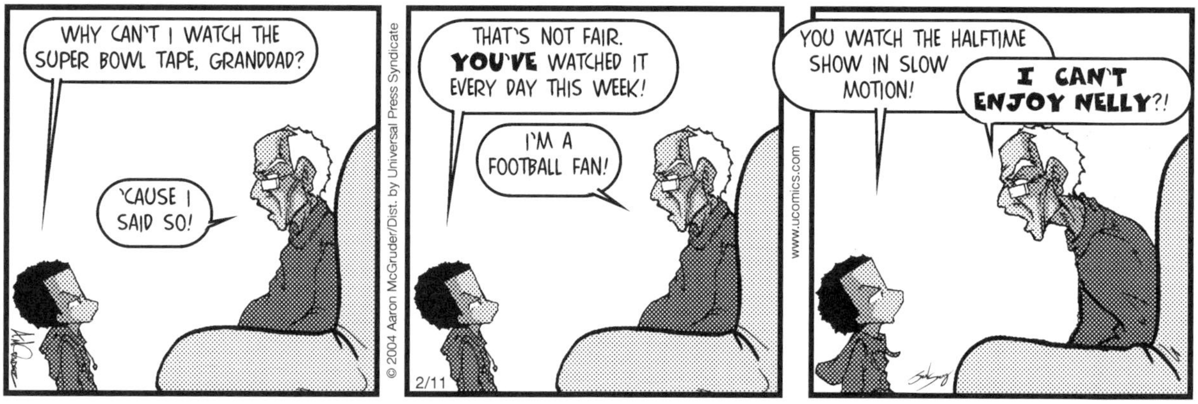
WHY CAN'T I WATCH THE SUPER BOWL TAPE, GRANDDAD?
'CAUSE I SAID SO!
© 2004 Aaron McGruder/Dist. by Universal Press Syndicate
THAT'S NOT FAIR. YOU'VE WATCHED IT EVERY DAY THIS WEEK!
I'M A FOOTBALL FAN!
2/11
www.ucomics.com
YOU WATCH THE HALFTIME SHOW IN SLOW MOTION!
I CAN'T ENJOY NELLY?!

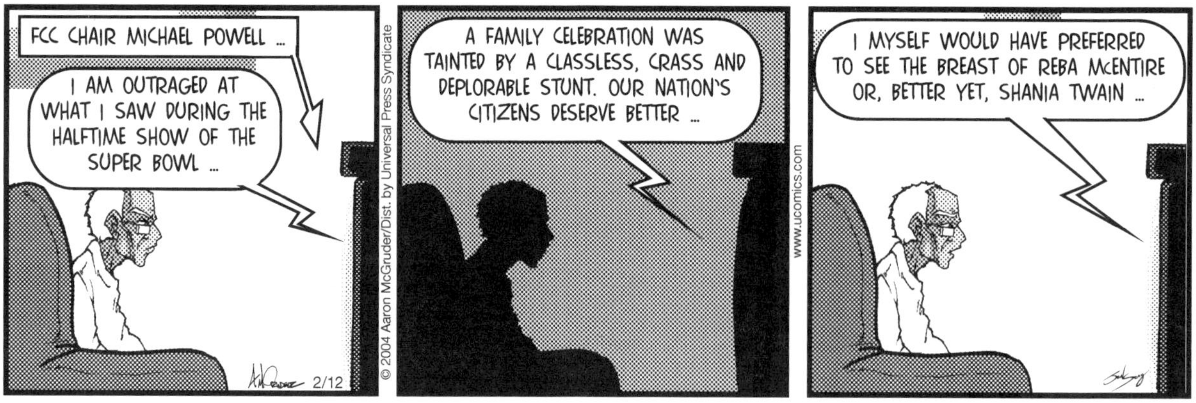
FCC CHAIR MICHAEL POWELL ...
I AM OUTRAGED AT WHAT I SAW DURING THE HALFTIME SHOW OF THE SUPER BOWL ...
2/12
© 2004 Aaron McGruder/Dist. by Universal Press Syndicate
A FAMILY CELEBRATION WAS TAINTED BY A CLASSLESS, CRASS AND DEPLORABLE STUNT. OUR NATION'S CITIZENS DESERVE BETTER ...
www.ucomics.com
I MYSELF WOULD HAVE PREFERRED TO SEE THE BREAST OF REBA McENTIRE OR, BETTER YET, SHANIA TWAIN ...

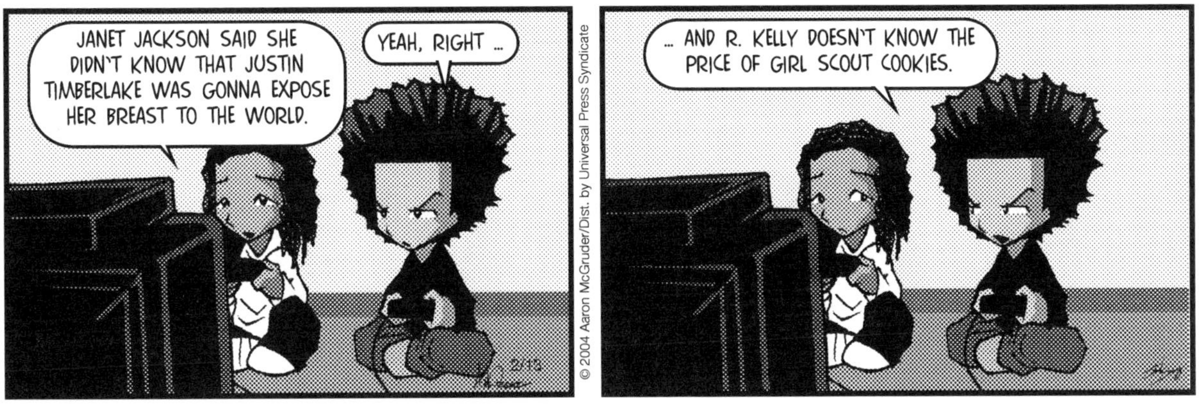
JANET JACKSON SAID SHE DIDN'T KNOW THAT JUSTIN TIMBERLAKE WAS GONNA EXPOSE HER BREAST TO THE WORLD.
YEAH, RIGHT ...
... AND R. KELLY DOESN'T KNOW THE PRICE OF GIRL SCOUT COOKIES.
2/13
© 2004 Aaron McGruder/Dist. by Universal Press Syndicate

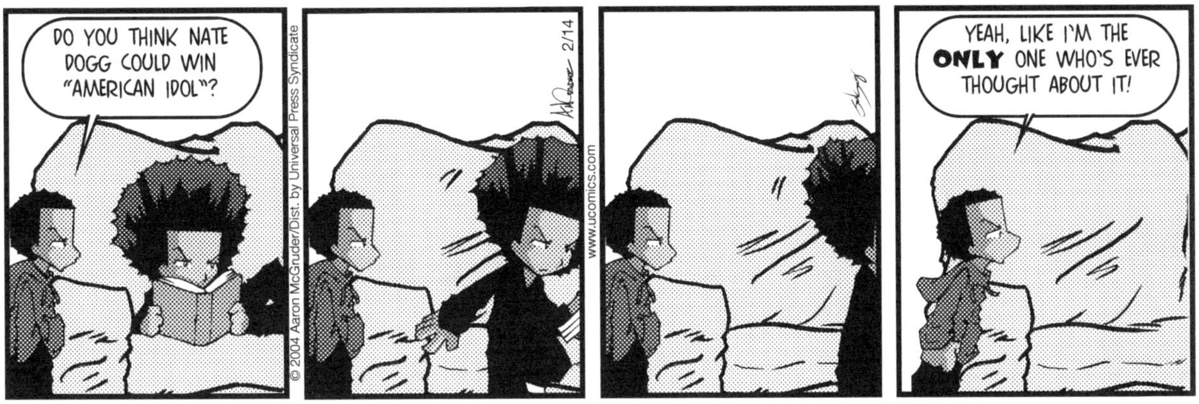
DO YOU THINK NATE DOGG COULD WIN "AMERICAN IDOL"?
YEAH, LIKE I'M THE **ONLY** ONE WHO'S EVER THOUGHT ABOUT IT!
2/14
© 2004 Aaron McGruder/Dist. by Universal Press Syndicate
www.ucomics.com

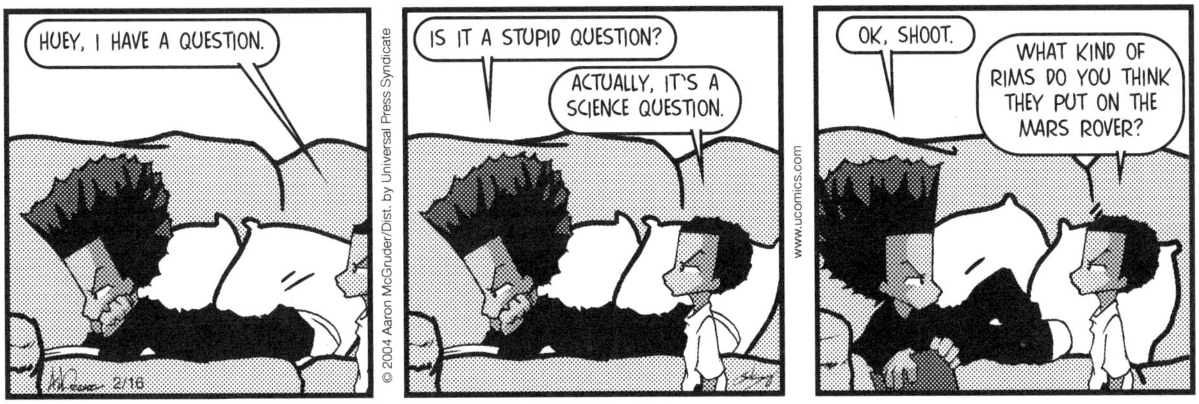
HUEY, I HAVE A QUESTION.
IS IT A STUPID QUESTION?
ACTUALLY, IT'S A SCIENCE QUESTION.
OK, SHOOT.
WHAT KIND OF RIMS DO YOU THINK THEY PUT ON THE MARS ROVER?
2/16
© 2004 Aaron McGruder/Dist. by Universal Press Syndicate
www.ucomics.com

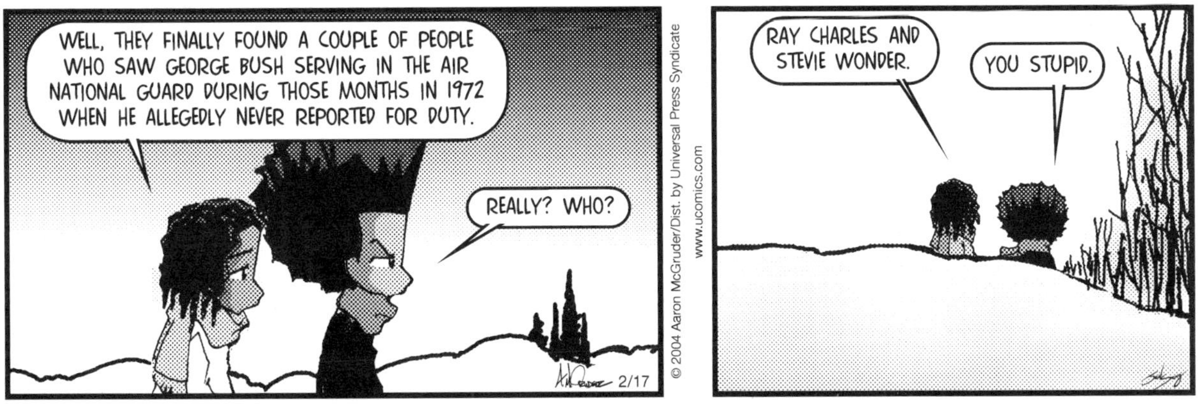
WELL, THEY FINALLY FOUND A COUPLE OF PEOPLE WHO SAW GEORGE BUSH SERVING IN THE AIR NATIONAL GUARD DURING THOSE MONTHS IN 1972 WHEN HE ALLEGEDLY NEVER REPORTED FOR DUTY.
REALLY? WHO?
RAY CHARLES AND STEVIE WONDER.
YOU STUPID.
2/17
© 2004 Aaron McGruder/Dist. by Universal Press Syndicate
www.ucomics.com

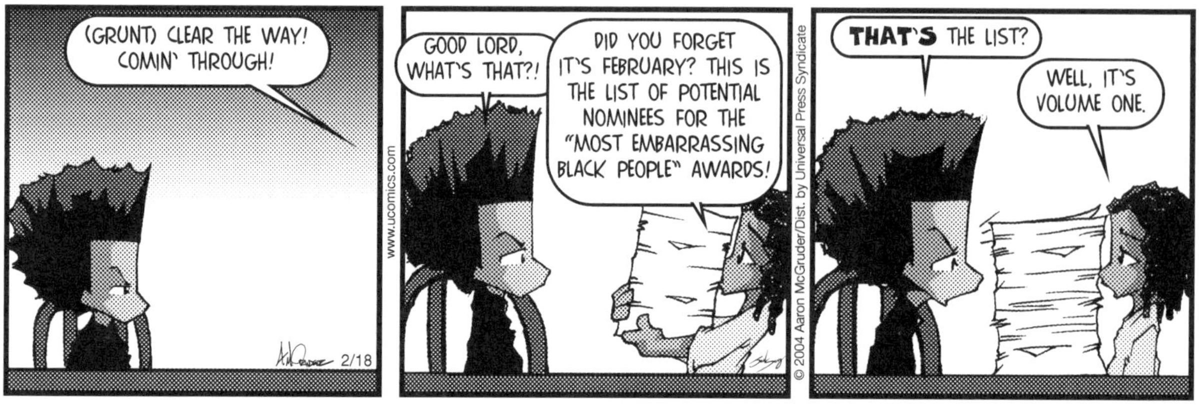
(GRUNT) CLEAR THE WAY! COMIN' THROUGH!
GOOD LORD, WHAT'S THAT?!
DID YOU FORGET IT'S FEBRUARY? THIS IS THE LIST OF POTENTIAL NOMINEES FOR THE "MOST EMBARRASSING BLACK PEOPLE" AWARDS!
THAT'S THE LIST?
WELL, IT'S VOLUME ONE.
2/18

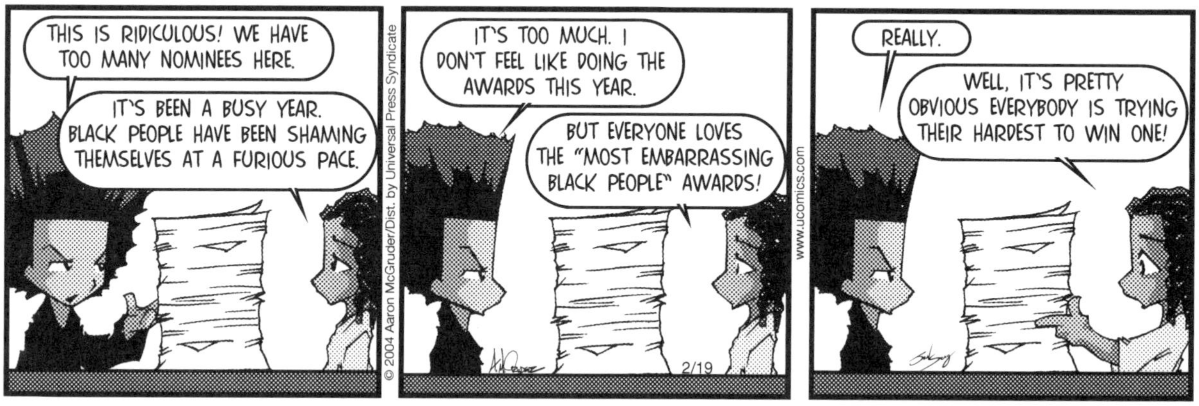
THIS IS RIDICULOUS! WE HAVE TOO MANY NOMINEES HERE.
IT'S BEEN A BUSY YEAR. BLACK PEOPLE HAVE BEEN SHAMING THEMSELVES AT A FURIOUS PACE.
IT'S TOO MUCH. I DON'T FEEL LIKE DOING THE AWARDS THIS YEAR.
BUT EVERYONE LOVES THE "MOST EMBARRASSING BLACK PEOPLE" AWARDS!
REALLY.
WELL, IT'S PRETTY OBVIOUS EVERYBODY IS TRYING THEIR HARDEST TO WIN ONE!
2/19

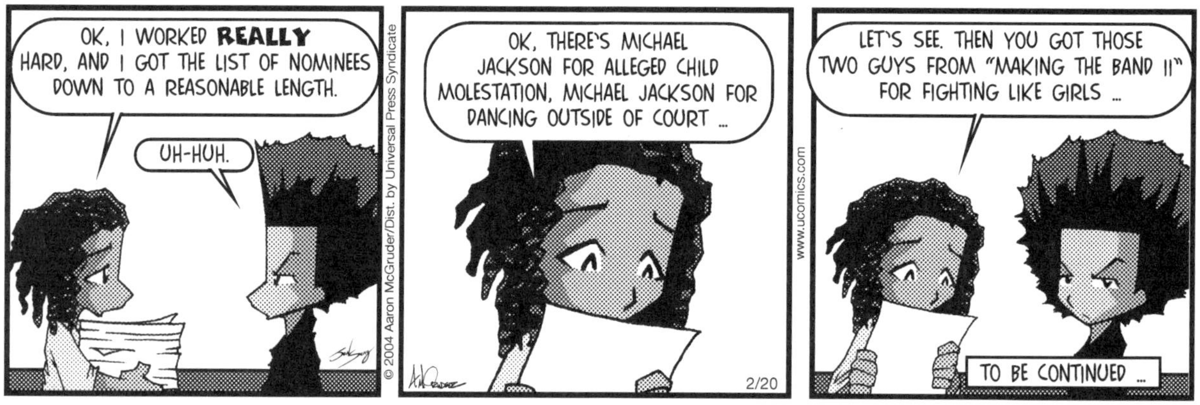
OK, I WORKED **REALLY** HARD, AND I GOT THE LIST OF NOMINEES DOWN TO A REASONABLE LENGTH.
UH-HUH.
OK, THERE'S MICHAEL JACKSON FOR ALLEGED CHILD MOLESTATION, MICHAEL JACKSON FOR DANCING OUTSIDE OF COURT ...
LET'S SEE. THEN YOU GOT THOSE TWO GUYS FROM "MAKING THE BAND II" FOR FIGHTING LIKE GIRLS ...
TO BE CONTINUED ...
2/20

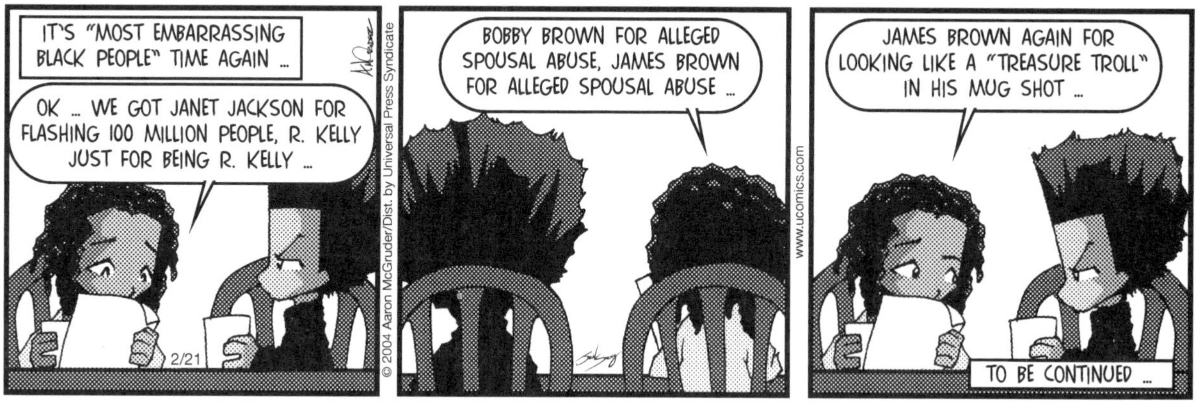
IT'S "MOST EMBARRASSING BLACK PEOPLE" TIME AGAIN ...
OK ... WE GOT JANET JACKSON FOR FLASHING 100 MILLION PEOPLE, R. KELLY JUST FOR BEING R. KELLY ...
BOBBY BROWN FOR ALLEGED SPOUSAL ABUSE, JAMES BROWN FOR ALLEGED SPOUSAL ABUSE ...
JAMES BROWN AGAIN FOR LOOKING LIKE A "TREASURE TROLL" IN HIS MUG SHOT ...
TO BE CONTINUED ...
2/21

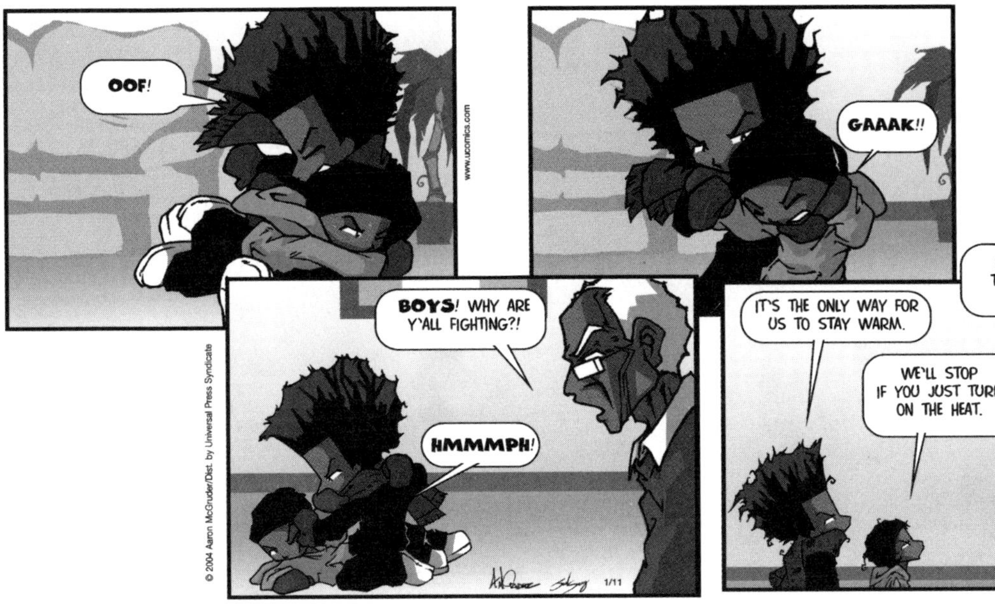
OOF!
www.ucomics.com
GAAAK!!
© 2004 Aaron McGruder/Dist. by Universal Press Syndicate
BOYS! WHY ARE Y'ALL FIGHTING?!
HMMMPH!
1/11
IT'S THE ONLY WAY FOR US TO STAY WARM.
WE'LL STOP IF YOU JUST TURN ON THE HEAT.
IT'S OKAY. JUST TRY NOT TO BLEED ON MY CARPET.

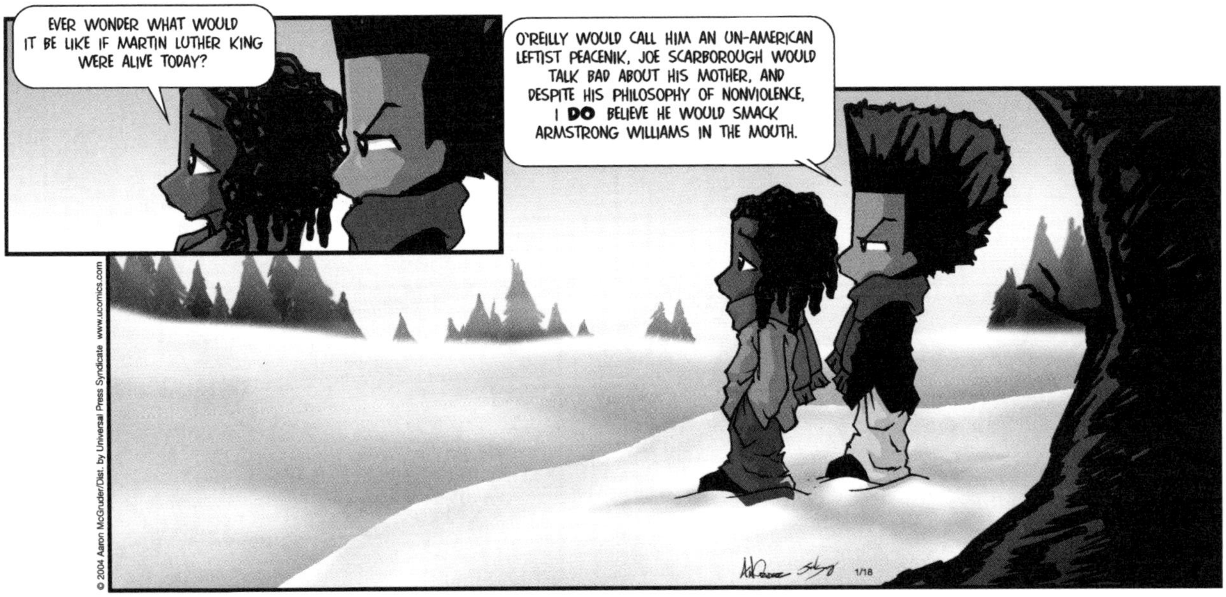
EVER WONDER WHAT WOULD IT BE LIKE IF MARTIN LUTHER KING WERE ALIVE TODAY?
O'REILLY WOULD CALL HIM AN UN-AMERICAN LEFTIST PEACENIK, JOE SCARBOROUGH WOULD TALK BAD ABOUT HIS MOTHER, AND DESPITE HIS PHILOSOPHY OF NONVIOLENCE, I DO BELIEVE HE WOULD SMACK ARMSTRONG WILLIAMS IN THE MOUTH.
© 2004 Aaron McGruder/Dist. by Universal Press Syndicate www.ucomics.com
1/18

I'VE DECIDED THAT THE MUSIC INDUSTRY DOESN'T OFFER MUCH SECURITY, SO I'M WORKING ON COMEDY AS A BACKUP.
CHECK THIS OUT ... YOUR MOMMA IS SO DUMB, SHE SET THE HOUSE ON FIRE USING THE CD BURNER.
EH ... IT'S OKAY ...
www.ucomics.com www.boondocks.net
OKAY?! THAT WAS MY BEST JOKE!
IT DIDN'T CHALLENGE ME. I LIKE MY COMEDY TO EXPOSE THE FOLLY OF THE WORLD WE LIVE IN.
WE NEED MORE COMEDIANS USING HUMOR TO QUESTION THE STATUS QUO. GUYS WHO AREN'T AFRAID TO GET POLITICAL. RICHARD PRYOR, DICK GREGORY, GEORGE CARLIN, CHRIS ROCK — THAT KIND OF THING.
1/25
© 2004 Aaron McGruder/Dist. by Universal Press Syndicate
JOHN ASHCROFT'S MOMMA IS SO DUMB, SHE SET THE HOUSE ON FIRE USING THE CD BURNER.
NOW THAT'S FUNNY ...

HOW WILL FUTURE GENERATIONS REMEMBER THIS CURRENT ERA OF BLACK HISTORY?
WILL THERE BE ANYTHING TO SPEAK OF ASIDE FROM SLAIN RAPPERS, CIRCUS TRIALS OF SPOILED CELEBS, AND LACKLUSTER, CO-OPTED LEADERSHIP?
© 2004 Aaron McGruder/Dist. by Universal Press Syndicate
2/1
www.ucomics.com
THERE'S ALWAYS WAYNE BRADY, I GUESS ...
MAYBE THEY'LL JUST SHORTEN IT TO "BLACK HISTORY AFTERNOON" ...

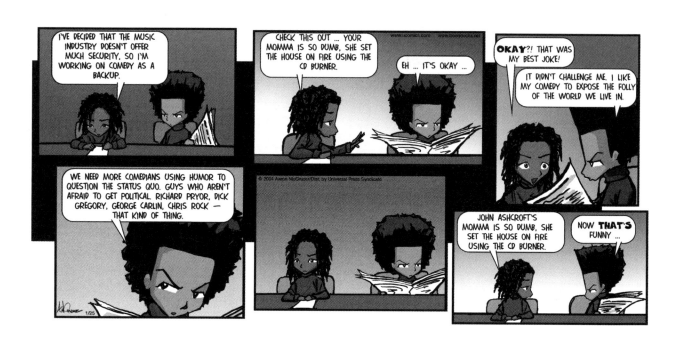

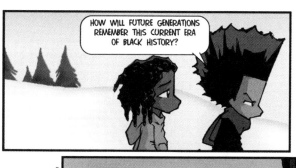

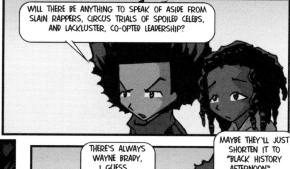

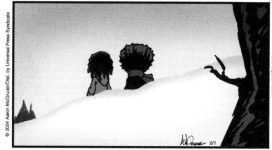

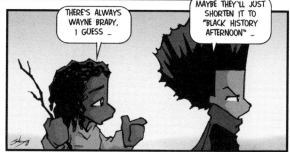

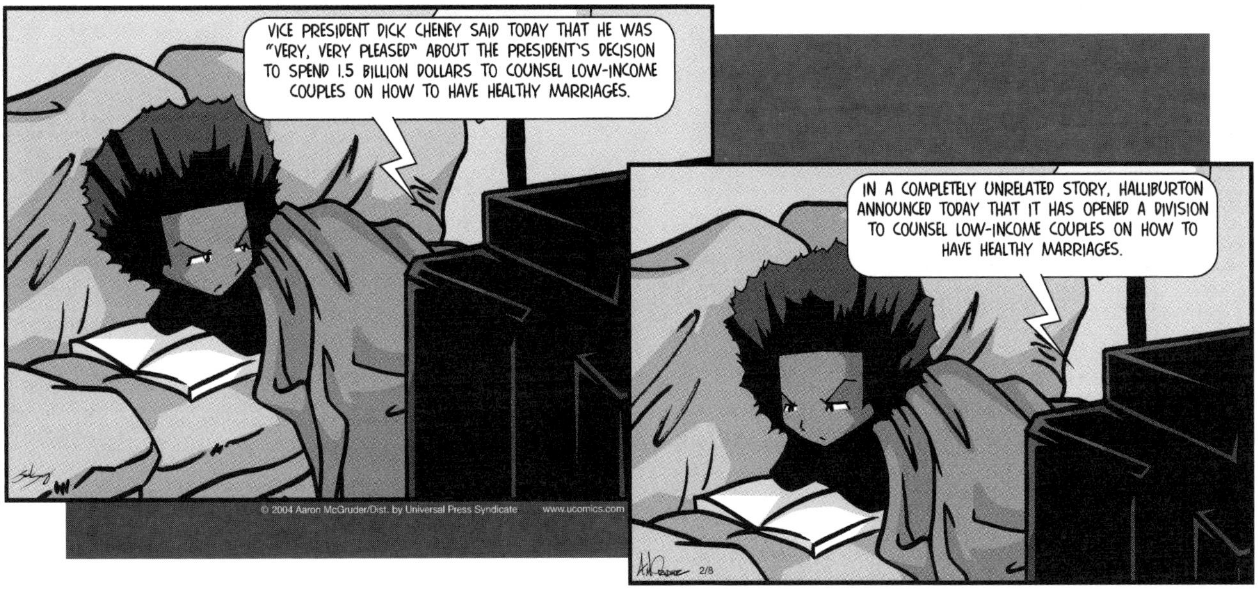
VICE PRESIDENT DICK CHENEY SAID TODAY THAT HE WAS "VERY, VERY PLEASED" ABOUT THE PRESIDENT'S DECISION TO SPEND 1.5 BILLION DOLLARS TO COUNSEL LOW-INCOME COUPLES ON HOW TO HAVE HEALTHY MARRIAGES.
IN A COMPLETELY UNRELATED STORY, HALLIBURTON ANNOUNCED TODAY THAT IT HAS OPENED A DIVISION TO COUNSEL LOW-INCOME COUPLES ON HOW TO HAVE HEALTHY MARRIAGES.
© 2004 Aaron McGruder/Dist. by Universal Press Syndicate www.ucomics.com
2/8

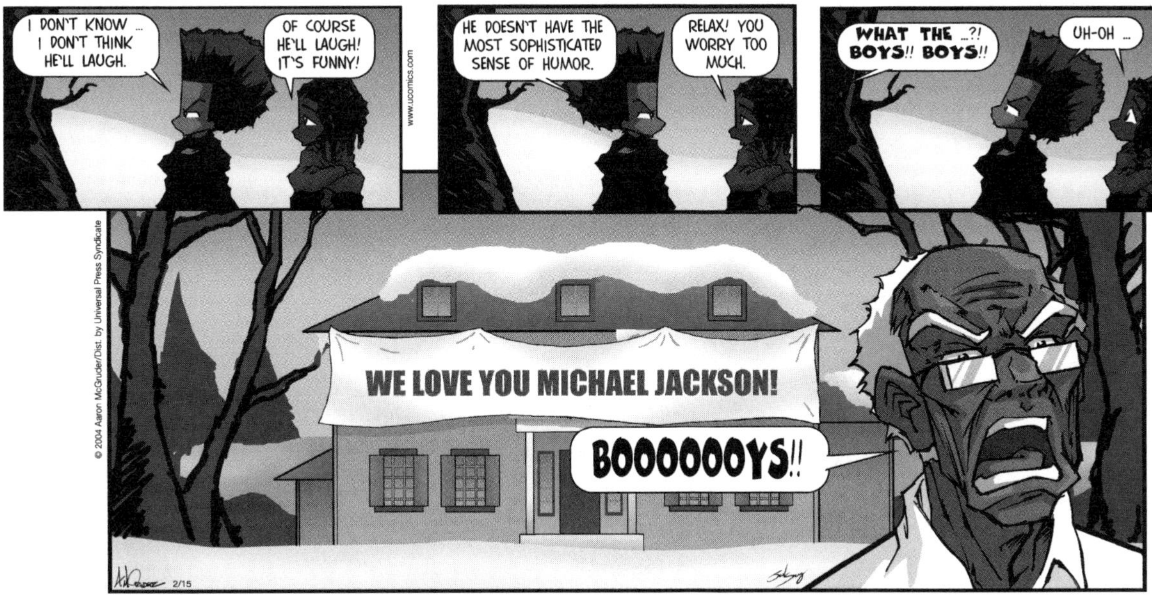
I DON'T KNOW ... I DON'T THINK HE'LL LAUGH.
OF COURSE HE'LL LAUGH! IT'S FUNNY!
HE DOESN'T HAVE THE MOST SOPHISTICATED SENSE OF HUMOR.
RELAX! YOU WORRY TOO MUCH.
WHAT THE ...?! BOYS!! BOYS!!
UH-OH ...
WE LOVE YOU MICHAEL JACKSON!
BOOOOOOYS!!
www.ucomics.com
© 2004 Aaron McGruder/Dist. by Universal Press Syndicate
2/15

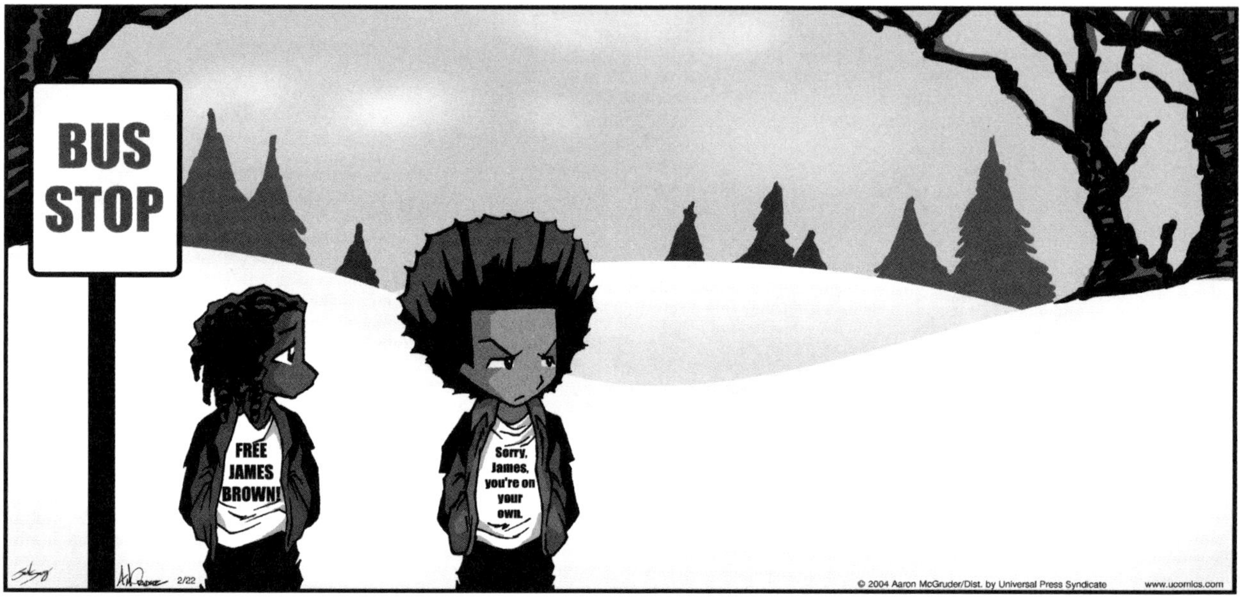
BUS STOP
FREE JAMES BROWN!
Sorry, James, you're on your own.
2/22
© 2004 Aaron McGruder/Dist. by Universal Press Syndicate
www.ucomics.com

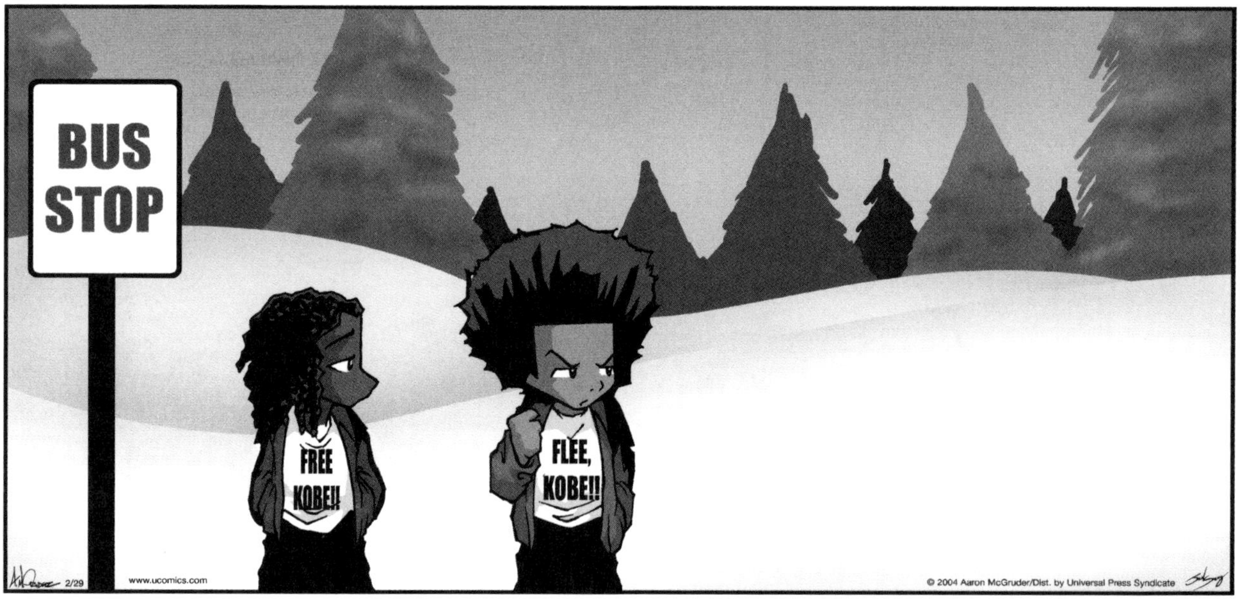
BUS STOP
FREE KOBE!!
FLEE, KOBE!!
2/29
www.ucomics.com
© 2004 Aaron McGruder/Dist. by Universal Press Syndicate

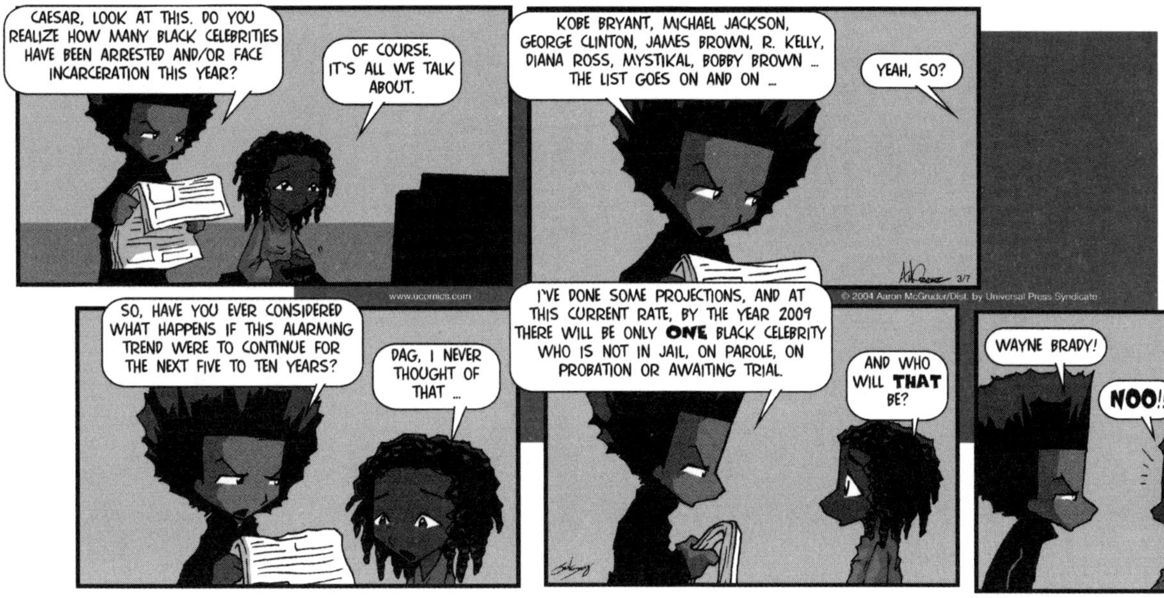
CAESAR, LOOK AT THIS. DO YOU REALIZE HOW MANY BLACK CELEBRITIES HAVE BEEN ARRESTED AND/OR FACE INCARCERATION THIS YEAR?
OF COURSE. IT'S ALL WE TALK ABOUT.
KOBE BRYANT, MICHAEL JACKSON, GEORGE CLINTON, JAMES BROWN, R. KELLY, DIANA ROSS, MYSTIKAL, BOBBY BROWN ... THE LIST GOES ON AND ON ...
YEAH, SO?
3/7
www.ucomics.com
© 2004 Aaron McGruder/Dist. by Universal Press Syndicate
SO, HAVE YOU EVER CONSIDERED WHAT HAPPENS IF THIS ALARMING TREND WERE TO CONTINUE FOR THE NEXT FIVE TO TEN YEARS?
DAG, I NEVER THOUGHT OF THAT ...
I'VE DONE SOME PROJECTIONS, AND AT THIS CURRENT RATE, BY THE YEAR 2009 THERE WILL BE ONLY **ONE** BLACK CELEBRITY WHO IS NOT IN JAIL, ON PAROLE, ON PROBATION OR AWAITING TRIAL.
AND WHO WILL **THAT** BE?
WAYNE BRADY!
NOO!!

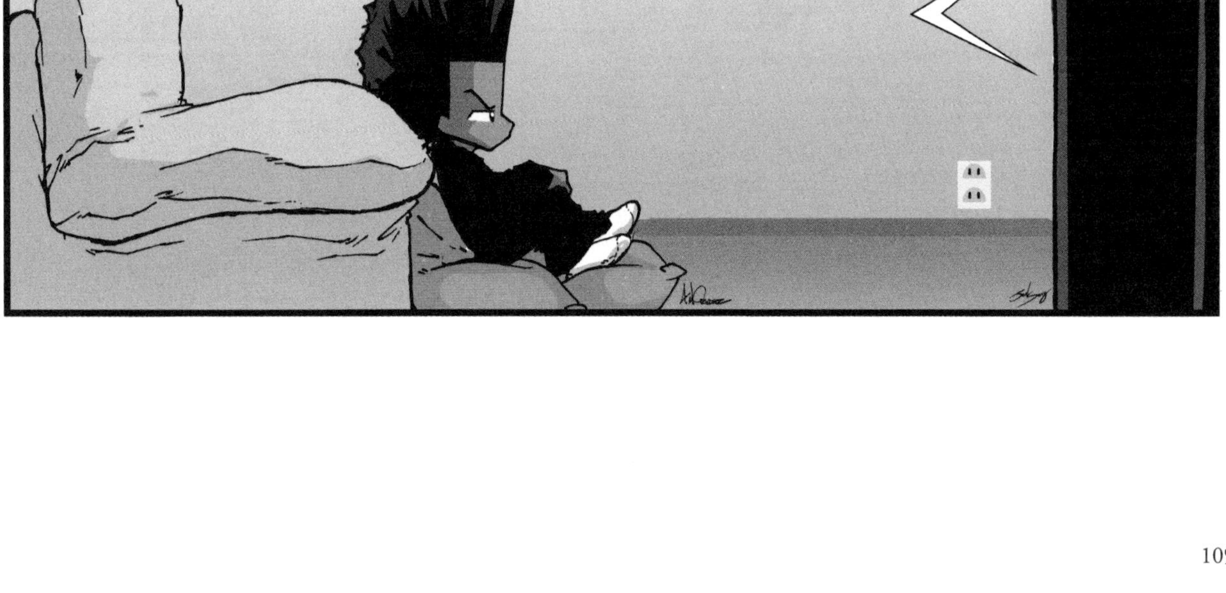
3/14 www.ucomics.com © 2004 Aaron McGruder/Dist. by Universal Press Syndicate
THIS WEEK ON A VERY SPECIAL EPISODE OF NBC'S "THE APPRENTICE" ...
... AND SINCE WE'VE DECIDED IT'S CONSIDERABLY MORE COST-EFFICIENT TO PRODUCE THIS SHOW IN MEXICO, YOU'RE **ALL** FIRED ...

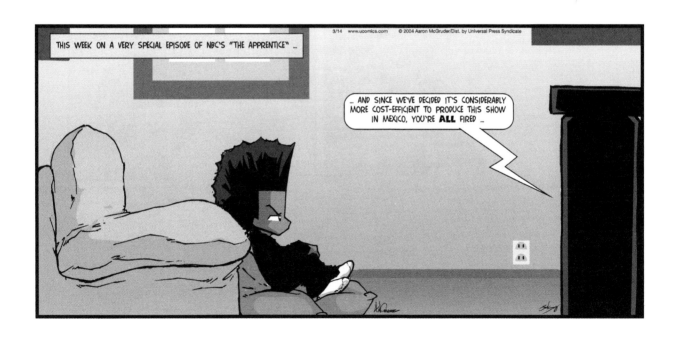

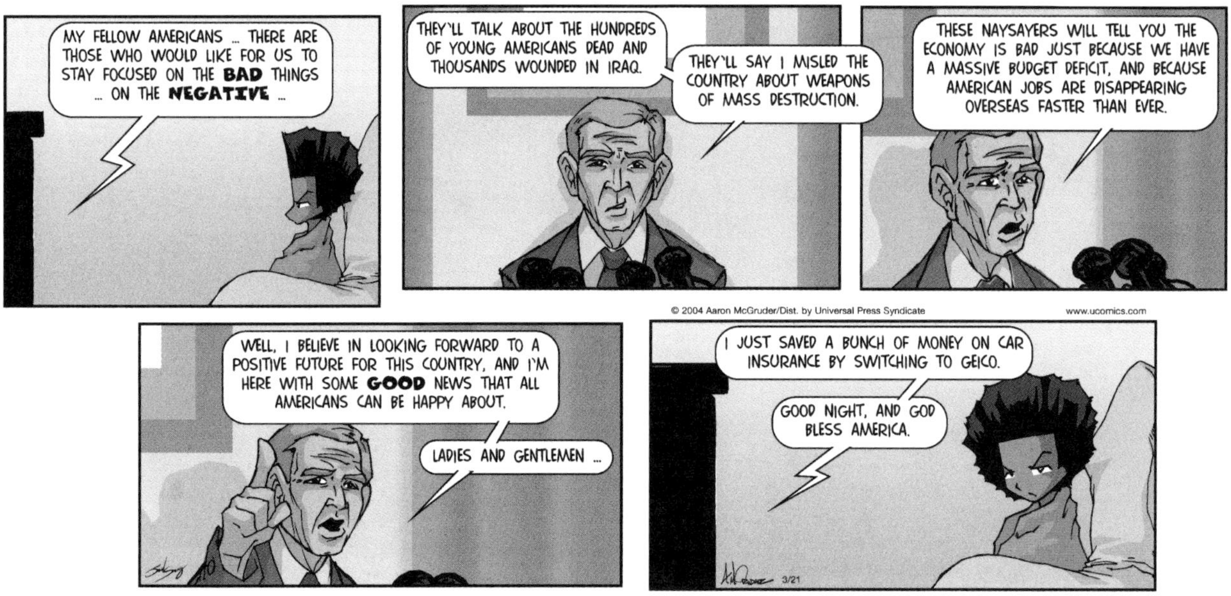
MY FELLOW AMERICANS ... THERE ARE THOSE WHO WOULD LIKE FOR US TO STAY FOCUSED ON THE BAD THINGS ... ON THE NEGATIVE ...
THEY'LL TALK ABOUT THE HUNDREDS OF YOUNG AMERICANS DEAD AND THOUSANDS WOUNDED IN IRAQ.
THEY'LL SAY I MISLED THE COUNTRY ABOUT WEAPONS OF MASS DESTRUCTION.
THESE NAYSAYERS WILL TELL YOU THE ECONOMY IS BAD JUST BECAUSE WE HAVE A MASSIVE BUDGET DEFICIT, AND BECAUSE AMERICAN JOBS ARE DISAPPEARING OVERSEAS FASTER THAN EVER.
WELL, I BELIEVE IN LOOKING FORWARD TO A POSITIVE FUTURE FOR THIS COUNTRY, AND I'M HERE WITH SOME GOOD NEWS THAT ALL AMERICANS CAN BE HAPPY ABOUT.
LADIES AND GENTLEMEN ...
I JUST SAVED A BUNCH OF MONEY ON CAR INSURANCE BY SWITCHING TO GEICO.
GOOD NIGHT, AND GOD BLESS AMERICA.
3/21

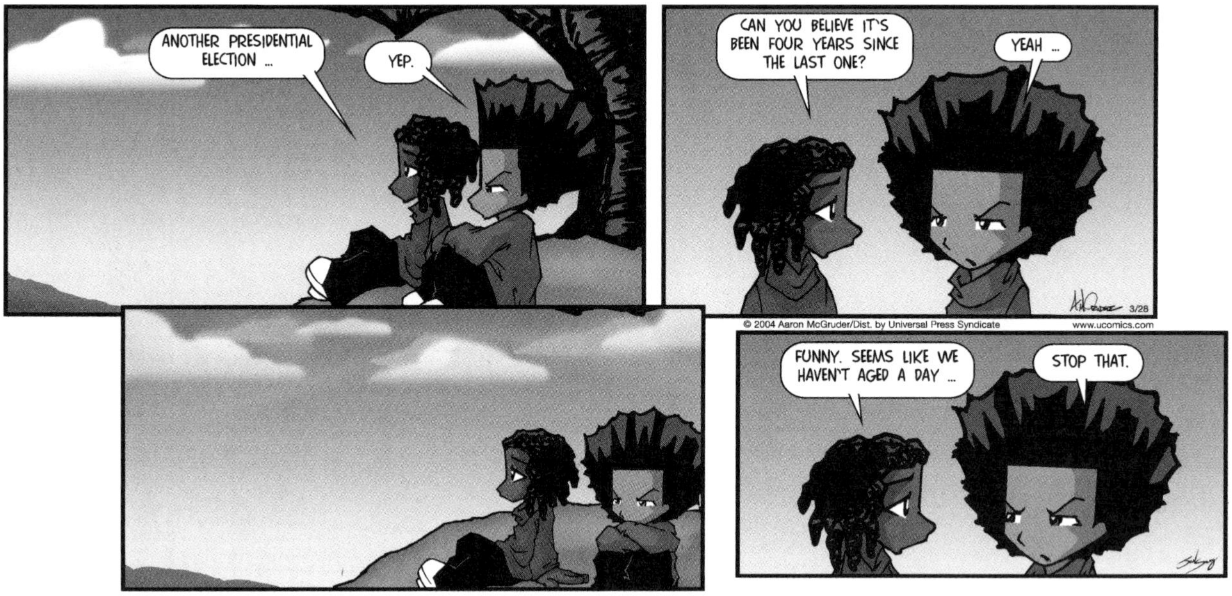
ANOTHER PRESIDENTIAL ELECTION ...
YEP.
CAN YOU BELIEVE IT'S BEEN FOUR YEARS SINCE THE LAST ONE?
YEAH ...
3/28
FUNNY. SEEMS LIKE WE HAVEN'T AGED A DAY ...
STOP THAT.

... I'M JUST SAYIN', IT MIGHT BE EASIER FOR EVERYBODY IF THEY JUST CONVERTED HIS **HOUSE** INTO A COURTROOM WITH, LIKE, A LITTLE JAIL IN THE BACK YARD ...
LEAVE BOBBY BROWN ALONE ...
© 2004 Aaron McGruder/Dist. by Universal Press Syndicate
www.ucomics.com
4/11

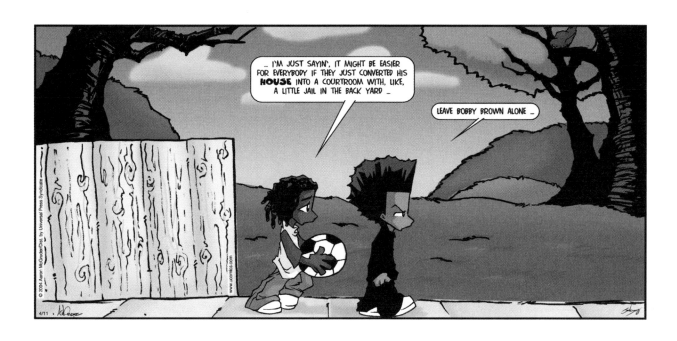

To the Reader:

Due to a publication error, the following installment of this feature, which was originally slated for October 3, 2004, is running today.

We apologize for the inconvenience.

I CAN'T BELIEVE THEY FINALLY FOUND OSAMA BIN LADEN ...
AND SO SOON BEFORE THE ELECTION.
YOU SUSPECT SOMETHING ... CONSPIRATORIAL?
IT'S TOO MUCH OF A COINCIDENCE. THEY'VE HAD HIM FOR A WHILE, AND THEY'RE BRINGING HIM OUT AT THE MOMENT OF GREATEST POLITICAL ADVANTAGE.
MAN ... WHO COULD HAVE **POSSIBLY** SEEN THIS COMING ...
NOT ME.
© 2004 Aaron McGruder/Dist. by Universal Press Syndicate www.ucomics.com
4/25

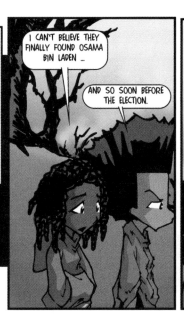

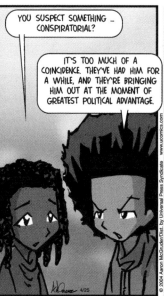

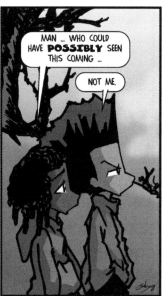

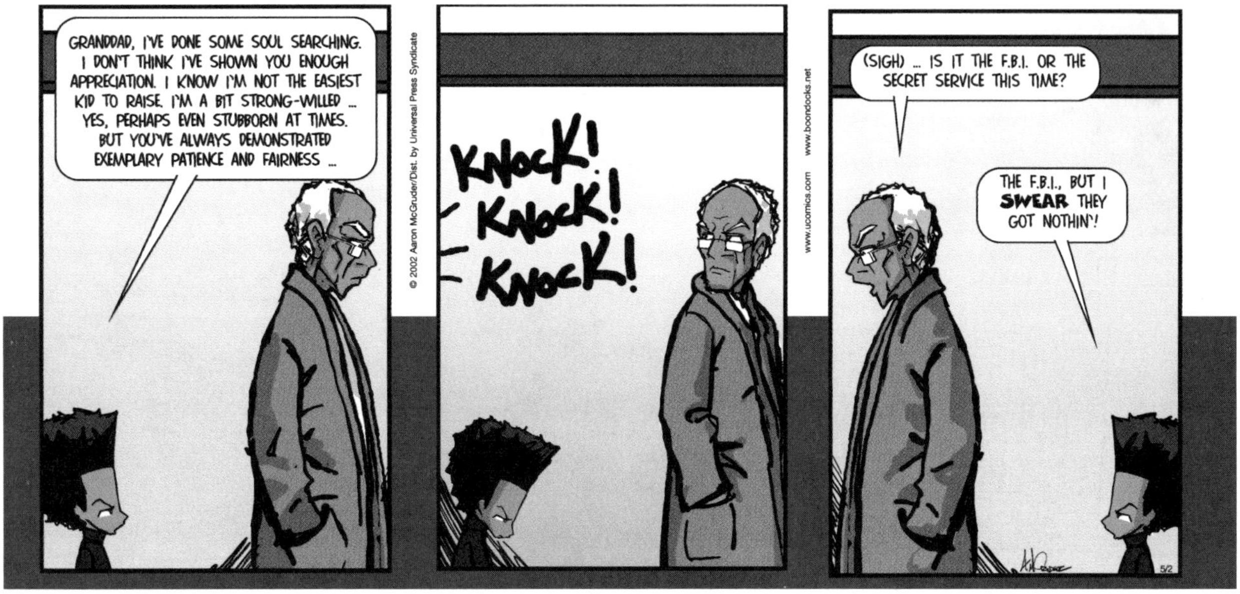
GRANDDAD, I'VE DONE SOME SOUL SEARCHING. I DON'T THINK I'VE SHOWN YOU ENOUGH APPRECIATION. I KNOW I'M NOT THE EASIEST KID TO RAISE. I'M A BIT STRONG-WILLED ... YES, PERHAPS EVEN STUBBORN AT TIMES. BUT YOU'VE ALWAYS DEMONSTRATED EXEMPLARY PATIENCE AND FAIRNESS ...
© 2002 Aaron McGruder/Dist. by Universal Press Syndicate
KNOCK! KNOCK! KNOCK!
www.ucomics.com www.boondocks.net
(SIGH) ... IS IT THE F.B.I. OR THE SECRET SERVICE THIS TIME?
THE F.B.I., BUT I SWEAR THEY GOT NOTHIN'!
5/2

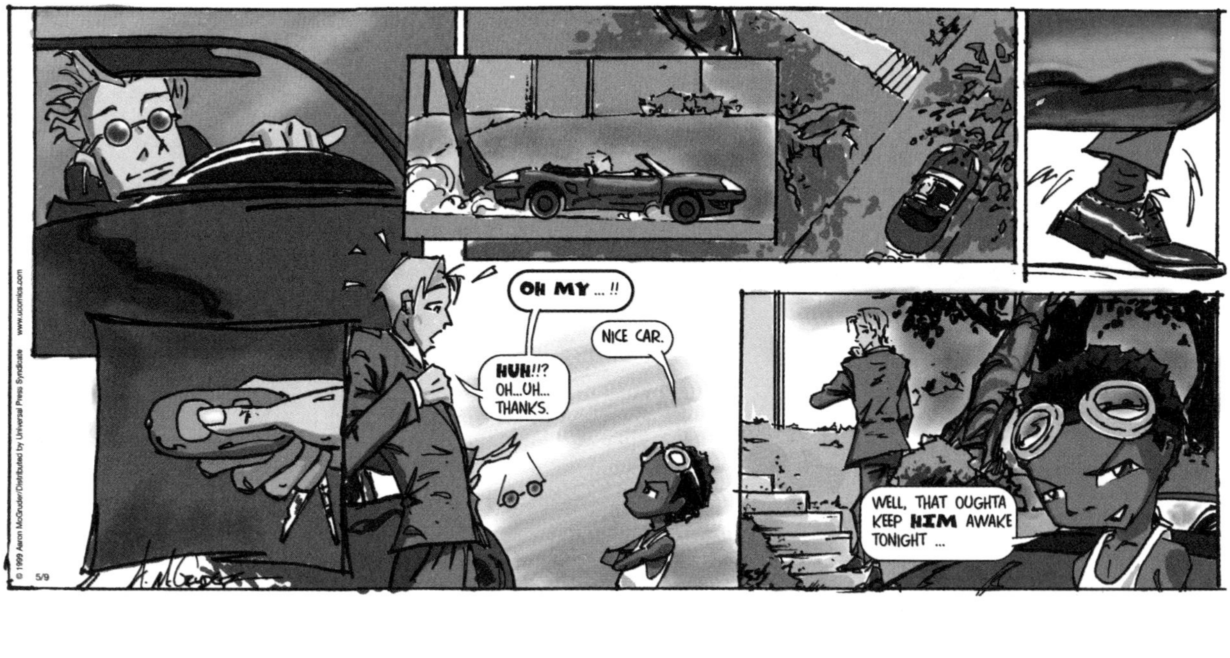
© 1999 Aaron McGruder/Distributed by Universal Press Syndicate www.ucomics.com
5/9
OH MY ... !!
HUH!!? OH...UH... THANKS.
NICE CAR.
WELL, THAT OUGHTA KEEP HIM AWAKE TONIGHT ...

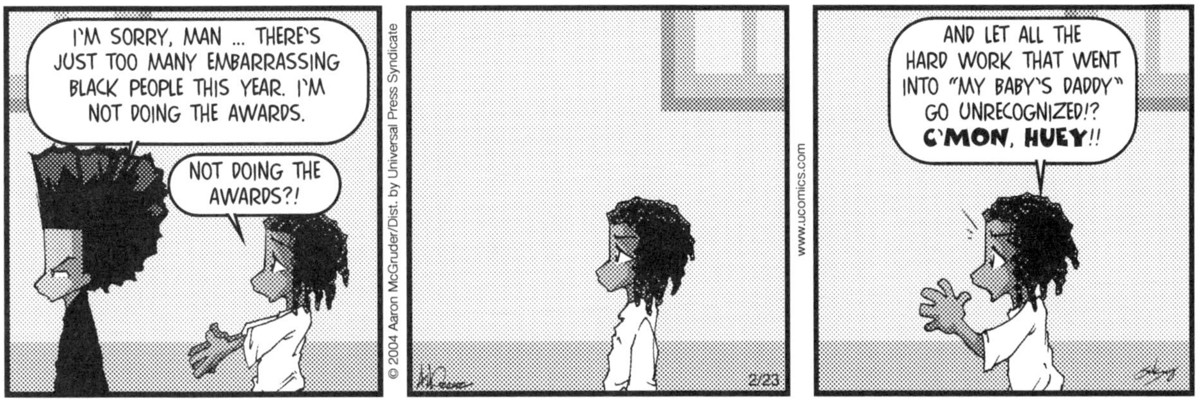
I'M SORRY, MAN ... THERE'S JUST TOO MANY EMBARRASSING BLACK PEOPLE THIS YEAR. I'M NOT DOING THE AWARDS.
NOT DOING THE AWARDS?!
AND LET ALL THE HARD WORK THAT WENT INTO "MY BABY'S DADDY" GO UNRECOGNIZED!? **C'MON, HUEY**!!
© 2004 Aaron McGruder/Dist. by Universal Press Syndicate
www.ucomics.com
2/23

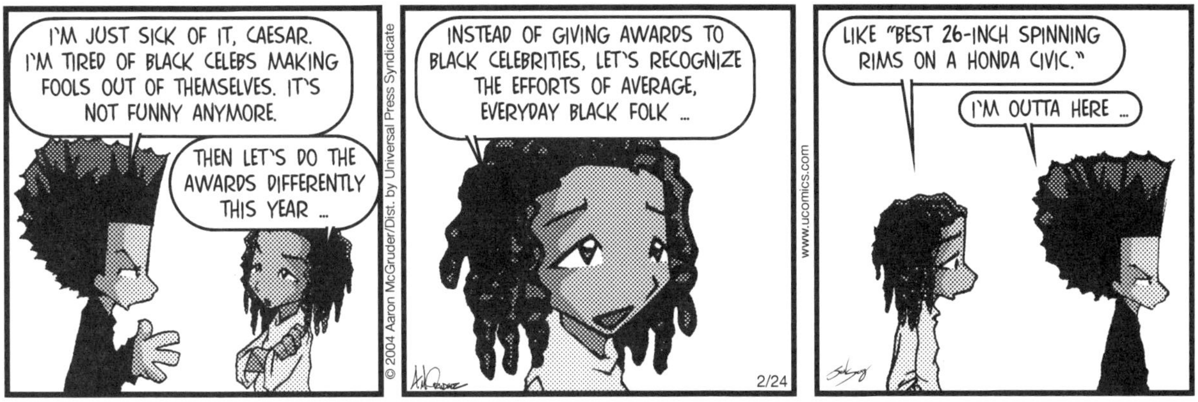
I'M JUST SICK OF IT, CAESAR. I'M TIRED OF BLACK CELEBS MAKING FOOLS OUT OF THEMSELVES. IT'S NOT FUNNY ANYMORE.
THEN LET'S DO THE AWARDS DIFFERENTLY THIS YEAR ...
INSTEAD OF GIVING AWARDS TO BLACK CELEBRITIES, LET'S RECOGNIZE THE EFFORTS OF AVERAGE, EVERYDAY BLACK FOLK ...
LIKE "BEST 26-INCH SPINNING RIMS ON A HONDA CIVIC."
I'M OUTTA HERE ...
© 2004 Aaron McGruder/Dist. by Universal Press Syndicate
www.ucomics.com
2/24

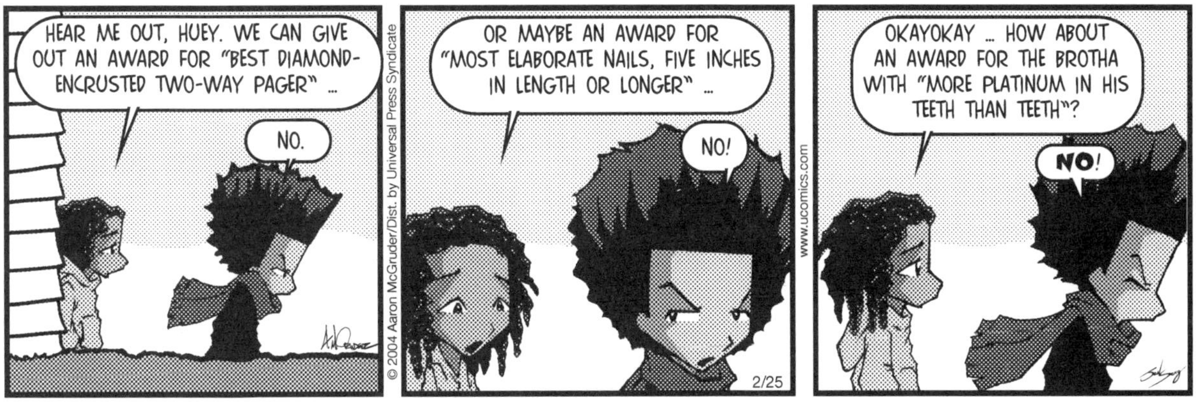
HEAR ME OUT, HUEY. WE CAN GIVE OUT AN AWARD FOR "BEST DIAMOND-ENCRUSTED TWO-WAY PAGER" ...
NO.
OR MAYBE AN AWARD FOR "MOST ELABORATE NAILS, FIVE INCHES IN LENGTH OR LONGER" ...
NO!
OKAYOKAY ... HOW ABOUT AN AWARD FOR THE BROTHA WITH "MORE PLATINUM IN HIS TEETH THAN TEETH"?
NO!
© 2004 Aaron McGruder/Dist. by Universal Press Syndicate
www.ucomics.com
2/25

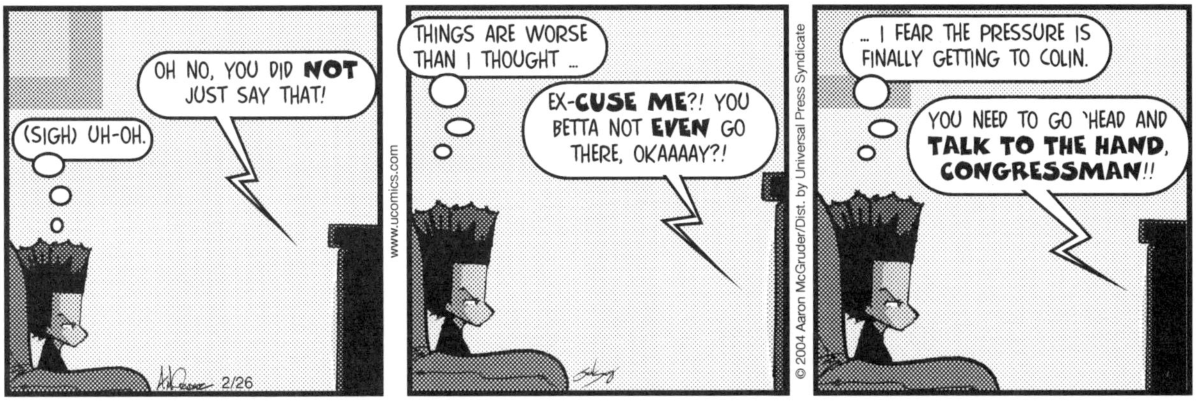
OH NO, YOU DID **NOT** JUST SAY THAT!
(SIGH) UH-OH.
THINGS ARE WORSE THAN I THOUGHT ...
EX-**CUSE ME**?! YOU BETTA NOT **EVEN** GO THERE, OKAAAAY?!
... I FEAR THE PRESSURE IS FINALLY GETTING TO COLIN.
YOU NEED TO GO 'HEAD AND **TALK TO THE HAND, CONGRESSMAN**!!
www.ucomics.com
© 2004 Aaron McGruder/Dist. by Universal Press Syndicate
2/26

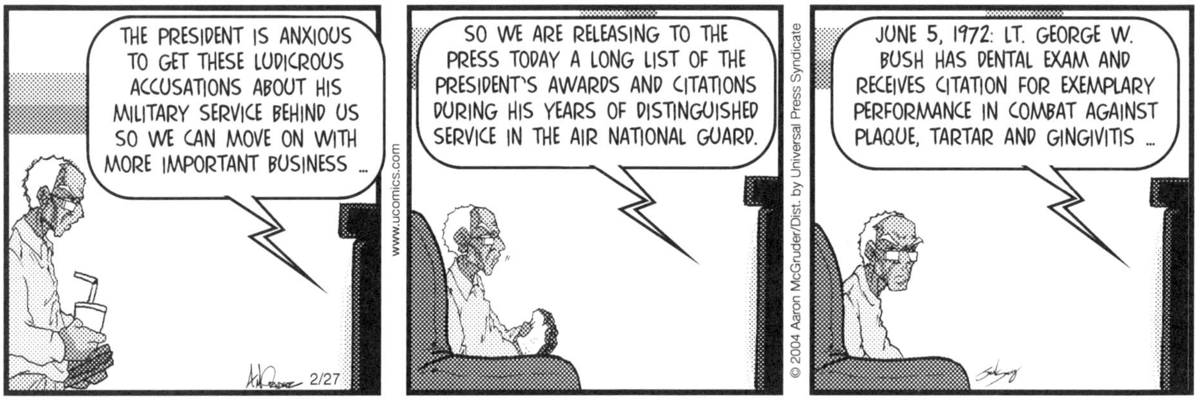
THE PRESIDENT IS ANXIOUS TO GET THESE LUDICROUS ACCUSATIONS ABOUT HIS MILITARY SERVICE BEHIND US SO WE CAN MOVE ON WITH MORE IMPORTANT BUSINESS ...
SO WE ARE RELEASING TO THE PRESS TODAY A LONG LIST OF THE PRESIDENT'S AWARDS AND CITATIONS DURING HIS YEARS OF DISTINGUISHED SERVICE IN THE AIR NATIONAL GUARD.
JUNE 5, 1972: LT. GEORGE W. BUSH HAS DENTAL EXAM AND RECEIVES CITATION FOR EXEMPLARY PERFORMANCE IN COMBAT AGAINST PLAQUE, TARTAR AND GINGIVITIS ...
2/27
www.ucomics.com
© 2004 Aaron McGruder/Dist. by Universal Press Syndicate

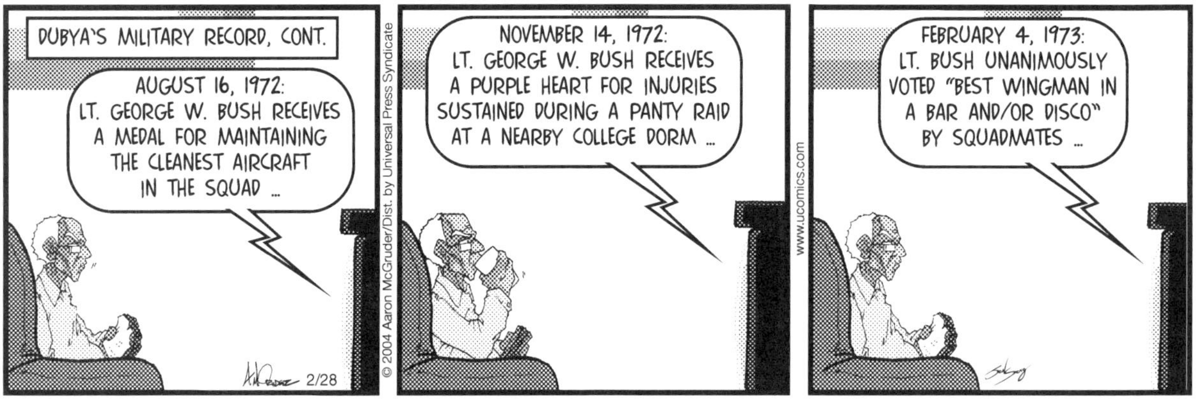
DUBYA'S MILITARY RECORD, CONT.
AUGUST 16, 1972: LT. GEORGE W. BUSH RECEIVES A MEDAL FOR MAINTAINING THE CLEANEST AIRCRAFT IN THE SQUAD ...
NOVEMBER 14, 1972: LT. GEORGE W. BUSH RECEIVES A PURPLE HEART FOR INJURIES SUSTAINED DURING A PANTY RAID AT A NEARBY COLLEGE DORM ...
FEBRUARY 4, 1973: LT. BUSH UNANIMOUSLY VOTED "BEST WINGMAN IN A BAR AND/OR DISCO" BY SQUADMATES ...
2/28
© 2004 Aaron McGruder/Dist. by Universal Press Syndicate
www.ucomics.com

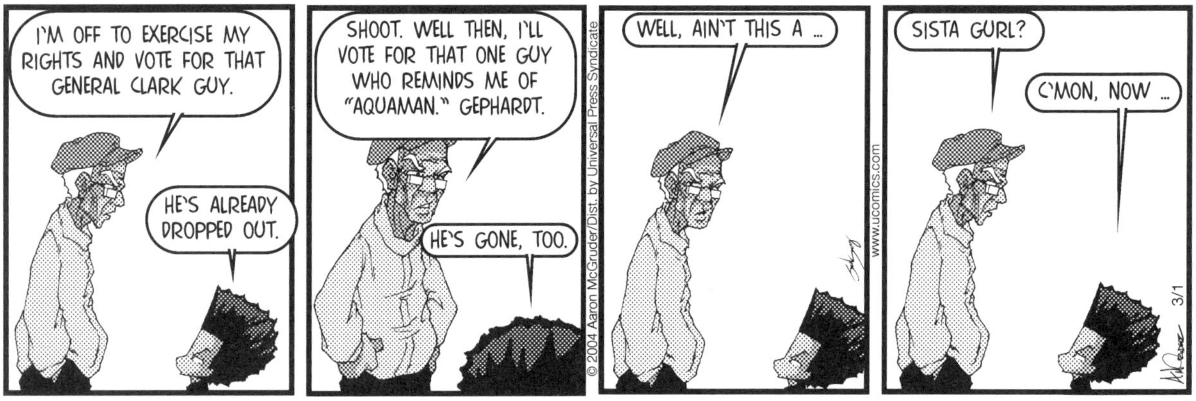
I'M OFF TO EXERCISE MY RIGHTS AND VOTE FOR THAT GENERAL CLARK GUY.
HE'S ALREADY DROPPED OUT.
SHOOT. WELL THEN, I'LL VOTE FOR THAT ONE GUY WHO REMINDS ME OF "AQUAMAN." GEPHARDT.
HE'S GONE, TOO.
WELL, AIN'T THIS A ...
SISTA GURL?
C'MON, NOW ...
3/1
© 2004 Aaron McGruder/Dist. by Universal Press Syndicate
www.ucomics.com

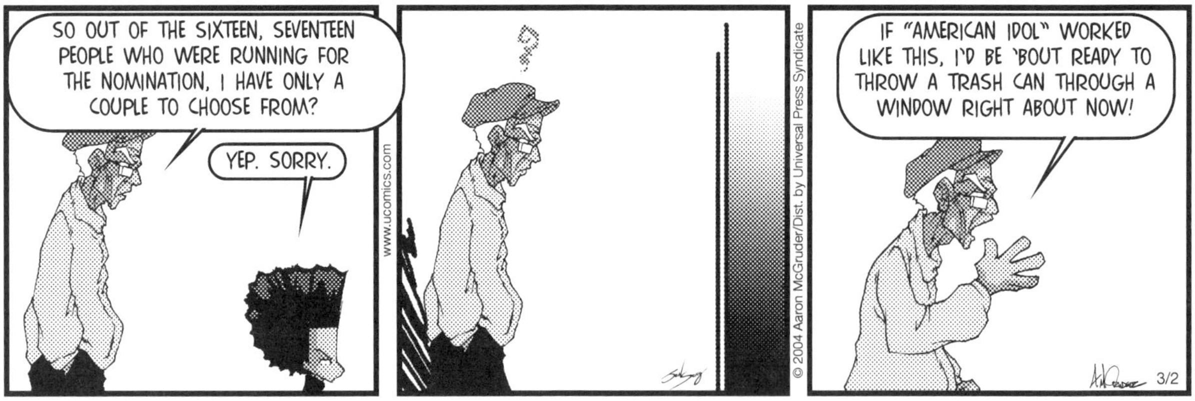
SO OUT OF THE SIXTEEN, SEVENTEEN PEOPLE WHO WERE RUNNING FOR THE NOMINATION, I HAVE ONLY A COUPLE TO CHOOSE FROM?
YEP. SORRY.
?
IF "AMERICAN IDOL" WORKED LIKE THIS, I'D BE 'BOUT READY TO THROW A TRASH CAN THROUGH A WINDOW RIGHT ABOUT NOW!
3/2
www.ucomics.com
© 2004 Aaron McGruder/Dist. by Universal Press Syndicate

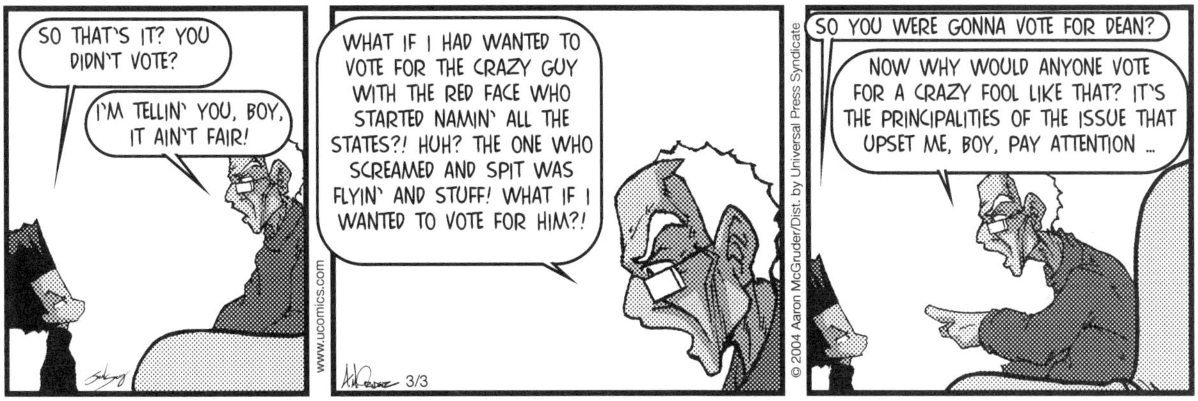
SO THAT'S IT? YOU DIDN'T VOTE?
I'M TELLIN' YOU, BOY, IT AIN'T FAIR!
www.ucomics.com
WHAT IF I HAD WANTED TO VOTE FOR THE CRAZY GUY WITH THE RED FACE WHO STARTED NAMIN' ALL THE STATES?! HUH? THE ONE WHO SCREAMED AND SPIT WAS FLYIN' AND STUFF! WHAT IF I WANTED TO VOTE FOR HIM?!
3/3
© 2004 Aaron McGruder/Dist. by Universal Press Syndicate
SO YOU WERE GONNA VOTE FOR DEAN?
NOW WHY WOULD ANYONE VOTE FOR A CRAZY FOOL LIKE THAT? IT'S THE PRINCIPALITIES OF THE ISSUE THAT UPSET ME, BOY, PAY ATTENTION ...

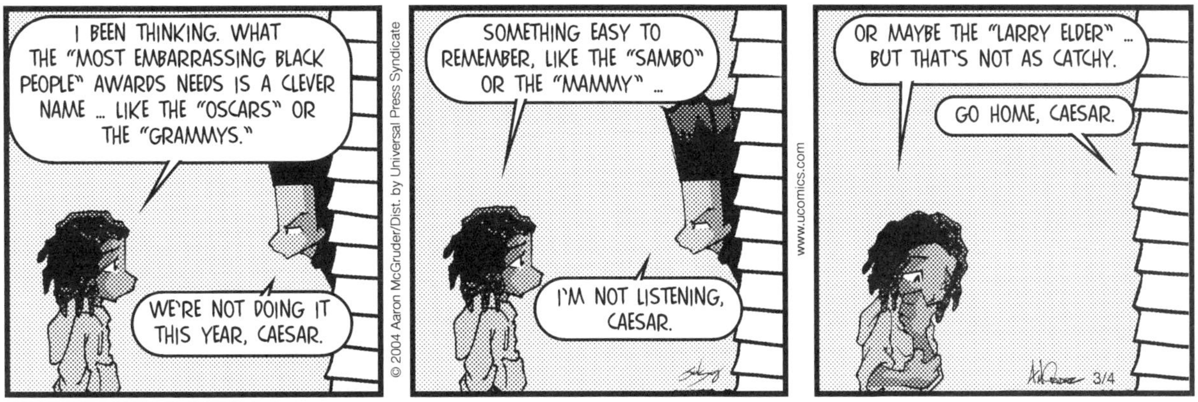
I BEEN THINKING. WHAT THE "MOST EMBARRASSING BLACK PEOPLE" AWARDS NEEDS IS A CLEVER NAME ... LIKE THE "OSCARS" OR THE "GRAMMYS."
WE'RE NOT DOING IT THIS YEAR, CAESAR.
© 2004 Aaron McGruder/Dist. by Universal Press Syndicate
SOMETHING EASY TO REMEMBER, LIKE THE "SAMBO" OR THE "MAMMY" ...
I'M NOT LISTENING, CAESAR.
www.ucomics.com
OR MAYBE THE "LARRY ELDER" ... BUT THAT'S NOT AS CATCHY.
GO HOME, CAESAR.
3/4

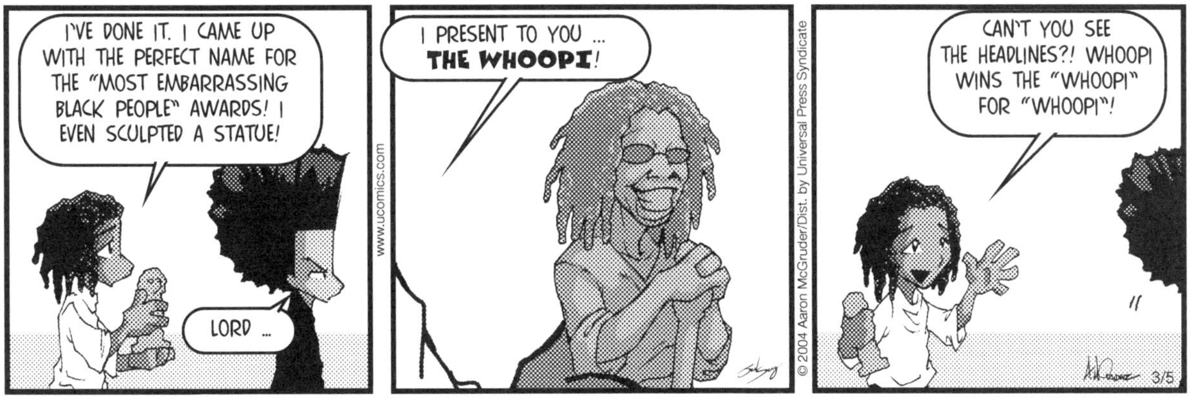
I'VE DONE IT. I CAME UP WITH THE PERFECT NAME FOR THE "MOST EMBARRASSING BLACK PEOPLE" AWARDS! I EVEN SCULPTED A STATUE!
LORD ...
www.ucomics.com
I PRESENT TO YOU ... THE WHOOPI!
© 2004 Aaron McGruder/Dist. by Universal Press Syndicate
CAN'T YOU SEE THE HEADLINES?! WHOOPI WINS THE "WHOOPI" FOR "WHOOPI"!
3/5

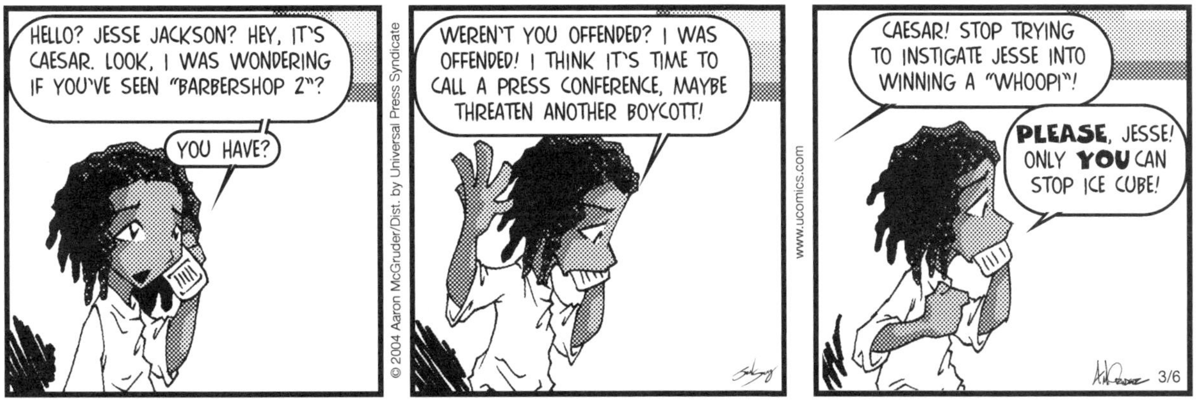
HELLO? JESSE JACKSON? HEY, IT'S CAESAR. LOOK, I WAS WONDERING IF YOU'VE SEEN "BARBERSHOP 2"?
YOU HAVE?
© 2004 Aaron McGruder/Dist. by Universal Press Syndicate
WEREN'T YOU OFFENDED? I WAS OFFENDED! I THINK IT'S TIME TO CALL A PRESS CONFERENCE, MAYBE THREATEN ANOTHER BOYCOTT!
www.ucomics.com
CAESAR! STOP TRYING TO INSTIGATE JESSE INTO WINNING A "WHOOPI"!
PLEASE, JESSE! ONLY YOU CAN STOP ICE CUBE!
3/6

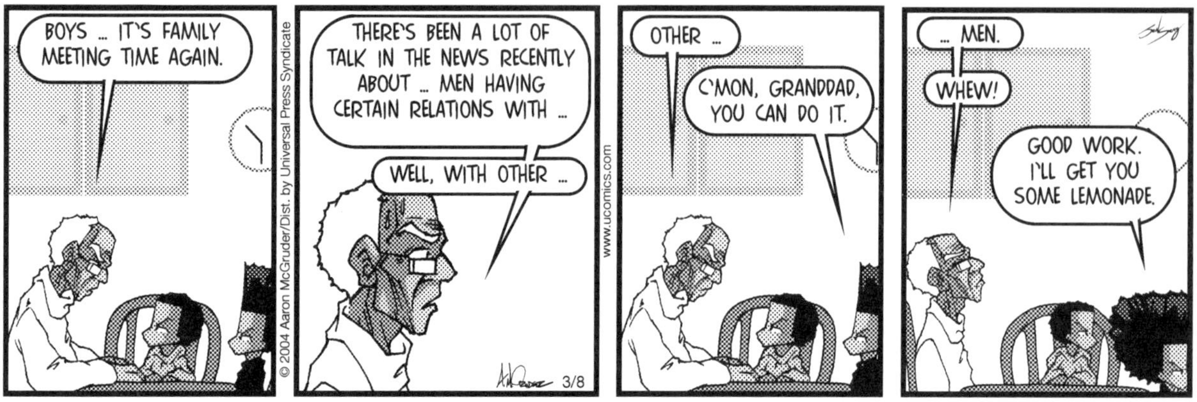
BOYS ... IT'S FAMILY MEETING TIME AGAIN.
© 2004 Aaron McGruder/Dist. by Universal Press Syndicate
THERE'S BEEN A LOT OF TALK IN THE NEWS RECENTLY ABOUT ... MEN HAVING CERTAIN RELATIONS WITH ...
WELL, WITH OTHER ...
3/8
www.ucomics.com
OTHER ...
C'MON, GRANDDAD, YOU CAN DO IT.
... MEN.
WHEW!
GOOD WORK. I'LL GET YOU SOME LEMONADE.

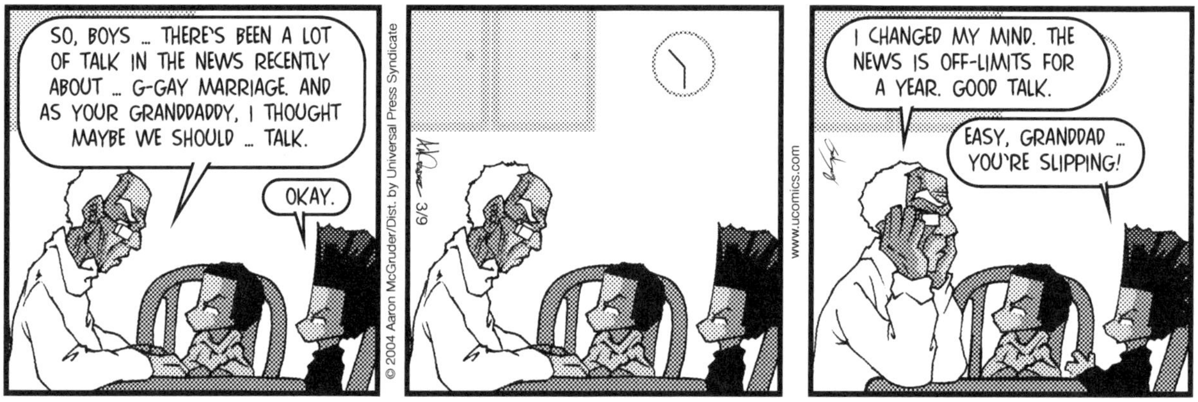
SO, BOYS ... THERE'S BEEN A LOT OF TALK IN THE NEWS RECENTLY ABOUT ... G-GAY MARRIAGE. AND AS YOUR GRANDDADDY, I THOUGHT MAYBE WE SHOULD ... TALK.
OKAY.
© 2004 Aaron McGruder/Dist. by Universal Press Syndicate
3/9
www.ucomics.com
I CHANGED MY MIND. THE NEWS IS OFF-LIMITS FOR A YEAR. GOOD TALK.
EASY, GRANDDAD ... YOU'RE SLIPPING!

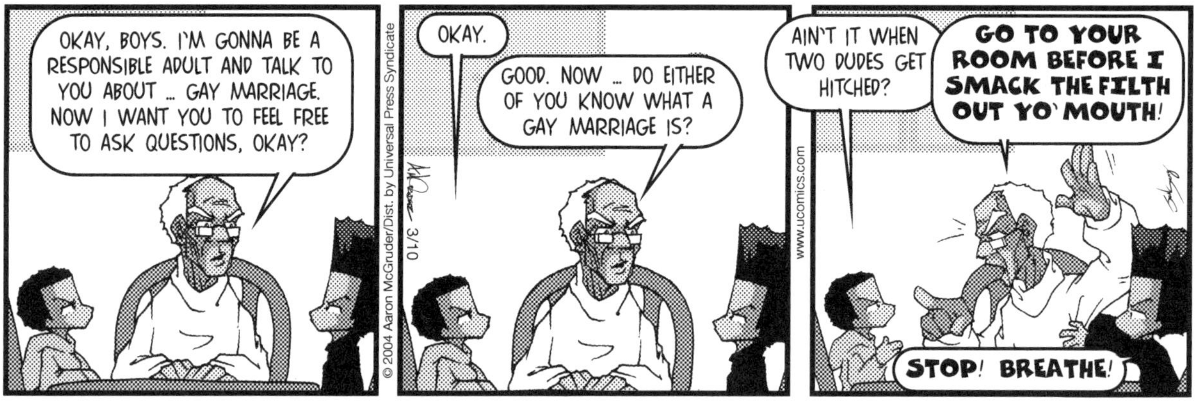
OKAY, BOYS. I'M GONNA BE A RESPONSIBLE ADULT AND TALK TO YOU ABOUT ... GAY MARRIAGE. NOW I WANT YOU TO FEEL FREE TO ASK QUESTIONS, OKAY?
© 2004 Aaron McGruder/Dist. by Universal Press Syndicate
OKAY.
GOOD. NOW ... DO EITHER OF YOU KNOW WHAT A GAY MARRIAGE IS?
3/10
www.ucomics.com
AIN'T IT WHEN TWO DUDES GET HITCHED?
GO TO YOUR ROOM BEFORE I SMACK THE FILTH OUT YO' MOUTH!
STOP! BREATHE!

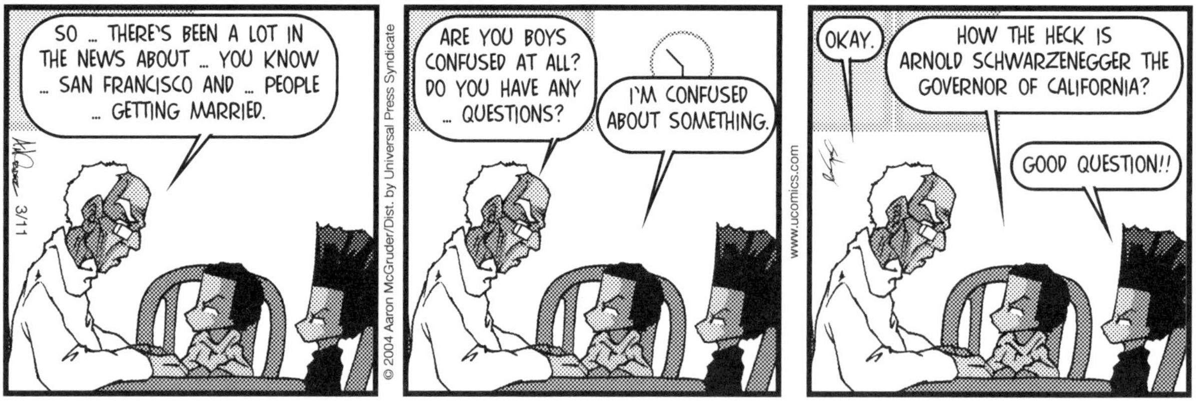
SO ... THERE'S BEEN A LOT IN THE NEWS ABOUT ... YOU KNOW ... SAN FRANCISCO AND ... PEOPLE ... GETTING MARRIED.
3/11
© 2004 Aaron McGruder/Dist. by Universal Press Syndicate
ARE YOU BOYS CONFUSED AT ALL? DO YOU HAVE ANY ... QUESTIONS?
I'M CONFUSED ABOUT SOMETHING.
www.ucomics.com
OKAY.
HOW THE HECK IS ARNOLD SCHWARZENEGGER THE GOVERNOR OF CALIFORNIA?
GOOD QUESTION!!

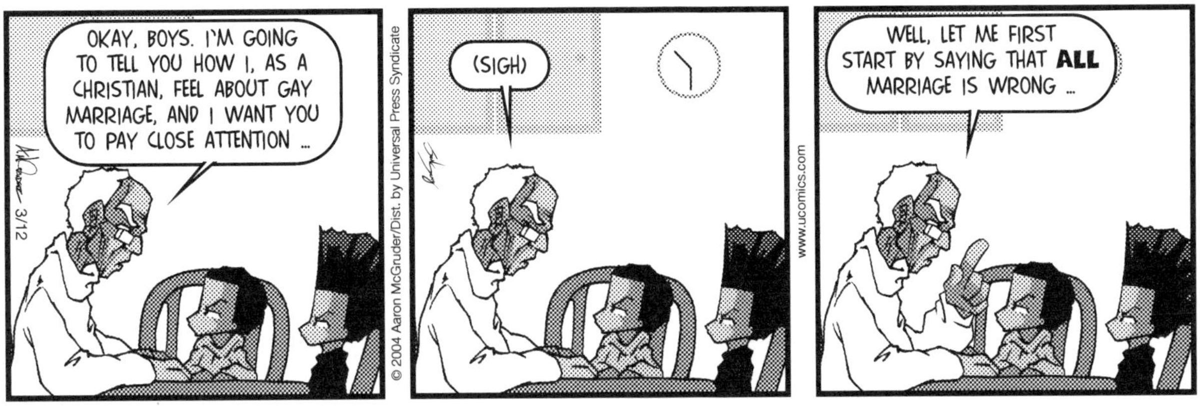
OKAY, BOYS. I'M GOING TO TELL YOU HOW I, AS A CHRISTIAN, FEEL ABOUT GAY MARRIAGE, AND I WANT YOU TO PAY CLOSE ATTENTION ...
3/12
© 2004 Aaron McGruder/Dist. by Universal Press Syndicate
(SIGH)
www.ucomics.com
WELL, LET ME FIRST START BY SAYING THAT **ALL** MARRIAGE IS WRONG ...

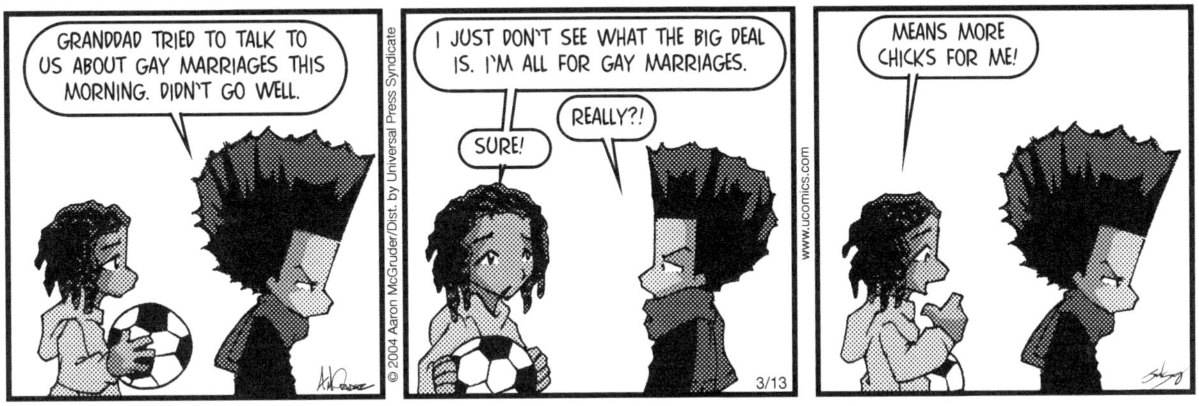
GRANDDAD TRIED TO TALK TO US ABOUT GAY MARRIAGES THIS MORNING. DIDN'T GO WELL.
© 2004 Aaron McGruder/Dist. by Universal Press Syndicate
I JUST DON'T SEE WHAT THE BIG DEAL IS. I'M ALL FOR GAY MARRIAGES.
SURE!
REALLY?!
3/13
www.ucomics.com
MEANS MORE CHICKS FOR ME!

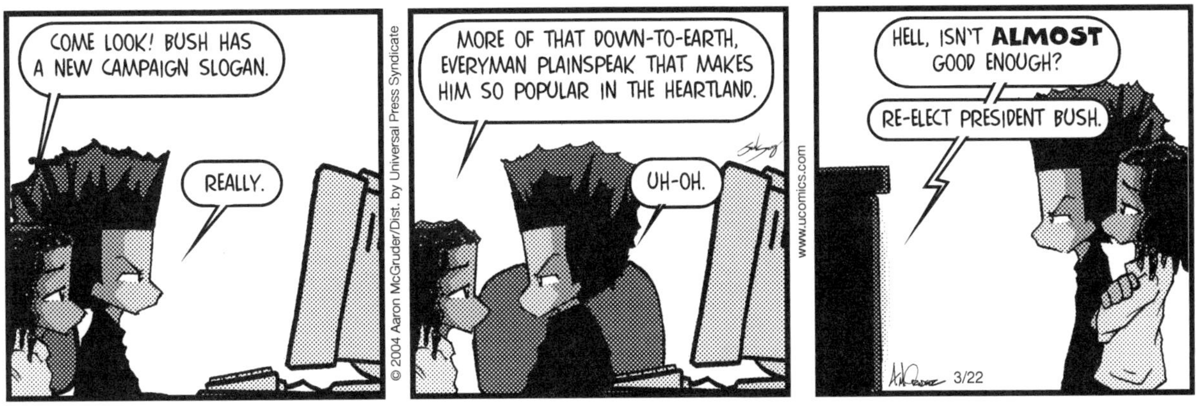
COME LOOK! BUSH HAS A NEW CAMPAIGN SLOGAN.
REALLY.
© 2004 Aaron McGruder/Dist. by Universal Press Syndicate
MORE OF THAT DOWN-TO-EARTH, EVERYMAN PLAINSPEAK THAT MAKES HIM SO POPULAR IN THE HEARTLAND.
UH-OH.
www.ucomics.com
HELL, ISN'T **ALMOST** GOOD ENOUGH?
RE-ELECT PRESIDENT BUSH.
3/22

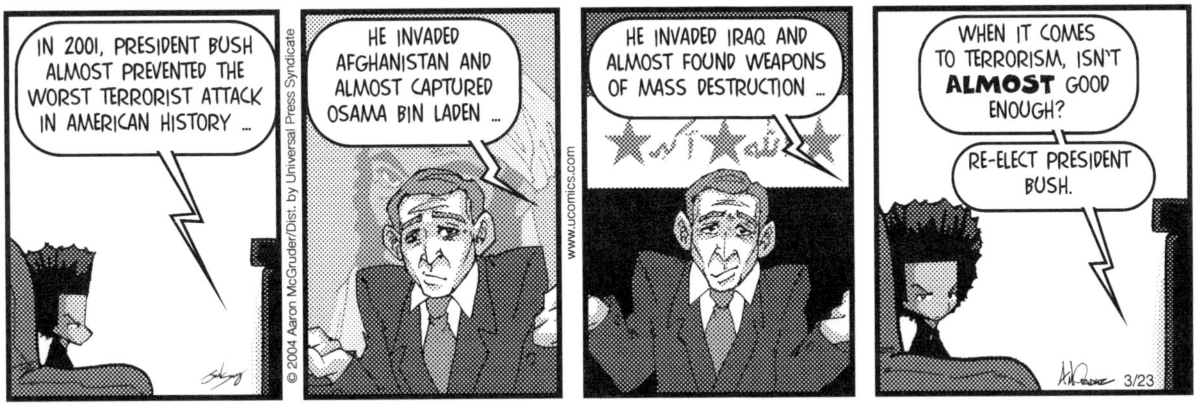
IN 2001, PRESIDENT BUSH ALMOST PREVENTED THE WORST TERRORIST ATTACK IN AMERICAN HISTORY ...
© 2004 Aaron McGruder/Dist. by Universal Press Syndicate
HE INVADED AFGHANISTAN AND ALMOST CAPTURED OSAMA BIN LADEN ...
www.ucomics.com
HE INVADED IRAQ AND ALMOST FOUND WEAPONS OF MASS DESTRUCTION ...
WHEN IT COMES TO TERRORISM, ISN'T **ALMOST** GOOD ENOUGH?
RE-ELECT PRESIDENT BUSH.
3/23

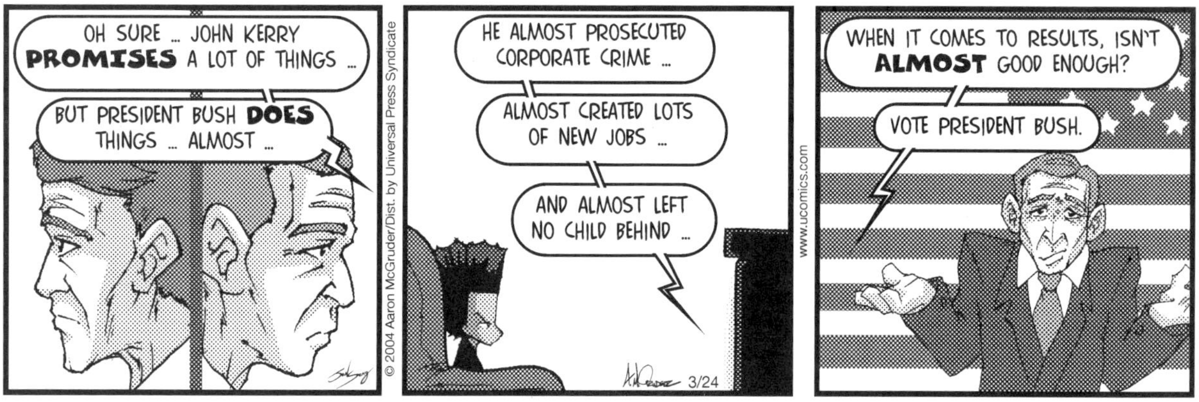
OH SURE ... JOHN KERRY **PROMISES** A LOT OF THINGS ...
BUT PRESIDENT BUSH **DOES** THINGS ... ALMOST ...
© 2004 Aaron McGruder/Dist. by Universal Press Syndicate
HE ALMOST PROSECUTED CORPORATE CRIME ...
ALMOST CREATED LOTS OF NEW JOBS ...
AND ALMOST LEFT NO CHILD BEHIND ...
3/24
www.ucomics.com
WHEN IT COMES TO RESULTS, ISN'T **ALMOST** GOOD ENOUGH?
VOTE PRESIDENT BUSH.

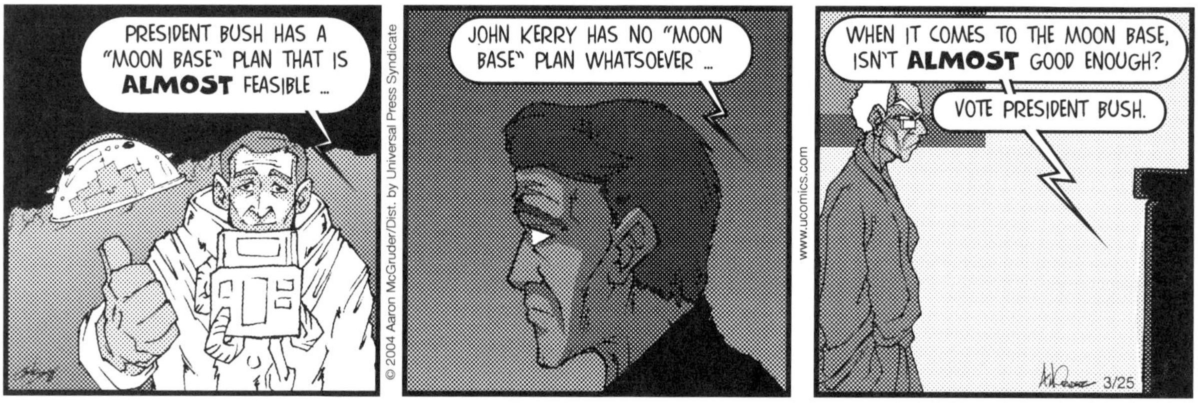
PRESIDENT BUSH HAS A "MOON BASE" PLAN THAT IS **ALMOST** FEASIBLE ...
© 2004 Aaron McGruder/Dist. by Universal Press Syndicate
JOHN KERRY HAS NO "MOON BASE" PLAN WHATSOEVER ...
www.ucomics.com
WHEN IT COMES TO THE MOON BASE, ISN'T **ALMOST** GOOD ENOUGH?
VOTE PRESIDENT BUSH.
3/25

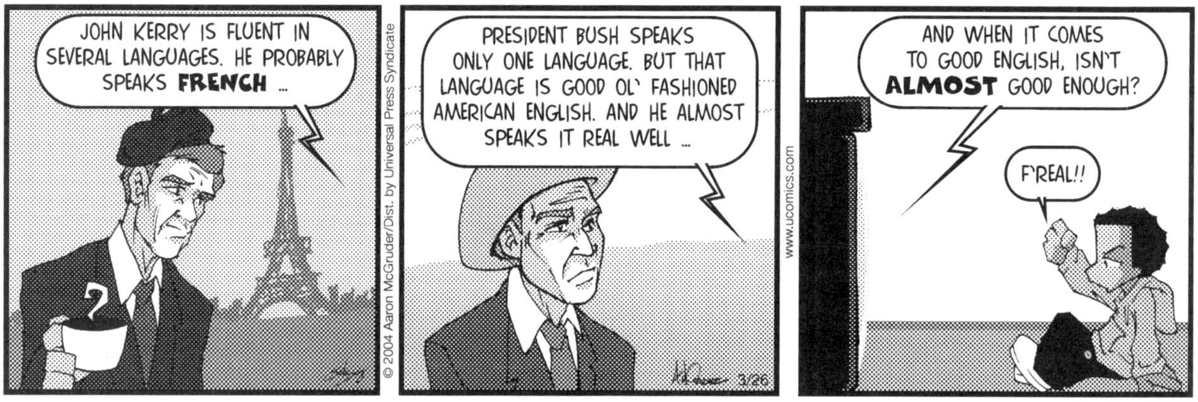
JOHN KERRY IS FLUENT IN SEVERAL LANGUAGES. HE PROBABLY SPEAKS **FRENCH** ...
© 2004 Aaron McGruder/Dist. by Universal Press Syndicate
PRESIDENT BUSH SPEAKS ONLY ONE LANGUAGE. BUT THAT LANGUAGE IS GOOD OL' FASHIONED AMERICAN ENGLISH. AND HE ALMOST SPEAKS IT REAL WELL ...
3/26
www.ucomics.com
AND WHEN IT COMES TO GOOD ENGLISH, ISN'T **ALMOST** GOOD ENOUGH?
F'REAL!!

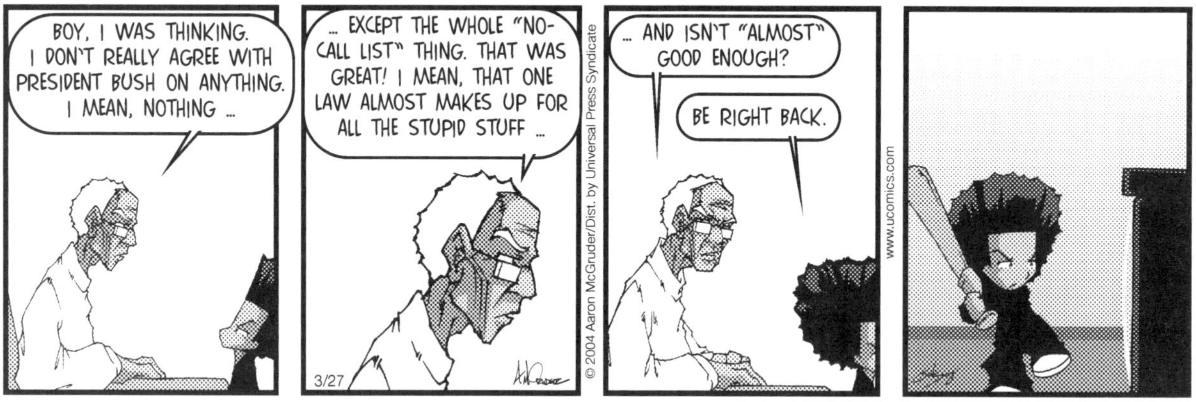
BOY, I WAS THINKING. I DON'T REALLY AGREE WITH PRESIDENT BUSH ON ANYTHING. I MEAN, NOTHING ...
... EXCEPT THE WHOLE "NO-CALL LIST" THING. THAT WAS GREAT! I MEAN, THAT ONE LAW ALMOST MAKES UP FOR ALL THE STUPID STUFF ...
3/27
© 2004 Aaron McGruder/Dist. by Universal Press Syndicate
... AND ISN'T "ALMOST" GOOD ENOUGH?
BE RIGHT BACK.
www.ucomics.com

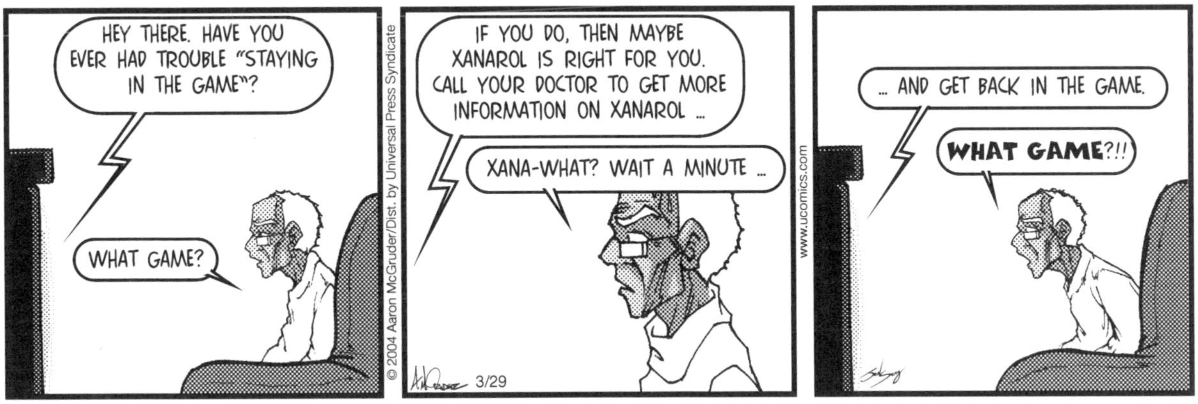
HEY THERE. HAVE YOU EVER HAD TROUBLE "STAYING IN THE GAME"?
WHAT GAME?
© 2004 Aaron McGruder/Dist. by Universal Press Syndicate
3/29
IF YOU DO, THEN MAYBE XANAROL IS RIGHT FOR YOU. CALL YOUR DOCTOR TO GET MORE INFORMATION ON XANAROL ...
XANA-WHAT? WAIT A MINUTE ...
www.ucomics.com
... AND GET BACK IN THE GAME.
WHAT GAME?!!

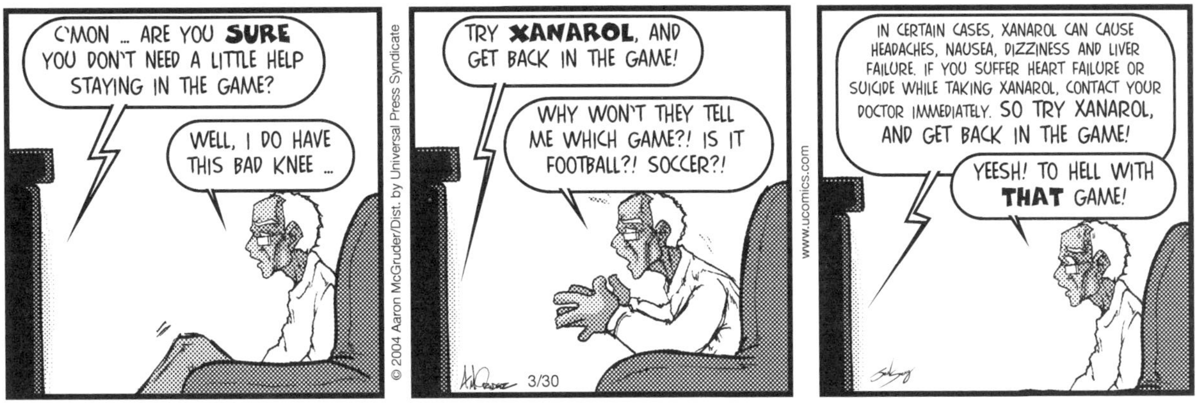
C'MON ... ARE YOU SURE YOU DON'T NEED A LITTLE HELP STAYING IN THE GAME?
WELL, I DO HAVE THIS BAD KNEE ...
© 2004 Aaron McGruder/Dist. by Universal Press Syndicate
TRY XANAROL, AND GET BACK IN THE GAME!
WHY WON'T THEY TELL ME WHICH GAME?! IS IT FOOTBALL?! SOCCER?!
3/30
www.ucomics.com
IN CERTAIN CASES, XANAROL CAN CAUSE HEADACHES, NAUSEA, DIZZINESS AND LIVER FAILURE. IF YOU SUFFER HEART FAILURE OR SUICIDE WHILE TAKING XANAROL, CONTACT YOUR DOCTOR IMMEDIATELY. SO TRY XANAROL, AND GET BACK IN THE GAME!
YEESH! TO HELL WITH THAT GAME!

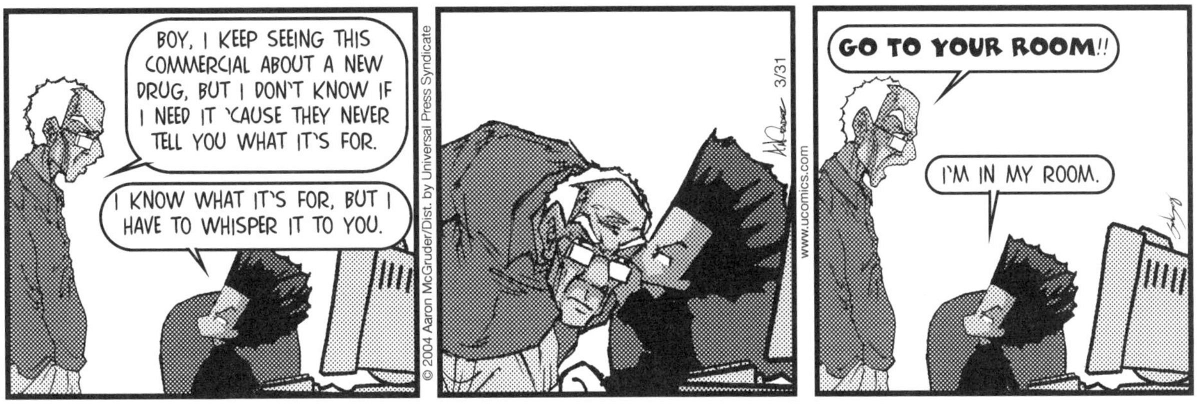
BOY, I KEEP SEEING THIS COMMERCIAL ABOUT A NEW DRUG, BUT I DON'T KNOW IF I NEED IT 'CAUSE THEY NEVER TELL YOU WHAT IT'S FOR.
I KNOW WHAT IT'S FOR, BUT I HAVE TO WHISPER IT TO YOU.
© 2004 Aaron McGruder/Dist. by Universal Press Syndicate
3/31
www.ucomics.com
GO TO YOUR ROOM!!
I'M IN MY ROOM.

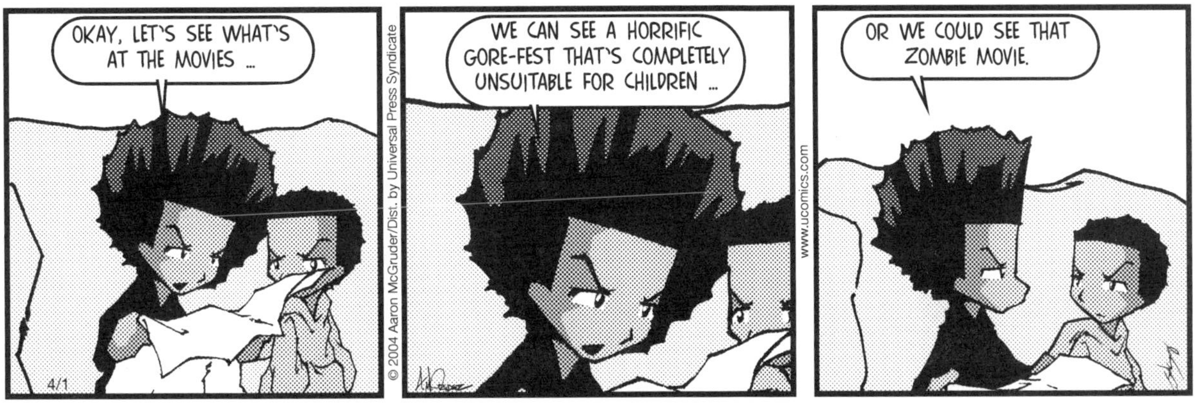
OKAY, LET'S SEE WHAT'S AT THE MOVIES ...
4/1
© 2004 Aaron McGruder/Dist. by Universal Press Syndicate
WE CAN SEE A HORRIFIC GORE-FEST THAT'S COMPLETELY UNSUITABLE FOR CHILDREN ...
www.ucomics.com
OR WE COULD SEE THAT ZOMBIE MOVIE.

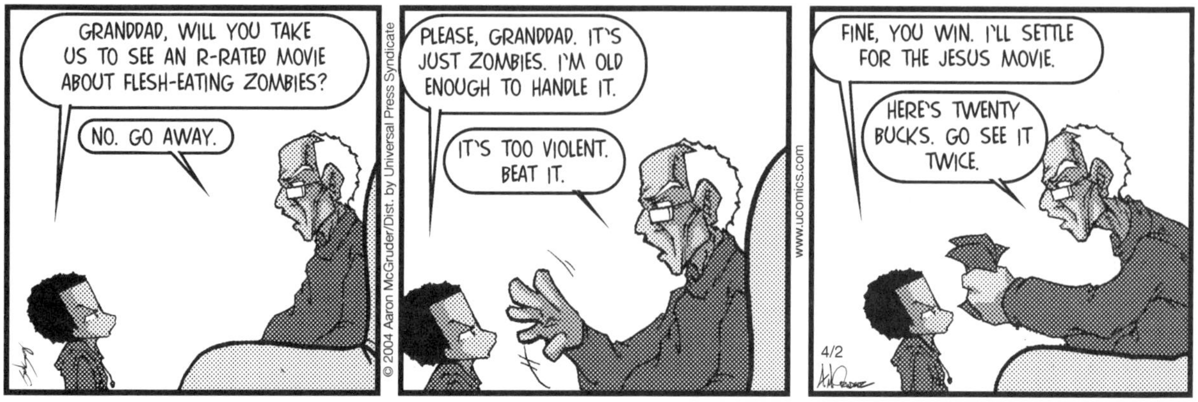
GRANDDAD, WILL YOU TAKE US TO SEE AN R-RATED MOVIE ABOUT FLESH-EATING ZOMBIES?
NO. GO AWAY.
© 2004 Aaron McGruder/Dist. by Universal Press Syndicate
PLEASE, GRANDDAD. IT'S JUST ZOMBIES. I'M OLD ENOUGH TO HANDLE IT.
IT'S TOO VIOLENT. BEAT IT.
www.ucomics.com
FINE, YOU WIN. I'LL SETTLE FOR THE JESUS MOVIE.
HERE'S TWENTY BUCKS. GO SEE IT TWICE.
4/2

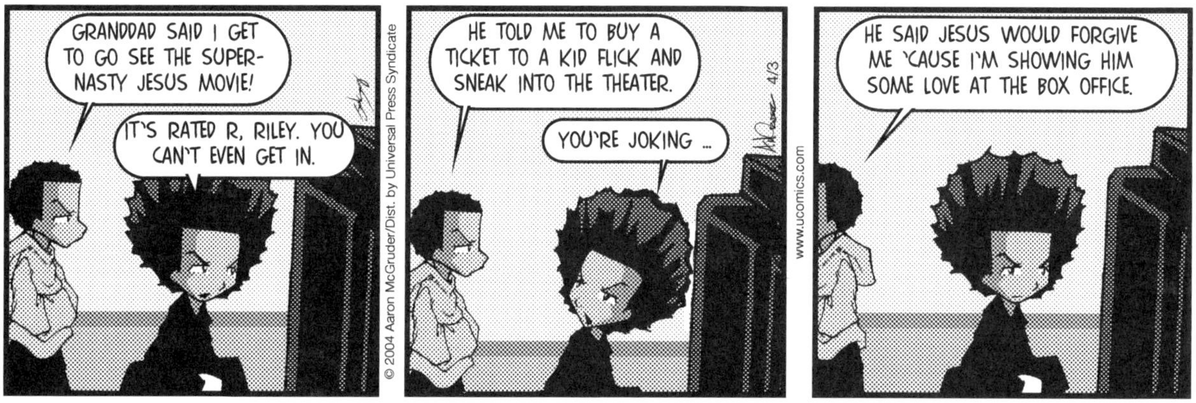
GRANDDAD SAID I GET TO GO SEE THE SUPER-NASTY JESUS MOVIE!
IT'S RATED R, RILEY. YOU CAN'T EVEN GET IN.
© 2004 Aaron McGruder/Dist. by Universal Press Syndicate
HE TOLD ME TO BUY A TICKET TO A KID FLICK AND SNEAK INTO THE THEATER.
YOU'RE JOKING ...
4/3
www.ucomics.com
HE SAID JESUS WOULD FORGIVE ME 'CAUSE I'M SHOWING HIM SOME LOVE AT THE BOX OFFICE.

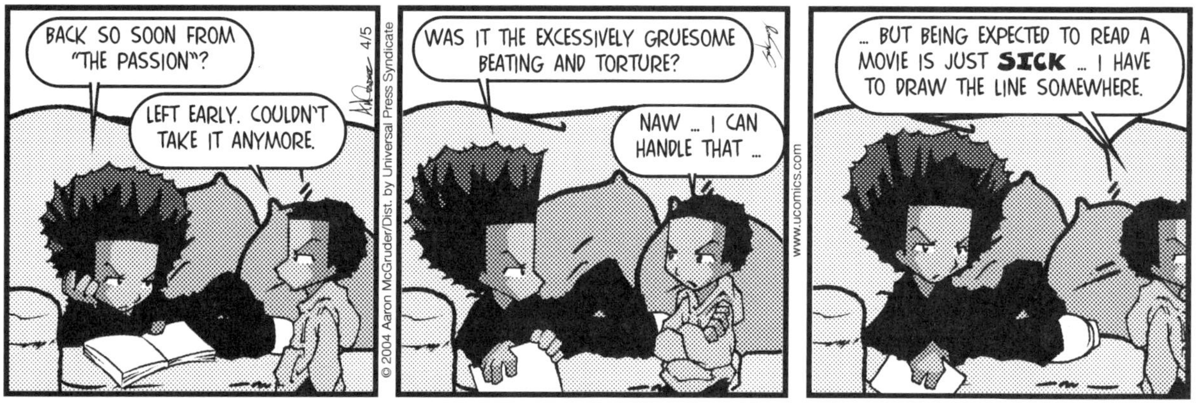
BACK SO SOON FROM "THE PASSION"?
LEFT EARLY. COULDN'T TAKE IT ANYMORE.
4/5
© 2004 Aaron McGruder/Dist. by Universal Press Syndicate
WAS IT THE EXCESSIVELY GRUESOME BEATING AND TORTURE?
NAW ... I CAN HANDLE THAT ...
www.ucomics.com
... BUT BEING EXPECTED TO READ A MOVIE IS JUST SICK ... I HAVE TO DRAW THE LINE SOMEWHERE.

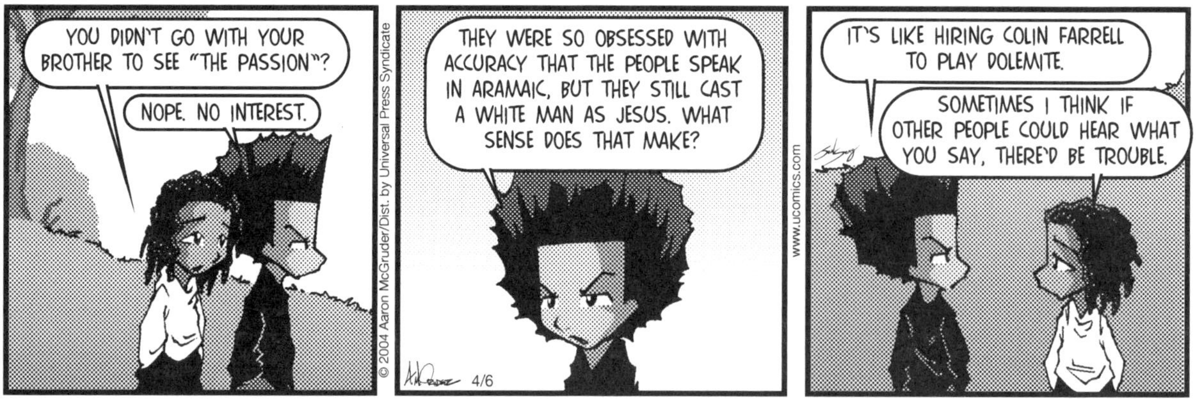
YOU DIDN'T GO WITH YOUR BROTHER TO SEE "THE PASSION"?
NOPE. NO INTEREST.
© 2004 Aaron McGruder/Dist. by Universal Press Syndicate
THEY WERE SO OBSESSED WITH ACCURACY THAT THE PEOPLE SPEAK IN ARAMAIC, BUT THEY STILL CAST A WHITE MAN AS JESUS. WHAT SENSE DOES THAT MAKE?
4/6
www.ucomics.com
IT'S LIKE HIRING COLIN FARRELL TO PLAY DOLEMITE.
SOMETIMES I THINK IF OTHER PEOPLE COULD HEAR WHAT YOU SAY, THERE'D BE TROUBLE.

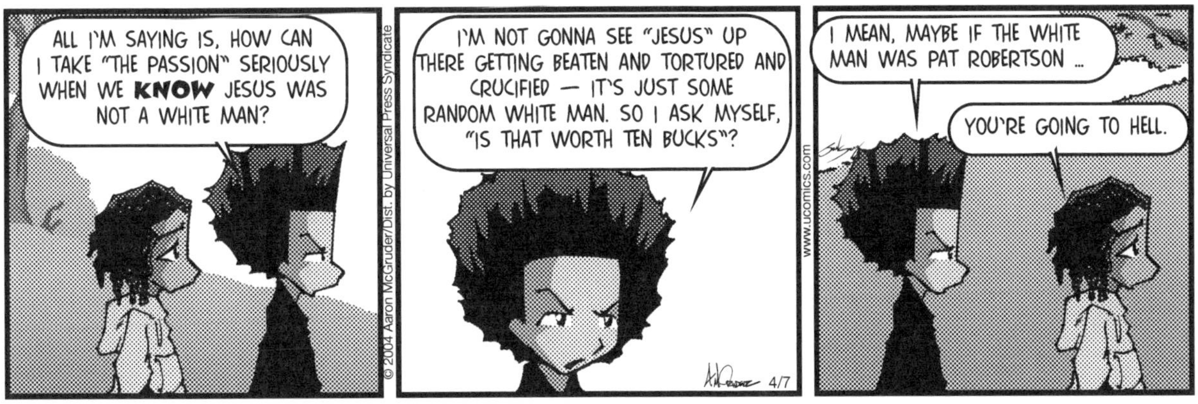
ALL I'M SAYING IS, HOW CAN I TAKE "THE PASSION" SERIOUSLY WHEN WE **KNOW** JESUS WAS NOT A WHITE MAN?
I'M NOT GONNA SEE "JESUS" UP THERE GETTING BEATEN AND TORTURED AND CRUCIFIED — IT'S JUST SOME RANDOM WHITE MAN. SO I ASK MYSELF, "IS THAT WORTH TEN BUCKS"?
I MEAN, MAYBE IF THE WHITE MAN WAS PAT ROBERTSON ...
YOU'RE GOING TO HELL.
© 2004 Aaron McGruder/Dist. by Universal Press Syndicate
www.ucomics.com

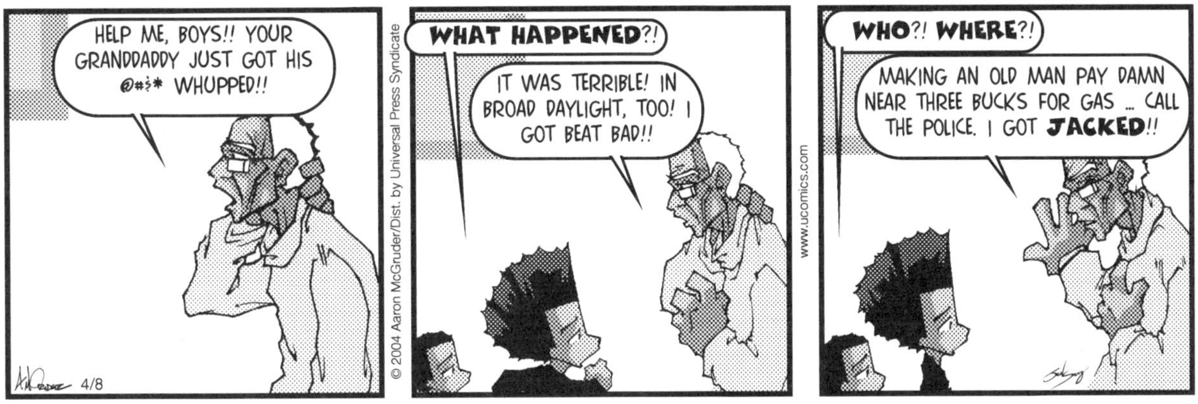
HELP ME, BOYS!! YOUR GRANDDADDY JUST GOT HIS @#$* WHUPPED!!
WHAT HAPPENED?!
IT WAS TERRIBLE! IN BROAD DAYLIGHT, TOO! I GOT BEAT BAD!!
WHO?! **WHERE**?!
MAKING AN OLD MAN PAY DAMN NEAR THREE BUCKS FOR GAS ... CALL THE POLICE. I GOT **JACKED**!!
© 2004 Aaron McGruder/Dist. by Universal Press Syndicate
www.ucomics.com

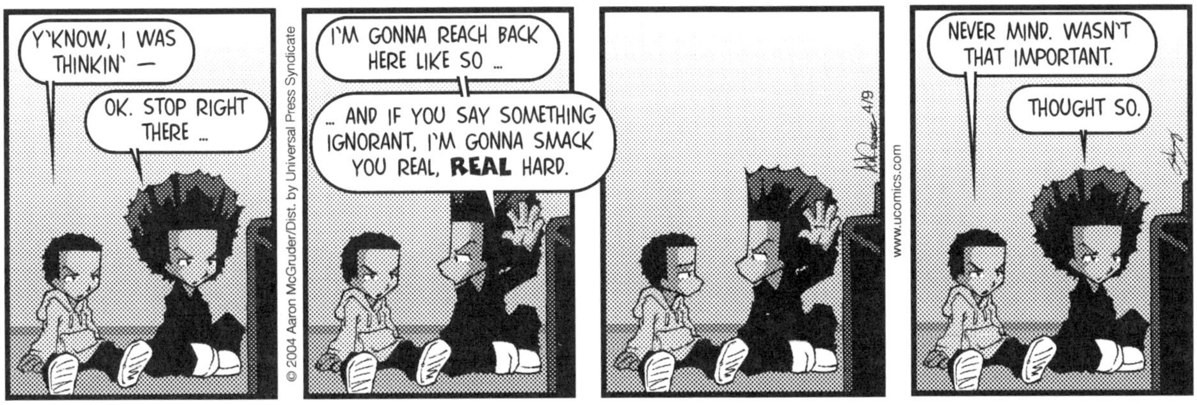
Y'KNOW, I WAS THINKIN' —
OK. STOP RIGHT THERE ...
I'M GONNA REACH BACK HERE LIKE SO ...
... AND IF YOU SAY SOMETHING IGNORANT, I'M GONNA SMACK YOU REAL, **REAL** HARD.
NEVER MIND. WASN'T THAT IMPORTANT.
THOUGHT SO.
© 2004 Aaron McGruder/Dist. by Universal Press Syndicate
www.ucomics.com

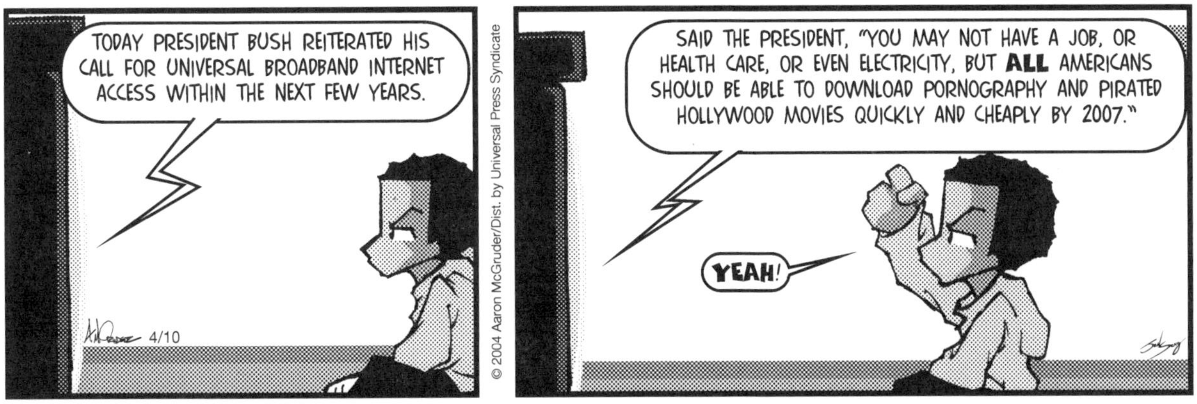
TODAY PRESIDENT BUSH REITERATED HIS CALL FOR UNIVERSAL BROADBAND INTERNET ACCESS WITHIN THE NEXT FEW YEARS.
SAID THE PRESIDENT, "YOU MAY NOT HAVE A JOB, OR HEALTH CARE, OR EVEN ELECTRICITY, BUT **ALL** AMERICANS SHOULD BE ABLE TO DOWNLOAD PORNOGRAPHY AND PIRATED HOLLYWOOD MOVIES QUICKLY AND CHEAPLY BY 2007."
YEAH!
© 2004 Aaron McGruder/Dist. by Universal Press Syndicate

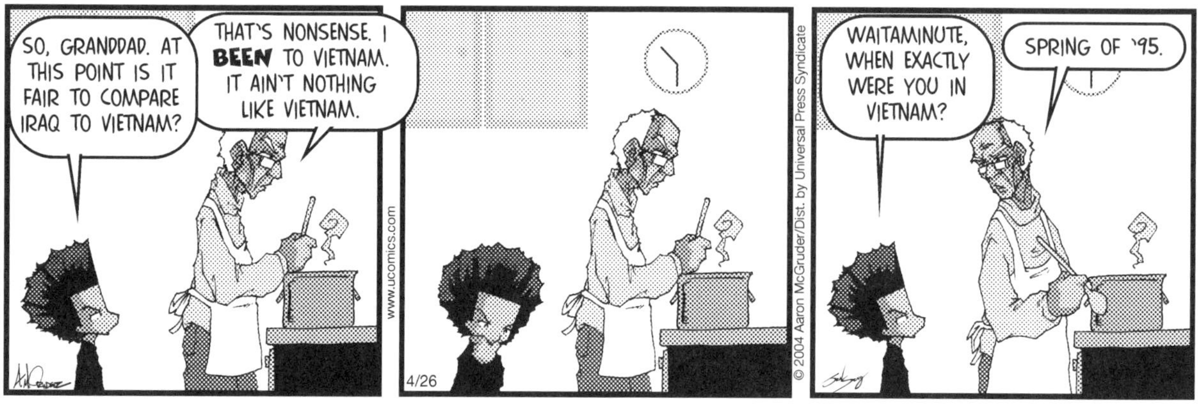
SO, GRANDDAD. AT THIS POINT IS IT FAIR TO COMPARE IRAQ TO VIETNAM?
THAT'S NONSENSE. I **BEEN** TO VIETNAM. IT AIN'T NOTHING LIKE VIETNAM.
WAITAMINUTE, WHEN EXACTLY WERE YOU IN VIETNAM?
SPRING OF '95.
www.ucomics.com
4/26
© 2004 Aaron McGruder/Dist. by Universal Press Syndicate

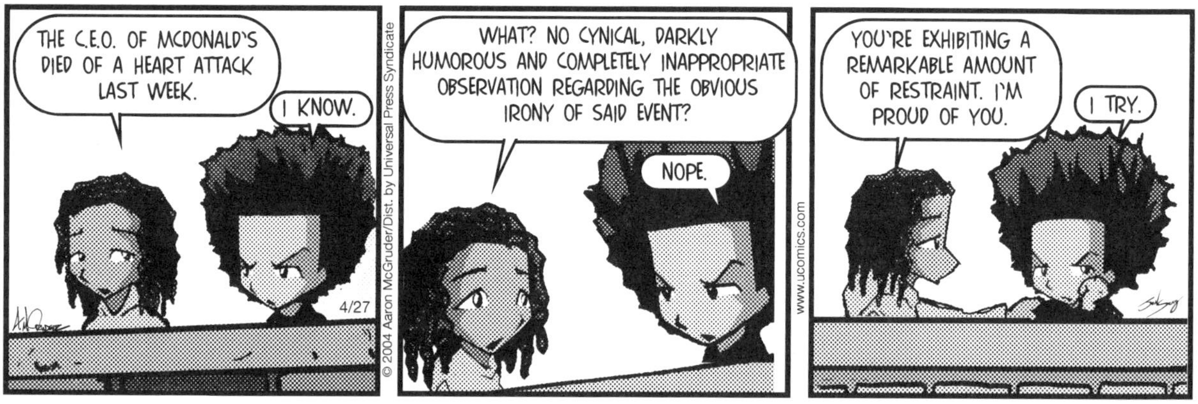
THE C.E.O. OF MCDONALD'S DIED OF A HEART ATTACK LAST WEEK.
I KNOW.
4/27
WHAT? NO CYNICAL, DARKLY HUMOROUS AND COMPLETELY INAPPROPRIATE OBSERVATION REGARDING THE OBVIOUS IRONY OF SAID EVENT?
NOPE.
YOU'RE EXHIBITING A REMARKABLE AMOUNT OF RESTRAINT. I'M PROUD OF YOU.
I TRY.
© 2004 Aaron McGruder/Dist. by Universal Press Syndicate
www.ucomics.com

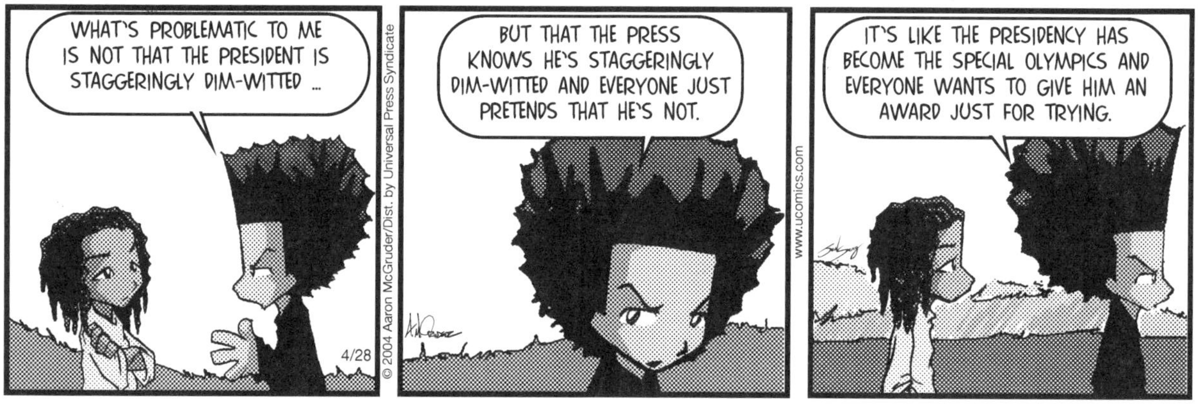
WHAT'S PROBLEMATIC TO ME IS NOT THAT THE PRESIDENT IS STAGGERINGLY DIM-WITTED ...
4/28
BUT THAT THE PRESS KNOWS HE'S STAGGERINGLY DIM-WITTED AND EVERYONE JUST PRETENDS THAT HE'S NOT.
IT'S LIKE THE PRESIDENCY HAS BECOME THE SPECIAL OLYMPICS AND EVERYONE WANTS TO GIVE HIM AN AWARD JUST FOR TRYING.
© 2004 Aaron McGruder/Dist. by Universal Press Syndicate
www.ucomics.com

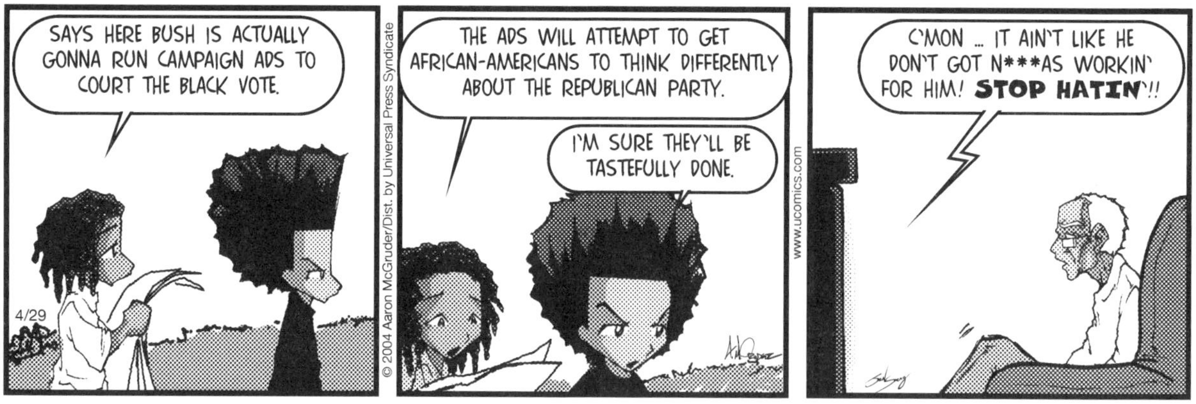
SAYS HERE BUSH IS ACTUALLY GONNA RUN CAMPAIGN ADS TO COURT THE BLACK VOTE.
4/29
THE ADS WILL ATTEMPT TO GET AFRICAN-AMERICANS TO THINK DIFFERENTLY ABOUT THE REPUBLICAN PARTY.
I'M SURE THEY'LL BE TASTEFULLY DONE.
C'MON ... IT AIN'T LIKE HE DON'T GOT N***AS WORKIN' FOR HIM! **STOP HATIN'**!!
© 2004 Aaron McGruder/Dist. by Universal Press Syndicate
www.ucomics.com

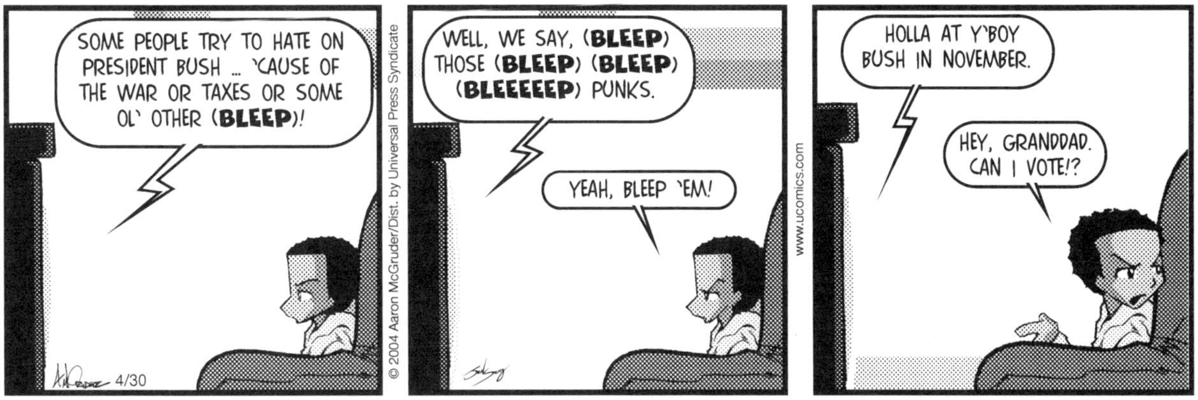
SOME PEOPLE TRY TO HATE ON PRESIDENT BUSH ... 'CAUSE OF THE WAR OR TAXES OR SOME OL' OTHER (BLEEP)!
4/30
© 2004 Aaron McGruder/Dist. by Universal Press Syndicate
WELL, WE SAY, (BLEEP) THOSE (BLEEP) (BLEEP) (BLEEEEEP) PUNKS.
YEAH, BLEEP 'EM!
www.ucomics.com
HOLLA AT Y'BOY BUSH IN NOVEMBER.
HEY, GRANDDAD. CAN I VOTE!?

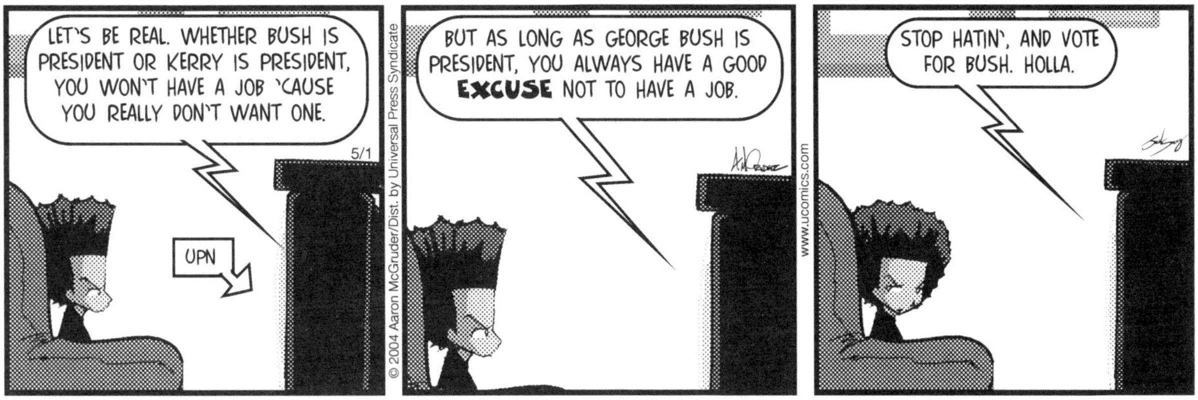
LET'S BE REAL. WHETHER BUSH IS PRESIDENT OR KERRY IS PRESIDENT, YOU WON'T HAVE A JOB 'CAUSE YOU REALLY DON'T WANT ONE.
5/1
UPN
© 2004 Aaron McGruder/Dist. by Universal Press Syndicate
BUT AS LONG AS GEORGE BUSH IS PRESIDENT, YOU ALWAYS HAVE A GOOD EXCUSE NOT TO HAVE A JOB.
www.ucomics.com
STOP HATIN', AND VOTE FOR BUSH. HOLLA.

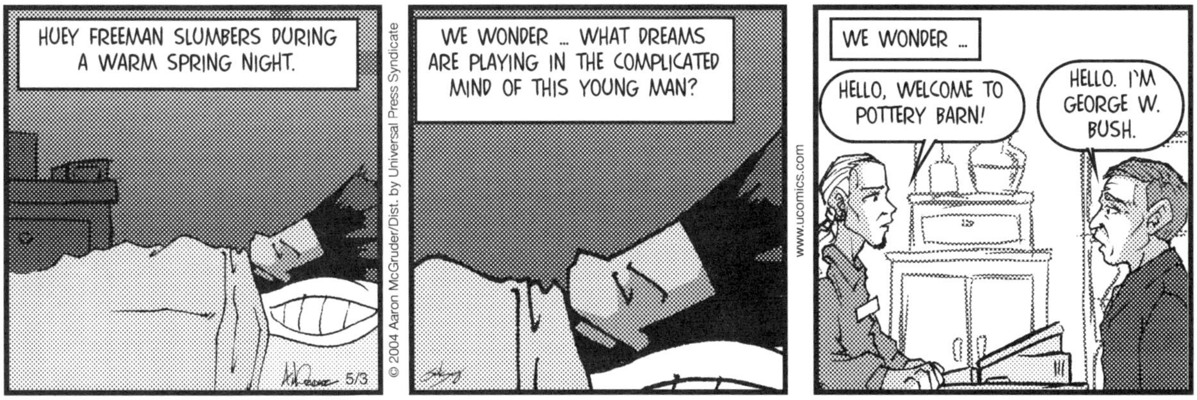
HUEY FREEMAN SLUMBERS DURING A WARM SPRING NIGHT.
5/3
© 2004 Aaron McGruder/Dist. by Universal Press Syndicate
WE WONDER ... WHAT DREAMS ARE PLAYING IN THE COMPLICATED MIND OF THIS YOUNG MAN?
www.ucomics.com
WE WONDER ...
HELLO, WELCOME TO POTTERY BARN!
HELLO. I'M GEORGE W. BUSH.

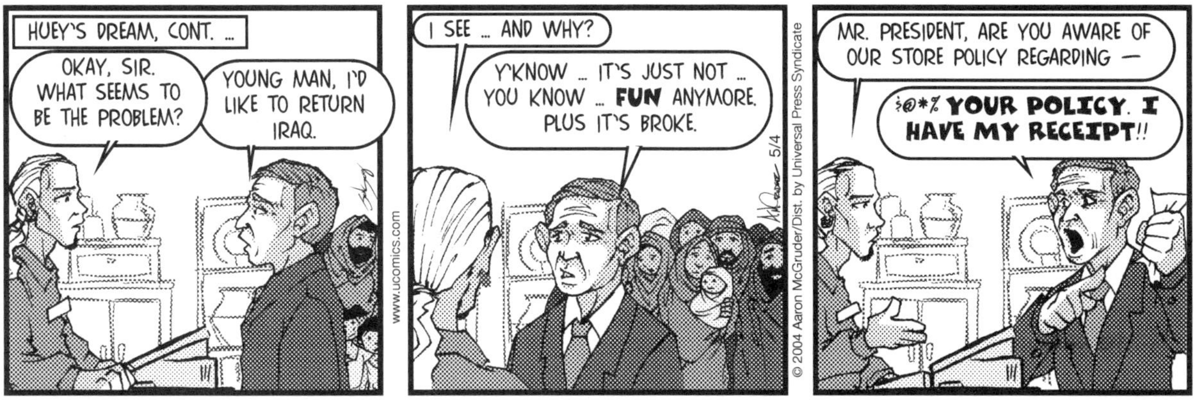
HUEY'S DREAM, CONT. ...
OKAY, SIR. WHAT SEEMS TO BE THE PROBLEM?
YOUNG MAN, I'D LIKE TO RETURN IRAQ.
www.ucomics.com
I SEE ... AND WHY?
Y'KNOW ... IT'S JUST NOT ... YOU KNOW ... FUN ANYMORE. PLUS IT'S BROKE.
5/4
© 2004 Aaron McGruder/Dist. by Universal Press Syndicate
MR. PRESIDENT, ARE YOU AWARE OF OUR STORE POLICY REGARDING —
$@*% YOUR POLICY. I HAVE MY RECEIPT!!

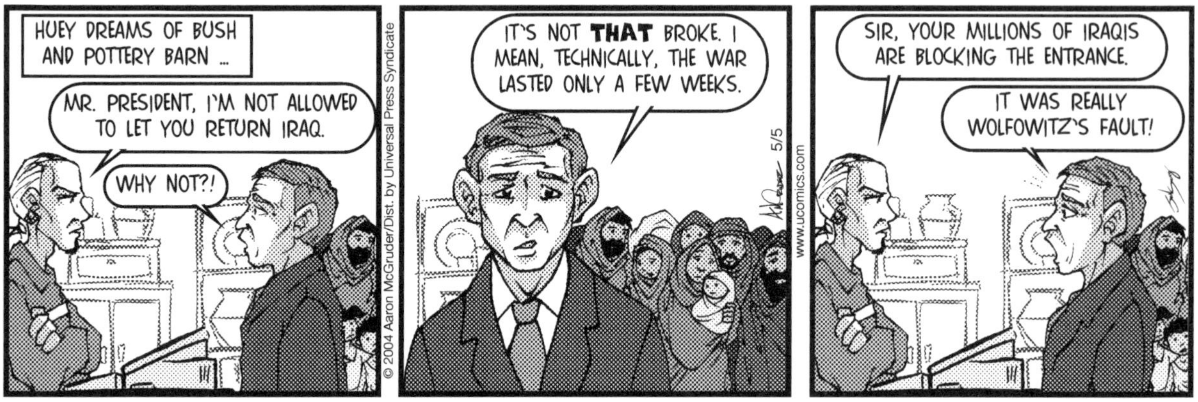
HUEY DREAMS OF BUSH AND POTTERY BARN ...
MR. PRESIDENT, I'M NOT ALLOWED TO LET YOU RETURN IRAQ.
WHY NOT?!
© 2004 Aaron McGruder/Dist. by Universal Press Syndicate
IT'S NOT THAT BROKE. I MEAN, TECHNICALLY, THE WAR LASTED ONLY A FEW WEEKS.
5/5
www.ucomics.com
SIR, YOUR MILLIONS OF IRAQIS ARE BLOCKING THE ENTRANCE.
IT WAS REALLY WOLFOWITZ'S FAULT!

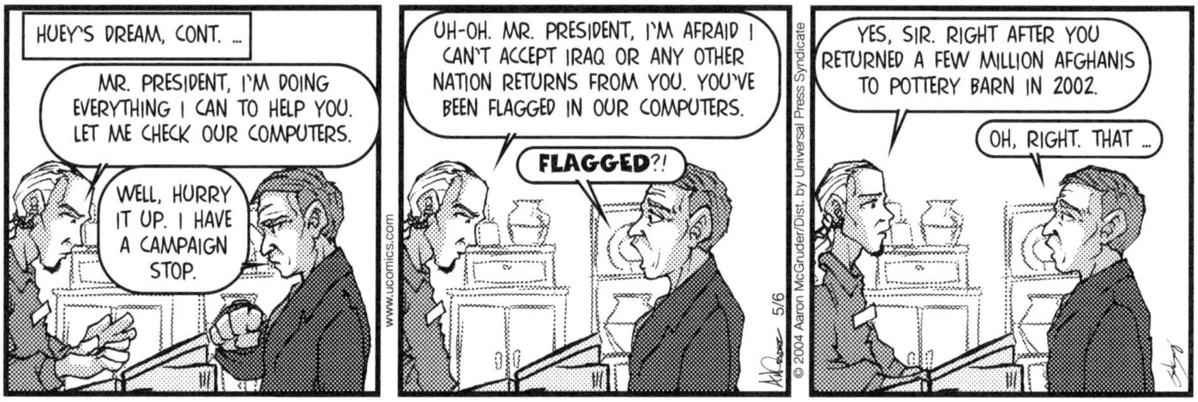
HUEY'S DREAM, CONT. ...
MR. PRESIDENT, I'M DOING EVERYTHING I CAN TO HELP YOU. LET ME CHECK OUR COMPUTERS.
WELL, HURRY IT UP. I HAVE A CAMPAIGN STOP.
www.ucomics.com
UH-OH. MR. PRESIDENT, I'M AFRAID I CAN'T ACCEPT IRAQ OR ANY OTHER NATION RETURNS FROM YOU. YOU'VE BEEN FLAGGED IN OUR COMPUTERS.
FLAGGED?!
5/6
© 2004 Aaron McGruder/Dist. by Universal Press Syndicate
YES, SIR. RIGHT AFTER YOU RETURNED A FEW MILLION AFGHANIS TO POTTERY BARN IN 2002.
OH, RIGHT. THAT ...

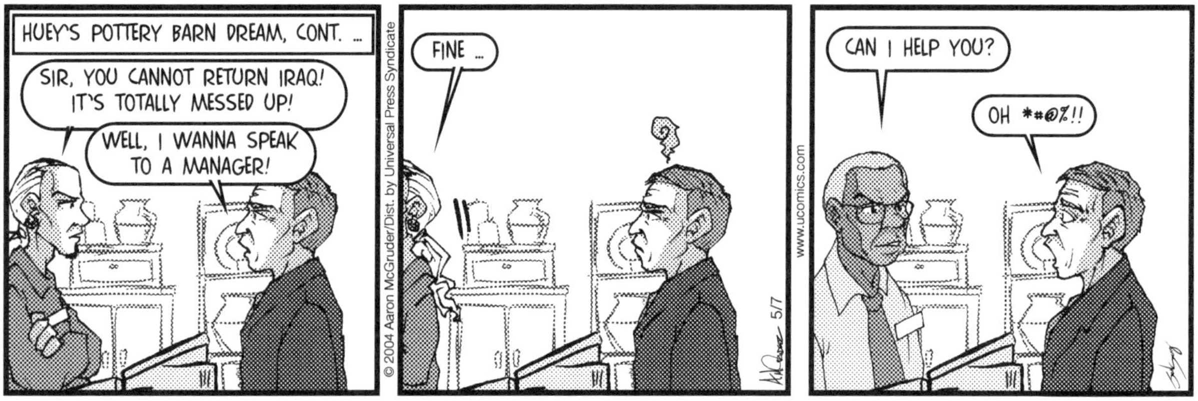
HUEY'S POTTERY BARN DREAM, CONT. ...
SIR, YOU CANNOT RETURN IRAQ! IT'S TOTALLY MESSED UP!
WELL, I WANNA SPEAK TO A MANAGER!
© 2004 Aaron McGruder/Dist. by Universal Press Syndicate
FINE ...
5/7
www.ucomics.com
CAN I HELP YOU?
OH *#@%!!

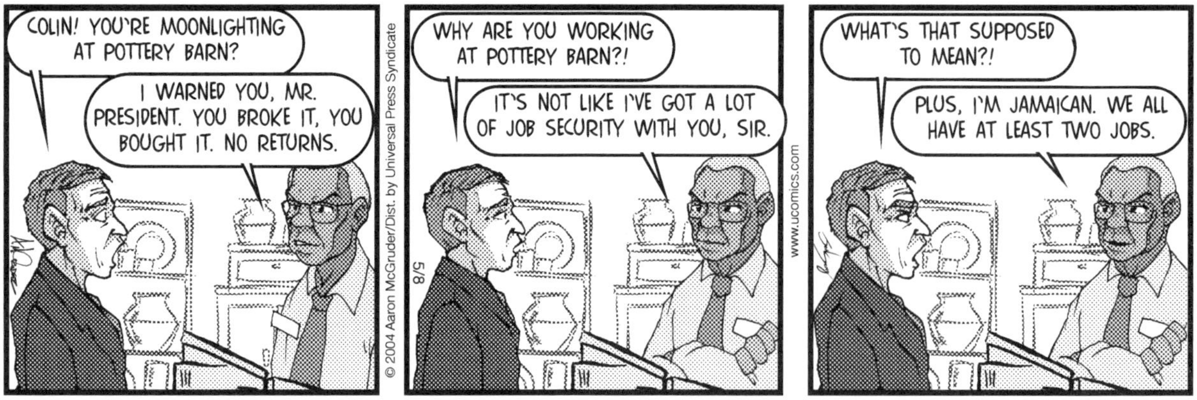
COLIN! YOU'RE MOONLIGHTING AT POTTERY BARN?
I WARNED YOU, MR. PRESIDENT. YOU BROKE IT, YOU BOUGHT IT. NO RETURNS.
© 2004 Aaron McGruder/Dist. by Universal Press Syndicate
5/8
WHY ARE YOU WORKING AT POTTERY BARN?!
IT'S NOT LIKE I'VE GOT A LOT OF JOB SECURITY WITH YOU, SIR.
www.ucomics.com
WHAT'S THAT SUPPOSED TO MEAN?!
PLUS, I'M JAMAICAN. WE ALL HAVE AT LEAST TWO JOBS.

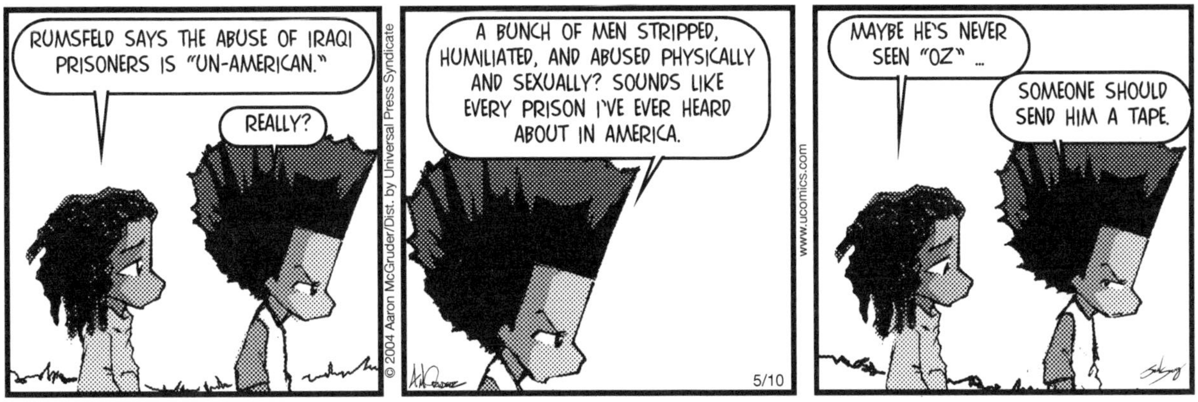
RUMSFELD SAYS THE ABUSE OF IRAQI PRISONERS IS "UN-AMERICAN."
REALLY?
© 2004 Aaron McGruder/Dist. by Universal Press Syndicate
A BUNCH OF MEN STRIPPED, HUMILIATED, AND ABUSED PHYSICALLY AND SEXUALLY? SOUNDS LIKE EVERY PRISON I'VE EVER HEARD ABOUT IN AMERICA.
5/10
www.ucomics.com
MAYBE HE'S NEVER SEEN "OZ" ...
SOMEONE SHOULD SEND HIM A TAPE.

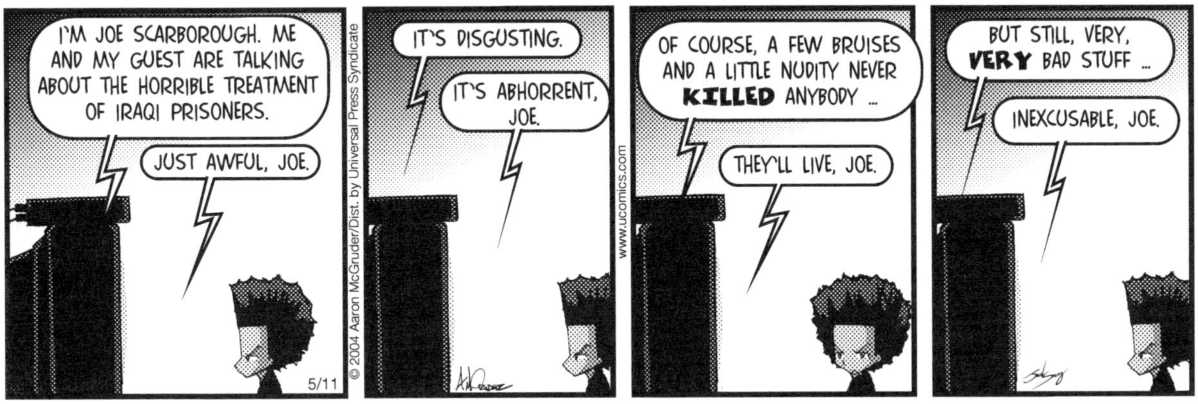
I'M JOE SCARBOROUGH. ME AND MY GUEST ARE TALKING ABOUT THE HORRIBLE TREATMENT OF IRAQI PRISONERS.
JUST AWFUL, JOE.
5/11
© 2004 Aaron McGruder/Dist. by Universal Press Syndicate
IT'S DISGUSTING.
IT'S ABHORRENT, JOE.
www.ucomics.com
OF COURSE, A FEW BRUISES AND A LITTLE NUDITY NEVER **KILLED** ANYBODY ...
THEY'LL LIVE, JOE.
BUT STILL, VERY, **VERY** BAD STUFF ...
INEXCUSABLE, JOE.

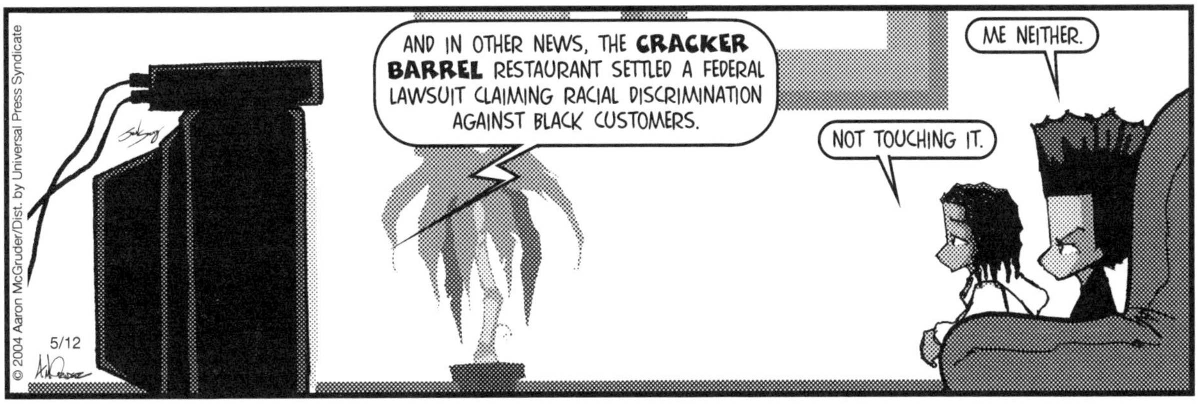
© 2004 Aaron McGruder/Dist. by Universal Press Syndicate
5/12
AND IN OTHER NEWS, THE **CRACKER BARREL** RESTAURANT SETTLED A FEDERAL LAWSUIT CLAIMING RACIAL DISCRIMINATION AGAINST BLACK CUSTOMERS.
NOT TOUCHING IT.
ME NEITHER.

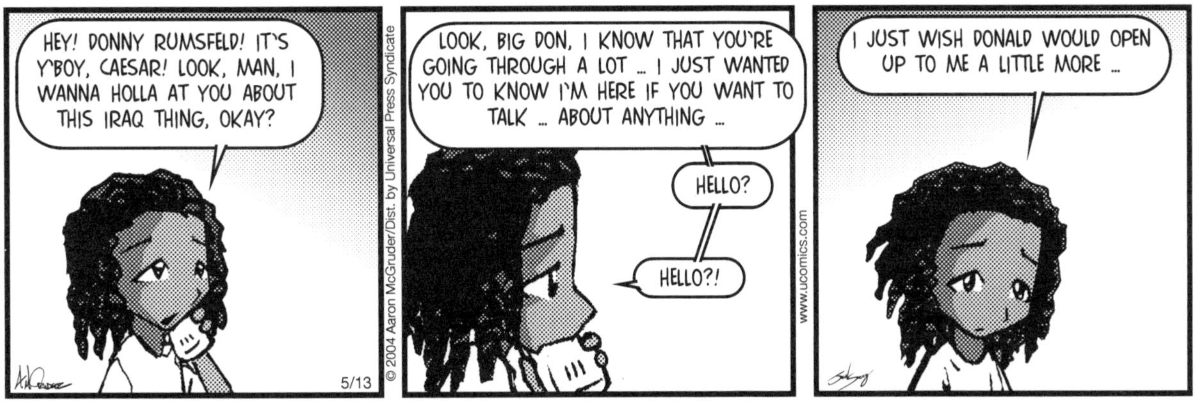
HEY! DONNY RUMSFELD! IT'S Y'BOY, CAESAR! LOOK, MAN, I WANNA HOLLA AT YOU ABOUT THIS IRAQ THING, OKAY?
5/13
© 2004 Aaron McGruder/Dist. by Universal Press Syndicate
LOOK, BIG DON, I KNOW THAT YOU'RE GOING THROUGH A LOT ... I JUST WANTED YOU TO KNOW I'M HERE IF YOU WANT TO TALK ... ABOUT ANYTHING ...
HELLO?
HELLO?!
www.ucomics.com
I JUST WISH DONALD WOULD OPEN UP TO ME A LITTLE MORE ...

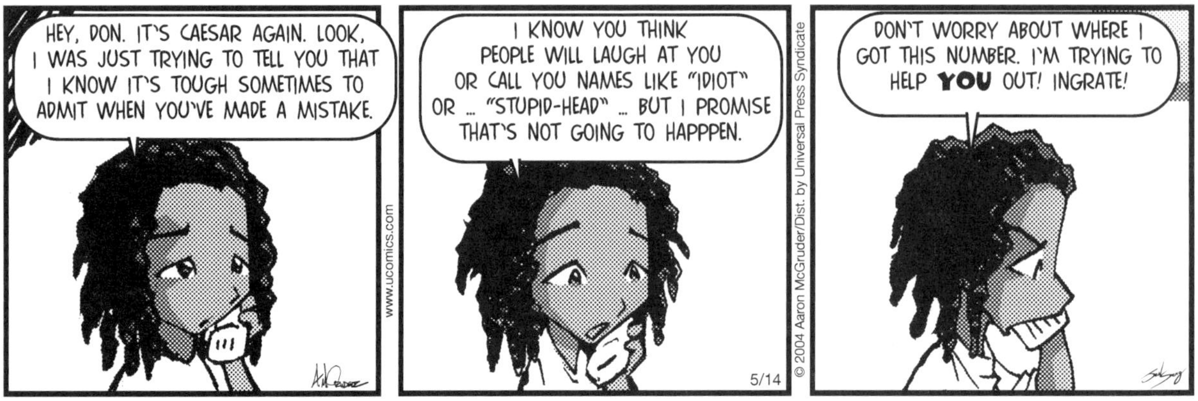
HEY, DON. IT'S CAESAR AGAIN. LOOK, I WAS JUST TRYING TO TELL YOU THAT I KNOW IT'S TOUGH SOMETIMES TO ADMIT WHEN YOU'VE MADE A MISTAKE.
www.ucomics.com
I KNOW YOU THINK PEOPLE WILL LAUGH AT YOU OR CALL YOU NAMES LIKE "IDIOT" OR ... "STUPID-HEAD" ... BUT I PROMISE THAT'S NOT GOING TO HAPPPEN.
5/14
© 2004 Aaron McGruder/Dist. by Universal Press Syndicate
DON'T WORRY ABOUT WHERE I GOT THIS NUMBER. I'M TRYING TO HELP **YOU** OUT! INGRATE!

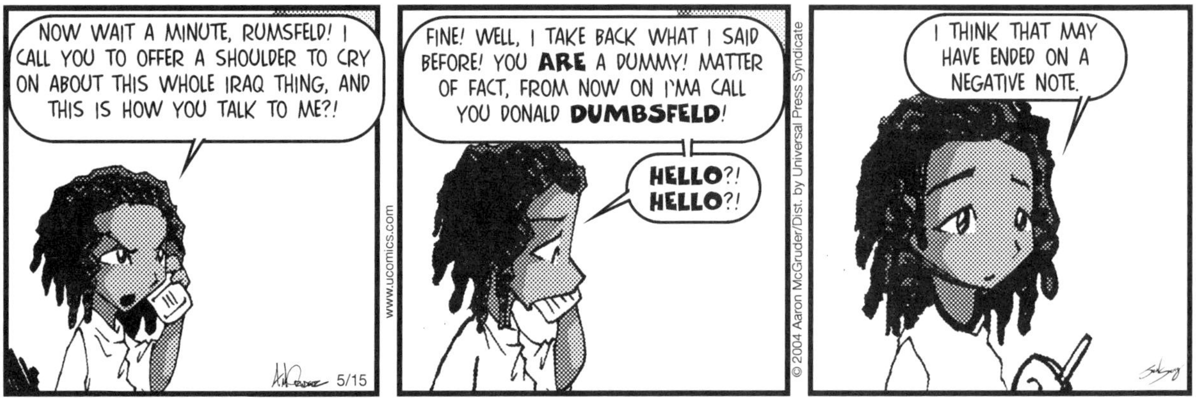
NOW WAIT A MINUTE, RUMSFELD! I CALL YOU TO OFFER A SHOULDER TO CRY ON ABOUT THIS WHOLE IRAQ THING, AND THIS IS HOW YOU TALK TO ME?!
5/15
www.ucomics.com
FINE! WELL, I TAKE BACK WHAT I SAID BEFORE! YOU **ARE** A DUMMY! MATTER OF FACT, FROM NOW ON I'MA CALL YOU DONALD **DUMBSFELD**!
HELLO?! **HELLO**?!
© 2004 Aaron McGruder/Dist. by Universal Press Syndicate
I THINK THAT MAY HAVE ENDED ON A NEGATIVE NOTE.

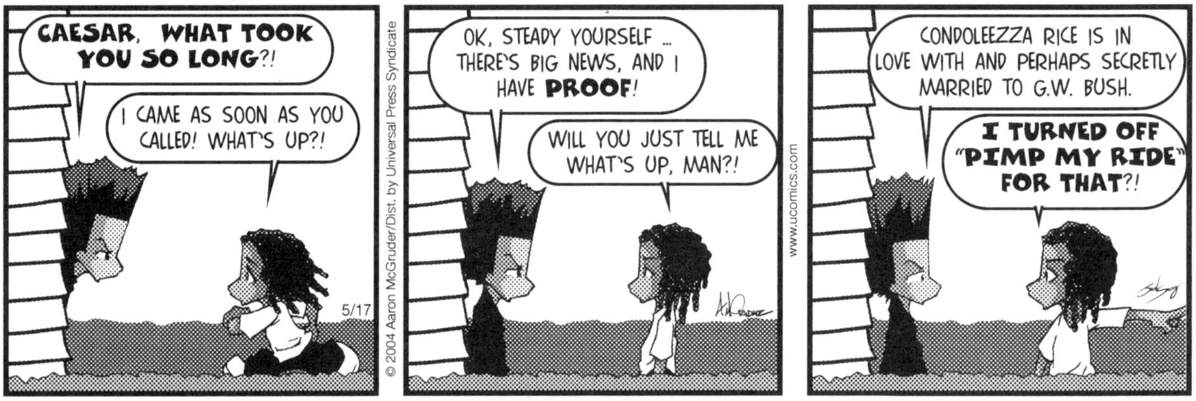
CAESAR, **WHAT TOOK YOU SO LONG**?!
I CAME AS SOON AS YOU CALLED! WHAT'S UP?!
5/17
© 2004 Aaron McGruder/Dist. by Universal Press Syndicate
OK, STEADY YOURSELF ... THERE'S BIG NEWS, AND I HAVE **PROOF**!
WILL YOU JUST TELL ME WHAT'S UP, MAN?!
www.ucomics.com
CONDOLEEZZA RICE IS IN LOVE WITH AND PERHAPS SECRETLY MARRIED TO G.W. BUSH.
I TURNED OFF "PIMP MY RIDE" FOR THAT?!

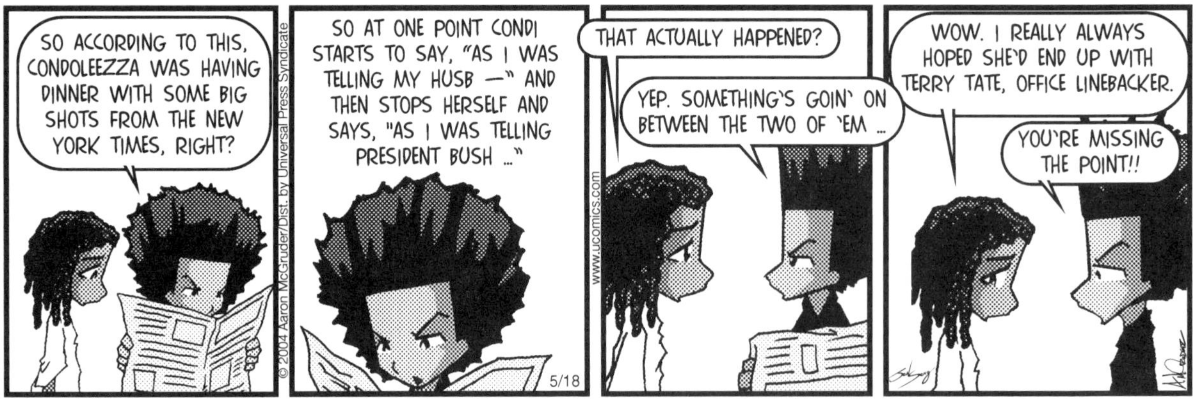
SO ACCORDING TO THIS, CONDOLEEZZA WAS HAVING DINNER WITH SOME BIG SHOTS FROM THE NEW YORK TIMES, RIGHT?
© 2004 Aaron McGruder/Dist. by Universal Press Syndicate
SO AT ONE POINT CONDI STARTS TO SAY, "AS I WAS TELLING MY HUSB —" AND THEN STOPS HERSELF AND SAYS, "AS I WAS TELLING PRESIDENT BUSH ..."
5/18
www.ucomics.com
THAT ACTUALLY HAPPENED?
YEP. SOMETHING'S GOIN' ON BETWEEN THE TWO OF 'EM ...
WOW. I REALLY ALWAYS HOPED SHE'D END UP WITH TERRY TATE, OFFICE LINEBACKER.
YOU'RE MISSING THE POINT!!

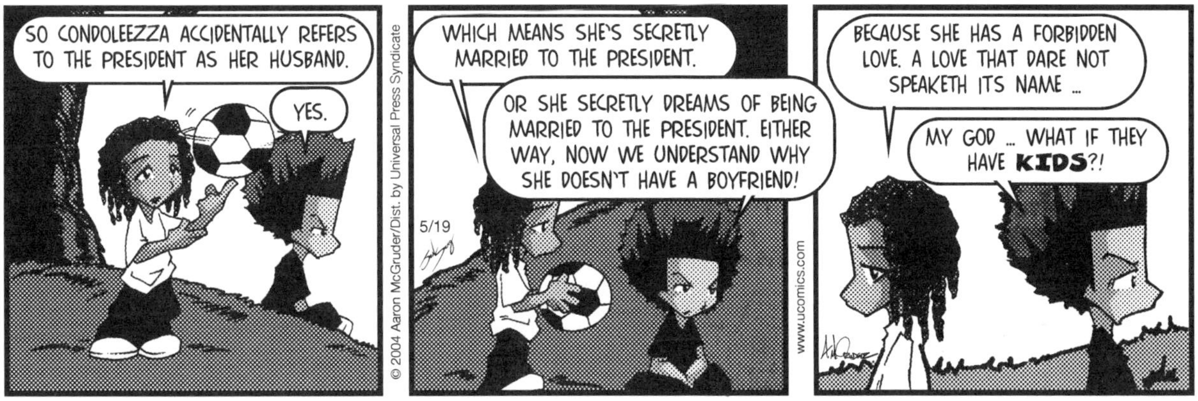
SO CONDOLEEZZA ACCIDENTALLY REFERS TO THE PRESIDENT AS HER HUSBAND.
YES.
© 2004 Aaron McGruder/Dist. by Universal Press Syndicate
WHICH MEANS SHE'S SECRETLY MARRIED TO THE PRESIDENT.
OR SHE SECRETLY DREAMS OF BEING MARRIED TO THE PRESIDENT. EITHER WAY, NOW WE UNDERSTAND WHY SHE DOESN'T HAVE A BOYFRIEND!
5/19
www.ucomics.com
BECAUSE SHE HAS A FORBIDDEN LOVE. A LOVE THAT DARE NOT SPEAKETH ITS NAME ...
MY GOD ... WHAT IF THEY HAVE **KIDS**?!

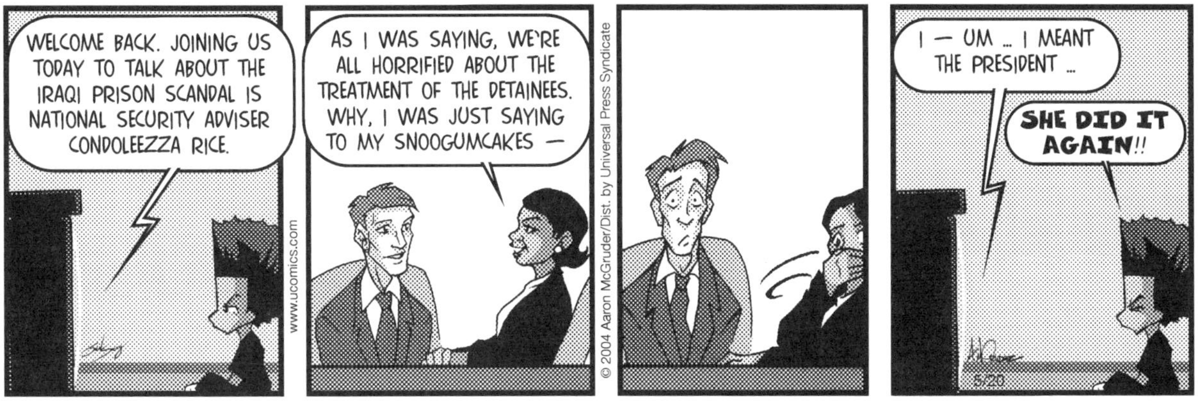
WELCOME BACK. JOINING US TODAY TO TALK ABOUT THE IRAQI PRISON SCANDAL IS NATIONAL SECURITY ADVISER CONDOLEEZZA RICE.
www.ucomics.com
AS I WAS SAYING, WE'RE ALL HORRIFIED ABOUT THE TREATMENT OF THE DETAINEES. WHY, I WAS JUST SAYING TO MY SNOOGUMCAKES —
© 2004 Aaron McGruder/Dist. by Universal Press Syndicate
I — UM ... I MEANT THE PRESIDENT ...
SHE DID IT AGAIN!!
5/20

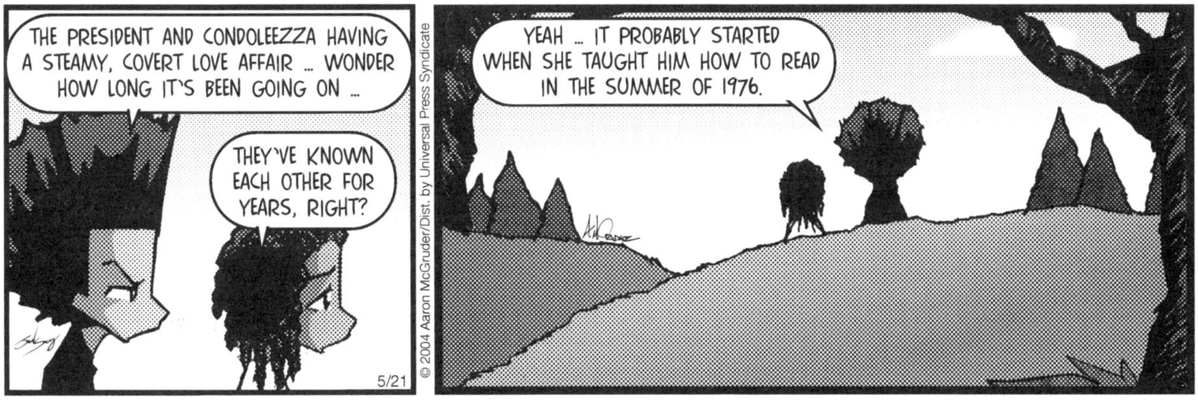
THE PRESIDENT AND CONDOLEEZZA HAVING A STEAMY, COVERT LOVE AFFAIR ... WONDER HOW LONG IT'S BEEN GOING ON ...
THEY'VE KNOWN EACH OTHER FOR YEARS, RIGHT?
5/21
© 2004 Aaron McGruder/Dist. by Universal Press Syndicate
YEAH ... IT PROBABLY STARTED WHEN SHE TAUGHT HIM HOW TO READ IN THE SUMMER OF 1976.

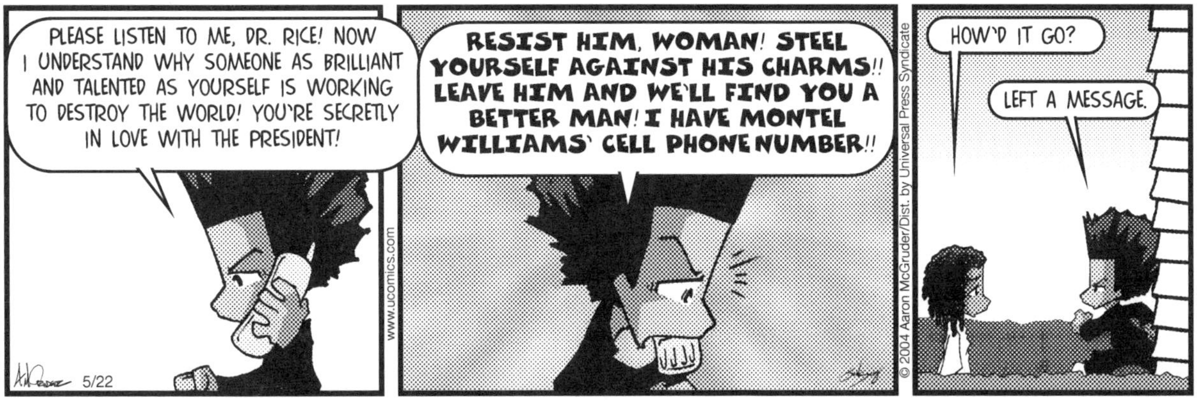
PLEASE LISTEN TO ME, DR. RICE! NOW I UNDERSTAND WHY SOMEONE AS BRILLIANT AND TALENTED AS YOURSELF IS WORKING TO DESTROY THE WORLD! YOU'RE SECRETLY IN LOVE WITH THE PRESIDENT!
5/22
www.ucomics.com
RESIST HIM, WOMAN! STEEL YOURSELF AGAINST HIS CHARMS!! LEAVE HIM AND WE'LL FIND YOU A BETTER MAN! I HAVE MONTEL WILLIAMS' CELL PHONE NUMBER!!
© 2004 Aaron McGruder/Dist. by Universal Press Syndicate
HOW'D IT GO?
LEFT A MESSAGE.

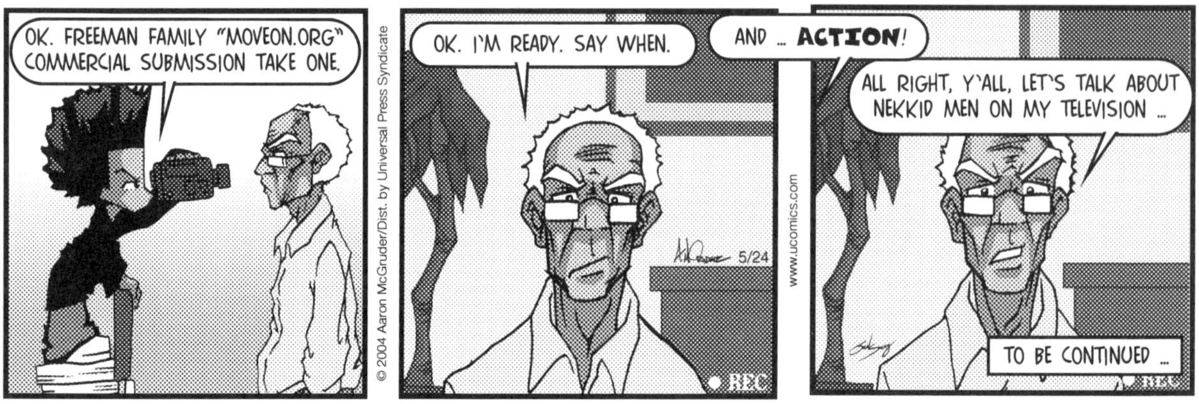
OK. FREEMAN FAMILY "MOVEON.ORG" COMMERCIAL SUBMISSION TAKE ONE.
OK. I'M READY. SAY WHEN.
5/24
© 2004 Aaron McGruder/Dist. by Universal Press Syndicate
AND ... ACTION!
ALL RIGHT, Y'ALL, LET'S TALK ABOUT NEKKID MEN ON MY TELEVISION ...
www.ucomics.com
TO BE CONTINUED ...

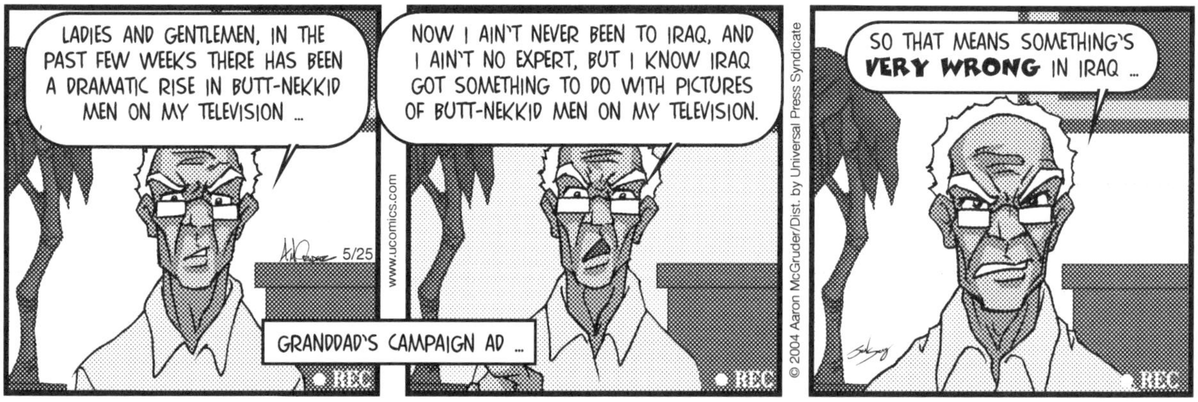
LADIES AND GENTLEMEN, IN THE PAST FEW WEEKS THERE HAS BEEN A DRAMATIC RISE IN BUTT-NEKKID MEN ON MY TELEVISION ...
5/25
www.ucomics.com
GRANDDAD'S CAMPAIGN AD ...
NOW I AIN'T NEVER BEEN TO IRAQ, AND I AIN'T NO EXPERT, BUT I KNOW IRAQ GOT SOMETHING TO DO WITH PICTURES OF BUTT-NEKKID MEN ON MY TELEVISION.
© 2004 Aaron McGruder/Dist. by Universal Press Syndicate
SO THAT MEANS SOMETHING'S VERY WRONG IN IRAQ ...

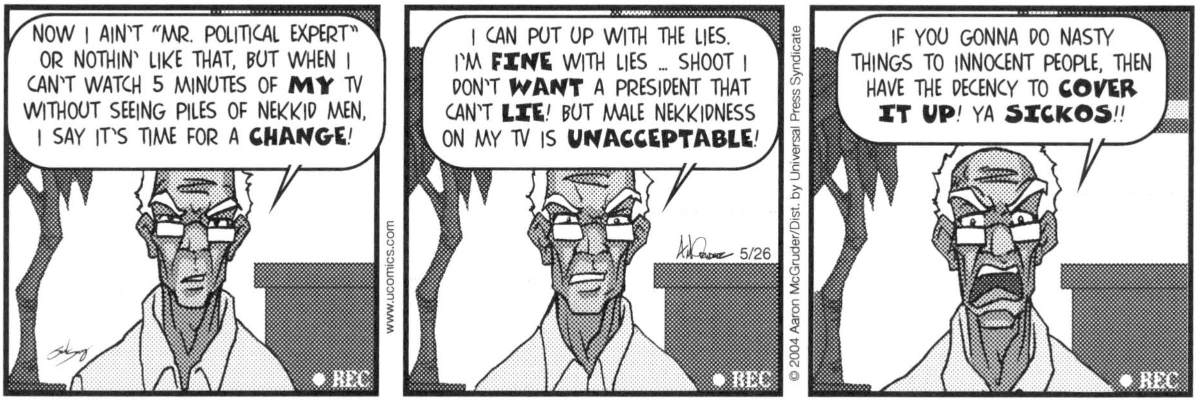
NOW I AIN'T "MR. POLITICAL EXPERT" OR NOTHIN' LIKE THAT, BUT WHEN I CAN'T WATCH 5 MINUTES OF MY TV WITHOUT SEEING PILES OF NEKKID MEN, I SAY IT'S TIME FOR A CHANGE!
www.ucomics.com
I CAN PUT UP WITH THE LIES. I'M FINE WITH LIES ... SHOOT I DON'T WANT A PRESIDENT THAT CAN'T LIE! BUT MALE NEKKIDNESS ON MY TV IS UNACCEPTABLE!
5/26
© 2004 Aaron McGruder/Dist. by Universal Press Syndicate
IF YOU GONNA DO NASTY THINGS TO INNOCENT PEOPLE, THEN HAVE THE DECENCY TO COVER IT UP! YA SICKOS!!

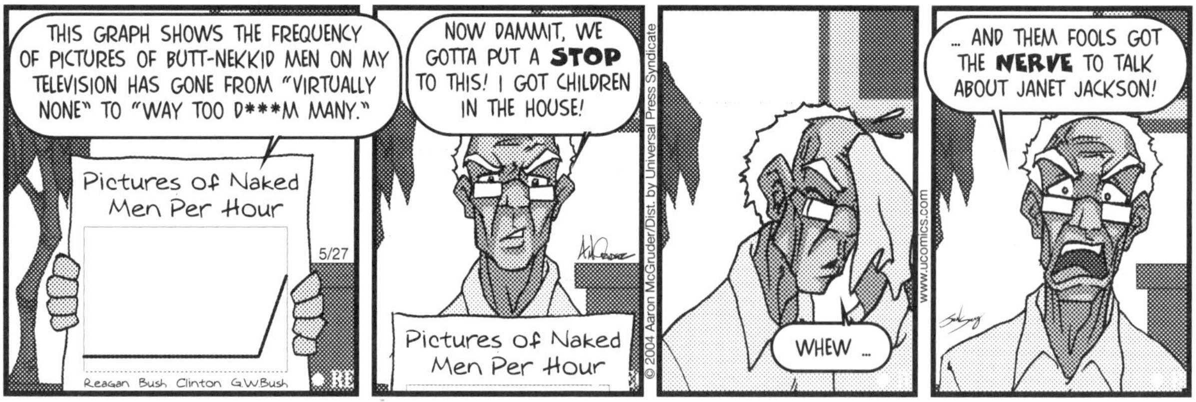
THIS GRAPH SHOWS THE FREQUENCY OF PICTURES OF BUTT-NEKKID MEN ON MY TELEVISION HAS GONE FROM "VIRTUALLY NONE" TO "WAY TOO D***M MANY."
Pictures of Naked Men Per Hour
Reagan Bush Clinton G.W.Bush
5/27
NOW DAMMIT, WE GOTTA PUT A STOP TO THIS! I GOT CHILDREN IN THE HOUSE!
Pictures of Naked Men Per Hour
© 2004 Aaron McGruder/Dist. by Universal Press Syndicate
WHEW ...
www.ucomics.com
... AND THEM FOOLS GOT THE NERVE TO TALK ABOUT JANET JACKSON!

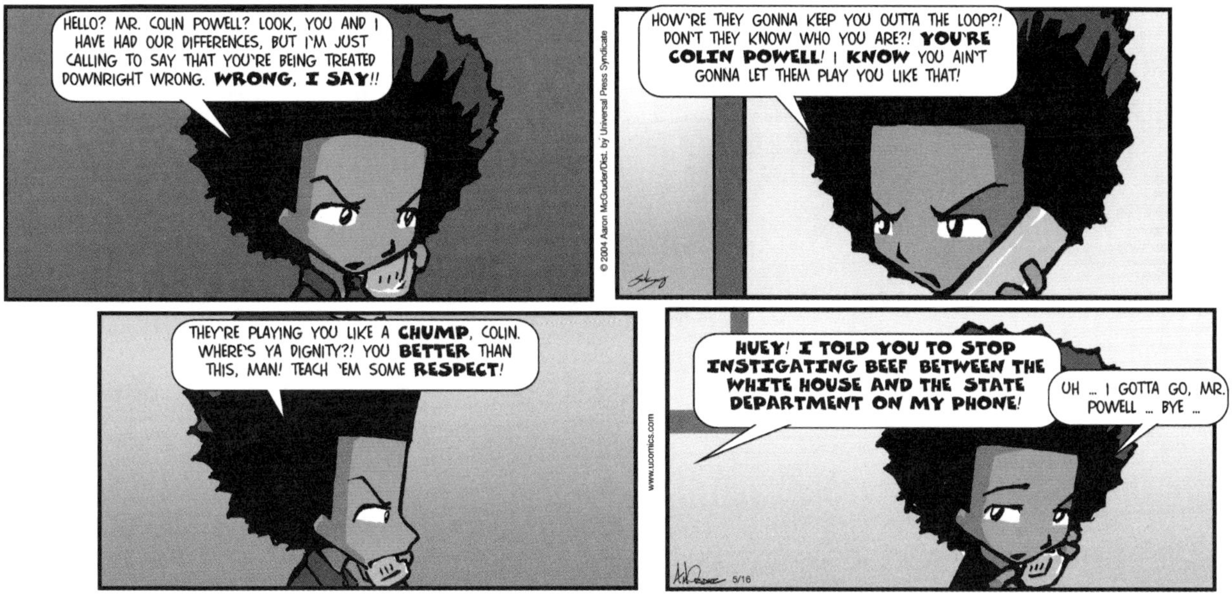
HELLO? MR. COLIN POWELL? LOOK, YOU AND I HAVE HAD OUR DIFFERENCES, BUT I'M JUST CALLING TO SAY THAT YOU'RE BEING TREATED DOWNRIGHT WRONG. **WRONG, I SAY**!!
© 2004 Aaron McGruder/Dist. by Universal Press Syndicate
HOW'RE THEY GONNA KEEP YOU OUTTA THE LOOP?! DON'T THEY KNOW WHO YOU ARE?! **YOU'RE COLIN POWELL**! I **KNOW** YOU AIN'T GONNA LET THEM PLAY YOU LIKE THAT!
THEY'RE PLAYING YOU LIKE A **CHUMP**, COLIN. WHERE'S YA DIGNITY?! YOU **BETTER** THAN THIS, MAN! TEACH 'EM SOME **RESPECT**!
www.ucomics.com
HUEY! I TOLD YOU TO STOP INSTIGATING BEEF BETWEEN THE WHITE HOUSE AND THE STATE DEPARTMENT ON MY PHONE!
UH ... I GOTTA GO, MR. POWELL ... BYE ...
5/16

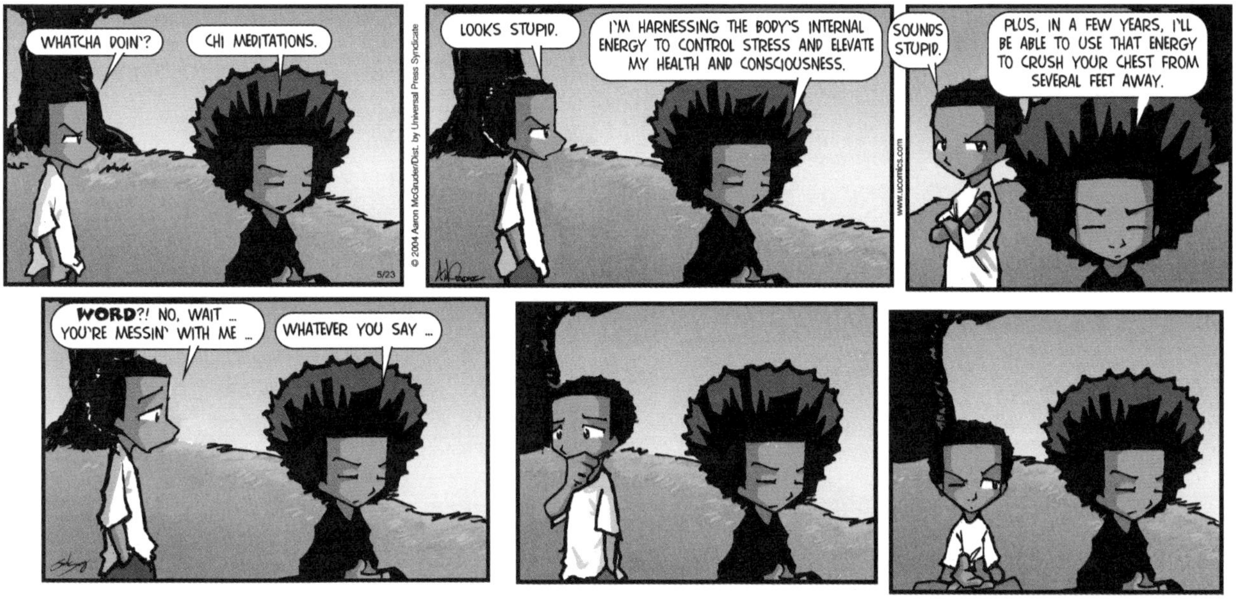
WHATCHA DOIN'?
CHI MEDITATIONS.
5/23
© 2004 Aaron McGruder/Dist. by Universal Press Syndicate
LOOKS STUPID.
I'M HARNESSING THE BODY'S INTERNAL ENERGY TO CONTROL STRESS AND ELEVATE MY HEALTH AND CONSCIOUSNESS.
SOUNDS STUPID.
PLUS, IN A FEW YEARS, I'LL BE ABLE TO USE THAT ENERGY TO CRUSH YOUR CHEST FROM SEVERAL FEET AWAY.
www.ucomics.com
WORD?! NO, WAIT ... YOU'RE MESSIN' WITH ME ...
WHATEVER YOU SAY ...

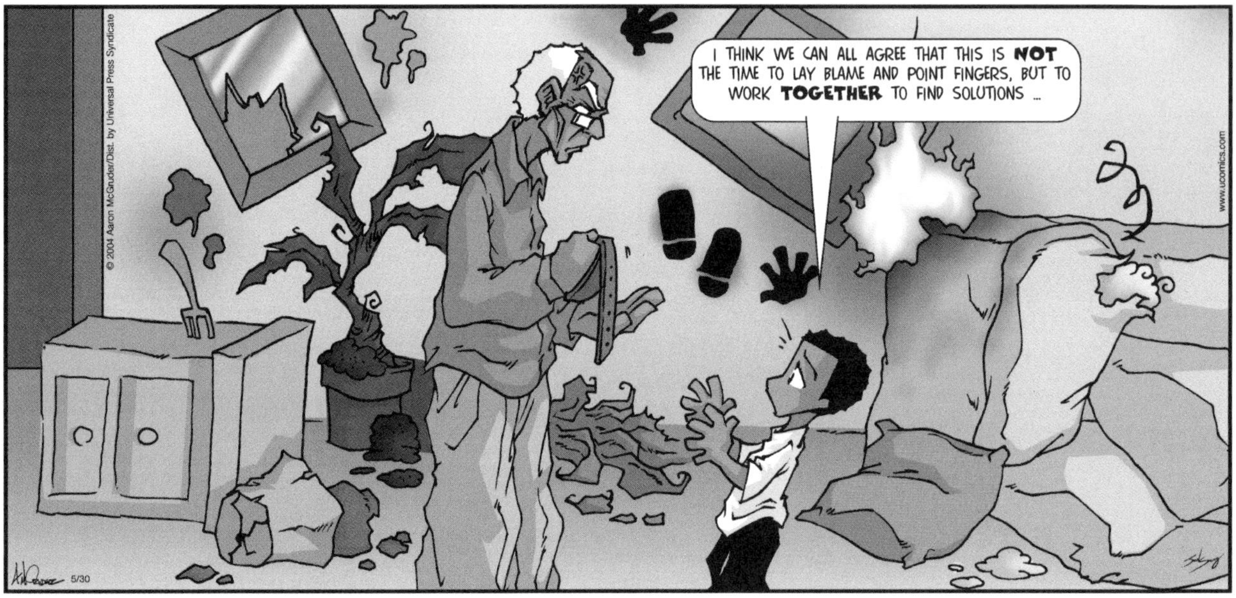
© 2004 Aaron McGruder/Dist. by Universal Press Syndicate
I THINK WE CAN ALL AGREE THAT THIS IS **NOT** THE TIME TO LAY BLAME AND POINT FINGERS, BUT TO WORK **TOGETHER** TO FIND SOLUTIONS ...
www.ucomics.com
5/30

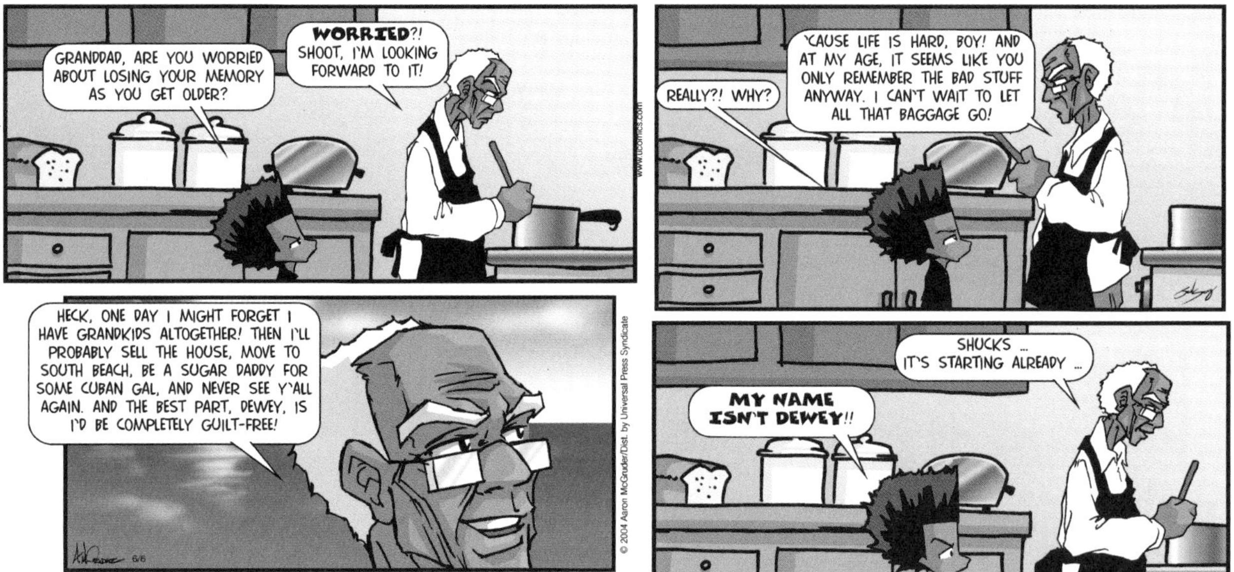
GRANDDAD, ARE YOU WORRIED ABOUT LOSING YOUR MEMORY AS YOU GET OLDER?
WORRIED?! SHOOT, I'M LOOKING FORWARD TO IT!
www.ucomics.com
REALLY?! WHY?
'CAUSE LIFE IS HARD, BOY! AND AT MY AGE, IT SEEMS LIKE YOU ONLY REMEMBER THE BAD STUFF ANYWAY. I CAN'T WAIT TO LET ALL THAT BAGGAGE GO!
HECK, ONE DAY I MIGHT FORGET I HAVE GRANDKIDS ALTOGETHER! THEN I'LL PROBABLY SELL THE HOUSE, MOVE TO SOUTH BEACH, BE A SUGAR DADDY FOR SOME CUBAN GAL, AND NEVER SEE Y'ALL AGAIN. AND THE BEST PART, DEWEY, IS I'D BE COMPLETELY GUILT-FREE!
© 2004 Aaron McGruder/Dist. by Universal Press Syndicate
6/6
MY NAME ISN'T DEWEY!!
SHUCKS ... IT'S STARTING ALREADY ...

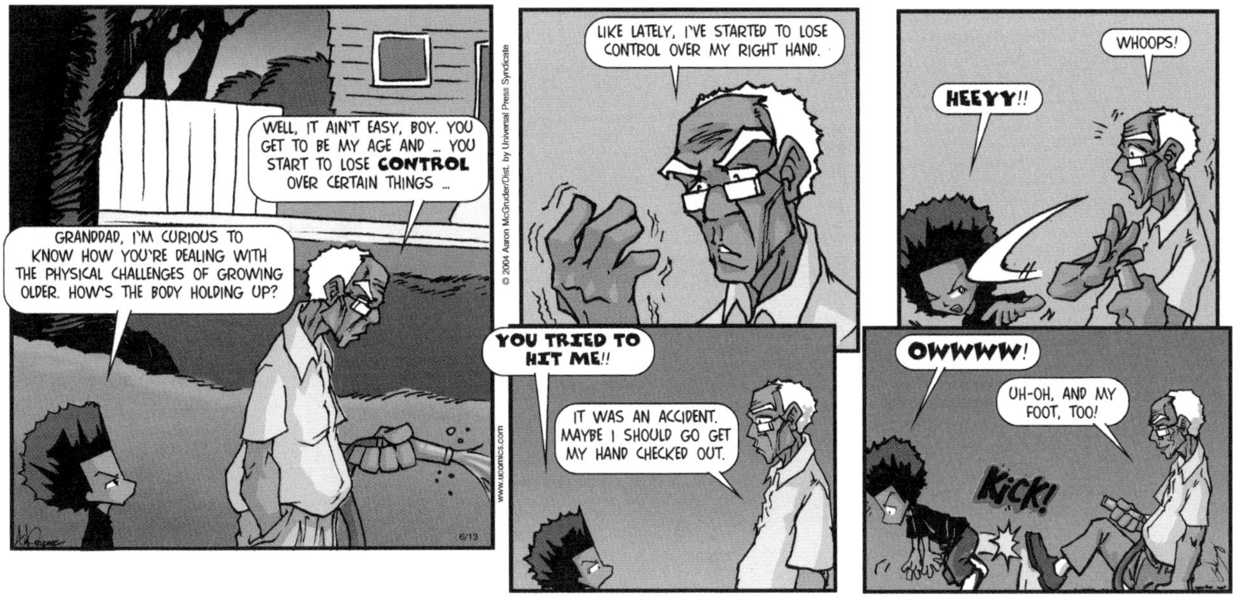
GRANDDAD, I'M CURIOUS TO KNOW HOW YOU'RE DEALING WITH THE PHYSICAL CHALLENGES OF GROWING OLDER. HOW'S THE BODY HOLDING UP?
WELL, IT AIN'T EASY, BOY. YOU GET TO BE MY AGE AND ... YOU START TO LOSE **CONTROL** OVER CERTAIN THINGS ...
© 2004 Aaron McGruder/Dist. by Universal Press Syndicate
www.ucomics.com
6/13
LIKE LATELY, I'VE STARTED TO LOSE CONTROL OVER MY RIGHT HAND.
HEEYY!!
WHOOPS!
YOU TRIED TO HIT ME!!
IT WAS AN ACCIDENT. MAYBE I SHOULD GO GET MY HAND CHECKED OUT.
OWWWW!
UH-OH, AND MY FOOT, TOO!
KICK!

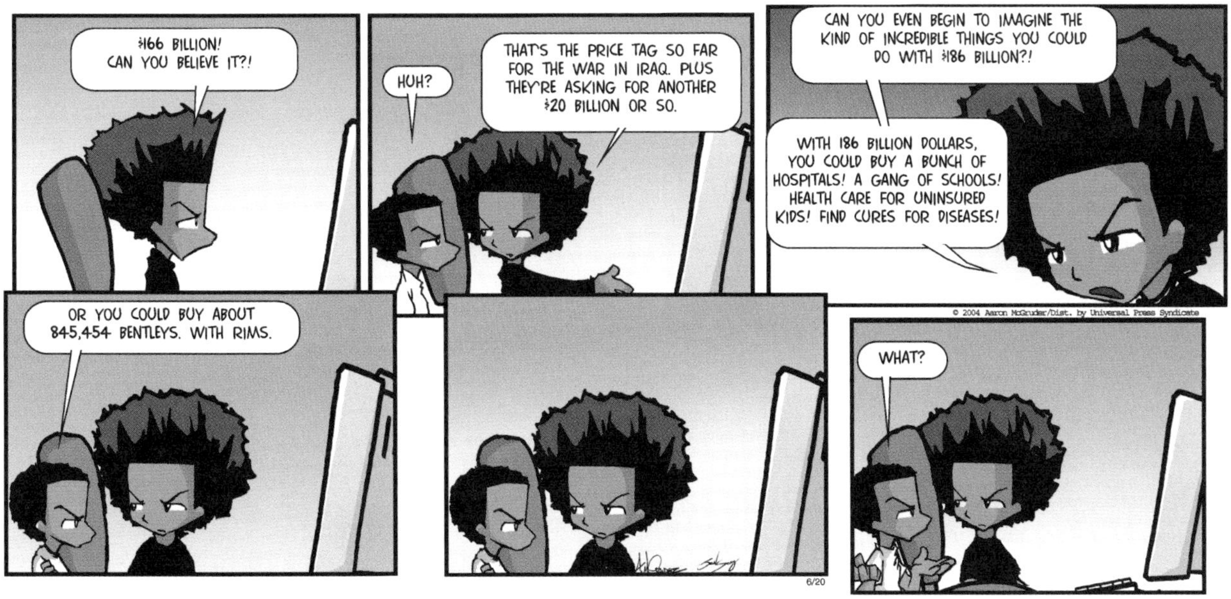
$166 BILLION! CAN YOU BELIEVE IT?!
HUH?
THAT'S THE PRICE TAG SO FAR FOR THE WAR IN IRAQ. PLUS THEY'RE ASKING FOR ANOTHER $20 BILLION OR SO.
CAN YOU EVEN BEGIN TO IMAGINE THE KIND OF INCREDIBLE THINGS YOU COULD DO WITH $186 BILLION?!
WITH 186 BILLION DOLLARS, YOU COULD BUY A BUNCH OF HOSPITALS! A GANG OF SCHOOLS! HEALTH CARE FOR UNINSURED KIDS! FIND CURES FOR DISEASES!
© 2004 Aaron McGruder/Dist. by Universal Press Syndicate
OR YOU COULD BUY ABOUT 845,454 BENTLEYS. WITH RIMS.
6/20
WHAT?

BUSH'S NUMBERS DON'T LOOK GREAT ...
THEY'LL NO DOUBT RESPOND WITH A SOPHISTICATED PROPAGANDA ASSAULT TO SWAY THE SAVVY AMERICAN VOTING PUBLIC.
www.ucomics.com
6/27
© 2004 Aaron McGruder/Dist. by Universal Press Syndicate
JOHN KERRY DOESN'T LIKE PRESIDENT BUSH.
AND NEITHER DO THE TERRORISTS!!
THAT'S BECAUSE PRESIDENT BUSH FIGHTS TERRORISTS. SO IF JOHN KERRY DOESN'T LIKE PRESIDENT BUSH, WHO DOES HE LIKE?
John Kerry
SUPPORTS TERRORISM.
...and that's a FACT!

I'M GEORGE W. BUSH, AND I APPROVE THIS MESSAGE ...
© 2004 Aaron McGruder/Dist. by Universal Press Syndicate
RECENTLY, URBAN YOUTH HAVE BEEN RECEIVING A LOT OF MESSAGES ABOUT VOTING. SOME OF IT MAY BE CONFUSING ...
www.ucomics.com
IS THERE READING INVOLVED? HOW DO I WORK THE VOTING MACHINE? AM I LEGALLY ALLOWED TO VOTE IF I'M A FELON?
POLITICS IS VERY COMPLICATED, AND IF YOU'RE UNSURE ABOUT THE ISSUES OR YOUR VOTING STATUS, YOU COULD BE EMBARRASSED, EVEN ARRESTED, IF YOU TRY TO VOTE.
BUT I'M ON PAROLE!!
AND DEPENDING ON WHERE YOU LIVE, YOUR VOTE MAY NOT EVEN COUNT! SO BEFORE YOU GET UP AND GO ALL THE WAY TO THE POLLS, ASK YOURSELF ... IS IT REALLY WORTH IT?
NO WAY, HOMIE!!
Voting:
It Ain't Worth It, Homie!
Paid for by Bush/Cheney for President

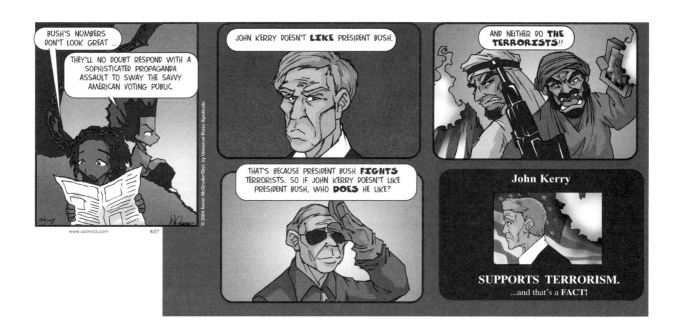

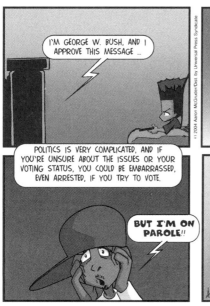

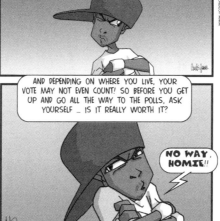

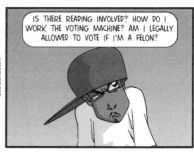

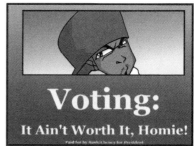

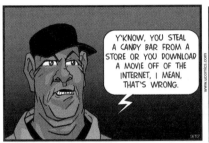

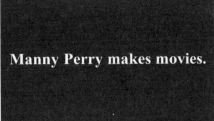

Y'KNOW, YOU STEAL A CANDY BAR FROM A STORE OR YOU DOWNLOAD A MOVIE OFF OF THE INTERNET, I MEAN, THAT'S WRONG.
Manny Perry makes movies.
A LOT OF PEOPLE PUT A LOT OF TIME, ENERGY, EFFORT AND, IN MY SITUATION, LIVES ON THE LINE.
... THEY'RE DOING ALL THAT AND THEN SOME PERSON JUST COMES ALONG AND HITS A COUPLE OF BUTTONS AND REAPS ALL THAT BENEFIT.
IT'S JUST ... IT'S JUST NOT RIGHT.
Put an end to piracy.
GET TO THE MOVIE ALREADY!!!
WE ARE SO WRONG.
www.ucomics.com
© 2004 Aaron McGruder/Dist. by Universal Press Syndicate

(SIGH) ... YET ANOTHER INNOCENT VICTIM OF INTERNET PIRACY ...
PEOPLE COME UP TO ME AND THEY SAY, "YOUR BOOTLEGS ARE SO CLEAR, AND YOU NEVER SEE ANYONE WALKING IN FRONT OF THE SCREEN" ... AND THAT LETS ME KNOW MY WORK IS APPRECIATED.
RUFUS "SPIELBERG" JENKINS BOOTLEGS MOVIES.
BOOTLEGGERS RISK JAIL TO BRING YOU CHEAP MOVIES AT HOME THE DAY THEY COME OUT IN THE THEATER - SOMETIMES EARLIER ...
THEN SOME NERD PUTS IT ON THE INTERNET, AND NOW ANYONE CAN JUST HIT A FEW BUTTONS AND REAP ALL THAT BENEFIT.
IT'S ... IT'S JUST NOT RIGHT ...
Bootlegged movies. They're worth 20 bucks for 3 DVDs.
© 2004 Aaron McGruder/Dist. by Universal Press Syndicate
www.ucomics.com

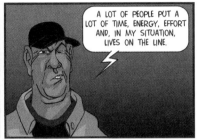

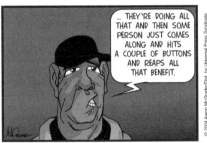

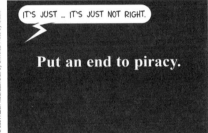

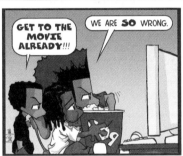

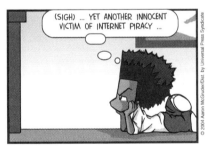

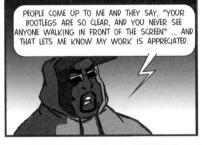

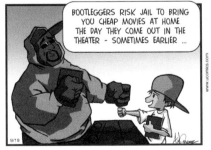

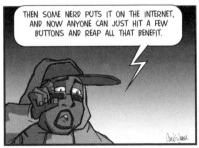

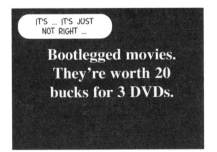

© 2004 Aaron McGruder/Dist. by Universal Press Syndicate
BAM!
www.ucomics.com
9/26
"ONLY IN AMERICA"

INFORMAL POLL
HONK ONCE FOR KERRY
TWICE FOR BUSH!
10/3
www.ucomics.com
INFORMAL POLL
HONK ONCE FOR KERRY
TWICE FOR BUSH!
HONK! HONK!
INFORMAL POLL
HONK ONCE FOR KERRY
TWICE FOR BUSH!
© 2004 Aaron McGruder/Dist. by Universal Press Syndicate
INFORMAL POLL
HONK ONCE FOR KERRY
TWICE FOR BUSH!

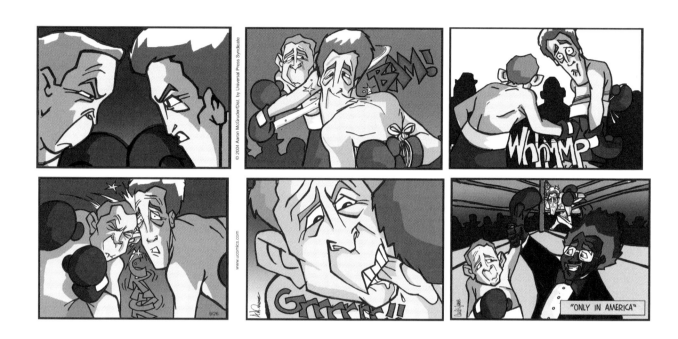

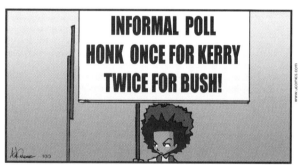

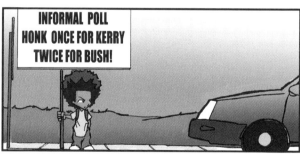

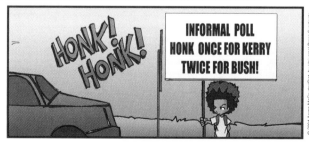

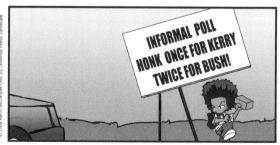

WE'VE GOTTA SUPPORT KERRY!
NEVER!!
HE'S ALL WE'VE GOT!
FOOL! HE VOTED FOR THE WAR IN IRAQ, WHICH MAKES HIM EVIL, STUPID, OR BOTH!
YOU'RE BEING SHORTSIGHTED AND STUBBORN! WE CAN'T LET BUSH WIN!
THE LESSER OF TWO EVILS IS STILL EVIL!
www.ucomics.com
MORAL COMPROMISE IS UNACCEPTABLE!
IF BUSH WINS, MORE GOOD PEOPLE WILL DIE IN THIS STUPID WAR!
10/10
AAARRRGH!!
© 2004 Aaron McGruder/Dist. by Universal Press Syndicate
Y'KNOW, YOU'RE THE ONLY PERSON I KNOW WHOSE INTERNAL DEBATES BECOME VIOLENT.
I HATE ELECTION YEARS ...

HELLO?
MR. JONES. IT'S HUEY. YOU READY?
© 2004 Aaron McGruder/Dist. by Universal Press Syndicate
YOUNG MAN, I TOLD YOU LAST TIME THIS ISN'T FUNNY. YOU'RE GOING TO GET US BOTH INTO TROUBLE.
LAST TIME, I PROMISE. HOLD ON.
THIS IS BUSH.
MR. PRESIDENT, PLEASE HOLD FOR DARTH VADER.
www.ucomics.com
PRESIDENT BUSH, THIS IS DARTH VADER ... I WANTED TO THANK YOU FOR HELPING SPREAD EVIL THROUGHOUT THE GALAXY!
UH ... THANK YOU, LORD VADER!
10/17

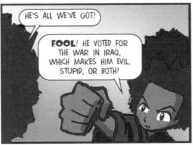

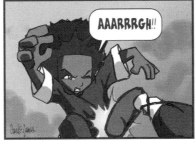

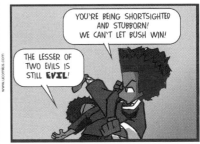

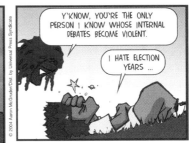

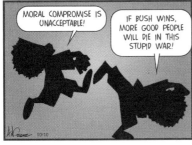

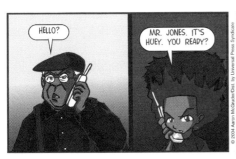

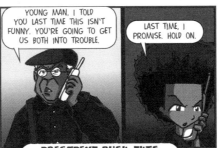

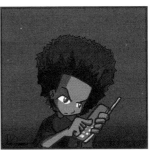

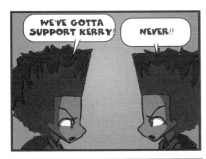

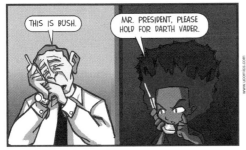

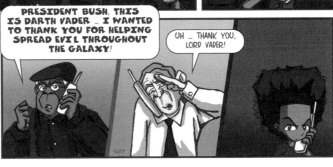

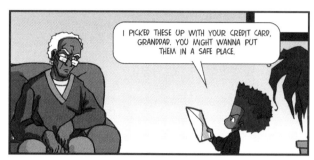

I PICKED THESE UP WITH YOUR CREDIT CARD, GRANDDAD. YOU MIGHT WANNA PUT THEM IN A SAFE PLACE.
WHAT IS IT?
I'M NOT TRYING TO BE OVERLY PESSIMISTIC ABOUT THE ELECTION. IT'S JUST A PRECAUTION.
NON-REFUNDABLE, ONE-WAY AIRPLANE TICKETS TO CANADA!!
BETTER TO HAVE IT AND NOT NEED IT, THAN TO NEED IT AND NOT HAVE IT, I ALWAYS SAY.
© 2004 Aaron McGruder/Dist. by Universal Press Syndicate
www.ucomics.com
10/24

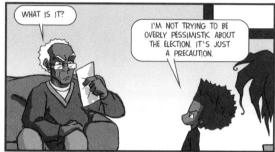

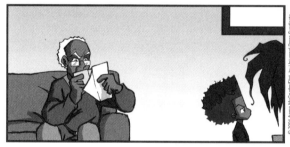

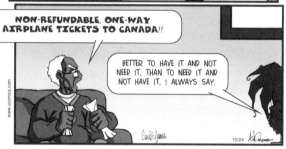

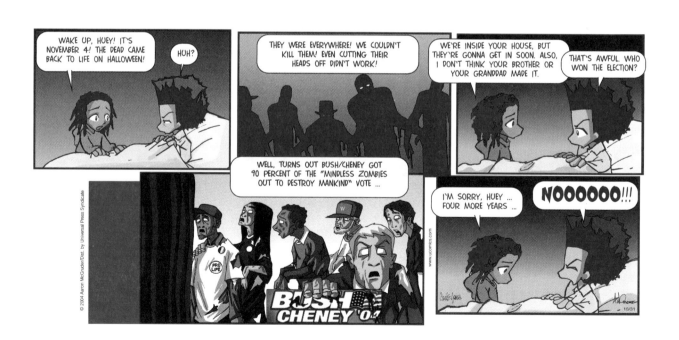

WAKE UP, HUEY! IT'S NOVEMBER 4! THE DEAD CAME BACK TO LIFE ON HALLOWEEN!
HUH?
THEY WERE EVERYWHERE! WE COULDN'T KILL THEM! EVEN CUTTING THEIR HEADS OFF DIDN'T WORK!
WE'RE INSIDE YOUR HOUSE, BUT THEY'RE GONNA GET IN SOON. ALSO, I DON'T THINK YOUR BROTHER OR YOUR GRANDDAD MADE IT.
THAT'S AWFUL. WHO WON THE ELECTION?
WELL, TURNS OUT BUSH/CHENEY GOT 90 PERCENT OF THE "MINDLESS ZOMBIES OUT TO DESTROY MANKIND" VOTE ...
PRO LIFE
BUSH CHENEY '04
I'M SORRY, HUEY ... FOUR MORE YEARS ...
NOOOOOO!!!
© 2004 Aaron McGruder/Dist. by Universal Press Syndicate
www.ucomics.com
10/31

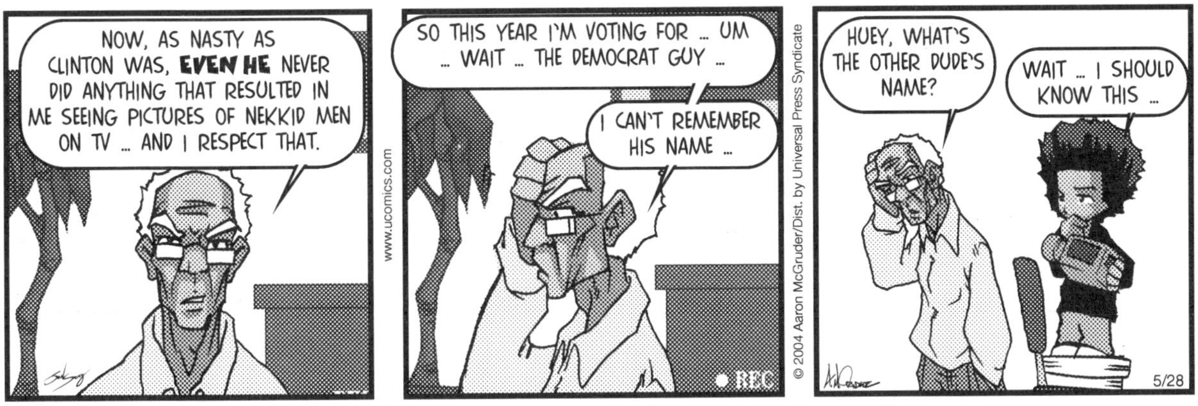
NOW, AS NASTY AS CLINTON WAS, **EVEN HE** NEVER DID ANYTHING THAT RESULTED IN ME SEEING PICTURES OF NEKKID MEN ON TV ... AND I RESPECT THAT.
www.ucomics.com
SO THIS YEAR I'M VOTING FOR ... UM ... WAIT ... THE DEMOCRAT GUY ...
I CAN'T REMEMBER HIS NAME ...
● REC
© 2004 Aaron McGruder/Dist. by Universal Press Syndicate
HUEY, WHAT'S THE OTHER DUDE'S NAME?
WAIT ... I SHOULD KNOW THIS ...
5/28

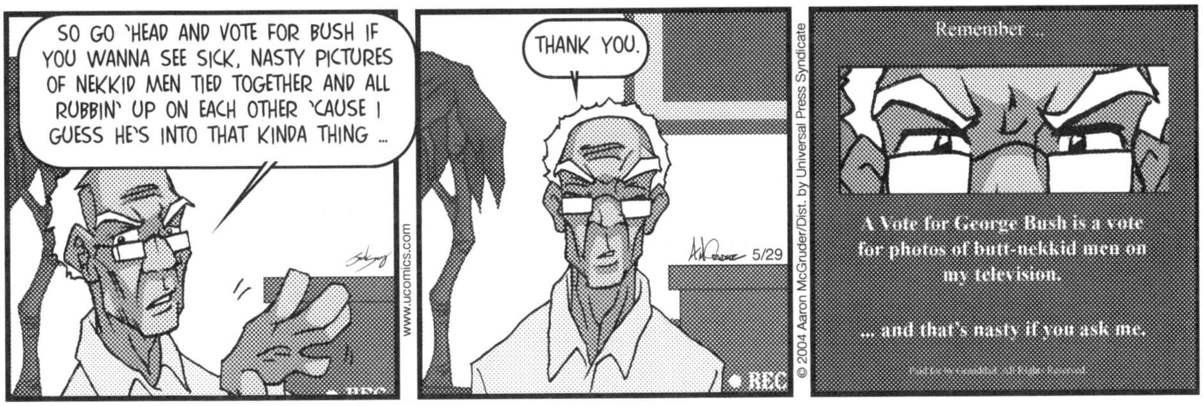
SO GO 'HEAD AND VOTE FOR BUSH IF YOU WANNA SEE SICK, NASTY PICTURES OF NEKKID MEN TIED TOGETHER AND ALL RUBBIN' UP ON EACH OTHER 'CAUSE I GUESS HE'S INTO THAT KINDA THING ...
www.ucomics.com
THANK YOU.
5/29
● REC
© 2004 Aaron McGruder/Dist. by Universal Press Syndicate
Remember ...
A Vote for George Bush is a vote for photos of butt-nekkid men on my television.
... and that's nasty if you ask me.

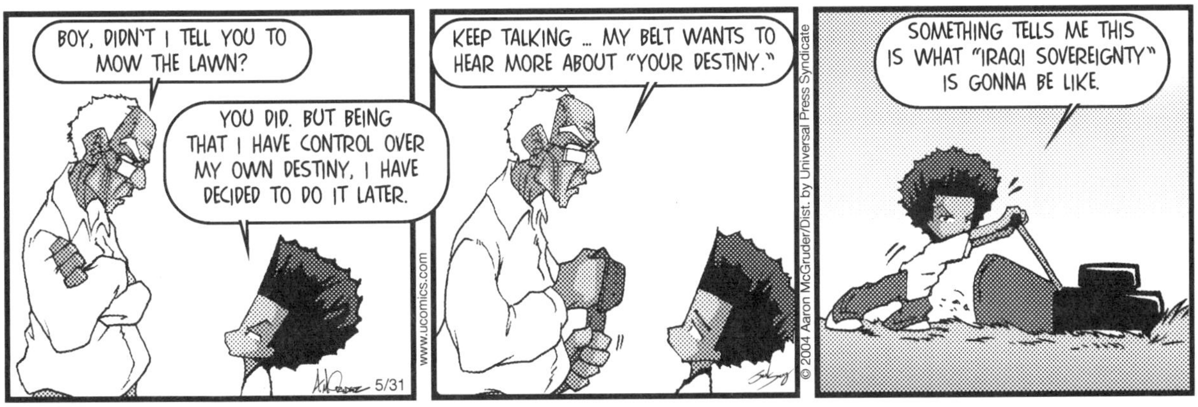
BOY, DIDN'T I TELL YOU TO MOW THE LAWN?
YOU DID. BUT BEING THAT I HAVE CONTROL OVER MY OWN DESTINY, I HAVE DECIDED TO DO IT LATER.
5/31
www.ucomics.com
KEEP TALKING ... MY BELT WANTS TO HEAR MORE ABOUT "YOUR DESTINY."
© 2004 Aaron McGruder/Dist. by Universal Press Syndicate
SOMETHING TELLS ME THIS IS WHAT "IRAQI SOVEREIGNTY" IS GONNA BE LIKE.

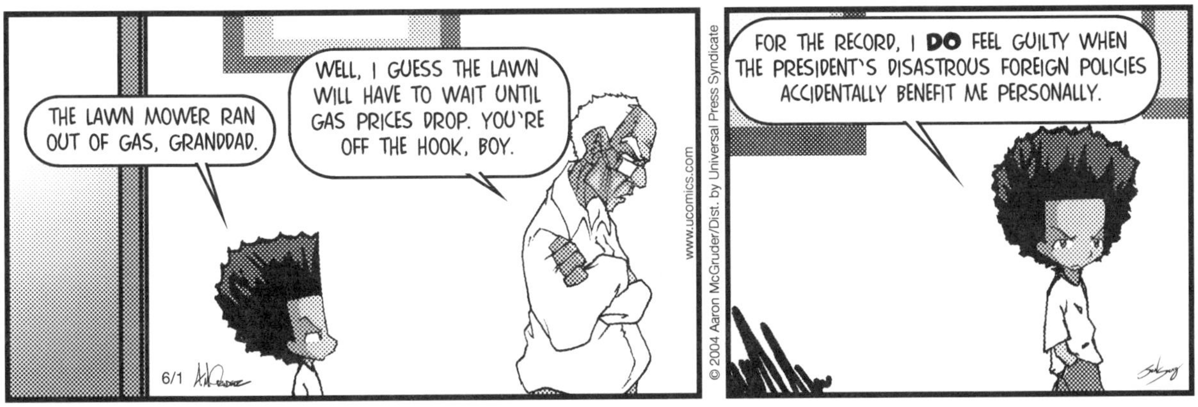
THE LAWN MOWER RAN OUT OF GAS, GRANDDAD.
WELL, I GUESS THE LAWN WILL HAVE TO WAIT UNTIL GAS PRICES DROP. YOU'RE OFF THE HOOK, BOY.
6/1
www.ucomics.com
© 2004 Aaron McGruder/Dist. by Universal Press Syndicate
FOR THE RECORD, I **DO** FEEL GUILTY WHEN THE PRESIDENT'S DISASTROUS FOREIGN POLICIES ACCIDENTALLY BENEFIT ME PERSONALLY.

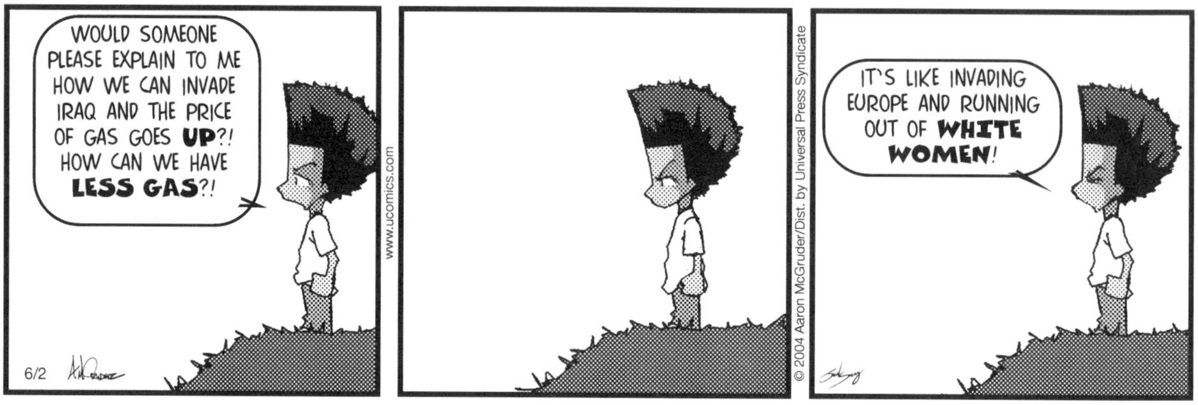
WOULD SOMEONE PLEASE EXPLAIN TO ME HOW WE CAN INVADE IRAQ AND THE PRICE OF GAS GOES **UP**?! HOW CAN WE HAVE **LESS GAS**?!
6/2
www.ucomics.com
© 2004 Aaron McGruder/Dist. by Universal Press Syndicate
IT'S LIKE INVADING EUROPE AND RUNNING OUT OF **WHITE WOMEN**!

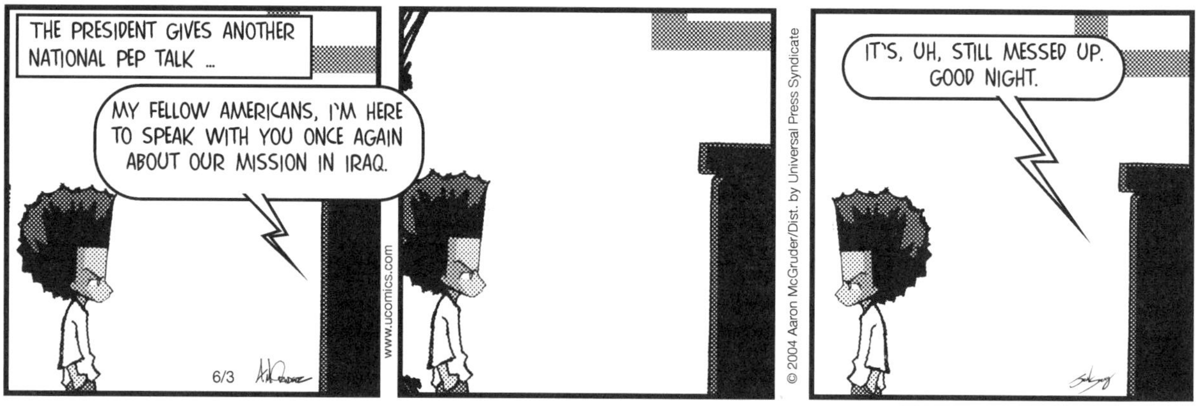
THE PRESIDENT GIVES ANOTHER NATIONAL PEP TALK ...
MY FELLOW AMERICANS, I'M HERE TO SPEAK WITH YOU ONCE AGAIN ABOUT OUR MISSION IN IRAQ.
6/3
www.ucomics.com
© 2004 Aaron McGruder/Dist. by Universal Press Syndicate
IT'S, UH, STILL MESSED UP. GOOD NIGHT.

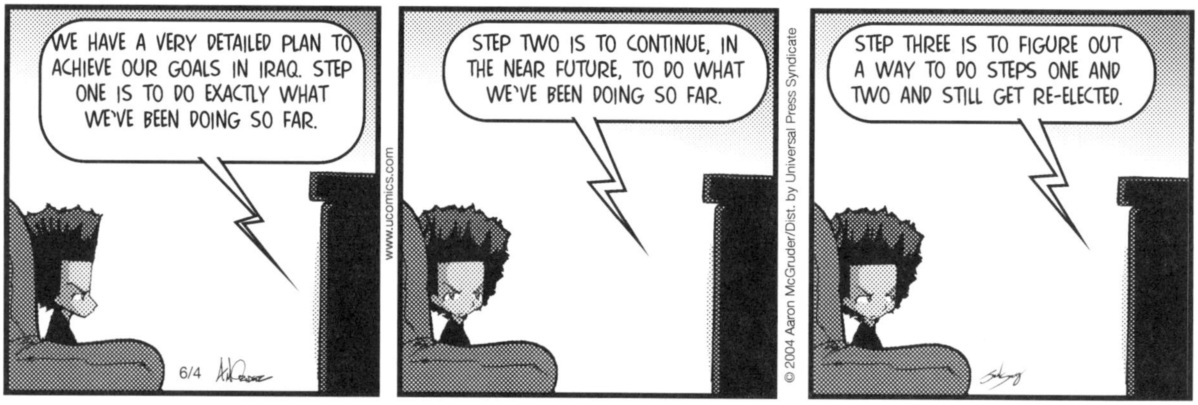
WE HAVE A VERY DETAILED PLAN TO ACHIEVE OUR GOALS IN IRAQ. STEP ONE IS TO DO EXACTLY WHAT WE'VE BEEN DOING SO FAR.
6/4
www.ucomics.com
STEP TWO IS TO CONTINUE, IN THE NEAR FUTURE, TO DO WHAT WE'VE BEEN DOING SO FAR.
© 2004 Aaron McGruder/Dist. by Universal Press Syndicate
STEP THREE IS TO FIGURE OUT A WAY TO DO STEPS ONE AND TWO AND STILL GET RE-ELECTED.

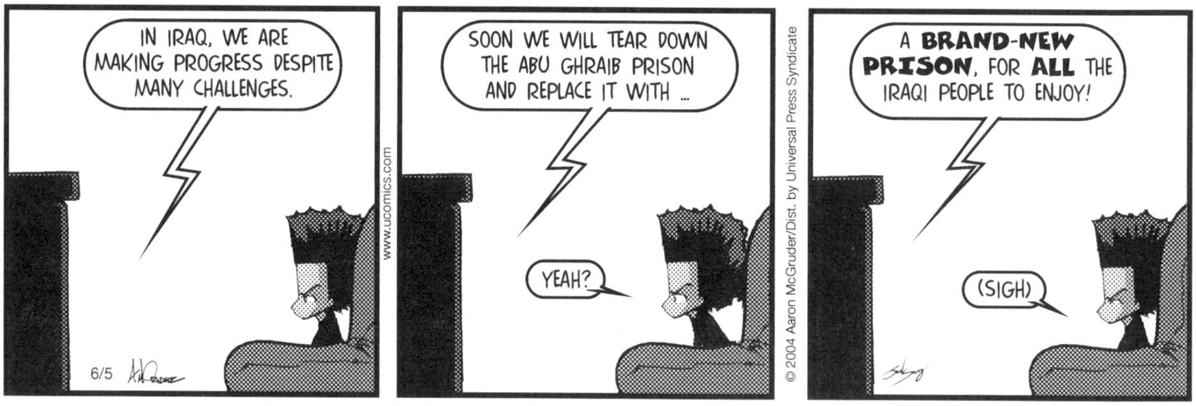
IN IRAQ, WE ARE MAKING PROGRESS DESPITE MANY CHALLENGES.
6/5
www.ucomics.com
SOON WE WILL TEAR DOWN THE ABU GHRAIB PRISON AND REPLACE IT WITH ...
YEAH?
© 2004 Aaron McGruder/Dist. by Universal Press Syndicate
A **BRAND-NEW PRISON**, FOR **ALL** THE IRAQI PEOPLE TO ENJOY!
(SIGH)

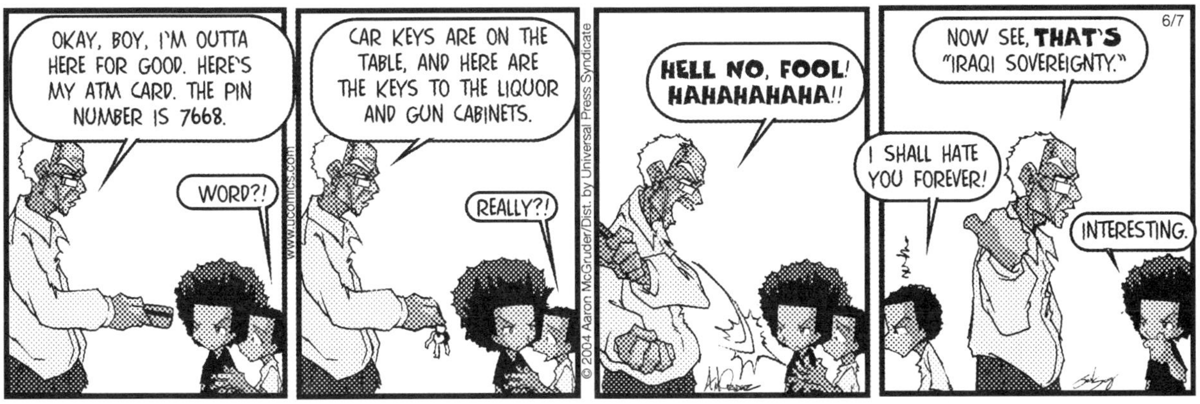
OKAY, BOY, I'M OUTTA HERE FOR GOOD. HERE'S MY ATM CARD. THE PIN NUMBER IS 7668.
WORD?!
www.ucomics.com
CAR KEYS ARE ON THE TABLE, AND HERE ARE THE KEYS TO THE LIQUOR AND GUN CABINETS.
REALLY?!
© 2004 Aaron McGruder/Dist. by Universal Press Syndicate
HELL NO, FOOL! HAHAHAHAHA!!
6/7
NOW SEE, THAT'S "IRAQI SOVEREIGNTY."
I SHALL HATE YOU FOREVER!
INTERESTING.

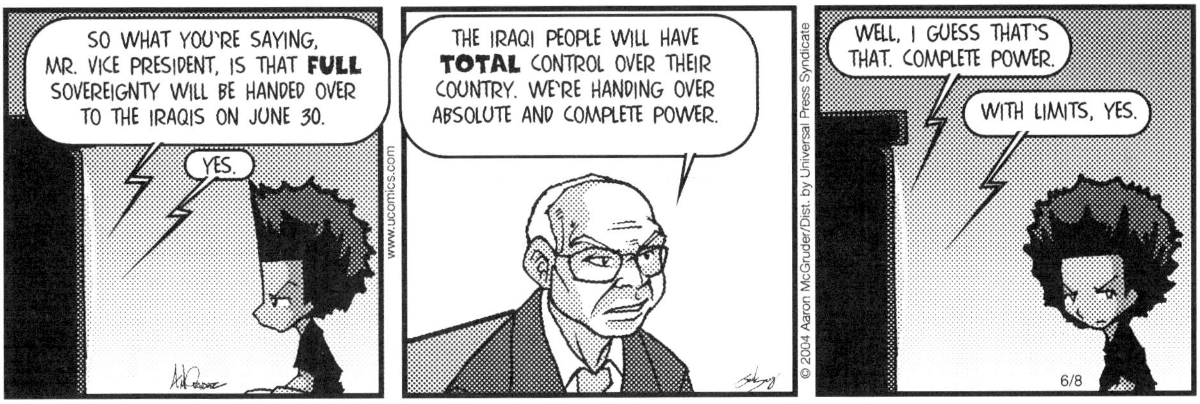
SO WHAT YOU'RE SAYING, MR. VICE PRESIDENT, IS THAT FULL SOVEREIGNTY WILL BE HANDED OVER TO THE IRAQIS ON JUNE 30.
YES.
www.ucomics.com
THE IRAQI PEOPLE WILL HAVE TOTAL CONTROL OVER THEIR COUNTRY. WE'RE HANDING OVER ABSOLUTE AND COMPLETE POWER.
© 2004 Aaron McGruder/Dist. by Universal Press Syndicate
WELL, I GUESS THAT'S THAT. COMPLETE POWER.
WITH LIMITS, YES.
6/8

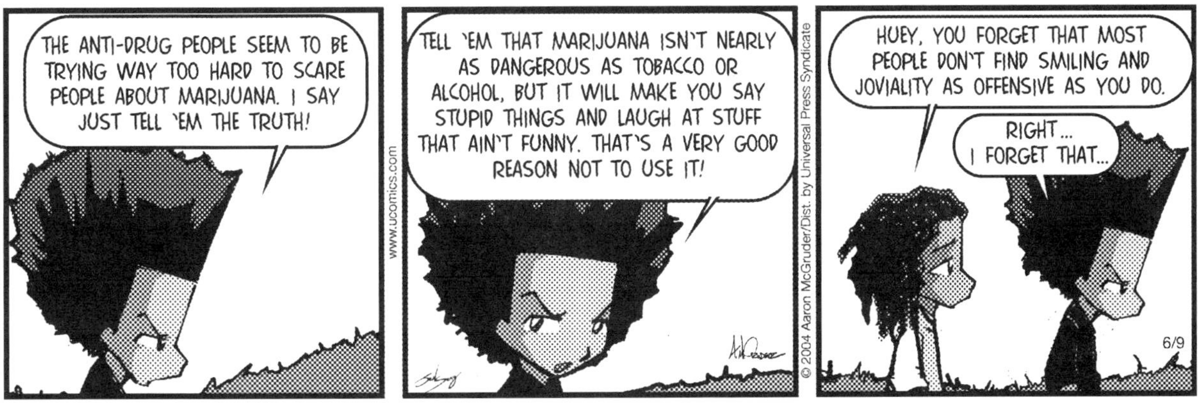
THE ANTI-DRUG PEOPLE SEEM TO BE TRYING WAY TOO HARD TO SCARE PEOPLE ABOUT MARIJUANA. I SAY JUST TELL 'EM THE TRUTH!
www.ucomics.com
TELL 'EM THAT MARIJUANA ISN'T NEARLY AS DANGEROUS AS TOBACCO OR ALCOHOL, BUT IT WILL MAKE YOU SAY STUPID THINGS AND LAUGH AT STUFF THAT AIN'T FUNNY. THAT'S A VERY GOOD REASON NOT TO USE IT!
© 2004 Aaron McGruder/Dist. by Universal Press Syndicate
HUEY, YOU FORGET THAT MOST PEOPLE DON'T FIND SMILING AND JOVIALITY AS OFFENSIVE AS YOU DO.
RIGHT... I FORGET THAT...
6/9

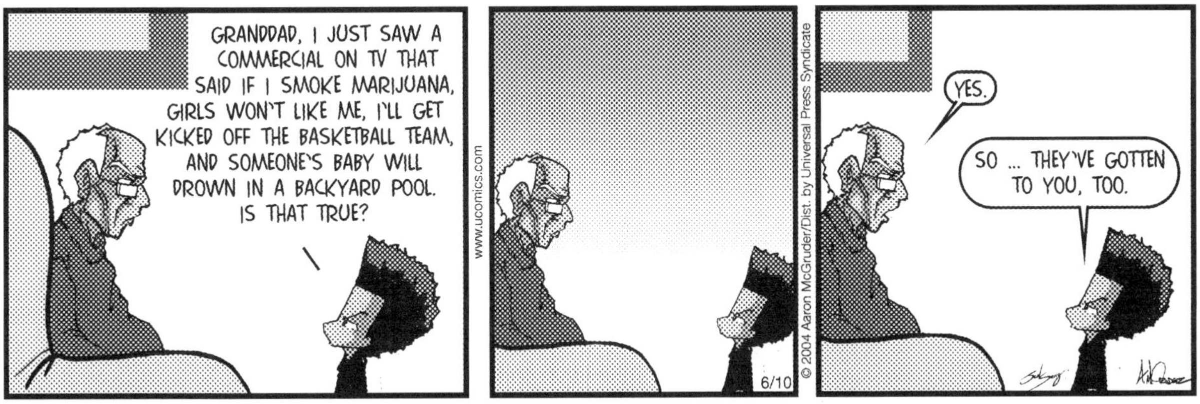
GRANDDAD, I JUST SAW A COMMERCIAL ON TV THAT SAID IF I SMOKE MARIJUANA, GIRLS WON'T LIKE ME, I'LL GET KICKED OFF THE BASKETBALL TEAM, AND SOMEONE'S BABY WILL DROWN IN A BACKYARD POOL. IS THAT TRUE?
www.ucomics.com
6/10
© 2004 Aaron McGruder/Dist. by Universal Press Syndicate
YES.
SO ... THEY'VE GOTTEN TO YOU, TOO.

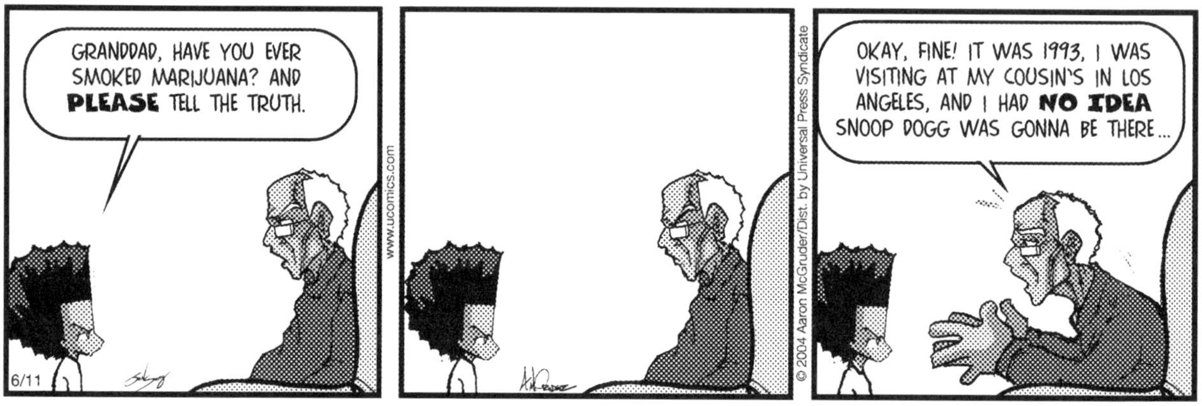
GRANDDAD, HAVE YOU EVER SMOKED MARIJUANA? AND **PLEASE** TELL THE TRUTH.
OKAY, FINE! IT WAS 1993, I WAS VISITING AT MY COUSIN'S IN LOS ANGELES, AND I HAD **NO IDEA** SNOOP DOGG WAS GONNA BE THERE ...
6/11
www.ucomics.com
© 2004 Aaron McGruder/Dist. by Universal Press Syndicate

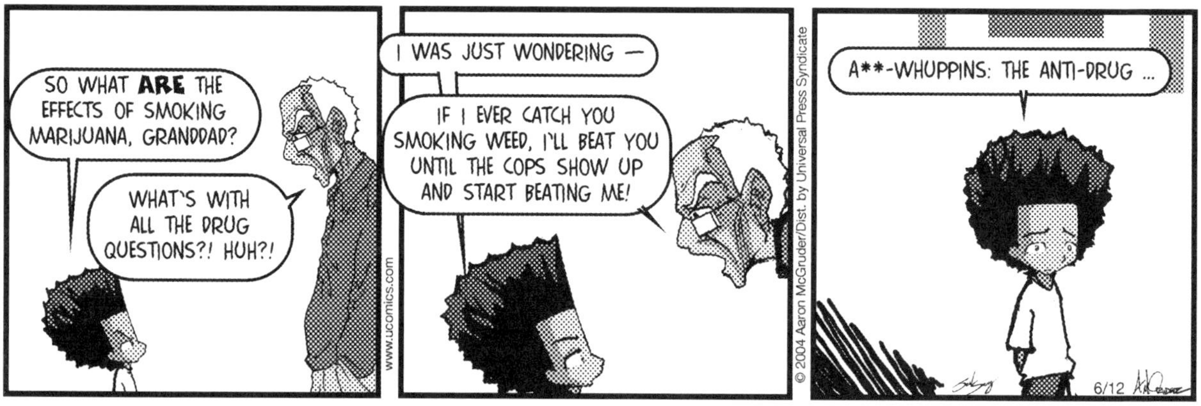
SO WHAT **ARE** THE EFFECTS OF SMOKING MARIJUANA, GRANDDAD?
WHAT'S WITH ALL THE DRUG QUESTIONS?! HUH?!
I WAS JUST WONDERING —
IF I EVER CATCH YOU SMOKING WEED, I'LL BEAT YOU UNTIL THE COPS SHOW UP AND START BEATING ME!
A**-WHUPPINS: THE ANTI-DRUG ...
6/12
www.ucomics.com
© 2004 Aaron McGruder/Dist. by Universal Press Syndicate

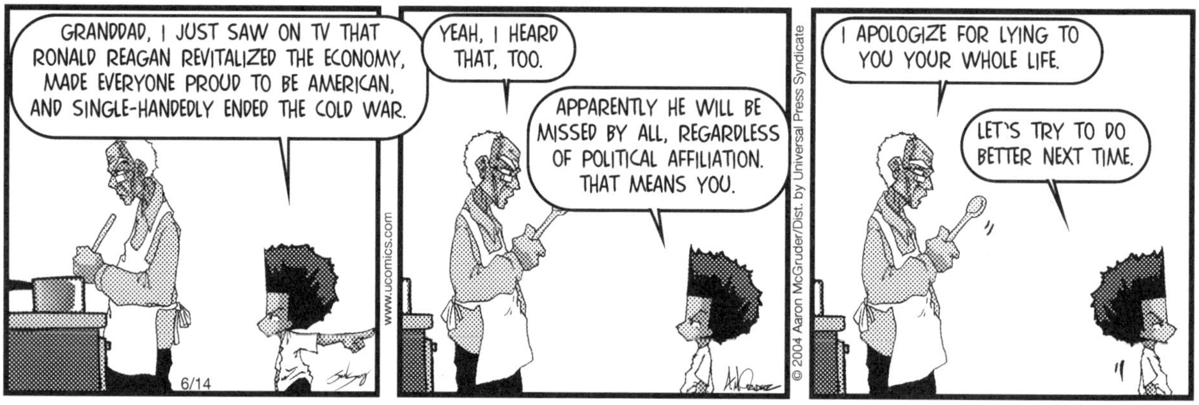
GRANDDAD, I JUST SAW ON TV THAT RONALD REAGAN REVITALIZED THE ECONOMY, MADE EVERYONE PROUD TO BE AMERICAN, AND SINGLE-HANDEDLY ENDED THE COLD WAR.
YEAH, I HEARD THAT, TOO.
APPARENTLY HE WILL BE MISSED BY ALL, REGARDLESS OF POLITICAL AFFILIATION. THAT MEANS YOU.
I APOLOGIZE FOR LYING TO YOU YOUR WHOLE LIFE.
LET'S TRY TO DO BETTER NEXT TIME.
6/14
www.ucomics.com
© 2004 Aaron McGruder/Dist. by Universal Press Syndicate

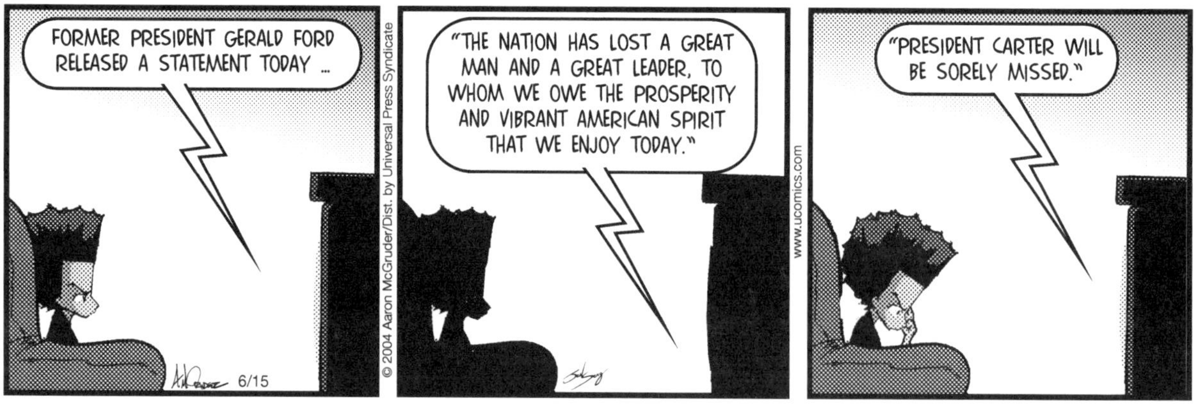
FORMER PRESIDENT GERALD FORD RELEASED A STATEMENT TODAY ...
"THE NATION HAS LOST A GREAT MAN AND A GREAT LEADER, TO WHOM WE OWE THE PROSPERITY AND VIBRANT AMERICAN SPIRIT THAT WE ENJOY TODAY."
"PRESIDENT CARTER WILL BE SORELY MISSED."
6/15
© 2004 Aaron McGruder/Dist. by Universal Press Syndicate
www.ucomics.com

To the Reader:

This feature was found not to be in keeping with the national mood of "selective memory" regarding the Reagan presidency, and some of its content may have been altered to make it more fit for public viewing.

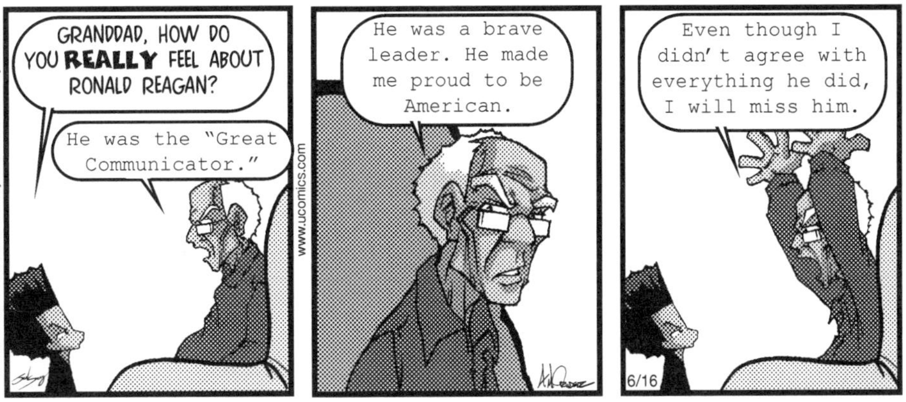
© 2004 Aaron McGruder/Dist. by Universal Press Syndicate
GRANDDAD, HOW DO YOU **REALLY** FEEL ABOUT RONALD REAGAN?
He was the "Great Communicator."
www.ucomics.com
He was a brave leader. He made me proud to be American.
Even though I didn't agree with everything he did, I will miss him.
6/16

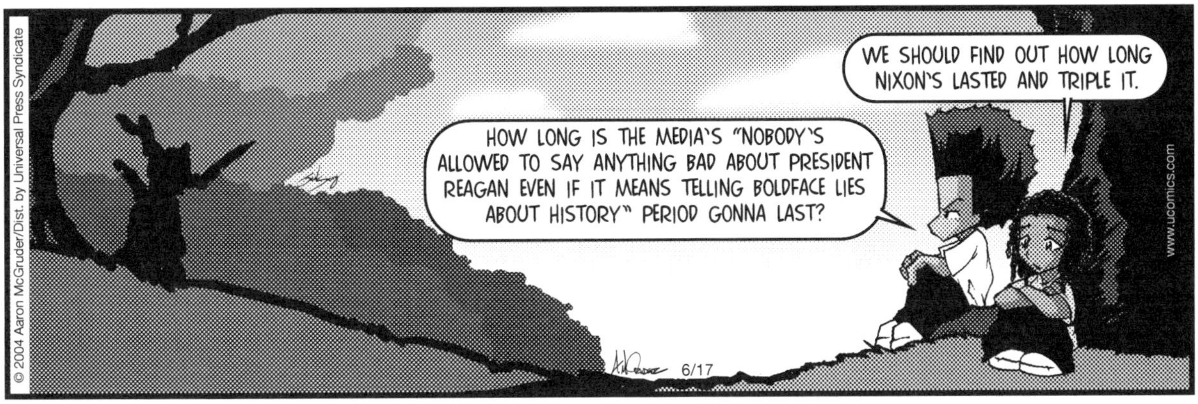
© 2004 Aaron McGruder/Dist. by Universal Press Syndicate
HOW LONG IS THE MEDIA'S "NOBODY'S ALLOWED TO SAY ANYTHING BAD ABOUT PRESIDENT REAGAN EVEN IF IT MEANS TELLING BOLDFACE LIES ABOUT HISTORY" PERIOD GONNA LAST?
WE SHOULD FIND OUT HOW LONG NIXON'S LASTED AND TRIPLE IT.
www.ucomics.com
6/17

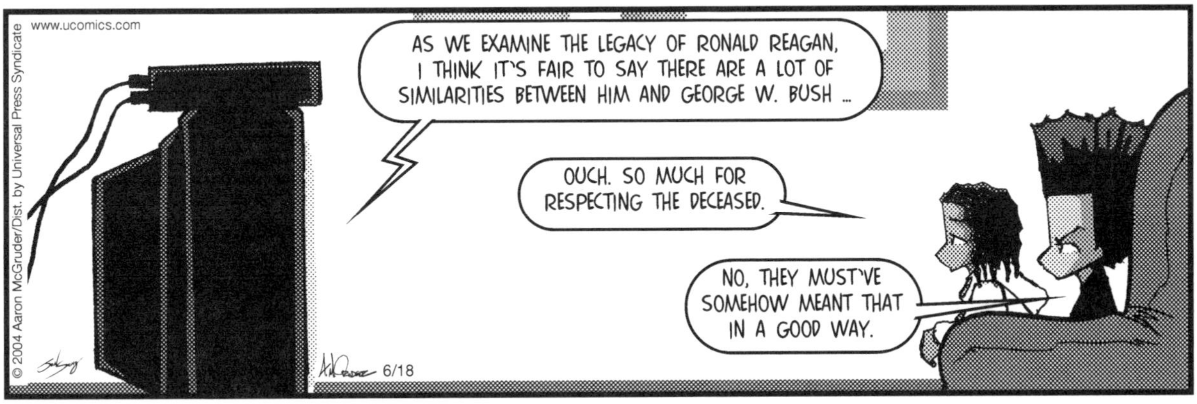
© 2004 Aaron McGruder/Dist. by Universal Press Syndicate
www.ucomics.com
AS WE EXAMINE THE LEGACY OF RONALD REAGAN, I THINK IT'S FAIR TO SAY THERE ARE A LOT OF SIMILARITIES BETWEEN HIM AND GEORGE W. BUSH ...
OUCH. SO MUCH FOR RESPECTING THE DECEASED.
NO, THEY MUST'VE SOMEHOW MEANT THAT IN A GOOD WAY.
6/18

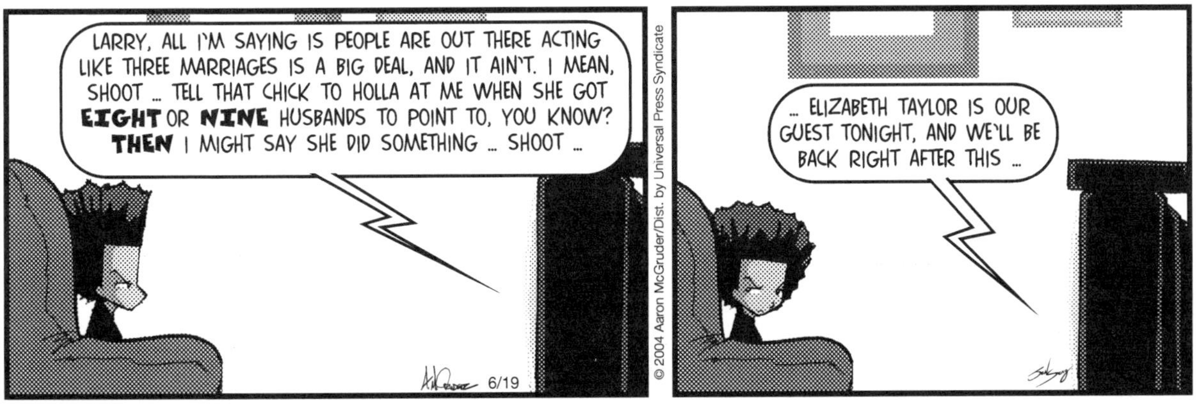
LARRY, ALL I'M SAYING IS PEOPLE ARE OUT THERE ACTING LIKE THREE MARRIAGES IS A BIG DEAL, AND IT AIN'T. I MEAN, SHOOT ... TELL THAT CHICK TO HOLLA AT ME WHEN SHE GOT **EIGHT** OR **NINE** HUSBANDS TO POINT TO, YOU KNOW? **THEN** I MIGHT SAY SHE DID SOMETHING ... SHOOT ...
6/19
© 2004 Aaron McGruder/Dist. by Universal Press Syndicate
... ELIZABETH TAYLOR IS OUR GUEST TONIGHT, AND WE'LL BE BACK RIGHT AFTER THIS ...

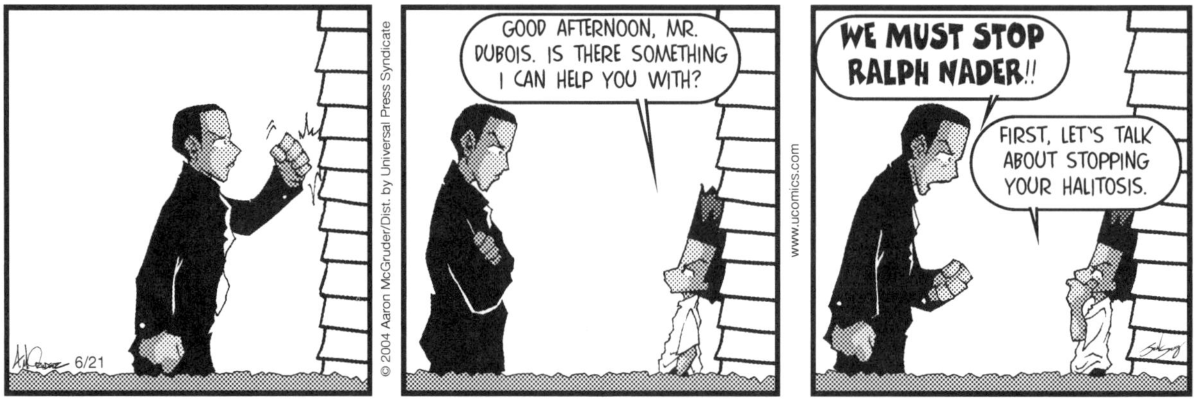
6/21
© 2004 Aaron McGruder/Dist. by Universal Press Syndicate
GOOD AFTERNOON, MR. DUBOIS. IS THERE SOMETHING I CAN HELP YOU WITH?
www.ucomics.com
WE MUST STOP RALPH NADER!!
FIRST, LET'S TALK ABOUT STOPPING YOUR HALITOSIS.

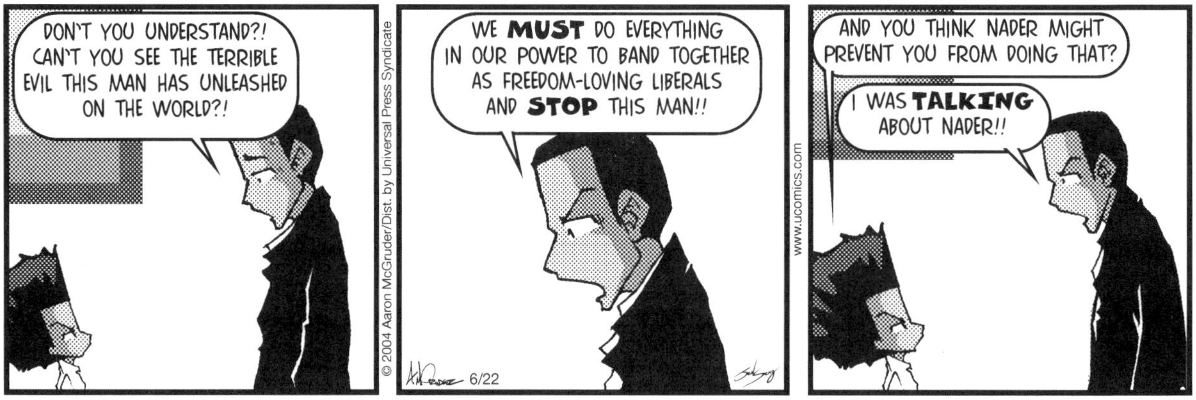
DON'T YOU UNDERSTAND?! CAN'T YOU SEE THE TERRIBLE EVIL THIS MAN HAS UNLEASHED ON THE WORLD?!
© 2004 Aaron McGruder/Dist. by Universal Press Syndicate
6/22
WE MUST DO EVERYTHING IN OUR POWER TO BAND TOGETHER AS FREEDOM-LOVING LIBERALS AND STOP THIS MAN!!
www.ucomics.com
AND YOU THINK NADER MIGHT PREVENT YOU FROM DOING THAT?
I WAS TALKING ABOUT NADER!!

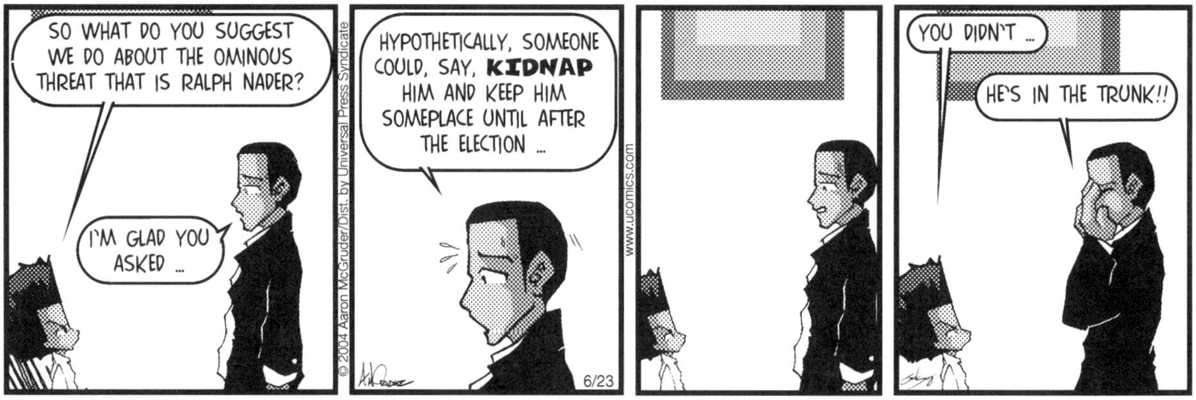
SO WHAT DO YOU SUGGEST WE DO ABOUT THE OMINOUS THREAT THAT IS RALPH NADER?
I'M GLAD YOU ASKED ...
© 2004 Aaron McGruder/Dist. by Universal Press Syndicate
HYPOTHETICALLY, SOMEONE COULD, SAY, KIDNAP HIM AND KEEP HIM SOMEPLACE UNTIL AFTER THE ELECTION ...
6/23
www.ucomics.com
YOU DIDN'T ...
HE'S IN THE TRUNK!!

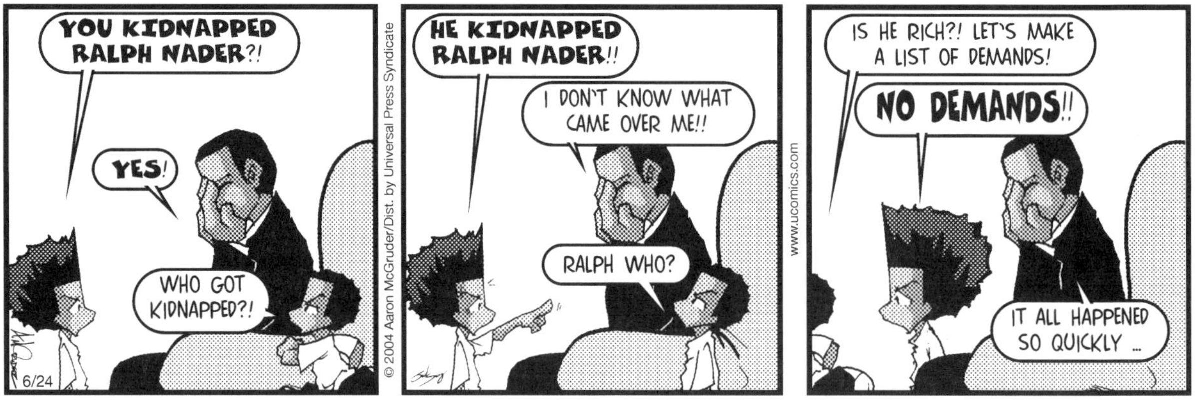
YOU KIDNAPPED RALPH NADER?!
YES!
WHO GOT KIDNAPPED?!
6/24
© 2004 Aaron McGruder/Dist. by Universal Press Syndicate
HE KIDNAPPED RALPH NADER!!
I DON'T KNOW WHAT CAME OVER ME!!
RALPH WHO?
www.ucomics.com
IS HE RICH?! LET'S MAKE A LIST OF DEMANDS!
NO DEMANDS!!
IT ALL HAPPENED SO QUICKLY ...

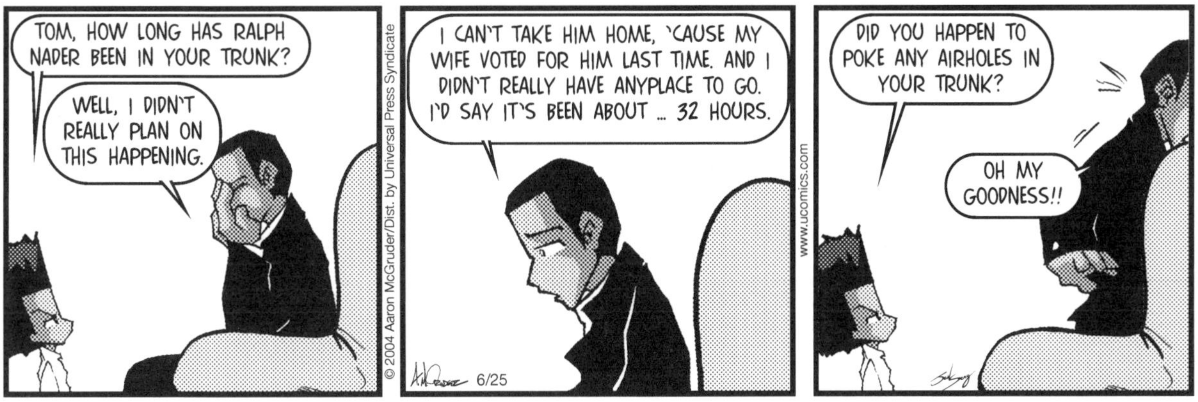
TOM, HOW LONG HAS RALPH NADER BEEN IN YOUR TRUNK?
WELL, I DIDN'T REALLY PLAN ON THIS HAPPENING.
© 2004 Aaron McGruder/Dist. by Universal Press Syndicate
I CAN'T TAKE HIM HOME, 'CAUSE MY WIFE VOTED FOR HIM LAST TIME. AND I DIDN'T REALLY HAVE ANYPLACE TO GO. I'D SAY IT'S BEEN ABOUT ... 32 HOURS.
6/25
DID YOU HAPPEN TO POKE ANY AIRHOLES IN YOUR TRUNK?
OH MY GOODNESS!!
www.ucomics.com

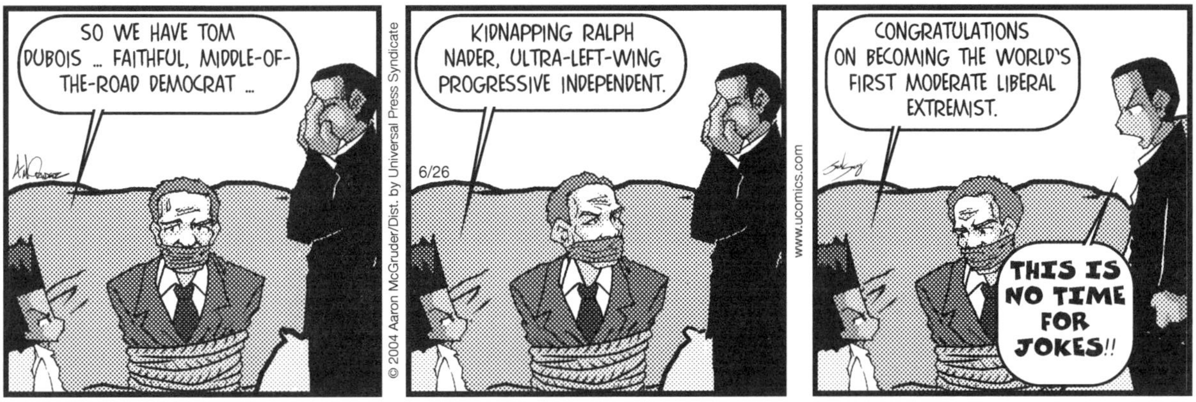
SO WE HAVE TOM DUBOIS ... FAITHFUL, MIDDLE-OF-THE-ROAD DEMOCRAT ...
© 2004 Aaron McGruder/Dist. by Universal Press Syndicate
KIDNAPPING RALPH NADER, ULTRA-LEFT-WING PROGRESSIVE INDEPENDENT.
6/26
CONGRATULATIONS ON BECOMING THE WORLD'S FIRST MODERATE LIBERAL EXTREMIST.
www.ucomics.com
THIS IS NO TIME FOR JOKES!!

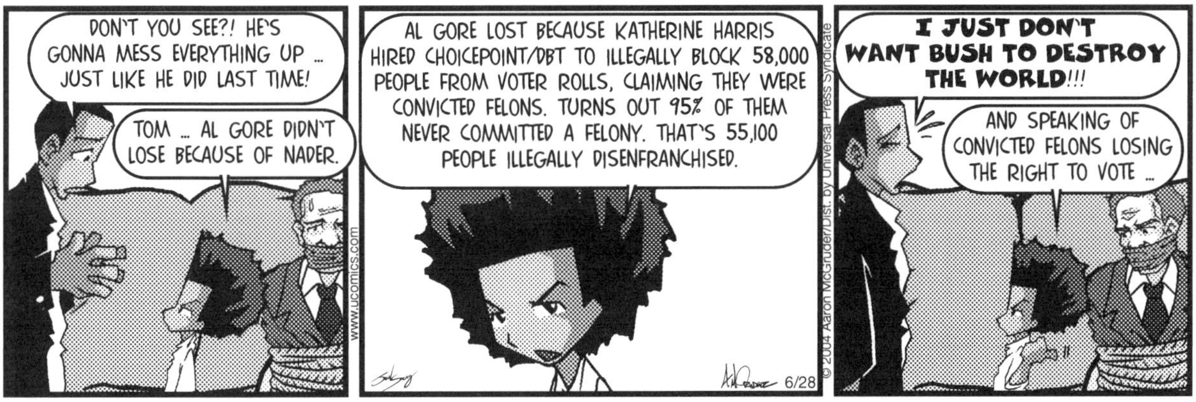
DON'T YOU SEE?! HE'S GONNA MESS EVERYTHING UP ... JUST LIKE HE DID LAST TIME!
TOM ... AL GORE DIDN'T LOSE BECAUSE OF NADER.
www.ucomics.com
AL GORE LOST BECAUSE KATHERINE HARRIS HIRED CHOICEPOINT/DBT TO ILLEGALLY BLOCK 58,000 PEOPLE FROM VOTER ROLLS, CLAIMING THEY WERE CONVICTED FELONS. TURNS OUT 95% OF THEM NEVER COMMITTED A FELONY. THAT'S 55,100 PEOPLE ILLEGALLY DISENFRANCHISED.
6/28
© 2004 Aaron McGruder/Dist. by Universal Press Syndicate
I JUST DON'T WANT BUSH TO DESTROY THE WORLD!!!
AND SPEAKING OF CONVICTED FELONS LOSING THE RIGHT TO VOTE ...

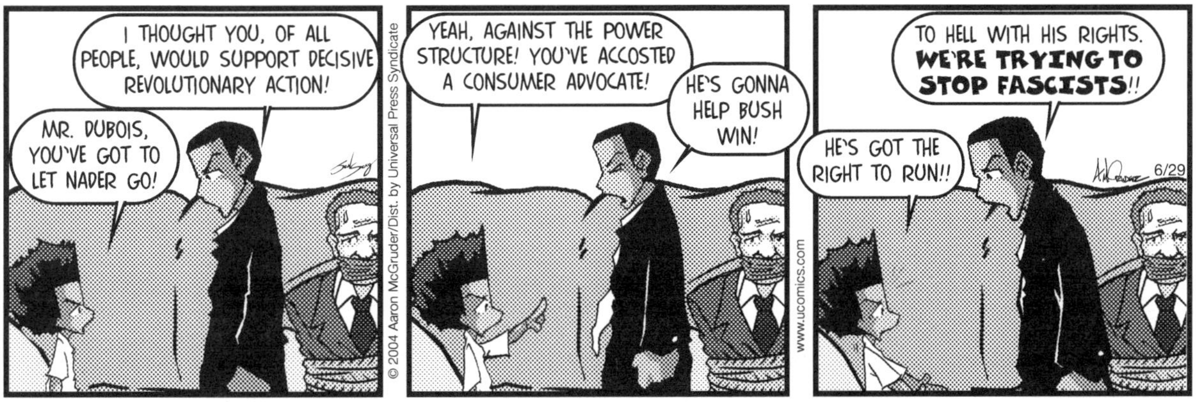
I THOUGHT YOU, OF ALL PEOPLE, WOULD SUPPORT DECISIVE REVOLUTIONARY ACTION!
MR. DUBOIS, YOU'VE GOT TO LET NADER GO!
© 2004 Aaron McGruder/Dist. by Universal Press Syndicate
YEAH, AGAINST THE POWER STRUCTURE! YOU'VE ACCOSTED A CONSUMER ADVOCATE!
HE'S GONNA HELP BUSH WIN!
www.ucomics.com
TO HELL WITH HIS RIGHTS. WE'RE TRYING TO STOP FASCISTS!!
HE'S GOT THE RIGHT TO RUN!!
6/29

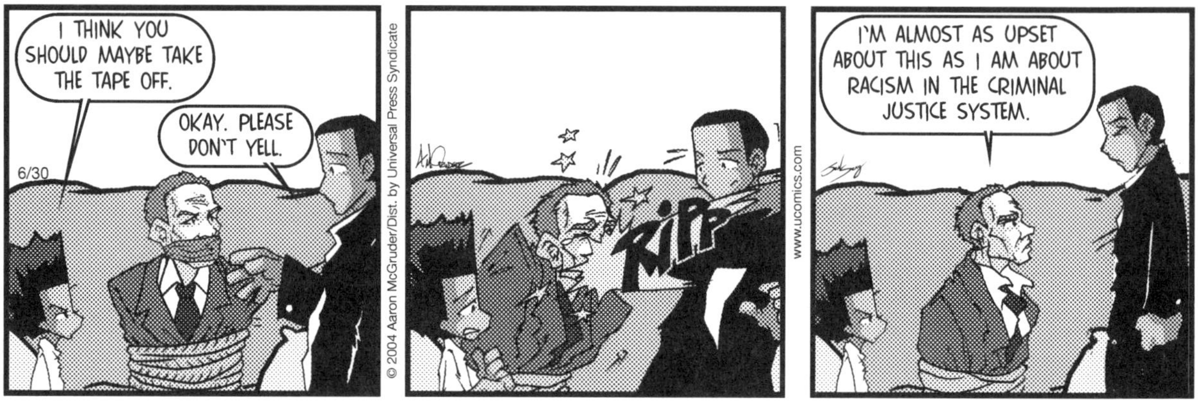
I THINK YOU SHOULD MAYBE TAKE THE TAPE OFF.
OKAY. PLEASE DON'T YELL.
6/30
© 2004 Aaron McGruder/Dist. by Universal Press Syndicate
RIPP
www.ucomics.com
I'M ALMOST AS UPSET ABOUT THIS AS I AM ABOUT RACISM IN THE CRIMINAL JUSTICE SYSTEM.

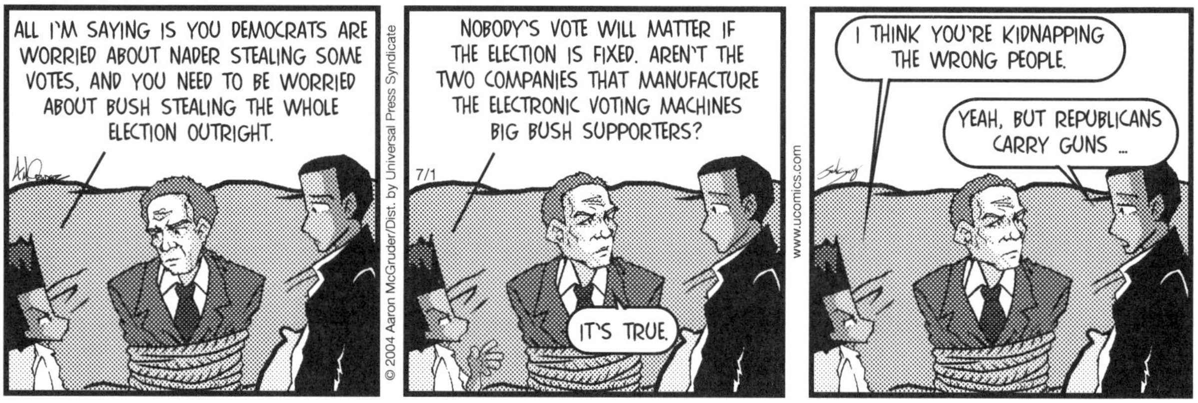
ALL I'M SAYING IS YOU DEMOCRATS ARE WORRIED ABOUT NADER STEALING SOME VOTES, AND YOU NEED TO BE WORRIED ABOUT BUSH STEALING THE WHOLE ELECTION OUTRIGHT.
© 2004 Aaron McGruder/Dist. by Universal Press Syndicate
NOBODY'S VOTE WILL MATTER IF THE ELECTION IS FIXED. AREN'T THE TWO COMPANIES THAT MANUFACTURE THE ELECTRONIC VOTING MACHINES BIG BUSH SUPPORTERS?
7/1
IT'S TRUE.
www.ucomics.com
I THINK YOU'RE KIDNAPPING THE WRONG PEOPLE.
YEAH, BUT REPUBLICANS CARRY GUNS ...

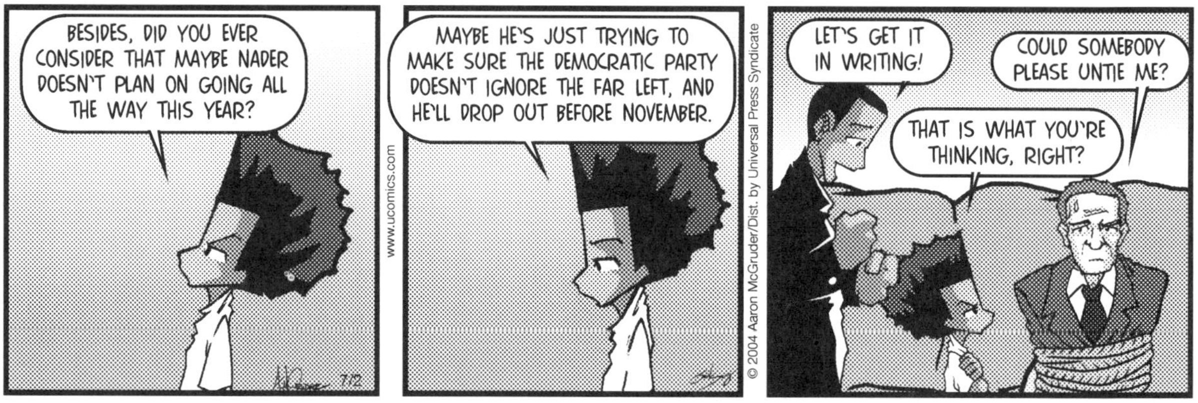
BESIDES, DID YOU EVER CONSIDER THAT MAYBE NADER DOESN'T PLAN ON GOING ALL THE WAY THIS YEAR?
7/2
www.ucomics.com
MAYBE HE'S JUST TRYING TO MAKE SURE THE DEMOCRATIC PARTY DOESN'T IGNORE THE FAR LEFT, AND HE'LL DROP OUT BEFORE NOVEMBER.
© 2004 Aaron McGruder/Dist. by Universal Press Syndicate
LET'S GET IT IN WRITING!
COULD SOMEBODY PLEASE UNTIE ME?
THAT IS WHAT YOU'RE THINKING, RIGHT?

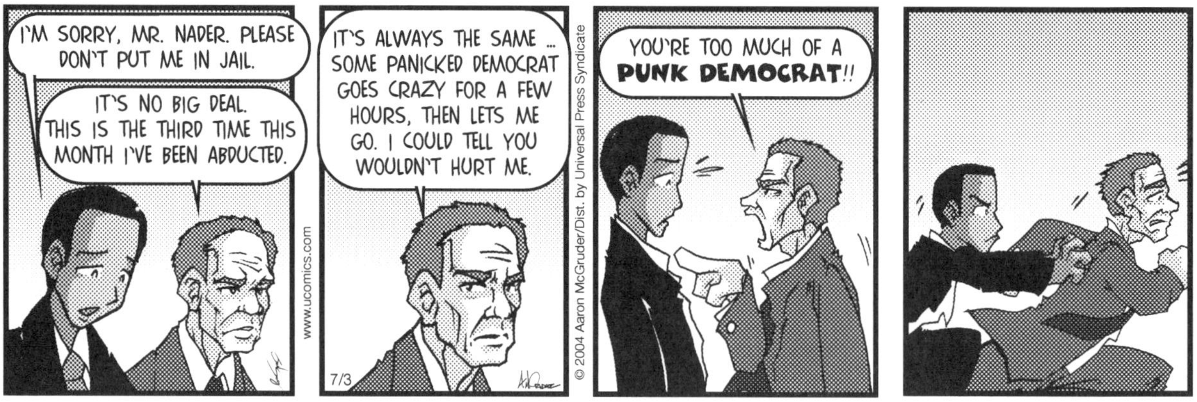
I'M SORRY, MR. NADER. PLEASE DON'T PUT ME IN JAIL.
IT'S NO BIG DEAL. THIS IS THE THIRD TIME THIS MONTH I'VE BEEN ABDUCTED.
www.ucomics.com
IT'S ALWAYS THE SAME ... SOME PANICKED DEMOCRAT GOES CRAZY FOR A FEW HOURS, THEN LETS ME GO. I COULD TELL YOU WOULDN'T HURT ME.
7/3
© 2004 Aaron McGruder/Dist. by Universal Press Syndicate
YOU'RE TOO MUCH OF A PUNK DEMOCRAT!!

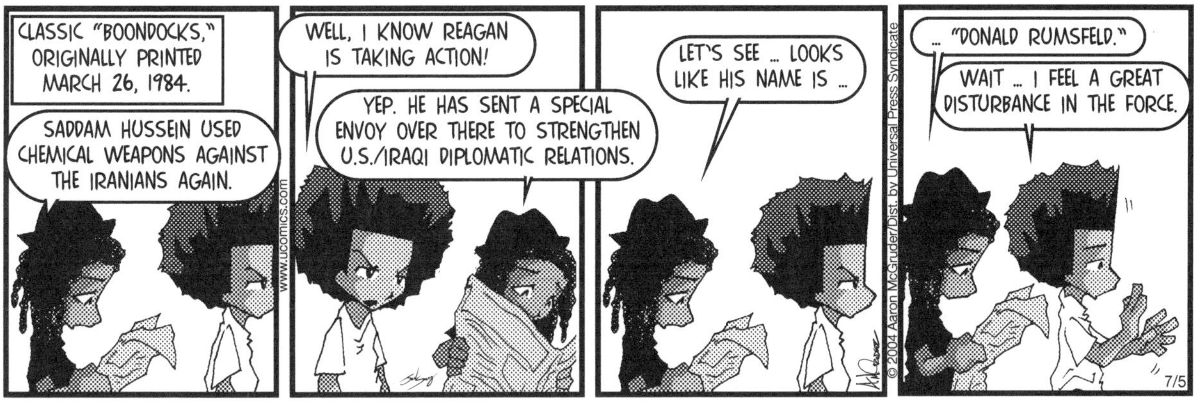
CLASSIC "BOONDOCKS," ORIGINALLY PRINTED MARCH 26, 1984.
SADDAM HUSSEIN USED CHEMICAL WEAPONS AGAINST THE IRANIANS AGAIN.
www.ucomics.com
WELL, I KNOW REAGAN IS TAKING ACTION!
YEP. HE HAS SENT A SPECIAL ENVOY OVER THERE TO STRENGTHEN U.S./IRAQI DIPLOMATIC RELATIONS.
LET'S SEE ... LOOKS LIKE HIS NAME IS ...
© 2004 Aaron McGruder/Dist. by Universal Press Syndicate
... "DONALD RUMSFELD."
WAIT ... I FEEL A GREAT DISTURBANCE IN THE FORCE.
7/5

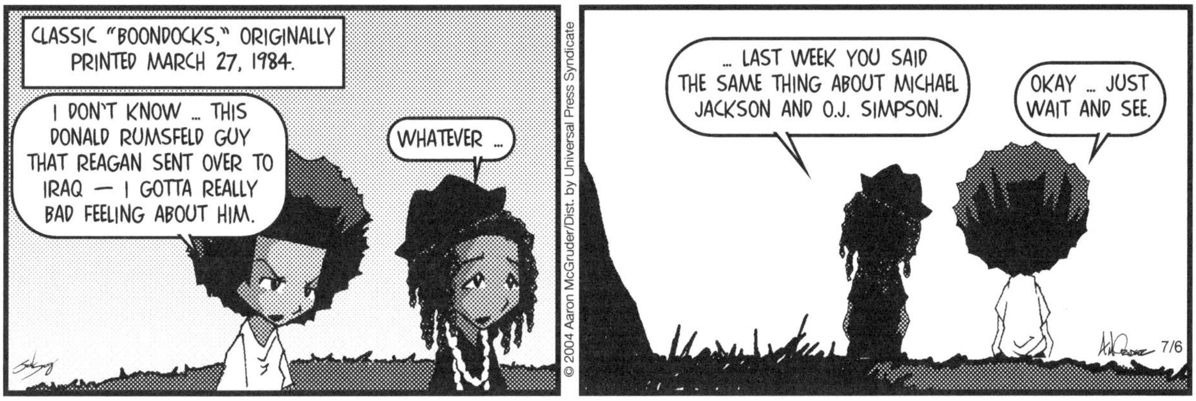
CLASSIC "BOONDOCKS," ORIGINALLY PRINTED MARCH 27, 1984.
I DON'T KNOW ... THIS DONALD RUMSFELD GUY THAT REAGAN SENT OVER TO IRAQ — I GOTTA REALLY BAD FEELING ABOUT HIM.
WHATEVER ...
© 2004 Aaron McGruder/Dist. by Universal Press Syndicate
... LAST WEEK YOU SAID THE SAME THING ABOUT MICHAEL JACKSON AND O.J. SIMPSON.
OKAY ... JUST WAIT AND SEE.
7/6

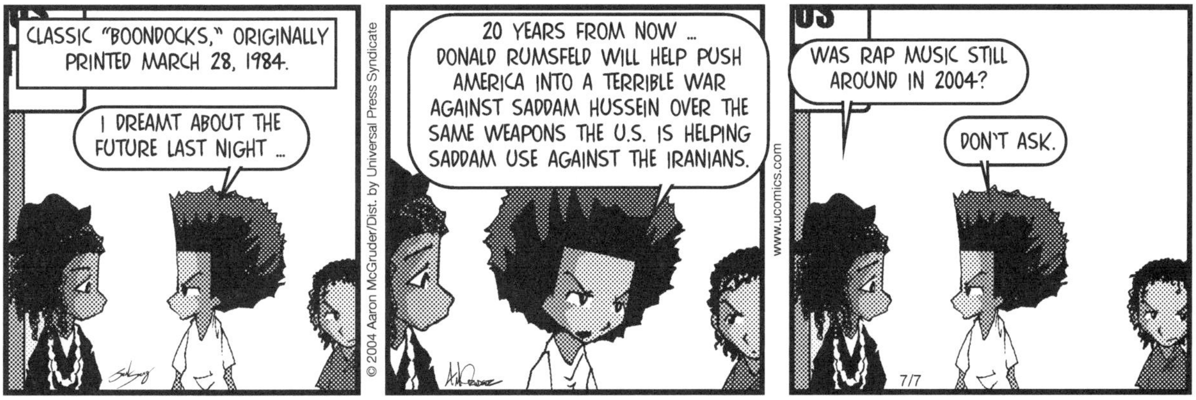
CLASSIC "BOONDOCKS," ORIGINALLY PRINTED MARCH 28, 1984.
I DREAMT ABOUT THE FUTURE LAST NIGHT ...
© 2004 Aaron McGruder/Dist. by Universal Press Syndicate
20 YEARS FROM NOW ... DONALD RUMSFELD WILL HELP PUSH AMERICA INTO A TERRIBLE WAR AGAINST SADDAM HUSSEIN OVER THE SAME WEAPONS THE U.S. IS HELPING SADDAM USE AGAINST THE IRANIANS.
www.ucomics.com
WAS RAP MUSIC STILL AROUND IN 2004?
DON'T ASK.
7/7

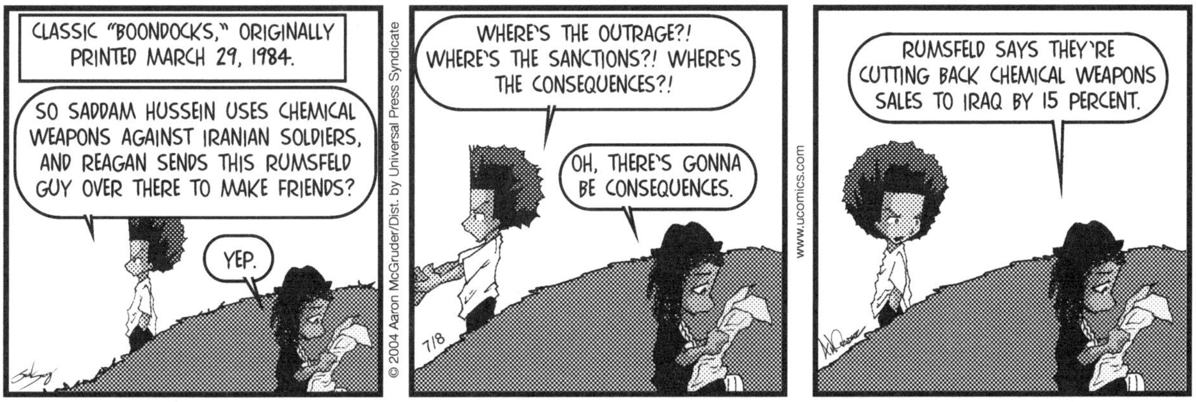
CLASSIC "BOONDOCKS," ORIGINALLY PRINTED MARCH 29, 1984.
SO SADDAM HUSSEIN USES CHEMICAL WEAPONS AGAINST IRANIAN SOLDIERS, AND REAGAN SENDS THIS RUMSFELD GUY OVER THERE TO MAKE FRIENDS?
YEP.
© 2004 Aaron McGruder/Dist. by Universal Press Syndicate
WHERE'S THE OUTRAGE?! WHERE'S THE SANCTIONS?! WHERE'S THE CONSEQUENCES?!
OH, THERE'S GONNA BE CONSEQUENCES.
7/8
www.ucomics.com
RUMSFELD SAYS THEY'RE CUTTING BACK CHEMICAL WEAPONS SALES TO IRAQ BY 15 PERCENT.

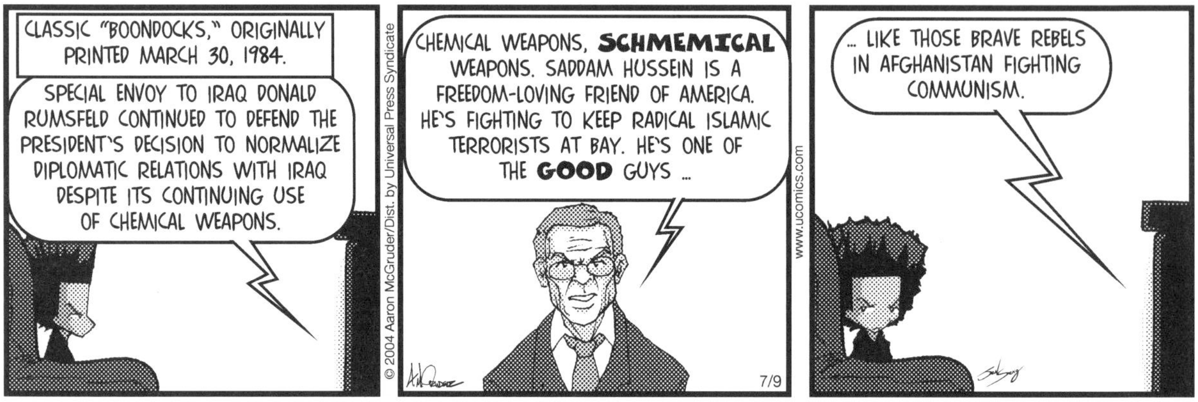
CLASSIC "BOONDOCKS," ORIGINALLY PRINTED MARCH 30, 1984.
SPECIAL ENVOY TO IRAQ DONALD RUMSFELD CONTINUED TO DEFEND THE PRESIDENT'S DECISION TO NORMALIZE DIPLOMATIC RELATIONS WITH IRAQ DESPITE ITS CONTINUING USE OF CHEMICAL WEAPONS.
CHEMICAL WEAPONS, **SCHMEMICAL** WEAPONS. SADDAM HUSSEIN IS A FREEDOM-LOVING FRIEND OF AMERICA. HE'S FIGHTING TO KEEP RADICAL ISLAMIC TERRORISTS AT BAY. HE'S ONE OF THE **GOOD** GUYS ...
... LIKE THOSE BRAVE REBELS IN AFGHANISTAN FIGHTING COMMUNISM.
© 2004 Aaron McGruder/Dist. by Universal Press Syndicate
www.ucomics.com
7/9

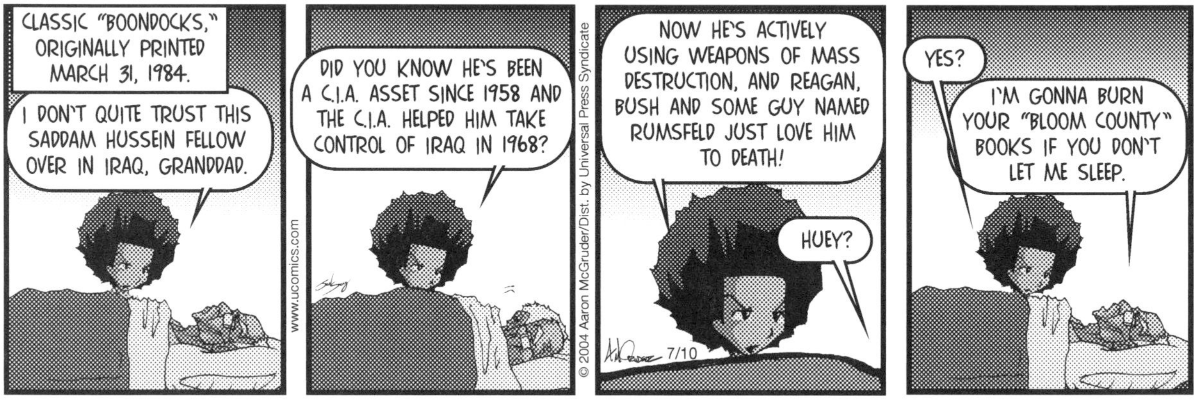
CLASSIC "BOONDOCKS," ORIGINALLY PRINTED MARCH 31, 1984.
I DON'T QUITE TRUST THIS SADDAM HUSSEIN FELLOW OVER IN IRAQ, GRANDDAD.
DID YOU KNOW HE'S BEEN A C.I.A. ASSET SINCE 1958 AND THE C.I.A. HELPED HIM TAKE CONTROL OF IRAQ IN 1968?
NOW HE'S ACTIVELY USING WEAPONS OF MASS DESTRUCTION, AND REAGAN, BUSH AND SOME GUY NAMED RUMSFELD JUST LOVE HIM TO DEATH!
HUEY?
YES?
I'M GONNA BURN YOUR "BLOOM COUNTY" BOOKS IF YOU DON'T LET ME SLEEP.
www.ucomics.com
© 2004 Aaron McGruder/Dist. by Universal Press Syndicate
7/10

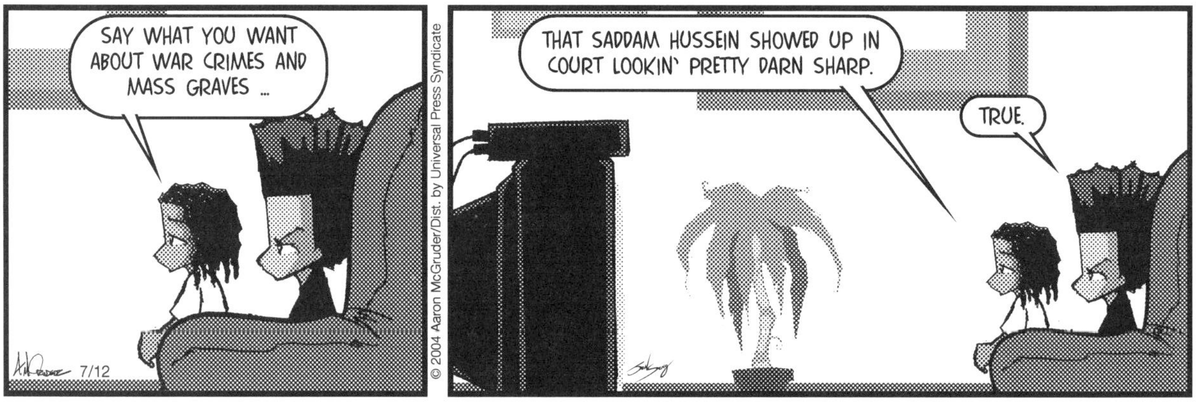
SAY WHAT YOU WANT ABOUT WAR CRIMES AND MASS GRAVES ...
THAT SADDAM HUSSEIN SHOWED UP IN COURT LOOKIN' PRETTY DARN SHARP.
TRUE.
7/12
© 2004 Aaron McGruder/Dist. by Universal Press Syndicate

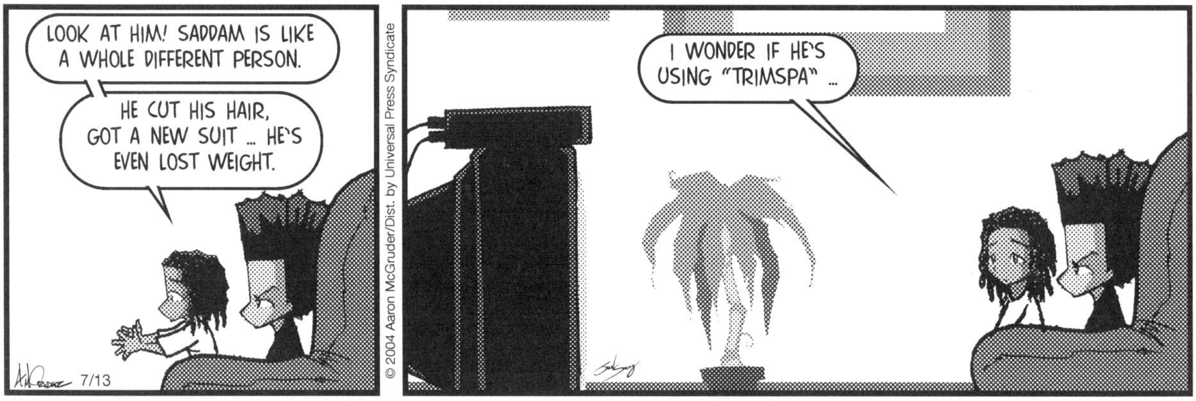
LOOK AT HIM! SADDAM IS LIKE A WHOLE DIFFERENT PERSON.
HE CUT HIS HAIR, GOT A NEW SUIT ... HE'S EVEN LOST WEIGHT.
I WONDER IF HE'S USING "TRIMSPA" ...
7/13
© 2004 Aaron McGruder/Dist. by Universal Press Syndicate

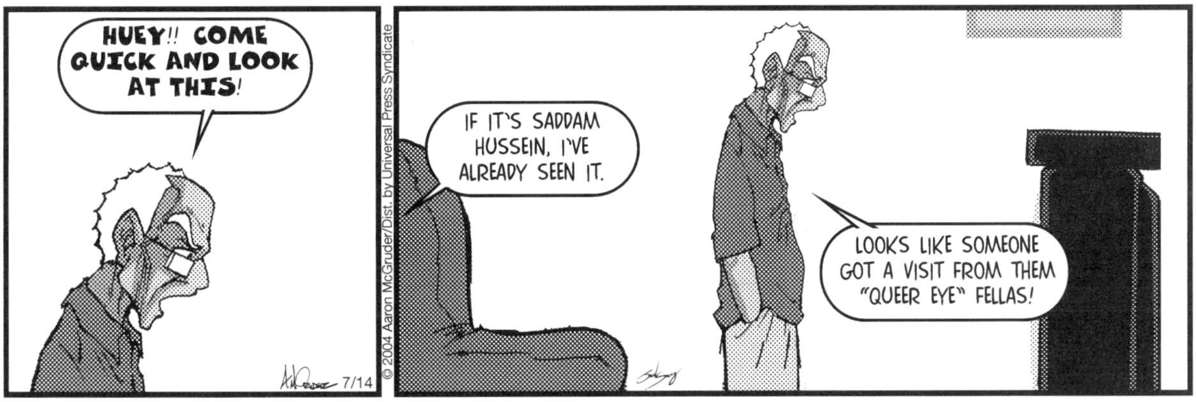
HUEY!! COME QUICK AND LOOK AT THIS!
IF IT'S SADDAM HUSSEIN, I'VE ALREADY SEEN IT.
LOOKS LIKE SOMEONE GOT A VISIT FROM THEM "QUEER EYE" FELLAS!
7/14
© 2004 Aaron McGruder/Dist. by Universal Press Syndicate

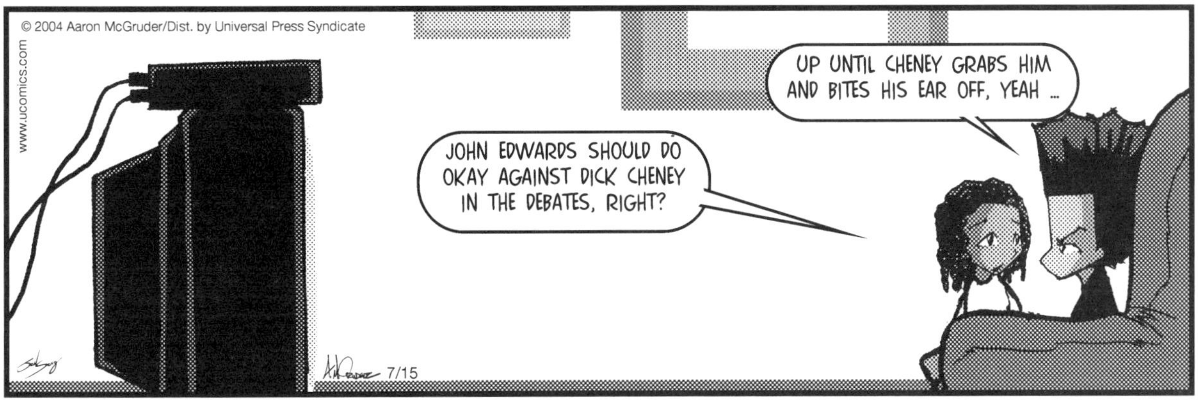
© 2004 Aaron McGruder/Dist. by Universal Press Syndicate
www.ucomics.com
JOHN EDWARDS SHOULD DO OKAY AGAINST DICK CHENEY IN THE DEBATES, RIGHT?
UP UNTIL CHENEY GRABS HIM AND BITES HIS EAR OFF, YEAH ...
7/15

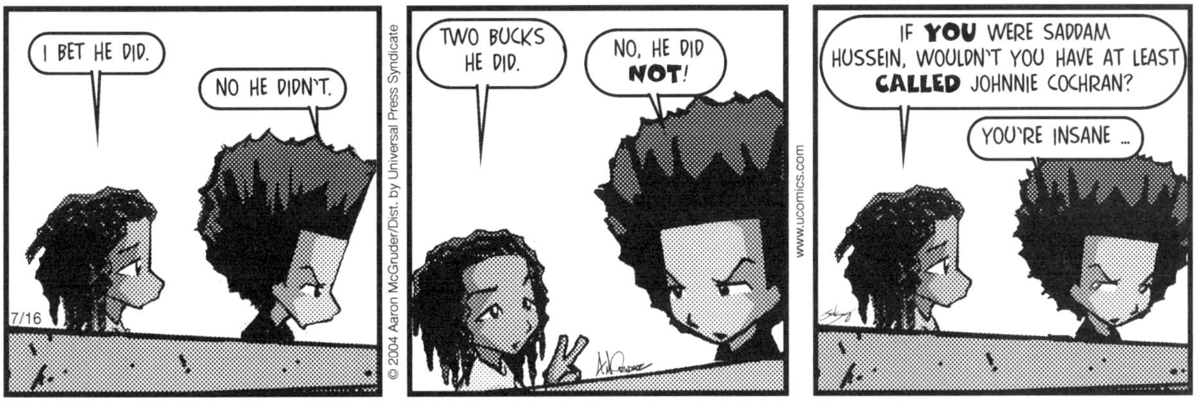
I BET HE DID.
NO HE DIDN'T.
7/16
© 2004 Aaron McGruder/Dist. by Universal Press Syndicate
TWO BUCKS HE DID.
NO, HE DID NOT!
www.ucomics.com
IF YOU WERE SADDAM HUSSEIN, WOULDN'T YOU HAVE AT LEAST CALLED JOHNNIE COCHRAN?
YOU'RE INSANE ...

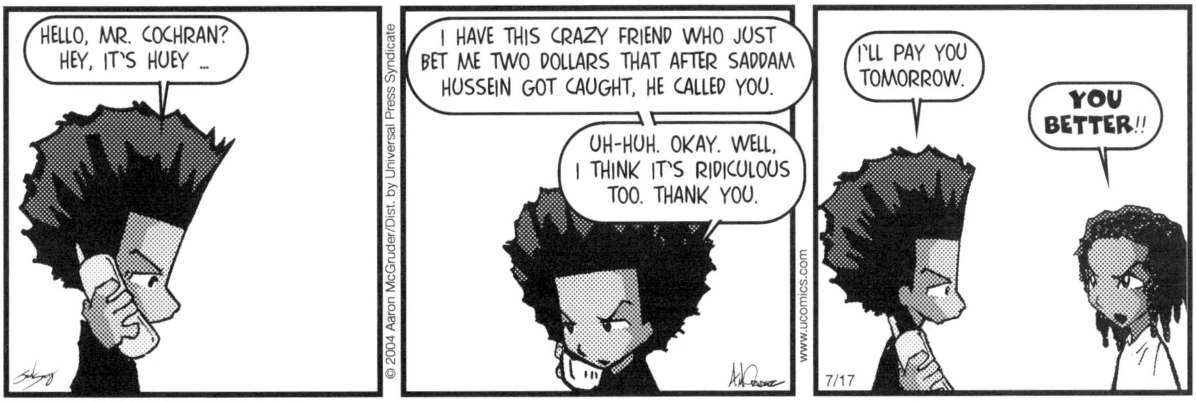
HELLO, MR. COCHRAN? HEY, IT'S HUEY ...
© 2004 Aaron McGruder/Dist. by Universal Press Syndicate
I HAVE THIS CRAZY FRIEND WHO JUST BET ME TWO DOLLARS THAT AFTER SADDAM HUSSEIN GOT CAUGHT, HE CALLED YOU.
UH-HUH. OKAY. WELL, I THINK IT'S RIDICULOUS TOO. THANK YOU.
www.ucomics.com
I'LL PAY YOU TOMORROW.
YOU BETTER!!
7/17

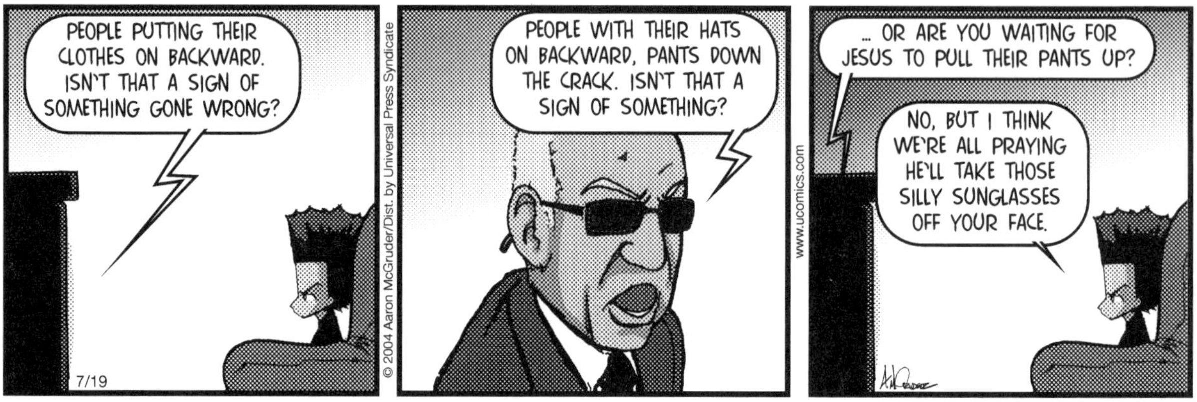
PEOPLE PUTTING THEIR CLOTHES ON BACKWARD. ISN'T THAT A SIGN OF SOMETHING GONE WRONG?
7/19
© 2004 Aaron McGruder/Dist. by Universal Press Syndicate
PEOPLE WITH THEIR HATS ON BACKWARD, PANTS DOWN THE CRACK. ISN'T THAT A SIGN OF SOMETHING?
www.ucomics.com
... OR ARE YOU WAITING FOR JESUS TO PULL THEIR PANTS UP?
NO, BUT I THINK WE'RE ALL PRAYING HE'LL TAKE THOSE SILLY SUNGLASSES OFF YOUR FACE.

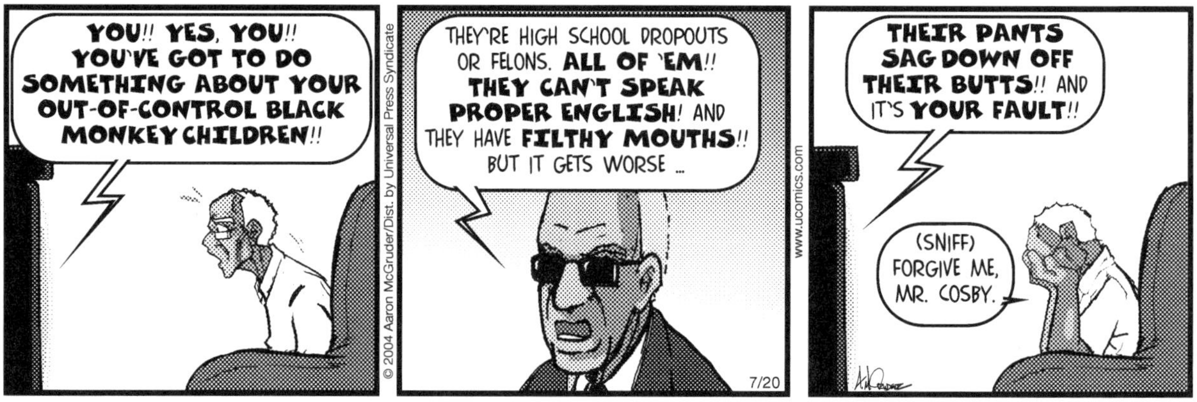
YOU!! YES, YOU!! YOU'VE GOT TO DO SOMETHING ABOUT YOUR OUT-OF-CONTROL BLACK MONKEY CHILDREN!!
© 2004 Aaron McGruder/Dist. by Universal Press Syndicate
THEY'RE HIGH SCHOOL DROPOUTS OR FELONS. ALL OF 'EM!! THEY CAN'T SPEAK PROPER ENGLISH! AND THEY HAVE FILTHY MOUTHS!! BUT IT GETS WORSE ...
7/20
www.ucomics.com
THEIR PANTS SAG DOWN OFF THEIR BUTTS!! AND IT'S YOUR FAULT!!
(SNIFF) FORGIVE ME, MR. COSBY.

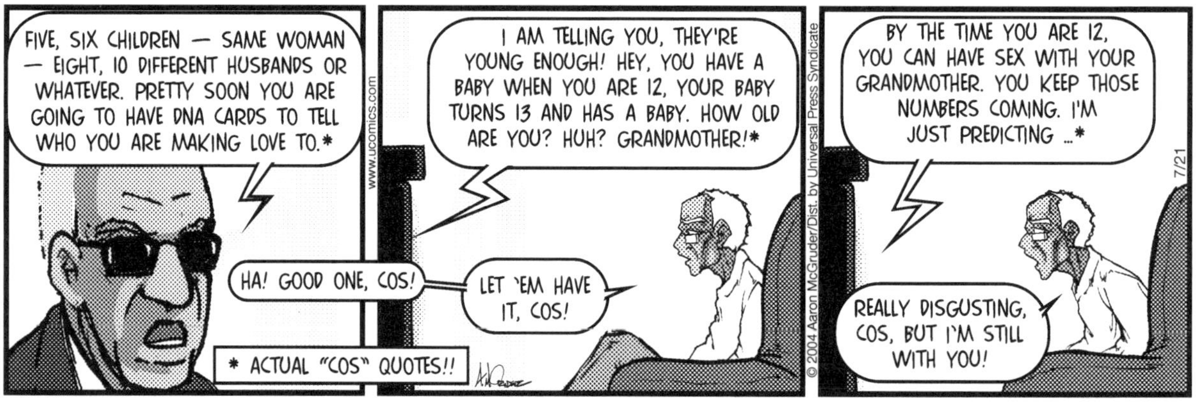
FIVE, SIX CHILDREN — SAME WOMAN — EIGHT, 10 DIFFERENT HUSBANDS OR WHATEVER. PRETTY SOON YOU ARE GOING TO HAVE DNA CARDS TO TELL WHO YOU ARE MAKING LOVE TO.*
www.ucomics.com
I AM TELLING YOU, THEY'RE YOUNG ENOUGH! HEY, YOU HAVE A BABY WHEN YOU ARE 12, YOUR BABY TURNS 13 AND HAS A BABY. HOW OLD ARE YOU? HUH? GRANDMOTHER!*
HA! GOOD ONE, COS!
LET 'EM HAVE IT, COS!
* ACTUAL "COS" QUOTES!!
© 2004 Aaron McGruder/Dist. by Universal Press Syndicate
BY THE TIME YOU ARE 12, YOU CAN HAVE SEX WITH YOUR GRANDMOTHER. YOU KEEP THOSE NUMBERS COMING. I'M JUST PREDICTING ...*
7/21
REALLY DISGUSTING, COS, BUT I'M STILL WITH YOU!

To the Reader:

Within the past few days this newspaper has received 23,457 complaints regarding this feature's current sensitive subject matter.

www.ucomics.com

For the record, this publication has the utmost respect for Bill Cosby, while we believe the creator of this feature is an obnoxious, foul-mouthed hooligan who probably needs to pull his pants up.

We now rejoin this feature, already in progress …

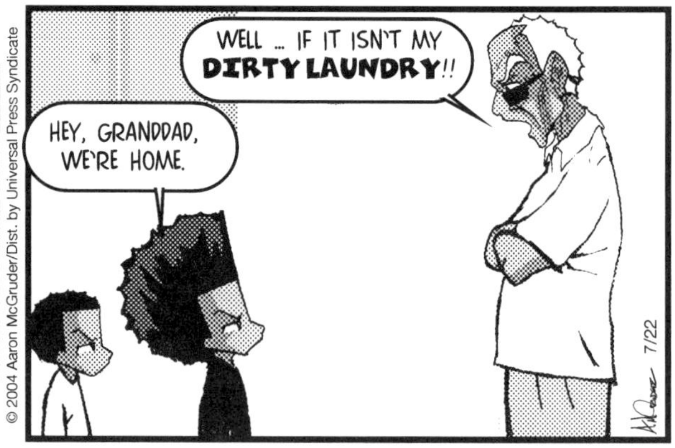
© 2004 Aaron McGruder/Dist. by Universal Press Syndicate
HEY, GRANDDAD, WE'RE HOME.
WELL ... IF IT ISN'T MY DIRTY LAUNDRY!!
7/22

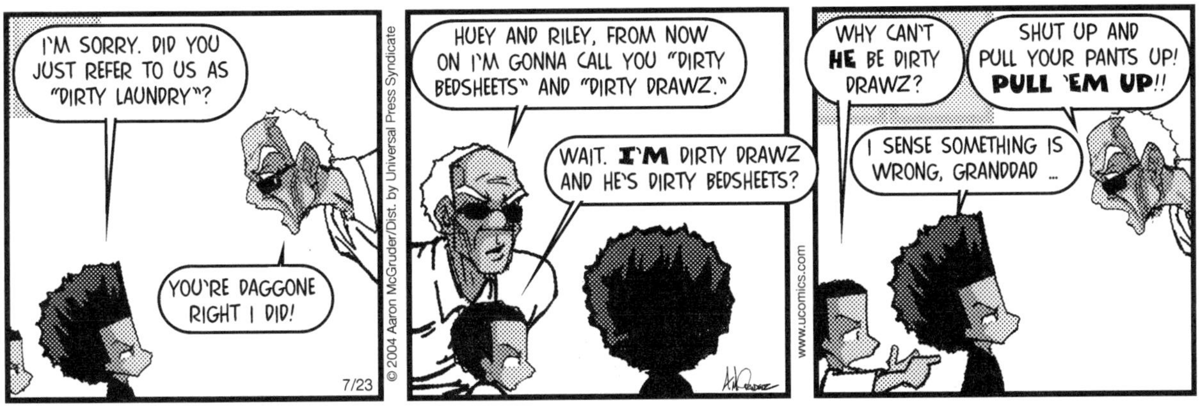
I'M SORRY. DID YOU JUST REFER TO US AS "DIRTY LAUNDRY"?
YOU'RE DAGGONE RIGHT I DID!
7/23
© 2004 Aaron McGruder/Dist. by Universal Press Syndicate
HUEY AND RILEY, FROM NOW ON I'M GONNA CALL YOU "DIRTY BEDSHEETS" AND "DIRTY DRAWZ."
WAIT. I'M DIRTY DRAWZ AND HE'S DIRTY BEDSHEETS?
www.ucomics.com
WHY CAN'T HE BE DIRTY DRAWZ?
SHUT UP AND PULL YOUR PANTS UP! PULL 'EM UP!!
I SENSE SOMETHING IS WRONG, GRANDDAD ...

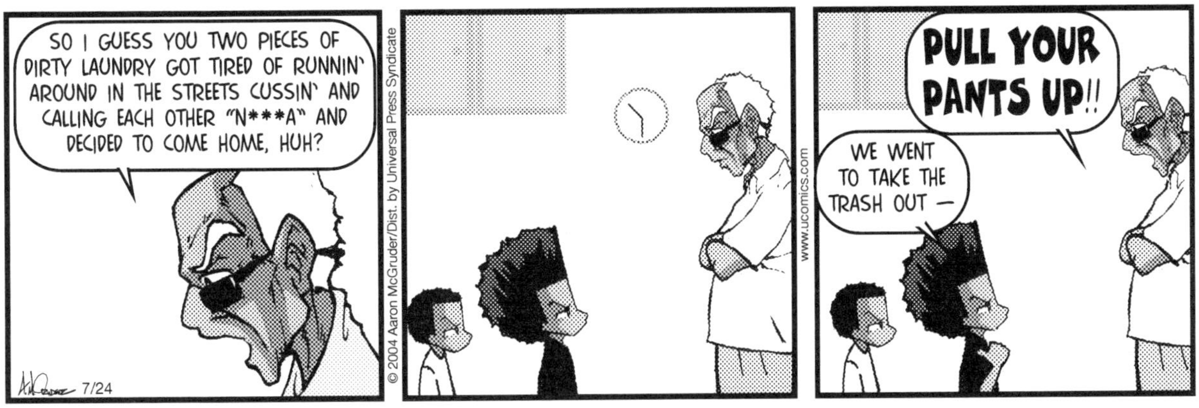
SO I GUESS YOU TWO PIECES OF DIRTY LAUNDRY GOT TIRED OF RUNNIN' AROUND IN THE STREETS CUSSIN' AND CALLING EACH OTHER "N***A" AND DECIDED TO COME HOME, HUH?
7/24
© 2004 Aaron McGruder/Dist. by Universal Press Syndicate
www.ucomics.com
PULL YOUR PANTS UP!!
WE WENT TO TAKE THE TRASH OUT —

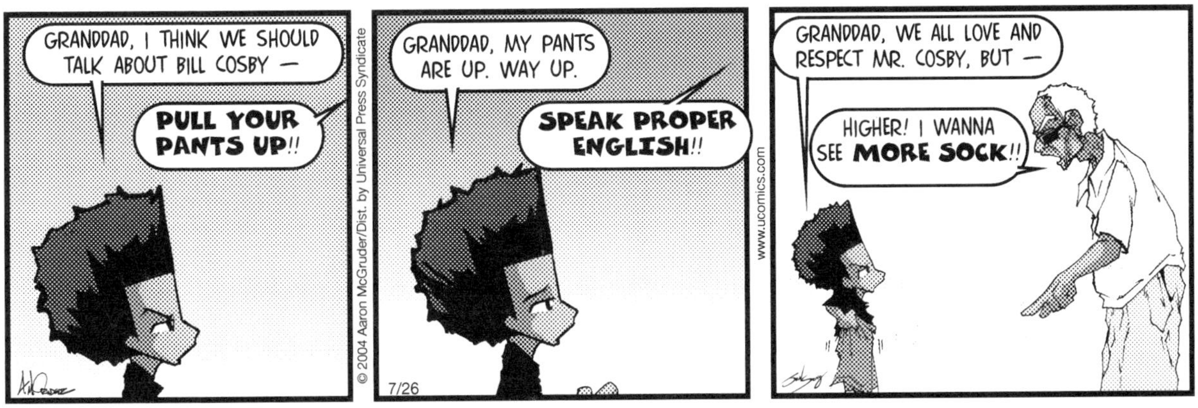
GRANDDAD, I THINK WE SHOULD TALK ABOUT BILL COSBY —
PULL YOUR PANTS UP!!
© 2004 Aaron McGruder/Dist. by Universal Press Syndicate
GRANDDAD, MY PANTS ARE UP. WAY UP.
SPEAK PROPER ENGLISH!!
7/26
www.ucomics.com
GRANDDAD, WE ALL LOVE AND RESPECT MR. COSBY, BUT —
HIGHER! I WANNA SEE MORE SOCK!!

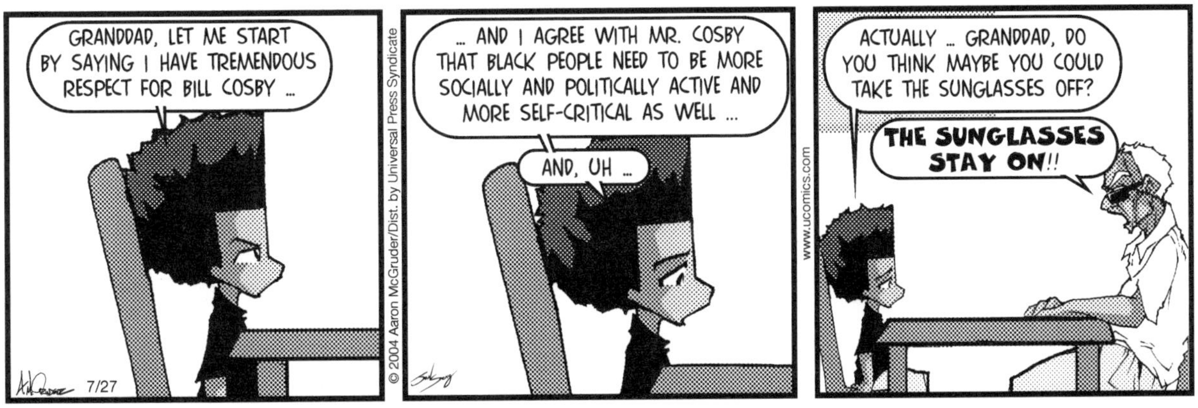
GRANDDAD, LET ME START BY SAYING I HAVE TREMENDOUS RESPECT FOR BILL COSBY ...
7/27
© 2004 Aaron McGruder/Dist. by Universal Press Syndicate
... AND I AGREE WITH MR. COSBY THAT BLACK PEOPLE NEED TO BE MORE SOCIALLY AND POLITICALLY ACTIVE AND MORE SELF-CRITICAL AS WELL ...
AND, UH ...
www.ucomics.com
ACTUALLY ... GRANDDAD, DO YOU THINK MAYBE YOU COULD TAKE THE SUNGLASSES OFF?
THE SUNGLASSES STAY ON!!

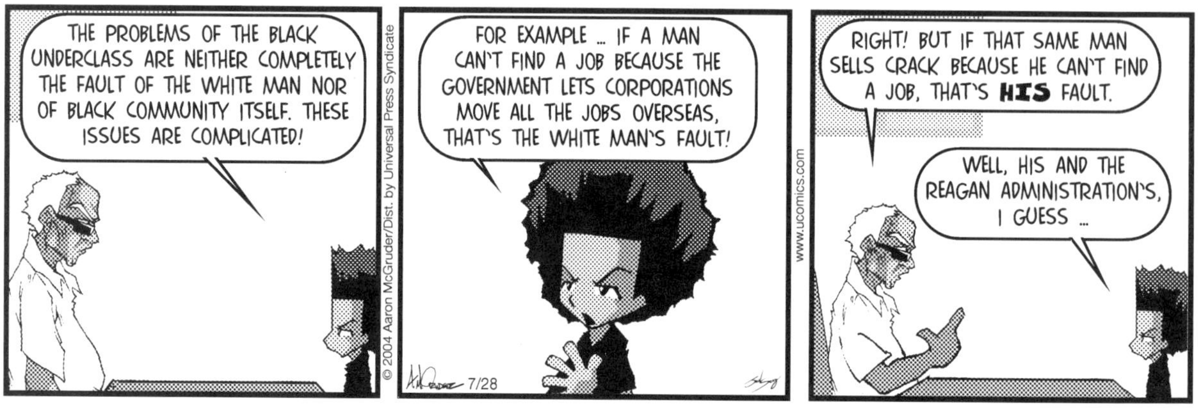
THE PROBLEMS OF THE BLACK UNDERCLASS ARE NEITHER COMPLETELY THE FAULT OF THE WHITE MAN NOR OF BLACK COMMUNITY ITSELF. THESE ISSUES ARE COMPLICATED!
© 2004 Aaron McGruder/Dist. by Universal Press Syndicate
FOR EXAMPLE ... IF A MAN CAN'T FIND A JOB BECAUSE THE GOVERNMENT LETS CORPORATIONS MOVE ALL THE JOBS OVERSEAS, THAT'S THE WHITE MAN'S FAULT!
7/28
RIGHT! BUT IF THAT SAME MAN SELLS CRACK BECAUSE HE CAN'T FIND A JOB, THAT'S **HIS** FAULT.
WELL, HIS AND THE REAGAN ADMINISTRATION'S, I GUESS ...
www.ucomics.com

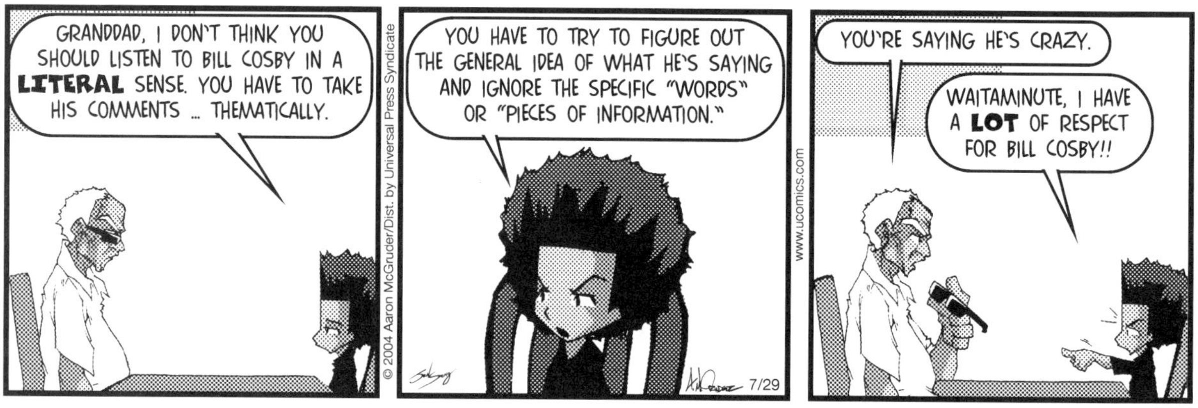
GRANDDAD, I DON'T THINK YOU SHOULD LISTEN TO BILL COSBY IN A **LITERAL** SENSE. YOU HAVE TO TAKE HIS COMMENTS ... THEMATICALLY.
© 2004 Aaron McGruder/Dist. by Universal Press Syndicate
YOU HAVE TO TRY TO FIGURE OUT THE GENERAL IDEA OF WHAT HE'S SAYING AND IGNORE THE SPECIFIC "WORDS" OR "PIECES OF INFORMATION."
7/29
YOU'RE SAYING HE'S CRAZY.
WAITAMINUTE, I HAVE A **LOT** OF RESPECT FOR BILL COSBY!!
www.ucomics.com

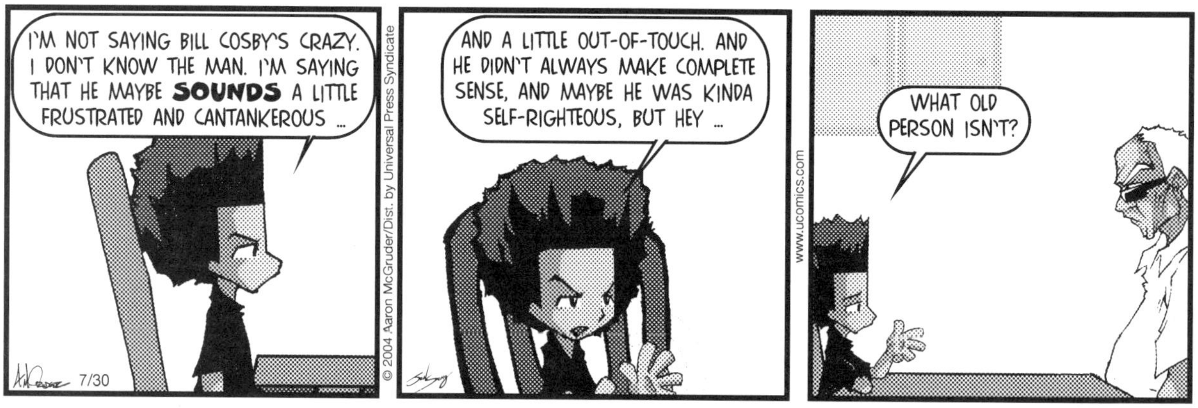
I'M NOT SAYING BILL COSBY'S CRAZY. I DON'T KNOW THE MAN. I'M SAYING THAT HE MAYBE **SOUNDS** A LITTLE FRUSTRATED AND CANTANKEROUS ...
7/30
© 2004 Aaron McGruder/Dist. by Universal Press Syndicate
AND A LITTLE OUT-OF-TOUCH. AND HE DIDN'T ALWAYS MAKE COMPLETE SENSE, AND MAYBE HE WAS KINDA SELF-RIGHTEOUS, BUT HEY ...
WHAT OLD PERSON ISN'T?
www.ucomics.com

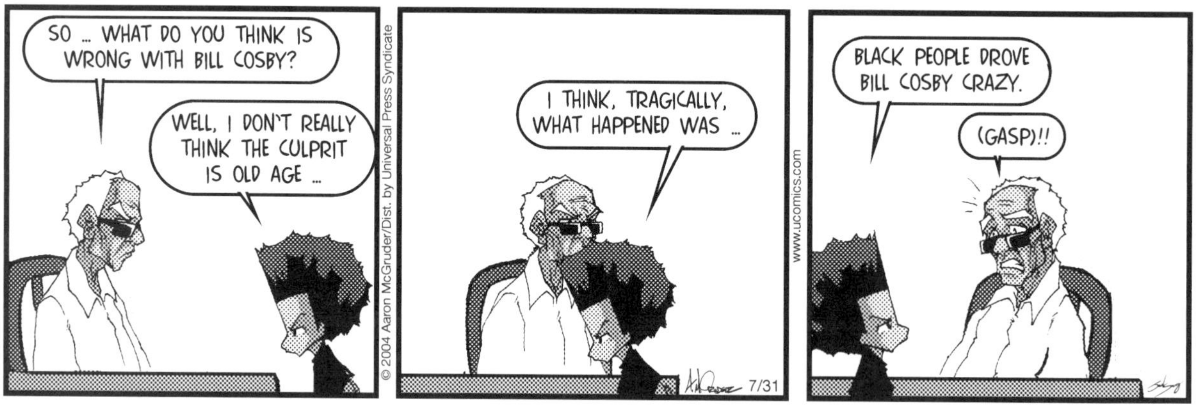
SO ... WHAT DO YOU THINK IS WRONG WITH BILL COSBY?
WELL, I DON'T REALLY THINK THE CULPRIT IS OLD AGE ...
© 2004 Aaron McGruder/Dist. by Universal Press Syndicate
I THINK, TRAGICALLY, WHAT HAPPENED WAS ...
7/31
BLACK PEOPLE DROVE BILL COSBY CRAZY.
(GASP)!!
www.ucomics.com

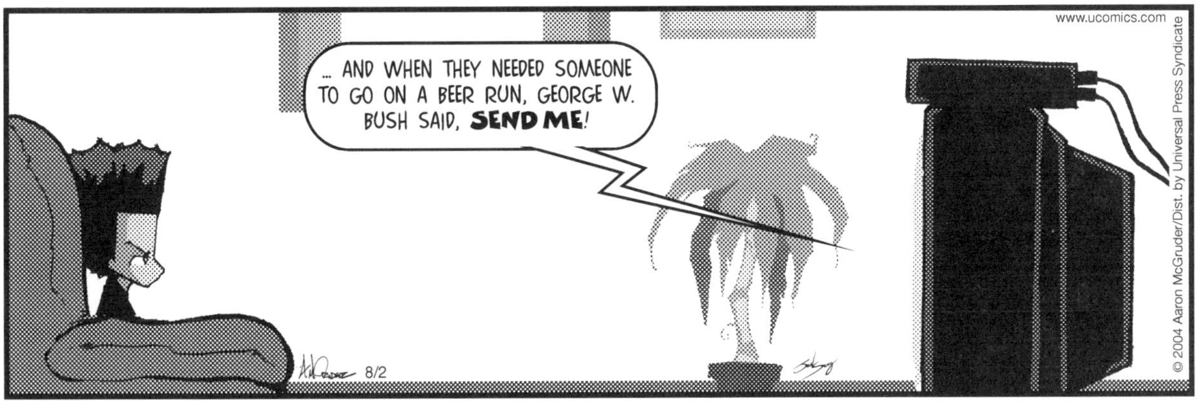
... AND WHEN THEY NEEDED SOMEONE TO GO ON A BEER RUN, GEORGE W. BUSH SAID, **SEND ME**!
www.ucomics.com
© 2004 Aaron McGruder/Dist. by Universal Press Syndicate
8/2

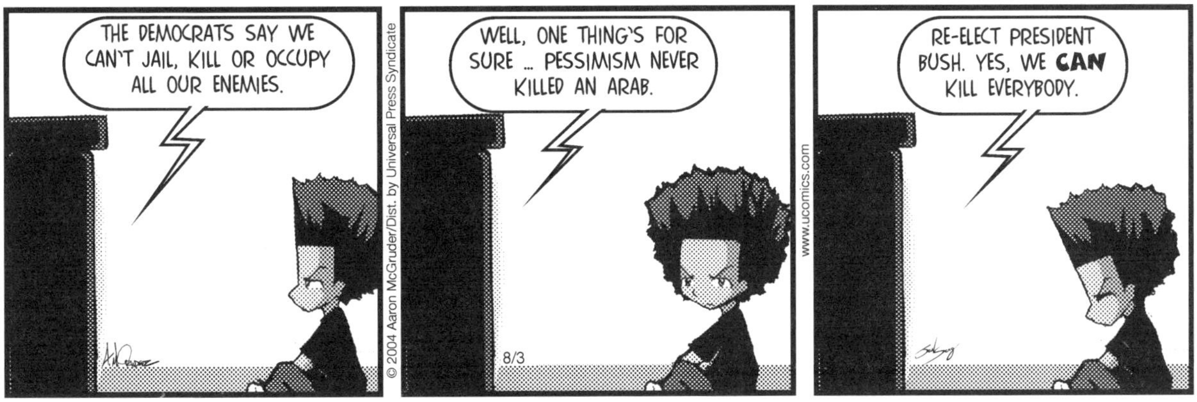
THE DEMOCRATS SAY WE CAN'T JAIL, KILL OR OCCUPY ALL OUR ENEMIES.
WELL, ONE THING'S FOR SURE ... PESSIMISM NEVER KILLED AN ARAB.
RE-ELECT PRESIDENT BUSH. YES, WE **CAN** KILL EVERYBODY.
© 2004 Aaron McGruder/Dist. by Universal Press Syndicate
www.ucomics.com
8/3

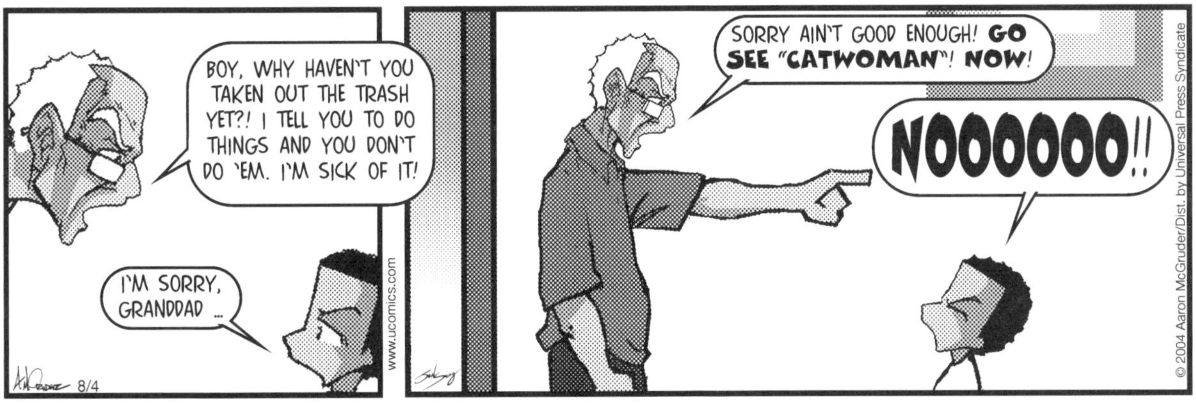
BOY, WHY HAVEN'T YOU TAKEN OUT THE TRASH YET?! I TELL YOU TO DO THINGS AND YOU DON'T DO 'EM. I'M SICK OF IT!
I'M SORRY, GRANDDAD ...
SORRY AIN'T GOOD ENOUGH! **GO SEE "CATWOMAN"! NOW**!
NOOOOOO!!
www.ucomics.com
© 2004 Aaron McGruder/Dist. by Universal Press Syndicate
8/4

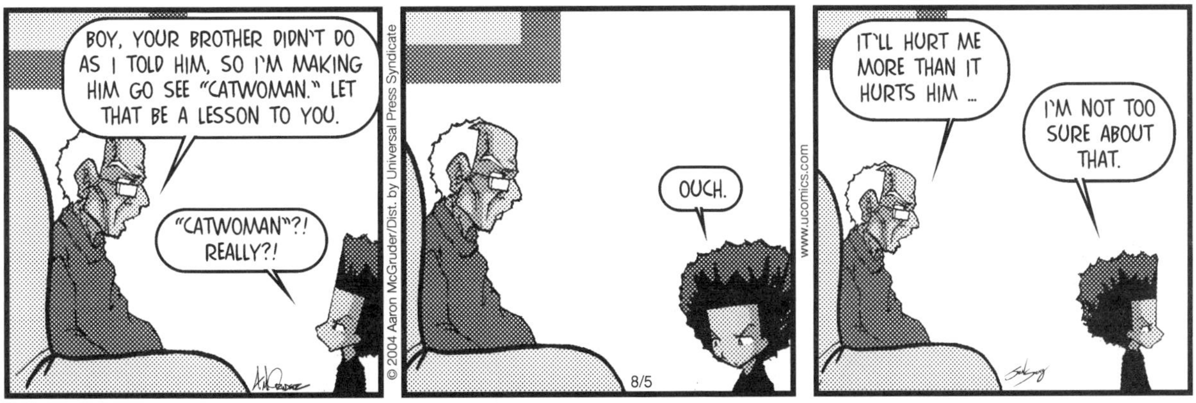
BOY, YOUR BROTHER DIDN'T DO AS I TOLD HIM, SO I'M MAKING HIM GO SEE "CATWOMAN." LET THAT BE A LESSON TO YOU.
"CATWOMAN"?! REALLY?!
OUCH.
IT'LL HURT ME MORE THAN IT HURTS HIM ...
I'M NOT TOO SURE ABOUT THAT.
© 2004 Aaron McGruder/Dist. by Universal Press Syndicate
www.ucomics.com
8/5

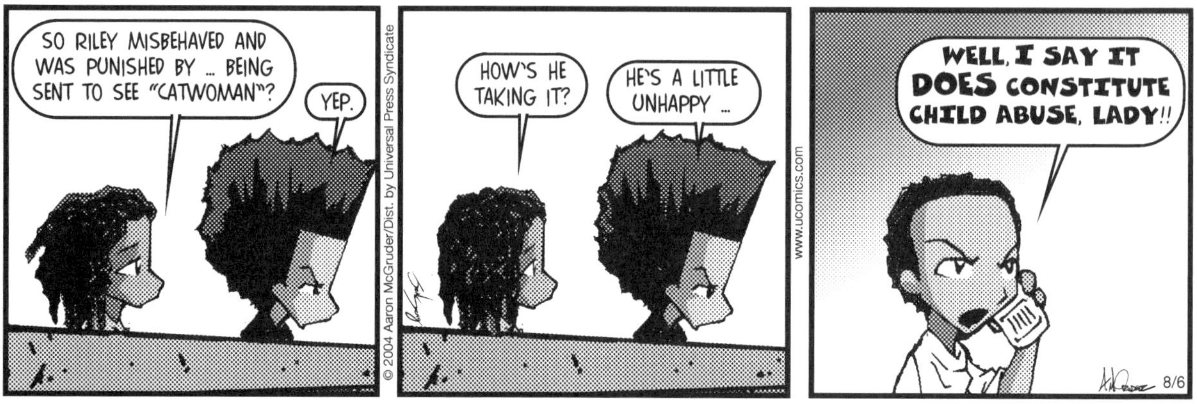
SO RILEY MISBEHAVED AND WAS PUNISHED BY ... BEING SENT TO SEE "CATWOMAN"?
YEP.
© 2004 Aaron McGruder/Dist. by Universal Press Syndicate
HOW'S HE TAKING IT?
HE'S A LITTLE UNHAPPY ...
www.ucomics.com
WELL, I SAY IT DOES CONSTITUTE CHILD ABUSE, LADY!!
8/6

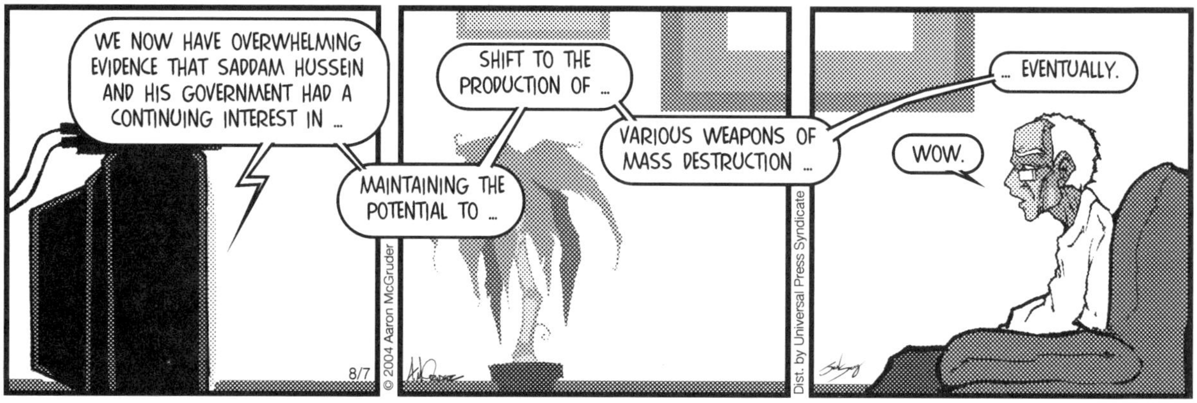
WE NOW HAVE OVERWHELMING EVIDENCE THAT SADDAM HUSSEIN AND HIS GOVERNMENT HAD A CONTINUING INTEREST IN ...
8/7
© 2004 Aaron McGruder
MAINTAINING THE POTENTIAL TO ...
SHIFT TO THE PRODUCTION OF ...
VARIOUS WEAPONS OF MASS DESTRUCTION ...
Dist. by Universal Press Syndicate
... EVENTUALLY.
WOW.

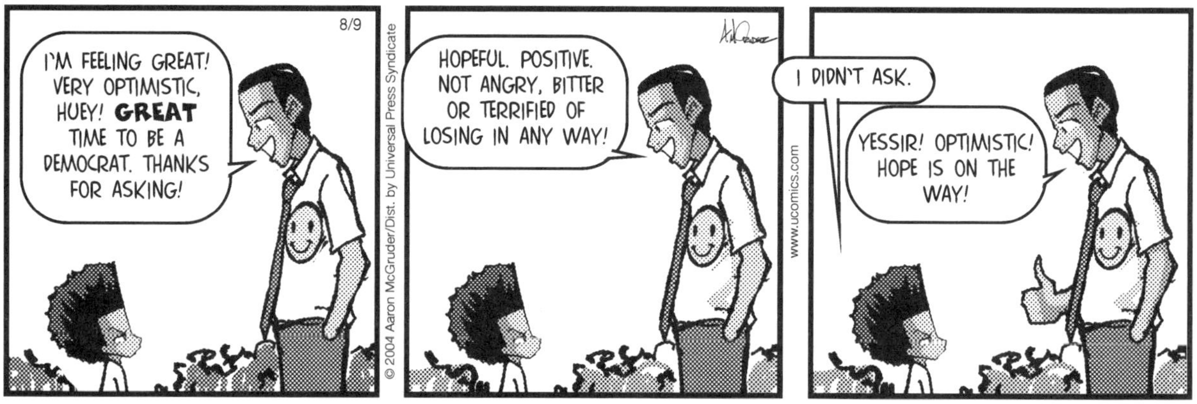
8/9
I'M FEELING GREAT! VERY OPTIMISTIC, HUEY! GREAT TIME TO BE A DEMOCRAT. THANKS FOR ASKING!
© 2004 Aaron McGruder/Dist. by Universal Press Syndicate
HOPEFUL. POSITIVE. NOT ANGRY, BITTER OR TERRIFIED OF LOSING IN ANY WAY!
www.ucomics.com
I DIDN'T ASK.
YESSIR! OPTIMISTIC! HOPE IS ON THE WAY!

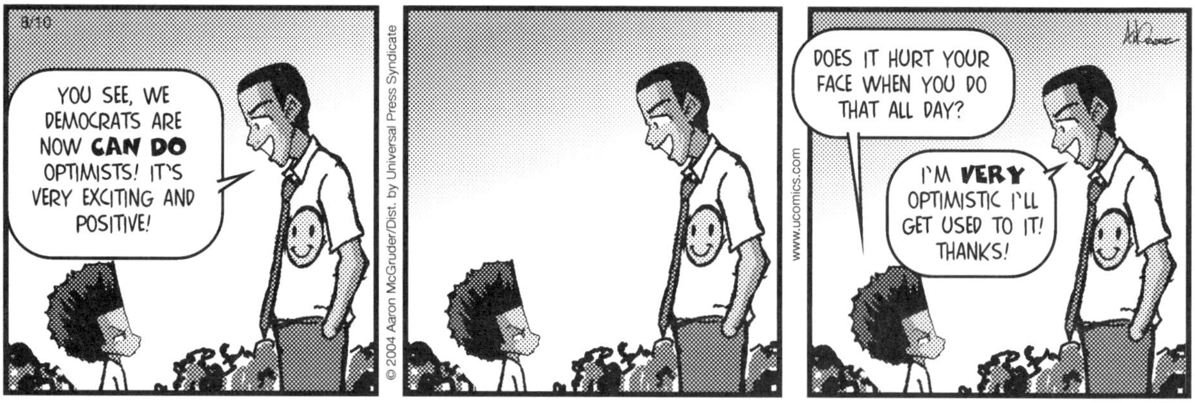
8/10
YOU SEE, WE DEMOCRATS ARE NOW CAN DO OPTIMISTS! IT'S VERY EXCITING AND POSITIVE!
© 2004 Aaron McGruder/Dist. by Universal Press Syndicate
www.ucomics.com
DOES IT HURT YOUR FACE WHEN YOU DO THAT ALL DAY?
I'M VERY OPTIMISTIC I'LL GET USED TO IT! THANKS!

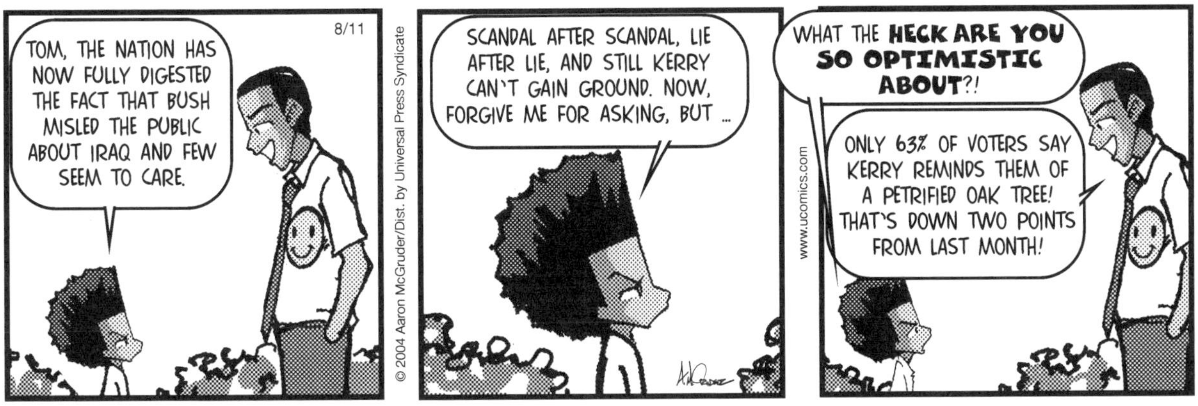
8/11
TOM, THE NATION HAS NOW FULLY DIGESTED THE FACT THAT BUSH MISLED THE PUBLIC ABOUT IRAQ AND FEW SEEM TO CARE.
© 2004 Aaron McGruder/Dist. by Universal Press Syndicate
SCANDAL AFTER SCANDAL, LIE AFTER LIE, AND STILL KERRY CAN'T GAIN GROUND. NOW, FORGIVE ME FOR ASKING, BUT ...
WHAT THE HECK ARE YOU SO OPTIMISTIC ABOUT?!
www.ucomics.com
ONLY 63% OF VOTERS SAY KERRY REMINDS THEM OF A PETRIFIED OAK TREE! THAT'S DOWN TWO POINTS FROM LAST MONTH!

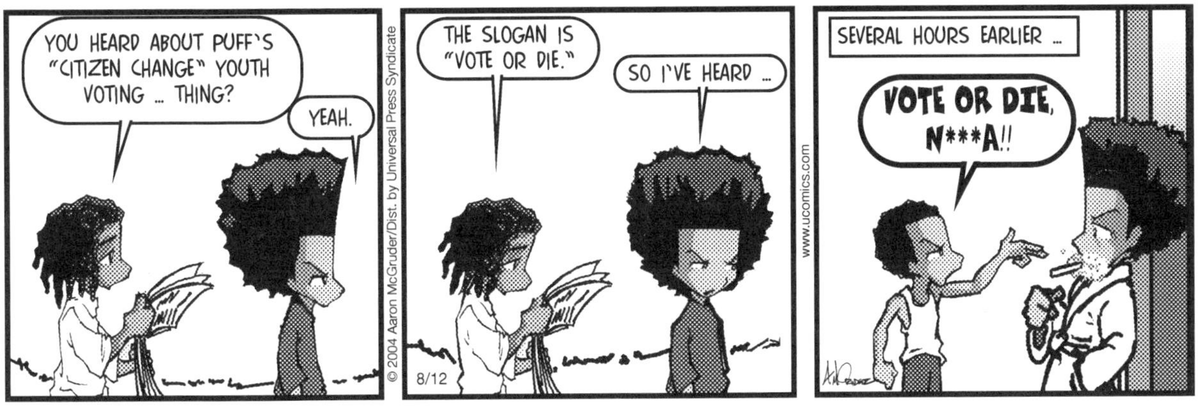
YOU HEARD ABOUT PUFF'S "CITIZEN CHANGE" YOUTH VOTING ... THING?
YEAH.
© 2004 Aaron McGruder/Dist. by Universal Press Syndicate
THE SLOGAN IS "VOTE OR DIE."
SO I'VE HEARD ...
8/12
SEVERAL HOURS EARLIER ...
VOTE OR DIE, N***A!!
www.ucomics.com

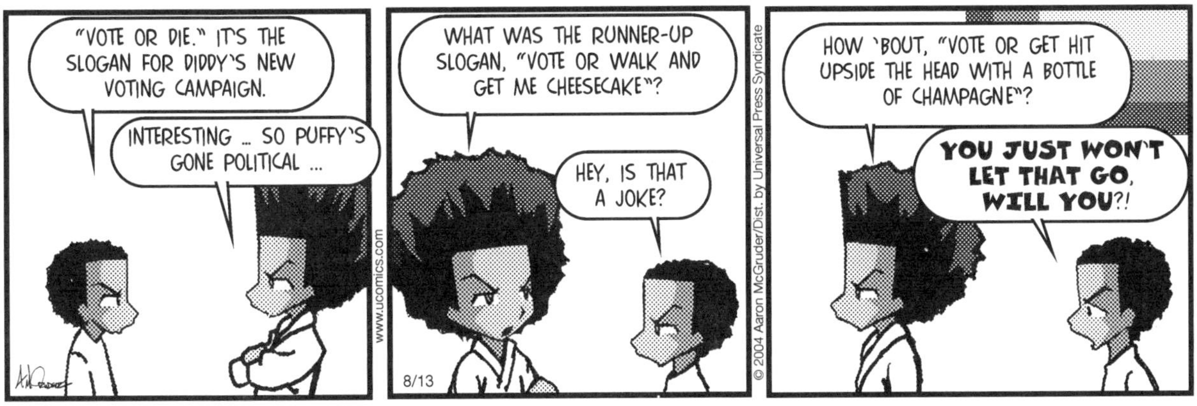
"VOTE OR DIE." IT'S THE SLOGAN FOR DIDDY'S NEW VOTING CAMPAIGN.
INTERESTING ... SO PUFFY'S GONE POLITICAL ...
www.ucomics.com
WHAT WAS THE RUNNER-UP SLOGAN, "VOTE OR WALK AND GET ME CHEESECAKE"?
HEY, IS THAT A JOKE?
8/13
© 2004 Aaron McGruder/Dist. by Universal Press Syndicate
HOW 'BOUT, "VOTE OR GET HIT UPSIDE THE HEAD WITH A BOTTLE OF CHAMPAGNE"?
YOU JUST WON'T LET THAT GO, WILL YOU?!

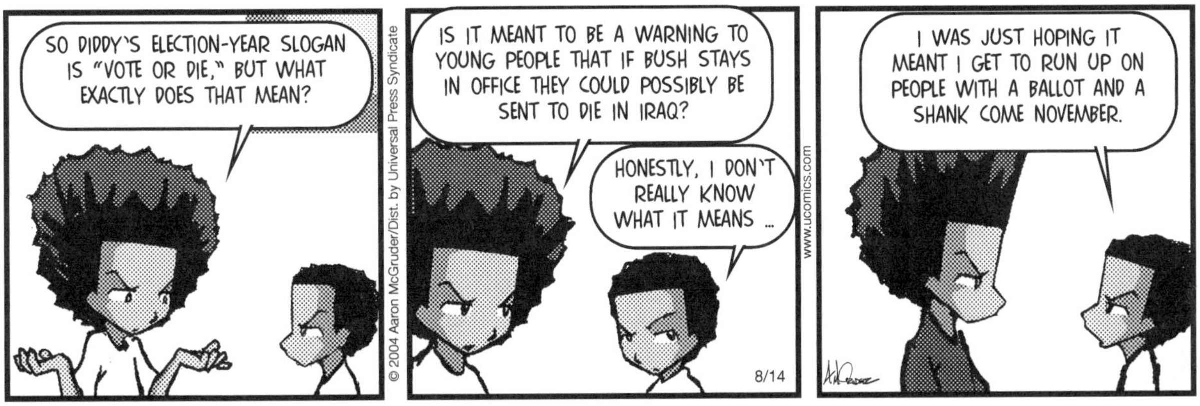
SO DIDDY'S ELECTION-YEAR SLOGAN IS "VOTE OR DIE," BUT WHAT EXACTLY DOES THAT MEAN?
© 2004 Aaron McGruder/Dist. by Universal Press Syndicate
IS IT MEANT TO BE A WARNING TO YOUNG PEOPLE THAT IF BUSH STAYS IN OFFICE THEY COULD POSSIBLY BE SENT TO DIE IN IRAQ?
HONESTLY, I DON'T REALLY KNOW WHAT IT MEANS ...
8/14
www.ucomics.com
I WAS JUST HOPING IT MEANT I GET TO RUN UP ON PEOPLE WITH A BALLOT AND A SHANK COME NOVEMBER.

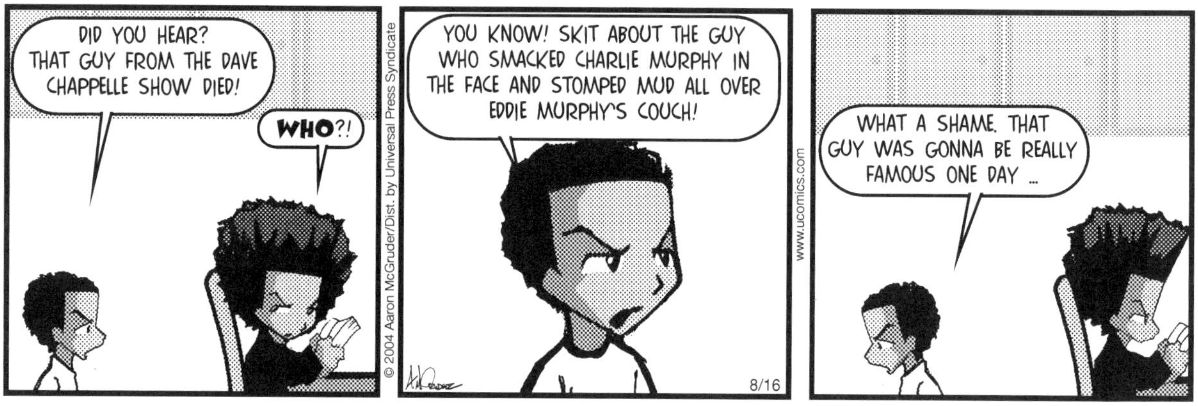
DID YOU HEAR? THAT GUY FROM THE DAVE CHAPPELLE SHOW DIED!
WHO?!
YOU KNOW! SKIT ABOUT THE GUY WHO SMACKED CHARLIE MURPHY IN THE FACE AND STOMPED MUD ALL OVER EDDIE MURPHY'S COUCH!
WHAT A SHAME. THAT GUY WAS GONNA BE REALLY FAMOUS ONE DAY ...
© 2004 Aaron McGruder/Dist. by Universal Press Syndicate
www.ucomics.com
8/16

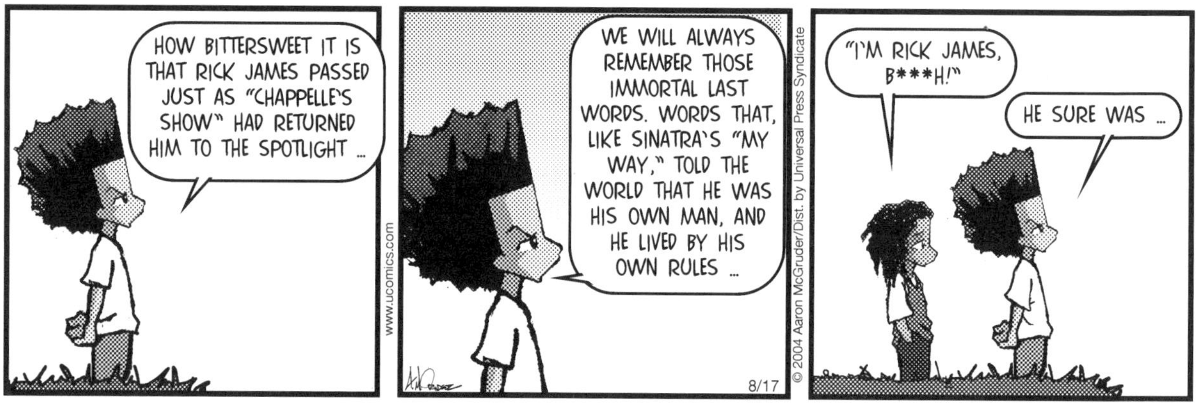
HOW BITTERSWEET IT IS THAT RICK JAMES PASSED JUST AS "CHAPPELLE'S SHOW" HAD RETURNED HIM TO THE SPOTLIGHT ...
WE WILL ALWAYS REMEMBER THOSE IMMORTAL LAST WORDS. WORDS THAT, LIKE SINATRA'S "MY WAY," TOLD THE WORLD THAT HE WAS HIS OWN MAN, AND HE LIVED BY HIS OWN RULES ...
"I'M RICK JAMES, B***H!"
HE SURE WAS ...
www.ucomics.com
© 2004 Aaron McGruder/Dist. by Universal Press Syndicate
8/17

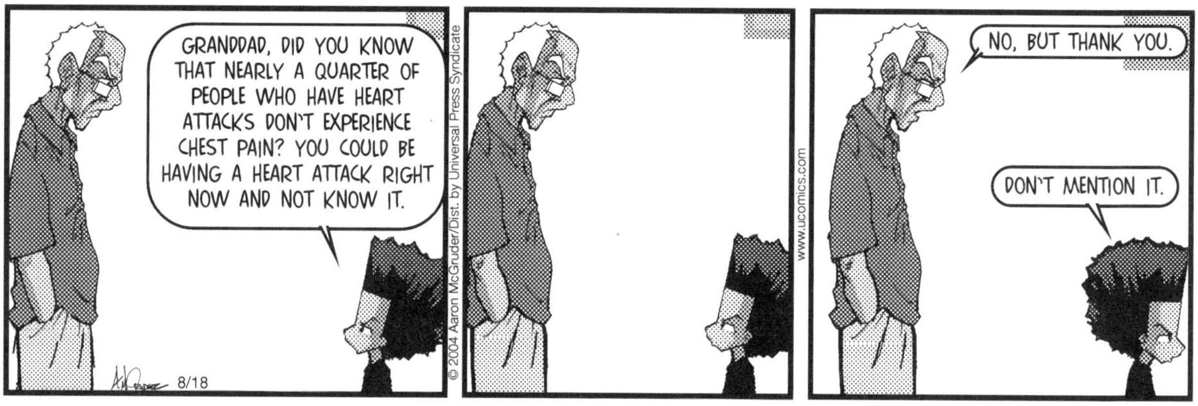
GRANDDAD, DID YOU KNOW THAT NEARLY A QUARTER OF PEOPLE WHO HAVE HEART ATTACKS DON'T EXPERIENCE CHEST PAIN? YOU COULD BE HAVING A HEART ATTACK RIGHT NOW AND NOT KNOW IT.
NO, BUT THANK YOU.
DON'T MENTION IT.
8/18
© 2004 Aaron McGruder/Dist. by Universal Press Syndicate
www.ucomics.com

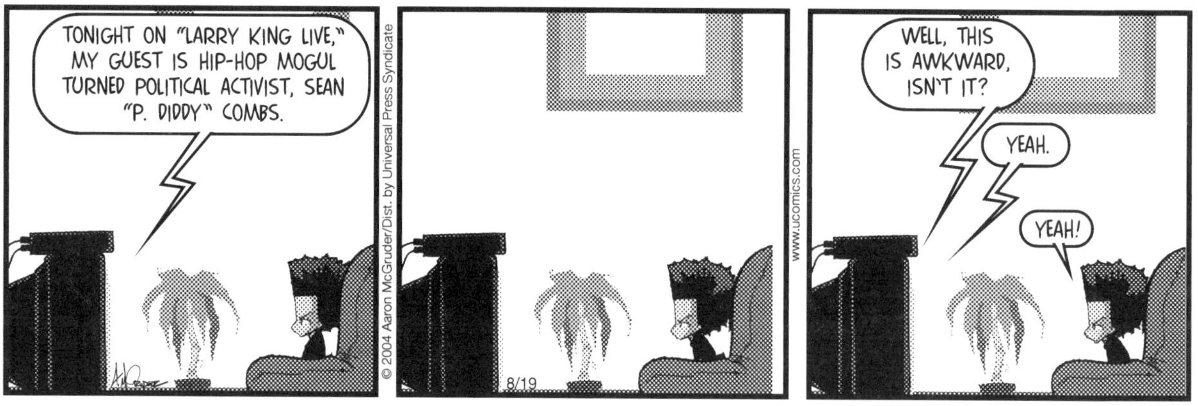
TONIGHT ON "LARRY KING LIVE," MY GUEST IS HIP-HOP MOGUL TURNED POLITICAL ACTIVIST, SEAN "P. DIDDY" COMBS.
WELL, THIS IS AWKWARD, ISN'T IT?
YEAH.
YEAH!
© 2004 Aaron McGruder/Dist. by Universal Press Syndicate
www.ucomics.com
8/19

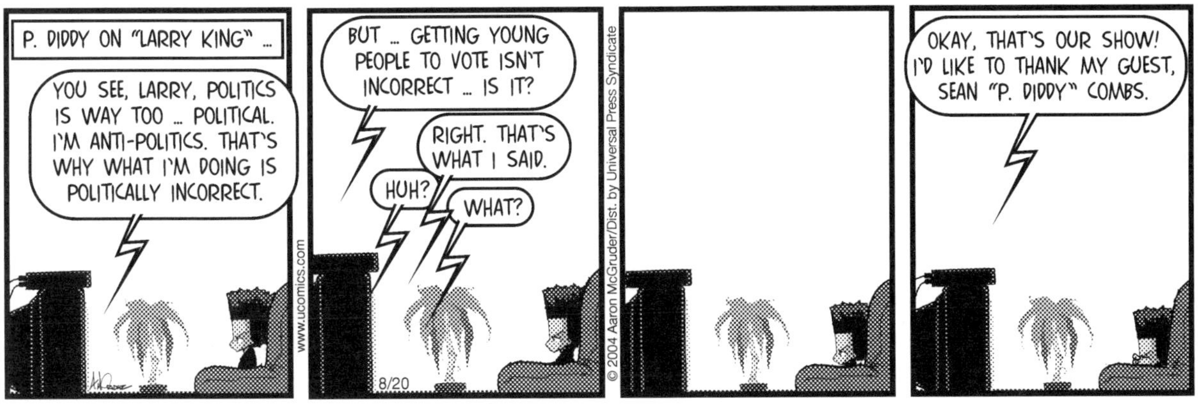
P. DIDDY ON "LARRY KING" ...
YOU SEE, LARRY, POLITICS IS WAY TOO ... POLITICAL. I'M ANTI-POLITICS. THAT'S WHY WHAT I'M DOING IS POLITICALLY INCORRECT.
www.ucomics.com
BUT ... GETTING YOUNG PEOPLE TO VOTE ISN'T INCORRECT ... IS IT?
RIGHT. THAT'S WHAT I SAID.
HUH?
WHAT?
8/20
© 2004 Aaron McGruder/Dist. by Universal Press Syndicate
OKAY, THAT'S OUR SHOW! I'D LIKE TO THANK MY GUEST, SEAN "P. DIDDY" COMBS.

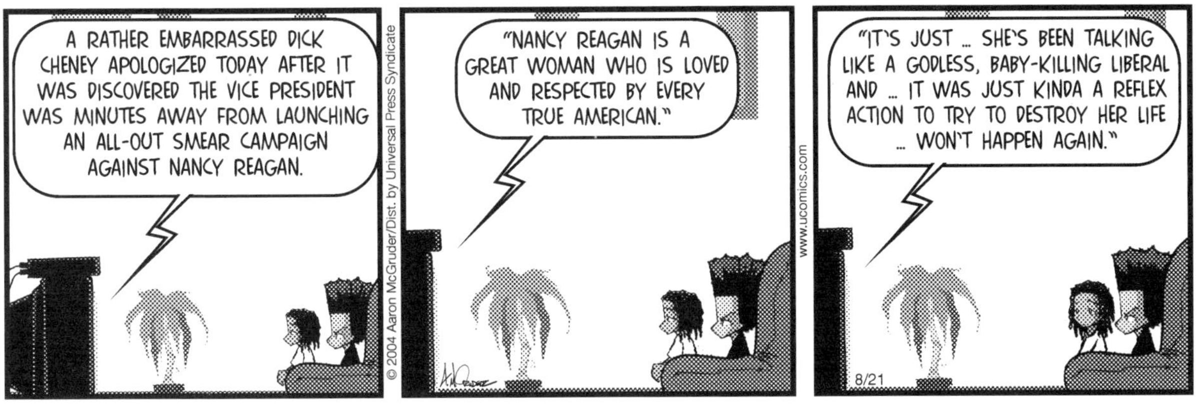
A RATHER EMBARRASSED DICK CHENEY APOLOGIZED TODAY AFTER IT WAS DISCOVERED THE VICE PRESIDENT WAS MINUTES AWAY FROM LAUNCHING AN ALL-OUT SMEAR CAMPAIGN AGAINST NANCY REAGAN.
© 2004 Aaron McGruder/Dist. by Universal Press Syndicate
"NANCY REAGAN IS A GREAT WOMAN WHO IS LOVED AND RESPECTED BY EVERY TRUE AMERICAN."
www.ucomics.com
"IT'S JUST ... SHE'S BEEN TALKING LIKE A GODLESS, BABY-KILLING LIBERAL AND ... IT WAS JUST KINDA A REFLEX ACTION TO TRY TO DESTROY HER LIFE ... WON'T HAPPEN AGAIN."
8/21

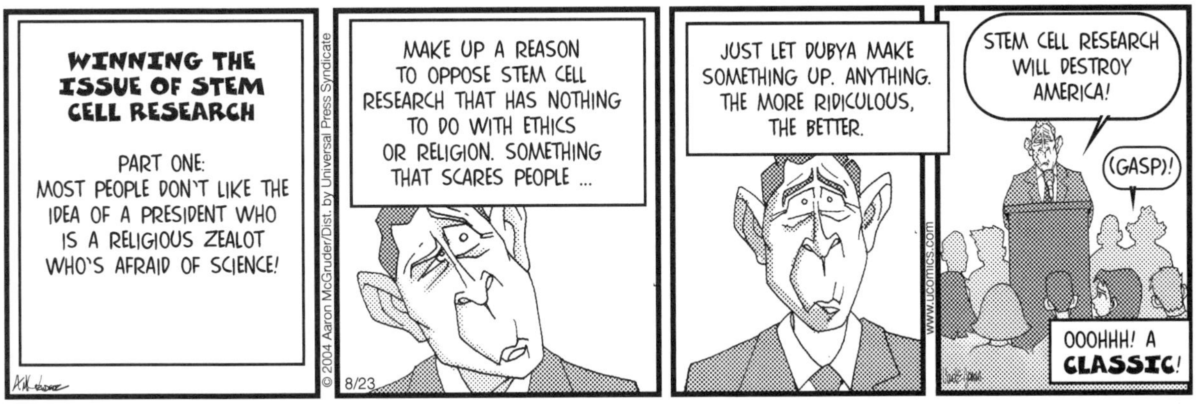
WINNING THE ISSUE OF STEM CELL RESEARCH
PART ONE: MOST PEOPLE DON'T LIKE THE IDEA OF A PRESIDENT WHO IS A RELIGIOUS ZEALOT WHO'S AFRAID OF SCIENCE!
© 2004 Aaron McGruder/Dist. by Universal Press Syndicate
MAKE UP A REASON TO OPPOSE STEM CELL RESEARCH THAT HAS NOTHING TO DO WITH ETHICS OR RELIGION. SOMETHING THAT SCARES PEOPLE ...
8/23
JUST LET DUBYA MAKE SOMETHING UP. ANYTHING. THE MORE RIDICULOUS, THE BETTER.
STEM CELL RESEARCH WILL DESTROY AMERICA!
(GASP)!
www.ucomics.com
OOOHHH! A CLASSIC!

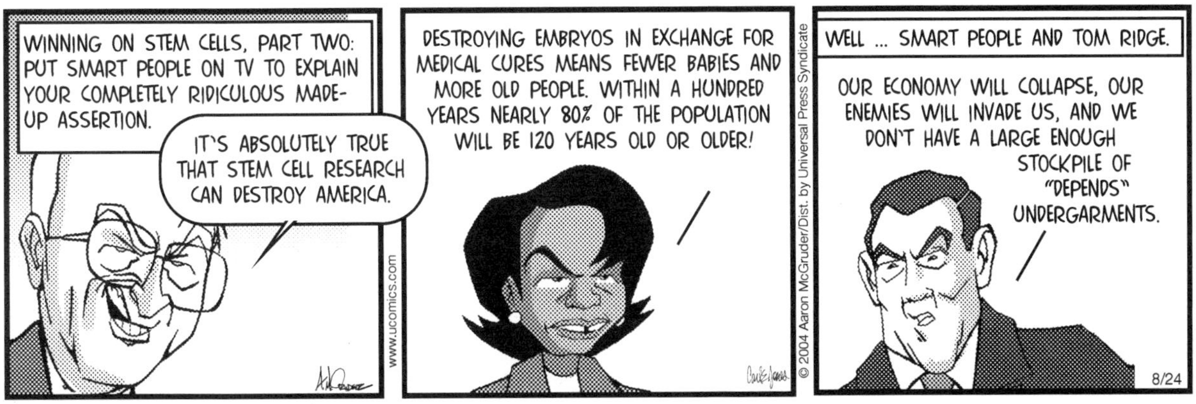
WINNING ON STEM CELLS, PART TWO: PUT SMART PEOPLE ON TV TO EXPLAIN YOUR COMPLETELY RIDICULOUS MADE-UP ASSERTION.
IT'S ABSOLUTELY TRUE THAT STEM CELL RESEARCH CAN DESTROY AMERICA.
www.ucomics.com
DESTROYING EMBRYOS IN EXCHANGE FOR MEDICAL CURES MEANS FEWER BABIES AND MORE OLD PEOPLE. WITHIN A HUNDRED YEARS NEARLY 80% OF THE POPULATION WILL BE 120 YEARS OLD OR OLDER!
© 2004 Aaron McGruder/Dist. by Universal Press Syndicate
WELL ... SMART PEOPLE AND TOM RIDGE.
OUR ECONOMY WILL COLLAPSE, OUR ENEMIES WILL INVADE US, AND WE DON'T HAVE A LARGE ENOUGH STOCKPILE OF "DEPENDS" UNDERGARMENTS.
8/24

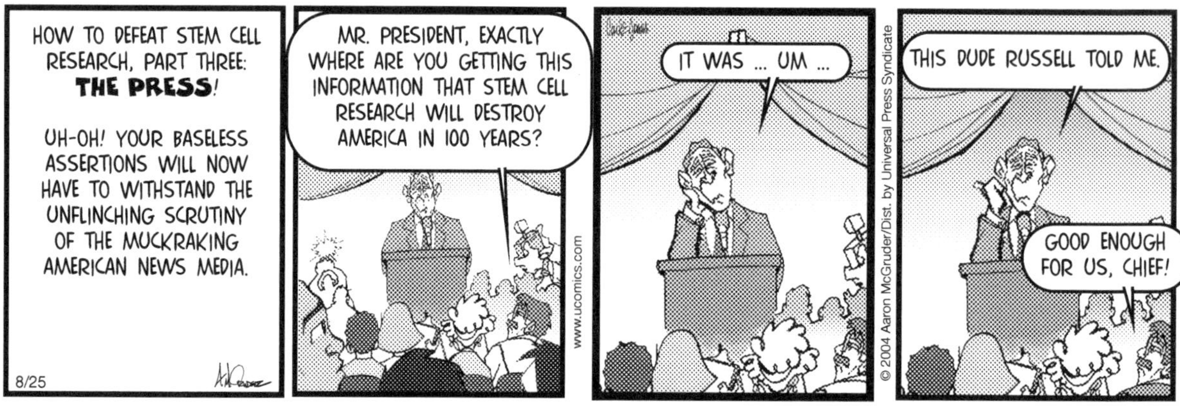
HOW TO DEFEAT STEM CELL RESEARCH, PART THREE: THE PRESS!
UH-OH! YOUR BASELESS ASSERTIONS WILL NOW HAVE TO WITHSTAND THE UNFLINCHING SCRUTINY OF THE MUCKRAKING AMERICAN NEWS MEDIA.
8/25
MR. PRESIDENT, EXACTLY WHERE ARE YOU GETTING THIS INFORMATION THAT STEM CELL RESEARCH WILL DESTROY AMERICA IN 100 YEARS?
www.ucomics.com
IT WAS ... UM ...
© 2004 Aaron McGruder/Dist. by Universal Press Syndicate
THIS DUDE RUSSELL TOLD ME.
GOOD ENOUGH FOR US, CHIEF!

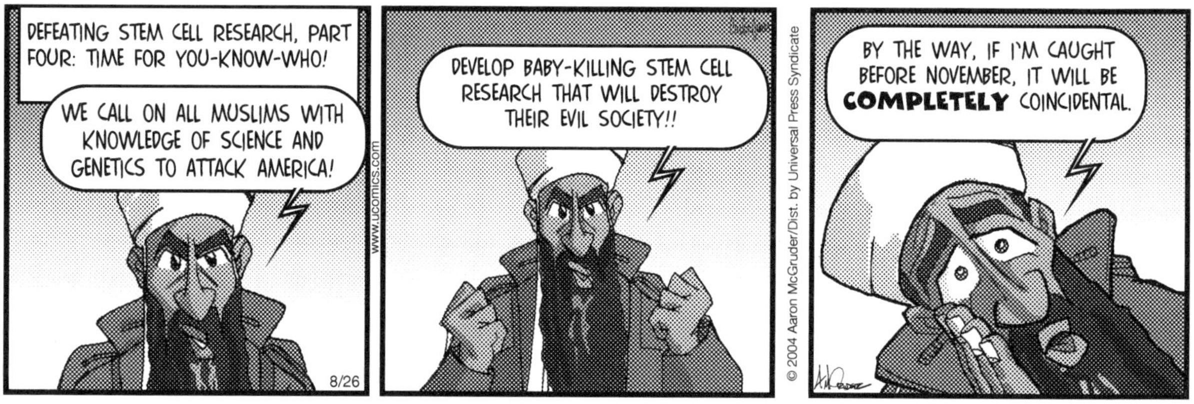
DEFEATING STEM CELL RESEARCH, PART FOUR: TIME FOR YOU-KNOW-WHO!
WE CALL ON ALL MUSLIMS WITH KNOWLEDGE OF SCIENCE AND GENETICS TO ATTACK AMERICA!
8/26
www.ucomics.com
DEVELOP BABY-KILLING STEM CELL RESEARCH THAT WILL DESTROY THEIR EVIL SOCIETY!!
© 2004 Aaron McGruder/Dist. by Universal Press Syndicate
BY THE WAY, IF I'M CAUGHT BEFORE NOVEMBER, IT WILL BE COMPLETELY COINCIDENTAL.

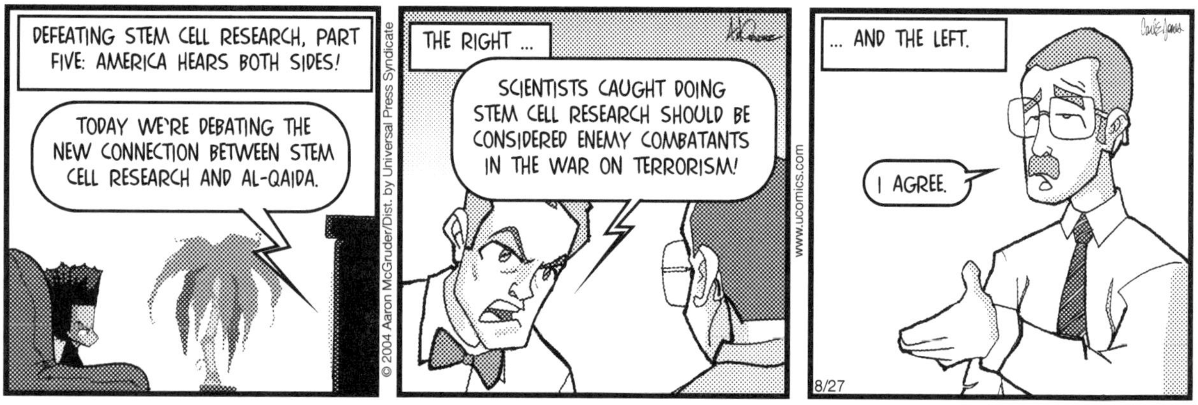
DEFEATING STEM CELL RESEARCH, PART FIVE: AMERICA HEARS BOTH SIDES!
TODAY WE'RE DEBATING THE NEW CONNECTION BETWEEN STEM CELL RESEARCH AND AL-QAIDA.
© 2004 Aaron McGruder/Dist. by Universal Press Syndicate
THE RIGHT ...
SCIENTISTS CAUGHT DOING STEM CELL RESEARCH SHOULD BE CONSIDERED ENEMY COMBATANTS IN THE WAR ON TERRORISM!
www.ucomics.com
... AND THE LEFT.
I AGREE.
8/27

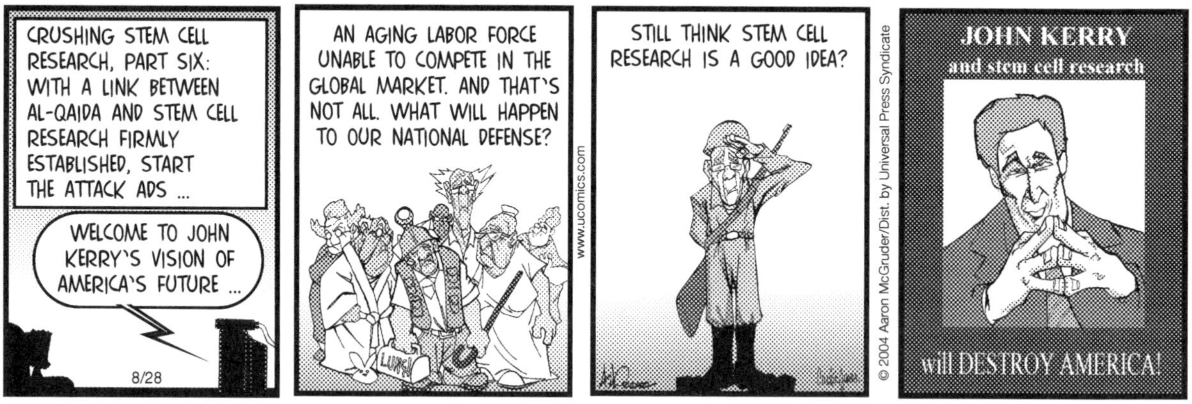
CRUSHING STEM CELL RESEARCH, PART SIX: WITH A LINK BETWEEN AL-QAIDA AND STEM CELL RESEARCH FIRMLY ESTABLISHED, START THE ATTACK ADS ...
WELCOME TO JOHN KERRY'S VISION OF AMERICA'S FUTURE ...
8/28
AN AGING LABOR FORCE UNABLE TO COMPETE IN THE GLOBAL MARKET. AND THAT'S NOT ALL. WHAT WILL HAPPEN TO OUR NATIONAL DEFENSE?
www.ucomics.com
STILL THINK STEM CELL RESEARCH IS A GOOD IDEA?
© 2004 Aaron McGruder/Dist. by Universal Press Syndicate
JOHN KERRY
and stem cell research
will DESTROY AMERICA!

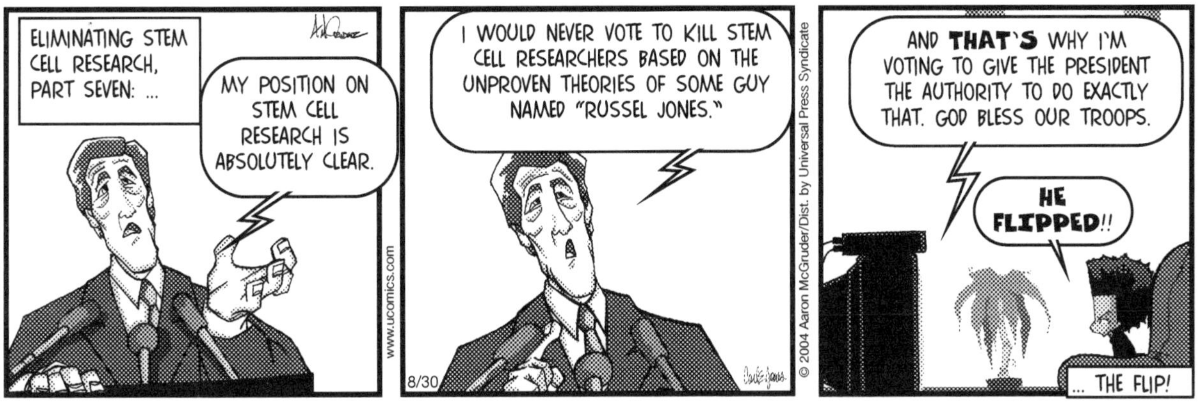
ELIMINATING STEM CELL RESEARCH, PART SEVEN: ...
MY POSITION ON STEM CELL RESEARCH IS ABSOLUTELY CLEAR.
www.ucomics.com
I WOULD NEVER VOTE TO KILL STEM CELL RESEARCHERS BASED ON THE UNPROVEN THEORIES OF SOME GUY NAMED "RUSSEL JONES."
8/30
© 2004 Aaron McGruder/Dist. by Universal Press Syndicate
AND **THAT'S** WHY I'M VOTING TO GIVE THE PRESIDENT THE AUTHORITY TO DO EXACTLY THAT. GOD BLESS OUR TROOPS.
HE FLIPPED!!
... THE FLIP!

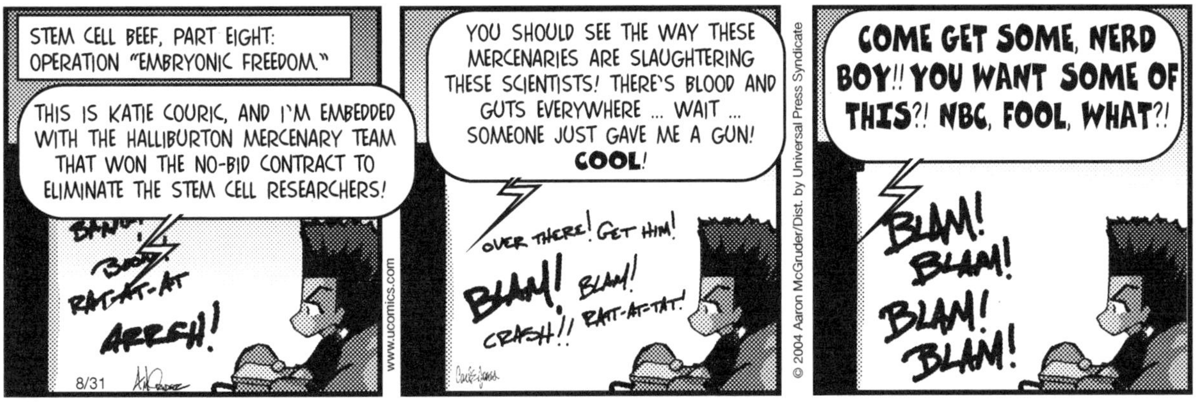
STEM CELL BEEF, PART EIGHT: OPERATION "EMBRYONIC FREEDOM."
THIS IS KATIE COURIC, AND I'M EMBEDDED WITH THE HALLIBURTON MERCENARY TEAM THAT WON THE NO-BID CONTRACT TO ELIMINATE THE STEM CELL RESEARCHERS!
RAT-AT-AT
ARRGH!
8/31
www.ucomics.com
YOU SHOULD SEE THE WAY THESE MERCENARIES ARE SLAUGHTERING THESE SCIENTISTS! THERE'S BLOOD AND GUTS EVERYWHERE ... WAIT ... SOMEONE JUST GAVE ME A GUN! **COOL**!
OVER THERE! GET HIM!
BLAM! BLAM!
CRASH!! RAT-AT-TAT!
© 2004 Aaron McGruder/Dist. by Universal Press Syndicate
COME GET SOME, NERD BOY!! YOU WANT SOME OF THIS?! NBC, FOOL, WHAT?!
BLAM! BLAM! BLAM! BLAM!

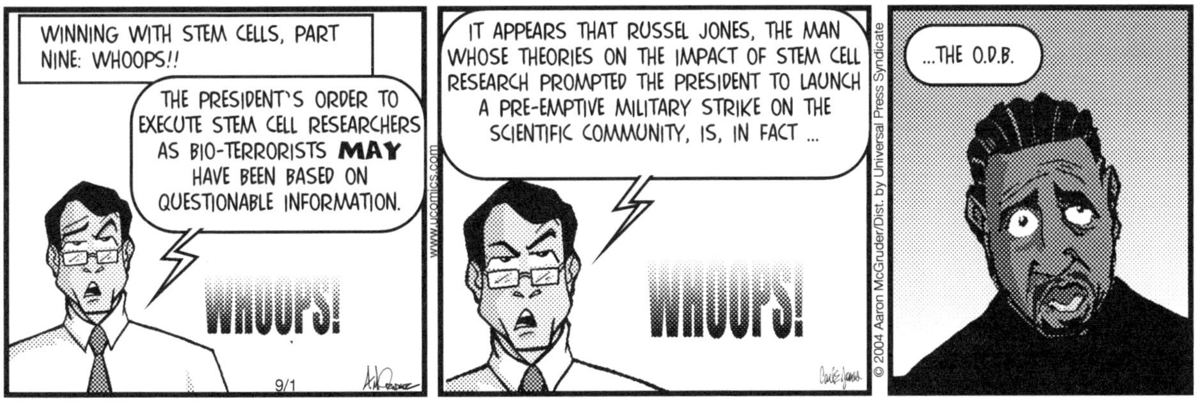
WINNING WITH STEM CELLS, PART NINE: WHOOPS!!
THE PRESIDENT'S ORDER TO EXECUTE STEM CELL RESEARCHERS AS BIO-TERRORISTS **MAY** HAVE BEEN BASED ON QUESTIONABLE INFORMATION.
WHOOPS!
9/1
www.ucomics.com
IT APPEARS THAT RUSSEL JONES, THE MAN WHOSE THEORIES ON THE IMPACT OF STEM CELL RESEARCH PROMPTED THE PRESIDENT TO LAUNCH A PRE-EMPTIVE MILITARY STRIKE ON THE SCIENTIFIC COMMUNITY, IS, IN FACT ...
WHOOPS!
© 2004 Aaron McGruder/Dist. by Universal Press Syndicate
...THE O.D.B.

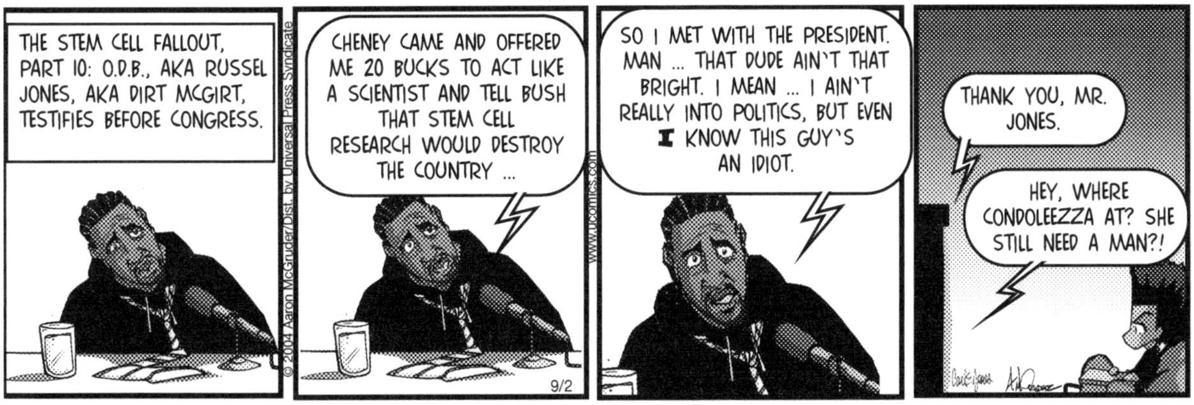
THE STEM CELL FALLOUT, PART 10: O.D.B., AKA RUSSEL JONES, AKA DIRT MCGIRT, TESTIFIES BEFORE CONGRESS.
© 2004 Aaron McGruder/Dist. by Universal Press Syndicate
CHENEY CAME AND OFFERED ME 20 BUCKS TO ACT LIKE A SCIENTIST AND TELL BUSH THAT STEM CELL RESEARCH WOULD DESTROY THE COUNTRY ...
9/2
www.ucomics.com
SO I MET WITH THE PRESIDENT. MAN ... THAT DUDE AIN'T THAT BRIGHT. I MEAN ... I AIN'T REALLY INTO POLITICS, BUT EVEN **I** KNOW THIS GUY'S AN IDIOT.
THANK YOU, MR. JONES.
HEY, WHERE CONDOLEEZZA AT? SHE STILL NEED A MAN?!

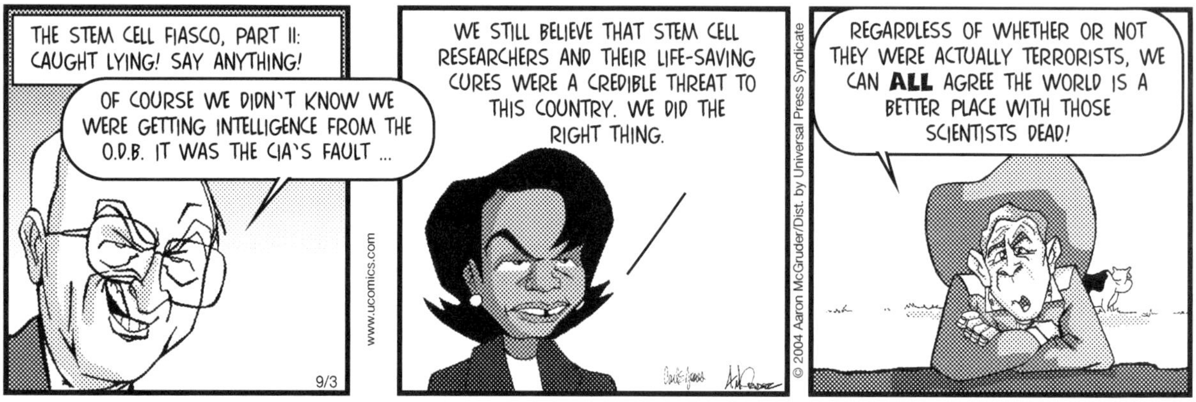
THE STEM CELL FIASCO, PART 11: CAUGHT LYING! SAY ANYTHING!
OF COURSE WE DIDN'T KNOW WE WERE GETTING INTELLIGENCE FROM THE O.D.B. IT WAS THE CIA'S FAULT ...
WE STILL BELIEVE THAT STEM CELL RESEARCHERS AND THEIR LIFE-SAVING CURES WERE A CREDIBLE THREAT TO THIS COUNTRY. WE DID THE RIGHT THING.
REGARDLESS OF WHETHER OR NOT THEY WERE ACTUALLY TERRORISTS, WE CAN **ALL** AGREE THE WORLD IS A BETTER PLACE WITH THOSE SCIENTISTS DEAD!
9/3
www.ucomics.com
© 2004 Aaron McGruder/Dist. by Universal Press Syndicate

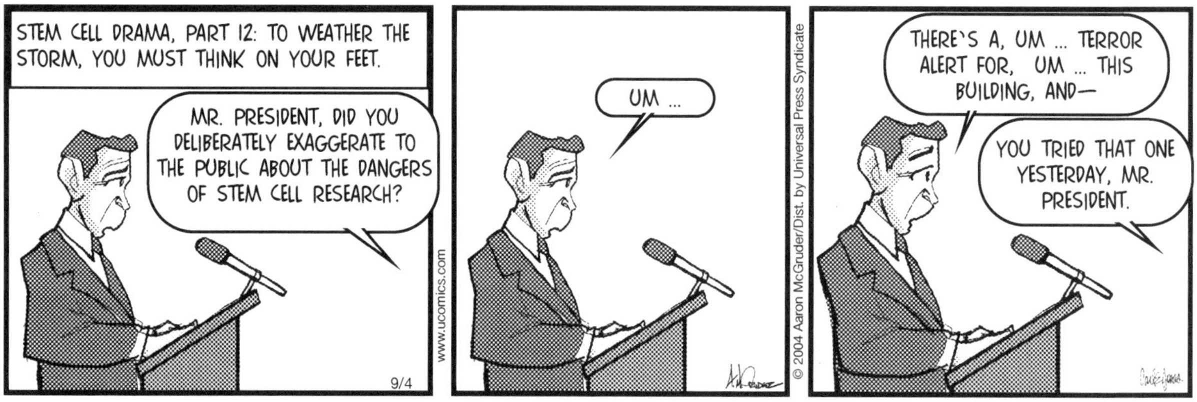
STEM CELL DRAMA, PART 12: TO WEATHER THE STORM, YOU MUST THINK ON YOUR FEET.
MR. PRESIDENT, DID YOU DELIBERATELY EXAGGERATE TO THE PUBLIC ABOUT THE DANGERS OF STEM CELL RESEARCH?
UM ...
THERE'S A, UM ... TERROR ALERT FOR, UM ... THIS BUILDING, AND—
YOU TRIED THAT ONE YESTERDAY, MR. PRESIDENT.
9/4
www.ucomics.com
© 2004 Aaron McGruder/Dist. by Universal Press Syndicate

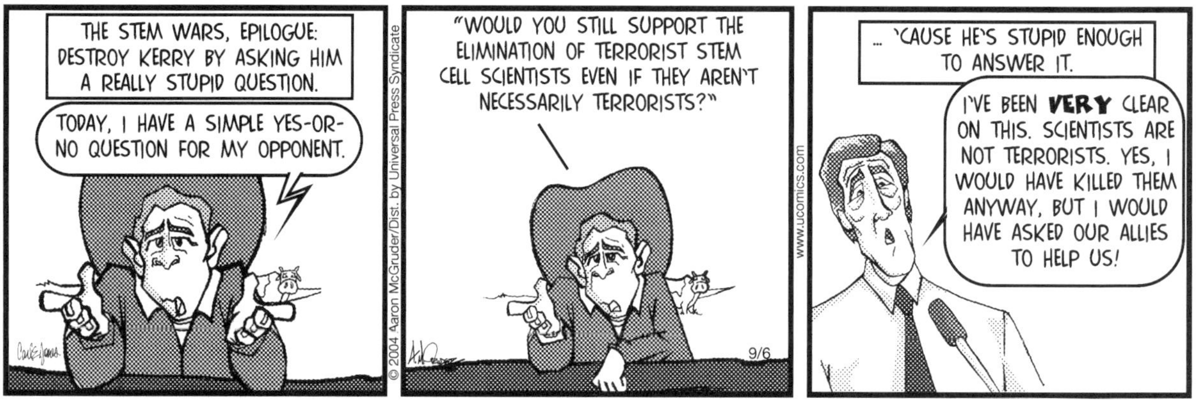
THE STEM WARS, EPILOGUE: DESTROY KERRY BY ASKING HIM A REALLY STUPID QUESTION.
TODAY, I HAVE A SIMPLE YES-OR-NO QUESTION FOR MY OPPONENT.
"WOULD YOU STILL SUPPORT THE ELIMINATION OF TERRORIST STEM CELL SCIENTISTS EVEN IF THEY AREN'T NECESSARILY TERRORISTS?"
... 'CAUSE HE'S STUPID ENOUGH TO ANSWER IT.
I'VE BEEN **VERY** CLEAR ON THIS. SCIENTISTS ARE NOT TERRORISTS. YES, I WOULD HAVE KILLED THEM ANYWAY, BUT I WOULD HAVE ASKED OUR ALLIES TO HELP US!
9/6
© 2004 Aaron McGruder/Dist. by Universal Press Syndicate
www.ucomics.com

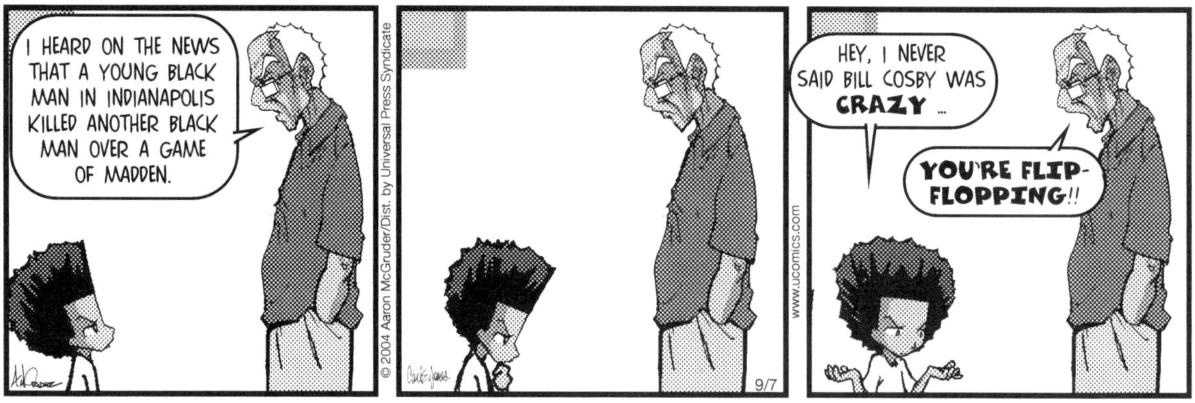
I HEARD ON THE NEWS THAT A YOUNG BLACK MAN IN INDIANAPOLIS KILLED ANOTHER BLACK MAN OVER A GAME OF MADDEN.
HEY, I NEVER SAID BILL COSBY WAS **CRAZY** ...
YOU'RE FLIP-FLOPPING!!
9/7
© 2004 Aaron McGruder/Dist. by Universal Press Syndicate
www.ucomics.com

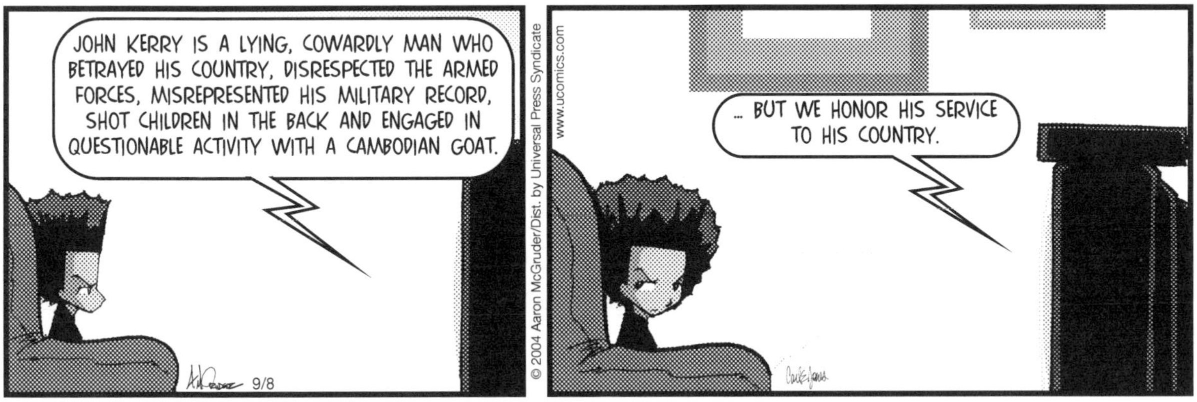
JOHN KERRY IS A LYING, COWARDLY MAN WHO BETRAYED HIS COUNTRY, DISRESPECTED THE ARMED FORCES, MISREPRESENTED HIS MILITARY RECORD, SHOT CHILDREN IN THE BACK AND ENGAGED IN QUESTIONABLE ACTIVITY WITH A CAMBODIAN GOAT.
9/8
© 2004 Aaron McGruder/Dist. by Universal Press Syndicate www.ucomics.com
... BUT WE HONOR HIS SERVICE TO HIS COUNTRY.

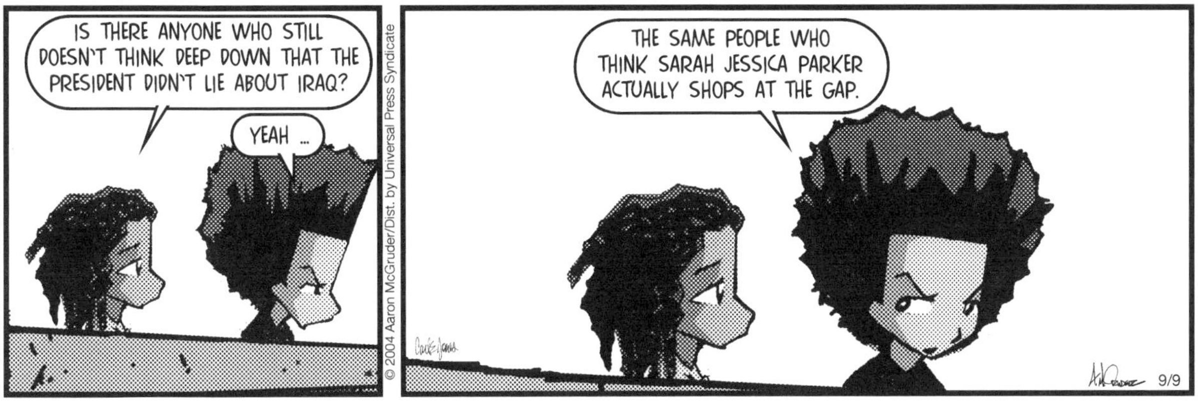
IS THERE ANYONE WHO STILL DOESN'T THINK DEEP DOWN THAT THE PRESIDENT DIDN'T LIE ABOUT IRAQ?
YEAH ...
© 2004 Aaron McGruder/Dist. by Universal Press Syndicate
THE SAME PEOPLE WHO THINK SARAH JESSICA PARKER ACTUALLY SHOPS AT THE GAP.
9/9

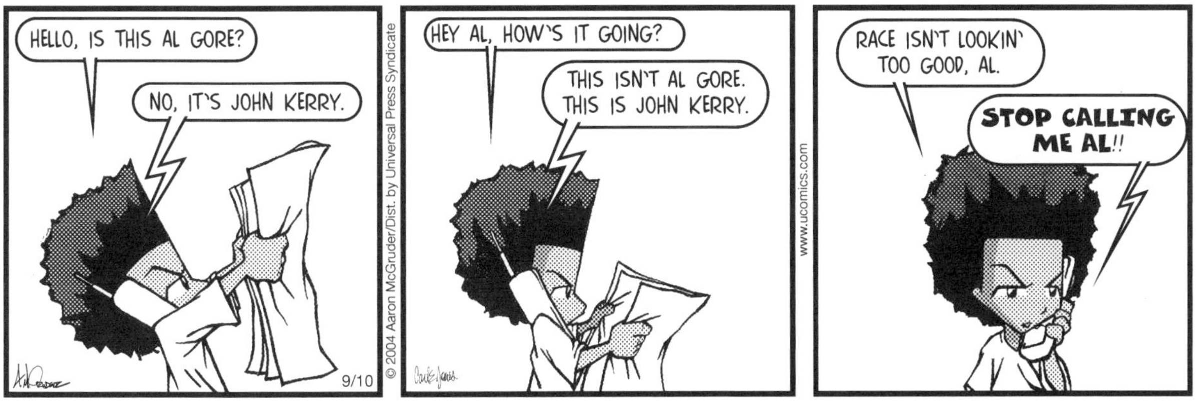
HELLO, IS THIS AL GORE?
NO, IT'S JOHN KERRY.
9/10
© 2004 Aaron McGruder/Dist. by Universal Press Syndicate
HEY AL, HOW'S IT GOING?
THIS ISN'T AL GORE. THIS IS JOHN KERRY.
www.ucomics.com
RACE ISN'T LOOKIN' TOO GOOD, AL.
STOP CALLING ME AL!!

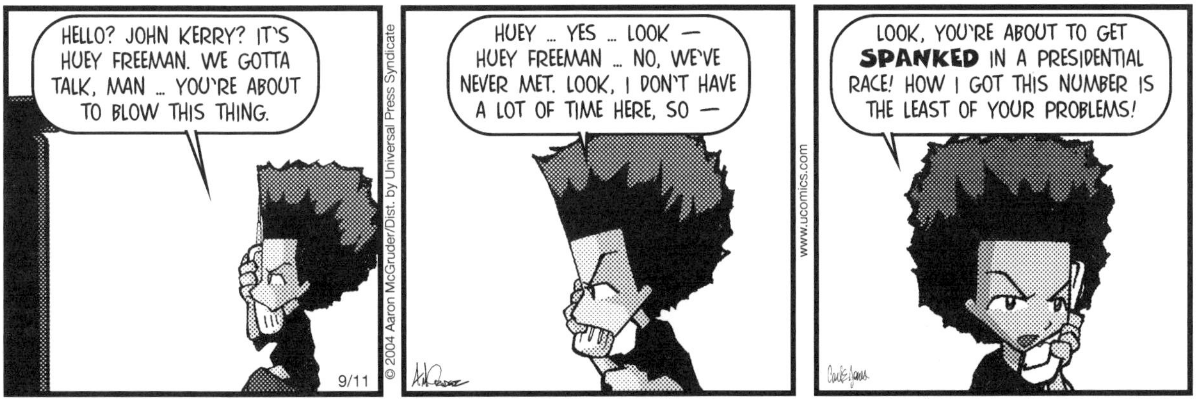
HELLO? JOHN KERRY? IT'S HUEY FREEMAN. WE GOTTA TALK, MAN ... YOU'RE ABOUT TO BLOW THIS THING.
9/11
© 2004 Aaron McGruder/Dist. by Universal Press Syndicate
HUEY ... YES ... LOOK — HUEY FREEMAN ... NO, WE'VE NEVER MET. LOOK, I DON'T HAVE A LOT OF TIME HERE, SO —
www.ucomics.com
LOOK, YOU'RE ABOUT TO GET SPANKED IN A PRESIDENTIAL RACE! HOW I GOT THIS NUMBER IS THE LEAST OF YOUR PROBLEMS!

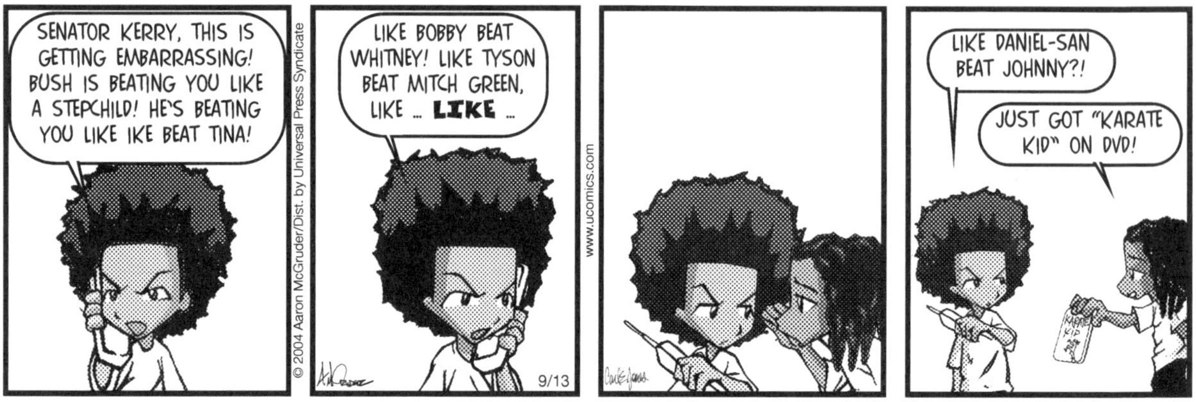
SENATOR KERRY, THIS IS GETTING EMBARRASSING! BUSH IS BEATING YOU LIKE A STEPCHILD! HE'S BEATING YOU LIKE IKE BEAT TINA!
© 2004 Aaron McGruder/Dist. by Universal Press Syndicate
LIKE BOBBY BEAT WHITNEY! LIKE TYSON BEAT MITCH GREEN, LIKE ... **LIKE** ...
9/13
www.ucomics.com
LIKE DANIEL-SAN BEAT JOHNNY?!
JUST GOT "KARATE KID" ON DVD!

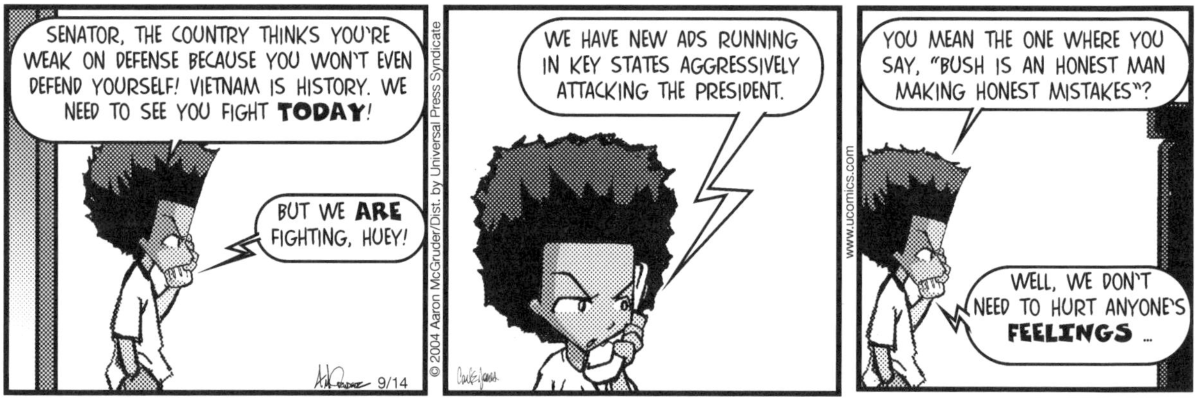
SENATOR, THE COUNTRY THINKS YOU'RE WEAK ON DEFENSE BECAUSE YOU WON'T EVEN DEFEND YOURSELF! VIETNAM IS HISTORY. WE NEED TO SEE YOU FIGHT **TODAY**!
BUT WE **ARE** FIGHTING, HUEY!
9/14
© 2004 Aaron McGruder/Dist. by Universal Press Syndicate
WE HAVE NEW ADS RUNNING IN KEY STATES AGGRESSIVELY ATTACKING THE PRESIDENT.
www.ucomics.com
YOU MEAN THE ONE WHERE YOU SAY, "BUSH IS AN HONEST MAN MAKING HONEST MISTAKES"?
WELL, WE DON'T NEED TO HURT ANYONE'S **FEELINGS** ...

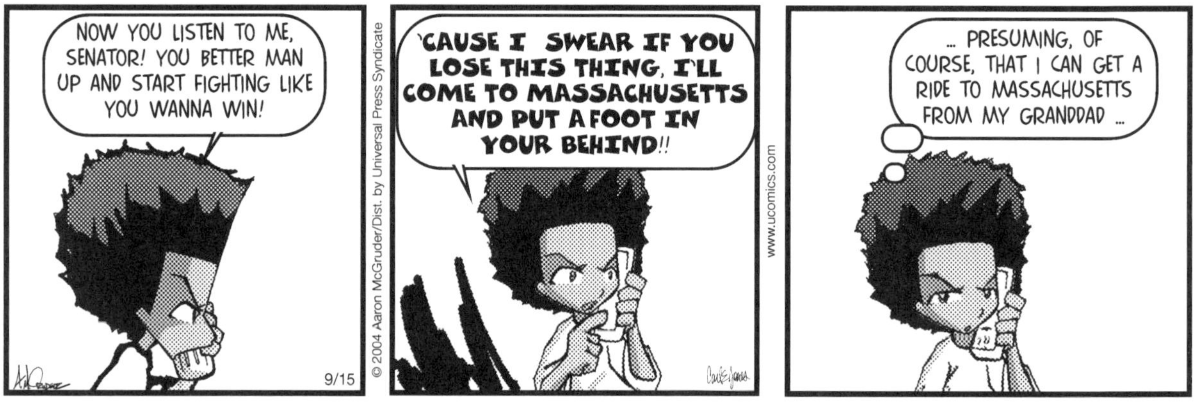
NOW YOU LISTEN TO ME, SENATOR! YOU BETTER MAN UP AND START FIGHTING LIKE YOU WANNA WIN!
9/15
© 2004 Aaron McGruder/Dist. by Universal Press Syndicate
'CAUSE I SWEAR IF YOU LOSE THIS THING, I'LL COME TO MASSACHUSETTS AND PUT A FOOT IN YOUR BEHIND!!
www.ucomics.com
... PRESUMING, OF COURSE, THAT I CAN GET A RIDE TO MASSACHUSETTS FROM MY GRANDDAD ...

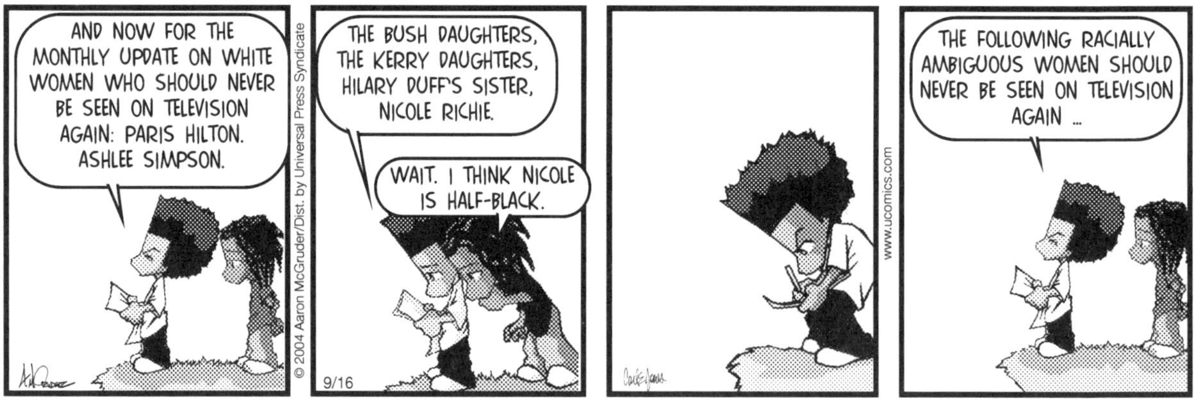
AND NOW FOR THE MONTHLY UPDATE ON WHITE WOMEN WHO SHOULD NEVER BE SEEN ON TELEVISION AGAIN: PARIS HILTON. ASHLEE SIMPSON.
© 2004 Aaron McGruder/Dist. by Universal Press Syndicate
THE BUSH DAUGHTERS, THE KERRY DAUGHTERS, HILARY DUFF'S SISTER, NICOLE RICHIE.
WAIT. I THINK NICOLE IS HALF-BLACK.
9/16
www.ucomics.com
THE FOLLOWING RACIALLY AMBIGUOUS WOMEN SHOULD NEVER BE SEEN ON TELEVISION AGAIN ...

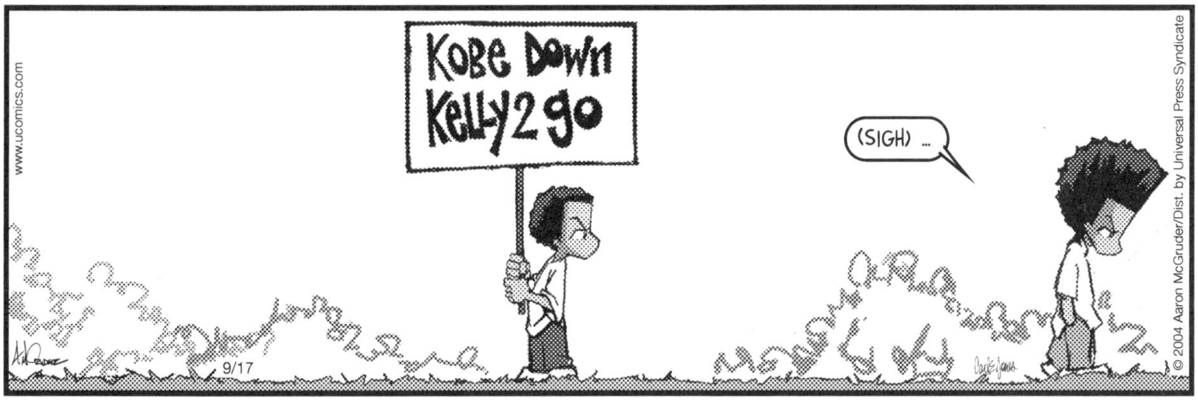
Kobe Down
Kelly 2 go
(SIGH) ...
9/17
www.ucomics.com
© 2004 Aaron McGruder/Dist. by Universal Press Syndicate

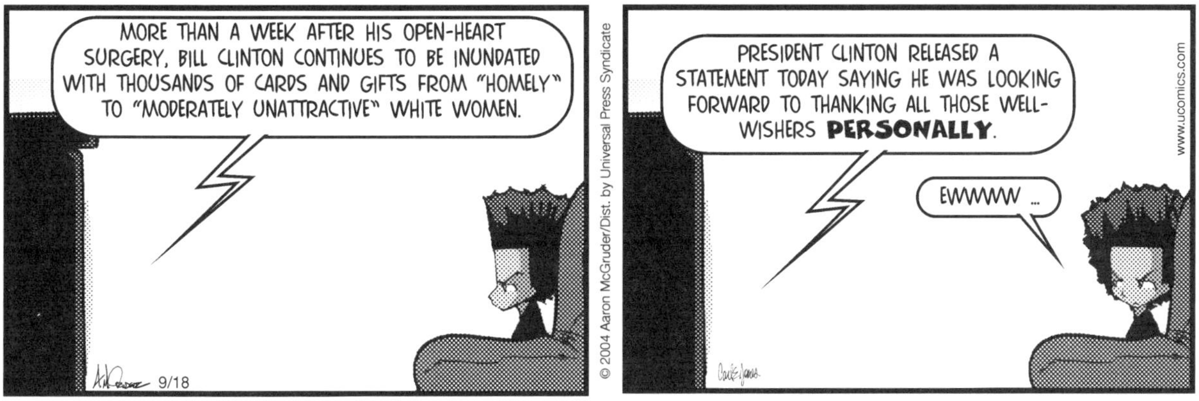
MORE THAN A WEEK AFTER HIS OPEN-HEART SURGERY, BILL CLINTON CONTINUES TO BE INUNDATED WITH THOUSANDS OF CARDS AND GIFTS FROM "HOMELY" TO "MODERATELY UNATTRACTIVE" WHITE WOMEN.
9/18
© 2004 Aaron McGruder/Dist. by Universal Press Syndicate
PRESIDENT CLINTON RELEASED A STATEMENT TODAY SAYING HE WAS LOOKING FORWARD TO THANKING ALL THOSE WELL-WISHERS **PERSONALLY**.
EWWWW ...
www.ucomics.com

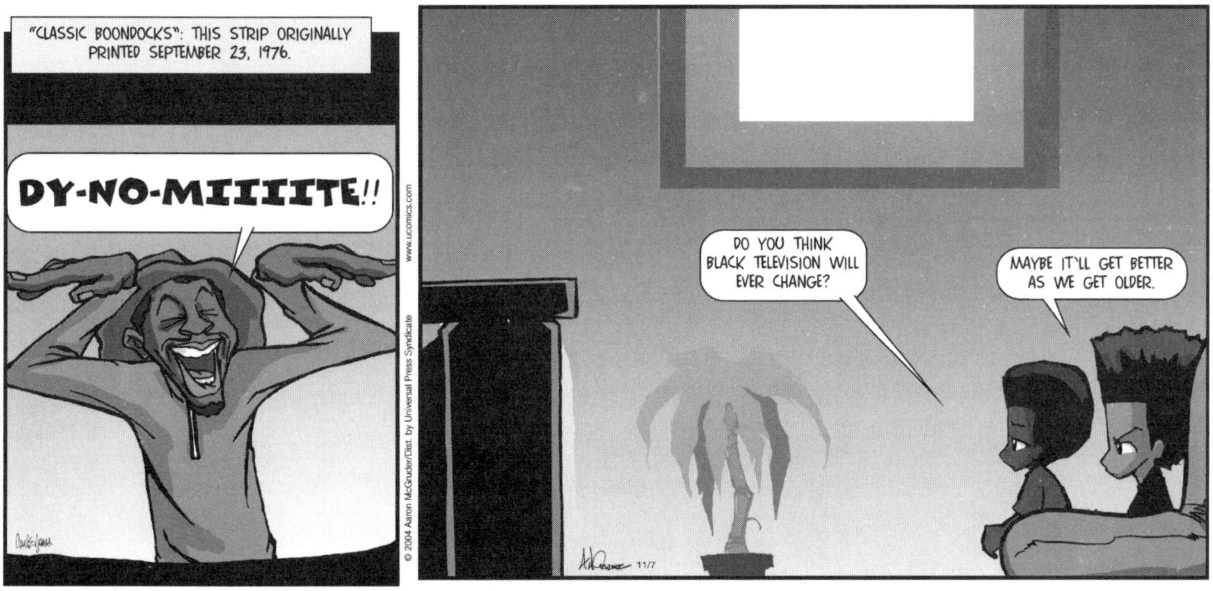
"CLASSIC BOONDOCKS": THIS STRIP ORIGINALLY PRINTED SEPTEMBER 23, 1976.
DY-NO-MIIIIITE!!
www.ucomics.com
© 2004 Aaron McGruder/Dist. by Universal Press Syndicate
DO YOU THINK BLACK TELEVISION WILL EVER CHANGE?
MAYBE IT'LL GET BETTER AS WE GET OLDER.
11/7

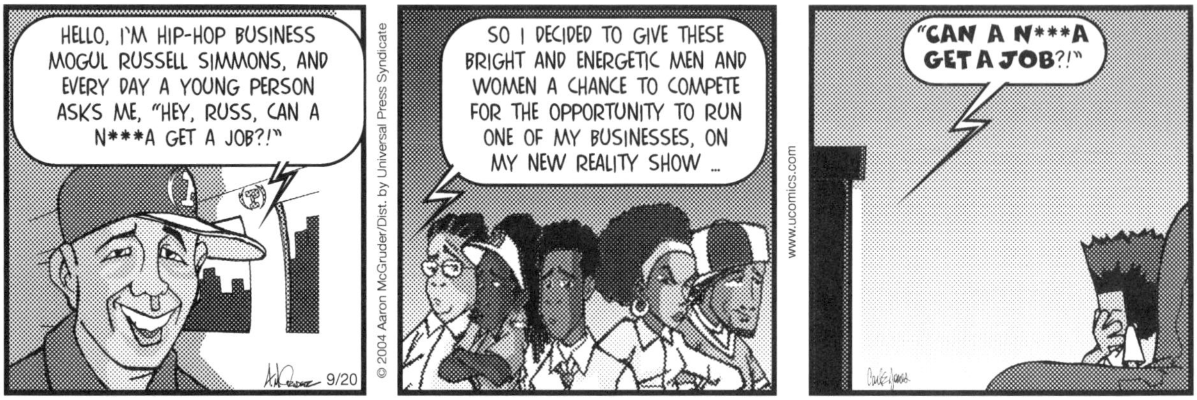
HELLO, I'M HIP-HOP BUSINESS MOGUL RUSSELL SIMMONS, AND EVERY DAY A YOUNG PERSON ASKS ME, "HEY, RUSS, CAN A N***A GET A JOB?!"
9/20
© 2004 Aaron McGruder/Dist. by Universal Press Syndicate
SO I DECIDED TO GIVE THESE BRIGHT AND ENERGETIC MEN AND WOMEN A CHANCE TO COMPETE FOR THE OPPORTUNITY TO RUN ONE OF MY BUSINESSES, ON MY NEW REALITY SHOW ...
www.ucomics.com
"CAN A N***A GET A JOB?!"

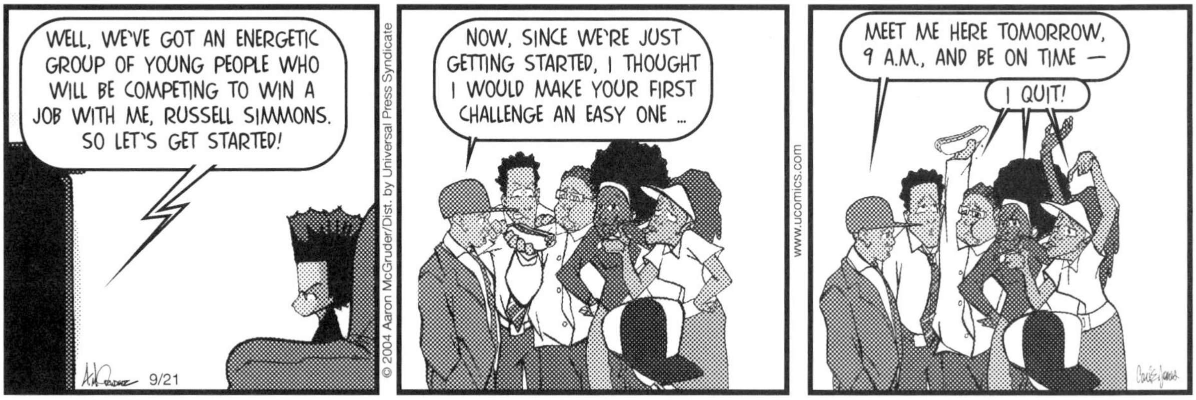
WELL, WE'VE GOT AN ENERGETIC GROUP OF YOUNG PEOPLE WHO WILL BE COMPETING TO WIN A JOB WITH ME, RUSSELL SIMMONS. SO LET'S GET STARTED!
9/21
© 2004 Aaron McGruder/Dist. by Universal Press Syndicate
NOW, SINCE WE'RE JUST GETTING STARTED, I THOUGHT I WOULD MAKE YOUR FIRST CHALLENGE AN EASY ONE ...
www.ucomics.com
MEET ME HERE TOMORROW, 9 A.M., AND BE ON TIME —
I QUIT!

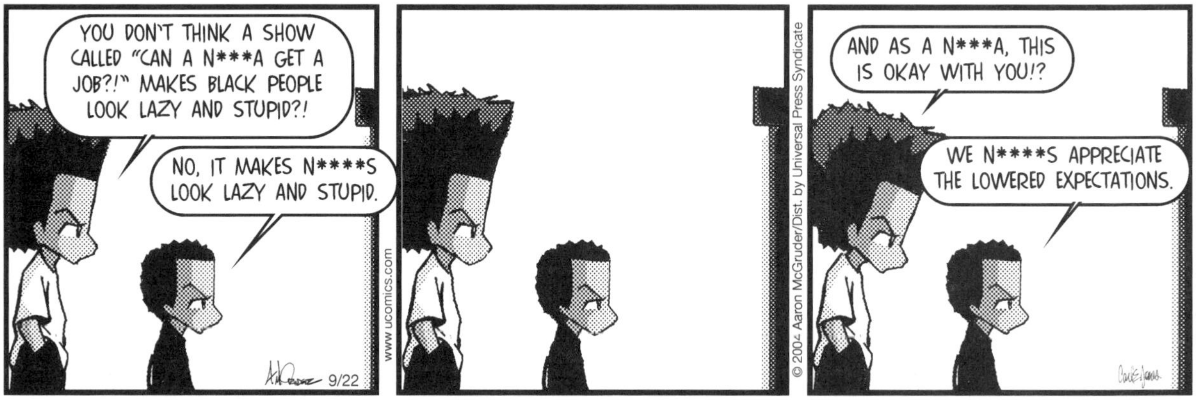
YOU DON'T THINK A SHOW CALLED "CAN A N***A GET A JOB?!" MAKES BLACK PEOPLE LOOK LAZY AND STUPID?!
NO, IT MAKES N****S LOOK LAZY AND STUPID.
9/22
www.ucomics.com
© 2004 Aaron McGruder/Dist. by Universal Press Syndicate
AND AS A N***A, THIS IS OKAY WITH YOU!?
WE N****S APPRECIATE THE LOWERED EXPECTATIONS.

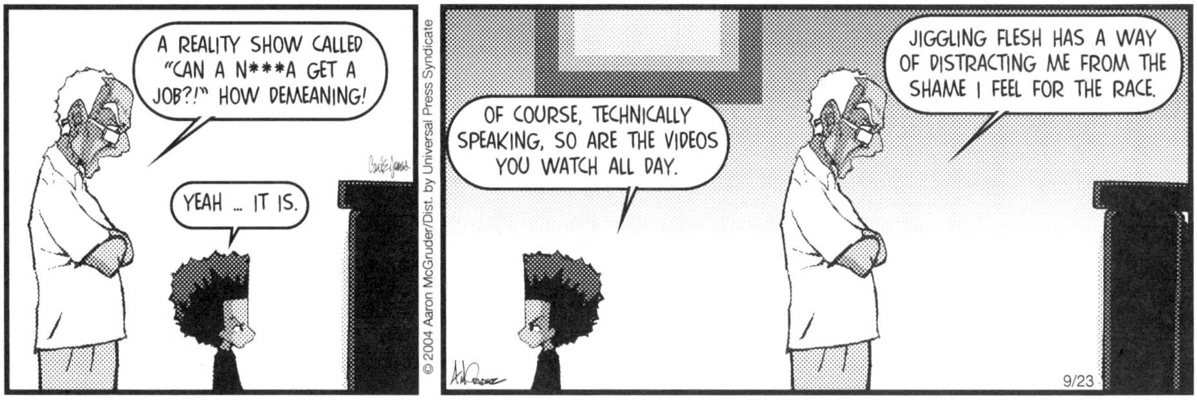
A REALITY SHOW CALLED "CAN A N***A GET A JOB?!" HOW DEMEANING!
YEAH ... IT IS.
© 2004 Aaron McGruder/Dist. by Universal Press Syndicate
OF COURSE, TECHNICALLY SPEAKING, SO ARE THE VIDEOS YOU WATCH ALL DAY.
JIGGLING FLESH HAS A WAY OF DISTRACTING ME FROM THE SHAME I FEEL FOR THE RACE.
9/23

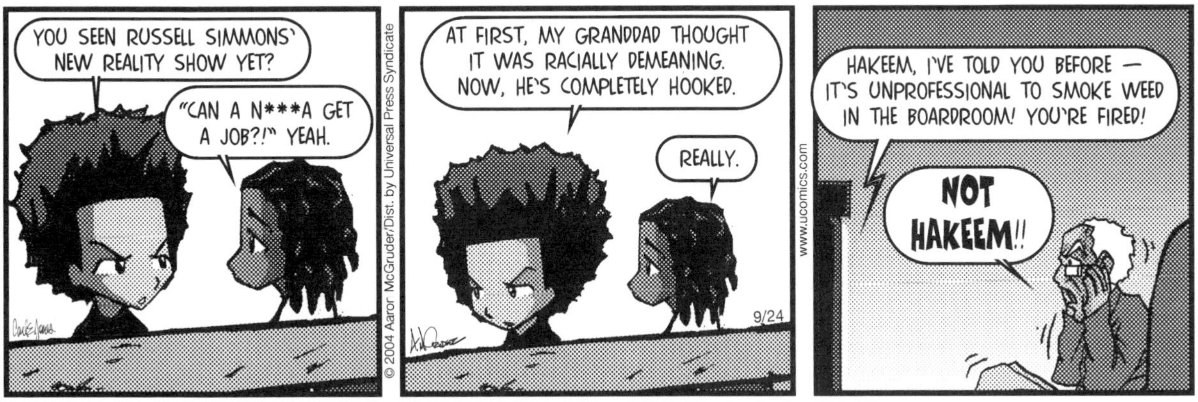
YOU SEEN RUSSELL SIMMONS' NEW REALITY SHOW YET?
"CAN A N***A GET A JOB?!" YEAH.
© 2004 Aaron McGruder/Dist. by Universal Press Syndicate
AT FIRST, MY GRANDDAD THOUGHT IT WAS RACIALLY DEMEANING. NOW, HE'S COMPLETELY HOOKED.
REALLY.
9/24
www.ucomics.com
HAKEEM, I'VE TOLD YOU BEFORE — IT'S UNPROFESSIONAL TO SMOKE WEED IN THE BOARDROOM! YOU'RE FIRED!
NOT HAKEEM!!

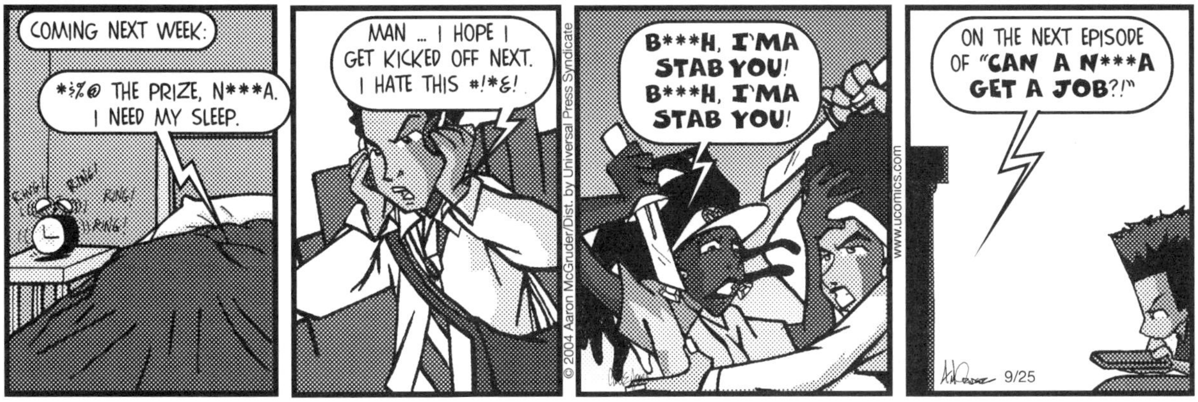
COMING NEXT WEEK:
*$%@ THE PRIZE, N***A. I NEED MY SLEEP.
RING! RING! RING! RING!
MAN ... I HOPE I GET KICKED OFF NEXT. I HATE THIS #!*&!
© 2004 Aaron McGruder/Dist. by Universal Press Syndicate
B***H, I'MA STAB YOU! B***H, I'MA STAB YOU!
www.ucomics.com
ON THE NEXT EPISODE OF "CAN A N***A GET A JOB?!"
9/25

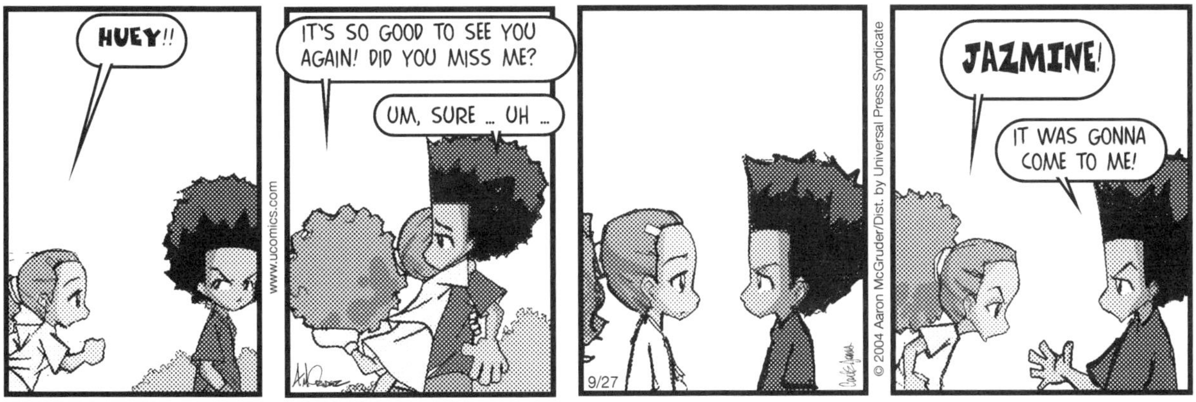
HUEY!!
www.ucomics.com
IT'S SO GOOD TO SEE YOU AGAIN! DID YOU MISS ME?
UM, SURE ... UH ...
9/27
© 2004 Aaron McGruder/Dist. by Universal Press Syndicate
JAZMINE!
IT WAS GONNA COME TO ME!

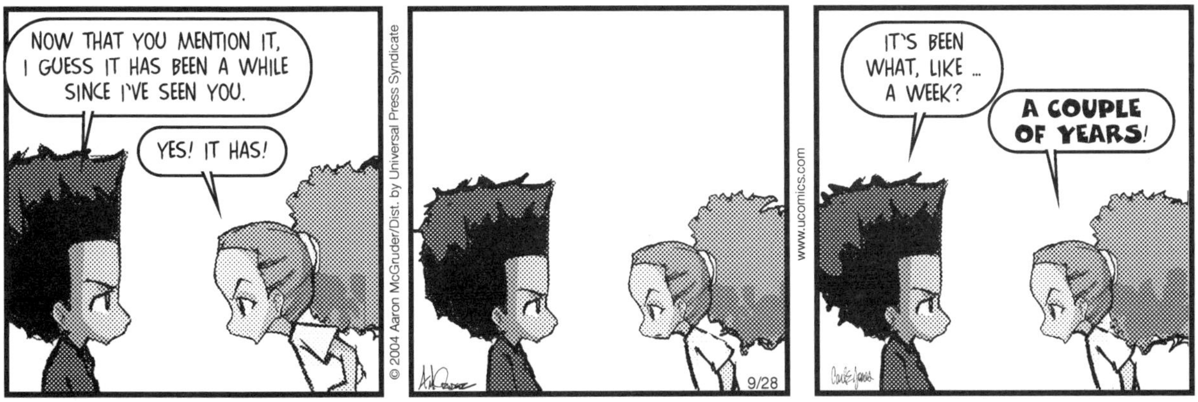
NOW THAT YOU MENTION IT, I GUESS IT HAS BEEN A WHILE SINCE I'VE SEEN YOU.
YES! IT HAS!
© 2004 Aaron McGruder/Dist. by Universal Press Syndicate
9/28
www.ucomics.com
IT'S BEEN WHAT, LIKE ... A WEEK?
A COUPLE OF YEARS!

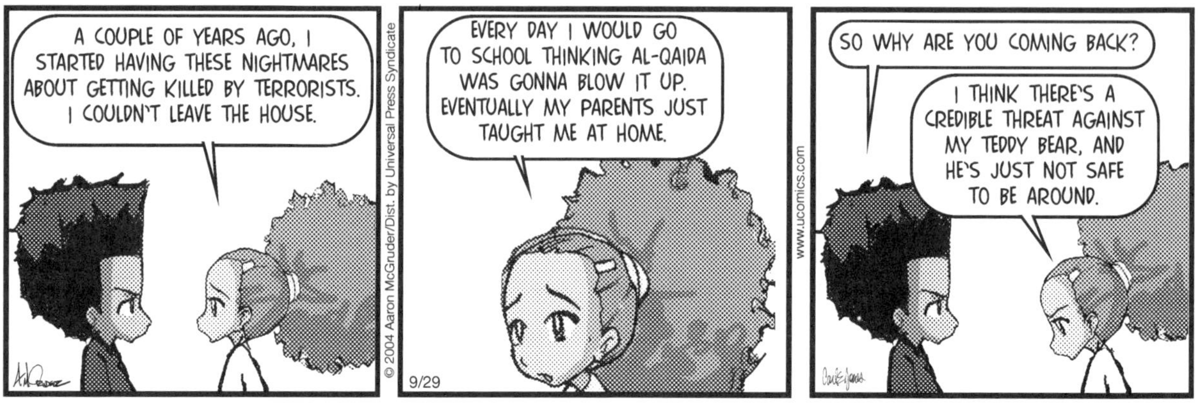
A COUPLE OF YEARS AGO, I STARTED HAVING THESE NIGHTMARES ABOUT GETTING KILLED BY TERRORISTS. I COULDN'T LEAVE THE HOUSE.
© 2004 Aaron McGruder/Dist. by Universal Press Syndicate
EVERY DAY I WOULD GO TO SCHOOL THINKING AL-QAIDA WAS GONNA BLOW IT UP. EVENTUALLY MY PARENTS JUST TAUGHT ME AT HOME.
9/29
www.ucomics.com
SO WHY ARE YOU COMING BACK?
I THINK THERE'S A CREDIBLE THREAT AGAINST MY TEDDY BEAR, AND HE'S JUST NOT SAFE TO BE AROUND.

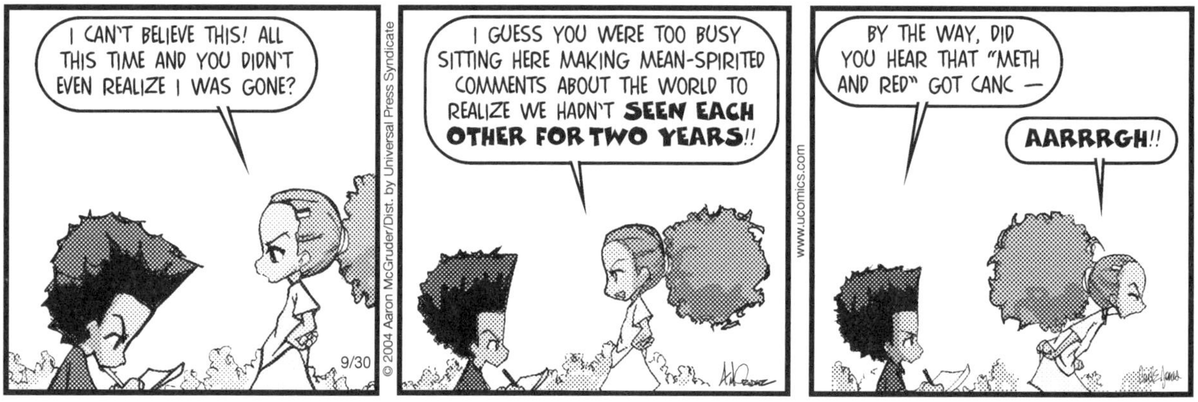
I CAN'T BELIEVE THIS! ALL THIS TIME AND YOU DIDN'T EVEN REALIZE I WAS GONE?
9/30
© 2004 Aaron McGruder/Dist. by Universal Press Syndicate
I GUESS YOU WERE TOO BUSY SITTING HERE MAKING MEAN-SPIRITED COMMENTS ABOUT THE WORLD TO REALIZE WE HADN'T SEEN EACH OTHER FOR TWO YEARS!!
www.ucomics.com
BY THE WAY, DID YOU HEAR THAT "METH AND RED" GOT CANC —
AARRRGH!!

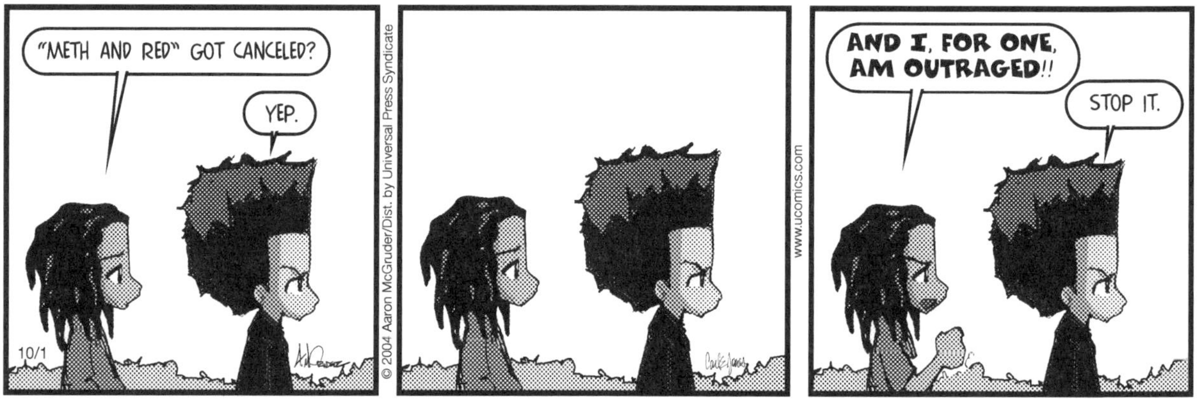
"METH AND RED" GOT CANCELED?
YEP.
10/1
© 2004 Aaron McGruder/Dist. by Universal Press Syndicate
www.ucomics.com
AND I, FOR ONE, AM OUTRAGED!!
STOP IT.

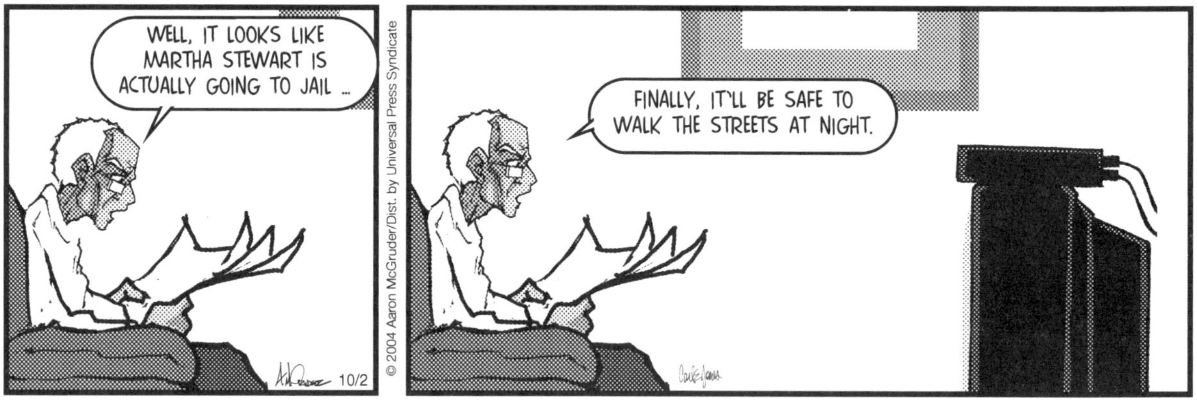
WELL, IT LOOKS LIKE MARTHA STEWART IS ACTUALLY GOING TO JAIL ...
10/2
© 2004 Aaron McGruder/Dist. by Universal Press Syndicate
FINALLY, IT'LL BE SAFE TO WALK THE STREETS AT NIGHT.

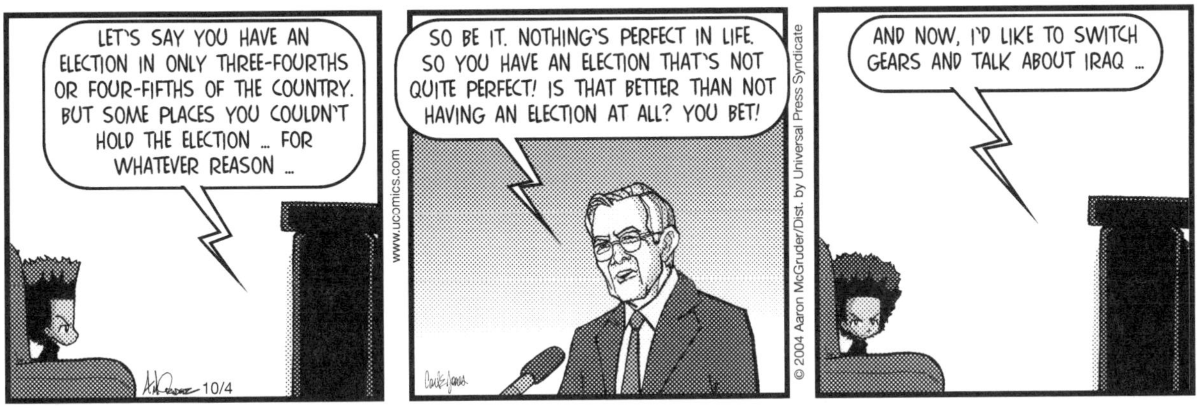
LET'S SAY YOU HAVE AN ELECTION IN ONLY THREE-FOURTHS OR FOUR-FIFTHS OF THE COUNTRY. BUT SOME PLACES YOU COULDN'T HOLD THE ELECTION ... FOR WHATEVER REASON ...
10/4
www.ucomics.com
SO BE IT. NOTHING'S PERFECT IN LIFE. SO YOU HAVE AN ELECTION THAT'S NOT QUITE PERFECT! IS THAT BETTER THAN NOT HAVING AN ELECTION AT ALL? YOU BET!
© 2004 Aaron McGruder/Dist. by Universal Press Syndicate
AND NOW, I'D LIKE TO SWITCH GEARS AND TALK ABOUT IRAQ ...

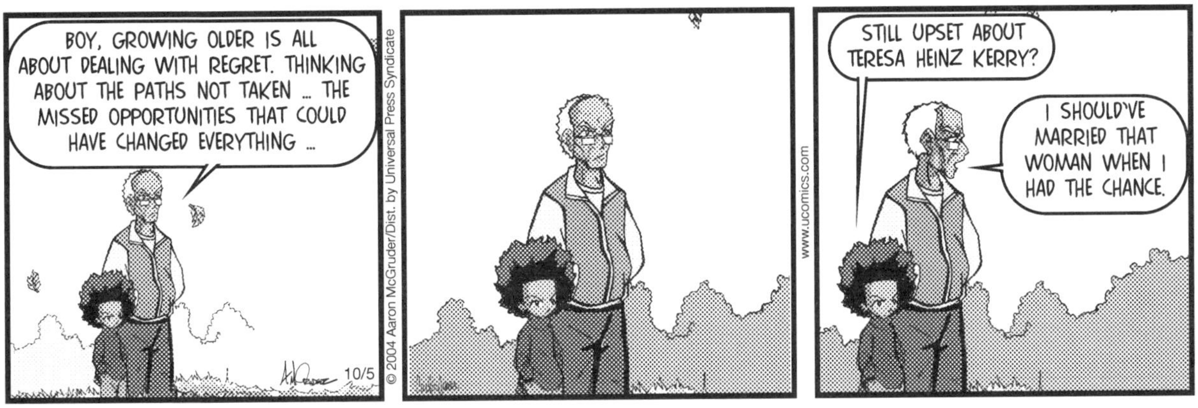
BOY, GROWING OLDER IS ALL ABOUT DEALING WITH REGRET. THINKING ABOUT THE PATHS NOT TAKEN ... THE MISSED OPPORTUNITIES THAT COULD HAVE CHANGED EVERYTHING ...
10/5
© 2004 Aaron McGruder/Dist. by Universal Press Syndicate
STILL UPSET ABOUT TERESA HEINZ KERRY?
I SHOULD'VE MARRIED THAT WOMAN WHEN I HAD THE CHANCE.
www.ucomics.com

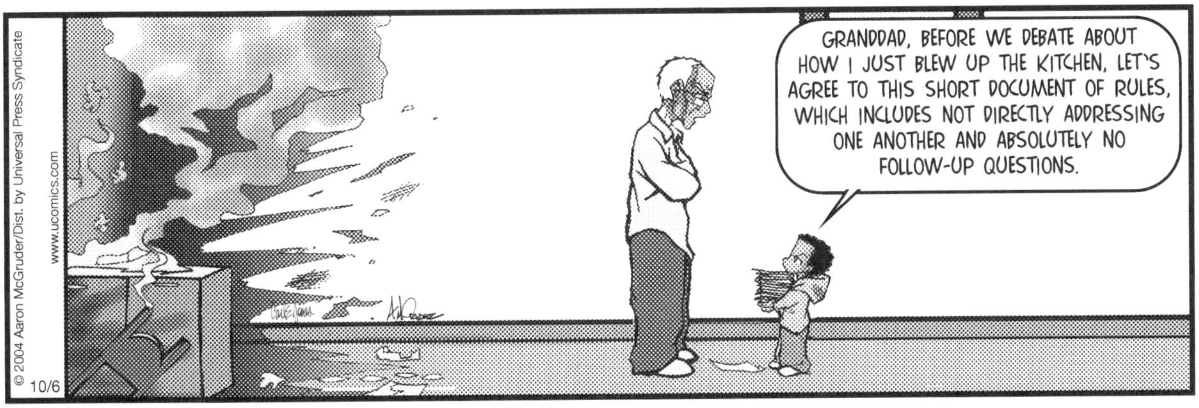
© 2004 Aaron McGruder/Dist. by Universal Press Syndicate
www.ucomics.com
10/6
GRANDDAD, BEFORE WE DEBATE ABOUT HOW I JUST BLEW UP THE KITCHEN, LET'S AGREE TO THIS SHORT DOCUMENT OF RULES, WHICH INCLUDES NOT DIRECTLY ADDRESSING ONE ANOTHER AND ABSOLUTELY NO FOLLOW-UP QUESTIONS.

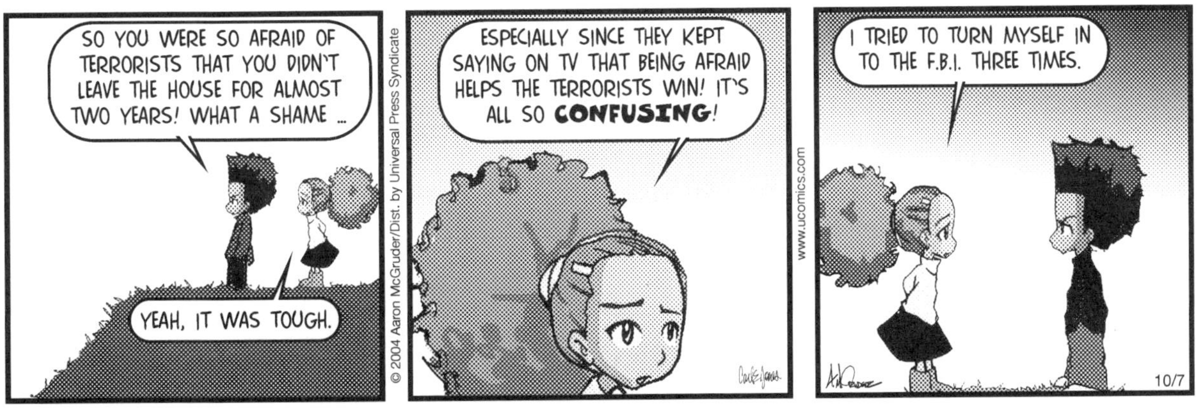
SO YOU WERE SO AFRAID OF TERRORISTS THAT YOU DIDN'T LEAVE THE HOUSE FOR ALMOST TWO YEARS! WHAT A SHAME ...
YEAH, IT WAS TOUGH.
© 2004 Aaron McGruder/Dist. by Universal Press Syndicate
ESPECIALLY SINCE THEY KEPT SAYING ON TV THAT BEING AFRAID HELPS THE TERRORISTS WIN! IT'S ALL SO CONFUSING!
www.ucomics.com
I TRIED TO TURN MYSELF IN TO THE F.B.I. THREE TIMES.
10/7

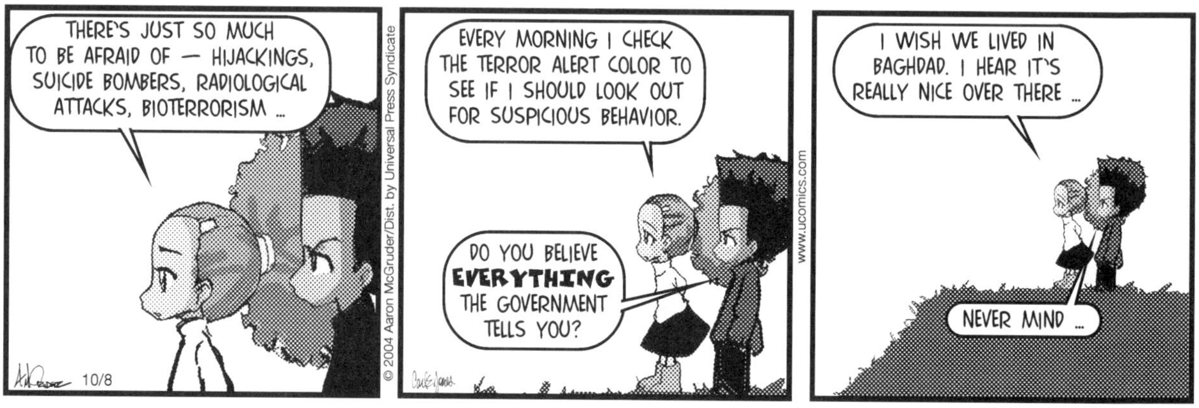
THERE'S JUST SO MUCH TO BE AFRAID OF — HIJACKINGS, SUICIDE BOMBERS, RADIOLOGICAL ATTACKS, BIOTERRORISM ...
10/8
© 2004 Aaron McGruder/Dist. by Universal Press Syndicate
EVERY MORNING I CHECK THE TERROR ALERT COLOR TO SEE IF I SHOULD LOOK OUT FOR SUSPICIOUS BEHAVIOR.
DO YOU BELIEVE EVERYTHING THE GOVERNMENT TELLS YOU?
www.ucomics.com
I WISH WE LIVED IN BAGHDAD. I HEAR IT'S REALLY NICE OVER THERE ...
NEVER MIND ...

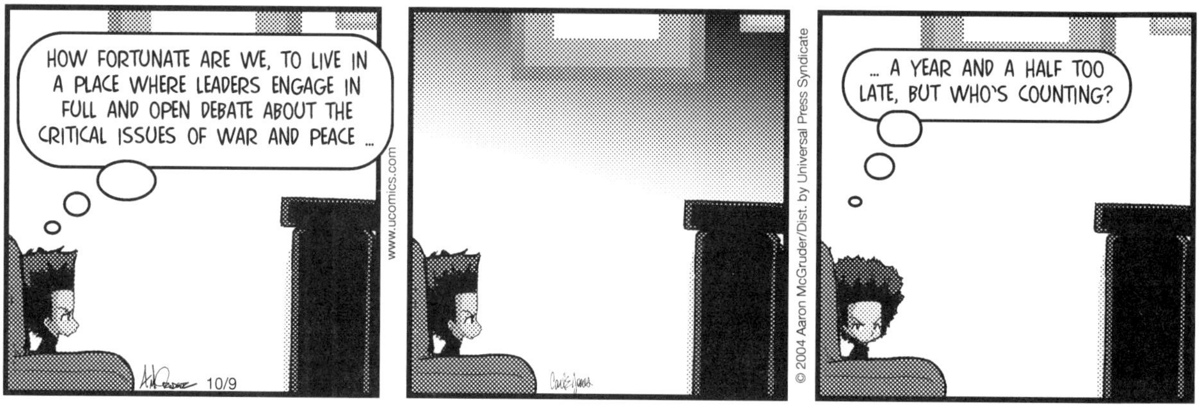
HOW FORTUNATE ARE WE, TO LIVE IN A PLACE WHERE LEADERS ENGAGE IN FULL AND OPEN DEBATE ABOUT THE CRITICAL ISSUES OF WAR AND PEACE ...
10/9
www.ucomics.com
© 2004 Aaron McGruder/Dist. by Universal Press Syndicate
... A YEAR AND A HALF TOO LATE, BUT WHO'S COUNTING?

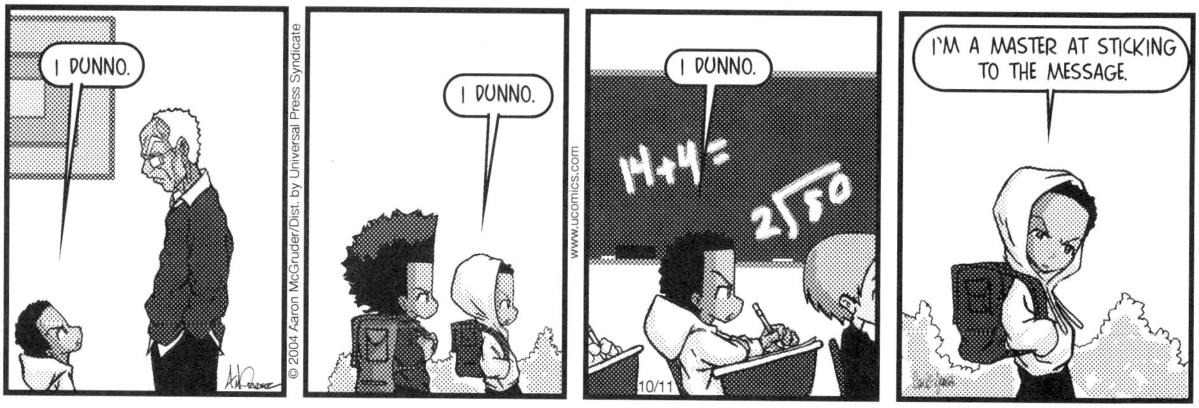
I DUNNO.
© 2004 Aaron McGruder/Dist. by Universal Press Syndicate
I DUNNO.
www.ucomics.com
I DUNNO.
14+4=
2⟌50
10/11
I'M A MASTER AT STICKING TO THE MESSAGE.

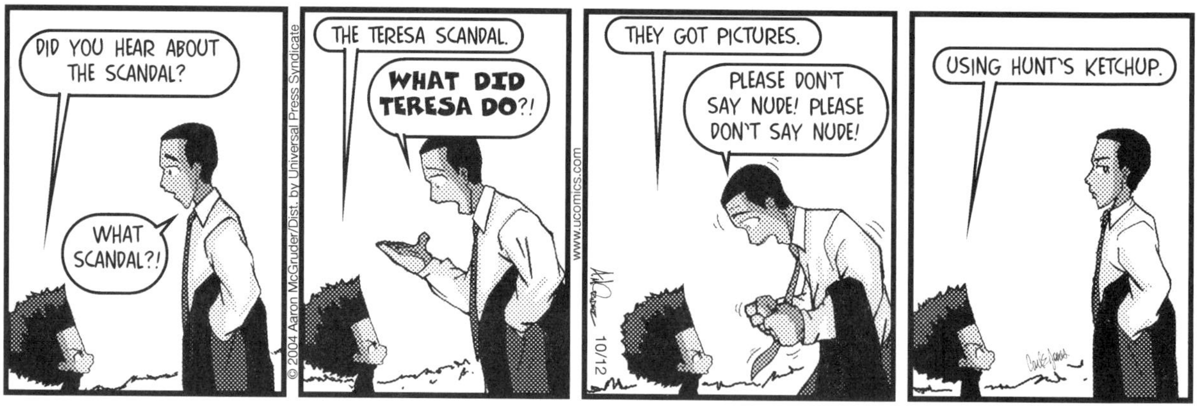
DID YOU HEAR ABOUT THE SCANDAL?
WHAT SCANDAL?!
© 2004 Aaron McGruder/Dist. by Universal Press Syndicate
THE TERESA SCANDAL.
WHAT DID TERESA DO?!
www.ucomics.com
10/12
THEY GOT PICTURES.
PLEASE DON'T SAY NUDE! PLEASE DON'T SAY NUDE!
USING HUNT'S KETCHUP.

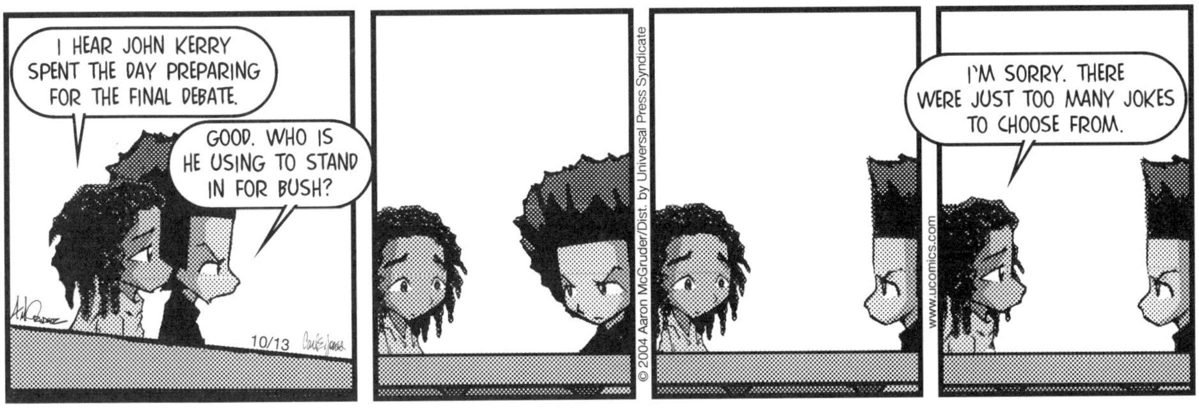
I HEAR JOHN KERRY SPENT THE DAY PREPARING FOR THE FINAL DEBATE.
GOOD. WHO IS HE USING TO STAND IN FOR BUSH?
10/13
© 2004 Aaron McGruder/Dist. by Universal Press Syndicate
www.ucomics.com
I'M SORRY. THERE WERE JUST TOO MANY JOKES TO CHOOSE FROM.

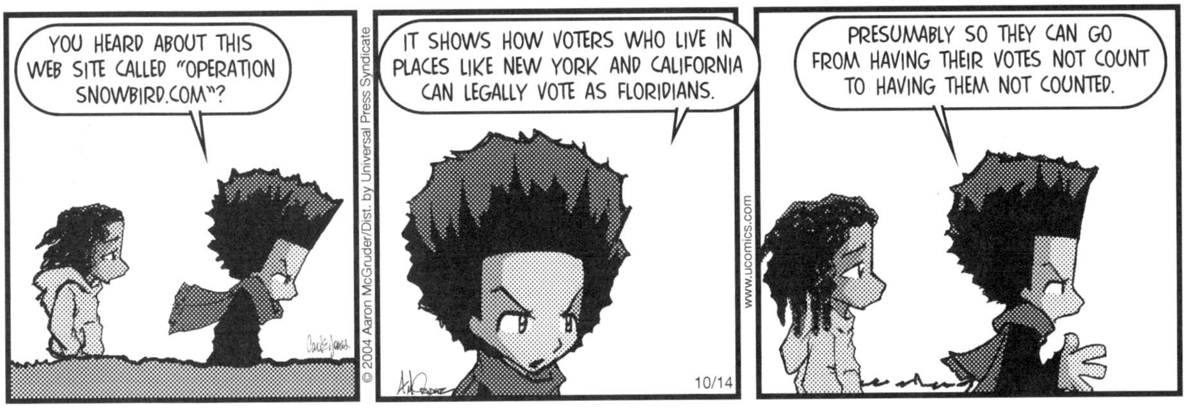
YOU HEARD ABOUT THIS WEB SITE CALLED "OPERATION SNOWBIRD.COM"?
© 2004 Aaron McGruder/Dist. by Universal Press Syndicate
IT SHOWS HOW VOTERS WHO LIVE IN PLACES LIKE NEW YORK AND CALIFORNIA CAN LEGALLY VOTE AS FLORIDIANS.
10/14
www.ucomics.com
PRESUMABLY SO THEY CAN GO FROM HAVING THEIR VOTES NOT COUNT TO HAVING THEM NOT COUNTED.

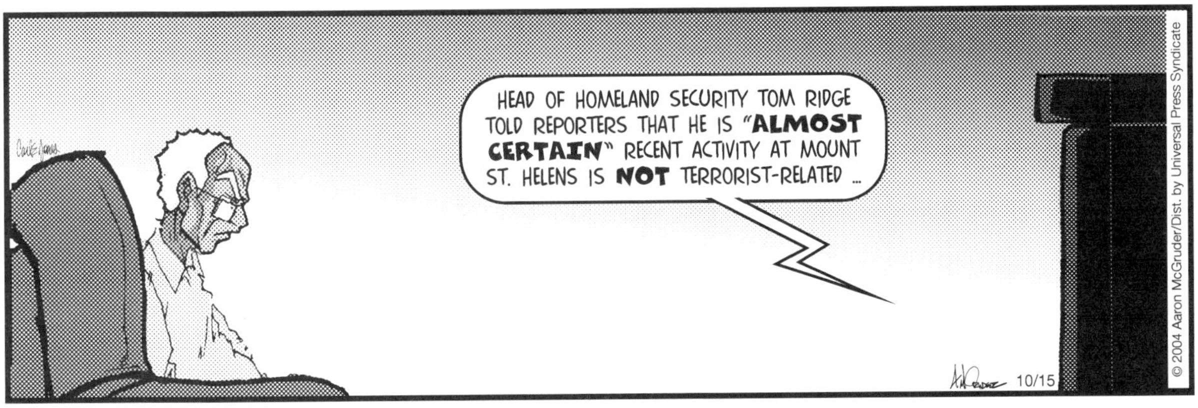
HEAD OF HOMELAND SECURITY TOM RIDGE TOLD REPORTERS THAT HE IS "**ALMOST CERTAIN**" RECENT ACTIVITY AT MOUNT ST. HELENS IS **NOT** TERRORIST-RELATED ...
10/15
© 2004 Aaron McGruder/Dist. by Universal Press Syndicate

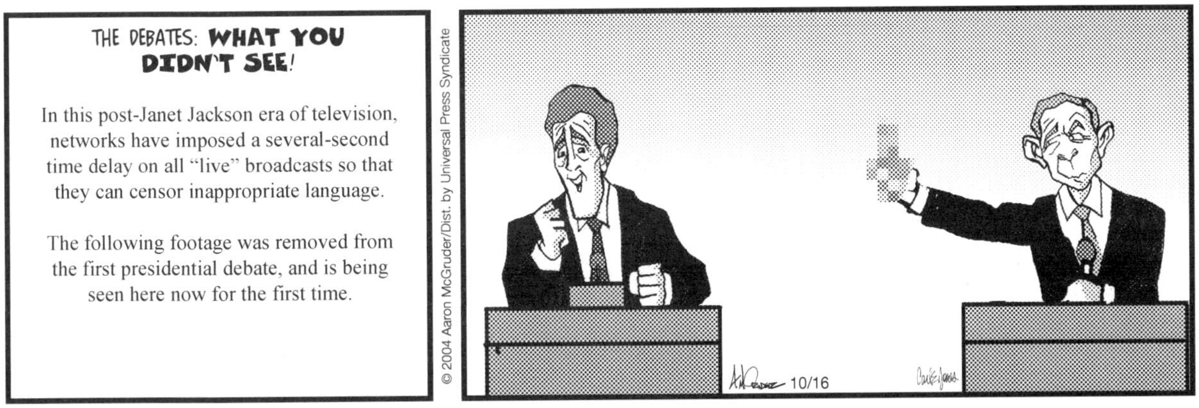
THE DEBATES: **WHAT YOU DIDN'T SEE**!
In this post-Janet Jackson era of television, networks have imposed a several-second time delay on all "live" broadcasts so that they can censor inappropriate language.
The following footage was removed from the first presidential debate, and is being seen here now for the first time.
© 2004 Aaron McGruder/Dist. by Universal Press Syndicate
10/16

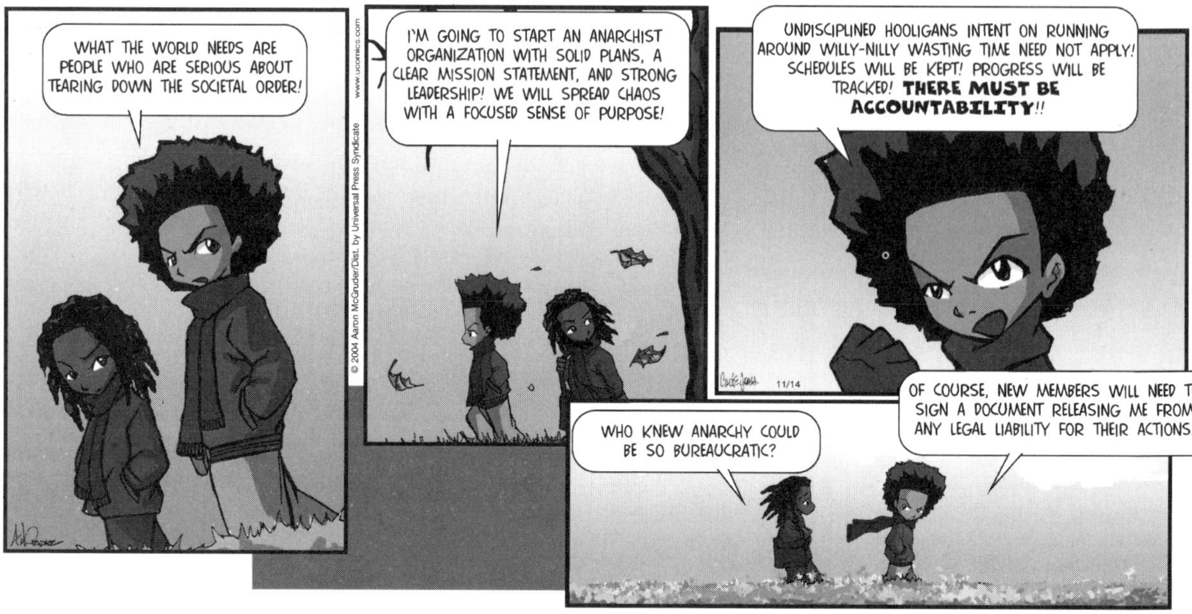
WHAT THE WORLD NEEDS ARE PEOPLE WHO ARE SERIOUS ABOUT TEARING DOWN THE SOCIETAL ORDER!
© 2004 Aaron McGruder/Dist. by Universal Press Syndicate
www.ucomics.com
I'M GOING TO START AN ANARCHIST ORGANIZATION WITH SOLID PLANS, A CLEAR MISSION STATEMENT, AND STRONG LEADERSHIP! WE WILL SPREAD CHAOS WITH A FOCUSED SENSE OF PURPOSE!
UNDISCIPLINED HOOLIGANS INTENT ON RUNNING AROUND WILLY-NILLY WASTING TIME NEED NOT APPLY! SCHEDULES WILL BE KEPT! PROGRESS WILL BE TRACKED! THERE MUST BE ACCOUNTABILITY!!
11/14
OF COURSE, NEW MEMBERS WILL NEED TO SIGN A DOCUMENT RELEASING ME FROM ANY LEGAL LIABILITY FOR THEIR ACTIONS.
WHO KNEW ANARCHY COULD BE SO BUREAUCRATIC?

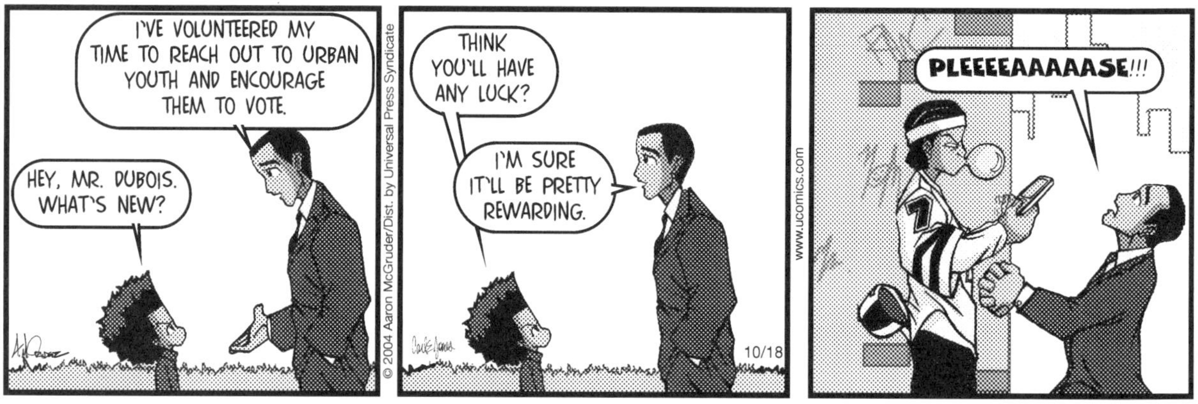
HEY, MR. DUBOIS. WHAT'S NEW?
I'VE VOLUNTEERED MY TIME TO REACH OUT TO URBAN YOUTH AND ENCOURAGE THEM TO VOTE.
© 2004 Aaron McGruder/Dist. by Universal Press Syndicate
THINK YOU'LL HAVE ANY LUCK?
I'M SURE IT'LL BE PRETTY REWARDING.
10/18
www.ucomics.com
PLEEEEAAAAASE!!!

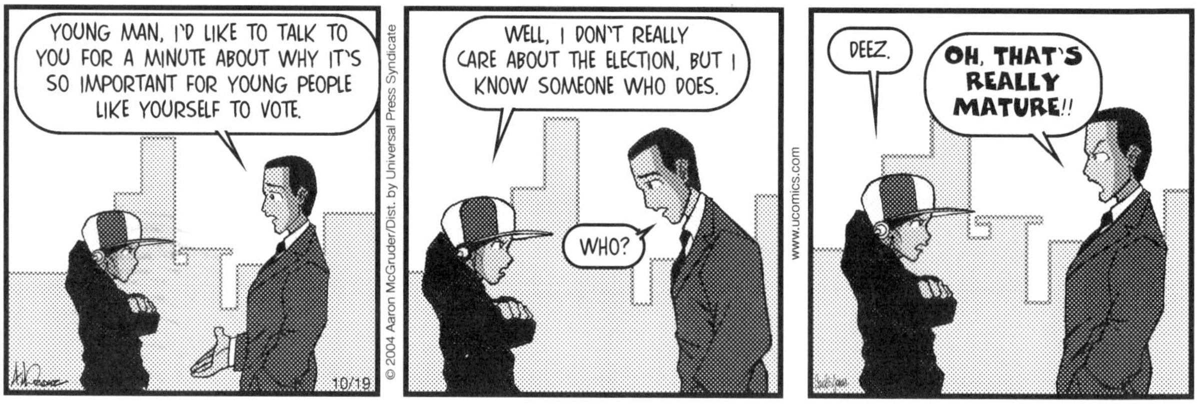
YOUNG MAN, I'D LIKE TO TALK TO YOU FOR A MINUTE ABOUT WHY IT'S SO IMPORTANT FOR YOUNG PEOPLE LIKE YOURSELF TO VOTE.
10/19
© 2004 Aaron McGruder/Dist. by Universal Press Syndicate
WELL, I DON'T REALLY CARE ABOUT THE ELECTION, BUT I KNOW SOMEONE WHO DOES.
WHO?
www.ucomics.com
DEEZ.
OH, THAT'S REALLY MATURE!!

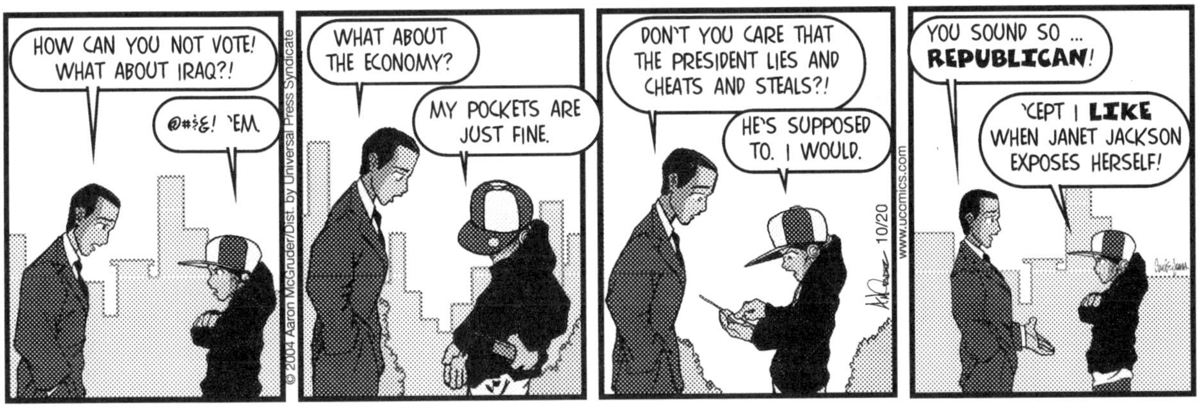
HOW CAN YOU NOT VOTE! WHAT ABOUT IRAQ?!
@#$&! 'EM.
© 2004 Aaron McGruder/Dist. by Universal Press Syndicate
WHAT ABOUT THE ECONOMY?
MY POCKETS ARE JUST FINE.
DON'T YOU CARE THAT THE PRESIDENT LIES AND CHEATS AND STEALS?!
HE'S SUPPOSED TO. I WOULD.
10/20
www.ucomics.com
YOU SOUND SO ... **REPUBLICAN**!
'CEPT I **LIKE** WHEN JANET JACKSON EXPOSES HERSELF!

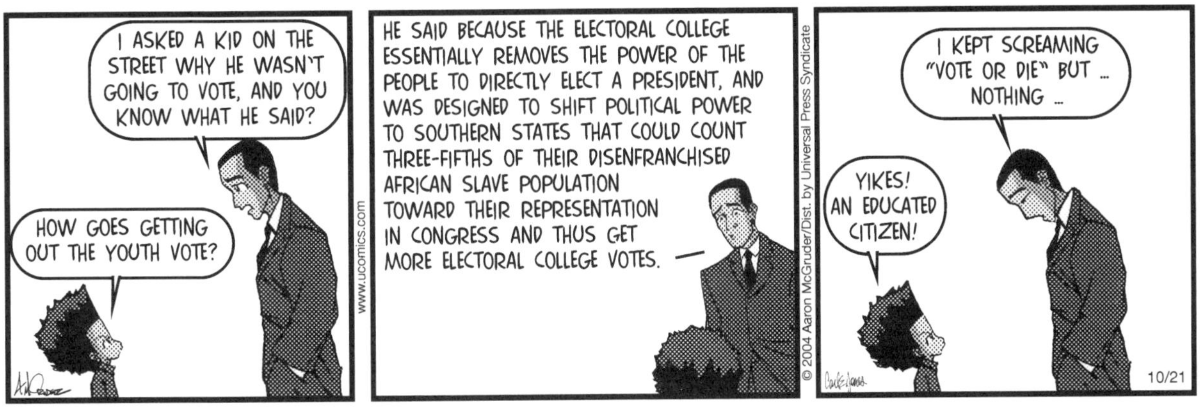
I ASKED A KID ON THE STREET WHY HE WASN'T GOING TO VOTE, AND YOU KNOW WHAT HE SAID?
HOW GOES GETTING OUT THE YOUTH VOTE?
www.ucomics.com
HE SAID BECAUSE THE ELECTORAL COLLEGE ESSENTIALLY REMOVES THE POWER OF THE PEOPLE TO DIRECTLY ELECT A PRESIDENT, AND WAS DESIGNED TO SHIFT POLITICAL POWER TO SOUTHERN STATES THAT COULD COUNT THREE-FIFTHS OF THEIR DISENFRANCHISED AFRICAN SLAVE POPULATION TOWARD THEIR REPRESENTATION IN CONGRESS AND THUS GET MORE ELECTORAL COLLEGE VOTES.
© 2004 Aaron McGruder/Dist. by Universal Press Syndicate
I KEPT SCREAMING "VOTE OR DIE" BUT ... NOTHING ...
YIKES! AN EDUCATED CITIZEN!
10/21

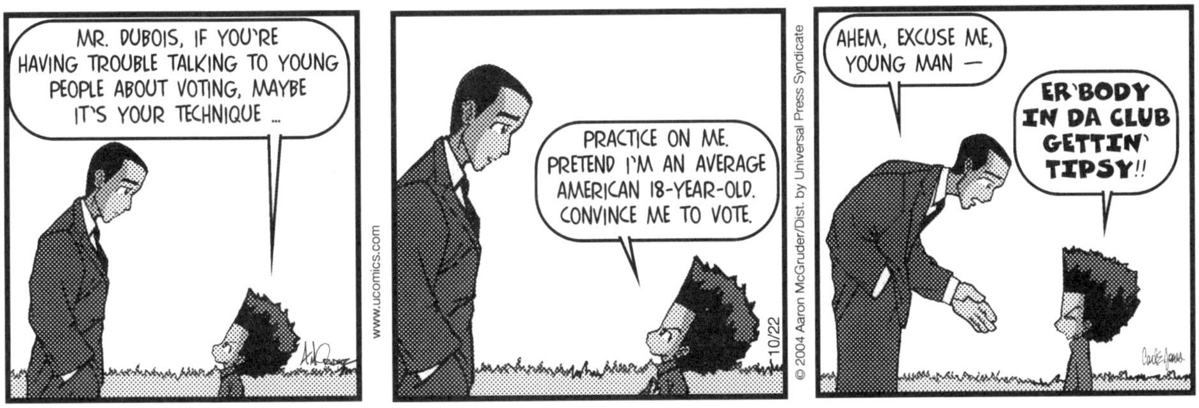
MR. DUBOIS, IF YOU'RE HAVING TROUBLE TALKING TO YOUNG PEOPLE ABOUT VOTING, MAYBE IT'S YOUR TECHNIQUE ...
www.ucomics.com
PRACTICE ON ME. PRETEND I'M AN AVERAGE AMERICAN 18-YEAR-OLD. CONVINCE ME TO VOTE.
10/22
© 2004 Aaron McGruder/Dist. by Universal Press Syndicate
AHEM, EXCUSE ME, YOUNG MAN —
ER'BODY IN DA CLUB GETTIN' TIPSY!!

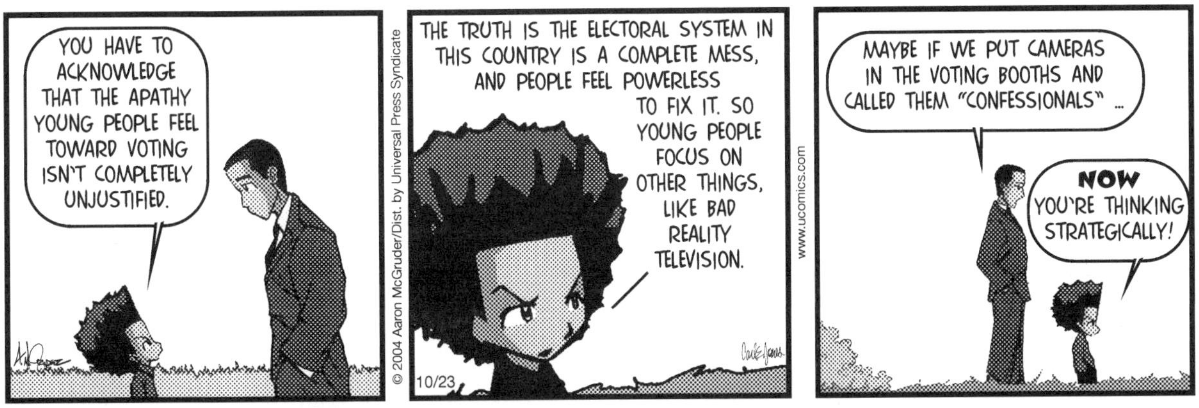
YOU HAVE TO ACKNOWLEDGE THAT THE APATHY YOUNG PEOPLE FEEL TOWARD VOTING ISN'T COMPLETELY UNJUSTIFIED.
© 2004 Aaron McGruder/Dist. by Universal Press Syndicate
THE TRUTH IS THE ELECTORAL SYSTEM IN THIS COUNTRY IS A COMPLETE MESS, AND PEOPLE FEEL POWERLESS TO FIX IT. SO YOUNG PEOPLE FOCUS ON OTHER THINGS, LIKE BAD REALITY TELEVISION.
10/23
www.ucomics.com
MAYBE IF WE PUT CAMERAS IN THE VOTING BOOTHS AND CALLED THEM "CONFESSIONALS" ...
NOW YOU'RE THINKING STRATEGICALLY!

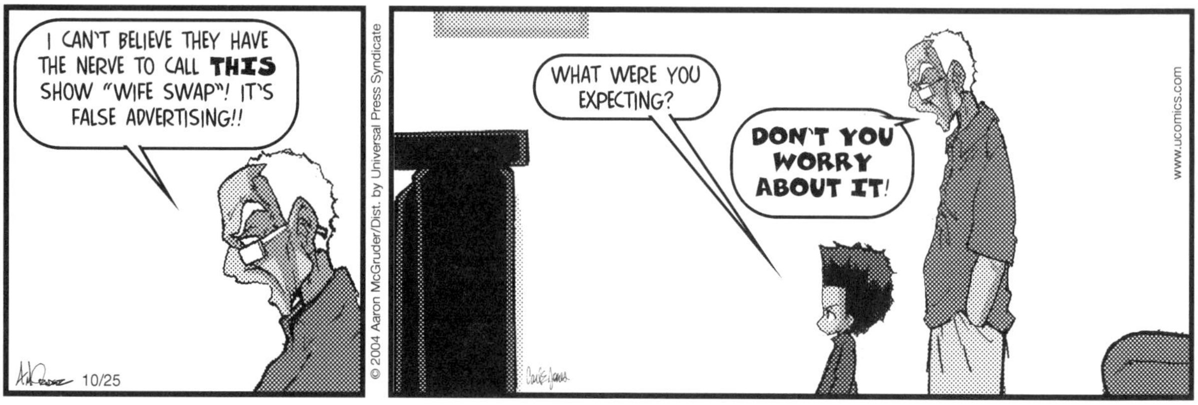
I CAN'T BELIEVE THEY HAVE THE NERVE TO CALL THIS SHOW "WIFE SWAP"! IT'S FALSE ADVERTISING!!
10/25
© 2004 Aaron McGruder/Dist. by Universal Press Syndicate
WHAT WERE YOU EXPECTING?
DON'T YOU WORRY ABOUT IT!
www.ucomics.com

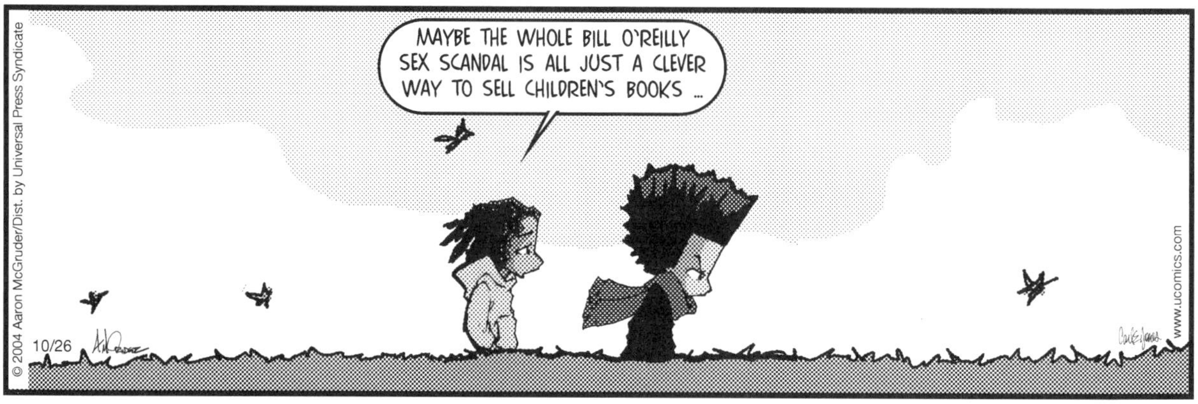
© 2004 Aaron McGruder/Dist. by Universal Press Syndicate
MAYBE THE WHOLE BILL O'REILLY SEX SCANDAL IS ALL JUST A CLEVER WAY TO SELL CHILDREN'S BOOKS ...
10/26
www.ucomics.com

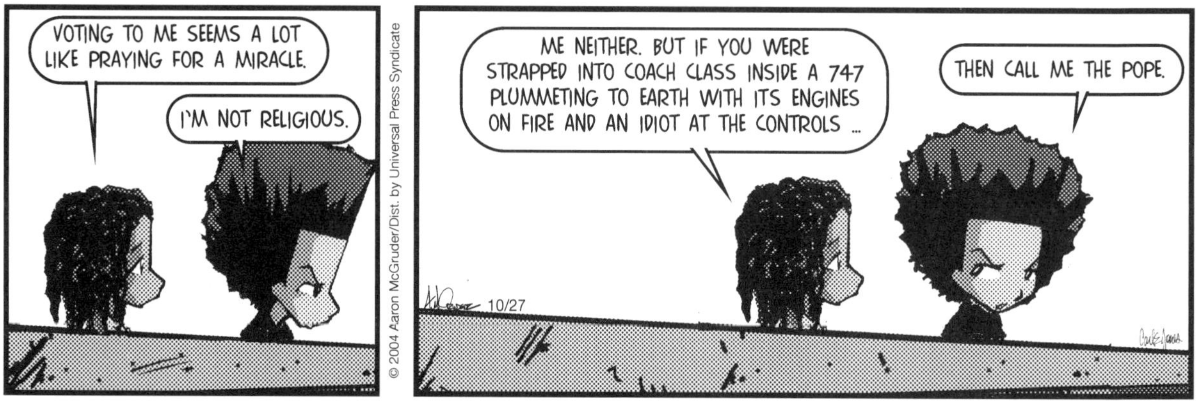
VOTING TO ME SEEMS A LOT LIKE PRAYING FOR A MIRACLE.
I'M NOT RELIGIOUS.
© 2004 Aaron McGruder/Dist. by Universal Press Syndicate
ME NEITHER. BUT IF YOU WERE STRAPPED INTO COACH CLASS INSIDE A 747 PLUMMETING TO EARTH WITH ITS ENGINES ON FIRE AND AN IDIOT AT THE CONTROLS ...
THEN CALL ME THE POPE.
10/27

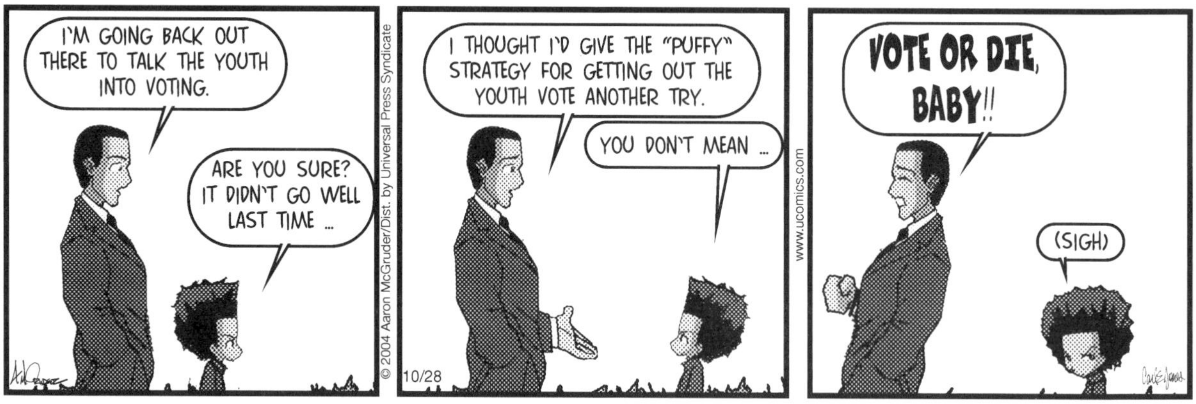
I'M GOING BACK OUT THERE TO TALK THE YOUTH INTO VOTING.
ARE YOU SURE? IT DIDN'T GO WELL LAST TIME ...
© 2004 Aaron McGruder/Dist. by Universal Press Syndicate
I THOUGHT I'D GIVE THE "PUFFY" STRATEGY FOR GETTING OUT THE YOUTH VOTE ANOTHER TRY.
YOU DON'T MEAN ...
10/28
www.ucomics.com
VOTE OR DIE, BABY!!
(SIGH)

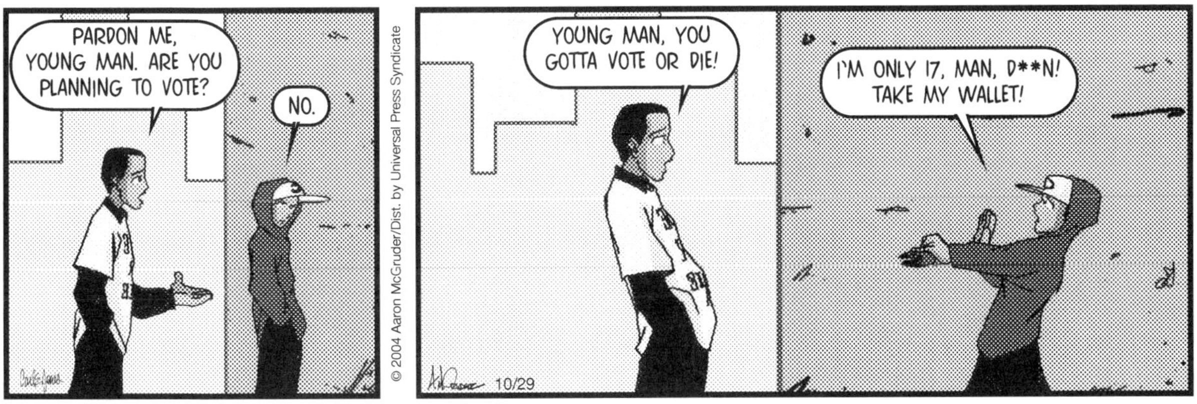
PARDON ME, YOUNG MAN. ARE YOU PLANNING TO VOTE?
NO.
© 2004 Aaron McGruder/Dist. by Universal Press Syndicate
YOUNG MAN, YOU GOTTA VOTE OR DIE!
I'M ONLY 17, MAN, D**N! TAKE MY WALLET!
10/29

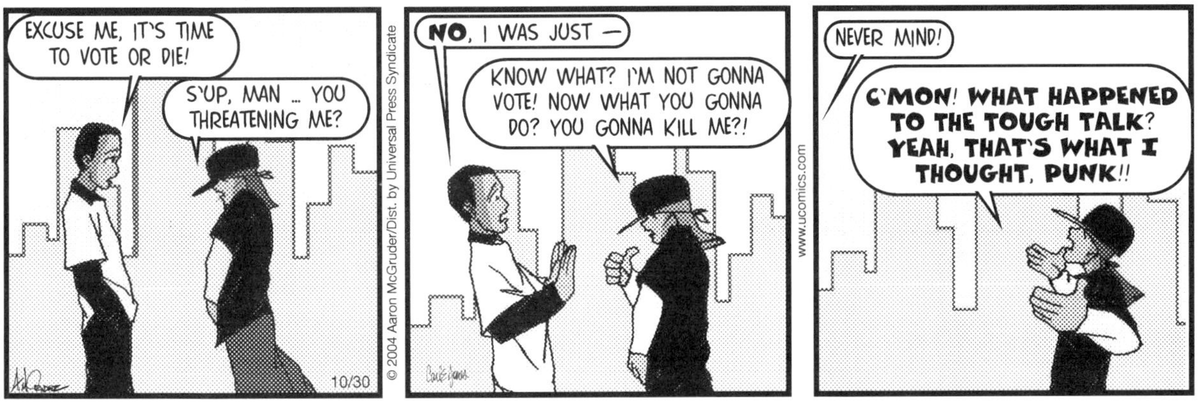
EXCUSE ME, IT'S TIME TO VOTE OR DIE!
S'UP, MAN ... YOU THREATENING ME?
10/30
© 2004 Aaron McGruder/Dist. by Universal Press Syndicate
NO, I WAS JUST —
KNOW WHAT? I'M NOT GONNA VOTE! NOW WHAT YOU GONNA DO? YOU GONNA KILL ME?!
www.ucomics.com
NEVER MIND!
C'MON! WHAT HAPPENED TO THE TOUGH TALK? YEAH, THAT'S WHAT I THOUGHT, PUNK!!

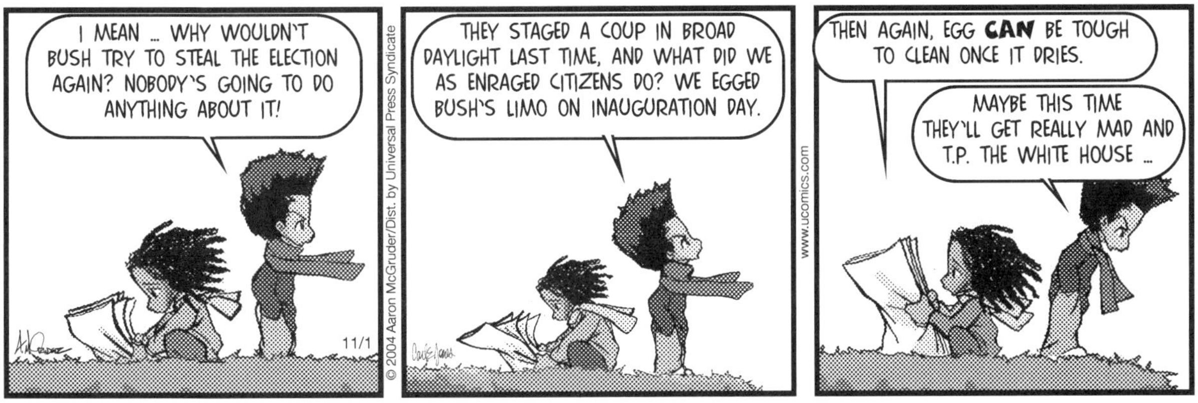
I MEAN ... WHY WOULDN'T BUSH TRY TO STEAL THE ELECTION AGAIN? NOBODY'S GOING TO DO ANYTHING ABOUT IT!
11/1
© 2004 Aaron McGruder/Dist. by Universal Press Syndicate
THEY STAGED A COUP IN BROAD DAYLIGHT LAST TIME, AND WHAT DID WE AS ENRAGED CITIZENS DO? WE EGGED BUSH'S LIMO ON INAUGURATION DAY.
www.ucomics.com
THEN AGAIN, EGG CAN BE TOUGH TO CLEAN ONCE IT DRIES.
MAYBE THIS TIME THEY'LL GET REALLY MAD AND T.P. THE WHITE HOUSE ...

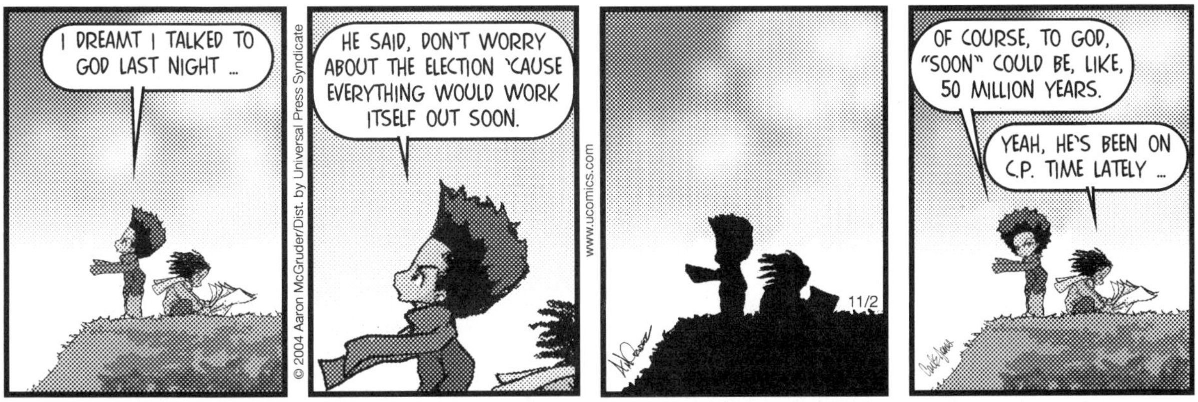
I DREAMT I TALKED TO GOD LAST NIGHT ...
© 2004 Aaron McGruder/Dist. by Universal Press Syndicate
HE SAID, DON'T WORRY ABOUT THE ELECTION 'CAUSE EVERYTHING WOULD WORK ITSELF OUT SOON.
www.ucomics.com
11/2
OF COURSE, TO GOD, "SOON" COULD BE, LIKE, 50 MILLION YEARS.
YEAH, HE'S BEEN ON C.P. TIME LATELY ...

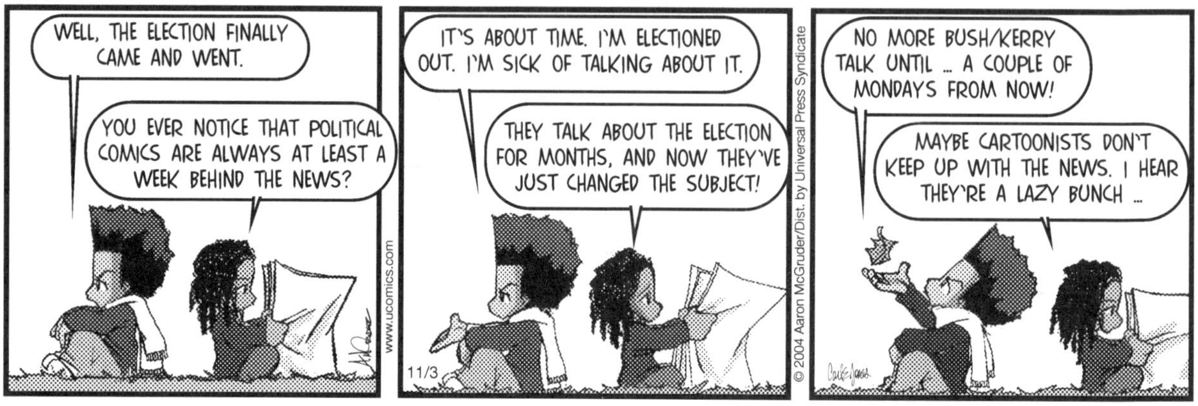
WELL, THE ELECTION FINALLY CAME AND WENT.
YOU EVER NOTICE THAT POLITICAL COMICS ARE ALWAYS AT LEAST A WEEK BEHIND THE NEWS?
www.ucomics.com
11/3
IT'S ABOUT TIME. I'M ELECTIONED OUT. I'M SICK OF TALKING ABOUT IT.
THEY TALK ABOUT THE ELECTION FOR MONTHS, AND NOW THEY'VE JUST CHANGED THE SUBJECT!
© 2004 Aaron McGruder/Dist. by Universal Press Syndicate
NO MORE BUSH/KERRY TALK UNTIL ... A COUPLE OF MONDAYS FROM NOW!
MAYBE CARTOONISTS DON'T KEEP UP WITH THE NEWS. I HEAR THEY'RE A LAZY BUNCH ...

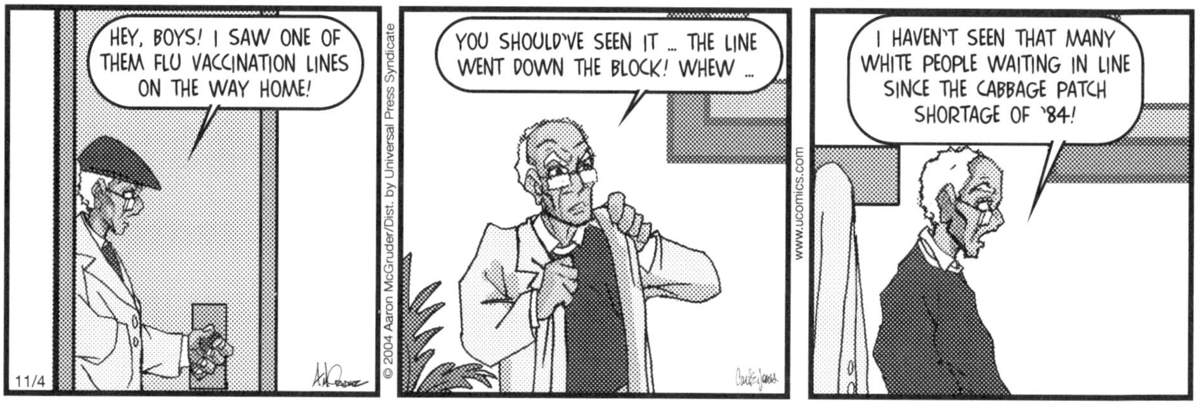
HEY, BOYS! I SAW ONE OF THEM FLU VACCINATION LINES ON THE WAY HOME!
11/4
© 2004 Aaron McGruder/Dist. by Universal Press Syndicate
YOU SHOULD'VE SEEN IT ... THE LINE WENT DOWN THE BLOCK! WHEW ...
www.ucomics.com
I HAVEN'T SEEN THAT MANY WHITE PEOPLE WAITING IN LINE SINCE THE CABBAGE PATCH SHORTAGE OF '84!

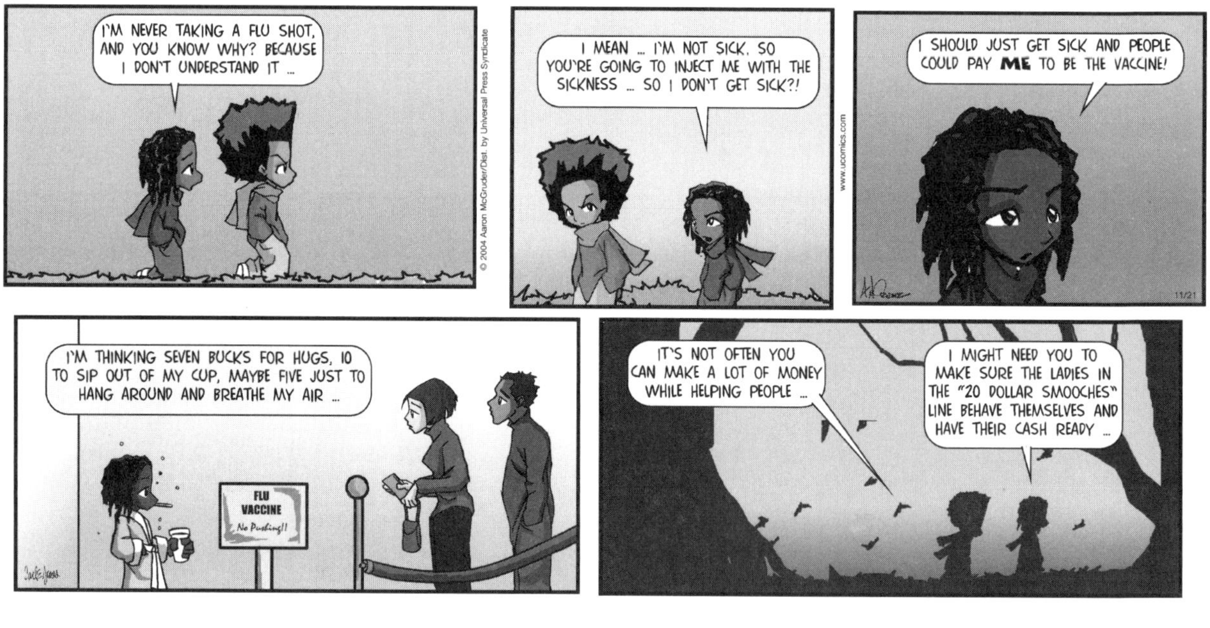
I'M NEVER TAKING A FLU SHOT, AND YOU KNOW WHY? BECAUSE I DON'T UNDERSTAND IT ...
© 2004 Aaron McGruder/Dist. by Universal Press Syndicate
I MEAN ... I'M NOT SICK, SO YOU'RE GOING TO INJECT ME WITH THE SICKNESS ... SO I DON'T GET SICK?!
www.ucomics.com
I SHOULD JUST GET SICK AND PEOPLE COULD PAY ME TO BE THE VACCINE!
11/21
I'M THINKING SEVEN BUCKS FOR HUGS, 10 TO SIP OUT OF MY CUP, MAYBE FIVE JUST TO HANG AROUND AND BREATHE MY AIR ...
FLU VACCINE
No Pushing!!
IT'S NOT OFTEN YOU CAN MAKE A LOT OF MONEY WHILE HELPING PEOPLE ...
I MIGHT NEED YOU TO MAKE SURE THE LADIES IN THE "20 DOLLAR SMOOCHES" LINE BEHAVE THEMSELVES AND HAVE THEIR CASH READY ...

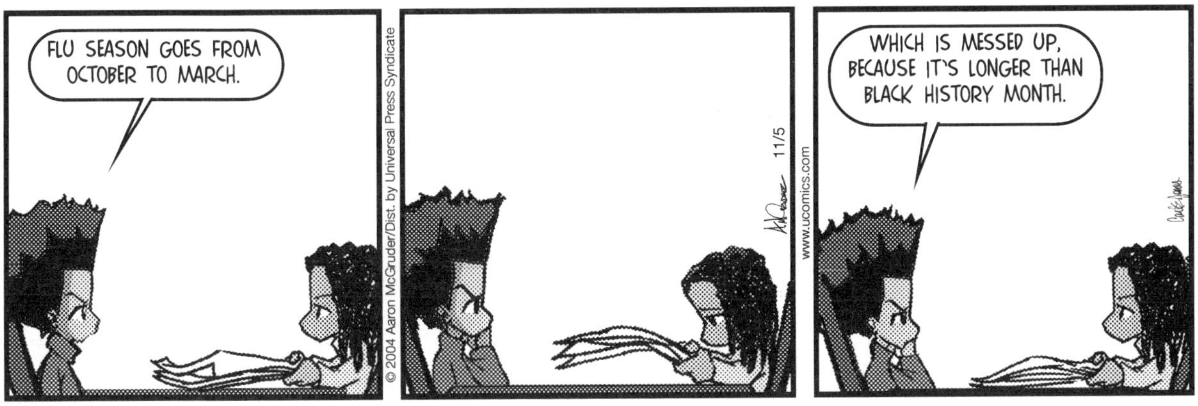
FLU SEASON GOES FROM OCTOBER TO MARCH.
© 2004 Aaron McGruder/Dist. by Universal Press Syndicate
11/5
www.ucomics.com
WHICH IS MESSED UP, BECAUSE IT'S LONGER THAN BLACK HISTORY MONTH.

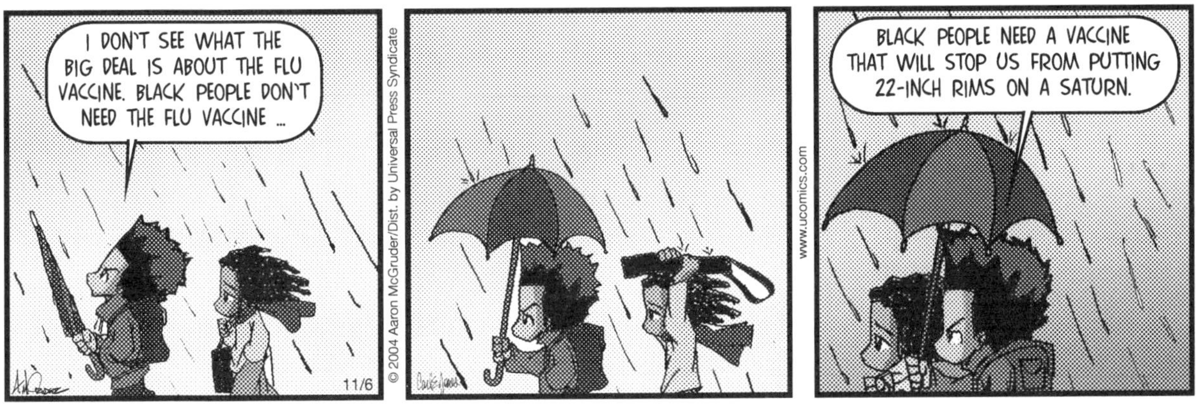
I DON'T SEE WHAT THE BIG DEAL IS ABOUT THE FLU VACCINE. BLACK PEOPLE DON'T NEED THE FLU VACCINE ...
11/6
© 2004 Aaron McGruder/Dist. by Universal Press Syndicate
www.ucomics.com
BLACK PEOPLE NEED A VACCINE THAT WILL STOP US FROM PUTTING 22-INCH RIMS ON A SATURN.

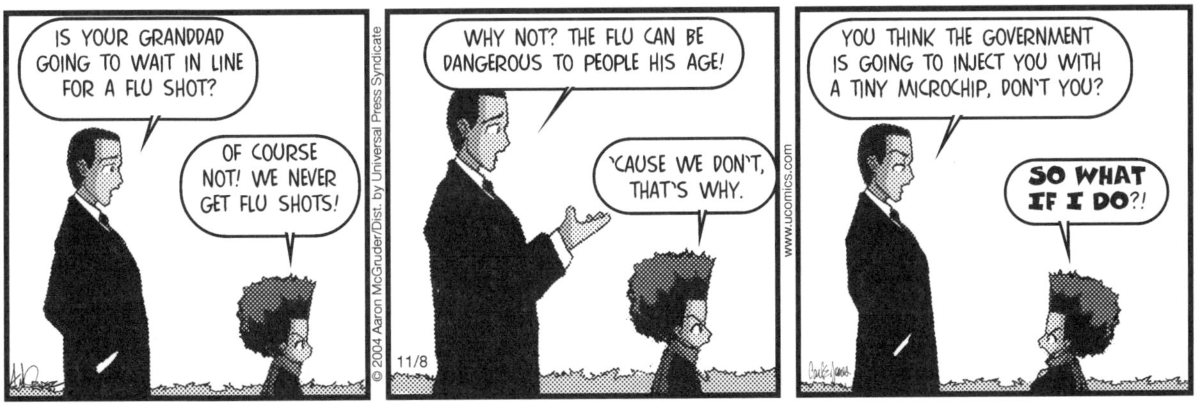
IS YOUR GRANDDAD GOING TO WAIT IN LINE FOR A FLU SHOT?
OF COURSE NOT! WE NEVER GET FLU SHOTS!
© 2004 Aaron McGruder/Dist. by Universal Press Syndicate
11/8
WHY NOT? THE FLU CAN BE DANGEROUS TO PEOPLE HIS AGE!
'CAUSE WE DON'T, THAT'S WHY.
www.ucomics.com
YOU THINK THE GOVERNMENT IS GOING TO INJECT YOU WITH A TINY MICROCHIP, DON'T YOU?
SO WHAT IF I DO?!

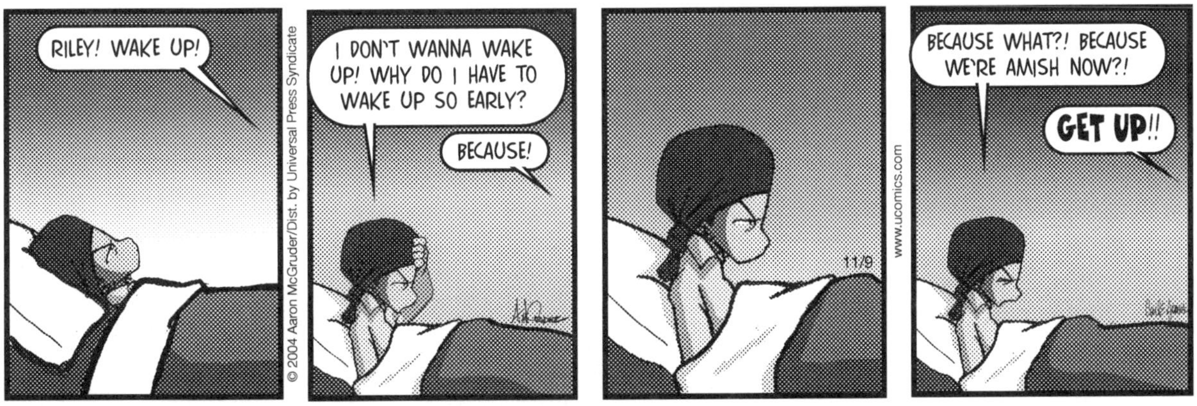
RILEY! WAKE UP!
© 2004 Aaron McGruder/Dist. by Universal Press Syndicate
I DON'T WANNA WAKE UP! WHY DO I HAVE TO WAKE UP SO EARLY?
BECAUSE!
11/9
www.ucomics.com
BECAUSE WHAT?! BECAUSE WE'RE AMISH NOW?!
GET UP!!

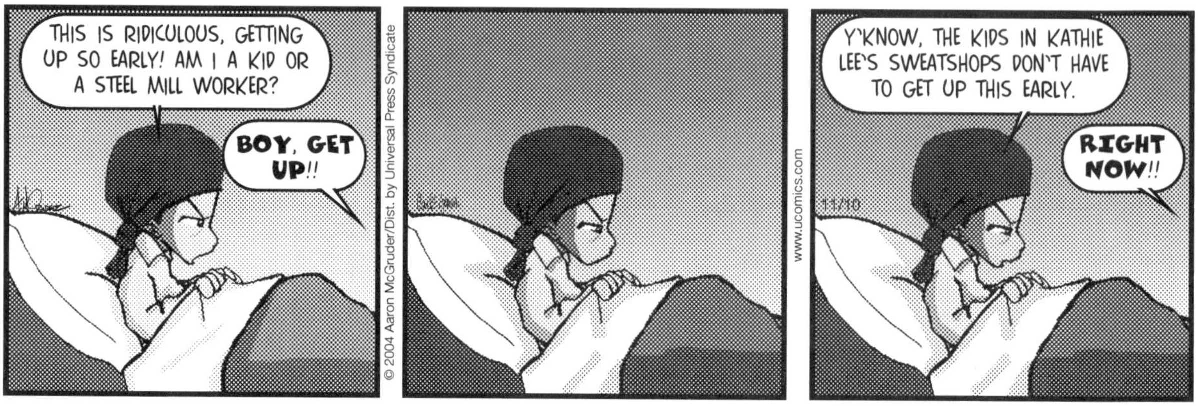
THIS IS RIDICULOUS, GETTING UP SO EARLY! AM I A KID OR A STEEL MILL WORKER?
BOY, GET UP!!
© 2004 Aaron McGruder/Dist. by Universal Press Syndicate
Y'KNOW, THE KIDS IN KATHIE LEE'S SWEATSHOPS DON'T HAVE TO GET UP THIS EARLY.
RIGHT NOW!!
11/10
www.ucomics.com

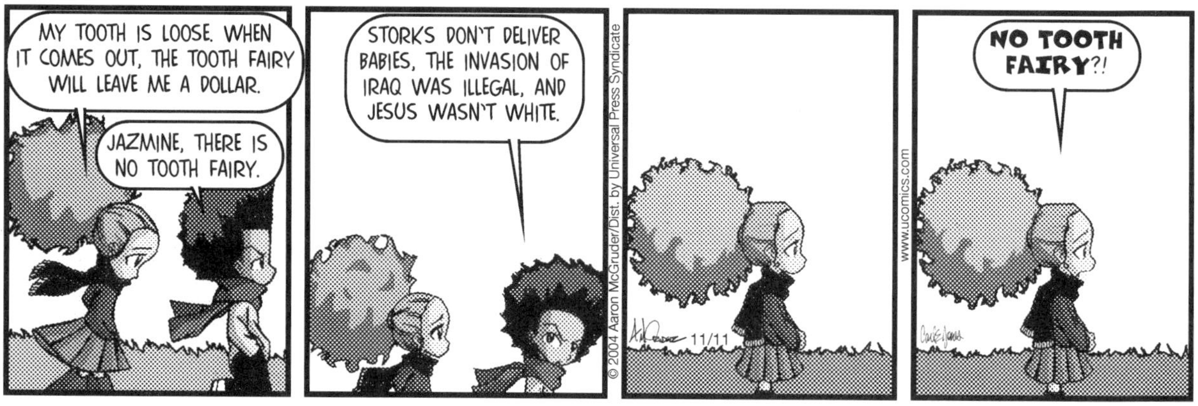
MY TOOTH IS LOOSE. WHEN IT COMES OUT, THE TOOTH FAIRY WILL LEAVE ME A DOLLAR.
JAZMINE, THERE IS NO TOOTH FAIRY.
STORKS DON'T DELIVER BABIES, THE INVASION OF IRAQ WAS ILLEGAL, AND JESUS WASN'T WHITE.
© 2004 Aaron McGruder/Dist. by Universal Press Syndicate
11/11
NO TOOTH FAIRY?!
www.ucomics.com

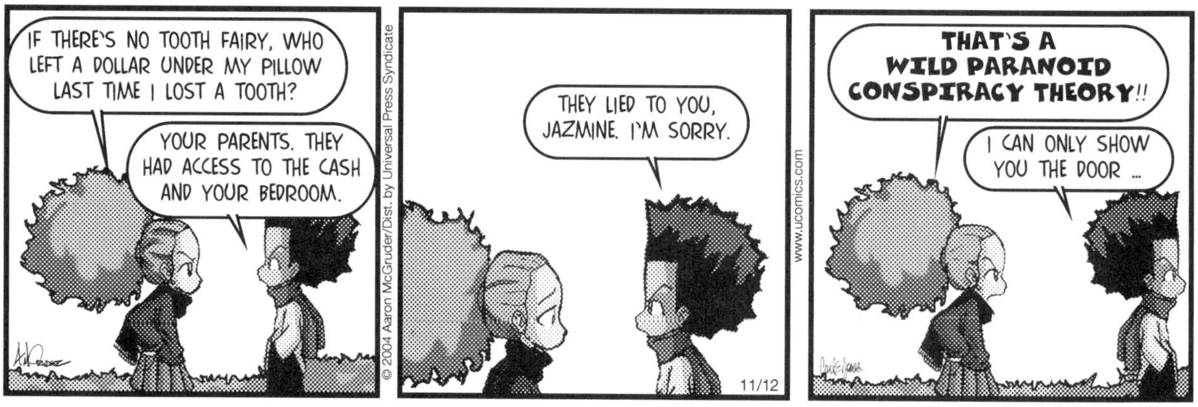
IF THERE'S NO TOOTH FAIRY, WHO LEFT A DOLLAR UNDER MY PILLOW LAST TIME I LOST A TOOTH?
YOUR PARENTS. THEY HAD ACCESS TO THE CASH AND YOUR BEDROOM.
© 2004 Aaron McGruder/Dist. by Universal Press Syndicate
THEY LIED TO YOU, JAZMINE. I'M SORRY.
11/12
THAT'S A WILD PARANOID CONSPIRACY THEORY!!
I CAN ONLY SHOW YOU THE DOOR ...
www.ucomics.com

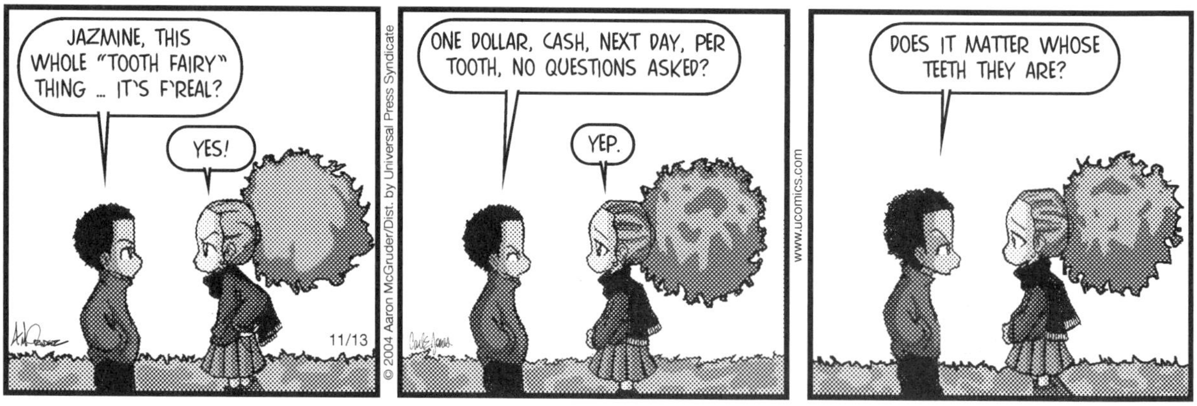
JAZMINE, THIS WHOLE "TOOTH FAIRY" THING ... IT'S F'REAL?
YES!
11/13
© 2004 Aaron McGruder/Dist. by Universal Press Syndicate
ONE DOLLAR, CASH, NEXT DAY, PER TOOTH, NO QUESTIONS ASKED?
YEP.
www.ucomics.com
DOES IT MATTER WHOSE TEETH THEY ARE?

ABOUT THE AUTHOR

Aaron McGruder is the creator of *The Boondocks.*
The Boondocks made its print debut in 1997 in *The Diamondback,* a student
newspaper at the University of Maryland, and now appears daily in more than
250 newspapers around the country and online at www.boondocks.net.
He is the coauthor of *Birth of a Nation: A Comic Novel.*
He lives in Los Angeles, California.

ALSO BY AARON McGRUDER

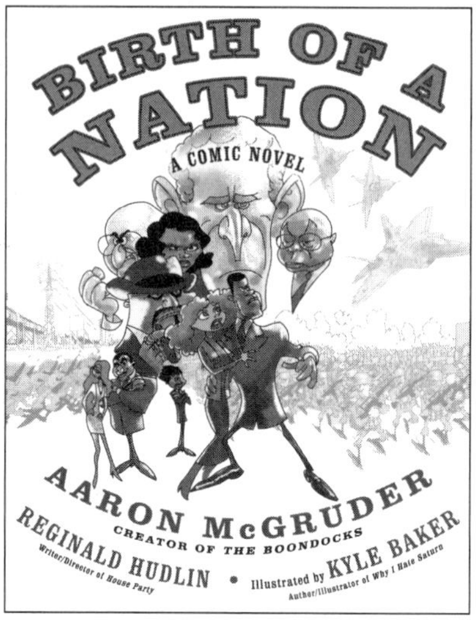
BIRTH OF A NATION
A COMIC NOVEL
AARON McGRUDER
CREATOR OF THE BOONDOCKS
REGINALD HUDLIN
Writer/Director of House Party
Illustrated by KYLE BAKER
Author/Illustrator of Why I Hate Saturn

A scathingly hilarious political satire that answers the burning question:
Would anyone care if East St. Louis seceded from the Union?
$13.95 paper (Canada: $21.00)
1-4000-8316-8

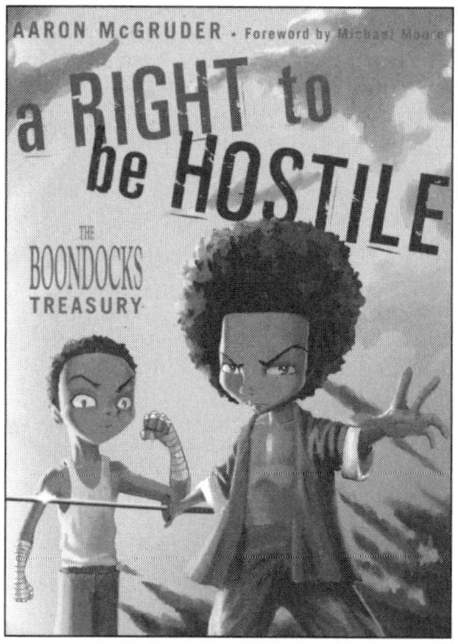
AARON McGRUDER • Foreword by Michael Moore
a RIGHT to be HOSTILE
THE BOONDOCKS TREASURY

The first big book of *The Boondocks,* with more than four years and 800 strips of one of the most influential, controversial, and funny comics ever to run in a daily newspaper.
$16.95 paper (Canada: $25.95)
1-4000-4857-5

Available from Three Rivers Press wherever books are sold
CrownPublishing.com